MONSTERS
AND
ANGELS

Surviving a Career in Music

Seymour Bernstein

DISTRIBUTED BY

7777 W. BLUEMOUND RD. P.O. BOX 13819 MILWAUKEE, WI 53213

Visit Hal Leonard Online at
www.halleonard.com

ISBN: 0-6340-7837-2

In memory of
my beloved mother

The Prelude
(1805)

The mind of man is framed even like the breath
And harmony of music. There is a dark
Invisible workmanship that reconciles
Discordant elements, and makes them move
In one society.

William Wordsworth

Contents

Preface

Monsters and Angels — Surviving a Career in Music is really about surviving life itself. In recounting my own survival, I hope to speak for all people, professional and otherwise, who strive to express their artistic passions. Self-expression through music is perhaps the deepest source of satisfaction available to mankind. Yet, the process through which our talent allows us free expression is fraught with difficulties. Chief among them is the struggle to achieve a balance between our artistic and personal selves. "Does my performance measure up to what others can do?" "Will I ever be recognized for my efforts?" "I can't live without my art; but how can I practice seriously and support myself at the same time?" These are some of the questions addressed in this book.

As everyone knows, parents, teachers, siblings, and friends shape and influence our lives for good and for ill. Survival, as I see it, depends to a great extent upon how successfully we learn to differentiate between the "angels" and "monsters" — those whose sole intent is to benefit us, and those who seem neurotically driven to dominate and control everyone within their grasp. Adulthood, however, has one distinctive privilege: it gives us the right to reject certain authority figures — even a parent, if need be.

My overview of music education and performing careers is not a positive one: composers and performers of the twentieth century are now separated from each other; ruthless managers have turned the performing scene into a veritable Armageddon; and some music critics demean music and performers and infect the public with the poison of their own boredom. Worst of all are certain teachers and managers who use their reputations and positions of power to demand sexual favors from young musicians.

On the positive side, amateur musicians protect the sacred art of music even more than most professionals do. There are, to be sure, dilettantes among them. But some amateurs have achieved the level of competence that we associate with professional musicians. They differ from professionals, however, in two respects: they make their living in non-musical fields, and they perform and compose for one reason only — a love of music, as the word amateur implies. Strange as it may seem, many professional musicians, caught up in the vicissitudes of careers, have all but forgotten their initial love of music.

To elevate serious amateurs to the status they deserve, I have placed them in a new category — the professional-amateur. The future of music is safe in their hands. In the end, it is they who will defend and promulgate music, not to gain public acclaim, but to benefit from and communicate music's harmonizing properties, and not for financial gain, but for the spiritual enlightenment which money cannot buy.

Genius always manifests itself, whatever the obstacles. But what of us non-geniuses? How do we find the courage to pursue our individual callings in the face of a society that bows to fame and money above everything else? I trust that others may find their own answers to this question as I relate my musical and personal experiences. For somehow, and in spite of everything, I have survived. I have shed my victim status and am now in control of my own destiny.

Often, people who have worked their way into positions of power have tried to undermine my efforts. One of them, a well-known writer, said to me, "Oh, have you done enough to write your memoirs?" Given his great accomplishments and generosity towards struggling gifted musicians, plus the fact that he admired my book *With Your Own Two Hands*, I thought he would have a clearer perspective about everyone's right to self-expression. Yet his question seemed to imply that while people like Artur Rubinstein have with good reason written their memoirs, who am I and what have I done that I should write mine? I am sure that my response, "Yes, I believe I have done enough," made him think I was as arrogant as my intention to write my memoirs.

This book is my answer to him. It affirms the right of all people, whatever their level of advancement, to develop and express their talents. Its chief purpose is to justify and encourage people like me who are not geniuses, and not world famous, but who are, nevertheless, imbued with an artistic passion which cries out for expression. It proposes that self-development and self-fulfillment are among life's greatest rewards. Ultimately, self-fulfillment reaches out beyond the self, enabling and inspiring us to contribute to others in countless ways. This giving of oneself, to be sure, brings the greatest rewards of all.

As I have discovered, the best antidote to rejection and discouragement is to marshal the courage to begin all over again. In the end, we and we alone know our strengths and weaknesses. Many of us are called. But to disagree with the last half of this familiar adage, we can be chosen, so long as our goals remain both idealistic and reasonable. With perseverance, we can, as the great scholar and classicist Gilbert Highet put it, "outsoar" our origins.

Acknowledgments

No person I have ever known has helped and supported me more than my dear friend Flora Levin. Her invaluable suggestions and the thoroughness with which she has edited my manuscripts have influenced my way of thinking in everything I do. Moreover, her own classical scholarship and treatises on ancient Greek music and her accomplishments as a musician and pianist are models which serve to inspire me in my own work. Words cannot adequately express my gratitude to her.

Alison Thomas, as consummate a writer and editor as she is a pianist and teacher, worked indefatigably in "fine-tuning" my manuscript for publication. Without her, this book could not have reached its final stage. I am deeply indebted to her.

Three other pupils helped me enormously: The eminent art critic and brilliant pianist Michael Kimmelman shared his extraordinary expertise with me. I cannot say how privileged I felt to have been his pupil for the better part of a year. Donald Shaw read the manuscript several times and offered me suggestions with the same sensitivity and logic that marks his poetic playing. And Mark Riggleman proved himself to be is virtuosic on the computer as he is on the keyboard. My thanks to him for scanning the photographs into my manuscript.

Special thanks to the pianist and photographer Christian A. Pohl for allowing me to use his photograph "Twilight in Freiberg," which appears on the cover.

I am also grateful to the following pupils, friends, and colleagues who have made significant contributions to this book: Michel Bayard, Raj Bhimani, Marieanne Colas, Gia Comolli, Roger Dettmer, Lorraine Glickstein, Marcia Goode, Richard Goode, Gabriel Gordon, Irene Grau, David Hassler, Myles Jordan, John Joswick, David Karp, David Leisner, Samuel R. Levin, Ferdinand Liva, Jeffrey Middleton, Nakcheung Paik, Claire Preston, Mark Preston, Richard Preston, Sylvia Rosenberg, Lydia Seifter, Dean Stein, Baylis Thomas, Sarah Thornblade, Ludwig Tomescu, Ben Verdery, Adelaide Weismann, and Mitchell Zeidwig.

List of Photographs

PART 1:
LEAVE-TAKING

I have never attended a farewell recital. But I know that such an event with a famous artist can be a somber affair. While I was no candidate for such high drama on the occasion of my own farewell recital, I anticipated that some people close to me would be shocked by my decision. After all, it is no small thing to stop giving solo recitals after nearly a lifetime of performing. If there was anything I wanted to avoid, it was an emotional scene: family members, friends, and pupils all mourning over the end of my solo career. My own emotions, I thought, would be quite enough to deal with. Considering all of this, I had long ago made up my mind to keep secret the fact that this was my farewell recital.

It was not an easy decision. I agonized over it for almost two years, weighing the pros and cons a thousand times. No one ever had to lecture me about the benefits of practicing — how acquiring that laser beam concentration necessary to survive a performance can have a positive effect upon everything you do. After all, I wrote a book on the subject.[*] Though I had terrible bouts of pre-performance anxiety, like most performers, I had learned at least to tolerate them. And while the business end of performing was always antithetical to my nature, I learned to deal with ruthless managers and agents.

One thing influenced my decision more than anything else: I wanted to compose and to write, but I found it nearly impossible to do so while practicing four to six hours a day for performances and also teaching. I would never give up teaching. It was, and still is, not only my chief passion, but also the mainstay of my income. I remember telltale signs that indicated a need for a radical change in my life: I would be deeply involved in composing something and resented having to stop to prepare for a performance. Performing had to go.

---

[*] *With Your Own Two Hands* (New York: G. Schirmer, 1981).

Musical time is an experience unto itself. Each composition creates its own time-frame. The performer gets the feeling that universal and biological time bow to musical time. At my farewell recital, time seemed to stretch out indefinitely. Each piece, each phrase seemed to progress at a painfully slow pace, heedless of my own desire to bring my solo career to an end. When finally the *coda* of Liszt's *Funerailles* was upon me, I was filled with a storm of contradictory feelings. The last flickering torments of doubt collided with a heightened sense of relief. And to my utter surprise, a wave of nostalgia, as powerful as the sentiments within the music itself, battled for supremacy. It was like looking back for a final glimpse at something that was a vital part of my life. Was it possible that the performer within me did not want to let go? In a very real sense, it was the performer who maintained his concentration through all of this. My musical self and my automatic pilot kept the playing intact, while my personal self relived all the conflicts of the previous two years.

All that I have been describing lasted only a minute or two. And like those moments when reality flashes upon you and surprises you by far exceeding all expectations, I suddenly found myself in the final measures of Liszt's *Funerailles*. Two dark menacing chords followed by one sinister *staccato* octave deep in the bass, and the first half of my recital was over. During the silence that followed, my hands remained motionless over the surface of the keys, while the audience, on its part, seemed not to breathe at all. Suddenly, there was a roar that fairly shook me out of my reverie.

Everyone, I believe, welcomes applause as a generous expression of approbation. Yet, like most performers, I am hypercritical of my playing. I have also suffered those serpent-like waves of insecurity known only to those who dare to do impossible things — like performing music in public. Inevitably, then, applause means only one thing to me: somehow, by the grace of God perhaps, I got away with it. I still had a large work of my own to perform, but I actually looked forward to it. Placing it at the end of my farewell recital was my declaration of a new life.

It is often difficult to know what is best for ourselves. Even after I firmly decided to give up solo performing, I suffered ambivalence, fear, and even guilt: ambivalence in wondering whether my need to be creative was a rationalization for escaping the anxieties of performing; fear of charting new territories at the age of fifty-one (I considered myself then, as I do now, merely a novice at composing and writing); and guilt in wondering if I had the right to relinquish my responsibilities as an interpreter of music. Such ghosts of indecision haunted me for some time. While I drew some measure of comfort from having read Dr. Johnson's justification of his own retirement, "No man is so well qualified to leave public life as he who has long tried it and known it well," still, a gnawing question remained: How long, and how well must a person know public life before leaving it?

Another question troubled me even more: What if I made the wrong decision? If world-renowned figures have doubted their own intentions, how, then, could I trust mine? In searching for the right answer, I turned to the activity I knew best — performing. If I have learned anything at all from practicing in preparation for a performance, it is that self-doubt can lead to positive action. In other words, pre-concert anxiety can motivate the kind of practicing that enables you to survive a performance — in spite of your nervousness. Looking at it the other way around, I have always suspected that some performers who botch up their performances from a lack of practicing simply don't get nervous enough! At any rate, like sediment that drops gradually to the bottom of a vessel leaving the liquid clear, so, too, did my doubts finally fall away, allowing me a clear vision of the course which I felt compelled to follow. Fear or inadequacy aside, I would discipline myself and learn whatever skills were necessary to compose and to write. If, in the end, I concluded that I had made the wrong decision, I could always return to performing. Whatever the risk, whatever doubts remained, I was resolved to end my solo career.

PRECIOUS BOND

Funerailles, which ended the first half of my farewell recital, was preceded by my own transcription of the Organ Toccata and Fugue in *D* minor by Bach, and two works by Beethoven — the Bagatelles Op. 126 (among my favorite pieces in all of music) and the Polonaise Op. 89. After the intermission, I was to premiere one of my own multimedia works, *American Pictures at an Exhibition*. It is a long and difficult piece, and I was prepared to give it my best. However, nothing is more demanding than interpreting time-honored masterpieces. By comparison, then, having to play my own work, difficult though it was, did not pose too great a challenge to me. When I came to the end of *Funerailles*, therefore, I had the feeling that I had already said farewell to a major part of my career. In view of this, it was quite a different person who returned to the green room. I believe it was the first time in all of my performing experiences that I breathed a sigh of relief during the intermission.

American Pictures at an Exhibition was a sequel to my previously published work *New Pictures at an Exhibition*. Both works were written in collaboration with my former pupil, Owen Lewis, now Dr. Lewis, a prominent psychiatrist in New York City. As a young man of sixteen, "Oven" (as his late grandmother, of Russian-Jewish descent, pronounced it) was bursting with talent — and not just for music. At one lesson, he shyly handed me a poem called *Chez Chagall*, inspired by the murals at the Metropolitan Opera House at Lincoln Center. Though he was but half my age, his gifts as a pianist and this new evidence of the creative fire that burned within him kindled a deep bond between us.

As for Owen's poem, I found it impressive enough to send to *Seventeen Magazine*. Thinking that he was too young and too inexperienced to handle a possible rejection, I kept this a secret from him. To my surprise, a contract arrived, almost by return mail, and with it, a check for $25.00. Owen was positively euphoric. With this vote of confidence from a major publication, the young poet spread his wings. Other poems, and a novel, too, poured out of him. Approximately three years later, we began our collaboration on the two works mentioned above.

American Pictures, some thirty minutes long, is a multimedia work comprising ten piano pieces and ten poems — all inspired by American paintings from three centuries of art. Owen, sitting stage right, did the recitations of his own poems. The paintings were projected onto a large screen at center stage, and the piano was positioned to the left of it. For the segment "American Gothic," Owen and I switched roles: he accompanied me at the piano, while I, sporting a straw hat and wire-rimmed glasses, like the farmer in the painting, sang and also tap-danced to a song we wrote together, "Ain't pullin' but a tale o' what's there." Given the seriousness of the first half of my farewell recital, the audience was at once shocked and amused — to such an extent, in fact, that my singing and Owen's playing could hardly be heard over the roar of laughter. Standing up in my somewhat dubious role as a singer (unlike my earlier, more successful attempts at singing) gave me the unique advantage of viewing the entire audience. To this day I shall never forget that sea of open-mouthed faces. By all appearances, everyone was having a good time. And with my own sense of liberation from the solo stage mounting at every moment, no one had a better time than I did.

A Perspective on Humor

Many serious people have a penchant for humor. Even such a figure as Chopin was well-known for his mimicry of friends, colleagues, and pupils — among them some prominent persons of the day in the world of music, art, and literature. I, personally, have always found it liberating to laugh at my own seriousness. It helps me to place not only my work but also my whole life in proper perspective. While most of my friends and pupils accept my joking around privately, some of them were shocked by my departure from formality on the stage of a major concert hall. One friend and one pupil in particular saw my antics in *American Pictures at an Exhibition* as a defiance of concert stage protocol. Although my singing and tap dance routine were extreme departures from accepted concert decorum, they were not meant to be a defiance of the formality of which I am speaking. Rather, they grew out of a spontaneous response to the painting "American Gothic," and the general format that Owen and I had devised. Once we had created that format, Owen and I consciously decided to inject this absurdly humorous segment into the performance as a kind of exclamation point to contrast with the more serious segments which surrounded it. In short, we conceived *American Pictures* as a theater piece. Everything associated with it, therefore, was in keeping with this decision — my singing and tap dancing included.

My critical friend and my pupil, however, seemed to take my singing and dancing as a personal affront, not relating them to the theatrical context of the work. A tug of war started: I saw in their criticisms a lack of understanding of that part of me which enjoys parody, mimicry, and whimsy — even in public. They, on the other hand, kept insisting that I had overstepped the boundaries of propriety. After hours of bickering, I got angry with them for wanting to deny me the right to pause in my work and have a good laugh at myself. I accused them of being stodgy, and I suggested that it would be good for them to let their own hair down occasionally.

As far as stage deportment is concerned, I have always thought that the overly formal decorum adopted by most performers can militate against the very spontaneity which they hope to achieve. In giving my own recitals, I have often altered this formality by at least speaking to my audiences about the music and my own responses to it.

When you are close to someone, his or her criticism can penetrate right to the core of your emotional world, especially if you are criticized moments after a performance. It can stir up a tempest of present and past feelings. My friend's opposing voice might well have been that of my own father, who attempted to snuff out the child within me. Paradoxically, one of the qualities I love in this friend is his own capacity for just plain silliness. He keeps this a private matter, however, and would not dream of exhibiting it in public. I, on the other hand, have something of the performer in me, even off-stage. Being conscious of this, I have always tried to integrate my personal self with my professional self. For me to alter this extroversive tendency just to please someone else would be to betray my own personality. In the final analysis, most of us have preconceived notions of how we would like others to act. These notions play a vital role in determining who attracts or repels us.

5

Part 1: Leave-Taking

Without ruling out the value of criticism, one's inner voice is often the true guide to follow. I can recall how often throughout my life I followed my own convictions in opposition to sound and well-meant advice. In doing so, I trusted that those who gave me advice respected me sufficiently not only to allow me, but, more importantly, to encourage me to be faithful to my true nature.

CRITICISMS AND COMPLIMENTS

All of this raises the thorny issue of criticism and compliments. When you actually ask for criticisms, such as I did after a run-through of *American Pictures at an Exhibition* in my New York City studio, you must be prepared to hear a gamut of responses. On that occasion, there was, at first, a conspicuous silence, perhaps due to shyness or embarrassment. Little by little, though, everyone's self-consciousness eased somewhat, and comments began to fly back and forth. They ranged from whole-hearted praise (which pleased Owen and me greatly) to expressions of shock and disapproval, these being aimed mainly at my dancing and singing antics. There were also a few of those comments which, because of their evasiveness, ended up saying nothing at all: "It was fascinating!" "What an interesting work!" or "My, all of those notes. The piece must have taken you forever to write!"

"He's criticizing me, and not my playing!"

Nothing, of course, is more awkward than forcing yourself to say something positive about someone's performance which you may actually have disliked. Thus, empty phrases such as "I can't believe what you did!" or "You're really too much!" are attempts to skirt the issue of criticism without offending the person in question. I have always found it difficult to criticize a performance by a colleague or a pupil that I felt was below an acceptable standard. Through the years, though, I have come to the following conclusion: It is a sign of love and respect to speak your true feelings to another person. One thing to remember, however, is never to offer criticism unless you are asked to do so. (This proviso does not apply to pupils, who, of course, need criticism as a part of instruction.) The other thing is to become, as it were, the person you are criticizing and to take into yourself his or her feelings. Yet, however sensitive and tactful you try to be, you may inadvertently offend the person whom you criticize. I should like to offer what I think is a possible reason for this: Music is a person's soul, inseparable from him. It follows, then, that criticism leveled at someone's playing may be taken more personally than musically. For example, suppose you criticize a friend for rushing uncon-

6

trollably on fast passages. Your friend may think "I'm being told in effect that I am an unstable person, given to a lack of control." In other words, criticisms of our performances — musical and otherwise — carry with them personal connotations.

On the occasions when people criticize my performances, I accept the fact that I, the person, made a musical error in judgment, I chose the wrong method of practicing this or that passage, and I alone miscalculated an interpretive approach to a phrase or even to an entire piece. On the other hand, a compliment from someone whose opinion I trust becomes as it were symbolic of a personal triumph. Whatever the case, I would always like to be told the truth. For how else can I improve a performance or a creative act, both of which are governed by my own thought processes? Moreover, how can I maintain a sufficiently high standard of performance unless someone points out the bad as well as the good in all that I do? If I am performing, for example, it all comes down to this: I will not be a victim of circumstance. Should something go wrong during my perform-ance, I cannot blame the piece, the piano, or the audience members for coughing. I alone am responsible for everything I do — before, during, and after the performance. Momentary inconsistencies and human failings notwithstanding, *I perform the way I practice*. And even when a fingering that a teacher gave me proves to be unreliable, I, and not my teacher, am to blame. For it was I who accepted my teacher's fingering, and along with that acceptance I must take full responsibility for its outcome.

Some people avoid mentioning your playing entirely, or they may direct their comments to the music itself. Nothing infuriates a performer more than a music critic who wastes precious space pontificating about some historical detail concerning the music and then adds a perfunctory sentence or two about the performance. Speaking about being infuriated — I once played Op. 111 by Beethoven for a very fine pianist. Her beautiful Hamburg Steinway model "B," with its warm, resonant sound and responsive action, seemed to be the ideal vehicle for that transcendent piece. After the final *C* major chord had died away, I asked what she thought of my performance. She looked at me with a perfectly blank expression and exclaimed, "What a beautiful piece!" And without pausing, she added, "Would you like tea with your pastry?" To my ears, this sounded like a non sequitur. When finally her question had registered upon me, I replied, "Yes, tea will be fine." I ate the pastry, drank the tea, and engaged in some small talk. When it was time to leave, I thanked her for listening to me and for the refreshments.

Once outside, the voices of doubt began to undermine my confidence: "I must not have played as well as I thought. In fact, it must have been so bad that she could only comment on the piece and not on my playing." By the following day, however, I was less critical of myself and more so of her. Even if she had not liked my playing, I reasoned, she might have found at least one measure to comment on. The more I thought about it, the more furious I became.

Beethoven's Op. 111 *is* beautiful, but I played it for the pianist in question for reasons other than having her laud Beethoven's masterpiece. Why did she respond to my playing with such empty words? Thinking about it now, I can only conjecture as to the reasons: Perhaps she had her own concept of Op. 111, a concept which she may have thought I had violated; she may not have liked my playing; or she may even have been jealous of my performance. If the last was true, then focusing upon the piece instead of my performance of it may have been her way of disguising her own feelings of competitiveness. It is also possible that she was not familiar with Op. 111; her superficial comment, then, may have been her attempt to hide her ignorance. Or she may sincerely have thought that my performance revealed the beauty of the piece and that no further words were necessary. But given the circumstances of my playing for her, I felt that she treated my best efforts inconsiderately and superficially.

On the other hand, I would rather hear "What a beautiful piece" than a hypocritical phrase such as "You're absolutely fantastic!" — this, from a person who clearly thought the performance totally unacceptable. Try to compliment such people after their own performances, and you yourself may be accused of being hypocritical.

> For neither man nor angel can discern
> Hypocrisy, the only evil that walks
> Invisible.[*]

It is natural, I believe, for us all to want some sort of recognition for our efforts. There is nothing like well-chosen words of praise or a phrase of encouragement to lift our spirits and promote our confidence. The sad truth is that our best performances may go unheeded, even by those closest to us. And occasionally, even though someone wishes to applaud us, he or she may in fact feel that we are above praise. Such people find it embarrassing, therefore, to say what they assume to be all too obvious. There may also be delayed responses to our efforts, as I had occasion to experience in Seoul, Korea, during a State Department tour.

One evening I was invited to a music-lover's home, and was asked to

---

[*] Milton, *Paradise Lost*, 3-683-5.

play informally. I remember that occasion in particular because of the assemblage of well-known musicians and literary people, including one of Korea's foremost poets. The piano, an old upright, was practically unmanageable. My performance, therefore, was far from my best. Afterwards, at a banquet in my honor, I tried to hide my discontent with myself at the way I performed. The fact that not a single person commented upon my playing or even caught my eye did not help matters any. Finally, after a half hour or so, the poet, who was sitting opposite me, said something in Korean to my interpreter. Judging from her impassive expression, I assumed that she was commenting on the delectable food that we were all enjoying. I was stunned, therefore, when my interpreter translated her words: "The poet has just told me that she was so moved by your playing that she wishes to die!" With this, the poet's eyes met mine, and the warmth and sincerity of her feelings came pouring out to me. The ice had been broken, and the others present offered their comments about my playing, which helped considerably to allay my sense of failure.

Losing Credibility

As I have learned from experience, nothing weakens my credibility more than complimenting certain pupils who suffer from a whole range of problems, including low self-esteem, guilt for not practicing properly, or a dislike of their performance. Such pupils often lose all objectivity as to what is good or bad in their playing. I may be totally unaware that certain pupils are battling with such feelings — that is, until I compliment them about something in their playing which I truly admire. In an instant, an inner dissatisfaction with themselves may turn into outward hostility towards me. Once, a highly self-critical pupil who had just given one of the finest recitals I have ever heard greeted my words of enthusiasm backstage with just one word of her own: "Hypocrite!"

When I first became aware that compliments unsettled certain pupils, I stopped complimenting all of my pupils entirely. In time, though, I realized that my pupils' reaction to compliments was their problem, and not mine. Besides, in acting counter to my feelings, I was really being untruthful to myself and to my pupils as well. Therefore, if I like something in a pupil's playing, I say so — whether this distresses a pupil or not. Whatever the consequences, being truthful, as I have discovered, is always the best course to follow. I have had many heart-to-heart discussions with my pupils to help them overcome their low self-esteem. In time, they can gain an overall objectivity about what is good in their playing, and what needs further attention.

Part 1: Leave-Taking

There have been occasions when pupils, convinced that their playing was unacceptable and that their talents were hopelessly limited, have interpreted my compliments as a ploy to gain sexual favors from them. Whenever I suspect this to be the case, I ask pupils outright why they think I have complimented them. One pupil actually confessed to the very thing I feared: he thought that my compliments were a ploy. According to what I sense in a pupil, I have on occasion come right out with the truth: "Just in case this may apply to you, I wish to state categorically that my compliments are not meant to imply anything beyond strictly musical concerns." Quite obviously, pupils confronted with such a statement are stunned at first. While some are relieved, others may feel insulted or even disappointed. In the final analysis, however, most of my pupils are heartened to know that my interest in them lies solely in their personal and musical well-being, and in no other area.

A teacher, of course, can fall in love with a pupil — and vice versa. And I am certainly no exception. But teachers who use their position to demand sexual favors from their pupils are not only immoral, but they also demean the very art they practice.

"At last, someone is truthful to me!"

Talent and self-doubt often go hand-in-hand. A possible reason for this may be that truly gifted people have flashes of perfection which subsequently elude them. Having a star within your reach and having it constantly slip from your grasp can induce feelings of frustration and insecurity. This, coupled with an undisciplined nature, can cause musicians to lose all objectivity about themselves and others. This may explain why certain monstrous teachers attract such large classes of gifted pupils. Their reservoirs of knowledge notwithstanding, such teachers are masters of sadistic comments designed to undermine their pupils' self-confidence and make them subservient to their own malevolent intentions. A self-deprecating pupil, whose playing is assessed by his or her teacher as having nothing to recommend it — "You have no technique, you do not know how to phrase, your tone is harsh," etc. — thinks, "At last, someone is telling me the truth!" The longer such a pupil continues to study with a destructive teacher, the more pronounced will the respective sadistic and masochistic tendencies become: the teacher, having found a willing victim, grows increasingly dominant and vicious; the pupil, harboring the worst opinion of him or herself, becomes hopelessly entangled in the teacher's web of destructiveness.

EDUCATIONAL SCHISM

My decision to end my solo career ought not to have been a surprise to anyone. After all, I did more than simply talk about wanting to compose and to write. Only a year before my farewell recital, I presented a program on that very same stage devoted exclusively to my own works. I intended it to be a public declaration of my desire to be more than solely a performing pianist. I walked out to center stage, bowed, and spontaneously said to my large audience, "This is the happiest day of my life!" Yet few people knew why I was happy. And even when I made my feelings known, those close to me had their own responses to that occasion: "I'm glad you're doing what makes you happy, but it certainly would be nice to hear you play a Beethoven sonata." Others were sarcastic: "There you go again trying to be a modern-day Scriabin!"

A few friends expressed their opinions concerning my decision to replace solo performing with composing and writing. "But you are creative in the way you perform and teach," was the comment I heard most frequently. The hours spent in discussions concerning the differences between re-creating (performing) and creating (composing, writing, etc.) resulted in the same divergence of opinion with which we began our conversations. In the end, only my friends and colleagues who were themselves creative understood what I always assumed to be an obvious point — namely, that while a performance or a piano lesson may contain certain creative attributes, the word creative ought to be reserved for people who do, in fact, create something — people who literally inscribe notes, words, or artistic shapes onto a blank piece of paper or canvas, and then develop them according to their own creative bent.

I believe that this controversy derives from the schism that exists now between composing and performing — a schism which I believe began in the late nineteenth century. Formerly, it was unthinkable to separate composing and performing, as virtually all composers until then did both. That Prokofiev and Rachmaninoff were, in my opinion, the last of the great composer-pianists, raises the following question: Why hasn't any other twentieth century virtuoso created anything comparable to what those two masters have left us?

Conservatories and colleges of music seem to perpetuate this schism. Their programs of study speak for themselves: you audition either as a composition (or theory) major, or a performance major — but rarely both. The composer and the performer who, formerly, lived in harmony within the same person are now two distinct entities, with an ever-increasing air of rivalry growing between them. Instrumentalists often think that composers are inept at the keyboard, while composers look upon instru-

11

mentalists and singers as being uncreative. Fostered by the schism in music schools, these stereotypical views seem to reflect the condition of the two professions with considerable accuracy: insufficient keyboard training and unfamiliarity with the very instruments they write for, on the part of some composers, and a total lack of interest in trying to compose, on the part of performers. Quite obviously, such deficiencies among composers and performers limit their effectiveness in their respective fields. Specialization exacts a price beyond that of limiting one's musical growth. For in the long run, it can hinder personal development as well.

"You don't love me any more!"

Creativity, however, has its own hazard: it can actually threaten personal relationships. Simply by having no time for long telephone conversations, dinners, and social functions, for example, you can induce feelings of rejection and jealousy in a person close to you. I have suffered greatly over this whole issue. No matter how much I have tried to keep a balance between my work and social activities, I have inadvertently disappointed or hurt some family members and friends. The truth is, my creative passions are stronger than my social needs. In fact, they seem to be autonomous at times and actually dictate the course of my life. When this occurs, I feel that I have no other recourse than to seek solitude in order to define those surging currents within me. Yet only my closest friends understand my need for seclusion.

Love, it has been said, wants only what is best for the other person. Though I have tried to live up to this precept, I have unwittingly estranged certain people I love simply because my work made it impossible for me always to be available to them. Curiously, none of this conflict occurred during the years when I was performing; then, everyone close to me accepted my priest-like existence as a matter of course. After my farewell recital, however, and when I began writing my book, close friends who never had an inclination to do anything creative apparently failed to understand my need for solitude. They actually saw my focus on creative projects as a rejection of them. When finally my book was published, one friend voiced her pent up annoyance: "I liked you better before you wrote your book." If love can be defined as wanting only what is best for the other person, what was the meaning of this remark? I sensed that my friend resented, and was even competitive with, my success.

As I discovered, there is nothing like a work in progress to reveal the true status of your relationships. Is it not ironic that the closer you draw to your artistic self, the more you may alienate others? Doing the best job you know how, in whatever you do, requires consistent and unswerving devotion — even at the expense of social intimacy. And no less a personal devotion is required of a friend who claims to love you. It saddened me to learn that my friend apparently did not really want what was best for me.

"Practicing is more important to me than you are!"

I believe that each person's field of interest ought to be the chief priority in that person's life, and that love itself can be measured by the degree to which one person encourages another in the pursuit of such priorities. I have always wondered, therefore, why one's spouse or a close friend would say, "You seem to be more devoted to your practicing than you are to me!" Should someone say that to me, I would wholeheartedly agree with his or her observation: "Practicing *is* more important to me than you are. For were I to forgo my practicing, and with it, the pure nourishment of myself, then one thing is predictable: I would not be fit to be devoted to you or to anyone else." Practicing can also be a viable means of avoiding certain people. But in harmonious relationships, it is, as I see it, the pooling together of individual passions — be it the study of music or some other equally compelling subject — that constitutes the chief requisite of a successful relationship. In other words, if there is something more to relationships than sexual attraction, it must surely be the shared devotion to individual achievements as well as common interests. Not that devotion to work alone or the encouragement of it will ensure everlasting happiness. But at least relationships are more likely to flourish when their focus is on the profound things in life of which humans are the mere instruments.

For the Sake of My Pupils

While I decided to give up my solo career, I had no intention of giving up performing entirely. I fully intended to continue playing chamber music, exploring a repertory that was close to my heart. Doing this, I would not have to perform from memory, which for me, at least, always required many extra hours of practicing. I also intended to continue playing my own works in public. In moderation, then, performing would remain a vital part of my life. The point is, I wanted to keep on practicing. And there is nothing like a commitment to a performance to make one achieve this end. Besides, I could not in good conscience expect my pupils to strive towards the highest standards of performance without setting some sort of example myself. That many of my present pupils have never heard me play a solo recital is a fact that most of them have learned to understand and to accept.

Pupils, of course, tend to emulate their teachers. To this day, when the torments of performing seem unendurable, pupils will occasionally threaten to end their performing careers as I did. I counsel them as one who has, himself, suffered anguish on the stage a thousand times over. I remind them that I gave up performing in order to compose and write, and that they ought to have something equally compelling to take the place of performing. Otherwise, to quit without having a justifiable reason for doing so would be to give in to their weakness.

The act of performing takes on many guises. Some musical devotees are simply not emotionally suited to perform publicly. My friend and pupil, Flora Levin, a recognized scholar in ancient Greek music, is one such person. To her, playing for me at piano lessons is tantamount to performing. Her bi-weekly lessons, therefore, motivate her best practicing. Music is so important to her that she would probably practice dedicatedly even without lessons. Steeped in ancient Greek thought, she knows full well the harmonizing effects of synthesizing feeling, thinking, physical coordination, and sensory perception. In short, practicing makes her feel good about herself. She was the ideal person to help me write *With Your Own Two Hands.*

If I have gained anything at all from my life as a solo performer, it is that I became intimate with all of the problems that my own pupils encounter, the chief one being that to perform is to meet conflict head on. Doing this, confronting and then dissolving conflict, molds the personality. Difficult as performing is, I would want all of my pupils to experience those profound benefits that result from hard and consistent work. But were a pupil ever to be beckoned to another calling — one of comparable challenge — then I would be the first to help plan a farewell recital.

Why Compose?

Were I to single out the chief reason for ending my solo performing career, I would say that I wanted time to follow in a direction which music itself suggested. As I see it, musical creativity is a natural outgrowth of practicing and performing. In other words, the process of integrating music into our hearts and minds ought to awaken a creative voice within us. There is striking evidence about this in Bach's "Sincere Instructions," the preface to his Two and Three Part Inventions. Obviously, he intended us "to learn to play cleanly in two parts" (and later in three), "and at the same time, not only to compose good inventions, but to develop them well." Bach then makes it clear that in the process, the serious student ought to acquire "a taste for the elements of composition." If I understand Bach properly, the study of his inventions has a purpose beyond the development of interpretive and technical skills; its more significant role is to guide our hand as we compose our own "inventions." In my case, I felt ready to tap those resources lying deep within me, and even risk the unknown for the sake of my total development.

As far as I was concerned, I delayed too long in making that decision. Without shifting the blame to anyone, I believe that my piano teachers' indifference towards composing diminished my own enthusiasm about it. Only once, when I was fourteen, did my teacher at the time, Herman Holzman, actually give me a composition assignment: "Write a barcarole," he suggested (he had first, of course, to explain to me what a barcarole was). "Now compose a theme and write three variations on it." So inspired was I to be asked to express something totally original that I wrote four barcaroles, and six variations on my theme. Alas, when I changed teachers a year later, I was, from that time on, groomed exclusively for the concert stage. Though I continued to write little pieces and poems, my teachers showed only a superficial interest in them. Subsequently, without feedback of any kind, these creative endeavors ceased entirely.

Rarely will a music teacher today suggest that composing can spark a deeper understanding of music, or, what is even more important, promote a student's personal growth. Moreover, it is generally accepted that if you are destined to compose, you'll do it anyway — even without encouragement: "No one had to tell Schubert to write a song every day of his life," a piano teacher told a pupil who inquired about learning the rudiments of composition. This may be true of certain creative individuals. But as my experience has proved, it is far more common for creative impulses to lie dormant "within the secret chambers of the soul," as Plato put it. It then remains for a teacher to lead them out, which is in fact the definition of the word "education." Sometimes it takes only the simplest encouragement from a teacher or a colleague to lead out the best in us.

All of us, I believe, ought to do whatever is necessary to be worthy of our gifts, to give life the best fight we know how. I followed my calling, therefore, not merely to be published, but for the joy of honest effort; not for public recognition, but to know that I could continue to grow; and not for self-satisfaction alone, but to make myself fit to benefit others — especially my pupils. For what better example could I set for my pupils than to strive constantly to develop my own talent? As I see it, the very act of confronting the creative side of my nature has a meaning beyond composing and writing itself: it is the only way I know of justifying my life. As Otto Rank said, "For the artist, his calling is not a means of livelihood, but life itself....He does not practice his calling, but is it."

"I feel you ought to know!"

There are certain people who either begrudge whatever modest successes we may achieve, or else secretly rejoice at our failures. Concerning the latter, I am reminded of a well-known maxim of La Rochefoucauld's: "There is something in the misfortune of our friends that is not altogether displeasing." Living, as they do, with a sense of failure about themselves, such people wait for that opportune moment when they can bring us down to their own wretched state. As a rule, they are among the gossip mongers of the world. After my farewell recital, which these people saw as an indication of defeat on my part, a few of them buzzed their opinions as to why I quit the stage: "He was probably getting too old!" "He gave up because his career wasn't going anywhere!" "He lost his nerve!" The last comment was a particularly sensitive issue with me, since the very same thought had crossed my mind during that anguished time when I contemplated my farewell recital. In light of my drastic decision, perhaps this interpretation was unavoidable.

It all proved that musicians could be just as petty and vicious as anyone else, although one wonders why the humanity that is music does not influence all those who practice it. Occasionally, friends or pupils would pass on remarks of this kind to me in what they thought was a spirit of devotion. Little did they know, however, that I did not see this as devotion at all. And much to their embarrassment, I felt compelled to explain what I consider to be a fundamental rule in human behavior: Never pass on second-hand negative information to the person to whom it applies.

This has nothing to do, of course, with sharing confidences with a friend, which, on occasion, may even include harsh criticisms of others. Whoever has not spoken disparagingly about another person, let him cast the first stone! We have all, at times, expressed our disapproval or discontent about someone to an intimate friend. In its best sense, this is a way of formulating an opinion, and testing it out on someone you trust. If you go further, and actually confront the person who is the subject of your criticism, then two things are achieved. First, it is actually a way of expressing your high regard for that person, of saying in effect, "I admire you, but certain behavior problems on your part are making me uncomfortable." And second, the very fact that you can openly and sincerely verbalize your true feelings elevates the substance of your remarks above that of cheap gossip.

Few things are more destructive of a friendship, however, than the passing on of a confidence, when someone to whom you have confided something suddenly turns tattler. Of all the ignoble traits in human beings, tattling must surely be one of the lowest. A tattler is, to be sure, a betrayer, and betrayers reveal their mal-intent as soon as they pass on negative information, whether they were sworn to secrecy or not. However well-meaning a tattler may claim to be — "I feel you ought to know!" "I'm going to tell you in order to protect you!" etc. — there is, as I see it, some hostile or self-serving intent beneath the veneer of so-called devotion. In fact, tattlers are known to exaggerate and distort facts in order to serve their own ends. For whatever reason, and however you look at it, nothing justifies the passing on of negative information to anyone.

The Demons Within

Shortly after my leave-taking, one of my pupils was offered his first concert tour, which included concerto dates. Judging from the tone of our conversation, I assumed that he was asking for my opinion as to whether he was ready to meet such a challenge. He happened to be one of those musicians whose ambitions far exceed their preparedness. He was not ready for such a tour, and I told him so. In an instant, he was on the attack. He not only disagreed with my assessment of his preparedness, but he also voiced his suspicions as to what he thought motivated that assessment: "You're discouraging me from accepting the tour because you never had a big career!"

Most teachers would dismiss a pupil for being so impertinent. But I have always held to the belief that whatever the disagreement, a breakup should be the last resort. Although I was deeply hurt by his remark, I feel that teachers can be just as effective as caring parents by exercising patience in the face of such rebelliousness. Besides, he was sufficiently gifted, intelligent, and personable to have warranted my patience and forgiveness for over twenty years. He and I were very close. Our relationship was marked by seriousness and an abundance of good humor.

To return to our difficulty, I tried in all fairness to view his comment from the proper perspective. Quite obviously, the infrequency of my public performances before my leave-taking could result in my being accused of sour grapes: "He gave up because his career wasn't going anywhere." My pupil, however, ought to have known the real reasons for my leave-taking, for I had often discussed with him my desire to develop my creative gifts. And besides, even if what he said had been true, it was insensitive of him to blurt it out as he did.

We discussed this. But after an hour or so of attempting to reason with him, I found that he still would not admit to his lack of preparedness. That he would so misconstrue my advice, and, in the process, cast aspersions upon my integrity, went far beyond my patience. As I saw it, he secretly felt guilty about his lack of preparedness, and he converted his guilt into hostility towards me.

Interestingly, this pupil had often passed on negative information to me. In this area, he always admitted to his mal-intent. As a matter of fact, he often spoke openly of his personal battles with his "demons," as he called them, who "seem to rule my behavior!" Accordingly, any criticism of him from me qualified me for "demonship." By discouraging him from accepting the tour, I touched the nerve center of his laziness and irresponsibility about practicing — the two chief demons of his own making. I saw his audacious outburst towards me as the consequence of my having penetrated to the core of his discontent.

As it happened, my pupil accepted the tour anyway. His unpreparedness notwithstanding, he could at least boast that he was a legitimate touring concert artist — which was, I believe, more important to him than the standard of his playing. He returned home with glowing accounts of his success. Because self-deceptive people are rarely objective about themselves, I could not trust his evaluation of his playing. The years which followed were marked by one deception upon another — to himself, to music, and to me. Finally, his repeated transference to me of his self-hatred led to the dissolution of our relationship.

Though we had no contact for around seven years, I knew from mutual friends that he had gone on to establish a successful career as a teacher, and a modest, but also successful, career in performing. When he was forty, he contracted AIDS. Speaking about teachers being surrogate parents, I felt as though my own son were dying. I visited him near the end. All discontent from the past vanished. The visit was marked by apologies, forgiveness, and tears. I lost a child.

EARLY STIRRINGS

With the playing of my farewell recital, all ghosts of indecision vanished — never to return again. While most of my family members and close friends were profoundly saddened by my decision to quit the solo stage, they gave me, nevertheless, their abiding love and support. My mother, however, was not in the least surprised by my decision, for she remembered how creative I had been as a child.

Children express creative impulses more freely than adults do. Because they have not as yet been taught to suppress their feelings, they scribble their drawings or make up little poems without inhibition. Everyone expects children to do these things, and family members and teachers alike show genuine enthusiasm for all such spontaneous creations. The year I spent in kindergarten, for instance, was devoted exclusively to self-expression. We were all given paper and crayons and encouraged to give free reign to our creative urges. For most students, however, everything changes from first grade on. Crayons are replaced with a curriculum which often bypasses self-expression entirely. Regarding those creative impulses in children which continue to surface from time to time, it is quite common for adults to see them as passing phases of childhood.

The Chalk Box

My own early school years proved to be the exception to the rule. All of my creative gifts, musical and otherwise, were enthusiastically encouraged both at home and during the eight years I spent in grade school. For one thing, my 6th grade homeroom teacher, Mrs. Ar, was, to my good fortune, the art teacher as well. Under her guidance and encouragement, my talent for art flourished — to such an extent, in fact, that I won first prize in an all-state poster contest.

One day, while she was lecturing to the class about Africa, she asked me to create jungle scenes on a large roll of brown paper taped along the entire length of the classroom. To this day, I can still recall those tingling sensations which are so much a part of the creative process. And I can still see and also feel the powdery surface of those multi-colored pieces of chalk lying row-upon-row in a large wooden box. For all intents and purposes, I was the Douanier Rousseau. Tropical growths, animals and birds of unknown species — all came tumbling out of my imagination. Thereafter, I created other murals for each country under discussion.

As I think back to that time, I marvel at the naturalness with which those dream-like figures streamed out of my subconscious mind. But I marvel even more at the fact that Mrs. Ar allowed me to do this during the formal part of the teaching day. That most of the students seemed more interested in watching me than listening to her seemed not to faze her in the slightest. In time we all got caught up with our facts. As far as Mrs. Ar was concerned, she clearly defined her own pedagogical priorities: one student, at least, would preserve his creative fire.

Once I entered high school, however, not a single teacher took notice of my creative talents. I played the piano a great deal, to be sure. But what of my paintings and poems, and my general need to create? Was I now to think that being creative had nothing to do with growing up?

Inner Voices

Creative expression now became my private domain. Even when nothing in particular stimulated me, still, notions, ideas, and inspirations coursed through my head. In my childish imagination, I viewed these stirrings as belonging to a secret world within me, a world where an inner voice whispered commands. It was the voice of some nameless authority, and I simply had to obey it. It compelled me to convert feelings into forms and structures. For example, every occasion, were it a birthday, an anniversary, or a death in the family, inspired a poem. On a less lofty level, I also built model airplanes, wove elaborate objects out of beads, designed terrariums, and even tried my hand at photography.

None of these activities, of course, would have been possible without a conducive home environment. To be sure, I was given material things — a piano, paper and paints, and a modest allowance for photographic supplies. But all of this was eclipsed by something far more important — the love, support, and enthusiasm of my mother and sisters. All was not perfect, however: I had a lot of difficulty with my father.

Being the only boy in a household dominated by women, and having a father who seemed like a stranger to me, could very easily have had its drawbacks. In my case, however, fate intervened in my favor. When I was six, Frank Lozowick began courting my eldest sister, Lillian. Shortly afterwards, Saul Armm declared his affections for my middle sister, Sylvia. Both Frank and Saul became my brothers-in-law when I was twelve. And, finally, my youngest sister, Evelyn, married Arthur Zorn when I was seventeen.

As far as I was concerned, I had three sisters plus three bona fide brothers. They took me with them to functions of all sorts — ball games, the circus, the movies. And they treated me to meals in restaurants where I was introduced to new and exotic-tasting dishes. They also delighted in buying me things — toys and games of every description, and construction kits that fired my imagination. In fact, it was Saul who bought me my first camera, a so-called box camera, consisting quite literally of a simple black box and a shutter.

Darkroom in the Cellar

Seeing the prints of the first roll of film taken with my box camera triggered a passionate interest in photography — one which has lasted throughout most of my adult life. From the moment I saw those prints, I acquired a wide-eyed enthusiasm for everything associated with taking and processing pictures. Soon, a small storage area in the cellar became my darkroom. By fastening a latch on the inside of the door, I made it serve another function as well — that of a secluded sanctuary. Having my own room in a rather crowded household was no small thing to a twelve-year-old boy. I spent hours there, experimenting with and improving the various techniques used in photographic processing. At other times, I simply sat there, lost in my own thoughts. How often I heard my mother's voice calling me to dinner, I cannot say. "I'm coming, I'm coming," I would scream back from my haven in the basement. But in all truth, I had no intention of coming until I had finished processing the roll of negatives freshly immersed in the developer. Besides, I relished every moment I could find to be alone in my sanctuary.

Years later, when I was twenty-five, and through no design of my own, photography actually became a semi-profession. As it happened, the portraits I took of my musician friends in New York City often appeared in concert brochures. Before long, other musicians, and concert managers, too, took notice of them. One day, a pianist telephoned me and asked for a sitting. "This has got to be a hoax call!" I thought. But as he continued to ask questions, and especially when he inquired about my fee, I suddenly realized that I had a prospective customer on my hands.

As a portrait photographer, I may have lacked certain professional skills, and I certainly did not have the kind of lights and other equipment that one finds in professional studios. But I did have one important asset: being a musician myself enabled me to "talk music" with my musical subjects. I was, therefore, able to elicit from them that flash of naturalness, that "divine moment" which all photographers watch for and try to capture. Occasionally, when subjects were particularly self-conscious, I suspended the sessions temporarily and asked them to play or sing for me. Once they resumed posing, they were invariably more in touch with themselves.

On one occasion, when the tenor Charles Bressler seemed particularly ill at ease, I went to the piano and accompanied him on the first few songs from Schumann's *Dichterliebe*. Secretly, but with the best intentions, I turned on my tape machine before going to the piano. Returning, then, to the photographic session, I played back the tape to him. His utter surprise and his total absorption in listening to his own singing produced spectacular results: self-consciousness gave way to animated facial expressions which showed Charles at his best.

In time, taking portraits of musicians became profitable enough to help pay my rent. While it was certainly unusual to be paid for something I did out of sheer love and interest, there was, nevertheless, something unsettling about it. The fact is, I simply could not equate self-expression with money. As a result, fees handed me for performing, teaching, or taking portraits of musicians, while satisfying a need for economic security in one sense, embarrassed me in another. It was like being paid for the privilege of loving something.

21

To this day, I continue to feel uneasy about accepting fees. It is not that I am impractical: I do, after all, quote fees for engagements and to new pupils; I even pluck up enough courage to be business-like with some pupils who cancel lessons far too frequently. Yet I do this with a pervading sense of uneasiness. I feel easier offering scholarships or reduced lesson fees to gifted pupils who can barely eke out a living — a seemingly never-ending problem. In spite of parental trepidation, and in spite of all that is written concerning the difficulties of making a living in music, there seems to be an ever-increasing influx of young aspiring musicians — all devoted to an art that scarcely promises economic security. Because I pursued my passions unconditionally, and because I know what it is to live on pasta alone, my heart goes out to such pupils. The irony is, however, that by reducing my fees, and sometimes suspending them altogether, I have occasionally placed myself in a position similar to that of the very pupils I help!

THINK IT, DO IT

In certain people, and more so in children, thought and action are one and the same. I remember, for example, spiraling a football better than other boys in my neighborhood. No one taught me how to do this; I simply imagined the football soaring through space, and as if by magic, my entire body harnessed itself to actualize my concept.

Similarly, the overwhelming beauty within music scrolled through my whole being in search of an outlet. For one thing, it chose my fingers, which, of course, had subsequently to be trained. But it also found a comfortable habitat within my vocal cords, activating them as naturally as breathing itself. Without training, I sang in a clear, resonant voice, and loud enough, I thought, to be heard at the far ends of the earth. I sang everywhere — in school, in the synagogue, and at social functions. And I remember enjoying the expressions of approval on the faces of my audiences. They took me seriously, and showed complete absorption in what I was doing.

Music was life: the hours spent at the piano, the songs we sang in school, and the march music which Mrs. Conlin, one of my teachers, thumped out on that old grand piano as we filed into the auditorium for assembly programs — all became a living part of my daily routine. Hymns, especially, filled me with deep emotion. Even today, the simplest harmonic progression elicits a corresponding spiritual association, and with it, an inclination to bow my head in prayer. Small wonder, then, that I loved to attend religious services in churches — not for religious reasons, but rather for the sheer inspiration of listening to the choir and the organ. At such moments, music *was* my religion. Through it, I thought, God spoke to me in a language which even so-called religious people could not comprehend.

"I Hear America Singing"

The grade school which I attended, Chancellor Avenue School, was separated from Weequahic High School by a lawn some one hundred feet wide. In fact the classroom windows overlooked those of the high school. Three times a week throughout the school term the high school chorus rehearsed *I Hear America Singing* — that rapturous choral work by Howard Hanson set to a poem by Walt Whitman. Considering my proclivity for vocal music, it is not difficult to imagine how those sounds affected me. The melodies and harmonies floating across the courtyard, and especially the harmonic progression to the line, "The varied carols I hear," all fell upon my ear in waves of ecstasy. Time and time again my homeroom teacher, Mrs. Eagen, was obliged to call me to attention, so transported was I by the music. I imagined myself accompanying that chorus, an image which did nothing much to restore my concentration on my studies. That I actually fulfilled this fantasy at the age of sixteen was a fact I could hardly believe. Whether the choral conductor, Mrs. Archer, was equally enthralled with this work, or whether she simply had a limited repertory, I cannot say. I only know that life took on a different meaning when she handed me the Hanson score on the very first day of rehearsal. To live out my childhood fantasy, to soar on the piano while surrounded by vocal sounds, brought me a happiness unlike anything I had ever known.

The Ultimate Gift: Freedom to Experiment

The spontaneity that guided my hand in creating murals in school found another outlet on the keyboard: chords that defied analysis, elaborate configurations, and swirling *glissandi* — all constituted my own language for improvising sound dramas. Invariably, they began softly and slowly, and subsequently grew into a storm of torrential passages up and down the entire length of the keyboard. Then the intensity slowly subsided and gave way to a calm after the storm.

As I think back to my childhood, I cannot say what occupied my time more — improvising or sight-reading. I remember one thing in particular, though: discovering the music department of the Newark Public Library when I was fifteen. Like an awe-struck archaeologist in the presence of a find, I stood transfixed before the seemingly endless shelves of musical treasures. Every Saturday morning thereafter I took the local bus to the library and staggered home under a mountain of scores: solo and chamber music works, vocal scores, piano reductions and transcriptions of orchestral works and operas — I hungrily devoured all of them and replaced them with new scores on the following Saturday. Though I sight-read and improvised for hours on end, no one in the family seemed disturbed; nor did anyone criticize me for not practicing my lesson assignment. This I did anyway in my own good time.

Not all children are given the freedom to express themselves as I was. Often when children suspend their practicing to improvise or to sight-read, well-meaning parents, even performers among them, will cry out, "Stop that fooling around, and get on with your practicing!" No one, of course, would rule out the importance of supervision in a child's musical development. But to forbid "fooling around" entirely stifles the creative bent in a child and ultimately inhibits musical development. Someone in the family must exercise a balance between freedom — what a child feels like doing, and discipline — what music requires of us all. It is not easy to find the right kind of supervision. The responsibility falls upon the teacher to be constantly alert and make whatever suggestions are necessary.

No one in my home supervised my practicing. And while I did a lot of fooling around, I did manage to learn a great deal of repertory. To begin with, I adored my teachers, and I would do anything whatsoever to please them. Moreover, I loved the pieces they assigned to me; whatever period, whatever style, each one was a new musical universe. These two things, then — my desire to please my teachers and my love of music — were the chief factors that motivated me to practice.

My Beloved Mama

And someone else motivated me — my mother. She adored listening to me play. She would often leave her cooking and come over to the piano with requests for her favorite pieces. It seems that when she was a child, she begged to have piano lessons. Unfortunately, her family was too poor to afford them. Nevertheless she taught herself to play certain pieces by ear, and she would, on occasion, delight me by playing one of them. It was a maudlin piece, replete with tremolos, like a silent film accompaniment.

My mother, Nellie Haberman, was born in Warsaw, Poland, in 1895. She was the next to the youngest of seven children — four girls and three boys. She was only three years old when the Habermans immigrated to the United States. The family settled in the Harlem district of Manhattan. She met and married my father in 1913 when she was eighteen, the very year that her mother was dying of diabetes. Sadly, the marriage ceremony took place at her mother's bedside.

My beloved mother at eighty.
(Photo by Seymour Bernstein)

At seven with my dog Scottie.

I mentioned earlier that I had three older sisters. But before I was born, my mother conceived a fourth girl who unfortunately died at birth. Close relationships between mothers and sons are not unusual. But the fact that four girls preceded me perhaps made my appearance all the more special. It also contributed to my being rather spoiled.

By the time I was in my teens, my mother thought that I was simply too idealistic for my own good. Never one to interfere in my life, she voiced loud complaints, nevertheless, about certain pupils who she thought were taking advantage of my generosity. "Stop being so good to everyone," she would say. "Look after yourself for a change!"

However perturbed my mother may have appeared at such moments, there was a part of her which *shepped nachas* (Yiddish for experienced pleasure) from everything I did — my generous ways included. All of my artistic aptitudes were her joys. And she wanted everyone else to know about them, too. When I was three, for example, she had me sing, dance, and recite poems for practically everyone who came into the house. She was not a stage mother, by any means. On the contrary! Stage mothers dominate, control, and exploit their children for their own selfish ends. My mother, being the proverbial earth mother, was careful never to place her own interests above my own. She held to this unconditionally, even at the expense of her own creature comforts.

Seeing me perform as a child, one might have thought I was a perfect angel. But in all truth, I could be just as naughty as any other little boy — a fact to which my sisters, especially, can testify. Their recollections of my childhood pranks paint me as being more devilish than angelic. I taunted them mercilessly, and I took impish delight in hiding behind walls and suddenly jumping out at them. I nearly frightened my poor sister Sylvia to death once doing this. My mother did not take it lightly, and administered the occasional spanking.

Punishment from a parent defines other things, too. Spankings from my father, for example, whose very presence terrified me, increased my hatred of him; while those from my mother, although they certainly were not pleasant, were somehow tolerable and soon forgotten. I sensed that her anger signified merely another aspect of her love for me, in which reprimand was meted out justly and fairly. Reprimands aside, my mother knew that her Sonny had special gifts, and she was willing to go to any extreme to protect them. If this necessitated her siding with me against my father, then so be it. Little did she know, however, that opposing my father on my account merely aggravated the strained relationship that already existed between him and me. In fact, the conflict with my father may have precipitated the devilish aspects of my behavior.

Music, the Strongest Signal

Of all the artistic signals which took possession of me from early childhood on, music was the strongest one. We did not own a piano until I was six, but I remember visits to Aunt Ethel's apartment, where I had my first encounter with an old upright piano. While family conversation resounded all around me, I picked out melodies with my index finger. Instantly I was transported into a magical world of my own making. Even though I was only four, I knew I belonged in that world. There was something about caressing those keys that enabled me then, as it does now, to "touch the sky."*

Fascination, when it is allowed to run its course, can grow into a passion. So it was that my passion for music took possession of me at the age of six, when the parents of my brother-in-law Frank gave us their upright player piano. To have a keyboard all to myself, to be able to experiment with musical sounds as often as I wished, filled me with an indescribable happiness. My mother, seeing my total absorption in the piano, took it upon herself to find me a piano teacher. This was quite a tall order for someone who knew nothing whatsoever about music education. She simply queried each person who came into the house — the milkman included. "My daughter gives piano lessons," he responded. And that was how I came to have my first piano teacher. Lessons were arranged for Saturday mornings. The fee was 50 cents for an hour. I was by that time a little more than six years old.

My first piano lesson was like the beginning of life itself. My teacher, Rita Robey, was, according to my childish fantasy, a goddess with supernatural powers in her fingers. I emulated everything she did — her facial expressions included. My chief intent was to delight and please her, so that when she assigned me two or three pieces from a particular book, I learned the entire book within the week. She did not realize this until one day, when she asked me to sight-read a new piece, I simply played it from the beginning to the end from memory. Fortunately for me, she was astute enough to supply me from then on with ample repertory to satisfy my insatiable appetite for music. Curiously, various pieces I encountered sounded familiar to me — like re-establishing a lost relationship. When I discovered an arrangement of Schubert's song *Ständchen* (Serenade), for example, it seemed as if I was reliving some experience from the past. To my ears, it was the most beautiful piece in the whole world. No amount of

---

* Sappho (Bergk, 37), translated by Flora R. Levin:
  I never dreamt
  that with my own two hands
  I could touch the sky.

repetitions could satisfy my craving for it. Nor did it ever occur to me that anyone else in the house was listening to my playing. My mother, though, became alarmed at one point. Awakened early one Sunday morning by the mournful strains of the Serenade, she rushed downstairs to find her *zeenala* (Yiddish for "little son") weeping at the piano. Puzzled, and delighted, she simply took me in her arms and wept along with me.

While I had no idea how to practice, I communed, so to speak, with each piece available to me. As a result, I did in part what all good practicers ought to do: I sight-read continually and approached music spontaneously, repeating entire pieces or sections of them over and over again simply to satisfy my love of them. The fact that my technique did not keep pace with my enthusiasm did not seem to faze me in the slightest. My sole intent was to express myself, however inaccurate and innocent the results may have been. The whole world seemed contained at that keyboard, a world in which the composers whispered their secrets to me. Since no one at home opposed my enthusiasm, I spent as much time at the piano as I wished. There were, of course, relatively few hours after school when I could practice the piano, which made having to go to Hebrew school an unmitigated torment. On weekends, though, I sat at the piano most of the day, and it confused me when my mother or father would occasionally tell me to leave the piano and go out to play, as though I were missing out on life by spending too much time at the piano. What, in fact, constituted life, I wondered — the social world, or the world at the piano? Everyone else seemed to think that it was the former. But as far as I was concerned, music, far from being an escape from life, was life itself. Although my mother was never caught up in anything whatsoever which might have led her to a similar realization, she somehow understood everything that music meant to me, and that ultimately music was my destiny. She saw to it that nothing and no one would obstruct my path in fulfilling all that she thought I was meant to be.

Thus did I spend my childhood expressing my passion for music without having the slightest notion of what a career in music actually meant. Nor did my teacher ever so much as suggest that I might be qualified to have a career. Not being a performer herself, she knew nothing at all about how to prepare me for performing in public. Small wonder, then, that my technique was sorely neglected. For I believe that only teachers who perform or have performed themselves are best qualified to teach performing skills to their students. But while Rita Robey and my other early teachers failed me in this area, they certainly compensated for it in another: love, encouragement, inspiration — all these things they gave me in abundance. I, in turn, reciprocated their love in the only way I knew how — by practicing to the best of my ability. I practiced so diligently that I somehow found my own solutions to technical problems; unorthodox fingerings and hand positions notwithstanding, I at least was able to get through my pieces in some respectable fashion. It was not unusual for me to have ten or more pieces ready to perform at any given time. In fact, I was far more comfortable playing for people than I was talking with them. For music, even more than language, supplied me with a viable means of communication — one which was not only direct, but also natural for me.

First Crime!

As everyone knows, a lack of conscious understanding can very easily subvert the very things we do naturally. One day, my teacher actually assigned me a piece to be memorized for the following lesson. She wrote the word "by," meaning "by memory," on the upper right hand margin of my music. I knew, of course, what the word "memorize" meant. But, still, I had not the slightest notion of what I was expected to do in order to memorize music consciously. I suddenly became self-conscious about a process which had previously been automatic. Each time I opened my music and saw the word "by" scrawled on the top of the page, I experienced both anxiety and embarrassment at my own ignorance. Since the piano was my exclusive domain, it never occurred to me to ask my mother, sisters, or brothers-in-law for assistance. My childish sensibilities told me only one thing: I had, somehow, to remove this irritant from my life.

One day, then, when I was sure no one was watching, I erased the word "by" from my music. Even as I did so, I knew I was committing an unpardonable crime — and a pre-meditated one, at that. As I think about it now, I am appalled at how desperation and confusion led me to erase my teacher's instruction. It drives home how much responsibility teachers bear and the consequences of their ignorance. In my case, I stopped playing from memory altogether. I also wondered why my teacher never made mention of my having erased the word "by," which I kept on doing after each lesson. Was I actually getting away with my crime? Or was her silence, in effect, an admission of her inability to teach memorization? At nine, of course, I could not imagine my goddess teacher having any deficiencies at all. It was my own deficiency, my own crime, and I had to keep it a secret from everyone. Needless to say, my progress was seriously hindered by guilt and confusion.

First Trauma

As I soon discovered, there is no substitute for methodical practicing. I was still nine years old when, at a moment's notice, a teacher in school asked me to perform a solo on an assembly program. Saying yes to playing for others, and always doing it well, had been my habit. This time, however, the vastness of the darkened auditorium, plus the memory problems I had been battling with, made me self-conscious from the start. Nevertheless I dashed into an arrangement of *The Flight of the Bumblebee* by Rimsky Korsakoff with my customary zeal. That I stopped abruptly in the middle of the piece was as much a shock to me as it must have been to my audience. My embarrassment was heightened by the beam of a spotlight aimed at me. I waved my arms frantically so as to signal the person in the control booth. But the spotlight persisted, like an accusing finger, and all the while my spirit shrank in disgrace. Unable to bear my shame one moment longer, I dashed from the piano and sought refuge in the darkened auditorium. Nor did my shame lessen when the spotlight finally went out.

As though my sense of failure was not punishment enough, I had also to endure a sharp reprimand from the teacher who had asked me to perform. Passing me in the hall later that same day, she stopped me abruptly. Fire shot from her eyes. Placing both of her hands upon my shoulders, she shook me violently and shouted, "How dare you stop like that right in the middle of a piece! You ruined my program!" Totally crushed, I responded as might any other little boy of nine; I simply lowered my head and began to cry. Not that my tears diminished the teacher's anger in the slightest. She shook me several more times, muttered something under her breath, and stormed away.

Determination

My own sense of failure and the teacher's irrational response to my memory lapse traumatized me for some time afterwards. In fact it was months before I was able to play in school again, or anywhere, for that matter. In time, though, I drew several conclusions that helped me to understand why the breakdown occurred: one was what I mentioned earlier — that I simply did not know how to memorize music; the second was an awareness of just how vulnerable I could be while performing for others. Concerning the first, I eventually learned the proper procedures for memorizing music. Concerning the second, the truth is that my sense of vulnerability merely increased through the years, this being one of the more unpleasant corollaries of performing. That I continued to perform in public, in spite of the threat to my security, led me to a third conclusion.

31

Perhaps I had something, at least, of what it takes to be a performer: if not a phenomenal talent, then certainly enough courage and perseverance to compensate for whatever I lacked; if not a perfect technique, then at least one that was adequate enough to express my deepest feelings about music. By the time I was fifteen and met my first serious teacher, Clara Husserl, I knew one other thing: performing was a challenge I was going to meet head-on. Whatever difficulties I would encounter, however long it would take, I would perfect, as far as possible, the skills necessary to survive a performance. I sensed something else, too, something that sparked my determination throughout my life: through this process, I would strengthen the person, as well as the musician.

I have concluded that the capacity for hard and consistent work is the greatest gift of all — a gift that can make a modestly talented musician sound prodigious. For when one stops to think about it, nothing worthwhile in life can escape the "refiner's fire" (Malachi, 3.2), that organizational beauty and logic which results more from devotion and application than from native gifts alone. Devoted practicers, therefore, are worthy of the most extravagant praise: though they are just as fearful as anyone else, they can eventually perform heroic feats in front of others; though they have modest gifts, they can, nevertheless, rise above their own limitations to Olympian heights and even make significant contributions to the world. In the words of Gilbert Highet:

> And one certain truth about the great works of the mind — inventions, philosophical systems, poems and plays, pictures and music, scientific discoveries and political institutions — is that many of them were made by men who started life in ordinary, even unfavorable, situations and then far outsoared their origins.*

Determination alone, then, is the fuel that propels us to transcend our shortcomings. Without it, nothing worthwhile can be accomplished; without it, a career in music is not possible.

A Time of Innocence

I do not intend to bore my readers with reminiscences about how much better life was in the good old days. But I should like to mention one thing:

---

* Gilbert Highet, *Man's Unconquerable Mind* (New York: Columbia University Press, 1954, 12th printing, 1970) p. 33.

the 1930s was, by today's standards, a time of innocence. And innocent, too, was the manner in which my family spent its leisure hours. Even though New York City theaters and concert halls were at the most forty-five minutes away from Newark, we could neither afford to attend such functions, nor were my parents and sisters particularly interested in doing so.

A Saturday evening, for instance, might be spent at home listening to the radio, singing around the upright piano, trying out the latest dance steps, or, if the weather permitted, roller-skating on the intersection of Keer Avenue and Schley Street. The four corners were cordoned off; children, teenage couples, and adults, too, roller-skated for hours on end under the glow of the street lamp. There were no sophisticated skates in those days. Ours had four wheels and were made entirely of aluminum. They clipped onto our shoes by means of small side brackets which threaded onto a long, key-controlled screw. Turning the key clockwise guided the brackets towards each other and tightly against the protruding rims of our shoes. Alas, scabbed and scarred knees testified to the fact that this was not the safest means of diversion; a skate would fall off, a wheel would jam, or we might inadvertently roll over a segment of uneven pavement. Any of these things, and we would take a spill. All told, those skates were as hard on us as their wheels were on the street pavement. But if I did injure myself, I could always count upon my mother's healing powers to make everything better.

Butter Kuchen

All of us, I think, have our own particular associations with people we love, as we do with certain objects or events. Not surprisingly, I came to associate my mother with *Kuchen*, a butter-yeast cake which she laced with chocolate, cinnamon, and nuts. The cake seemed to symbolize her nature. The very manner in which my mother labored over its preparation — the kneading of the dough, the way it rose and filled the refrigerator overnight, and, above all, her cheerful attitude during the whole ritual — epitomized the atmosphere of wholesomeness, goodness, and motherly protection that I was fortunate to experience. I still see myself, literally at my mother's apron strings, pleading for a taste of that raw, butter-flavored yeast dough. "You'll get a stomachache," my mother warned me. But she gave me a sizeable chunk of the dough anyway, and sometimes, even a second piece. Ingesting that dough was, in a sense, like absorbing all the goodness of my mother. To me, that *Kuchen* was the essence of what we imagine a mama to be.

In November of 1990 my mother developed heart failure and lay in a coma in a Florida hospital. Suddenly in the middle of the night, she opened her eyes only long enough to say to me "I love you." She never spoke another word. It was her final bequest, a spiritual treasure which I cherish. She spent the last five days of her life in a hospice. I lived in the room with her and held her hand as she died on December 2nd. She was 95. The most comforting words came from my sister Sylvia, who summed up my mother's life: "Mother lived totally for your benefit, not merely *for* you, but *through* you. By helping you to fulfill yourself, she justified her own life. I'm sure she saw you as her greatest accomplishment."

Self-sacrifice does not always result in positive ends. Some parents who live through their children ruin their lives, and everyone else's. My mother's love for her *zeenala*, however, defined love as it was meant to be. I have already stated how that love influenced me. But I also see it as having had the most positive effects upon my mother — even beyond her sense of personal gratification. For just as misery is self-generating, so, too, is love; and love can propel itself into a life-sustaining force that promotes health and well-being. Thus I believe that my mother's love for me actually prolonged her life, that it sustained her through some difficult times, and that it kept her mind razor sharp until the coma silenced it some five days before her death.

I am the greatest beneficiary of that love. Whatever I have accomplished in life, whatever I have been able to contribute to others, I owe mostly to my beloved mother.

THE DARK CLOUD

Clearly, to have had such a mother, three sisters, and three surrogate brothers, all of whom loved and supported me, was good fortune. As one might imagine, it served to create a foundation of security and confidence from which I draw today. It served another purpose too — that of lessening the devastating effects of a dark cloud that hovered over me from early childhood on. It saddens me to say that the dark cloud was my own father.

Born in Russia in 1885, my father, like my mother, was one of seven children, three girls and four boys. He was fifteen when he came to the United States. During his processing at the immigration office on Ellis Island, he spoke his name, "Max Blisnak," as clearly as he could. But because of his Russian-Yiddish accent, the immigration officer could understand neither "Blisnak" nor his attempt at pronouncing each letter of the name. In desperation, then, my father arbitrarily chose the name "Bernstein," which the officer finally understood and recorded.

Unable to support himself at first, my father lived in an attic room in Newark, New Jersey, in the home of his sister Ethel and her husband

Beryl. He continued to live there even after he married my mother thirteen years later. He first went into the burlap bag business and later became a scrap metal dealer. Finally, when he became more solvent, he and my mother moved into a cold water flat on Bergen Street in Newark, the apartment where I was born.

Like so many fathers, he had a concept of just the kind of a person his son ought to be. But the fact is, I was the antithesis of his concept. The effects of this were blatantly apparent — at least to me: he was morose, severe, and angry in most of his dealings with me. For one thing, he would not tolerate conversation or my boyish joviality at the dinner table. Stern rebukes such as "Stop talking, and eat!" or "Act like a man!" were quite common. When his scoldings went unheeded, a slap in the face would squelch my exuberance and induce a stomachache, besides.

One evening we had a guest for dinner, a business acquaintance of my father's from Holland. Afterwards we stood around the living room, my father towering over me, and his friend towering over him. It was my father who initiated the discussion — something about my being too sensitive and not manly enough. The Dutchman sized up my ten-year-old frame and arrived at what he thought was a perfect solution: "You should train to be a feather-weight boxer," he said, his eyes sparkling with a sort of diabolical glee. "You certainly have the physique for it!" I cannot recall my father's reply, but I remember shrinking into the floor in utter horror and embarrassment.

Desperate people clutch at straws, and my father, seeing my artistic development as being contrary to all that constitutes manliness, would no doubt have taken seriously any suggestion whatsoever that might reverse things. Whatever the reason, he arrived home a few days later with a pair of boxing gloves. One glance at them and panic overtook me. It got worse when my brother-in-law Frank fastened them around my wrists and took me outside to the back yard for my first boxing lesson. He jabbed me lightly to my right shoulder, fully expecting me to retaliate, or at least defend myself. When I did neither, he jabbed me so hard that I was knocked over and burst into tears. That was it for the lesson. So much for toughening me up.

Becoming a Jew

Regarding my religious training, my father had strong ideas about this, too: I was to become a "real Jew" — whatever that meant. When I was six, the same year I began taking piano lessons, a venerable rabbi came to the house to begin tutoring me. With his white beard falling down to his vest, his wide-brimmed hat, and his long black coat, which seemed to touch the floor as he walked, he certainly cut a menacing figure at first. When he spoke, however, his eyes gleamed and his voice revealed a gentle, loving nature. As the lessons progressed, I developed a genuine affection for him, which prompted me, I am sure, to learn my *alef-bet* (the first two letters in the Hebrew alphabet) in record time. Both he and my father were delighted with my progress.

The following year, my father enrolled me in Hebrew school. It was adjacent to an orthodox synagogue which my father attended only once or twice a year during the High Holy Days of *Rosh Hashana* and *Yom Kippur*. The class comprised approximately ten students ranging in age from seven to around fifteen. Lessons lasted from 4 to 5 PM — Monday through Friday. It ought to have been a stimulating and productive experience. Yet the course consisted only in teaching us to read and write Hebrew and Yiddish and to recite certain Hebrew prayers from memory. *What* we read or recited seemed inconsequential; we merely parroted the rabbi in a mindless, albeit somewhat efficient, manner. To make matters worse, each year brought with it a new crop of beginning students — and always of disparate ages. This necessitated having to start the course all over again. It was pointless to explain this to my father. As far as he was concerned, I would invent anything at all to avoid going to Hebrew school.

I cannot say with what bitterness and resentment I trudged each day to Hebrew school. With the time it took to walk there and return home, in addition to the lesson itself, more than two precious hours were lost to me entirely — hours in which I would have preferred to practice, to work at my various hobbies, or simply to play out of doors with my friends. Pleadings to my mother were of no avail. She knew better than to oppose my father on religious matters. In the end, it was a question of either going to Hebrew school, or facing my father's wrath.

It did not take very long for me to discover the purpose of this mindless, mechanical instruction: we were to make our fathers proud of us by being able to read any section whatsoever of the High Holy Day prayers at services in the synagogue. I can still hear my father prompting me with "louder, louder!" And I can see him exchanging proud glances with all the men standing around me. I, of course, could only think of the price I had to pay to make my father proud of me. Those were moments when I hated him more than at any other time.

By the time I was nine, I was already wrestling with severe conflicts. On the one hand, my father would brook no discussion concerning Hebrew school: "You'll continue, and that's that!" On the other hand, he seemed bent on erasing the joy and wide-eyed wonder of my childhood. I saw him as a dragon who, when aroused, would consume me in fire. To defy him was unthinkable. Though a dragon, he was still my father, and aren't fathers god-like figures whose every command must be obeyed? "Hide your hatred," I thought, "or certainly that real God up there will find a way to punish you!" I paid a heavy price for repressing my loathing of my father; persistent headaches, stomachaches, and various other neurotic symptoms were some of the consequences I suffered. Shameful as it sounds, I often wished my father and the rabbis dead. The more I entertained such thoughts, the more guilt-ridden I became.

Parents are teachers, and there are even more bad parents than there are bad piano teachers. I spent a good deal of adult life unlearning what my father and several piano teachers taught me. Bad piano teachers can be replaced, of course. But parents and children are biologically chained together. A parent can disown a child, or vice versa, but biology can't be denied.

"Come back when you're thirteen!"

To put it bluntly, my father and I were stuck with each other. And as far as being a teacher is concerned, he was the proverbial hopeless case. On the other hand, I must concede that some of his innocent attempts at sex education are some of the most amusing memories of my childhood. An example of this occurred when I was eleven and trying my best to handle something my sister Evelyn's boyfriend Arnie told me — that men peed into women, and that's how come women got pregnant and had babies. Disgusted and horrified, I rushed to my mother hoping sincerely that she would repudiate all of this: "Arnie was only teasing me, wasn't he, Ma?"

My poor mother was completely taken aback. Much as she was sympathetic and adaptable to all of my needs, this was simply too much for her to deal with. Although she had been living in the United States since she was three, she had retained much of the old world. For one thing, sex and all discussions concerning it were taboo. Under the circumstances, then, she did an admirable job in containing herself. Her response to me was, no doubt, similar to what her own mother might have said: "Ask your father!"

We lived then at 350 Keer Avenue in Newark, New Jersey. It was a modest home having two floors plus a basement and an attic. It was Sunday morning, and my father was on the second floor leisurely shaving himself. I knocked at the bathroom door, timidly to be sure, and he ushered me in just as he was scraping away the soap from his face. I sat on the flush cover close to the sink where I could see his face. I then repeated to him what Arnie had told me. Suddenly, the razor froze in its tracks. It appeared to me as though a long silence ensued. When finally he found his voice, he said with an artificial calm, "Come back when you're thirteen!" And without so much as a glance in my direction, he went right on shaving. Being far more perplexed than when I first approached my mother, I simply slunk out of the bathroom.

Life to a child is a constant series of kaleidoscopic vignettes, and by the following morning, I had completely forgotten what Arnie had told me. Then a few days later, the doorbell rang. It was a delivery man with a huge carton of Bernar McFadden Health Books. Being an inquisitive little boy, I tore open the carton and took in all six books at once. I was particularly fascinated by the fold-out models showing the skeletal and muscular properties of the human body. Data on various illnesses and their cures flashed by. Then I came upon a section entitled "Intercourse." Since that word was unfamiliar to me, I bypassed this section entirely.

That this health encyclopedia was my father's answer to my question never so much as crossed my mind until some ten years later. Concerning what Arnie told me, I eventually discovered the truth about this from my friends. In those days, neither parents nor our educational system knew how to deal with this delicate subject.

Becoming a Man

While I was not a man according to my father's criteria, I would soon be sanctioned as one anyway — at least according to Jewish law. I was twelve, and there was much discussion and excitement concerning my upcoming *bar mitzvah*, the Jewish rite of passage from boyhood to manhood. As far as I was concerned, however, it meant only one thing: liberation from Hebrew school.

Attending Hebrew school from Monday through Friday was trying enough. But now, my father ordered me to attend services at the synagogue every Saturday morning as well. *Shabbes*, the Jewish Sabbath beginning Friday evening and lasting until sundown on Saturday, was the day reserved for *bar mitzvah* ceremonies. And since my own *bar mitzvah* was a year hence, my father thought I would benefit from watching other boys go through the ritual.

Weekends, of course, were the only days I had free from school. It was a time for music, for creative projects, and for sheer fun. Now, according to my father's new dictum, I would have to spend six days of every week in my least favorite place — the synagogue. If six years of wasted time in Hebrew school was my father's first error in judgment, "the last error shall be worse than the first," to quote the Bible itself. A circle of rebellion which had been slowly building up within me was now complete. I knew that a violent confrontation was imminent.

Rabbi Cohen, the chief rabbi of the synagogue, tutored all the boys and girls for their *bar* and *bas mitzvahs*. While everything about the school and the synagogue was hateful to me, one aspect of my new training proved to be surprisingly pleasurable. It was the part of the *bar mitzvah* service which called for chanting. All music affected me deeply — whether it was playing my favorite pieces on the piano or intoning the sacred text of the Torah. Since neither the Torah nor the text itself had any significance to me whatsoever, I looked upon the whole experience as merely another opportunity to raise my voice in song. I was doing very well, and the rabbi seemed pleased, when one day I had the misfortune of mispronouncing a word. In an instant, a large gnarled hand shot out across the sacred text and slapped me on the cheek. I remember being more insulted than hurt, and I bit my lower lip to keep from crying. From that moment on, I knew I had two dragons to deal with.

In fact I developed a fear of most older men, with the exception of my brothers-in-law. For example, I would go on an errand for my mother to the drugstore. It was one those general stores in which you could buy practically anything. I remember the ice cream counter on one side where you could buy a fudge sundae with real whipped cream for fifteen cents. The proprietor was a charming man and always greeted me with warmth and affection. One look at him, though, and a defensive mechanism was set into motion: I tightened up inside and I would blush for no apparent reason. I had the same reaction in the presence of other proprietors of stores, male teachers in school, and even older male relatives. At nine, I had no notion of what caused those symptoms. Thinking about it now, I believe that I transferred a fear of my father to most older men.

Two things helped me shed this neurosis: One was my father's death; the other was the satisfying relationships I enjoyed with my brothers-in-law, my surrogate brothers. The attention they lavished upon me compensated for my father's total lack of personal involvement with me. Had it not been for them, I might very well have retained this neurosis throughout my life.

The day of my *bar mitzvah* arrived. I would imagine that an average boy or girl of thirteen would view that day with a sense of joy and accomplishment. To me, however, it was fraught with as much anxiety as were those later days of important piano recitals. While most performers are subject to pre-concert nerves, even without having had a *bar mitzvah*, I have often wondered whether the sheer panic I felt while standing on that pulpit may, in fact, have remained with me throughout my performing

The *bar mitzvah* man at thirteen.

career. As far as performing is concerned, musicians can learn to play well in spite of their nervousness simply by taking certain preventative measures. Years of performing experience have taught me about the importance of having tryouts, for example, with one of them being at the concert site, if possible. But now at my *bar mitzvah* ceremony, an entire year of having been merely an observer proved to be no substitute whatsoever for the real thing, any more than being a member of the audience can prepare a musician for the stage. Imagine, then, how I felt, suddenly finding myself standing on the pulpit of a synagogue and staring down at the Torah — all for the very first time. And the fact that I was the center of attention in front of an overflowing audience certainly did not help matters any. Becoming a man...? That was the very last thing I could identify with. Only one thought crossed my mind: If I did not do well, if I were to forget any part of the ceremony, it was not God's retribution I feared, but, in a very real sense, that of my father and Rabbi Cohen. The latter stood at my right, appearing more as a threat than a support. "Boinstein, vhat's de matter mit you, Boinstein — are you sick or something?" he muttered in alarm as I began intoning the first of a long series of prayers in a barely audible voice. I stood my ground, though, in spite of a pasty mouth, a tight knot in the middle of my stomach, and the rabbi. The ceremony seemed to last forever. It included recitations in Hebrew, chanting from the Torah, and two speeches, one in Yiddish and one in English. In my innocence, I thought that the final words of my speech meant liberation from seven years of my own kind of bondage — a leave-taking at thirteen. Then, however, the circumstances were far different from those of my farewell recital. For one thing, there was a dragon waiting in the wings. And my farewell to Hebrew school was the very last thing he had in mind.

Confrontation

That night, during a celebration dinner at home, my *bar mitzvah* ceremony was quite naturally the chief subject under discussion. In the best of spirits, and with that sense of relief which performers come to know so well, I expressed my happiness at never having to attend Hebrew school again. With this, my father put down his knife and fork. "What!" he shouted, "You think your Hebrew training is over just because you were *bar mitzvahed*?" I felt myself grow pale in utter disbelief. That he expected me to continue going to Hebrew school was the very last thing I could have predicted. In an instant, years of repressed rage exploded, and before I knew it, my speaking voice took on all the power which it had lacked on the pulpit. "I'll never go back there, never!" I shouted. "You can punish me, you can say whatever you like, but you'll never make me go back to that school — ever again!"

I thought my father was going to kill me. His fists came crashing down on either side of his dinner plate, sending shock waves the length of the dining room table. His body recoiled against the back of his armchair. And in another instant, the momentum sent him and the chair backwards, spilling him onto the floor.

While my mother and three sisters all rushed to my father's aid, I sat frozen in my seat with only one thought in mind: "I've killed my father!" But he was neither dead nor injured. The chair was righted, and the patriarch, having been helped to his feet, took his seat once again at the head of the table.

When some moments had gone by, and my father seemed to have regained his composure, my mother spoke up. As I have said, she never opposed my father on religious matters, but now his stance must have tried her patience to the breaking point: "Seven years, Max — seven years! Why should he continue on in Hebrew school? After all, he's not going to become a rabbi. It's enough. He should have more time to practice, and to be in the fresh air. No more Hebrew school, and that's final!" My father, still dealing with the humiliation of having tumbled to the floor, must have found the added burden of my mother's protestations too much to handle. Whatever the reason, his temper was entirely defused. And in a meek voice, no longer that of a dragon, he responded quite simply, "All right, all right," and went on eating.

Everything changed after that. Conceding to my mother was tanta- mount to acknowledging her control over my destiny. The fact that the dragon was brought to submission ought to have brought me a sense of relief. But it caused my father to erupt even more often and violently, and the cloud grew even darker.

My Son, the Junkman

Since I was the only boy in the family, my father quite naturally looked forward to having me in his business. When I was fourteen, he insisted that I spend the summer working in his junkyard. I found it abhorrent, and no doubt my feelings were written all over my face. This, of course, did nothing to improve our relationship. As the summer months wore on, my father grew ever more irritable in all of his dealings with me. I particularly dreaded the times when we were alone, such as during coffee breaks and lunches. Then, the silence between us merely heightened the tension that already existed. If anything good came out of my brief encounter with the scrap metal business, it was that my passion for music and my determination to make it my life's work grew stronger than ever. It proved how opposition can strengthen one's resolve. In fact I have always thought that my father's total disinterest in my musical ambitions made me practice all the harder.

My parents would have enjoyed an ideal relationship had it not been for me. From the time of the chair-falling incident on the day of my *bar mitzvah*, my mother opposed my father on almost all issues where I was concerned. She knew that practicing was a vital part of my life, and she let my father and everyone else in the family know that my need to practice had to take precedence over everything else. I marvel to this day how she managed to maintain a balance between her devotion to me and her obligations to my father and sisters.

Everything seemed to be going comparatively smoothly until one spring night when I was fifteen. My father approached me about working again in his junkyard that summer. Fortunately, my mother was not far away, and she announced to my father, "He's going to practice during the summer, so forget about him working for you or for anyone else — and that's that!" My father didn't take that too well and he argued this point with my mother: "He ought to be working at something during the summer," as though practicing was not work. "It won't hurt him to learn what life is like outside of the house. Besides, he should be earning some money, like other boys do." My mother handled his obstinacy in the only way she knew how. When my father returned home from work the following evening, she did not prepare dinner for him. My father had lost ground once again, and all because of his musician son.

Three Daughters and a Pianist
At whatever price to his vanity, my father had finally to accept the fact that my destiny lay in music, and not in the junk business. When in my late teens I began winning contests and gaining a modest recognition as a pianist in New Jersey and New York City, his attitude changed considerably. From that point on, he became surprisingly generous in his support of my musical activities. He was not rich, by any means, but there was always money for whatever I needed — the rental of halls, managerial fees, clothing, etc. But even though he went through the motions of supporting me, something within him could never wholeheartedly accept my choice of career. I remained an anomaly to him — and he to me. In fact, when he was asked how many children he had, his reply was always the same: "I have three daughters and a pianist!" There was more than irony in his reply. Brought up in a society that frowned upon music as a career for a man, he was deeply distressed that his own son was a

musician. Similarly, I was embarrassed to tell my teachers and my musical friends that my father was a junkman. We were caught in a hopeless web of incompatibility — to such an extent, in fact, that I can recall only one circumstance in which I was not uncomfortable in my father's presence, and that was when we listened to one particular radio program together.

In spite of all the differences between us, my father and I had one thing in common — sentimentality. He, more than I, would often weep openly at the slightest provocation. Every Sunday afternoon he and I listened to a radio program entitled "The Greatest Story Ever Told." It was an ongoing series recounting incidents in the life of Jesus. Listening to a radio program, of course, precludes conversation, and this was no doubt the fundamental reason why it was the only pleasurable thing we ever did together. At any rate, when the voice of Jesus spoke in parables at the end of each half-hour segment, my father sobbed uncontrollably. If only we had not been strangers to each other, if only I had had more courage, I would have asked him why he wept: was he secretly drawn to Christianity, or was he simply responding to the significance of the parable? Considering that my father had so little connection with me and my aspirations, I also found it more bizarre than touching that he wept when he listened to me play certain pieces: was he moved by the music, did he regret his past behavior towards me, or was he finally proud of his son, the pianist?

He is gone, now, and I will never know the answers to these questions. He died of liver cancer in July, 1964, at the age of seventy-nine. I was thirty-seven. Ironically, my father, so far-removed from me in life, died in my arms. Near the end, I was the only person whom he allowed to perform certain hygienic necessities which he could no longer handle, though he once slapped me when he thought I had overstepped the boundaries of propriety.

It was not until I was around fifty that I was finally able to utter the truth of my feelings: I hated my father. Even today, the mere thought of him invokes a montage of unpleasant images from my childhood:

He is about to leave the house to go deep-sea fishing with his friends. I plead with him to take me along. He ignores me. I am left with an overwhelming sense of rejection — a theme that repeats itself throughout our relationship.

I see him in the cellar of our home in Newark, determined to teach our full-grown police dog, Scottie, to stand on his hind legs. He holds a large shovel in one hand, and grasps Scottie's collar with the other. But Scottie, like me, cannot satisfy my father's expectations. I can still hear the howls of pain as the shovel comes crashing down repeatedly on Scottie's haunches. My father's sadistic rage is mounting, and I scream, "Stop it! Stop it!" But he ignores me and continues to beat Scottie.

And finally, there are images I can never forget: I am three, perhaps four. I'm with my father in the bathroom of our apartment on Payne Avenue in Newark. He's toilet-training me. I see he has an erection. Now I am six. We are alone in the living room on Keer Avenue. I am sitting on his lap on the sofa. He is stroking my genitalia.

I believe my father lived in fear that I remembered these episodes. His general irritability, his attempts to suffocate my nature, and his constant habit of avoiding my glance all seemed to be symptomatic of this. I see his behavior towards me as a protracted psychological shovel-beating, a futile attempt on his part to beat down the past in the hope of obliterating it entirely. It was not I, of course, whom he psychologically, and sometimes physically, beat. Rather, I became in his eyes a symbol of his guilt for the things he had done to me. He wasn't punishing me or Scottie; he was punishing himself.

Curiously, no one else in the family suspected what had gone on repeatedly between me and my father. They attributed the tension existing between us to my father's disappointment at not having me in his business, and to a general incompatibility. Besides, my father affected a certain normalcy when in the presence of my mother and sisters — a normalcy such as might have existed between any father and son. He even addressed me as "pal" (he pronounced it "pel"), as though he and I were the best of friends. I remember as a child actually wincing at the very sound of that name. If anything, his calling me "pel" merely intensified the emptiness of our relationship.

I am now profoundly saddened to think that I never knew that sweet exchange that can exist between a father and son. Instead, I had to cope daily with my father's neuroses, which he transferred to me through his actions, his words, or simply by the look in his eye. Small wonder, then, that I wept more profusely at his passing than did my mother and sisters — not out of love or affection, by any means, but rather for the father I never had.

Solitude

As I see it, people have to do something in life that draws them out of themselves — something apart from the monotony of daily routine and petty considerations. My father had no self-consuming interest whatsoever, and nothing, therefore, to divert him from his own pain. I, at least, was able to lose myself entirely in my practicing and all of my creative projects. Apart from the support I drew from my mother, sisters, and brothers-in-law, I also had a surrogate family consisting of teachers and stimulating friends. In their presence, all conscious thoughts of my father vanished.

When I reached my thirties, I established a retreat in Maine, a sublime home on a cliff looking out to the Atlantic. I refer to it as my Shangri-La. There I spend months in seclusion, months during which I am able to tap the best within me. During such hours of reflection, I have been able to gain a perspective on all that transpired between me and my father. Recently, a neighbor, knowing of my predilection for long stretches of solitude during the summer months, offered her own observation on this subject: "You must really love yourself to spend all of that time alone!" "I suppose I do," I answered, much to her astonishment. To admit that you love yourself sufficiently must come as a shock to those who have never faced themselves in solitude. Paradoxically, my capacity to draw close to people, and even my right to do so, is, to my way of thinking, a direct result of the work that I do when I am alone. For what better thing can a person contribute to others than that rarified knowledge gained through self-discovery?

Was it childhood abuse that made me turn inward? I cannot answer this question, for people turn inward without ever having been abused. In a broader sense, when profound thinkers attempt to define those highly complex nuances which characterize life's survivors, or works of art, the whole construct changes with the next individual, the next work of art. I feel certain however, that genetic programming or environmental influences alone were not the only factors which helped me to survive. I am referring not only to the problems with my father, but to my career as well.

Because my thoughts about this are closely related to music, I should first like to express my views regarding musical creations. While I might see a Bach Cantata as a manifestation of God's voice, I know that it was not God who created it, but a person. As my friend Flora Levin put it, "Music is the meaning and value given to a world not of God's creation, but of man's."

The point is, works of art, like healthy, productive people, do not simply appear by God's decree. On the contrary! Most artistic creations are the result of human struggle. Easy answers usually come to those who never make an attempt to out-soar their limitations.

If solitude can reveal the best that is within us, how does a person develop the capacity to be alone? And how do we muster the energy, the patience, and the sheer motivation to follow a project through to its end? In my opinion, it all begins with the establishment of a sense of dignity about yourself. Though my father tried to diminish my dignity, I fought him to the end to preserve it. As a boy, it seemed to me that preserving my dignity was, in a sense, preserving my life.

Having a sense of dignity enables people to know their place in the scheme of things. Inexperienced performers, for example, should be encouraged to program whatever they wish. But when they show a lack of technical security and suffer frequent memory slips, they could turn failure into success simply by playing less difficult pieces and using their music when they perform in public.

The stage is like life itself — one vast battlefield where performers learn survival tactics. In life, the battle commences from early childhood on. To be sure, we have to deal with the enemy from within — our own destructive selves. And there is the enemy from without — people who want to make us prey to their destructive impulses.

Children, of course, see parents and teachers as all-loving, all-supporting. Until I was about five years old, my own child-like innocence and trust veiled any such notion of destructiveness on the part of my father. On the contrary! Anything that went wrong between us I thought to be my fault. In other words, all feelings which deviated from that embryonic bliss from which I was not so far removed indicated my own questionable behavior. I must have done something to displease my father. I was just plain bad.

Forgiveness

It is especially disillusioning to discover human failings in a parent or a teacher, not to mention coming face to face with our own frailties. The question is, does a confrontation with our frailties teach us to understand them and, subsequently, to forgive them in others?

I do not believe that forgiveness is always a virtue. Moreover, I see the word forgiveness intrinsically connected to another — "responsibility." These two words, "forgiveness" and "responsibility," interact in a never-ending stream of conflicts. In my opinion, children, being too young to be responsible to anyone or to anything, ought to be forgiven for practically everything. But adults...? Ought adults to be forgiven for being irresponsible, for creating chaos and causing emotional or even physical pain in others?

On this issue, I side with Roger Carbury, that steadfast and highly moral character in Anthony Trollope's novel *The Way We Live Now*. While there is much of the intractable in Carbury, his virtues, nevertheless, are sufficiently impressive to inspire my forgiveness of this fault. At any rate, early in the novel, when Carbury has real cause to believe that his close friend may win the woman whom he himself loves, Trollope briefly but firmly expounds upon forgiveness:

> Roger Carbury did not quite believe in the forgiveness of injuries. If you pardon all the evil done to you, you encourage others to do you evil! If you give your cloak to him who steals your coat, how long will it be before your shirt and trowsers will go also?

One argument would be that people who repeatedly act irresponsibly and do hurtful things to others do not behave like adults to begin with. Though I might rationally accept this fact about my father, I have difficulty, nevertheless, in forgiving him. At this point it ceases to matter to me why and how his emotional development got stunted, and what the circumstances of his own childhood were that led to this. As far as I am concerned, irresponsible people ought to be categorically rejected for two important reasons: the first is an obvious one — self-preservation; the second is that irresponsible people may reverse their behavior rather than bear the pain of rejection. I have seen the positive effects of rejection in my relationships with various pupils, for example. Just as rejection is deserved, forgiveness is earned. In other words, forgiveness ought to be reserved only for those who make an attempt, at least, to act responsibly.

Conflict is not always a bad thing. As a matter of fact, psychologists tell us that it is indispensable to the development of the personality. Whether the good effects of my own conflict with my father have outweighed the bad, I cannot say.

No Ticket, No Praying!

I have learned one important thing about the painful experiences with my father — that they will never go away. My father's tyranny over me, the things he did to me when I was a mere child, remain barriers around which I will have to veer all of my life. Moreover, the mere thought of an Orthodox Jewish service stirs up a veritable tempest within me. An incident which occurred shortly after my father's death did nothing to endear organized religion to me. As it happened, my father changed his membership to another temple after he and my mother moved to Millburn, New Jersey. In the pain and confusion that followed his death, none of us was aware, or even cared, that his membership had expired. It was once again the High Holy Days, and my mother felt a strong compulsion to say *Yiskor* (a prayer for the dead chanted during the service of *Yom Kippur*, the day of atonement) in memory of my father. My mother's wish, of course, was stronger than my aversion to the synagogue, so I agreed wholeheartedly to escort her there.

Upon entering the foyer of the temple, we were confronted by a row of stern-looking men sitting at a long table and wrapped in *tallithim* (Jewish prayer shawls). "Where's your membership card?" one of them asked. Knowing nothing about the custom of presenting a ticket before entering a temple, as one would do to attend a concert, I explained the circumstances of our being there — that my father had died recently, that he had been a member of the temple for more than ten years, and that my mother wanted to say *Yiskor* in his memory. I might as well have been giving them the weather forecast, for they sat there with impassive expressions. Finally, the one in the center who had originally spoken to us fairly barked a reply: "Sorry, you can't go in without a membership card!"

His unreasonable manner, and, I am sure, my years of sublimated rebellion against Hebrew school training, instantly transported me back to that explosive scene at the dinner table on the day of my *bar mitzvah*. As a matter of fact, neither before this incident nor since have I ever experienced a rage of such intensity. My shouts of "Hypocrites!" echoed throughout the temple proper and disrupted the service itself. Had it not been for the restraint of a policeman on duty, I most certainly would have overturned the table at which the men were sitting and hurled it at them. Almost at once, a dozen or so men rushed out of the service to see what all of the disturbance was about. One of them, who happened to be the owner of a local supermarket, knew my mother well. He was mortified to see her standing there crying. While I told him what had happened, he darted glances over his shoulder at the men who were still sitting sternly at their table. Moved and angry, he insisted that we use his own tickets to gain entrance to the temple. My poor mother, hysterical with grief and embarrassment, thanked him for his kindness. She did finally say *Yiskor*, while I stood silently beside her, still white with rage.

My mother never again asked me to take her to the *Yom Kippur* service. Nor have I ever again attended a religious service in a temple.

Regrets and Reflections

Certain of my feelings towards my father have gone through transformations. He no longer frightens me. Rather, I see him as a pitiful, misdirected man whose chief passions were making money and playing cards. I have regrets, too. One is that I never asked him about his own childhood. Perhaps he was abused by *his* father, and so — the sins of the father.

Most people, I believe, are victims of their early environment. But because human nature is so complex, it is difficult to pinpoint the reasons why one person succumbs to childhood maltreatment, while another rises above it. In thinking about my own childhood, I would like to stress two things in particular which I believe helped me to survive my father's tyranny.

The first point, which I touched on previously, concerns my acceptance of the irrevocable fact that the past, and all the images associated with it, will remain in my memory forever. The second concerns my ability to create a life for myself apart from my family. I did this almost entirely by pursuing my passion for music, a passion which left me little time to dwell upon the past. Whatever measures we take, however, and no matter how hard we work at eradicating the past, we carry it around with us throughout our lives. Painful as the truth may be, therefore, I have chosen to face the fact of my childhood abuse, and get on with my life.

All of this is not unlike dealing with pre-performance anxiety. As I see it, performers have two choices: either they deplete their energies trying to rid themselves of nervousness, or else they accept it for what it is — an indication of being responsible to their art, to themselves, and to others. Thus, responsible performers, those who are prepared to the best of their ability, are quite open about their *right to be nervous*. Seeing pre-concert nervousness as a natural concomitant of performing, they invest their energy where it is really needed — in their practicing. In the end, responsible musicians play well, in spite of their nervousness.

If it is any help to others who battle with problems similar to the ones I have discussed, I would like to stress one more fact: working at something larger than we are, like music, enables us to create a harmony within ourselves. We are then "in a position, if not to eliminate, at least in some way to counter-balance the discords pressing in on us from outside," as Goethe said.

The memories of my father occasionally flood back and overwhelm me as though they are happening at the moment. But I'm good at repression and at creating defensive mechanisms. One image helps me a great deal: I imagine myself living in a protective dome, one that has become increasingly impenetrable. Through its translucent walls, I can discern the dove from the raven. Sadly, I see my own father as one of the ravens. Psychologically, at least, I have had to disown him, as I have certain friends, managers, and teachers. They are all there, outside of the dome, but they cannot enter my world. I am convinced that the only antidote to negative influences from the past or present is the ability to immerse oneself in some worthwhile and satisfying activity. And this, fundamentally, is the reason why I teach people to practice conscientiously.

THE STATUS OF MY CAREER

My artistic experiences in childhood might best be described as having been natural and spontaneous. These are no substitutes, however, for the kind of practicing that can prepare a gifted young musician for a career in music. The inescapable truth is that my technical growth did not keep pace with my musical comprehension. This, and all the other deficits I have mentioned, finally caught up with me. As a result, by the time I entered my teens, memory fears loomed up like serpents ready to strike at unpredictable moments. The fact that I eventually overcame much of this fear through deductive reasoning and by sheer perseverance ought to encourage other musicians who may be grappling with this same problem. One thing that conscientious practicing teaches you is that difficulties which may at first seem insurmountable can be overcome through clear thinking and by consistent effort. The fact that I actually succeeded in performing difficult programs with a minimum of mishaps, and even received critical praise for my efforts, is, as far as I am concerned, nothing short of a miracle.

Around the time of my farewell recital, my career was a modest one. In fact, I never had the kind of career enjoyed by some of my esteemed colleagues. Critics often commented about this in their reviews:

Tokyo — 1960:
If it is Seymour Bernstein's aspiration — and I venture to guess that it is — to rise into the ranks of the world's great pianists, it rests not with him, but with the world to make this aspiration come true. (Hans Pringsheim)

New York — 1969:
If his recital yesterday afternoon in Alice Tully Hall was not merely one of those freakishly great days that good pianists sometimes enjoy, Seymour Bernstein is ready to break out into a wider circle of attention. (Donal Henahan)

New York — 1978 (from the review of my farewell recital):
It is a pity that, given the modesty of his bearing and the subtlety of his art, Seymour Bernstein will probably never be as widely appreciated as are dozens and dozens of lesser pianists. (Joseph Horowitz)

While it is embarrassing for me to quote these glowing reviews (heaven knows, I have had my share of bad ones, too), nevertheless, they confirm

51

the status of my career. To begin with, it would be unfair to hold the world accountable for my not having risen "into the ranks of the world's great pianists." Frankly speaking, if anyone is to blame for this, it is I: while I aspired to having a performing career, I never wanted to have a major one; I never wanted to "break out into a wider circle of attention," nor did it faze me in the slightest that I was never as appreciated as "dozens and dozens of lesser pianists." And why? In the first place, I never thought my talent warranted such acclaim. Secondly, everything associated with careers — traveling, dealing with managers, coping with inferior pianos, constantly being urged to indulge in career-building tactics, such as being seen in the right places in order to meet the right people, etc., etc. — all of this was, and still is, repugnant to me. In matters of repertory, too, I was firm and inflexible and would simply not play the game. For example, I did not enter certain competitions when the required repertory neither suited my temperament nor added to my total development. I could no sooner draw close to certain pieces than I could to certain people.

I once forfeited a contract with a major recording company simply because I could not bring myself to learn the repertory required of me:

> PRODUCER (after hearing a tape recording of a recital I
> gave in Alice Tully Hall):
> You don't have to be told how well you play. But the truth
> is, artistry doesn't sell records. Of course, if you would be
> willing to learn all the *Etudes tableaux* of Rachmaninoff
> [the one in *E* flat minor was included on my tape], then
> we might talk business.

A big record company will rarely sign up a performer who is not a superstar — unless, of course, it serves a commercial purpose. In this case, the inclusion in their catalogue of all the *Etudes tableaux* happened to be one of the company's high priorities. "There is nothing like a big package deal to entice customers," the producer told me. But since learning all of these pieces was the very last thing I wanted to do at that time, we never did "talk business."

The sickening realization that emerged during the early stages of my career was that certain producers, managers, and teachers succeed in dominating, coercing, and controlling performers merely because performers say "yes" to everything. Desperate to find engagements, some performers will do absolutely anything to augment their careers, even when it is against their musical and personal well-being. In extreme cases, desperation can lead to a breakdown of moral and ethical principles.

You Pay, You Play!

Often, it is difficult to know right from wrong when making a musical or personal decision. Certainly I would not be critical of a pianist who agreed to learn the *Etudes tableaux*, even though he or she disliked them. In the following account, however, my decision to turn down a chance at the big time was predicated upon a principle, rather than on my own musical tastes:

The telephone rang. It was my manager:

MANAGER:
Are you sitting down? Kabi Laretei was scheduled to make her debut with the London Symphony Orchestra in Carnegie Hall on Wednesday (it was then Monday). I just received a telegram from her saying that she has pneumonia, of all things, and will have to cancel. How would you like to fill in for her?

S. B. (My heart skipped a beat, but I tried to maintain my composure):
What concerto would I have to play? (As though I knew them all!)

MANAGER:
You choose it: whichever one you like.

S. B. (I paused for a few seconds, trying to think of which concerto I could work up in two days):
Will the Liszt *E* flat do?

MANAGER:
Terrific! You're on. Now, there's one hitch: It will cost you $750!

This last remark from my manager caused a constriction in my chest, and with it, a building up of a familiar rage which once again triggered an association with my father. As a stalling tactic to regain my poise, I asked my manager to repeat what he had just said. In doing so, he added that the money would go to the manager of the orchestra. Almost before he reached the end of his sentence, my mouth seemed to form its own words:

S. B.:
Do you mean to tell me that I would have to pay for the privilege of performing with that orchestra? Even if you asked me for fifty cents, I would not be able to play one note under those circumstances. It's outrageous, and *you* are outrageous for suggesting that I be a party to this!

MANAGER:
Come on, get with it! You're in the twentieth century! You know very well it would cost you more money to rent a concert hall and give a recital in New York City. I'm offering you an opportunity to make your debut in Carnegie Hall with a first-rate orchestra. And you have the nerve to quibble over $750! If you won't play the game, then don't expect to have a career in music!

His last sentence was the only thing with which I could identify. I would not "play the game." Rather than compromise my principles, I preferred to forfeit engagements, and, instead, to stay home and practice; to draw close to the one thing in my life which embodied the highest principles of all — music. This was, of course, something which my manager could never understand.

The orchestra found a replacement without the slightest difficulty. And I am sure that several people, my manager included, shared the spoils of $750. Not long after this altercation, I broke with him entirely.

Not playing the game certainly has its drawbacks. If you refuse to deal with managers, then you have to be your own representative. This, as I discovered, can be demeaning:

CONCERT REPRESENTATIVE in New Jersey (She answered the telephone on my first try):
Yes, we are booking chamber ensembles for our forthcoming season.

S. B.:
I am a member of a Trio which has been performing for years, now. Ironically, we have been engaged in practically every state in the United States with the exception of my own home state — New Jersey.

CONCERT REPRESENTATIVE:
Oh, you're from New Jersey?

S. B.:
Yes, I was born in Newark, and received all of my early training and performing experience there.

CONCERT REPRESENTATIVE:
I'm terribly sorry, but you see, we never hire musicians who live in New Jersey. All of our artists come from New York City!

I was left with self-recriminations for not having had the presence of mind to say that my colleagues and I were, actually, based in New York City. As it happened, we eventually performed several times in New Jersey — but never on that particular concert series.

COMING TO THE END OF THINGS
Considering all that I have related thus far, it is not hard to imagine why I viewed my farewell recital at the 92nd Street Y as a pinnacle of my career. To begin with, it was a novelty to perform in New York City without having to pay for it. Moreover, to be part of a major concert series in the Mecca of culture brought with it a certain prestige which, I am not ashamed to admit, I enjoyed. And considering the modest course which my career had taken up until that time, I could not help thinking that I had "arrived."

I received a lot of praise for that recital. I even thought that there were moments in which I exhibited more control and introspection than I was accustomed to doing in public. I also felt that I generated a special dramatic intensity in *Funerailles*. I might add that my having placed it on the program had nothing whatsoever to do with the farewell aspect of that recital. If I showed anguish in my facial expressions during its perform-ance, as some of my friends reported to me, this merely reflected my own emotional response to the music. There was nothing funereal in my feelings when I reached the intermission of that recital. On the contrary! I felt nothing but liberation. My heart quickened at the thought of beginning a whole new phase of my life — one in which my creative bent would have an outlet at last.

People really do come to the end of things, provided that they are alert to the signs when they appear. It then takes the courage and resolve of a warrior to draw the curtain over the past. But beyond doubts and fears, beyond what other people want for us, and even at the risk of making errors of judgment, we brandish our sword of conviction and follow our calling. In the end, we discover that hard-won victories can bring the greatest rewards, and that a farewell may be the prelude to a brighter future.

PART 2:
MONSTERS AND ANGELS

Because I have a passion for teaching, it seems only natural that I express my views on the subject. As a guide to students of all ages and levels of accomplishment, I wish to describe my own experiences with teachers — those who were angels, and others who were monsters capable of destructiveness of the worst sort. Ideally, a good music teacher ought to be both competent and humane. But I have concluded that a teacher's personal credentials are more important than his or her professional ones. For even though teachers may lack certain professional attributes, their positive and supportive attitudes bring out the best in us. A teacher whose sole intent is to benefit us will send us elsewhere to fill in the gaps.

Teachers are powerful figures. Ask your friends to name the people who have influenced them more than anyone else, and the chances are they will point to teachers. Music teachers, especially, can have an over-whelming influence on their pupils. This is not too surprising inasmuch as the study and performance of music activates our deepest emotional responses. Understandably enough, because music teachers help us to shape those responses, they can penetrate to the core of our emotional world. Thus one comment from a music teacher, however innocent it may be, is enough to uplift us or cast us down into a pit of depression.

I have always been aware of the powerful influence that I have over my own pupils. Depending on the degree of personal interaction, that influence can be as far-reaching as it is varied: friend, psychologist, or even lover — I can be any or all of these things to my pupils in real or imagined ways. I can also act as a surrogate parent and compensate for a parent's deficiencies. It is not unusual for children to love their music teachers even more than they do their own parents. The opposite is also true: teachers can play havoc with young, impressionable minds, exactly as do some parents.

Curiously, the reciprocal effect of this personal and musical interaction upon teachers is hardly ever discussed. In my own case, I am aware that I

57

go through a process of self-analysis with each pupil I teach. In fact, the relationships I have established with my pupils tend to exert a strong influence upon all of my other relationships.

ORIGINS OF TALENT

Performing musicians, professional and otherwise, are among those who embody the highest standards of human achievement. Discipline, sensitivity, and courage are only a few of the many attributes which performers live out before their audiences. While such powers are audible and visible to everyone, the origin of talent has remained a mystery. Recent studies, however, suggest that the human brain is programmed to respond to music. Moreover, neurosurgeons engaged in a comparative study of the brain have observed in musically gifted people an enlarged area in the right temporal lobe, an area known as the *planum temporale* — evidence that would support the theory that musical talent is genetically ordained. This is not to suggest that a musical potential, even when it is of genius calibre, will necessarily develop unassisted by training. Quite obviously, it takes a combination of good teaching and consistent practicing to achieve the promise of genetic programming.

Certainly not all musicians are born with the potential of a Mozart, nor can training alone be credited with producing such awesome accomplishments. Somewhere in between the genius and the trained musician are those who are mysteriously drawn to music, even without ever having been exposed to it in early childhood. Many such people are late bloomers; that is, they may suddenly have a compulsion to begin piano lessons in their teens, or even later in life. The question is, are such ardent music-lovers candidates for the kind of serious study which may lead to a career in music? I have a hunch that a love of music may actually indicate a *talent* for music. Or, as a scientist might put it, spontaneous responses to music may be signals sent by the right temporal lobe, signals which indicate nature's preparedness, at least. If we would "let nothing pass that would advantage us," as the Roman censor Cato put it, then perhaps we ought to heed those signals and take seriously our spontaneous emotional responses to things. For those responses may be beacons which point the way towards the very career for which we are ultimately suited.

CHOOSING YOUR MUSIC TEACHER

Teachers can aid us immeasurably in following music's calling. When we are young, our teachers are chosen for us. There comes a time, however, when we can choose our music teacher. In the process of making this choice, we confront our strengths and weaknesses. In other words, we may choose a teacher even as we would a friend, looking either for someone who caters to our weaknesses, or for someone who helps us overcome them. Music students who in secret never intend to take themselves seriously gravitate instinctively to undemanding teachers. The opposite obtains with more serious students: they seek out teachers who challenge them to "out-soar their origins."

In a third category are students who have a mounting history of failures due to psychological problems. One of the chief symptoms that I have noticed in such students is a general rebelliousness against authority figures. Somehow, though, and perhaps because they have reached the lowest level of a downward spiral, survival instincts surface which are stronger even than their self-destructiveness. Something makes them want to save themselves. They need then to find a teacher who will be willing to do extensive rehabilitation work with them. I have worked with problem students whom other teachers have thought to be unteachable. With an abundance of encouragement, love, and patience on my part, and a superhuman determination on theirs, I have occasionally helped them to lead happy and productive lives. How is this done? By teaching them how to absorb within their own natures the order, the harmony, and the sheer humanity that one finds within music itself.

Whether students are responsible or not, they may be laboring under certain psychological burdens which play an unconscious role in their choice of a teacher. For example, masochistic individuals consumed with self-loathing want always to be told how untalented they are and how poorly they play. To be sure, there is a plentiful supply of sadistic teachers in the music profession who can be counted upon to mete out that sort of desired punishment.

When I think back upon all of the teachers with whom I studied between the ages of six and forty, I am struck by the fact that almost all of them were chosen for me. My mother selected the first three, beginning with Rita Robey and ending with Clara Husserl, my first important teacher. After that, the directors of various music schools which I attended, however briefly, selected my teachers for me.

At seventeen, it suddenly occurred to me that I might approach teachers on my own. On occasion, some teachers were sufficiently impressed with my playing to approach me. My choices were predicated upon one criterion only: I wanted to study with someone who would improve my technique. I am saddened to say that not one of these teachers helped me in this respect. And strangely enough, in my search for the best guidance, it never occurred to me to weigh a teacher's personal credentials as I would his or her musical ones. As a result, only a few of the teachers

I came to know qualified for "angelhood." Others actually turned out to be "monsters" of the worst kind.

Nothing is more disillusioning than discovering that your teacher is a full-blown monster. At first, you pretend that it doesn't matter, so long as you make musical progress. Later, though, you discover that your musical self and your personal self are not separate entities, and that when your emotional world is adversely affected by a monster-teacher, so, too, is your musical one.

As far as parents are concerned, it is not uncommon for them to look the other way, even when they suspect that a monster is governing their child's musical training. Egos being what they are, many parents delude themselves into thinking that a teacher is "just wonderful" simply because they themselves made the choice. Like my father, who would not believe my accounts of the sheer hypocrisy which I confronted daily in Hebrew school, some parents who hear similarly disparaging reports about music teachers tend to suspect their own children of having an ulterior motive: "You'll do anything to avoid practicing!" Thus, when a prodigy of eight (who later became my pupil) returned home from his piano lessons with accounts of constant physical and emotional abuse on the part of his piano teacher, his mother accused him of fabricating the whole thing: "Don't talk such nonsense! He's the most highly respected teacher in this whole area. I know what you're up to; you would rather play baseball than practice!" The lessons continued for four more years, until this poor child was twelve. By that time, he was so traumatized that the effects have remained with him to this day.

Having Two or More Teachers

No matter how important a teacher or a person is in your life, he or she cannot possibly be all things to you. I therefore encourage my pupils to seek out other teachers from whom they may gain new insights. Let no one think that seeking someone else's opinion would weaken the relationship with one's primary teacher, any more than new acquaintances would jeopardize an existing friendship. On the contrary: when teachers demonstrate their wholehearted interest in wanting to expand their pupils' knowledge, it only strengthens their relationship. I am speaking mostly of advanced pupils, high school age or older, although some prodigies I know are flourishing under the guidance of more than one teacher. Because prodigies amass a large repertoire within one week, most teachers simply cannot find the time to hear everything at a single lesson. In such cases a second teacher can be extremely helpful, both to the student and to the main teacher. Certainly for ambitious students of any age who also compose, two or more lessons per week or the help of a second teacher is mandatory.

I have coached students enrolled in music schools who either wanted to expand their knowledge, or else felt that they were not getting the proper training. Some teachers approve of their students' seeking extra musical guidance; others, however, frown on any intervention in their pupils' musical training. In certain cases, insecurity or sheer incompetence can make teachers defensive, vicious, and aggressive. One teacher I know expelled her student from a major music school when she learned that that student was secretly playing for another teacher. Ideally, students ought to ask permission from their teachers to play for other musicians. But when permission is not granted, students and clandestine teachers face ethical questions. In my own case, my concern for gifted students' development overrides all other considerations. To make a play on an old adage, pupils in need stir my conscience indeed. If I can aid in their development, I feel compelled to do so, whether their teachers approve or not. In a larger sense, I feel that I am serving the cause of music itself. I would also urge the directors of music schools to institute a policy that will allow students to seek advice from whomever they wish. For in the final analysis, we are all students before our art.

Does contradictory information confuse pupils and impede their progress? Ultimately, not in the least. Pupils need to be taught that musicians have strong convictions about musical and technical issues, and that eventually they themselves must arrive at their own convictions. Teachers, like devoted friends, can serve as a proving ground for pupils, thus helping them sort out information, even though it may be contrary to their own beliefs. In the process, teachers may learn a great deal themselves. As I see it, the pupil, not the teacher, must make the final decision.

As it happens, I am not alone in teaching or coaching students who study with other teachers. It is common knowledge, for example, that many gifted students enrolled in prestigious music conservatories and music departments in universities seek help from other musicians. This indicates two things: The first is that whether a student's teacher is competent or not, it is, in the long run, extremely beneficial to have other opinions on musical and technical matters; the second is that music schools are notorious for assigning to their faculties musicians who are either incompetent, or who are monsters masquerading as teachers. Among them are well-known performers who know nothing whatsoever about teaching, "has-been" performers who are forced by circumstance to teach in order to make a living, and once-excellent teachers who have become jaded and bored. These casualties of the music world seek and often find a secure haven in music schools. Once there, they satisfy two needs: they find an ample supply of victims upon whom they can vent their rage and frustration, and they get paid for it, too!

Teacher Shopping

Students enrolled in schools are usually assigned a teacher. When, however, music students are free agents and can choose their own teachers, I advise them to go "teacher-shopping." In other words, I see no reason for a person to feel bound to study with a particular music teacher without having one or more trial lessons, any more than he or she is obliged to accept one doctor's diagnosis without getting a second or even a third opinion. The idea that pupils should audition teachers, even as teachers audition pupils, is a neglected concept in music education. I encourage each person who contacts me for lessons to teacher-shop, either before or after coming to me. Moreover, I strongly advise them against studying with any teacher who is defensive about this. I make it clear that the first lesson with me takes the form of mutual auditioning. When the lesson is over, we part without feeling obliged to make a commitment, one way or the other. I then ask the pupil to telephone me several days afterwards so that we may discuss our individual responses to one another. Should we feel enthusiastic about working together, then we can both agree to establish a permanent teacher-pupil relationship.

"You're not contest material!"

Because music epitomizes all that is human, it is difficult to believe some students' accounts of inhuman treatment on the part of their music teachers — especially those who are associated with music schools. Certain comments made by some faculty members who sit on juries during entrance auditions reveal what I believe are distorted notions about the kind of student they deem worthy of conservatory training. In one such instance, a young woman of twenty-eight, having failed her entrance audition for Juilliard, later consulted with one of the distinguished jury members. "At twenty-eight, you ought to have played a flawless audition," he told her. "But judging from the level of your playing, you are certainly no material for major competitions. And considering your age, you could not possibly get ready to enter them in two years!" (The age limit for most competitions is thirty.)

Are we to believe that being able to play now, or in the future, like those thoroughbred instrumentalists who enter international competitions is the only criterion for being admitted to that school? As far as I am concerned, any teacher who expresses such views is unfit to teach music altogether. On the face of it, it is commendable to reach the performance level which one hears from contestants at major competitions. And certainly schools such as Juilliard and the Curtis Institute have a right to hold to the highest standards of performance. But this brings up several questions: Should not so-called master teachers invest their faith in students who have not as yet reached that level, but who, nonetheless, exhibit the promise of doing so? And more importantly, why are time limits placed on something so personal and so varied as musical development? Ought not a musician strive for a high standard of performance as an ideal unassociated with anything else — especially competitions? Besides, with all of the books and articles written about the pitfalls of international competitions — how trying to win them can become an end in itself, even at the expense of musical growth and personal well being, and how technical proficiency often wins out over musicality — one must question the competence of any teacher who would point to competition-readiness as the main criterion for measuring a prospective student's worth. Moreover, it is common knowledge that many artists who have enjoyed, or are now enjoying, major careers were eliminated from the first rounds of big competitions. Other world-renowned musicians openly claim that they would "fall apart" under the pressure of those marathons. For example, the late Rudolph Serkin, who often adjudicated at major competitions, never missed an opportunity to tell the altogether shattered contestants afterwards that he himself would not have been able to play his best under that sort of pressure. One wonders, then, why he lent his name to something that reduces music to so many tugs of war in which potential artists are eliminated and cast into the bin of oblivion, some of them never to be heard of again.

In light of this, music schools ought to rethink their aims and policies: First, they should make it clear that music study yields personal as well as musical benefits; second, they ought to get rid of destructive, ignorant, and misdirected teachers whose professional reputations, ironically, ensnare the finest talents from all over the world; third, they ought to make interpretive issues and composing primary aims of music study, and not just the acquisition of fast, accurate fingers. Finally, the directors of some schools ought to be ashamed of themselves for expecting young, sensitive artists to play their best during auditions on inferior pianos. Experienced musicians know that the more talented a pianist is, the more unnerved he or she may become when having to cope with uneven actions and malfunctioning pedals. Moreover, how can serious students be expected to play their best when anticipating being stopped in the middle of a beautiful phrase? "Thank you. May we hear your etude, please?" The fact that some young performers are unperturbed by such impediments to serious music making may suggest that they are as insensitive to music as they are to their surroundings. Thus students who never strive for anything beyond playing flawlessly get into the finest music schools and win international competitions. The prize is won, the very institution which sanctioned such mechanical emptiness shares in the glory, and the circle of false values is completed.

Speaking about international competitions, I have been a jury member for several of them. While judges may disagree about who the winner should be, there is, nevertheless, common agreement about one thing: there has never before been such a vast supply of technically astounding performers. While no one can state with certainty the cause of this phenomenon, many theories have been proposed. One of them suggests a genetic transference of musical skills from one generation to another. A more generally accepted theory points to improved teaching methods. My own pet theory is that we are at once victims and beneficiaries of our electronic age: on the one hand, an addiction to mindless television programs and loud and vulgar videos and CDs can impede independent and creative thinking; on the other hand, the very same electronic media can bring the finest cultural presentations into any home, even in the remotest parts of the world. The positive effects of this are not difficult to imagine: watching TV, for example, and seeing a young pianist receive a gold medal and a check for $15,000 as the first prize winner of an international competition is quite enough to awaken a secret longing for stardom in the hearts and minds of aspiring young musicians. "I can do that, too," a young pianist might think. "It's simply a question of practicing six to eight hours a day." The pianist does practice, and he does gain extraordinary proficiency on his instrument. Moreover, with the added help of a dozen or more videotapes and recordings of the works he is practicing, he can derive stimulation and information from any number of the world's greatest performers. You merely press a button and "the way it is supposed to go" is now available to you as often as you like.

Grand Deception

One would think that jury and faculty members who have themselves experienced the rigors of auditions during their own student days would extend to young hopefuls an extra measure of understanding. Yet some members of the adjudicating committees in music schools can be especially cruel to less experienced performers. In one case, Mark Preston, a gifted violinist who had memory lapses during his recital for a master's degree at Juilliard — his teacher had neither taught him memory skills nor even suggested that he have tryouts before his recital — received comments from the chief violin teacher which ran something like this: "This young man has no talent. He should never have been admitted to Juilliard. Clearly, he is one of our mistakes." Imagine, if you will, what effect these comments had upon this student, who had already survived three years of schooling at Juilliard. He was now led to believe that his acceptance into the school and his passing grades for past performances and course work over a span of three years were now considered to represent a mistake in judgment on the part of the faculty. The result: he became so depressed that he could neither practice nor even play his violin for two years.

But he survived. He switched to the viola and is now a respected member of the DaPonte Quartet. Concerning the violin teacher, students by the dozens lined up in the hall outside her studio, hoping for twenty minutes of her time — that is, if she showed up at all. Until her recent death she reigned supreme at the "Taj Mahal," as Peter Mennin, the former president of Juilliard, referred to the new white marble building at Lincoln Center during his address at the opening ceremonies. To Harold Schonberg, however, who was then the chief music critic of *The New York Times*, the comparison had a prophetic note. He was quick to point out that the "Taj Mahal" is a tomb! In many respects, the school has functioned as one. And why? Because a few excellent teachers are outnumbered by incompetent ones. It takes more than white marble to nourish talents. Far from nourishing them, certain faculty members have promoted their demise. For many students, the school has become a mortuary of snuffed-out dreams, unnerving competitiveness, and music lessons which, for all intents and purposes, are musically dead. Faculty members who either cannot teach or have no more patience for it simply do not want to be bothered with remedial problems. Why work hard when you can inherit students whose techniques have already been perfected by other teachers? Sadly, the faculty and the school deprive themselves of the privilege of rearing potential artists. But in the final analysis, a rejection from such a school can actually be a student's gain.

Some students are not even sure why they are at Juilliard to begin with. Many have been driven to pursue music as a career by overly ambitious parents or former teachers. Life for some of the most gifted ones is a boring, routine affair which centers primarily upon preparing for big competitions. While they may secretly be contemptuous of competitions and of their teacher as well, they will never say so. To admit this would be to acknowledge their willingness to compromise their art and their personal development for something as insignificant as a prize, on the one hand, and to study with a famous teacher at any price, on the other. After graduation, however, many students reflect upon the past three or four years with a bitterness they won't easily forget. One such student summed up his feelings about certain faculty members as follows: "Gather them all together and bury them with toxic waste!" Is it not tragic that a music student is led to speak of his teachers in such a hostile fashion? It is a commentary on disillusionment, shattered dreams, and the betrayal of ideals.

"Can you think of a four letter word for 'love'?"

It was, to be sure, disillusionment and a betrayal of his ideals that Bruce Brundage, my former pupil, experienced at Juilliard in 1966. Gifted enough to receive a full scholarship, he was assigned to study with the late Beveridge Webster. Passionate about music, a hard worker, and a devoted student, Bruce fully expected to be given lessons of the highest order. While I would not advise anyone to attend this school now, I felt quite differently about it then. At that time, the glamour associated with Juilliard caused me to ignore what I knew about it: most of its artist faculty members were mere figureheads who knew nothing about teaching. As a result, many of their finest students sought help from outside of the school. The same situation exists today. I'm embarrassed to admit it, but I actually urged Bruce to take advantage of the school's reputation and endure whatever consequences might befall him.

After his first lesson, Bruce told me that Beveridge Webster seemed bored to death, and that he made no attempt to hide it. Attributing this to a low level of energy which anyone might experience on any given day, I urged him to be patient. But what he reported to me the following week could not be rationalized or excused on any grounds. It seemed that while he was pouring his heart out in the slow movement of a Mozart sonata, he heard pages rustling and assumed that Webster was leafing through the score. But when Bruce finished the movement and looked over at Webster, he found him poring over *The New York Times* crossword puzzle. Without a word about the Mozart, Webster asked him, "Can you think of a four letter word for 'love'?" Knowing of Bruce's proclivity for good fun, I at first thought that he was making this up. Soon though, I realized that he was not joking in the slightest. This actually occurred! Hardly believing that any music teacher was capable of such behavior, I questioned other pupils who were studying with Webster. Some confirmed the crossword puzzle story, while others had their own complaints. One pupil was put off by suggestive remarks made during lessons, while another told of Webster's drinking problem.

Incensed by the story, I made an appointment for both of us to speak with the dean, Gideon Waldrop. Certainly he would make Bruce realize that a scholarship in such a prestigious school is no small thing. No doubt he would assign him to a new teacher, and the whole unfortunate incident would soon be forgotten.

After Bruce related the crossword puzzle story, the dean's response was similar to what mine had been at first — utter disbelief. "That's preposterous," he exclaimed. "You must be making this up!" "Then why don't you send for Webster," I said to him seriously. "Let him defend himself in front of my pupil." At this, the dean became indignant: "That's out of the question. Even if the story were true, would you expect me to fire such an eminent artist, someone who has been teaching here for almost half a century?" I thought to myself, "Yes, he deserves to be fired." But I made no response, knowing full well that the dean would neither send for Webster nor fire him. For had Webster actually confessed to the charge against him, the news would have leaked out and the school's reputation would have been tarnished even more. As I reasoned, the dean had to hush up the incident at all costs.

I had another purpose in speaking to the dean that morning. I wanted him to confirm to my pupil that college teaching posts are contingent upon having degrees, that few degrees carry greater weight than those earned from Juilliard, and, finally, to persuade him to continue on in the school. "I cannot in good conscience tell your pupil these things," the dean replied in a more congenial tone. "For the truth is, approximately eighty percent of our artist faculty members have no degrees whatsoever!" This may not be the case now. But even today, well-known performers with or without degrees are often lured to the faculties of institutions solely because of the prestige associated with their names. I, for example, who have no degrees whatsoever, have been offered many posts in major institutions — all of which I turned down. Other competent musicians who, however, are not well-known have no chance of landing jobs without doctoral degrees.

Considering the seriousness of the charges directed against Beveridge Webster, it seemed odd to me that the dean did not at least assign my pupil to another teacher. I questioned him about this and learned that there was a rule forbidding pupils to change teachers in mid-term. Bruce would have to continue his lessons, and nothing more would be said or done about Webster's addiction to crossword puzzles. Bruce was so outraged that he withdrew from the school on the following day — and with my full approbation. We agreed that he could not continue studying in a school that would retain such a teacher on its faculty.

After the Juilliard fiasco, Bruce enrolled at Columbia University, where he spent two years pursuing a degree in Political Science. He then got seriously involved in a relationship and moved to Cleveland where he worked in sales and marketing for Republic Steel Corporation. He returned to New York City twelve years later to work as a Vice President at Bankers Trust. And then five years later, he joined Merck & Co. in New Jersey, where he is currently employed. Happily married and the father of three children, he bought a Steinway piano and continues to play for his own enjoyment. Regarding Beveridge Webster — evidently his pupils, and the school's administration as well, continued to tolerate his behavioral aberrations up until his retirement. In fact, he had even raised his fees, with no resistance from any quarter. As far as I know, no one else ever attempted to bring him to account for his actions. Most of the serious students in his class simply shrugged their shoulders and sought musical help from teachers outside of the school. Beveridge Webster died in 1999 at the age of ninety-one.

Fortunately, not all artist-teachers are guilty of such outrageous behavior. There are well-known performers who love to teach. Among them, there are some beneficent ones who use their influence in recommending their worthy students for engagements or teaching positions.

One important advantage of attending conservatories of music is that they provide an ideal training ground for students who may later join professional chamber music groups and orchestras. In fact it is usually required that all string, woodwind, brass, and percussion students play in one of the school orchestras and participate in chamber music groups — activities that are not readily available in the private sector. As Sylvia Rosenberg, the eminent violinist and master teacher, told me, "Playing a Beethoven symphony in an orchestra brings violin students closer to understanding Beethoven's solo works." But in my opinion, such benefits are hardly sufficient compensation to those unfortunate students who have been assigned to destructive or incompetent teachers.

Private Music Teachers

On the other hand, it is private music teachers who deserve, to a great extent, the credit for keeping the art of music alive. Practicing, reading, attending lectures and master classes, and often continuing to take music lessons themselves throughout their careers, private music teachers have done more to influence music students than all others in the profession. I myself have seen them gathering in droves at national, state, and local conventions where I have appeared as a clinician. In fact, the majority of contestants at international competitions are students of private teachers, most of whom happen to be women. The level of teaching has improved to such an extent that young virtuosi today under the guidance of these teachers have become, in many ways, far superior to their predecessors: they have better learning skills, keener ears, more facile and accurate techniques, and larger repertories than did young musicians in previous generations. More reason to laud private music teachers. For so long as they exist, music will never die.

The following accounts of certain piano teachers with whom I have studied stress the fact that musical growth at the expense of one's psychological and emotional stability is simply a losing proposition. Moreover, reputation alone must never be the chief criterion for choosing a music teacher; nor would one want to entrust the development of musical talent to an incompetent teacher who is "such a nice person!"

ALEX CHIAPPINELLI

When I was around the age of eleven, my mother decided that it was time I had a new teacher. I am not sure what precipitated her decision. Perhaps she sensed that I had reached an impasse in my musical development.

Alex Chiappinelli was a highly respected teacher in Newark, New Jersey. With his Italian accent, his expressive way of speaking, complete with hand gestures, his dark, luminous eyes, and the shock of thick black hair that set off his chiseled features, he was the typical Italian maestro.

I had to audition for him, of course, and I remember playing *Kamenoi Ostrow* by Anton Rubinstein, which I had learned on my own. He seemed to like it very much, which gave me confidence for what was to follow. The Maestro was very particular about scales and arpeggios, and he asked me to play some of them for him. I had not yet been taught to play scales, per se, but having encountered them in some of my pieces, I simply made them up on the spot. While they sounded lumpy, I no doubt played them loud and fast enough to hide the fact that I did not know the correct fingering. Accuracy aside, they at least had verve. Perhaps it was because of this alone that I passed the audition.

The Maestro was a strict disciplinarian. Whatever skills he lacked in teaching, he made up for by enforcing a regimen of hard, consistent practicing. His house, with pianos in almost every room, might well have been a music conservatory. And what pianos they were! Uprights with sticking keys and missing ivories, badly out of tune — they were hardly instruments upon which a novice might improve his or her playing. I recall that two or three of us would practice in the same room, all at the same time. Filtering out everyone else's playing was an exercise in concentration.

Nor did our efforts escape the Maestro's ear. It was common for him to roam from room to room, even during a pupil's private lesson. During such jaunts, he would pass on comments to this one or to that one, such as "Slower! Slower! Keep your rhythm! More articulation!" When, on occasion, he would catch a pupil conversing instead of practicing, his loud rebukes could be heard echoing from one end of the house to other. As a result, his students found it easier to practice than to risk the fire of his reprimands.

Private lessons were given on an old Steinway concert grand with an abnormally heavy action. I remember feeling defeated when trying to negotiate fast passages against all of that resistance. Even to this day, the very thought of it causes reflexive contractions of my forearm muscles. On the plus side, the piano had a large, resonant tone that inspired me whenever I played for the Maestro. Mr. "Chippinelli," which is how I pronounced his name, was always loving and encouraging to me. Yet he was not a constructive teacher, and he didn't play very well himself.

I also had class lessons in theory once a week, my first exposure to this subject. I remember being one of a dozen or so students squeezed together into a rather small room. The Maestro's home was too large and too antiquated to be heated properly, and I have vivid memories of shivering in the cold as I tried my best to focus upon the difference between major and perfect intervals. As in Hebrew school, most of the students were older and, therefore, far more advanced than I was. In fact, that whole Dickensian scene — the cold, musty room, the stern and unin-spiring theory teacher, the lack of individual attention, the group of older, rowdy boys who seized every moment to torment the teacher and the younger students — all reminded me of my unhappy days in Hebrew school.

400 Fingers

This was a most unfortunate time to be studying with the Maestro. He was in the process of organizing a marathon concert which would consist of twenty pianos, with two students playing at each piano. *400 FINGERS!* — as the posters announced. The concert was the talk of Newark long before it took place. The repertory included ensemble arrangements of the first movement of Beethoven's Fifth, and Overtures to *The Magic Flute*, *Semiramide*, and *Zampa*. There would also be concerti performed by the older, more advanced pupils. The orchestral accompaniments would be played on four pianos in addition to a small electronic keyboard called a Solovox — a forerunner of the synthesizer. Wired to giant speakers, and having organ-like stops plus a knee-operated lever for controlling dynamics, the Solovox sounded like a raucous, nasal pipe organ in need of repair. Nor did the vibrato stop help matters any. It will suffice to say that the introduction to the Tchaikovsky Concerto in *B* flat minor made one think of a nervous Wagnerian soprano.

What the Maestro had to shoulder in planning such an event can only be imagined. Besides soliciting twenty pianos, and purchasing or renting enough four-hand and eight-hand arrangements of music for forty pupils, he had also to teach each one of us the various parts. In addition, he had to organize practice sessions on as many pianos as might be assembled at any given time. Such rehearsals took place at the Griffith Piano Company, the New Jersey equivalent of the Steinway showroom in New York City. The directors of this company were extremely cooperative with the Maestro. And why shouldn't they have been? They trusted that the large number of music students coming to their showroom would increase the potential for selling their pianos. Though this reciprocal business arrangement did nothing much to promote the cause of music, it certainly benefited all parties concerned.

Considering the Maestro's responsibilities in organizing such a marathon concert, it was a wonder that he continued giving private lessons. He tried his best to focus upon solo repertory, but the music chosen for the marathon concert inevitably took precedence.

Ensemble at Any Price

The day of the dress rehearsal arrived. Whatever difficulties the Maestro had encountered during the arduous preparation for that event faded by comparison with the near impossibility of synchronizing eighty hands in the opening bars of Beethoven's Fifth. Standing exaggeratedly erect on his podium so as to compensate for his short stature, and with the fire of determination in his eyes, the Maestro might well have been Toscanini himself. An entire year of grooming us individually and in small groups was about to be put to the test. Eighty eyes were fixed upon him as he gave an energetic upbeat, and a swoop down of his baton for the downbeat to bring in the well-known repeated *G's,* followed by an *E* flat. Anyone who has ever attempted to play this motif in the four-hand arrangement knows well how difficult the ensemble can be. But eighty hands...? The poor Maestro! How he kept up his courage after hearing antiphonal *G's* as they might have sounded echoing through the Italian Alps was, to be sure, commendable in itself. But when he heard *E* flats repeating from various points on the stage long after he had signaled an abrupt silence, his expression of optimism changed to gloom. Several more attempts proved no more successful. Finally in desperation, he settled for an absolutely funereal tempo, in which, for safety, he beat an entire measure in advance before we entered.

Performing artists can be just as superstitious as anyone else. They say in the profession that when a dress rehearsal goes badly, the concert itself will be a success. And that is exactly what happened. At the concert that same evening, the Beethoven may have sounded like a dirge in *C* minor, but the repeated notes were synchronized, nonetheless. Concerning the rest of the program, we all played with a minimum of mistakes, and, generally speaking, we kept an even pulse. Some of the soloists played their concerti brilliantly, although there were moments when the piano sound could not compete with the electronic drone of the Solovox accompaniment. As a professional might say in jest about his or her own performance, "It may not have been good, but at least it was loud!"

CRITICAL TIMES

At thirteen, the year of my *bar mitzvah*, I took a stand against my father. And after seven years of piano lessons, with nothing to show for it save my ability to read music, I took a stand here, too. The Maestro was very much like my first teacher, in that he did nothing more than assign me new material each week. Why, then, waste my time and my parents' money when I could read music well enough to learn new repertory on my own?

Although my mother was distraught at my quitting piano lessons, she clearly understood the basis for my decision. While neither she nor I knew what to expect from a piano teacher, we reasoned that a piano lesson ought to consist of something more than merely turning pages for a pupil.

After the Maestro's triumph, many parents in the audience, fantasizing that their own children might someday accomplish a similar feat, clamored for lessons with him. It was not long before his popularity rose considerably. He was busy enough not to care whether one or more of his present students dropped out. Yet he was genuinely disappointed to learn that I would discontinue my lessons, and he made several attempts to lure me back to his class. My mind was made up, though; I was resolved to work on my own. As I see it now, it was a foolish decision to make considering that I was barely fourteen.

LUNCH TIME SAVIOR

Anyone who has ever taken piano lessons knows that the lessons themselves serve as a motivation to practice. Now, without a teacher, I began to spend less and less time at the piano. My mother noticed this, and became alarmed. As she reasoned, I needed a musical authority figure who would once again stimulate my interest. Without my knowledge, and acting on her instinctive need to protect me, she telephoned Dr. Herman Holzman, the director of music at the junior high school which I was then attending. I mentioned Herman Holzman earlier as being the only teacher who encouraged me to compose. In response to my mother's concern, he invited me to sight-read four-hand music with him during his own lunch break. His magnanimous gesture rekindled my enthusiasm for music and also afforded me an opportunity to show off my skill in sight-reading. Had it not been for Herman Holzman, I might never have gone back to serious music study.

One day, after a particularly pleasurable session, Herman Holzman showed me his own arrangement of the first movement of Tchaikovsky's Concerto in *B* flat minor. He had scored it for piano and band accompaniment. It was the one piece in particular which had overwhelmed me when I first heard it at the marathon concert. I knew then, of course, that its difficulties were far beyond my abilities. Now, however, with Herman Holzman's simplified arrangement, I was instantly fired up with the prospect of learning it. And what better person to study it with than the very man who made the arrangement! Quite naturally, then, I resumed taking regular lessons, with Herman Holzman. A few months later, I actually performed the work at a gala concert in school with Holzman conducting the band. We both enjoyed a handsome success which did much to motivate my interest in performing.

First Attempts at Composing

Having regular lessons again, I returned to my daily routine of practicing. Herman Holzman devoted a good part of every lesson to composing. Sparked by his arrangement of the Tchaikovsky Concerto, I made a modest attempt at arranging my favorite themes from Rachmaninoff's Concerto in *C* minor, for chorus and piano. I even wrote a poem to coincide with the meter of that rapturous second theme of the first movement. While it was, to be sure, gushing with teenage sentimentality, it nevertheless rekindled my early attempts at improvisation.

At fourteen, I had no notion of just how important these creative attempts were. Nor did Herman Holzman express anything more than mild enthusiasm for my accomplishments. Like my teachers before him, he merely assigned me new pieces to learn. But on the positive side, he was the only teacher I ever had who suggested different forms and styles of music to compose. By this time in my life, I had concluded that no one could help me solve my technical deficiencies. I would have to find answers and solutions on my own.

Clara Husserl (Aunt Clara).

None of this matters in the light of what Herman Holzman did for me. Were he alive today, I would tell him that those lunch-time sight-reading sessions were a source of spiritual nourishment that brought me back to musical life again. And I would express my gratitude to him for leading out my creative voices, however naive the results may have been. He gave freely of his time for only one reason — to see to it that I didn't turn my back on my musical talent. He may not have been the finest teacher, but he nevertheless offered me the best that was within him. Not all people excel in their chosen fields. Some people benefit others merely by being the personification of goodness. Herman Holzman was just that sort of person. For this I am eternally indebted to him.

CLARA HUSSERL

During my teenage years, no person apart from my mother influenced me more than Clara Husserl. She came into my life by chance, exactly as the milkman's daughter had. This time, my mother was visiting a friend in the hospital one day, and happened to mention the fact that she was in the process of looking for another piano teacher for her son. Someone in the room who was visiting with the patient spoke of one Clara Husserl as being "the best teacher in New Jersey!" This was all the recommendation my mother needed. That same evening, she telephoned Clara Husserl and arranged an audition for a few days later.

Aunt Clara, which is how I subsequently addressed her, was sixty-four when I first played for her. I performed Chopin's Polonaise in *A* flat, Op. 53, and very shabbily, as I recall. It had flair, though, and that was all that mattered to her. She accepted me as her pupil. But more than a pupil, I became, in effect, her musical child, and she, my musical mother. My adoration for her knew no bounds. Even to this day, the mere mention of her name reawakens my sadness at having lost her.

American born, of southern stock, Aunt Clara went to Vienna to study with the famed master teacher Theodore Leschetizky when she was seventeen. Being her pupil gave me a link to Beethoven himself, for Leschetizky studied with Czerny, and Czerny studied with Beethoven. Thus all of my pupils are amazed and charmed to learn that they are the musical great, great, great grandchildren of Beethoven. This lineage was further strengthened when I later studied with Alexander Brailowsky, who was Leschetizky's last pupil.

Aunt Clara was a magnificent pianist. I can still hear her warm, expressive phrasing, and see those quiet, strong fingers which seemed to fit the keyboard so naturally. "*Goldene Hände*" was how Professor Leschetizky referred to her hands, according to Aunt Clara's frequent accounts of her student days. I, of course, aspired to all of the qualities of sound and ease of execution which Aunt Clara demonstrated so beautifully. She looked impressive, too — more like a dowager queen than a piano teacher. But her clothing was something else. Her Victorian dresses with yards of tasseled scarves were always stained and wrinkled. One might have thought that she had extracted them from some musty old trunk in the attic. Her stature, however, more than compensated for this. As one can see from the photograph, she bore a striking resemblance to another Clara of historic fame — Clara Wieck Schumann.

Aunt Clara was married to Siegfried Husserl, a prominent Austrian physician. He, in turn, was a cousin of the world-renowned philosopher Edmund Husserl, whose very name strikes a note of awe in academic circles. Not that Aunt Clara or her four children felt overshadowed in the slightest by their inherited relationship to such an important personage. Each one of the Husserls excelled in his or her respective field. Franz, born in 1915, was an eminent psychiatrist. Adelaide, born in 1912, was an actress and was involved in a radio program for children. She married the violinist Diez Weismann. Paul, born in 1907, had a wide and varied career. A feature writer and reporter for *Time* and *Cinema Arts* magazines, he later became managing editor of *The March of Time*, which won an Academy Award for pioneering in-depth documentaries. During World War II, he served overseas as combat photographer under General Douglas MacArthur. After the war, he became Night News Editor of NBC in New York and film coordinator for the original "Today Show." Aunt Clara's eldest child, Hortense Husserl Monath, born in 1905, was the star of the family. A favorite pupil of Artur Schnabel and the first woman pianist to play with Arturo Toscanini and the NBC Symphony Orchestra, and with Bruno Walter and the New York Philharmonic (December 29, 1934), Hortense was a world figure in her thirties. I was in awe of her. Her very presence made me weak in the knees. Little did I know then that one day, she would come to me in desperate need.

Hortense Monath

Hortense Monath was neurotic and highly temperamental. For example, she thought nothing of canceling a scheduled appearance on the very day of the performance, thus leaving a conductor frantically trying to replace her at the very last minute. Everything that upset Hortense resulted in a phone call to her mother, calls which sometimes interrupted my piano lessons. Hortense would eventually burst into uncontrollable sobs, leaving poor Aunt Clara at her wits' end to know how to deal with her. In all truth, though, Aunt Clara was partly responsible for Hortense's behavior. She fawned upon her, as upon Paul, and her piano students, and sorely neglected her other children.

Hortense's first husband was Paul E. Monath, who provided her with a beautifully appointed villa in Vienna. Her last husband, Ira A. Hirschmann, whom everyone called "Dori," was a wealthy and shrewd businessman. A notorious "womanizer," Dori had a wide-ranging career which included being La Guardia's campaign adviser and a member of the Board of Higher Education. He was later appointed by FDR to the post of special inspector for the United Nations Relief and Rehabilitation Administration. In this post, he was instrumental in obtaining the release of tens of thousands of Rumanian concentration camp inmates during World War II. Dori was also an accomplished amateur pianist, good enough to have studied briefly with Artur Schnabel.

At the time I studied with Aunt Clara, the Hirschmanns occupied a luxurious duplex penthouse at 3 East 85th Street in New York City. Hortense's studio was on the top floor. In 1936 Hortense hatched a plan for a concert series in Town Hall entitled New Friends of Music. Dori adored Hortense and her playing, and offered to underwrite it. Luminaries such as Schnabel, Hindemith, and Stravinsky joined Hortense on the series. Dori, who held the purse strings and directed all advertising for New Friends, actually billed himself as its founder. Promoting himself above Hortense and Schnabel was inflammatory enough. But then he made a fatal blunder: At Hortense's suggestion, he appointed Henry Colbert, a cousin of Hortense's oldest friend, to the post of business manager. According to Dori, Colbert secretly and legally signed over all of the assets of New Friends to himself. He even had the door locks changed on the New Friends' offices in an attempt to force Dori out of the picture entirely. It all succeeded, and Dori in utter disgust formally resigned from New Friends. Hortense, on her part, was convinced that Dori and Colbert had conspired to cheat her out of money, leaving New Friends in a precarious position. Not surprisingly, then, discontent and hostility finally led Hortense to ask Dori for a divorce. It was not something that Dori wanted, for he still adored Hortense. Though broken-hearted, he eventually conceded to her wishes.

As though matters weren't bad enough, Colbert resigned from the directorship of New Friends. Hortense in her selfishness assumed that Dori would always be there to rescue her in all emergencies. But Dori finally had had enough of Hortense and New Friends. In 1952, one month before Hortense's final appearance in Town Hall, he left for Rumania to help resettle homeless Jews. Hortense, who begged him not to go, was now left with the overwhelming responsibility of running the series, a responsibility for which she was ill-equipped. Among other things, she now had to contend with meeting all expenses, both past and present. It was unfortunate enough that she had to cancel the rest of the 1952-1953 season. But worse than that, she lost everything — her apartment, her belongings, and even her Steinway concert grand. Had not Aunt Clara, her mother, been dead by that time, I am sure that all of this would have killed her. At any rate, Hortense was now left destitute. And with her long history of outrageous behavior, no one would come to her rescue.

One Sunday afternoon in 1955, shortly before I was to leave for my first State Department tour, I had just sat down in my New York City apartment to have a bowl of spaghetti, when the doorbell rang. I opened the door and gasped: there stood the specter of Aunt Clara, an apparition dressed in rags with straggly gray-streaked hair streaming over its face. Suddenly, the figure spoke: "Sonny, don't you remember me? I'm Hortense Monath. For the sake of my mother, who loved you, please help me!" The shock of seeing my one-time heroine reduced to such a deplorable state caused me to grow pale and mute. I ushered her in, of course, but I hardly knew how to act or what to say. Hortense had sought me out for a particular reason, and she lost no time in coming to the point. In a high-pitched, hysterical voice she told me that the board of the New Friends was holding her son Peter hostage in an office building in midtown Manhattan, and that they had stolen all of her money and even her clothing. Would I please lend her ten dollars so that she could take a taxi back to her hotel. One did not have to be a professional psychologist to know that poor Hortense was hopelessly paranoid. As one might imagine, I began to suffer my own delirium wondering how best to handle this situation.

I knew that I needed help in dealing with her. On a pretext I asked Hortense to wait in the hall outside of my apartment while I made a telephone call. Somehow she believed and trusted me, and she did as I asked. Alone in my apartment, I telephoned her brother, Franz Husserl, the psychiatrist. He told me that she was mentally ill, and that no one in the family was able to persuade her to commit herself to an institution. "The best thing you can do for her," he advised, "is to send her away. The police will finally take the necessary action and incarcerate her in a mental hospital." That Hortense's own brother could utter such a cruel statement was too much for me to bear. I ended our conversation as quickly as I could. A call to her son Peter also proved to no avail. "My mother has ruined my life," he told me. "I will have nothing more to do with her." Poor Peter, a victim of parental neglect, was hopelessly addicted to drugs. He himself was eventually abandoned by everyone and died at an early age.

Although Hortense was totally irrational and, for all I knew, even capable of harming me, she was, after all, Aunt Clara's daughter. I felt obliged to help her in whatever way I could. First, I hailed a taxi in order to take her to the office building where, she imagined, Peter was held hostage. It was Sunday and the building was closed, but an emergency bell on the outside of the building brought a superintendent to the door in a few moments. I explained the situation to him as best as I could, and he allowed us to go from floor to floor so as to prove to Hortense that the building was completely empty. The poor woman even searched in the restrooms before she was absolutely convinced that Peter was not there. With her fears now allayed, Hortense, momentarily at least, grew calm and projected a semblance of normalcy. I then gave her twenty dollars, all the money I had at that moment, and put her into a taxi. As I subsequently learned from her brother, she was, in fact, committed to an institution several days after I saw her and diagnosed as a paranoid schizophrenic. I heard nothing more about her for the better part of a year.

Then in May, 1956, my telephone rang. It was Hortense, sounding charming and quite normal. She said that her friend Martha Baird Rockefeller, who had also been a pupil of Schnabel, had come to her rescue. According to what Hortense told me, she paid for her psychotherapy, gave her money to return to Europe to reconstitute her performing career (this came to naught), and bought her a radio station on which Hortense could perform whenever she liked. "I'm certainly not going to use all of that time for myself," she told me. "I intend to feature you and some of my other musician friends as well. As soon as I get settled in my new apartment, you and I are going to have dinner together and discuss the whole thing." I was overjoyed to know that she was well and that she would perform again. It was, as I reasoned, a sign of her mental stability that she wanted to share performing time on her radio station with me and with others. But sadly, Adelaide Weismann, Hortense's surviving sister, suspects that everything Hortense told me concerning the radio program was mere fantasy. I was not able to ascertain the truth. I did discover, however, that for a brief period, and primarily due to Lithium, Hortense appeared to have recovered. It did not last long, though. Her psychological problems, complicated by an addiction to alcohol, soon led to another breakdown.

Only one week later, I happened to have a dental appointment and was browsing through *The New York Times* in the waiting room. Suddenly, I saw a photograph of Hortense on the obituary page and an accompanying article. She had been found dead in her New York City apartment. According to Peter, a combination of sleeping pills and alcohol caused her to smother in her sleep. She was fifty-two years old. Thus, sadly, ended the life of a person who at one time had the world at her fingertips.

Total Mentor

To return to Aunt Clara — being full of convictions about everything, musical and otherwise, she undertook the responsibility for my total development. For one thing, she supplied me with reading matter that would have challenged a Ph.D. candidate. How I at fifteen, having read only the books assigned to me in school, ever digested works by Nietzsche and Goethe, for example, astonishes me to this day. I would have been lost entirely had it not been for Aunt Clara's own comments, which filled the margins of practically every page. Taking the form of rebuttals and affirmations, they led me to understand, in part at least, the complicated subjects under discussion. Occasionally, some aspect of the text would inspire Aunt Clara to compose a poem which she would then scribble in a burst of inspiration onto the front or back pages of the book. To be sure, I was unsophisticated and given to extremes of sentimentality myself, yet even I winced at the awkward rhymes, the meter, and the naive content of those poems. And more than once, I felt compelled to utter out loud, "Oh, no...!"

Aunt Clara and I went everywhere together. It was she, for instance, who took me to Carnegie Hall for the first time, to hear the famed Artur Schnabel during his historic Beethoven cycle. Hortense and Mme. Schnabel, a well-known singer of *Lieder*, sat in a box to our right. Schnabel's performance of the *Waldstein* Sonata, as well as his imposing presence at the keyboard, has remained indelibly imprinted in my mind: the stillness of his body, the quiet, strong hands, and the extraordinary range of dynamics emanating from the piano — all reminded me of Aunt Clara's playing. As a matter of fact, Schnabel was himself a pupil of Leschetizky. And I remember thinking how fortunate I was to be in such good hands — and *goldene* ones at that!

The Censorious One

During this and other trips to New York City, everything Aunt Clara heard or saw became a subject for criticism. She may have looked regal, but her gravel-sounding voice was anything but that! Loudly opinionated, often to everyone's embarrassment, she was not a bit perturbed when the subjects of her cutting remarks were within earshot of everything she said. One evening, I remember, as we left her home on Clinton Avenue in Newark, we were both struck by the beauty of a full moon hanging over the spires of a church which stood directly across the street. Several people, including the minister, were standing by the church entrance. In an instant, Aunt Clara was all aflame about nature versus religion. Pointing accusingly at the church, and, by inference, at the minister himself, she shouted loudly enough for everyone to hear: "Sonny (she always called me by my family nickname), look at that moon. And those fools in there invent reasons to prove that God exists!"

Another time, while standing on a subway platform in New York City, we were within arm's length of a group of young women who were laughing uproariously. One of them, pitifully homely, brought attention to herself by laughing louder than all of the others. Aunt Clara wasted no time in composing a variation on a familiar aphorism. "Sonny," came the raspy voice, "beauty may be skin deep, but ugliness goes to the bone!" Fortunately for the poor woman, the roar of an oncoming train blotted out Aunt Clara's caustic remark.

Nor did concert-hall decorum inhibit Aunt Clara's proclivity for voicing whatever she might be feeling at the moment. Once, when a gifted young pianist from Newark broke down on the first descending chromatic scale in Chopin's Fantasie-Impromptu, she greeted this with a modest, "Hmpf!" But when he broke down a second time at the recapitulation, her patience wore thin. "He did it again!" she blurted out loudly enough for the performer to hear. I shudder to think what that poor young man must have felt at hearing such a comment from a member of the audience.

A Beer for Sonny

Having the best pupils in New Jersey, and basking in the glow of her own children's successes, Aunt Clara ought to have enjoyed her life to the fullest. Yet she clearly missed the intellectual climate of Vienna that she had experienced during her student days. At every opportunity, she tried to re-create that climate as best as she could. Vivid in her memory were the beer halls and the stimulating discussions held there among the Leschetizky pupils. She no doubt thought that her Sonny was deprived of something vital to his personal growth: Nietzsche, Goethe, and beer halls, too, would evidently improve my playing. Thus one evening, upon returning to Newark from one of our forays into New York City, Aunt Clara took me to a local bar around the corner from her home. To call it seedy would be a generous assessment of its appearance. Dirty and disheveled, it looked to be a hangout for Newark's low life. But all bars have beer on tap, and this was what interested Aunt Clara. I can scarcely imagine what the bartender and all of those derelicts must have thought at the sight of an elderly, aristocratic-looking woman and a teenaged boy sitting at a table guzzling beer. That I at fifteen was served at all was astonishing in itself. Aunt Clara, completely oblivious to the eyes upon us, calmly sipped her beer and proceeded to discuss the concert that we had attended that evening. After an hour or so, feeling quite satisfied that she had given her Sonny a sampling of Bohemian life, she decided to call it a night. She arose from her seat, went directly up to the bartender to pay him, and walked out with nonchalant dignity. I followed her, with a somewhat lighter step than that with which I had entered the bar.

Aunt Clara may have had her eccentric ways, but she was the paragon of piano playing. Whatever she assigned me, I learned. And if her ambitions for me far exceeded my capabilities, I was not aware of this in the slightest: Concerti by Mozart, Beethoven, Tchaikovsky, Schumann, and Liszt, all the difficult Beethoven sonatas, virtuoso works by Chopin and Liszt, and Schubert's *Wanderer* Fantasy, which she asked me to learn in one week for her yearly student recital — all of this, and more, I practiced and performed simply because she suggested it. Since everything was easy for her, she seemed totally unaware of all of the technical difficulties which this repertory posed. Occasionally, she suggested double-note exercises or etudes by Czerny and Cramer, for example. But she never explained to me how to practice them. As usual, though, I persevered and somehow managed to perform well. While I may have looked and sounded in control of my playing, my technical approach to the piano was anything but controlled. I remember the tell-tale pains in my forearms — indications of the wrong physical approach to the keyboard. Many performers, I subsequently discovered, consider it a sign of weakness to admit to technical difficulties or physical discomfort. I, too, was resigned to keep my own inadequacies and discomfort a secret from everyone — Aunt Clara included. As a result, I felt like a fraud. And like all frauds, I lived in fear of eventually being found out.

Summer Audiences

My lessons with Aunt Clara continued until I was eighteen years old. During those three years, she afforded me many opportunities to perform. If, for example, musicians visited her, or anyone who she thought might promote my career, she telephoned me to come to her home to perform for them. If she attended a meeting of a music organization, she always saw to it that they engaged me to play at a future time. And whenever she presented her own pupils in a formal recital, I was not only the featured soloist, but I also accompanied all of the concerti that her other pupils performed. This enabled me to learn the repertory and to improve my sight-reading. As one might imagine, all of these musical activities necessitated my being in Aunt Clara's home three or four times a week. It was a happy and productive time for me — that is, until the summer arrived.

Summer vacations with my parents ought to have been pleasurable occasions. But to me they meant separation from Aunt Clara and from my piano as well. But as I subsequently discovered, hotels had pianos, too. And finding one in a night club, recreation room, or even a bar was like being reunited with an old friend. Practicing in card rooms, however, has a special risk, as I had occasion to discover.

One afternoon during a week's stay with my parents in a hotel in Long Branch, New Jersey, I was practicing an Intermezzo by Brahms on an old upright piano. Whenever I practiced, I was always aware that I was performing for an audience — whether those present were consciously listening or not. On this occasion, I directed my musical passions toward four serious pinochle players who were at it some fifteen feet away. After a half an hour or so, during which some very annoyed glances flashed in my direction, one of the players had had quite enough. Obviously as unimpressed with Brahms as he was with me, he brought my practice session to an abrupt close by shouting, "Hey, who's your embalmer?"

There was another guest at the hotel, a slight, elderly woman who was far more appreciative of my Brahms. She introduced herself as Bessie Vasanska. In the course of conversation, I learned that she and her sister had participated in the last master class of Franz Liszt. After a little urging on my part, Bessie Vasanska went to the upright piano on which I had been practicing and played the Godowsky arrangement in thirds and sixths of Chopin's "Minute" Waltz. Though she must have been in her late eighties, or perhaps even older, her virtuosity was astonishing. As though that wasn't surprise enough, I subsequently learned that she was also a singer and had given recitals in which she played piano solos and then accompanied herself in *Lieder*. She then proceeded to sing and play Schumann's *Mondnacht* in such a way that tears formed in my eyes. We remained close friends until her death several years later.

One of the benefits of having been born in 1927 has been the privilege of meeting people who studied with or heard the great masters of the nineteenth century. When I was twenty, for example, I was invited to give a recital in a nursing home in Newark for intellectual Austrian women. On that occasion I performed an all Schubert and Brahms recital, including Op. 119 of Brahms. Afterwards, the director told me that one of their eldest residents had something urgent to tell me. I was escorted to an ancient woman with blazing eyes seated in a wheelchair. I was asked to kneel down so that she could whisper in my ear. And this is what I heard: "I attended Clara Schumann's funeral in Hanover, and there I heard

Brahms play his Op. 119." Hearing this, I ceased breathing. I had the feeling that I had been transported back to the nineteenth century. When I regained my poise, I asked her, "How did Brahms play?" "Not very well," she responded. "He made a lot of mistakes. You played it much better."

To return to my teenage summers, the following year, my mother gave me permission to rent a studio in Asbury Park, New Jersey, close to the hotel where we were then staying. It was an ideal arrangement: the studio had a fine seven-foot Steinway grand, and it was air-conditioned and completely private. I practiced every day for three or four hours, and then enjoyed the beach, good food, and all the youthful joys of summer.

My Teaching Career Begins

My fifteenth year was important to me in two respects: first, it introduced Aunt Clara into my life and, second, it marked the beginning of my teaching career. As it happened, Aunt Clara arranged for me to supervise the practicing of several of her young, gifted pupils. This proved to be extremely beneficial: the pupils began to play like young professionals, and I learned those teaching skills that have remained with me to this day. The pupils whom I supervised told their friends about me, and it was not long before I built up a class of private pupils. That I got paid for doing something that was both helpful and enjoyable was a novelty. Where my father was concerned, music seemed not to have been such a bad choice after all: I was actually earning some money for my efforts.

I have never thought that my pianistic gifts warranted a big career. But when it comes to teaching, I feel that I possess all the musical skills and personal attributes to be truly successful at it. In fact, with the first lesson I gave to one of Aunt Clara's students, I knew that I was destined to teach. To this day, it is the one activity which I feel I do better than anything else.

At fifteen, I could not say what pedagogical technique belonged to me naturally, or what was the result of Aunt Clara's influence. But I did know one thing: the relationship I had with her became a model for all my other relationships — with my pupils and my friends alike. In other words, I can unhesitatingly point to a music teacher as having influenced me more than anyone else.

The Griffith Artist Award

There is certainly no dearth of competitions today for gifted students. In fact the sheer number of them has now begun to diminish their importance insofar as building careers is concerned. During my student days, however, there were relatively few competitions. But the ones which did exist attracted a great deal of public attention. The major competition in

New Jersey was sponsored by the Griffith Music Foundation, of the piano store mentioned earlier. There were various categories, based upon a student's age and competence. A year earlier, at sixteen, I had entered the senior division, and barely passed with a mark of 80. Now, at seventeen, everything had changed: I had acquired a great deal of performing experience, thanks to Aunt Clara, and my playing had greatly improved. The previous year's low grade notwithstanding, I now set my sights on the top prize — the Griffith Artist Award.

By early May, Aunt Clara had gone off to her family compound, at Culver Lake, New Jersey. Siegfried was Dr. Husserl's name, and because the whole family had a passion for Wagner, they named the compound "Siegfried's Idyll." It consisted of a home for Aunt Clara and Dr. Husserl, and homes nearby for each one of the children. During that particular summer, Hortense Monath was living in seclusion there preparing three all-Mozart and Brahms programs for her New Friends of Music series in Town Hall. Aunt Clara had arranged for me to play in a community center in Culver Lake. I therefore received my first invitation to visit Siegfried's Idyll. The piano in Aunt Clara's home was in dreadful condition, not at all conducive to constructive practicing. Hortense had a Steinway concert grand in her home, yet she would not allow me to practice on it. She always behaved as though she were above everyone else. If anything, this merely increased my awe of her.

After my performance in Culver Lake, I returned to Newark and began serious practicing for the competition. It was during the Second World War, and life seemed like one prolonged desperate struggle. Most families were beset by tragic losses, separations became a way of life, and food rationing simply added to everyone's misery. My own family endured along with everyone else: My sister Sylvia's husband, Saul Armm, had been inducted into the army and was subsequently assigned to the combat engineers in Italy, while my youngest sister Evelyn's husband, Arthur Zorn, was an air force officer stationed in South America. To make matters worse, Sylvia was rearing a nine month old infant, Beryl, at the time that her husband received his orders for Italy.

In order to ease life somewhat for these two sisters, my parents decided that they should move in with us. Thus five adults, a child, and a Florey Brothers grand piano had all to be accommodated in a two-bedroom apartment. My sisters and nephew shared one of the two bedrooms, while I converted the dinette adjacent to the kitchen into my own room. Imagine, if you will, a grand piano, a full-sized silent keyboard formerly owned by Hortense Monath, a bed, a dresser, a desk, and a floor lamp — all crammed into a space approximately ten by seven feet. It was my sanctuary, nonetheless, and I was able to close the door and practice as long as I liked. Three years of living in such proximity resulted in a very close relationship between us. As far as my nephew Beryl was concerned, he related to me as if I had been his real father. In fact those special feelings which can exist between a father and a son have remained with us to this day.

I firmly believe that having to practice amidst the hustle and bustle of everyday family life forced me to acquire the skills of concentration that I enjoy today. I can still remember the various practice methods I invented in preparation for the competition — methods which enabled me to block out countless distractions. For example, I practiced each scale configuration of Bach's Prelude in *B* flat from Book 1 of *The Well-Tempered Clavier* in the following manner: I played the first two notes in tempo; I repeated them over and over again until they not only sounded even, but also felt comfortable; I then added each successive note until the entire passage fairly bubbled out of my fingers. Having succeeded in accomplishing this, I then practiced the passage backwards, beginning with the last two notes, then the last three, and so on. The whole time, I imagined myself performing the passage at the competition itself. I infused each repetition with intense musical energy. In other words, I instinctively did what I have since learned is indispensable when preparing for a performance: I practiced performing. This means, above everything else, that technique must be at the service of music's meaning, and not the other way around. As Artur Schnabel once explained to his son, who was questioning him about his repeating a passage two hundred times, "I wasn't practicing; I was making music!"

I practiced the difficult passages of the other two works on my audition program — the Ballade in *G* minor by Chopin, and *L'isle joyeuse* by Debussy — in a similar fashion. As to fortifying my memory in the Bach fugue, I invented something for this, too. With the aid of scotch tape, I constructed a one inch wide frame made of two layers of cardboard. It was large enough to frame an entire page of music. The vertical sides of the frame were open at the ends facing the music. I then cut out strips of black paper wide enough to cover a line of music, and inserted them into the verticals. The horizontal strips were moveable and could therefore be positioned wherever I wished. I alternately covered up the bass clef and treble clef lines, thus reading one clef while playing the other from memory. After a few days of this, I felt as though I had composed that fugue.

I spoke earlier of imagining myself as living under a protective dome, which nothing and no one could penetrate. As I practiced for that competition, my self-created dome functioned to full capacity. Nothing distracted me — neither my nephew Beryl, who was playing around the piano with his toys, nor the comings and goings of the family. The challenge of the competition, plus working completely on my own, brought out the best in me. As far as I was concerned, music was the only thing that existed so long as I sat at the piano. If it took ten hours a day to adapt my technique to the music's demands, then so be it. I was prepared to do whatever was required. And my family, for its part, never once complained about the bombardment of sound which filled that relatively small apartment from morning until night.

My work habits paid off. At the competition itself, I somehow struck a balance between musical feeling and physical comfort. As if by magic, technical difficulties vanished in a wave of emotional expression. That I was able to play better at the audition than in my own home was certainly a surprise to me. There was only one judge, and a very distinguished one at that — Rudolph Firkusny. When I finished playing, he leapt out of his chair, rushed over to me, and showered me with compliments. By the time I reached home, the director of the competition was on the telephone: "Mr. Firkusny was very impressed with you. In fact, he insisted upon giving you a mark of 100. We prevailed upon him, though, to lower it to 99. After all, you're only seventeen, and we think that there ought to be room for improvement. But congratulations: you have won the Griffith Artist Award, with honors."

I lost no time in telephoning Aunt Clara at her summer home. Her expression of joy still rings in my ears. She returned to Newark in time to attend the awards ceremony, which took place in a vast auditorium called the Mosque Theater, later renamed Symphony Hall. This was the hall where, ten years later, I played the Rachmaninoff *Rhapsody on a Theme of Paganini* with the New Jersey Symphony. With awards to be given to students in all the various categories of the competition, there were approximately 3,000 people in attendance. The Artist Award, reserved for the last, drew the greatest attention. Reporters flashed their cameras, and I received a standing ovation. My family and Aunt Clara were bursting with pride. We all celebrated until the wee hours of the morning. Social functions always brought out the best in my father. At such times there wasn't a hint of the dark side of his nature which always seemed present when we were alone. On this occasion, he was particularly happy and impressed by the public recognition I received. My award seemed finally to convince him that music should be my life's work.

I continued to study regularly with Aunt Clara until I was eighteen. News of her death reached me in 1952 while I was a soldier stationed in

Korea. That I could not be with her at the end, that I could not hold her hand as she passed from this world, has left me with unresolved feelings of sadness and loss. Moreover, I feel cheated not to have had the opportunity to tell her of the adventures I had, performing on the front lines during the war. Later, her absence was conspicuous at my New York City debut, and at the first concert of my own works. She would have had a great deal to say about everything — both good and bad. It is even likely that she would have blurted out her opinions during the performances themselves!

In another sense, however, Aunt Clara has always been at my side. I am aware that her vibrant spirit is with me even at this moment, guiding the writing of this book. So it is that a teacher can live on through the activities of a pupil. It is partly because of such relationships that music itself is perpetuated.

Leonard Bernstein

Aunt Clara had strong convictions about everything. Moreover, she stopped at nothing in her determination to implement them. When I was twenty-two, she attended a recital I gave in Newark a few years after I stopped having regular lessons with her. She was so enthusiastic about my playing that she decided then and there to set my career in motion. The following morning, she telephoned John Ortez, who was then the public relations director of the Baldwin Piano Company. Enticed by her charisma, as everyone else seemed to be, Mr. Ortez arranged an audition for me in two weeks. He was, as Aunt Clara informed me, a powerful figure in musical circles.

How many hours I practiced before that audition, I cannot begin to say. When the day finally arrived, Aunt Clara and I traveled to New York City by bus and train. When we finally arrived at our destination, I was completely numb with anxiety. I remember Mr. Ortez towering over me, and being as charming as he was large. I played for him the Polonaise in *F* sharp minor by Chopin, and *Gnomenreigen* (Dance of the Gnomes) by Liszt. Whether it was the result of endless hours of practicing, or my keen desire not to shame Aunt Clara, I played better than ever before. Mr. Ortez was extremely impressed, and so was Aunt Clara. Without so much as a word to us, he instructed his secretary to get Leonard Bernstein on the telephone. With this, Aunt Clara's eyes met mine, and our brows went up in disbelief. Word came back to Mr. Ortez, however, that Lenny (as everyone called him) was recuperating from an operation and would not be available for several weeks. Actually, I was much relieved to hear this news. For in all truth, I was neither pianistically nor psychologically ready to enter the "big time." Mr. Ortez, of course, had no inkling of how I really felt. As far as he was concerned, I was a finished pianist and ready for a career. As the following letter proves, he was determined to have Lenny hear that *other* Bernstein:

January 27, 1950
Dear Mrs. Husserl:
    I spoke to Lenny Bernstein yesterday, and he was most enthusiastic about Seymour Bernstein. He remembered meeting Seymour in Newark some time ago. He wants you to please write to him in February at 1050 Park Avenue, New York City, attention Miss Helen Coates, who is his personal secretary and advisor. She will make all the necessary arrangements for this meeting. I know that Miss Coates, in courtesy to us, will do all that she can to see that young Bernstein gets a well-deserved break. Frankly, I have never heard a better talent, and we must do something to help him.
        With kind, personal regards,
        Sincerely yours,
            Baldwin Piano Company
            John Ortez, Manager

I had actually met "Lenny" in Newark at a luncheon in his honor, at which I played the *Star-Spangled Banner*. He was utterly charming and complimentary to me. And he seemed delighted by the fact that I was introduced to him as "the other Bernstein."

Though I was thrilled by Mr. Ortez's enthusiasm, I didn't feel ready to play a concerto with Leonard Bernstein. And it worried me that if I played as well for him as I had for Mr. Ortez, Lenny might actually invite me to perform with him. By the time I read the above letter from Mr. Ortez, however, I had had time to reflect upon the situation. I reasoned that I could, if necessary, get a concerto ready given a sufficient amount of time. I therefore asked Aunt Clara to write to Helen Coates with the hope of setting up an audition with Lenny. Letters were exchanged between them. I then received the following communication from Helen Coates:

October 21, 1950

Dear Mr. Bernstein:

When I wrote to Mrs. Husserl last March, just before leaving for a stay of several months in Israel, I fully expected that Mr. Bernstein would be in New York this fall and would be able to give you an audition. Since then his plans have been changed, and he is remaining in Europe until January 1st, and after that he will be almost constantly busy on tour in the States until spring.

In the meantime, if you cared to play for me (Mr. Bernstein studied piano with me, as you may know), I would be glad to hear from you. If you should wish to do this, please get in touch with me, and I will be glad to arrange an appointment.

Sincerely,

Helen Coates

P.S. You may reach me by telephone in the evening (SA-2-7452)

Leonard Bernstein's teacher...? This all sounded very important to me. I lost no time in telephoning Helen Coates to arrange to play for her. If she liked my playing, I reasoned, then certainly she would see to it that Lenny engaged me.

I thought it was strange, though, that Helen Coates would take it upon herself to offer me an audition — unless, of course, Lenny had asked her to intervene. I wondered, too, why she mentioned that she had taught Lenny. Would I then be auditioning to study with her? The truth is, I wanted only one thing from Helen Coates — her influence in getting Lenny to listen to me. The exchange of letters, after all, was specifically about this.

The audition for Helen Coates proved to be disastrous in all respects. As soon as I began to play Brahms' Rhapsody in *E* flat, I suddenly felt like a rank amateur auditioning for a new teacher. My playing was self-conscious and technically sloppy. She made some superficial comments to me and asked me to play something else. The whole session was not only a waste of time, but worse than that, it presented me in the poorest possible light to the very person I wanted to impress. I felt certain that she would never recommend me to Lenny now that she had heard me play. Even if she had, I would not have been available for an audition or anything else, for that matter. For two months later, I was inducted into the army.

I almost always performed better than I thought. Many performers are as hard on themselves as I was, and still am. Apparently, Helen Coates was actually impressed with me. Years later, I actually played for Lenny — and very successfully at that. But first I have to backtrack a few years in order to pick up the thread of my formal piano studies.

LOUISE CURCIO

What did it mean to win the Griffith Artist Award? For one thing, the pressure was on: I was expected to be the paragon of perfection wherever I performed. Fortunately, though, this did not last too long, for I was replaced by another first place winner the following year. In the meantime, everyone paid a lot of attention to me; interviews appeared in local magazines, and various schools and organizations invited me to perform at special functions.

One day, shortly after the presentation of awards, I received a telephone call from someone who introduced herself as Louise Curcio, a piano teacher in Newark. She had heard from her pupils about my having won first place, and she began the conversation by congratulating me. But soon she revealed the real reason for her call. It seemed that she had a theory about a quality of tone which she recognized in the playing of certain world-renowned pianists — Vladimir Horowitz and Alexander Brailowsky among them. She called it the "dimensional tone." As she continued to talk, I gathered that the word "dimensional" referred to the tone's properties — namely, a tone that was resonant without hardness. Every pianist, I believe, aspires to produce such a tone. Louise Curcio then got right down to the crux of her call. Her own pupils, she told me, were not sufficiently advanced to implement her theory on the production of the dimensional tone. If I would be interested in working with her, she would give me three lessons a week on a full scholarship.

In spite of my breakthrough in preparation for the competition, I continued to be plagued by technical problems. Aunt Clara was inspiring, to be sure, but teaching technique was not one of her virtues. Thinking that Louise Curcio might have the answers to my technical problems, I eagerly accepted her offer. This was a foolish thing to do without finding out something about her. But I was young, painfully innocent, and open to adventure.

Louise Curcio had only partial vision and was considered to be functionally blind. Her sister, Mary, was totally blind and had a seeing-eye dog called Thelma. The truth is, I paid more attention to Thelma than I did the

Louise Curcio, center, flanked by her friend Margaret and myself at nineteen.

sisters. (As Sir Clifford Curzon's gardener in London once told him: "The more I know people, the more I love animals!")

Louise attributed her own and Mary's blindness to a congenital defect passed on to them by a syphilitic father. The two sisters lived in a modest two story home on the outskirts of Newark. The small rooms seemed to fit Louise's stature: she was short, thin, and bony; her hair was jet black, wiry, and streaked with gray; and her skin always looked as though it had been massaged with olive oil. Her black eyes had the vacant stare characteristic of blind people. Yet she saw outlines of things. As she spoke to you, she cocked her head to one side and strained her vision to search you out. Fortyish and single, Louise had an innocence about her such as one associates with nuns. In fact, the sparse and simple furnishings of her home, and especially the cell-like bedrooms upstairs, spotlessly clean and austere, and with a crucifix hanging over each bed, had all the earmarks of what I imagined a nunnery to be.

At eighteen, I was the perfect prey for a dominating woman teacher, and one who was single, at that. Because I had three lessons a week, I spent more time with Louise than with anyone else. But I preferred taking lessons, practicing, and reading to social activities. Paradoxically, my being president of my graduating class in grammar school, and later, something of a court musician throughout high school made me more popular than I actually cared to be. In fact I spent a great deal of time fending people off.

Considering how times have changed, it is difficult to imagine how naive I was at eighteen. In those days, I assumed that people liked me only because I played the piano. That some people may have been sexually attracted to me never crossed my mind. Tall, lean, and rather good looking, I came across as a charmer without even trying. I realized much later in life that certain "hangers-on" were interested in me for extra-musical reasons. The fact is, I was too dedicated to my music to read these signs correctly. I knew my pianistic limitations, and performance anxiety was never far away, so I spent most of my time working hard to overcome my weaknesses and fears. On many occasions, when the social demands of my friends made inroads upon my practicing, I asked my mother to intercept all telephone calls. At my suggestion, she would tell my friends that I was in seclusion for several weeks preparing for whatever engagement was on the horizon. I was always available, however, whenever Aunt Clara or Louise telephoned me. After all, they were the currents that fed my musical development. I was dependent upon them, and Louise, especially, took full advantage of this. As one might imagine, Aunt Clara was horrified at my having replaced her with "that blind nitwit," as she referred to Louise. Yet, like an understanding mother, she swallowed her pride and continued to support and encourage me. She remained on the sidelines, so to speak, waiting for her Sonny to act out what she thought was a most unfortunate phase in my development.

Color Hearing

Everything about Louise — her disability, her eccentricities, her over-powering convictions, and, especially, her dimensional tone theory — appealed to my romantic nature. I was particularly intrigued by the way she heard music. Interestingly, she possessed "color hearing," or *synesthesia*, from the Greek *syn* (with), and *aisthesis* (sensation). Color hearing is the result of a joint perception whereby the sense of hearing produces a subjective visual response — in Louise's case, color images. As she explained, every sound she heard, musical or otherwise, produced a color and a shape in her mind's eye. The sound of a spoon dropped on her kitchen floor, for instance, produced a black streak through a corresponding shape. Being a piano teacher, she learned to use these graphic images while listening to piano sounds: she not only *heard* percussive attacks on the piano, but she also *saw* them in the form of black streaks coursing through images produced by the tones. Conversely, warm, resonant sounds glowed with unobstructed radiant colors. To her, such tones lent dimensionality to a pianist's playing. The fact that her *synesthesia* confirmed her auditory responses impressed me, as it did many other people.

All told, though, my lessons with Louise were bizarre affairs. Sitting some ten feet away from the piano, where she could hear the full "dimensionality" of tones, she would interrupt my playing with comments and instructions. "Your elbow is too tight." "That's it; the color is purer, now." "Try tightening your fingers a little more." "Better, better!" In the final analysis, they were lessons on tone production for its own sake, completely divorced from music's meaning. Interpretation she left to me. Yet I was too inexperienced to be entrusted with the responsibility of interpreting time-honored masterpieces. And she, being a dreadful pianist, was of no help whatsoever when it came to devising fingerings, solving pedaling problems, or even demonstrating the simplest phrase. To be blunt about it, I was her guinea pig, and her attitude towards me was one of exclusive ownership throughout all of her experimentation. The more she expressed her gratification with my progress, the more enmeshed I became in her web.

Under the circumstances, one might think that my playing would have deteriorated. But the truth is, the opposite occurred. For one thing, having

94

to prepare three lessons a week for approximately four years necessitated my learning a vast amount of repertory. Moreover, being left to my own devices in matters of interpretation, fingering, and pedaling forced me to strengthen my own convictions in these areas. As for Louise's dimensional tone theory, although her method of implementing it was experimental and, in most cases, vague and even physically injurious, I nevertheless became more sensitive to sound and the physical sensations of producing it.

Silver

Having three lessons a week at no charge was no small thing. I was very grateful to Louise, and my devotion to her knew no bounds. I rode to my lessons on a bicycle that my father's business partner, Rhea Hirsch, had given me. I named the bicycle "Silver," after the Lone Ranger's horse. Along the way I purchased Jewish rye bread and cheese Danish pastries from a well-known bakery in Newark whose name, coincidentally, was Silver's. And what bread it was! The mere thought of it makes me salivate. It was always fresh, the crust was crisp, and each loaf was completely covered with large black poppyseeds. As for the cheese Danish, these were beyond anything I have ever tasted since. Once a week, the Curcios received these and other bounties — flowers, gifts, anything that could fit into the basket of my bike.

I mentioned earlier that one teacher cannot be all things to a student. Because I knew that there were serious gaps in my comprehension of music, I sought advice elsewhere — not only from pianists, but also from other instrumentalists, singers, and conductors. For example, Aunt Clara arranged for me to study all of the Beethoven sonatas for cello and piano with the cellist Maurice Eisenberg, who lived in Maplewood, New Jersey, a beautiful suburb of Newark. A disciple of Pablo Casals, Eisenberg was a well-known performer, and a magnetic personality. Playing these masterpieces with an artist of such stature was like being carried along on a tidal wave of dynamic energy. Technical passages that I sweated over at home seemed inconsequential in the wake of musical passion and a "do or die" attitude. When time permitted, Eisenberg coached me on my solo repertory. It was refreshing to address the music itself, and not merely to focus upon my muscular condition, which was the only thing that interested Louise during my lessons with her.

After the first lesson with Maurice Eisenberg, I could not wait to share with Louise all that he had taught me. Arriving at her home the following day, I rushed to the piano and demonstrated phrase by phrase my new musical concepts. Since I had had only the morning hours in which to work out the suggestions that Eisenberg had given me, my playing left a great deal to be desired. Nevertheless, I tried my best to demonstrate the essence of those suggestions, which, I believe, ought to have been discernible to any teacher generous enough to listen objectively. Far from being receptive and supportive, Louise quietly seethed with disapproval the whole time. When I finished demonstrating, she insisted that each and every one of the examples I played disclosed a deterioration in my playing. "I suppose you think that Eisenberg's suggestions have improved your playing," she blurted out, heatedly. "But the truth is, your playing has slipped backwards!" Her comments crushed me. I wanted to tell her that I only needed time to work out the suggestions, but I could not find my voice. I fully identified with Balzac, who, when his early attempts at writing elicited nothing but harsh criticisms from the press, wrote despairingly in his diary, "Why can't they see what I *will* be, just by the look in my eye!" Besides, I instinctively felt that anything I said in my defense would have been wasted on Louise. She was acting irrationally, out of sheer jealousy. In time, I thought, I would bring Louise over to my side: she would help me in her way, and humbly accept the fact that I needed help from others. My assessment, however, could not have been further from the mark. The monster had already laid her snare for me. She knew that her victim, being desperate for knowledge, would remain under her spell.

Intimacy

Gradually, and insidiously, Louise invited me to spend more and more time with her — especially in the evenings. To be fair about it, by not saying "no," I was partly to blame for the intimacy which followed. Yet, at that time, devotion and intimacy were one and the same. I was devoted to Aunt Clara, and I used to spend a great deal of time with her. So why should I not spend time with Louise? It was natural for me, therefore, to sit with her on her living room sofa and chat for hours on end. That she affectionately stroked my hair and massaged my neck seemed natural also. After all, I was brought up in an overtly affectionate environment, in which all family members kissed, hugged, and stroked one another as a matter of course. Louise's affectionate gestures, therefore, were in keeping with what I had experienced at home. And perhaps she, having led a sheltered and insulated life, meant only to express innocent affection. It is possible that her stroking me was the first overt sign of affection that she had ever expressed to a man.

Whatever her intent, my acquiescence encouraged her more than I intended. I became her exclusive property, not only musically, but also personally. As such, everyone who was close to me fell under her harsh criticism. "You know too many people," she would often complain. "Real artists live in solitude." I interpreted this to mean that I should be as anti-social as she was. She even went so far as to criticize my mother, whose slight Jewish accent, I believe, brought out Louise's anti-Semitic feelings. If ever I came close to socking a woman, it was when Louise ridiculed my mother for constantly saying, "Oh, my God!" And regarding my mother's taste in clothing, which everyone else thought was impeccable — "She dresses too ostentatiously!"

The Facts of Life

My mother, on her part, disliked Louise from the start. There was no logical reason for this — she simply had a sixth sense about every person who came into my life. In almost all instances, her instincts proved to be correct. As far as my relationship with Louise was concerned, she sensed that I was in danger. But never being one to interfere in my musical or personal life, she kept her feelings to herself. Finally, though, when certain gossip reached her ears and confirmed her hunch, she felt obliged to confront me on the subject: "Do you know that all of Newark is talking about your affair with your piano teacher?" "What?" I responded with utter surprise. "An affair with Louise? You must be kidding!" My mother, however, didn't think it was preposterous. "Putting two and six together" (one of her favorite expressions), she sincerely wondered what we did together evening after evening. I tried to explain to her something about that special relationship which can grow between a pupil and a teacher. I cited my relationship with Aunt Clara as an example of this; it was, as I knew, a relationship which my mother heartily approved of. But my mother was not to be swayed in the slightest. Aunt Clara's interest in me was aboveboard. But Louise? — her motives were anything but that! As my mother saw it, it was totally abnormal for an unmarried woman in her forties to spend so many evenings with a young man of eighteen.

My mother's inference left me in a state of confusion. I was that little boy again who, when asked to memorize a piece of music, became self-conscious about everything that had been natural and spontaneous. Immediately, the hair-stroking lost its innocence and charm. In fact, everything Louise did of a physical nature — taking my hand, touching my shoulder, etc. — took on a sexual connotation. "So that's it," I thought. "She wants to lure me into bed!" Nothing was ever the same again. From that time on, I was not only on guard with Louise, but subsequently with every teacher with whom I studied — male or female.

Partly due to my suspicions of Louise's motives and partly because of my busy life — I practiced six to eight hours a day, I had a class of pupils, and a modest social life — I began to spend less and less time at the

Curcio home. She was acutely aware of this, and her behavior towards me changed considerably. For one thing, she grew irritable, hostile, and harsh in her responses to my playing. I felt certain that because I was not fulfilling her romantic expectations, she intended to punish me in my most vulnerable area — my music making. The magic between us had vanished, and I secretly wanted to end the relationship as soon as possible. Yet I felt in debt to Louise for all the lessons she had given me. At least, I thought this was the reason that I continued to be a punching bag for a neurotic woman. It took years before I could discern the other reason.

Louise must have been very lonely before I came into her life. Because of her disability and her eccentric ways, people did not take to her too readily. And she, on her part, made no effort to befriend anyone — especially musicians. In fact, she was decidedly paranoid when it came to other teachers and instrumentalists, and she spoke of them as though they were the enemy. Anyone with knowledge posed a threat to Louise's security. For the truth is, she had only a limited knowledge of the repertory, and practically no ideas whatsoever concerning interpretation or any of the basic skills of keyboard technique. While musicians commonly agree that everything technical — the production of tone included — must be at the service of music, Louise deluded herself into believing the opposite: to her, the dimensional tone *was* music. Her theory served as a smoke screen to hide her deficiencies. It was her *raison d'être*, a validation for her very existence. And she used it to wield imaginary power in her delusionary world.

The Disciple

Louise intended from the beginning to use me for one purpose only — to make me into a channel through which her concepts of tone might be promulgated to the world. Because of her loneliness, and because she must have had a presentiment that life would pass her by without anyone's accepting her theory of the dimensional tone, I am sure that she latched onto me as a last resort. If she thought of herself as music's savior, then she saw me as her one and only disciple. And I was as obedient and responsible a disciple as any master might find. While I harbored many reservations about Louise and her theory, I nevertheless felt compelled to champion her cause out of sheer devotion. Besides, it would have reflected negatively upon me were I to be studying with someone whom I openly did not respect. There were many times at social gatherings of musicians, for instance, when I actually sermonized about the dimensional tone. I am sure I came on to my friends and colleagues exactly as Louise came on to me and to her other pupils: "Tone, for tone's sake!" In my secret heart, though, I neither fully understood Louise's theories, nor was I ever comfortable with the fact that she was musically ignorant.

Why did I continue to study with a teacher for whom I had so little respect? There is one simple explanation: I, like many students, was intent on idolizing my piano teachers, even when they did not deserve it. The other explanation is far more complex and painful to suggest: abused children often assume that they deserve abuse because they are just plain bad. So it is possible that in adulthood, I unconsciously continued to court abuse as a result of the unfortunate experiences of my childhood.

A Woman Scorned

My avoidance of evening intimacies with Louise must have hurt and frustrated her. Perhaps in retaliation, or as some sort of compensatory measure, she doubled her efforts to gain total control and ownership of me. She must have had fantasies of an ideal situation in which I would reject my family, friends, and colleagues and make her the center of my universe. Since nothing short of this would satisfy her, she grew more and more resentful of everyone and everything that interfered with the role she thought I ought to be playing in her life. I am sure that she saw our relationship as being one-sided: it was she who did all the giving, which included three free lessons a week, plus lunches, dinners, and hours of conversation. As I think about it now, I feel deep compassion for her suffering, and remorse for having unwittingly caused it. I see her trying to fill those caverns of insecurity and loneliness with delusions of grandeur almost too pitiful and too embarrassing to mention. "I am all things to him," she must have thought, "teacher, friend, cook, and even a potential lover. And how does he reciprocate? He not only seeks advice from other musicians, but he also courts people who are far beneath my intelligence and charm!" Emotionally stunted, Louise was simply too fragile for this world. She functioned well within the confines of her own environment. But in regard to the outside world and, especially, to all of her relationships, including the one with her sister, she saw herself as a victim of injustice. In thinking of me, her inner voice must have created a psychological construct of protection as a desperate attempt to ease her anguish — a construct in which I was the villain and she the helpless, guiltless party: "I deserve exclusive fidelity in return for all of my self-sacrifice." In reality, though, she behaved like a rejected woman — not only rejected but also betrayed, by the very person to whom she had entrusted the secrets of the dimensional tone, the person whom she had chosen to carry her message to the world. Inadvertently I became her Judas.

"You're not as good as they say!

As time went on, I became more and more wary of Louise's imperious habit of summarily dismissing all musical suggestions which other musicians had given me. As a matter of fact, she not only dismissed these suggestions, but she also discredited the musicians whose advice I sought. Even when I would quote supportive comments from others about my playing, these, too, she disparaged contemptuously. To cite one example, I tried out my Town Hall debut program at Montclair State Teachers College in New Jersey two weeks before the actual concert. It went extremely well, and I could hardly wait to tell Louise about it at my next lesson: "If only I could play like that in Town Hall," I told her, brimming over with excitement. "There were a number of faculty members there who had heard me through the years. You can't believe how enthusiastic they were. They all thought I had grown tremendously." Louise rolled her eyes upward and to the side, and with an unmistakable sneer she replied, "If I were you, I wouldn't take comments like that too seriously. After all, you're about to play an important recital. So even if you didn't play well, your friends would encourage you."

I spoke earlier of the various gifts I gave Louise in gratitude for the lessons she was giving me. I also did chores around her house — mowing the lawn, making whatever repairs I was able to manage, and hanging and then removing the screens and storm windows as the seasons required. While Louise appreciated all of this personal and practical attention, she had another sort of payment in mind, one which she no doubt had been devising all along. It was this: I, the chief proponent of the dimensional tone, was to give a public recital in Newark. She actually spoke of the recital as being the debut of her theory to the world. As such, she insisted upon writing the material for the leaflet. The heading — SEYMOUR BERNSTEIN and the DIMENSIONAL TONE — was followed by my bio:

> Seymour Bernstein began his quest for tone years ago. Believing the printed page with its notes and interpretive markings to be only the pattern for sound, he worked earnestly with Louise Curcio, an expert listener and guide, until, between them, they arrived at an effect so depth-giving that they called it the DIMENSIONAL TONE. Its natural beauty breathes life into every measure of music.

A single line followed about the awards I had won. Clearly, I was placed second to Louise and her Dimensional Tone.

The Steinway Basement

Few things are more problematic to a performing pianist than finding a suitable piano. The Griffith Piano Company rented out Steinway concert grands, but they were not kept in prime condition. We decided, therefore, to rent a concert grand directly from Steinway & Sons in New York City. Going to the famous Steinway basement and seeing all of the concert grands lined up like a regiment of soldiers was as thrilling then as it is now. Pianos, like people, have their own unique characteristics. That legendary figure, Bill Hupfer, who was then the chief technician of the concert grand department, often advised pianists as to which instrument he thought suited their particular style of playing. Imagine, then, what a privilege it was for me to have him help me in the selection process. As I went from piano to piano playing the same phrases so as to compare the sound and the touch of one piano to another, Bill listened with those miraculous ears which had earned him the status of "king of piano technicians." After ten minutes or so, when I was no closer to making my decision than when I entered the basement, Bill looked at me with a twinkle in his eye. And with a ceremonious gait, he walked over to CD-50 (all of the pianos had numbers stenciled on their lids), unlocked it and opened the lid on the full stick. "Try this one," he said, smiling.

Instantly, I felt this piano to be an extension of myself. Every subtlety of phrase, each technically demanding passage seemed to emanate from the piano at my slightest bidding. Even Louise was moved; her scowl gave way to a humanized smile. There was no question about it: this would be the piano for my recital. Bill told me later that CD-50 had been Schnabel's favorite piano for years. It no doubt was the very piano upon which Schnabel had played when I first heard him in Carnegie Hall. Louise and I then went upstairs to the rental office on the second floor to arrange as much practice time as I could be allowed on CD-50.

It was a joyous young pianist who wended his way back to Newark. To have been taken so seriously by a figure such as Bill Hupfer gave me a sense of having been accepted into a world which I had always thought was forbidden to me. That was not the last time I saw Bill Hupfer. He actually came out to Newark to tune and regulate my own piano. (I had long since replaced my Florey Brothers baby grand with a larger Steinway, a model "L.") Later, when I moved to New York City, he continued to service my piano there until his retirement in the 1970s. While we were not close socially, there was, nevertheless, a deep bond between us born of mutual respect for one another's gifts. He was generous to me, too. A month or so after Josef Hofmann died, the great pianist's silent keyboard, designed for him by Steinway, was left unclaimed in the Steinway basement. Bill offered it to me as a present. It was my chief treasure for years, and my constant companion on tours. Five years later, it was stolen out of a friend's car. Even now, its loss is incalculable.

Fate Snares the Monster!

Since the proposed concert I mentioned was to be Louise's debut, not mine, she insisted upon attending my practice sessions in the Steinway basement in order to check on the dimensionality of each tone I played. As the date for the recital drew nearer, I pointedly asked her not to come to any more of my rehearsals. "Finally, I have to be alone on that stage with CD-50, and you'll not be able to help me, then," I told her. Much to my relief, she found this reasonable enough. Her disciple, by this time, could be trusted to practice on his own.

The day of the concert arrived, and I awakened with that all too familiar whirlpool of anxiety churning in the pit of my stomach. Even before my mother served me breakfast, the doorbell rang. It was Western Union delivering a telegram from Steinway & Sons. "This must be one of Steinway's formalities," I thought. "They've sent me a telegram wishing me good luck." The true content of that telegram left me numb in disbelief. It seemed that the Steinway movers had gone on strike for the first time in Steinway's history. All deliveries were canceled! I rushed to the telephone to contact the rental office at Steinway. "Please don't worry," the woman in charge told me. "One of our concert grands happens to be in Paterson, New Jersey. We have already negotiated with New Jersey movers to deliver that piano to the auditorium where you will be performing. It will arrive early this afternoon." She assured me that it was a fine instrument, and that it came highly recommended by some other pianists. I believed her, and in a moment, I grew calm.

When the world-renowned cellist Gregor Piatigorsky told a group of his students backstage in Tanglewood that there are no heroes a moment before a recital, he was, of course, speaking for all performers. While I was very nervous on the day of that recital, I confess to having greeted the news of the Steinway strike with a certain sense of relief. To be sure, I loved CD-50. But not having it provided me with a watertight rationalization, should I not play my best. While I was ashamed of my response, still, the whole emergency served to lessen my anxiety. I would have enjoyed the hours before my recital had I not had a challenge before me far more demanding than the performance itself — that of having to tell Louise about the strike.

If ever a person gave proof of monster status, Louise did, both during that telephone conversation and in the hours preceding my recital. Heedless of the fact that it was I, after all, who had to do all of the playing, she greeted the news with an hysteria which said everything about her: "How can you produce a dimensional tone on a piano you don't even know? I insist that you call Steinway immediately and ask them to send you another telegram which I will dictate!"

At the time, it seemed easier to accede to her wishes rather than argue with her. My own embarrassment notwithstanding, I plucked up my courage and telephoned Steinway once again. The woman to whom I had just spoken was very cooperative and agreed to send the following telegram:

> The piano upon which this concert was prepared could not be delivered due to a truckers' strike. A substitute piano has been sent instead.

Later, Louise had a lawyer friend read this telegram from the stage moments before I walked out to perform. Quite obviously, her insistence on having that telegram read to a sold-out auditorium revealed her lack of faith in my ability to control a piano that she herself had not sanctioned. She covered her bases, so to speak, just in case I did not play well.

In the meantime, how she ranted and raved in the hall before my recital, I cannot begin to say. While I familiarized myself with the new instrument, Louise sat in the darkened auditorium and shouted comments such as "How can you play on such an uneven piano?" "The treble is so tinny!" "You're growing stiffer and stiffer!" Had I not experienced it, I would never have believed just how far a teacher could go in undermining a pupil's confidence just hours before a recital. All the while, I sincerely wondered whether it was the pianist or the piano that produced a dimensional tone. As far as Louise was concerned, there was no point in even trying: without a perfect piano, I was doomed to failure. More importantly, my failure would reflect upon her. Her reputation would be ruined, and I would be the cause of it.

Much to my relief, the father of one of Louise's pupils offered to drive her home. I then had two and a half hours in which to befriend the piano. Though not as sensitive as CD-50, it was, nevertheless, a fine instrument. Or perhaps it was the relief of finally being alone in the hall that made it seem so. At any rate, in an hour or so, my confidence was restored. At 7:30 PM, I retired backstage to dress for the occasion.

Stuck to the Keys

I have never resorted to rituals of any sort before a concert, but I certainly was not against anything of a practical nature that might improve my performance. On this occasion, therefore, I had with me a jar of egg white, of all things! As it happened, I had recently read an interview with the violinist Erica Morini. In it, she spoke of her own remedy for dealing with cold, clammy hands before a concert — that of rubbing egg white into them. Having always suffered from that slipping-sliding sensation on the keyboard, especially on the narrow black keys, I saw in Morini's remedy a possible solution to my own problem. Moments before I walked out on stage, therefore, I stood over a basin in my dressing room, unscrewed the jar of egg white, and poured the entire contents into my palms. Though I massaged and massaged, the thick gooey stuff stubbornly refused to be absorbed. "Perhaps it is only supposed to coat the palms," I reasoned. Then the obvious occurred to me: "Why hadn't I experimented with the egg white at one of my tryouts?" It was all too late now; there was a knock at my dressing room door; it was time to begin the recital. I took a deep breath and walked towards the stage entrance, my hands still coated with egg white.

Whatever one's physical condition may be, and whatever associative thoughts one may have before a concert, everything fades from consciousness with the first step onto the stage. One's coughs and sneezes cease (this is actually due to the secretion of adrenaline in the body), and even recent tragedies are instantly sublimated. As I bowed and sat down before the keyboard, therefore, I neither thought of Louise, the dimensional tone, nor the egg white coating my hands. I knew only one thing: I had to depress the first *D* minor chord of the Bach-Busoni Chaconne. Having done so, I proceeded to lift out of the first chord to prepare for the second. At that moment, however, I knew I was in serious trouble: The egg white might as well have been Elmer's glue; I was literally stuck to the keys and had to pull my fingers off of them. By the time I had finished the Chaconne, about fifteen minutes long, the greater part of the keyboard was coated with a thin layer of egg white. Somehow I reached the end of the Chaconne, and I doubt if my sticky situation was apparent to the audience. Needless to say, it was a relief to leave the stage. While I scrubbed my hands clean in my dressing room, the stage manager was at the same time washing an uncooked omelet off of the keyboard.

If a musician's preparation is three quarters of the battle in surmounting performance anxiety, the instrument itself must surely account for the remaining quarter. The piano turned out to be a fine instrument, which made Louise's histrionics and the second telegram from Steinway seem all the more absurd and unnecessary. Moreover, the acoustics of the hall were exceptional, helping me to achieve a wide range of dynamics. All in all, it was one of those ideal auditoriums which performers rarely encounter. With a seating capacity of nine hundred, it was housed in a magnificent neoclassical building. With its Corinthian columns and the gleaming white granite steps leading up to its ornate bronze doors decorated in bas-relief, it looked more like the Parthenon than the Mutual Benefit Life Insurance Company. Several years later, when I gave a second concert there, the building had been taken over by a Catholic school.

It is natural, I believe, to want to greet your teacher after an important recital. The entire audience, it seemed, filed past me afterwards. But Louise was nowhere in sight. Was she disappointed in my playing? Did I not play dimensionally? Should I have acknowledged her when I received a standing ovation — one which she might have felt belonged to her? These and other questions coursed through my mind. On the way home, I took stock of my playing. Apart from a slight memory slip in the final piece, the *Mephisto* Waltz by Liszt, from which I instantly recovered, the recital had gone well. Certainly, no one, not even Louise, would fault me for that. It was late when I arrived home, and I decided to wait until the morning to telephone her.

Eruption No. 2

I did not need to, though. At 10 AM, the telephone rang. It was Louise. There was hardly any exchange of conversation before she got right down to the point: "I didn't feel you played your best. There were percussive sounds, and uneven passages. As for the mishap in the Liszt, professional performers never have memory slips in public! You had better think twice before you undertake a career in music!"

When I described that turbulent scene at the dining room table after my *bar mitzvah*, I mentioned that there were a few occasions during my lifetime when my temper erupted like a volcano. This was one of those times. Years of anguish, confusion, and pent-up rage exploded in an outpouring of resentments. I began by reminding her that she and I had often heard our pianistic idols suffer memory slips in public — slips far worse than mine. I accused her of hypocrisy, and of being self-centered, hostile, and insensitive. And finally, I told her that my memory slip was the sort of thing that can happen to the most experienced performer, and that I had no intention of abandoning my aspirations to be performer. As I hung up the telephone, I knew that our relationship would never be the same again.

At first I felt relieved and vindicated to have told Louise outright exactly what I thought of her. But by the following day, my feisty mood gave way to a depression so intense that I could hardly function at all. The natural letdown that most performers experience after a concert plus the confrontation with Louise took a heavy toll on me. For there are few experiences in life more devastating than having an altercation with your teacher.

After several weeks, I began to take stock of things more objectively. At thirteen, when I stood up to my father, I did so with an underlying sense of doom: God will certainly strike me dead! At nineteen, however, having acquired greater confidence in myself, I felt very much the adult in standing up to this pernicious woman. Little did I know then that my whole experience with Louise was, in effect, basic training for dealing with another monster — one who made Louise seem like Florence Nightingale by comparison!

100 RECORDINGS

Surely only the masochist in me could explain why I continued to have anything at all to do with Louise. It shames me now to say that I continued my lessons with her, but only sporadically. Apart from psychological issues, there still remained two areas of unfinished business: recordings which I was in the process of making for the New Jersey Foundation for the Blind — a project that Louise had instituted, and a series of concerts at the Mosque Theater for which Louise and I had tickets. Feeling very resentful towards Louise, I was inclined to give away my ticket for the following concert. Fortunately, I did not act upon that impulse. For as it happened, that concert brought me into contact with one of the great figures in the musical world.

But first, to the recordings: these were to serve as an aid to blind students in deciphering the highly complex Braille symbols for music. Few things are more difficult than learning music by means of Braille. Like a computer language converted into embossed dots, Braille music requires a symbol for absolutely everything that a sighted musician takes for granted. For example, the data required to play a *B* flat would have to include the following information: the pitch name, its register on the keyboard, the rhythmic value, the interpretive dynamic, the fingering, its position in the phrase, etc., etc. Considering that a blind person can only play one hand at a time, the other hand being engaged in deciphering the Braille, it is not difficult to imagine how long it would take to learn a short, simple piece, much less a long, difficult one.

Louise, who had partial vision in one eye, learned music with the help of a telescopic lens. But she used Braille for reading books and for teaching several blind piano students. To facilitate the arduous learning process for blind pianists, she proposed a project whereby I would record a vast number of solo works and albums not available at that time. The project was sponsored by a grant given to the New Jersey Commission for the Blind by a wealthy philanthropist who was a friend of Louise's, Major M. C. Migel. He was the chairman of the board of the American Foundation for the Blind. The New Jersey Commission, then, turned over the grant to me as an honorarium for my efforts. The recordings were to become a part of a permanent collection at the Commission library and would be made available to blind students living in New Jersey.

Once Through

One day, a recording engineer named Matt arrived at my parents' apartment. He placed on my living room floor a Presto portable machine, which cut 33 rpm discs. In those days, of course, this was considered high-tech stuff. It did not seem so high-tech to me, though, when I made mistakes, for there could be no splicing whatsoever. Once through, and that was it! The discipline necessary to make those recordings taught me the real significance of concentration, not only during the recording sessions themselves, but especially during my practicing. In short, I had to fill every moment of my practice time with laser beam concentration. Learning a new program each week over a span of two years, and keeping up my own repertory besides, kept me at the piano for the better part of each day. It was pressure learning of the most stringent sort.

The repertory chosen for this project was taken from a vast number of unrecorded works, the music of which had been converted into Braille. Complete albums of Czerny, Cramer, and Burgmüller etudes, the entire *Album for the Young* by Schumann, plus countless solo pieces — these were among the huge list of works that I learned and recorded. As an aid to blind students, I would often precede the performance of a work by first recording certain technically difficult passages hands separately and then together — from slow to fast. For rhythmically complex passages, I set my metronome to a slow tempo. I allowed it to tick for one or two measures to set the tempo. I then counted out loud while playing the passage in question.

As any performer will tell you, there are few experiences more stressful than making a recording. In this case, I not only had to contend with the pressure of playing perfectly the first time, but I also was faced with the possibility of the machine jamming as it occasionally did — and often during my best performance. Moreover, the discs themselves were very expensive. With each mistake, I had a crisis of conscience. And whatever Matt would say to placate me, I continued to feel guilty each time my nerves got the better of me. On the few occasions when the recordings went well, Matt lingered on and allowed me to record my own repertory. I still have most of those discs. But as to the recordings that I made for the Commission, some discs were borrowed but never returned to the library. Finally, the entire collection of recordings vanished along with the Commission itself. I am comforted with the thought that the discs have probably remained in the hands of blind pianists. If this is so, then all of my efforts were not in vain.

FATEFUL MEETING

Exactly one week after my concert at the Mutual Benefit Life Insurance Company auditorium, Louise and I, with my dear friend Nikki Pickar-Greenberg, attended a recital at the Mosque Theater given by the famed pianist Alexander Brailowsky. As I mentioned earlier, Louise considered him to be a prime exemplar of the dimensional tone. She was, of course, not alone in her admiration of him: Brailowsky was a world-renowned figure at that time and had a following similar to that of Horowitz and Rubinstein. I had heard him perform in public many times. From the very first hearing, he became one of my pianistic idols.

After my stormy encounter with Louise, the very sight of her stirred up a tempest within me. But there is nothing like listening to a great artist to lessen tensions between people. As I perused the program, I was excited to note that Brailowsky planned to open his recital with the Bach-Busoni Chaconne, the same piece with which I had begun my recital. Moreover, the Steinway movers were still on strike, and Brailowsky had to perform on the same substitute piano that I had had to use. All of this prompted Nikki to insist that I go backstage after the concert and tell Brailowsky of these striking coincidences. It took a great deal of prodding on her part before I finally agreed to go. For I was always, as I have confessed, uneasy in the presence of famous people. I seriously wondered if I would be able to say anything at all once I found myself in the presence of Brailowsky.

After the recital, Nikki, Louise, and I waited in what seemed to be an endless line. Suddenly, I was actually face to face with my idol. I might as well have been on a stage and about to sound the first note of a recital, so anxious did I become in his presence. All of the pre-performance anxiety symptoms were there — shallow breathing, sweaty hands, and that dreadful sinking feeling in the pit of my stomach. I had all I could do to muster my courage in order to utter anything at all. Once I heard my own voice, though, I gained a bit more confidence. I proceeded to tell Brailowsky all about the strike and the Bach Chaconne. "You played on dat piano?" he responded, in a low, growling voice with a thick Russian accent. "And you also began with the Chaconne?" he added, his eyebrows raised like pointed gothic arches.

The ice had been broken. But as I reasoned, his last comment required some sort of response from me. What that response was, however, astonishes me even to this day. Had I planned it, I am sure I would never have had the courage to ask, "May I play the Chaconne for you one day?" I fully expected a polite "no," with an explanation such as, "I am too busy touring," or, "I do not have time to teach." But to my astonishment, Brailowsky did not hesitate a moment. He took my program, which I was nervously clutching at the time, autographed it for me, and added his address and telephone number. "I am going on tour soon," he replied as he handed the program back to me. "But if you will telephone me in three weeks, I will tell you when you may come to play the Chaconne."

Unexpected pleasures and fulfillments of dreams can often have a stupefying effect upon a person. I can only recall mumbling something to Brailowsky as I seemed to float away from him. Nor do I remember anything whatsoever of Nikki's and Louise's response other than their open-mouthed expressions.

Making this connection to Alexander Brailowsky had a profound effect upon me: it inspired me to redouble my efforts in practicing, and it gave me the courage to discontinue my lessons with Louise. Over the next two years, I occasionally played for her whenever I had decided to program new repertoire. My doing so was not motivated by devotion in the slightest. To be blunt about it, she was the most difficult person to play for, and I therefore used her to see if I could survive the challenge. At times she would invite a small audience to hear me. Her remarks after my performances were either perfunctory or acid. After two or three such experiences, I stopped contacting her entirely.

Through the years several excellent pianists studied with Louise. As with me, the poison of her own discontent created one breach after another. She died on January 1, 1987. Sadly, there were only six people at the funeral.

ALEXANDER BRAILOWSKY

Three weeks after I met Brailowsky at the Mosque Theater in Newark, I dialed the telephone number that he had written on my program. His wife Ela answered. Her voice was aristocratic and exceedingly gracious. Evidently Brailowsky had told her of our meeting backstage in Newark,

At twenty, during a lesson with Alexander Brailowsky in his
mansion at 107 East 64th Street, New York City.
(Photo by Seymour Bernstein)

for she was already prepared to give me a time when I might come to play for him.

Brailowsky lived in a magnificent five-story mansion at 107 East 64th Street in New York City. Standing before the door was even more anxiety-producing than waiting in line to meet him at the Mosque Theater. As I rang the bell, I was as pale as the snow on the sidewalk. Marie, the Brailowskys' French servant, opened the door. Her smile and her greeting in French disarmed me. Standing by was her husband, Joseph, who graciously took my coat. Still smiling, Marie beckoned me to a flight of steps leading up to the drawing room of the mansion. I was to wait there for the arrival of the master.

Palatial Ambience

The room in which I found myself made me temporarily forget the reason for my being there. Approximately forty by twenty-five feet, with a double-height ceiling, the room looked as though it had been lifted out of the Palais de Versailles. The first thing I noticed was the long sleek ebony Steinway concert grand. For all of its nine-foot length, it looked relatively small in that vast space. Behind it hung magnificent brocade drapes framing the windows facing East 64th Street. The drapes were pulled back in graceful folds by elegant sashes. One large oriental carpet covered most of the floor space, its thick padding providing that luxurious deeply-cushioned feeling. On the left side of the room stood a large sofa with a scalloped back, covered in coral velvet. A magnificently carved white marble fireplace occupied the center of the right wall. On its mantel stood a marble and bronze clock, which, I subsequently learned, had belonged to Napoleon Bonaparte. Hanging on the mirrored wall above the mantel was a striking portrait of a much younger Ela. Here and there, Louis XIV and XV chairs and tables added tasteful counterpoint to the larger pieces of furniture. Everything reflected a harmony of parts, like that of a Bach fugue.

I was standing in the middle of the room, transfixed by the splendor of my surroundings, when suddenly Brailowsky appeared from behind me. On stage, artists look bigger than life. But now, as the great pianist stood before me, I was amazed to see how short he actually was. He held out his hand and sported a clownish grin, quite literally from ear to ear. In an instant, my anxiety vanished. With sparkling warm eyes and a decidedly shy manner, he beckoned me to the piano. There, to my surprise, I found the artist bench turned up so high that I could not get my knees under the piano. Brailowsky chuckled at this and explained that he always sat very high because of his own particular proportions. I noticed at once that he had a short torso and long, spindly legs. I noticed, too, the early symptoms of osteoporosis, which grew into a serious problem as he got older. It took some two minutes of turning the knobs before I was able to lower the bench to my desired height. Once settled, I handed Brailowsky my score of the Bach-Busoni Chaconne and played it for him from beginning to end.

Having been somewhat in a trance from the moment I entered that home, I cannot say how I performed. I do remember, though, that Brailowsky positioned himself at the tail end of the concert grand during my performance. He rested the music on the lid of piano, crouched over it and turned each page as I played. When I finished, he walked around the full length of the piano and stood at my right with a gleeful expression. I, of course, leapt to my feet and stood facing him. His eyes were warm and expressive as he inquired, "Do you have a manager?" It was the same growling voice with the thick Russian accent that I remembered from backstage at the Mosque Theater. "No," I answered, and I wondered why he asked me that. "Do you play often in *pooblick?*" he then asked. "Very rarely," I replied, and I felt my cheeks grow red. "You must play in *pooblick* often." This sounded more like an admonition than advice. He then added, "You play very well. You must have a manager. Please telephone my manager and tell him I said he must manage you!"

This last statement alone summed up Brailowsky's naive understanding of the business end of music. Being at the pinnacle of his career, and having Ela to protect him from the outside world, he had no notion whatsoever of how difficult it was, and still is, to attract the interest of a concert manager. And I, being just as naive, actually telephoned his manager; that is, I left a message for him with his secretary. The fact that he never returned my call was not at all surprising. I am sure that he, like most concert managers, was bombarded daily with telephone calls from young hopefuls. To be truthful about it, I was somewhat relieved that he ignored my message. For however enthusiastic Brailowsky may have been about my playing, I knew that I was not ready to be launched into a concert career. Besides, I did not go to Brailowsky with the intention of soliciting references or engagements from him. That he thought my playing warranted the interest of his own manager was quite enough of a vote of confidence. I never attempted to communicate with his manager again; nor did Brailowsky ever inquire about it.

To return to the lesson, Brailowsky's comment about telephoning his manager seemed as unreal as was everything else. I thanked him and moved aside as he, still holding my score, sauntered to the piano. I quickly screwed up the bench again and the master seated himself at the keyboard. Placing the score of the Chaconne on the music desk, he turned to me and exclaimed, "Ven I played dis piece for Busoni...." "Busoni?" I thought. "He actually played the Chaconne for the composer himself!" I was so astonished at this, that I could hardly concentrate on Brailowsky's comments. It was like being privy to music history in the making. Brailowsky then proceeded to speak about and also demonstrate certain passages that Busoni had discussed with him. The sheer intensity of his tone left me spellbound. I was startled, then, when suddenly he turned to me and asked, "Do you have something by Chopin, perhaps?"

I had a reason to be startled. Brailowsky's popularity derived from one thing in particular: he was the first twentieth century pianist to perform all of the works of Chopin in one series of concerts. It was a feat that earned him a world-wide reputation, and which he repeated ten times in his career. Not that he restricted his repertory to Chopin. His recital programs were rich and varied, reflecting a wide range of styles and periods. I, personally, discovered the extent of his repertory: during the twenty-nine years I played for him, I never repeated a single piece, and whatever I brought to my lessons, he knew well enough to demonstrate. His accomplishment, though, of performing the entire Chopin cycle quite naturally categorized him as a Chopin pianist. He cut the figure of the grand romantic virtuoso, one who deservedly acquired a large and adoring public.

Imagine, if you will, how I felt, being asked to play Chopin for the world's most famous interpreter of this composer. While I had many works of Chopin in my repertory, I had thought it would be presumptuous on my part to perform them for Brailowsky. Now, however, to deny his request would be insulting to him, and would seem to suggest that I could not play a work by the composer who was, perhaps, closest to his heart. I plucked up my courage, therefore, and quite spontaneously played the Nocturne in *G* major, one of my favorite pieces. When I finished, he approached me more like a loving father than a world-renowned pianist: "Dis reminds me of my student days," he said, nostalgically. I suppressed an impulse to hug him out of sheer love and gratitude. To my surprise, he liked the Nocturne, and he said no more about it.

Ominous Ela

The lesson ended. Brailowsky walked slowly out of the drawing room and returned with Ela and his dog Chan, a large Manchurian chow. I have already spoken about my deep affection for animals. Little wonder that I had to restrain myself from greeting Chan first before shaking hands with Mme. Brailowsky. Ela, with her tight jet black hair parted down the middle, looked like an older version of the painting above the mantel.

Alexander Brailowsky with his dog Chan.
(Photo by Seymour Bernstein)

Alexander Brailowsky with Ela and Bambi.
(Photo by Seymour Bernstein)

Curiously, I felt an instant aversion to her. While she seemed to be warm and friendly, her voice, deep and aggressive in tone, and the look of torment in her eyes disquieted me from the start. More disturbing was her decidedly self-conscious demeanor. For during the entire time she remained in the room, she nervously smoothed down her hair with the fingers of both hands while simultaneously stealing glimpses of herself in the mirrored wall above the mantel. It was as if she harbored the illusion that the reflection might suddenly change to reveal her lost beauty and desirability. Oddly enough, she seemed oblivious to the fact that I was observing her gestures.

In all honesty, I was much relieved when she asked to be excused. In an instant, I rushed over to Chan, knelt down before him, and lovingly scratched his magnificent reddish brown mane — much to Brailowsky's delight. He himself spoke to Chan in a high falsetto voice, partly in Russian and partly in French. I had my camera with me, and Brailowsky allowed me to take many photographs of him with Chan. And with the help of a self-timer, I took a photograph of the three of us.

Suddenly I became aware that I might be overstaying my welcome. I stood up, reluctantly leaving Chan, and went over to the master to thank him. It then occurred to me that I had not as yet brought up the subject of payment for the lesson, although it seemed embarrassing to reduce that whole experience to money. Before I left home, my father had given me fifty dollars in cash, anticipating that Brailowsky's fee could be that much. Fifty dollars was a great deal of money in 1948. After thanking Brailowsky, I slipped my hand into my pants pocket, and, in a barely audible voice, asked him what his fee was. "I am very sorry," he said, trying to be more serious than he actually was. "I do not teach, and, therefore, I do not have a fee." As though anticipating what I would ask next, he added, "If you will telephone me in two weeks, I will hear you again." I was overwhelmed by this, and tears welled up in my eyes. Brailowsky embraced me warmly, and accompanied me downstairs. Marie and Joseph were waiting for us by the front door. While Joseph helped me on with my coat, Marie searched my face, perhaps pleased that color had returned to my cheeks. I had the feeling that they knew exactly why I was there, and I believe they were delighted to know that their master had found a young disciple. I thanked Brailowsky once again, embraced him a second time, and walked out onto East 64th Street. There was no happier young pianist in the whole world.

"Already there is something wrong!"

Lessons with Brailowsky ranged from hilarious to traumatizing. He was one of those performers who had no teaching experience. His idea of a lesson was to brush me aside and play the entire piece, or at least a good section of it. Once, for example, I mustered up enough courage to play Chopin's Ballade in *F* minor for him . In my opinion, no one has ever played the four Ballades as did Brailowsky. In his hands, they achieved a unity — like four chapters of a book. On this particular occasion, he took his customary position at the tail end of the concert grand. I took a deep breath, closed my eyes, and played the opening three repeated *G's* as sensitively as I was able. But before my left hand could make its entrance on the *E*, a dark, growling voice emanated from the far end of the piano: "Already there is something wrong!" — and the "*r's*" sounded more rolled than ever. Without another word, he ambled over, brushed me aside with what was now a familiar back-of-the-hand gesture, and sat at the keyboard. I stood to his left, fully expecting to hear what was wrong with the three *G's*. But instead, he played the entire Ballade as though he were on the stage of Carnegie Hall. While I tried my best to pay attention to each musical and technical detail, I found myself drawn into that nameless world of sound which does not admit of analysis. At the end of his performance, Brailowsky flashed me a particularly wide grin. And with an unmistakable air of having confirmed to himself just what an extraordinary artist he was, he exclaimed, "You see, dat's how it goes! Vat else have you voorked on?" And that was it! I never discovered what was wrong with those *G's*, nor did Brailowsky seem to be the slightest bit interested in hearing me play the rest of the Ballade. I simply went on to another piece.

While the incident seems humorous now, there was nothing humorous about it then. In fact, I felt so defeated at being summarily dismissed after the third note that I never performed that Ballade again. I'm quite sure Brailowsky never intended to diminish my confidence, for he loved me and admired my playing. Yet even supportive teachers can sometimes be hurtful. While I can still recall the inspiration of Brailowsky's performance, I nevertheless came away from that lesson with no more knowledge of the *F* minor Ballade than I had when I arrived.

Through the years, I have made light of this whole incident by simulating the scene both for my pupils and in "pooblick" during master classes. It never fails to elicit uproarious laughter. On one occasion, I was trying out a piece for my pupil Christopher Lewis. Being one of the funniest people I know, he seized the opportunity to turn the whole Ballade incident around. No sooner had I begun to play, than he stopped me abruptly with, "Already there is something *right!*" — and he rolled his "*r's*" exactly as he had heard me do during my imitations of Brailowsky.

A few more anecdotes are worth telling for their humor alone. They typify that special breed of performer who, while being totally ineffectual as a teacher, can be extremely funny. Once at a lesson, I asked Brailowsky how he pedaled the opening theme of the Waltz in *A* flat by Chopin. He looked at me quizzically and exclaimed, "I don't know how I pedal; I just pedal!" Similarly, in response to my asking him how he produced his full, resonant tone — indeed dimensional, he once again flashed me that vacant look of someone who has been confronted with a *non sequitur*: "Vat do you mean, how do I produce my tone? It is an expression of my soul!"

My Clowning Maître

Speaking about soulful expression, I once played for Brailowsky the posthumous Nocturne in *E* minor by Chopin. In all the years that I played for him, this was one of the few times that I was able to lose myself in a reverie of my own making. At the end of the piece, I held onto the final tones until they trailed off into the ether waves. Then, during the pregnant silence which followed, I slowly lowered my hands into my lap and remained motionless with my eyes closed for some ten seconds. "Now," I thought, "my master has finally heard me play my best. At last I have proved myself worthy of being his pupil."

I opened my eyes, fully expecting to see Brailowsky at his accustomed place at the tail end of the piano. But to my surprise, he was sitting on the drawing room floor, holding his head with both his hands and weaving back and forth as mourners do. As soon as I caught his eye he began to wail, "Oh, I am so sad! I have lost my best friend! Ohhhh!" I was open-mouthed, seeing my revered master in such a ridiculous pose, and hearing mournful wails instead of compliments. In a few seconds, however, we both howled with laughter. When we had regained our composure, he explained that I was far too sentimental in my interpretation of the Nocturne. Brailowsky then went to the piano to demonstrate his own approach to that piece: "Vhy do you play it so sadly?" he asked, while mimicking my exaggerated rubato. "It is a happy Nocturne!"

While I did not agree with his last comment, I did, however, modify my rubato in subsequent performances. The image of my master sitting on the floor remained with me for some time afterwards. And I could hardly keep from laughing out loud each time I performed that Nocturne in "pooblick."

Lifting My Fingering

Since I remained in awe of Brailowsky the entire time I studied with him, it never occurred to me that *he* might learn something from *me*. Once at a lesson, during my performance of the Hungarian Rhapsody No. 6 by Liszt, he stopped me abruptly after the following passage:

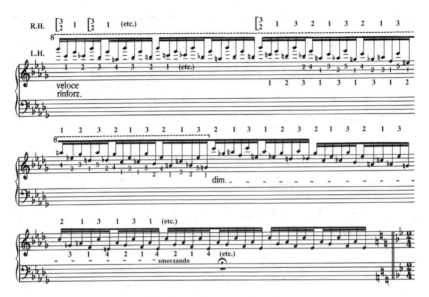

The large fingering is mine.

Walking over to me, and pointing to this cadenza in the music, he asked, "Vood you please play dis passage again?" Thinking that I may have learned a wrong note, I approached the passage more cautiously and deliberately. This time, I played it even better than I had before. All the while, Brailowsky hovered over the keyboard carefully examining my hands and looking every bit like a surgeon at an operation. Finishing the passage, I looked at my master inquiringly. "Very good," he growled. "Please continue." During the rest of my performance, I wondered why he had stopped me. I had to wait a week, though, before I learned the answer.

It was Brailowsky's annual appearance in Carnegie Hall. On that occasion, he ended the program with the very same Rhapsody that I had played for him a week earlier. As he played the cadenza passage in question, I noticed to my great delight that he redistributed the passage between his hands exactly as I did. My master had "lifted" my fingering! Was it professional pride or his altogether mysterious nature that prevented him from commenting upon my fingering at the lesson? Perhaps it was both. It would have been encouraging, however, had he complimented me on my successful redistribution. As it turned out, the incident passed without a word being exchanged.

Crisis and Success

Not all of my lessons with Brailowsky were humorous or easy-going affairs. In 1954, two weeks before my debut in Town Hall, I played *Feux d'artifice* (Fireworks) by Debussy for him. I had played this piece longer and knew it better than any of the other pieces on my program. That being the case, I had reserved my practicing of it until a few days before the recital. Admittedly, it was audacious of me to play it for my master off the top of my head, so to speak. I paid the price for it, too: it sounded superficial and uneven. Nothing, of course, escaped Brailowsky's miraculous ears. Almost with the last note, he proclaimed in a dark, accusing voice, "Dis piece is not ready for your debut!" — whereupon he turned on his heel and strode out of the drawing room. Needless to say, I was mortified. "I have offended my master," I thought, "and he will never teach me again."

As I continued to sit at the piano growing more and more dejected, Brailowsky returned with his Ela. Totally ignoring me, they exchanged some sentences in French — none of which I understood. It was Brailowsky who spoke first: "My wife used to play *Feux d'artifice*," he said rather proudly. "Would you please play it once again so that she can hear it?" I was surprised to learn that Ela had been a pianist. "So that's it," I thought. "He wants his wife to back up his decision in dismissing me." By this time I was so depressed that I began to play automatically, without the slightest thought or feeling. If anything, the opening section of Fireworks sounded even lumpier than the first time I played it. More French was exchanged, and then Ela spoke: "Would you please follow us to the third floor?" The Brailowskys then led me into the hall and up one flight of stairs. I had never been above the second floor before, and I was excited to be ushered into Brailowsky's studio. It was an elegant room, half the size of the drawing room, with a model "B" Hamburg Steinway angled into the near right corner. Looking towards the left, my eyes quickly took in a graceful Empire bed, which also served as a sofa. On the right wall, there was a large RCA radio-phonograph console. As I learned later, it was a gift from RCA Victor in token of Brailowsky's first platinum record — a symbol of one million records sold. The disc hung on the wall above the console, its frame a work of art in itself. The entire left wall was lined with bookcases and cabinets. The shelves were filled with rare books and a vast collection of leather-bound editions of music. The Brailowskys seated themselves in striped satin chairs by the windows and asked me to play *Fireworks* once again. The lighter action of this piano, coupled with the fact that it was my third time through, resulted in a much better performance. When I had finished, Brailowsky was all aglow, and his smile told me that he was pleased. Ela did all of the talking. "You see," she said proudly, "I told Sascha that the concert grand action was too heavy for you. My husband has very large and strong hands, and the action of the concert grand was made heavier for him. This Hamburg action is much more suited to your hands, and to your way of playing. You should always play for my husband on this piano." The whole time Brailowsky looked at Ela with loving approval. He then nodded to me to signify the end of the lesson.

The truth is, it was not the heavier action that had made me play poorly, but simply my lack of preparation. Regardless of its heaviness, I still preferred the sound of the concert grand to that of the Hamburg Steinway. At the time, though, it seemed much simpler to concur with Ela's appraisal of the situation. Besides, confessing that I had not practiced *Feux d'artifice* before my lesson would have added to my embarrassment.

Undercurrents

There were many unspoken feelings and thoughts that coursed between Ela and me. She communicated certain ones to me, though, by means of a look in her eye, a gesture, or a word. For one thing, I knew that she approved of my playing for her husband for a reason which I have not as yet mentioned: Around 1960, I began to notice marked signs of mental and physical deterioration in Brailowsky. I observed, too, that he was available to give me more frequent lessons, which could only mean one thing: his engagements had dwindled. Ela on her part seized every opportunity to make her husband feel wanted and admired. She knew full well that few people admired her husband as much as I did.

To Brailowsky, I represented the young generation of pianists whose playing, especially of the romantic repertory, he easily out-stripped. This boosted his ego. Apart from that special rubato that made his mazurkas, for instance, inimitable, he gleefully played chords that spanned a twelfth as easily as if they were octaves, and he chuckled sardonically when I had to resort to rolling or breaking them. This, of course, is a technical point of minor consequence. More importantly, he had been born close enough to the apex of the romantic era actually to have heard secondhand what Schumann and Brahms, for instance, said about this phrase or that tempo. And he had attended a recital at which Debussy himself played some of his own preludes. In fact, he gave me the program of that recital as a memento. In short, he was one of the last romantics. To hear him shape a phrase, or merely to be with him, was, to a nineteen-year-old young man, like stepping back in time. I felt at once privileged and frightened. For however diligently I may have practiced for those lessons, nerves invariably prevented me from playing my best. I lived in fear, therefore, that he would one day dismiss me forever. So when he walked out of the drawing room on this occasion, I thought the day had come. Even though he seemed pleased in the end, I imagined him thinking that I was a mistake, exactly as the violin teacher mentioned earlier thought of the young violinist.

The following morning, I began my practicing with *Fireworks*. In fact, I practiced it so diligently that it went flawlessly at my debut. Brailowsky did not come to that concert. Each time I bowed, or walked on or off of the stage, I glanced at the box seats where I knew he and Ela ought to have been sitting. While I was in a way relieved to see those seats empty (Brailowsky's presence would have added to my nervousness), I was convinced that my suspicions were now confirmed: Brailowsky was through with me. As it turned out, however, Ela telephoned me at around noon on the following day. She had waited until the reviews came out. "I had to restrain my husband from coming to your recital," she told me. "He has a dreadful cold, and the doctor forbade him to leave his bed." Whereupon my master got on the telephone and congratulated me for the wonderful reviews. He was not throwing me out after all. My heart sang again.

Deterioration

Whether Brailowsky's deterioration was due to senility or some other malady, I cannot say. As I recall, the symptoms became pronounced in the 1960s. Physically, the osteoporosis caused him to hunch even more, and he seemed more frail and was prone to respiratory infections. It was from pneumonia that he eventually died. Socially, he seemed always to be in a far away world. Yet during my lessons, he was vital in all respects. On the stage, however, his playing began to show the debilitating effects of whatever was wrong with him: his technique lost its accuracy and bravura, and his interpretations were illogical and marred by memory slips.

Poor Ela tried her best to boost his morale. And when he announced two recitals in Carnegie Hall in 1967 — a mixed program on February 22, and an all-Chopin recital on March 31 — she busily set about trying to recapture all of the excitement which his New York City appearances had always elicited from the public. For one thing, she asked me to photograph the poster displayed prominently on the billboard facing West 57th Street. The words SOLD OUT were pasted along the top of it. While I had a sense of foreboding about the whole affair, I nevertheless photographed my pupil Jim Pullman looking up at the poster, made an 8 x 10 enlargement of it, and gave it to my master. Brailowsky's eyes lit up when he saw the words SOLD OUT. It convinced him that the public had not forgotten him. He was too naive to know that this was all a publicity stunt, and that the recital was not, in fact, sold out.

Several years later I attended a debut recital in Carnegie when once again the words SOLD OUT were plastered everywhere. Such deception designed to draw in the public invariably ends up demeaning the artist and music itself. For all of this, we can thank greedy managers and artist representatives who claim to have their artists' best interests at heart. Regarding Brailowsky's concert, while the hall was not sold out, there was, nonetheless, a sizeable audience in attendance. I wished, though, that he had not performed at all. His playing was a mere shadow of what it once had been. The recital on March 31, 1967, was Brailowsky's last appearance in New York City.

Ela spent the better part of her life promoting and also protecting her husband's career. Finally, though, deception, like certain medications, loses its falsely protective cover. It was not long after this concert that Brailowsky's management and his recording company as well canceled his contracts. As Ela told me one day, it would have been more merciful had they placed a gun to her husband's head and pulled the trigger. Brailowsky lived for the stage alone. Without it, his life, in effect, was over. My coming to play for him once or twice a month did much to distract him from the depression that was creeping over him. Social encounters, too, lightened his spirits considerably. Knowing this, I took the Brailowskys on car trips in my Volkswagen "Beetle" during which my master sat beside me in the passenger seat. He was always light-hearted, and spent most of the trip mimicking the commercials on television, to which, evidently, he was addicted. The sight of this great artist clowning in such a fashion caused tears of laughter from Ela and me. One cannot be jovial all the time, however. I cannot say how painful it was to observe him sitting morosely in his drawing room, where the emptiness of his life cast him into a chasm of despair.

Occasionally, I invited the Brailowskys to dinner in my one-room studio apartment. I always prepared *kasha* with fried onions and mushrooms for him, as it was one of his favorite dishes. He also loved my two Siamese cats, Köchel and Sheila. There was no communicating with him so long as they sat on his lap. He cooed to them as he did to his own dogs. Before the advent of the burglar alarms now so prevalent in cars, my street was unusually quiet. In contrast to this, East 64th Street, where the Brailowskys lived, was a noisy thoroughfare to the Queensboro Bridge. Trucks, buses, and cars rumbled by the Brailowsky mansion day and night. While enjoying the peace and quiet of my small apartment, Brailowsky would often remark to Ela, "Oh, it is so quiet in Sighmore's house!" (He never learned to pronounce my name correctly.) "Well," I quickly responded, "why don't we switch homes? You

My pupil James Pullman in front of the poster at Carnegie Hall announcing
Brailowsky's final appearance in New York City.
(Photo by Seymour Bernstein)

live here, and I'll move into your mansion!" Such moments of humor cut through his depression. Then he was, if only temporarily, the maître I knew so well.

First Offense

Brailowsky was always at his best when I was playing for him. In fact, I once discussed with Ela the possibility of his accepting a modest class of pupils. But he could not tolerate most pianists — especially women. "They flail their elbows like the wings of a bird," he said, and he would imitate them exaggeratedly. He made it clear that I was, and would continue to be, his only pupil.

Only once in all the years I played for Brailowsky did he exhibit annoyance with me. The incident occurred during a lesson on Beethoven's Sonata Op. 110. It concerned the *ritardando* in the second movement:

Beethoven was not one of Brailowsky's specialties. When I was twenty-five, I brought him the Sonata Op. 111. He flatly refused to listen to it, and stated heatedly, "You must not play this vork until you are fifty!" Yet as I discovered, on February 10, 1927, when Brailowsky was thirty-one, he began a concert with this sonata in Peoria, Illinois. Curiously, he never performed it again. My feeling was that his particular gifts did not lend themselves to such transcendent works. This was not uncommon for a pianist of Brailowsky's vintage. Born in Kiev, Russia, in 1896, he received his early training at a time when artistic passions were not exactly tempered with scholarship. In fact, Brailowsky and Vladimir Horowitz were often sarcastically vocal about those "intellectuals" who claimed to be experts in playing late Beethoven and Schubert sonatas.

Brailowsky began taking piano lessons when he was five years old. His first teacher was his father, an amateur pianist. The lessons were confined to playing scales. In Brailowsky's own words:

> Oh! Such scales! Father made them a game, and, like a pace-
> maker, he carried me on and on. I would try to beat him in
> speed and accuracy, although I did not know at the time that
> he was really leading me on into what seemed like a delight-
> ful rivalry.
> (*The Etude*, June, 1925)

He goes on to say that very little was said to him about "tone and pieces." Nor was his training much different when he entered the Imperial Conservatory of Kiev three years later. His teacher, Pouchalsky, had studied with Theodore Leschetizky, so it seemed only natural that Brailowsky should follow in this tradition. At sixteen, then, Brailowsky went to Vienna to study with the world-renowned professor. As fate would have it, he was Leschetizky's last pupil.

To return to Op. 110, I doubted everything interpretive which my maître suggested because of one thing in particular: he had studied the Beethoven sonatas from the Hans von Bülow edition. While one can learn something from all editions, this one in particular is filled with distortions and inaccuracies of the worst kind. Seeing them, you get the feeling that von Bülow thought he understood the music better than Beethoven did. Concerning the *ritardando* in question, Brailowsky stopped me and demonstrated it in the most bizarre fashion. Instead of becoming gradually slower, which the word *ritardando* implies, he played all three measures abruptly slower, as one would do when seeing the words *ritenuto* or *ritenente*. Not only performers but even some composers confuse *ritardando* and *ritenuto*. Beethoven, however, was one composer who used these two words with explicit intent.

Being convinced that my maître was misreading Beethoven's indication, I could not in all conscience follow his advice. "Maître," I asked him. "Doesn't *ritardando* mean to grow slower gradually, and not to slacken the tempo abruptly?" Knowing of Brailowsky's vulnerability, I ought never to have said anything that would put him on the defensive. It was too late, however, and my question ignited a fuse: "No!" he roared like an aroused lion. "You must go slower as I showed you!"

The lesson continued, and I attributed his distracted state to a mood swing, something to which I was accustomed by this time. But as I subsequently discovered, it was far more serious than that. Ela, who always answered the telephone when I called to arrange a lesson, began to offer various excuses as to why her husband was unavailable: "I am so sorry, but Sascha is not here." "My husband has a cold, and it is difficult for him to speak." Finally, after six months of such stalling tactics, I asked her pointedly one day if something was wrong. "Well," she answered at once, "since you ask, I will tell you the truth: you offended my husband when you challenged the advice he gave you on Op. 110." "Offended him?" I responded in astonishment. "I would never intentionally offend your husband. I simply asked him a question about the word *ritardando*." I hated myself for pretending to be innocent, for I knew even at the time of the incident that there would be unpleasant repercussions. At any rate, Ela, wanting to make peace between Brailowsky and me, offered the following bit of advice: "Asking my husband a question was your first error in judgment. Don't you know that you must never question a Russian?" I apologized, of course, and asked if I might speak to Brailowsky. "One moment," she said in a friendly tone of voice. "I will ask him if he will speak to you."

A full minute went by, and finally I heard the familiar voice on the other end. "Hello, Sighmore," it growled. And with no pause whatsoever, he went right on with, "You must always listen to what I tell you and never oppose me!" He spoke in a sweet, loving tone which instantly warmed my spirit. I told him how sorry I was, and that I would never do that again. Another lesson was arranged, and from that time on he and I became even closer than before. Ela, on her part, grew more communicative with me. One day, after some fifteen years, I received an invitation to dinner.

Dinner in High Style

The dining room in the Brailowsky mansion, like everything else in the home, gave definition to the word "sumptuous." The crystal chandelier over the inlaid table, the antique wallpaper depicting American Indian scenes, the china and the silver — all were breathtakingly beautiful. Brailowsky, more hunched than ever and looking like a wizened elf, sat in an armchair at one end of the table; Ela sat at the other. Fritz, one of his two dachshunds, sat in Brailowsky's lap throughout the entire meal. Poor Chan, whom he adored, had recently died due to a freakish accident. It seems that the veterinarian had injected him with a mild sedative to calm him before cleaning his ears, and Chan died instantly of a heart attack. Brailowsky was grief-stricken, and Ela quickly purchased two dachshunds, Fritz and Bambi, who in no time at all occupied Brailowsky's affection. Fritz, though, was his favorite. He sat in Brailowsky's lap throughout the day, reluctantly leaving it to take an occasional walk. Fritz was very protective of his master, and growled at every person who came within a few feet of Brailowsky, Ela included. Interestingly, Fritz accepted me at once, and we all delighted in watching his tail wag whenever I approached Brailowsky.

Part 2: Monsters and Angels

During dinner, I was painfully self-conscious from the start. And the way that Ela overplayed her *grande dame* role did not put me at ease: "Are you enjoying the food?" "Do you want more?" "Why don't you want more?" Though stunningly dressed, Ela always looked haggard, with dark pools under her eyes. Even during dinner, she never ceased smoothing down her black hair. It was pitiful to watch her, and I always felt ill at ease in her presence.

It was time for dessert. Marie had baked a delectable *babka*, one of her specialties. After one taste, I swooned so conspicuously that I was sent home with the remainder of the *babka*, much to Marie's delight. Thereafter, each time Marie baked her *babkas*, Ela asked her to make an extra one just for me. It was, to be sure, a deeply touching gesture, one that was the forerunner of a whole series of generosities which Ela extended towards me.

A Wealth of Treasures

One evening in 1968, I was invited to dinner for a second time. Afterwards, Ela announced that there were two surprises waiting for me in her husband's studio on the third floor. All of us — the Brailowskys, Fritz, Bambi, and I — trudged up the stairs with great merriment. Once there, Ela went to a cabinet built into the bookcases. Rummaging through some scores, she produced the manuscript of Concerto No. 2 by Heitor Villa-Lobos, a work that the composer had written for, and dedicated to, Brailowsky. Villa-Lobos had once heard Brailowsky in Rio de Janeiro perform two concerti on the same program — the Tchaikovsky *B* flat minor and the Rachmaninoff *C* minor. He was so impressed by his playing that he decided to create another big romantic vehicle tailored to Brailowsky's virtuosic style. It was this score, then, that Ela handed me. With a sense of awe, I turned over the front cover and saw the following inscription:

MINISTERIO DA EDUCACAO E SAUDE
CONSERVATÓRIO NACIONAL DE CANTO ORFEONICO

Rio, 12/25/49
Cher Brailowsky,
    Voilà le Concerto que je vous avais promis. La partition
et matériel d'orchestre vous pouvez trouver à la Maison
Villa-Lobos Corp., 1585 Broadway, New York.
    Heureux 1950.
        Bien à vous,
            Villa-Lobos

128

*[Here is the Concerto that I promised you. You can find
the score and the orchestral parts at the Maison Villa-
Lobos Corp. Happy 1950. My best to you.]*

Ela explained, "With all of the big warhorses in my husband's repertory,
he never learned this concerto. Now, of course, he never will. Perhaps if it
interests you, you might première it with some major orchestra. But
whether you decide to study it or not, we would like you to have it."

And there was more. Going to another cabinet, Ela carefully extracted
a Japanese obi with great care. She took it to the Romanesque sofa and
slowly unrolled a few yards of it. Its beauty made me gasp. There, on a
field of woven black silk, was an array of multi-colored peacocks embroidered with real gold thread; emerald green and gold clouds floated behind
and around them. Ela then related the story of how they came to have the
obi. It seems that when Brailowsky performed in Japan in the 1920s, the
brother of the Emperor of Japan presented him with the obi as a gift,
purely out of admiration for his playing. It had been in the possession of
the imperial family for centuries. Since it did not blend in with the decor
of the Brailowsky home, and since the Brailowskys knew that my
apartment was decorated with oriental objets d'art, most of them gifts
received during my various state department tours to the Far East, the
Brailowskys now wanted me to have this rare heirloom.

Imagine how I felt on receiving two such treasures — as though being
the only pupil of one of the world's great pianists was not treasure enough
for a lifetime. I was speechless, and Brailowsky on his part seemed almost
breathless with excitement as he watched my responses to these gifts.
Sweet little Fritzie, responding to his master's infectious pleasure, barked
and wagged his tail in utter delight.

I tried to convey my thanks as well as I was able, my heart very full.
Even as I carried my gifts downstairs upon leaving the Brailowsky home
that evening, I had already decided to double my efforts on my master's
behalf. I had by that time been living in New York City for ten years. East
64th Street, therefore, was a mere bus trip across Central Park. I would
visit him more frequently and I would take him to concerts and
accompany him to libraries and museums. In short, I would find ways to
distract him from his unhappiness. I did, in fact, follow through with my
plan for years afterwards. But it saddens me to say that my best intentions
were cut short by Ela herself. For shortly afterwards her treacherous
behavior resulted in a painful rupture between me and my maître.

In the meantime, though, I devoured the Villa-Lobos score. The
writing, as I anticipated, was for large hands — like Brailowsky's. The

concerto was long, difficult, and thickly written for both the piano and orchestra. The work comprised four movements, the entire third movement being a cadenza for the piano. Everything about the piece — its themes, harmonic language, and the interplay between the piano and the orchestra — was of the romantic tradition. Thinking of a possible performance of it, I first checked with the publisher, G. Schirmer, to be sure that the full orchestral score and the instrumental parts were available. Having confirmed this, I then made the following decision: however difficult it was and however long it would take, I would learn the concerto and perform it as a testimonial to my beloved maître.

Debut with the Chicago Symphony

And how I worked on it...! It took months of consistent practicing to get the solo part into my fingers. Having done this, I set my sights on the orchestration. My own score included a piano reduction of the orchestral accompaniment. This turned out to be complex enough for twenty fingers! My reel-to-reel tape machine happened to have a superimposing device built into it. I set about, therefore, to record the orchestral reduction in two stages. When I completed this project, each note of the orchestral accompaniment was accurately recorded on the tape. After several more weeks of diligent practicing and experimentation with the placement of speakers, I was finally able to perform the solo part and synchronize it with my own tape recording of the accompaniment.

I was now ready to perform the concerto for Brailowsky. At the appointed time, I arrived at his home with my tape machine and speakers and busily set them up around the concert grand in the drawing room. Brailowsky and Fritzie sat on the sofa and watched with great interest and amusement as I crisscrossed wires under and around the piano. When all was set up, I turned on the tape machine and performed the entire concerto — the work which was inspired by Brailowsky's magnificent artistry. I had never before seen my maître so moved, and so impressed with my playing. In all modesty, I must say that it was a feat to learn both the solo part and the orchestral accompaniment. No one appreciated this more than Brailowsky. I felt that I had taken a step, at least, in giving him something in return for all that he had given me.

The following year, my manager arranged for me to play the United States première performance of this concerto, with the Chicago Symphony Orchestra in Orchestra Hall. My mother and several friends and pupils were there to share with me what was the most important engagement of my career up until that time. It was fortunate that I knew the orchestral accompaniment as well as I did, for as it happened, the first violin section skipped a full measure during the second movement. As if it had all been rehearsed in advance, I simply skipped along with them and went right on with the performance. The conductor, Irwin Hoffman, was very complimentary and expressed his desire to have me perform with him again. The critics, too, were enthusiastic. They seemed to like my playing more than they did the concerto. One critic expressed a desire to hear me again in a more standard work. While there seemed to be a strong potential for a re-engagement, my manager never took advantage of it.

Second Offense

It was in that same year, 1969, that Alice Tully Hall opened its doors at Lincoln Center. It was nine years since I had played a full recital in New York City. Whether the opening of the hall reawakened an urge to play again, or whether I fell prey to the glamour associated with performing in such a distinguished auditorium, I cannot say. Perhaps it was both. At any rate, I was the first pianist to book a date there — for September 26th. After posters were printed, and leaflets mailed out, Mark Schubart, who was then the president of Lincoln Center, telephoned me to say that the opening ceremonies to inaugurate the new Juilliard School were to be held in Alice Tully Hall on September 26th — the day I had reserved. Would I please consider moving my date. A Sunday in October was available, and he trusted that the new date would suit me. Lincoln Center would reprint all of my publicity and pay for all other expenses that might be incurred as a result of changing the date.

Under the circumstances, I could not refuse him. In time, everyone was informed of the new date — my personal contacts and all of the people on my mailing list — everyone, that is, except the person in charge of the computer at the ticket office. Due to some breakdown in communication, he or she had not been informed of the new date. As it happened, I myself went to the ticket office a week before my concert to draw two good seats for my Aunt Bessie. "Would you like to come into the office and see how the computer works?" the man in charge asked. In 1969 computers were a novelty, so I was extremely curious to see one in action. I was ushered through a door and into the area behind the ticket window. He went to the keyboard and typed in all of the necessary commands beginning with Event No. 1, the code number of my recital. He pressed "enter" and the computer brain was set into motion. After a brief whirring sound and a few blinking lights, the following message appeared on the monitor: *This recital has been canceled.*

I was horrified, and the computer operator for his part was speechless with embarrassment. I could only think of how many people must have

Alexander Brailowsky with Fritzie.
(Photo by Seymour Bernstein)

been turned away from that ticket window simply because the new date had not been properly entered into the computer. In spite of this, there were only fifty empty seats at my recital.

During the summer in Maine, I practiced the greater part of each day on that program. As October drew near, I grew more and more anxious. No one could help me, I reasoned; I, and I alone, would have to walk across that stage. In order to survive, I would have to draw strength from within myself far in advance of the occasion. I wrote to Brailowsky and explained to him that in order to muster up the necessary courage to go through with that recital, I would have to arrive at my own musical convictions, even at the risk of making the wrong decisions.

My letter to my master had exactly the same effect as had my questioning him about the *ritardando* in Op. 110. He neither answered my telephone messages, nor did he come to the concert. Only after he and Ela read my review in *The New York Times* did he communicate with me in the form of a telegram. Gradually, though, he forgave me, and once again I resumed my lessons with him.

Nurturing

In 1975, when I began writing my book *With Your Own Two Hands*, I wanted to interview Brailowsky about the psychology of performing. I knew, of course, that he might not be up to answering questions which required intellectual probing. Still, he exemplified that sort of performer who relies more on intuition than anything else. Depending upon Brailowsky's mood, I thought I might glean some information from him which might be helpful to all performers. Above everything else, though, I intended to make my maître feel wanted. And whether the interview was successful or not, I was resolved to treat it and Brailowsky as seriously as I was able.

It is clear to me now that Brailowsky was more to me than a musical maître. By accepting me as a musician, he also became the nurturing father I had always longed for. In the early stages of our relationship, I was primarily interested in seeking his approval. When he stormed out of the room after my unpracticed performance of *Feux d'artifice*, it was not only a musician rejecting a student, but on a deeper level, a father rejecting his son. At the time that I wanted to interview him, however, I was more mature and ready to return in kind all the love and encouragement which he had bestowed upon me for over twenty years. Like a devoted son, it was I who would now do the nurturing; I would forgive my father his faults and overlook his disabilities. The circle of giving and receiving would be complete.

Conspiracy and Ambush

I had, in a very real sense, earned my maître's approval for my musical accomplishments. Now, however, I sought his acceptance of my book, which was at that time in an embryonic stage. As it happened, by coincidence, the pianist Raymond Lewenthal had just written a book about practicing. Whereas his book had to do mainly with methods of practicing, my book viewed practicing as a self-integrating process. Raymond had spoken to me of his book from time to time, but I was unaware that he had actually completed it.

Raymond and I had been friends for some twenty-five years. I admired him for being both a brilliant pianist and a musical scholar. We often played for one another, and we also engaged in a great deal of humor. During our infrequent meetings (we were too busy to get together more than two or three times a year), I openly discussed the thesis of my book with him. He, on the other hand, was extremely competitive and secretive about everything associated with his career. It was not surprising, therefore, that he had finished his book without telling me, even as I was discussing my own book with him.

Raymond was a bitter, tormented person, a misanthrope if there ever was one. As frequently happens, such people find ways to punish everyone else for their misfortunes. But in truth he was his own worst enemy. During the time I knew him, the list of victims of his offensive and exploitative behavior swelled to alarming proportions. More often than not, he repelled the very people who admired his gifts and who wanted only to help him. Somehow, though, he liked me sufficiently to be on his best behavior with me; and I, for my part, always tried, but alas in vain, to soothe the savage in his breast.

I had met Raymond at a run-through for my New York City debut in 1954. Two years earlier, he had been attacked by a gang of hoodlums in Central Park. They robbed him and beat him so mercilessly that they shattered almost every bone in his shoulder and arm. This occurred at a time when Raymond's career was at a high point. A year in the hospital, followed by another year of therapy, took its toll on him professionally and personally: his manager canceled his contract, and his friends, being involved in their own careers, had no time to visit him in the hospital. One by one, all of his colleagues dropped away.

People, of course, have survived worse misfortunes than this without becoming misanthropic. Knowing Raymond as I did, I am sure he was emotionally and psychologically scarred long before he was attacked in Central Park, so that the attack merely exacerbated something unhealthy in his personality. At any rate, this was the person to whom I was introduced at the informal reception after my tryout. He and I had a stimulating conversation about music and careers. Later, to everyone's delight, we sight-read four-hand music. It went so well that we met shortly afterwards to explore the repertory. And thus began a long relationship that reached the sort of end which ought to have been predictable from the start.

Without concerts, and with only a smattering of pupils, Raymond was destitute. I set about, therefore, to champion his cause. I not only promoted his pianistic gifts wherever and whenever possible, but I also introduced him to my own patroness, Mildred Boos. Out of regard for me, she helped him in every way she could — buying him clothes, helping him with his living expenses, and paying his way to Europe where he began to perform again. Considering this, one would have thought that Raymond could not possibly see me in any other light save that of a staunch supporter. Yet even I was soon to become a victim of his treacherous nature.

Without so much as a hint to me, Raymond moved undercover, as it were, into the Brailowsky circle. He ostensibly was seeking Ela's help with some translations, but his real intention was to worm his way into her affections. Ela was easy prey for such a magnetic personality. She had, formerly, devoted all of her time to her husband's career, accompanying him on his world tours and handling his personal affairs. Now that her husband's career had ended, she must have whiled away the hours in utter boredom. One can well imagine, therefore, how thrilled she must have been by Raymond's advances. Talented, intelligent, and clever at languages, in addition to being tall and dark, he was just the sort of romantic figure to distract her from her misery. Having been a child actor, Raymond was adept at playing roles. I can hear him now flattering Ela and saying everything she wanted to hear.

Raymond was not only after Ela, but also the master himself. He asked Brailowsky, for example, to read his book on practicing. I cannot know for sure whether my maître was up to such a task or not. It is possible, of course, that he was able to concentrate on the manuscript during his lucid moments. On the face of it, there seemed nothing wrong with Raymond's presenting his book to Brailowsky. But the truth was that he knew of Brailowsky's mental deterioration. Moreover, he was openly contemptuous of Brailowsky's playing to the point of ridiculing him in my presence. It ought to have been just the opposite. Given Raymond's predilection for the romantic composers — the Liszt cycle he gave, for example, and his edition and recording of the piano works of Charles Alkan — he ought to have admired Brailowsky's proclivity for the romantics. But Raymond may possibly have seen his own weakness in Brailowsky's lack of affinity for Beethoven and Schubert. For it was not until Raymond was in his forties that he first performed a Beethoven sonata. At any rate, considering Raymond's outward contempt for Brailowsky's playing, one would hardly have thought that he would seek his opinion on a book about practicing. What else but Ela's contacts and financial support, then, could Raymond have desired? He knew a golden goose when he saw it; and it would be all his with me out of the way.

When I telephoned Ela to make an appointment to interview my maître, I had no idea that Raymond and the Brailowskys had become fast friends, nor had I any inkling that a conspiracy against me was already a *fait accompli.* "Come Wednesday evening at eight for tea and *babka,*" Ela suggested in a voice that gave not the slightest hint of anything unusual. "Afterwards, you can interview Sascha."

On the designated evening, I gathered together my manuscript, my list of questions, and my tape machine. I arrived punctually at eight at the Brailowsky mansion. Since Marie was busy in the kitchen, Joseph answered the door. He took my coat and beckoned me upstairs to the second floor. As I entered the dining room, I could hardly believe my eyes: there sat Raymond at the dining room table in the very seat which I usually occupied. I noticed at once that Marie was clearing the table of dinner dishes. "Why had I not been invited to dinner?" I wondered. Emotional responses invariably arouse corresponding physical sensations. At the moment that I experienced an undeniable sense of rejection, I felt that familiar constriction in my chest which often announces anxiety. My surprise and pleasure at seeing Raymond, however, enabled me to throw off this feeling almost at once. "What are you doing here?" I asked him in the high-pitched voice with which I usually greeted him. Curiously, he did not return my smile, which caused the constriction in my chest to return in full force. While I instinctively knew that something was wrong, the trusting side of my nature attributed Raymond's atypically cold greeting to his being shy in front of the Brailowskys. I shook hands with Ela, hugged my master, and scratched Fritzie, who, as usual, was sitting on Brailowsky's lap. A place was set for me at the table opposite Raymond. As I sat down, my mind raced ahead in a frenzy of speculations: What, in fact, was Raymond doing here? Perhaps Ela had found out we were friends. That must be it. She invited him here to help in the interview. As I entertained all of these possibilities, gracious and smiling Marie appeared out of the kitchen and served the *babka,* giving me a particularly generous slice. Ela poured the tea. "At least they waited for my arrival to have their *babka,*" I thought. "I wish I could follow Marie into the kitchen and disappear from this whole scene." As I picked up my fork to eat the *babka,* it all began.

Ela was the first to speak:

Ela, sneering, and with side glances towards Raymond:
"Tell us, Saymore (she had her own pronunciation of
my name), what is your book about?" ‾

S. B.:
"It is very difficult to explain. But, generally speaking,
it suggests that productive practicing can influence you in
non-musical areas."

Ela, eyeing Raymond and smiling sardonically:
"Oh?...you mean if I practice properly I can bake better
babka?"

With this, she and Raymond exchanged sneers once again. And Raymond
actually emitted an audible, "Hmpf!"

Brailowsky, with a warm, genuine smile and stroking
Fritzie *piu mosso*:
"You know, Sighmore, Raymond has written a book on
practicing. He showed it to me. It is a masterpiece! You
should not write another book about practicing. That is not
a nice thing to do. And besides, you cannot improve upon
what he has written."

The calm, almost automatic tone of my maître's voice led me to believe
that Ela and Raymond had put these notions into his head.

Raymond, ignoring Brailowsky and almost cutting off his
last word:
"How dare you write a book about practicing when you
knew that I had written one! You know very well that my
book is my security for my old age. How would you have
felt if I had played the Villa-Lobos Concerto before you
premiered it?"

I became aware instantly that I was the victim of an ambush. I felt sure
that Raymond had poisoned the Brailowskys against me by persuading
them that I wanted to corner the market on a book about practicing before
he, Raymond, could publish his book.

S. B.:
"Raymond, I cannot believe that this is happening. First, I had no idea that you had finished your book. And second, I discussed the thesis of my book with you long ago. You know that our books are totally different. Having known me for so many years, and considering all I have done for you, how can you now accuse me of competing with you? Besides, there are many books on the market about practicing. Neither you nor I can corner the market on this subject. As to the Villa-Lobos Concerto, I would have been thrilled if you had been engaged to play it around the time that I did."

Ela, gorging on her *babka* and leaving crumbs in her place setting:
"Do you have a publisher?"

S. B.:
"Of course not. My book is only partially completed."

Ela, still exchanging glances with her co-conspirator and obviously enjoying my discomfort:
"Well, Raymond has received some strong interest from publishers. I believe you ought to stop writing your book. You could never compete with what Raymond has written anyway."

I wanted to smash Ela's and Raymond's heads together, but I controlled my temper for Brailowsky's sake:

S. B.:
"I do not intend to stop writing my book, Madame, and I also do not intend to compete with Raymond, whom I have always admired and supported. And now, if you will excuse me, I believe I should go."

Ela seemed shocked and also disappointed when I announced my decision to leave. For I am sure that she had intended to make me squirm for a much longer period of time. As I got up from the table, Ela and Raymond remained in their seats and continued to exchange glances. Brailowsky, appearing to be unaware of the drama which had just unfolded, continued cooing to Fritzie. It was the first time in all the years that I visited the Brailowsky home that my maître did not accompany me to the front door. Joseph was there, however, with my coat in hand and his ever gracious smile. I rushed out of the mansion and into the street — furious, bewildered, and hurt. I knew that I would never see my maître again.

Torment

I hardly slept that night. My brain was on fire with confusion and torment. Why had Ela turned against me? And how could Raymond have behaved that way after twenty-five years of friendship? He had hurled other distorted accusations at me during that inquisition, one of them being a reference to the time some five years earlier when his mother died. Raymond was in South America functioning as the newly appointed director of a music conservatory. During his absence, his aged and ailing mother had moved into Raymond's studio apartment on the upper East Side of Manhattan. Friends of mine helped me to look after her. She was already in a weakened condition, and pining for her son merely exacerbated it. One evening, she died in her sleep.

It fell to me to telephone Raymond and deliver the sad news to him. He was devastated. Not being happy in his new post, he resigned from the school and left for New York City immediately. It is difficult enough to lose one's mother; but in Raymond's case, he had also lost his last remaining relative. In fact, he was so depressed that he could hardly function at all. My friends and I, therefore, helped with arrangements for the funeral. When Raymond wanted a last remembrance of his mother, I even agreed to his rather macabre request to photograph her as she lay in the coffin. Later, a pitifully small group accompanied Raymond and his mother's remains to the cemetery. Afterwards I took him back to my apartment and tried to comfort him as best as I could. Finally, I could not bear to have Raymond return to that lonely apartment where his mother had died. I therefore invited him to stay with me for several days. I canceled all of my teaching. Although I had an imminent performance to give of the Liszt Concerto in *E* flat, I refrained from practicing entirely. After three days of comforting him and trying to be a good friend, I gently told him that he would have to return home as I needed to go on with my professional life. After he left, I tried for several days to telephone him. Receiving no response, I began to fear the worst. When finally he telephoned me, I shouted at him, partly out of relief and partly out of desperation.

It was during that dreadful scene at the Brailowskys' that Raymond suddenly brought up the above incident. With eyes blazing in anger, he shouted loudly enough to cause Fritzie to bark: "You sent me home to sleep in the bed where my mother had died. As though that was not bad enough you screamed at me when I telephoned you!"

To have this unfair reprimand hurled at me five years after the event, and in the presence of the Brailowskys, shocked me into silence. I remember looking at Raymond in utter astonishment and contemplating the irony of it: I had for so many years tried to explain away to others his indefensible behavior. Now it had suddenly gathered force and was being directed at me, of all people.

I am sure that Brailowsky was an innocent pawn in a plot to belittle me. But Ela? What had I done to arouse that sort of behavior? "I will resolve it all in the morning," I thought. "I will telephone Ela, tell her some facts about Raymond, and help her see that she was taken in by his treachery. As for Raymond, he is, after all, a pitiful figure. He's so desperate to make money that he cannot brook any competition at all — not even from a friend. I will forgive him, of course. He's too wretched to be held accountable for his behavior."

I made two telephone calls the following morning — the first one to Ela. I asked her why she had invited Raymond to her home at a time when I had arranged to interview her husband, and how she could have been a party to an ambush. "Don't you dare tell *me* whom to invite to my own home!" she screamed. I learned nothing whatsoever of the reason for her complicity in the betrayal. If anything, the conversation with Ela merely intensified my anguish.

My second call was to Raymond. I left two messages for him on his answering machine. I never heard from him again.

Although I knew that my relationship with the Brailowskys and with Raymond was over, something within me refused to let go of the musical-paternal tie with my maître. Against my better judgment, I wrote to Ela several weeks later to ask permission to quote in my book something I once heard her say concerning careers in music — namely, "Music was never meant to be a business!" It was a powerful statement — one that was made by someone who knew, perhaps better than anyone else, all about the pitfalls associated with major careers. I also asked her permission to print a little waltz which Brailowsky had composed during his teenage years. This, I thought, would prove that many performing artists have a potential for composing. It was naive of me to have written a letter whose subject matter was the very cause of the ambush itself. Not surprisingly, then, I received the following reply:

July 5, 1975

Dear Mr. Bernstein,

As you well know, I have never considered myself a public figure, and, therefore, any "remarque" made by me in the privacy of my home should not be held for publication either under my own name or as the wife of a prominent pianist! Exactly the same applies to my husband.

As for the little page of music you speak about, it was meant as a youthful joke and cannot be considered "composing" which my husband never did.

Sincerely,

Ela Brailowsky

The tone of Ela's letter and the fact that she addressed me as "Mr. Bernstein" all amounted to one thing: a break in our relationship. As the days wore on, anger overrode all desire to continue to seek an amicable conclusion to this whole wretched affair. Raymond, as I reasoned, must have initiated the conspiracy against me, and Ela must certainly have considered the consequences of her behavior insofar as my relationship with her husband was concerned. With the collapse of her husband's career and her own sense of unfulfillment, she must have reached a point of utter desperation. After devoting most of her life to Brailowsky's career, did she not now deserve to satisfy her own secret cravings, and to establish a life for herself? Raymond's appearance in her life, therefore, could not have been better timed.

One thought caused me more grief than anything else: I would never see my beloved maître again. Since neither Ela nor Raymond would hear me out, I decided to write letters to each of them and to include duplicates so that each one would know what I wrote to the other. Heeding some good advice which Sir Clifford Curzon had given me in 1958, namely, "Never send a letter written in anger until you have slept on it for two nights," I waited not two nights, but three before making my decision. Upon re-reading them, I concluded that the tone wasn't strong enough, so I rewrote them and sent them off at once.

Being younger and less in control of my emotions, I expressed myself very vindictively. Not that I regret a single thing that I wrote, for both Ela and Raymond deserved the worst sort of reprimand. But I would now have been more circumspect in wording those letters. It is even possible that I might have followed the path rooted in ancient wisdom, which holds that "silence often speaks louder than words spoken in anger."

Be that as it may, in my letter to Ela I related some incidents from my relationship with Raymond, some of which I mentioned earlier. I also told her of a letter I wrote to Van Cliburn asking him to intervene on Raymond's behalf during the time when the Steinway company recalled their pianos which they had lent to various artists, Raymond included. Van Cliburn did contact a key person at Steinway with the result that Raymond was allowed to keep his piano. I then included a quote by the psychoanalyst Karen Horney which I had come upon while doing research for my book. In describing a particular type of neurotic nature, Karen Horney might well have been writing about Raymond:

> In the competitive struggles of our culture it is often expedient to try to damage a competitor in order to enhance one's own position of glory or to keep down a potential rival. The neurotic, however, is driven by a blind, indiscriminate and compulsive urge to disparage others. He may do this even though he realizes that the others would do him no actual harm, or even when their defeat is distinctly counter to his own interests. His feeling may be described as an articulate conviction that "no one but I shall succeed." There may be an enormous amount of emotional intensity behind his destructive impulses. For example, a man who was writing a play was thrown into a blind fury when he heard that a friend of his was also working on a play.[*]

The letter to Ela went on to chastise her for having arranged that Dostoyevskian plot over *babka*. "What a twist of fate," I told her, "that I should have been refused an interview with your husband, and that a person who has expressed nothing but contempt for his playing should have been granted one. He (Raymond) defiles the very sanctity of your husband's artistry by pretending to be interested in his opinions." I actually told Ela that I despised her for creating a situation which precluded all further contact with my maître. Finally, I ended the letter by telling her that I hoped never to see her again, that both she and Raymond were not worthy of my friendship, and that I was "convinced more than ever that you deserve one another." I signed the letter "Mr. Bernstein."

My letter to Raymond was much briefer than the one I wrote to Ela. In it, I told him that I had reached a point of "utter disgust in thinking that I

---

[*] Karen Horney, *The Neurotic Personality of Our Time*, New York: W. W. Norton, 1964, p. 193.

could have considered you and Ela my friends." The last sentence — "I exorcise both of you out of my system!" — summed up my feelings.

As for Ela, I confessed earlier to having disliked her from the start. Now, after twenty-nine years, I was relieved not to be playing games with her any longer. She played the proverbial role of the cat with a mouse with virtuosic expertise. For example, when I mentioned one evening during dinner that I had parked my Volkswagen directly outside their door, she exclaimed, "Oh, I am going to kill myself! We just gave our chocolate brown Porsche to our caretaker in Switzerland. It had everything in it — real leather seats, air-conditioning, and a stereo. If we had known you drove, we would have given it to you!" And when Brailowsky's manager from Spain visited him in New York City: "Oh, why didn't I think of inviting you here to play for him?" She had given me the manager's name and address months before and suggested that I write to him. I was to tell him of my association with Brailowsky and discuss the possibility of a tour in Spain. It would have been so simple for me to have played for him in the Brailowsky home, especially since I was Brailowsky's only pupil. But Ela, with her voracious appetite for controlling people and events, would constantly dangle such things in front of me. I never once asked her to use her influence on my behalf; it was always she who urged me to contact this manager or that conductor. Clearly she never intended to follow anything through. More often than not, people or actions which might have furthered my career were mentioned by her in hindsight only.

I received one more communication from Ela. In it, she told me something I already knew — namely, that her husband had read my letter, and that as a consequence of it, I could never again come into his presence. Ironically, on April 25, 1976, the very day on which I wrote the final word of my book *With Your Own Two Hands*, a pupil telephoned me with the sad news of my beloved maître's death. He was eighty. I grieved for his loss. And I grieved, too, to think that I never saw him again after that fateful evening. Curiously, in thinking of the effect that his death would have upon others, my first thought went to dear Fritzie, who I am sure must have succumbed to a broken heart. Ela, whose maiden name was Felicia Karczmar, died in New York City on March 5, 1993. She was eighty-five.

Raymond Lewenthal continued to be his own worst enemy. His master classes at the Manhattan School of Music, for instance, elicited protests from faculty members whose pupils he shattered with his indiscriminate and vicious comments. After his death in 1988, two books in manuscript form were found in his apartment — one of them being his book on practicing. It never did get published.

Part 2: Monsters and Angels

THE DUCHESS

In discussing Raymond Lewenthal, I made brief mention of my patroness, Mildred Boos. She took it upon herself to help as many young musicians as was possible. Mrs. Sterling F. Boos, as she was formally known, had a royal air about her which seemed to place her in another century. She loved music, and had a deep appreciation and respect for young people who worked diligently at their art. She was a handsome woman, around sixty, and widowed for about five years when I first met her. Having a cheerful disposition and a refreshing innocence about her, she seemed to delight in her wealth.

I first met Mrs. Boos in 1956 when I performed at her mansion at 9 East 72nd Street in New York City. The occasion was a poetry reading for which I was commissioned to write background music — my first commission, as a matter of fact. The poet was Patricia Benton, and the reading was done by the famous actress Blanche Yurka. But what really attracted Mrs. Boos' attention to me was the group of solos I performed on that program. She was so impressed, in fact, that she offered to help me right there and then. I was completely taken with her charm, enthusiasm, and generosity, not to mention the ambience of the storybook mansion in which I found myself.

And what a mansion it was! Having five floors, thirty-four rooms, and an elevator, it was one of the great homes in New York City. The music room, patterned after a French *palais*, was indescribably beautiful. Complete with a massive crystal chandelier, intricate bas-relief on the walls covered with gold leaf, and a Veronese self-portrait hanging over the seven-foot walnut Steinway which stood on a platform against the main wall, the room easily seated two hundred and fifty people. So impressive was the mansion that it was declared a Historical Site by the New York City Landmarks Association. In the 1970s, Mrs. Boos sold it to the Lycée Français, which also owns the adjoining townhouse at 7 East 72nd Street. Mrs. Boos had once owned that home as well. When number nine was sold, she gave me the walnut Steinway. It now stands in my New York City studio and is, as it always was, a magnificent piano.

Mrs. Boos was the sort of patroness whom many young musicians dream of meeting one day. Her generosity knew no bounds. Shortly after I performed in her home, for example, I received tickets to the Metropolitan Opera and the New York Philharmonic. For both of these series, she occupied the first tier center boxes, at the old "Met" in the West 30s, and in Carnegie Hall, where the Philharmonic performed at that time. After the performances, she treated me and her other guests to extravagant dinners where we all enjoyed stimulating conversations.

My patroness, Mrs. Sterling F. Boos, whom I called "Duchess."

Part 2: Monsters and Angels

At one such occasion, I learned that the mansion on East 72nd Street was a sanctuary devoted to a religious movement called "I Am." While Mrs. Boos may have been deeply involved in mysticism, she rarely spoke of it to me, nor did she ever once suggest that I follow her lead. Once, though, when we were driving up to Canada in her lavender Lincoln, I initiated a discussion on I Am. I asked her which religious figures she embraced. "All of them," she answered, in a very matter of fact tone. And then to my surprise she added, "Dear, St. Michael has been riding on the hood ever since we left." I could only blink my eyes and wonder. But as time proved, such mystical references were rare. Mrs. Boos concentrated almost entirely on the real world, and more specifically on my aspirations and the difficulties involved in making a career. She helped me in ways too numerous to mention, including paying my manager, Berenice Kazounoff, a retaining fee each month.

As we became more friendly, I found it ever more difficult to say the name "Boos" without making the obvious association with "booze." One day, I spontaneously addressed her as "Duchess," a title which, with her wealth and position, seemed to suit her ideally. How delighted she was, and how she laughed over this, I cannot begin to say. From that moment on and until her death, she was the Duchess, not only to me, but also to all of her "young friends," which is how she referred to the young musicians whom she helped.

Being the recipient of so much generosity, I felt obliged to do something in return, so I offered to play the organ at all of the Duchess' services. I could not possibly have known, of course, that I was the only one among her young friends who offered to do this. Considering the fact that those services were to the Duchess the *ne plus ultra* of her life, one can see what my gesture must have meant to her. From that moment on, she saw me as a gift sent to her from the spiritual world. I became her favorite among the veritable court of young aspiring musicians she had assembled. As such, I was given my own key to the mansion, and with it, the privilege of practicing there whenever I wished. Moreover, I was encouraged to arrange solo and chamber music recitals for myself and even to hold my student recitals there. All those in attendance were awestruck at the magnificence of the "Gold Room," as the music room was rightly called. The Duchess, who attended all of the performances, extended her welcome to everyone with the grace and breeding of a royal figure. For me, the late eighteenth century had come alive again, and I wondered what I had done to deserve such a blessing as this.

"Students," as the followers of I Am were called, attended services in a spacious room on the first floor. It contained a Baldwin grand piano

146

(there were four other pianos in the mansion) and an electronic organ. There was an altar at one end from which the Duchess directed services each Sunday and on special holidays. Dressed in a floor-length white satin, gold-braided cape fastened with an ornate gold clip, she cut a regal figure as she walked quickly through the door and onto the platform.

The Duchess and the students were dependent upon mediums who passed on to them psychic messages they received from a host of religious leaders and saints, both past and present. They were referred to as the "Masters." Anna, the Russian housekeeper, told me that the Masters gathered on the third floor of the mansion to hold their meetings, visible, of course, only to those with inner vision. "You must never go to the third floor," she warned. "It is forbidden." Her warning did nothing more than arouse my curiosity. So one day, on my way to having tea with the Duchess on the fifth floor, I set out a little earlier and brazenly pressed "3" on the elevator control panel. When the door opened, I found myself in a darkened corridor on the forbidden third floor. Wandering around, I suddenly came upon a room containing a large round high-glossed mahogany table surrounded by about a dozen tall brocade upholstered chairs. In the center of the table stood a large crystal vase holding a sizeable bouquet of freshly cut flowers. The crystal captured the intense light entering through large French windows, and bathed the table and chairs in a rainbow-colored canopy. This aura of light and the intense silence of the room conspired to send shivers down my spine. In the next instant, I was seized with guilt and terror. I had audaciously intruded into forbidden territory, the Holy of Holies, the inner sanctum of I Am. Surely the Duchess, or, for all I knew, the Masters themselves, would punish me for my impertinence. I rushed out of the room, down the corridor, and into the elevator so fast that I was breathless and pale when I arrived for tea. "I jogged across Central Park," I told the Duchess, who wondered why I was so out of breath.

Many mystical people have visions of various sorts. One Sunday when I played Debussy's *The Engulfed Cathedral* during a service, the Duchess went into a veritable trance, in which she was transported back in time to the island of Atlantis. According to her vision, I was a priest, and she, a priestess. She saw herself in a rowboat drifting away from Atlantis as it was sinking. The disturbing element in her vision was the fact that she had to leave me there to my fate. While embracing me she added, "But we are reunited again." And she wept with joy.

The Duchess was easily taken in by anyone who claimed to possess mystical powers. Thus she was always surrounded by charlatans who boasted of having this or that mystical power. And then there was the Inca

My first performance in the Duchess' mansion at 9 East 72nd Street in New York City. Blanche Yurka, left; Patricia Benton, right.

princess, or at least an incarnation of one, a beautiful exotic-looking woman with sleek black hair and a greasy tan complexion. Her tight-fitting and brightly-colored gowns embroidered with Indian designs accentuated a very sexy figure. She may have claimed to be a princess, but to my eyes, she looked like a royal hooker! What special claims this mysterious woman made, I never discovered. But I remember that she wormed her way into the Duchess' confidence to such an extent that she was invited to live in Scarsdale, where she actually slept in one of two beds in the Duchess' bedroom. While none of this sat well with me, it was not my place to point out what seemed obvious: that the princess was bent on exploiting the Duchess for all she was worth.

Then something strange happened, something totally out of keeping with what I knew of the Duchess. One day, while we were riding together in her car, she suddenly began asking leading questions concerning a close friend of mine: "Where did you meet him?" "Don't you think that you see each other too often?" "I wonder about his sexual orientation...!" This last comment lit a fuse, and my temper flared up: "Why are you asking me such questions? Tom and I are friends, and nothing more. You seem to be on a homosexual witch hunt!" I didn't regret my temper tantrum or anything that I had said up to that point. But I did regret what I added: "I might as well ask you why you allow a so-called princess to sleep next to you each night." The implication was clear enough, and the Duchess was taken aback. We continued to drive to our destination without exchanging another word. Nor did we ever discuss the subject again. In fact it was the only altercation we had during a friendship that lasted for more than four years.

I could only speculate as to why the Duchess engaged in that bizarre line of questioning about my friend. I thought that she felt guilty living with the princess under the bewildered glances of her three children and me. The truth is we all thought that the Duchess felt a sexual attraction for the princess, and that the princess was taking advantage of this. As it happened, the princess suddenly vanished three months later, never to be seen again.

Earlier, in speaking about Hortense Monath and her crises, I mentioned that Martha Baird Rockefeller had come to her rescue. Coincidentally, there existed in 1957 a foundation called the Martha Baird Rockefeller Aid to Music Program. Its purpose was to award grants to young performers for certain projects that the board felt would augment their careers. I auditioned before the board, and was awarded two such grants, in 1958 and 1959 respectively. The first one helped to defray my travel and living expenses during the six month period when I lived in

London and studied with Sir Clifford Curzon. Later, when I passed the BBC auditions in London and was offered a broadcast, I was awarded a second grant which enabled me to return to London in order to take advantage of this prestigious engagement.

Shortly before I left for my six months' stay in London, I happened to speak to the Duchess about my dream of performing in Europe one day. The grant that I had received, while it amply covered my living expenses, was hardly sufficient to defray the expenses of even one recital. A few days later, a special delivery letter arrived, its envelope sealed with wax. Inside was a letter from the Duchess together with a check for $5,000. "Use this money to make your debuts in Europe," the letter said. Needless to say, I was overwhelmed by the Duchess' gesture. Subsequently I made my debuts in London, Copenhagen, Amsterdam, Hamburg, and Paris. After each concert, the Duchess telephoned me long distance, eager to learn how it all went. Thus she and I remained in close contact during my entire stay in Europe.

While the Duchess used her mansion on East 72nd Street as a sanctuary and as a show place for cultural events of all sorts, she spent most of her time at her estate in Scarsdale where she lived with her three children — two sons, one slightly older and one slightly younger than I was, and a daughter my age. It was there that I spent Christmas holidays and occasional weekends in luxurious surroundings. Little did I realize how importantly Scarsdale was soon to figure in my life.

I was scheduled to perform at the National Gallery in Washington, D.C., four days after I returned from Europe. The Duchess thought, and I agreed with her, that if I went directly to my New York City studio, the telephone and other distractions would rob me of time and energy needed for practicing. Wouldn't it be better if I went to Scarsdale? It was a wonderful idea, and I happily took advantage of her suggestion. I arrived to a warm reception that I shall long remember. And I recall something else: photographs of me encased in extravagant frames rested and hung everywhere, their presence leaving no doubt in anyone's mind that I was the Duchess' favorite. It embarrassed me, mostly for the Duchess' children, but I said nothing about it. We all enjoyed a sumptuous dinner, and afterwards I had a lovely chat with the Duchess. It had been a long day, and I turned in early.

The Duchess and I were the first ones up the following morning. After breakfast, she asked if I would accompany her on a walk: "I want to show you something, dear." We went out of the front door and turned right. After a hundred yards or so, she led me to the front door of a Tudor home that was part of her estate. Standing in front of the closed door, she handed me a key: "It's yours," she said with a gleeful look in her eye. "You can do with it whatever you like."

One might think that I would have been overjoyed at hearing such a magnanimous offer. But interestingly enough, no sooner did I take the key from her than a sense of terror swept over me. I felt trapped, like the character "Alfie" in the movie of the same name. I tried, of course, to hide my true feelings and simulated an appearance of surprise and gratitude. Once through the front door and quaint entrance area, there were three steps leading down to a large sunken living room. In the center of the room and angled to the large stone fireplace stood a sleek ebony Imperial Bösendorfer concert grand with a high-gloss finish. French doors at the far end of the room opened out to a flagstone terrace with a stream flowing at its base and a wooded area beyond. Returning to the living room, we went up three steps to a dining room, completely furnished, and beyond this to a large kitchen with an adjoining pantry. Taking the stairs to the second floor, we explored all of the four furnished bedrooms. The master bedroom had a large, baronial fireplace. Back in the hallway, the Duchess opened the door of the linen closet, revealing an array of bedding and towels that looked like a display in a department store. There was a third floor, too, but the rooms there were empty. The Duchess explained that she had just spent $5,000 to have the imported roof tiles replaced.

Having wandered through all the rooms with the Duchess explaining this and that detail, we sat down on the sumptuous sofa in the living room. "This is your new home," she told me. "Keep your studio in New York City so that you may commute there whenever necessary. But you may live here forever, if you wish." I could do nothing but stare at her with glazed eyes, while my anxiety mounted with each second. The reasons for this were clear to me even then. The Duchess had been generous beyond my wildest dreams. Yet there was something demeaning in being the recipient of so much luxury. I was in conflict, too, about the social aspects of our relationship. Whenever I escorted the Duchess to public dinners and to various social events, I imagined that people thought of me as a gigolo. This was no fault of the Duchess: her intentions and her actions were entirely aboveboard. As she saw it, and as she explained to others, I was her young gifted protégé and a companion who happily escorted her to various functions. I drove her lavender Lincoln, affording her a sense of security and safety. I had accepted all of her invitations with no hesitation whatsoever, so she had no reason to suspect that I was suffering conflicts. And least of all could I tell her that I felt like a kept man.

Had I discussed my true feelings with the Duchess, I am sure she would have gone out of her way to free me of anything that would have added to my conflict. Even though I was in my thirties, I was far too immature to be so open and frank with her, or with anyone else, for that matter. I tried desperately to make my residence in Scarsdale productive, if not satisfying. I advertised for pupils, only to be threatened with a lawsuit from a neighbor who happened to be a lawyer. He informed me that I was in violation of a zoning rule. To be sure, I practiced and composed in complete privacy. But then there were dinners almost every evening in the Duchess' mansion at the far end of the expansive lawn between our respective homes. I could have said no to this, too. Yet I accepted all invitations simply because I felt it was expected of me. And there was something else — something which further aggravated my conflict: almost every day during the first month of my stay in Scarsdale, the doorbell would ring. There would be deliveries, including a TV set, an extravagant coffee server, a suede sports jacket, and other luxuries too numerous to mention. Far from inducing joy within me, each gift merely increased my discomfiture.

One evening, after a full year had gone by, I reached a point of desperation. It is a curious thing how taking one simple step over that invisible line separating one situation or one extreme from another will suddenly change a person's life. The time had come for me to take that step. I telephoned my brother-in-law, Saul Armm, and asked him to pick me up with his car and move me and my belongings out of Scarsdale and back to my studio in Manhattan. I might add that I left all the presents behind. I then went to the Duchess and told her that I was leaving. How her tears of shock and sadness flowed, I cannot begin to say.

Over the following weeks, letters arrived from the Duchess in which she pleaded with me to return. "Everything will be different," she wrote. "Come back to me, and we'll talk the whole thing through." Curiously, I read those letters as though they were meant for someone else. Feeling guilty for having caused the Duchess such anguish, and, at the same time, relieved to be living once again a free, unencumbered life, I saw those letters as a threat to my regained freedom. Once again I sought protection under that imaginary dome I mentioned earlier, and I decided not to answer them. Then one day, another letter arrived, this one sealed with wax. It contained three brief sentences: "I see that you won't come back to me. I have therefore asked my lawyers to rescind the legal arrangements I made on your behalf. I'm informing you of this in case they need you to sign some documents." Legal arrangements…? Perhaps the Duchess would have turned over the deed of the Tudor home to me in conjunction with a large inheritance. I would then have been secure for the rest of my life. Regarding the part in her letter about my having to sign documents, I am sure this was a final ploy to win me back; she hoped that I would think twice before forfeiting the promise of future security. The fact that no documents were ever sent to me seems to bear this out. At any rate, far from being lured by that last letter, I felt offended, and I ignored it as I had the previous ones.

It pains me to say that the Duchess was emotionally ill for the next five years of her life. Each year, though, I visited her during the Christmas holidays merely to show my gratitude to her for all she had given me. I said no to all of her other invitations. For the break, as I saw it, had to be a radical one.

For years afterwards, I was filled with remorse for having caused a dear and well-meaning person such an emotional upset. Given all of the conflicts, I felt there can be no justification for my having allowed that relationship to have advanced to the point where it eventually caused such grief and heartbreak. What else but greed, masked by false innocence on my part, could explain my behavior? To be sure, I fell prey to the lure of security and to having a safe haven in which to work, and I falsely justified it by pretending that I enjoyed my relationship with the Duchess: She helps me, and in return I provide companionship for her. But in truth, I hated myself for the role I played in her life. I can only trust that she and her children eventually forgave me.

After the Duchess's death, the entire estate in Scarsdale, including the Tudor home, was sold. I occasionally had contact with Bill, her younger son, who inherited his mother's predilection for mysticism. He claimed to have received psychic messages from her in which she declared her unconditional love for me. Both Bill and his brother have since died, leaving Marilyn, her children, and several grandchildren the sole family survivors.

I have learned two important lessons from this experience. One is to recognize the true meaning behind generosity: is it unconditional, or will there be a price to pay? The other lesson is to be aware of my own motives when extending generosity towards others.

GENEROSITY

Under different circumstances, the Scarsdale estate might have been a haven for me. But as it turned out, my guilt and the Duchess' spoken and implied needs turned it into a psychological battlefield. Through the years, I have observed that musicians tormented by low self-esteem can sink even lower when provided with conducive environments and economic security. For it is a sad fact of human nature that the generosity of others is not always received in the spirit with which it is given. As my own experience has taught me, it is one thing to be singled out for special favors, and quite another to feel worthy of them.

Generally speaking, my relationships with my pupils have been mutually rewarding. But I cannot begin to say how often my generosity to certain pupils and the modest sanctuaries I have offered them with my full heart have given rise to more resentment than gratitude. And why? They felt incapable of living up to what I expected of them. Free or extra lessons, gifts of music and even food and clothing when needed — all served to heighten their guilt for not practicing as they knew they should have. In fact, they saw all such offerings, including my sincere compliments about their playing, as a coercive ploy on my part to make them feel beholden to me — beholden enough to practice harder. To complicate matters even more, there is nothing like generosity to remind certain people of their own inability to provide for themselves, materially and otherwise. Having spent a lifetime trying to see my way through this psychological labyrinth, I have only recently begun to understand the problem from my pupils' standpoint. To begin with, some of them see the lessons themselves as ultimate gifts with which no other object or action can compare. Anything beyond this, even my offering them a glass of apple juice before, during, or after their lessons, embarrasses them and strikes them as gilding the lily. But should such pupils suffer guilt for not practicing properly, then any extra-musical gesture on my part results in their being suspicious of me: they think that I have ulterior motives. Paradoxical as it might seem, some pupils end up resenting me, not only for being generous to them, but also because my own industrious nature is too hard for them to match: "Save your ploys!" they seem to be thinking. "No matter how good you are to me, I can never be, nor do I even want to be, as devoted to my work as you are to yours!" Thus, some of my pupils have fluctuated between admiration for and dependency upon me, on the one hand, and resentment and seething hostility, on the other. The combination of the two can produce conflicts within them which, if anything, merely increase their sense of inadequacy.

It certainly is a reversal of anticipated responses when kindness and generosity provoke guilt and resentment in another person. People who have been imprisoned, for example, have been known to shun freedom when it is offered to them. Similarly, when poor practicers are supplied with the very things which ought to increase their motivation for productive work, the opposite may occur: even the faintest stirring of their former motivation may now actually collapse and die. In other words, generosity shown to the wrong people can make them retreat even further into a prison of their own making.

This condition actually befell a former pupil of mine whose talent, plus his family's tenuous financial circumstances, moved me to award him a full scholarship. He had motivation problems to begin with. But I sincerely hoped that my belief in his gifts, as symbolized by the scholarship, would spark him into serious practicing. Little did I know that the opposite would occur, that he would literally stop practicing entirely. After six months of his having made no progress whatsoever, I confronted him on the subject. That touched off an emotional upheaval on his part during which he confessed that he could never live up to the honor of being a scholarship pupil of mine. We discussed this heart to heart, and we came to the conclusion that it would be best for him to pay me whatever he could for the lessons. From that moment on, he began to practice productively.

Considering this example and others like it in which generosity simply backfires, I finally arrived at a viable method for dispensing favors to others. It takes the form of a frank and open discussion about my intentions and my pupils' feelings. Let us say that I wish to give a pupil a gift of a special edition of music which I know he cannot afford. The following is a close approximation of how I approach that pupil:

> Would you allow me to buy you the Bärenreiter edition of the Mozart Sonatas? Before you say yes or no, I wish to share with you something of my own experience in regard to receiving gifts from others. In almost all cases, my benefactors either requested outright, or subtly implied, reciprocity in some form or another — errands, social obligations, time-wasting telephone calls, and, in some cases, hints of expected sexual favors. It is natural, therefore, for you to wonder what my true motives are. I can only tell you this: I wish to give you this music unconditionally. I want nothing from you in return. I neither expect you to practice more — unless, of course, you want to — nor do I expect added favors from you to even out the score.
>
> Everyone knows that it is more difficult to receive than it is to give. This is primarily due to personal feelings of unworthiness on your part and mistrust for the giver. Should you be suffering from one or the other, then look upon my generosity as a challenge to overcome these problems. For the moment, try to transcend your suspicions of me and accept my gift unconditionally.

> Your acceptance will be my reward, for I will derive
> enormous pleasure from giving you this music. If you
> have a problem with this, then find a way to buy the
> edition yourself. Whatever you decide, is necessary for
> you to study from the finest edition available.

A declaration of this sort can induce suspicion in any pupil, but especially one who is suspicious to begin with: "My teacher doth protest his good intentions too much." Moreover, it is not difficult to imagine an opposite response — namely, that such a declaration may be interpreted as an open invitation for an intimacy which the pupil secretly wanted. But a pupil's interpretation of anything a teacher says or does is influenced by their interaction over a period of time. Furthermore, pupils usually can sense whether their teachers are sincere or not. If pupils are wary of their teachers to begin with, then even one hundred declarations of good intent will not erase their suspicion.

Suffice it to say that the discussions I have with my pupils almost always produce positive results. Most of them are able to accept my gifts without wondering and worrying about whether I have ulterior motives.

We have more to say about our destinies than we realize, or even want to realize. For indeed, to acknowledge the role that we can play in shaping and directing our lives is at once to assume the lion's share of responsibility for almost everything that happens to us. The reverse of this is to feel helpless and victimized, to expect others to do all of the providing and all of the protecting. To cite my own case, it was only when I tired of being a victim, when I rejected my managers and managed myself, and when I abandoned my performing career and gave heed to my creative calling, that I began to have a glimpse of that serenity which I have always longed for: not the sort of living death which some people mistakenly call serenity — that somnambulistic state in which the juices of secret aspirations dry up and cease to flow altogether; but rather, a serenity born out of the joy of accomplishment, the joy of making contributions to others, and the joy derived from mutually rewarding relationships.

MADAME ISABELLE VENGEROVA

In 1947, the year I met Alexander Brailowsky, my cousin Esther Burger and her husband Sol visited us one evening in Newark. Passionate lovers of music, they always had an eye out for anything that might further my career. On this particular occasion, they brought with them a business acquaintance who, like them, was an avid music lover. They had already told me on the telephone before they arrived that "Sydney Wortheim knows a lot of important people in the music world. You never can tell; he may do something for you."

Mr. Authority

Quite obviously, doing something for me was contingent upon hearing me play. I remember that I was not in particularly good performing condition at the time, but I tried my best, anyway. When I finished playing, Sydney Wortheim's response was positively explosive: "Fantastic! Fantastic!" he roared in a *basso profundo* voice, the intensity of which made his response sound more like an admonition than a compliment. I wasn't sure that my playing was "fantastic," but I was pleased that he liked it. He then asked a number of questions about my musical education: "What?" he exclaimed in surprise. "You're not enrolled in a music school? Why, that's preposterous! A person like you belongs in New York City. And I know just the school for you."

While my parents were relieved finally to meet someone who knew the field and who would guide their son's future, I wondered what all the fuss was about. They are talking about my destiny, I thought, and no one seems to be the slightest bit interested in knowing what I would like to do with my life. I was content to remain in Newark, and to continue studying with Brailowsky. In the one year since my graduation from high school, my routine of practicing six to eight hours per day was yielding results; my repertory was expanding, and my technique was slowly improving. Moreover, I was beginning to find more and more places to perform. Why change things now?

As everyone knows, young people can easily bend to family pressures. Children, for example, who are devoted to their parents may even go so far as to propose marriage to someone simply to fulfill their parents' expectations. Concerning Sydney Wortheim, he certainly came across as an authority figure. My parents and my cousins thought that I had better follow his advice. "He knows what he's talking about," my cousin Esther told me. "You'll see; he'll make your career!" It all sounded very convincing to me. So I finally decided to place myself in his hands.

Generally speaking, there are two types of music lovers who do not perform: those in the first category are humble in the face of music and performers; those in the second can be downright obnoxious. People of this latter type buy practically every recording on the market and feel that this alone earns them the status of a musical authority. Everyone, of course, is entitled to have opinions on all subjects, music included. As a matter of fact, the opinions of non-musicians have often benefited me more than those of my colleagues. Yet certain music lovers, like some music critics, sit in judgment on performers as though they themselves have studied music seriously and have been on the stage a countless number of times: "You can't take his Chopin seriously!" "She bangs!" "His 'Emperor' Concerto is completely out of style!" and on and on, ad nauseam.

Sydney Wortheim was just this sort of opinionated music lover. According to him, performers were categorized as either good guys or bad guys. And woe be unto any performer who fell into the second category! Fortunately for me, I was dubbed a good guy. Even when I did not play well for him, I could do no wrong. Having given me his stamp of approval, he lost no time in setting up an audition at the Mannes School of Music. I have no idea how he accomplished this, nor did I ever discover what his connection was to the Manneses. It was between semesters, and a person would have to have clout in order to set up an audition for just one pianist. He had *chutzpa*, though, and he certainly was one person who would rush in where angels feared to tread. Perhaps he telephoned Leopold Mannes and won him over with extravagant praise of me.

The Mannes School of Music

In 1947, the Mannes School of Music was housed in a brownstone on East 74th Street. David, Clara, and Leopold — father, mother, and son, respectively — were all active in running the school. All three attended my audition. David, the founder, was director emeritus, having passed on the reins to his son Leopold.

At my audition, I played the *Wanderer* Fantasy by Schubert and the Scherzo in *B* flat minor by Chopin in their entirety — and not too well, either. There was something about playing before Sydney Wortheim that always brought out the worst in me. Perhaps it was because I didn't trust his musical judgment. At any rate, I felt stiff, self-conscious, and altogether miserable during the entire audition. Afterwards, while I was coping with my own negative feelings about my playing, it came as a surprise to learn that the Manneses were very enthusiastic. Leopold, who did all of the talking, actually offered me a full scholarship. He spoke of sending me to the person he thought was the greatest teacher in the United States — Madame Isabelle Vengerova. I would have to audition for her, he told me, but that was a mere formality.

Most young musicians, no doubt, would have been overjoyed to have elicited such a response from the directors of a major music institution. But I greeted all of this with a mixture of happiness and apprehensiveness: If the Manneses and Sydney Wortheim are incapable of recognizing a fraud when they hear one, I thought, certainly this Vengerova woman —

whoever she is — will know it at once. I will be exposed at last.

I wish to comment briefly on how often I have assessed my playing and even my talent in harsh, critical terms. This was of course how I felt at that time. But as I reflect upon the past, I see clearly that it was my technical discomfort that made me think I didn't play well; it also made me feel like a fraud. But no doubt I played better than I thought, for in this case, I would not have been offered the scholarship.

In the 1940s, there were three teachers in New York City who had achieved legendary status — Rosina Lhèvinne, Olga Samaroff Stokowska, and Isabelle Vengerova. The first two taught at the Juilliard School; Mme. Vengerova taught at the Curtis Institute of Music in Philadelphia and at the Mannes School. Needless to say they each had their quota of illustrious pupils. To be accepted by any one of them was a signal of status — one that was looked upon favorably by managers, booking agents, and judges at competitions.

After graduating from high school, I knew one thing: higher education, which I had always prized, was something I would have to do without. For it would take practicing from morning until night to weed out all the weaknesses in my playing. And so I had led a cloistered life. As far as New York City was concerned, it may as well have been another planet. Apart from going to concerts occasionally, I knew nothing about musical life there, nothing about music schools, and I certainly had never heard the name of Mme. Vengerova. But as everyone kept insisting, New York City was the place to be if you wanted to have a career in music. So be it. I accepted the scholarship with much gratitude, and I intended to make the best of my new life in the big city.

It is quite natural, I believe, for students who aspire to careers in music to look upon their teachers as the center of their lives. With the exception of Louise, I loved all of my teachers. Even when I had occasional misgivings about them, as one might have with a parent or a friend, still, nothing shook my fundamental trust in them. I had a personal as well as a musical rapport with almost all of my teachers. Age differences notwithstanding, they were my best friends. I would go so far as to say that my veneration for most of my teachers bordered on hero-worship. A hero who was also a friend? What more could a person want from any relationship? Needless to say, then, my expectations for my new teacher were very high.

The Monster in Angel's Clothing

To be fair about it, Vengerova was extremely nice to me when I auditioned for her. An obese woman with dark, penetrating eyes, Madame extended her hand with aristocratic grace. "How do you do. *Mmn,*

Mr. Mannes has told me very nice things about you." Her thick Russian accent was punctuated by *mmns* which often preceded a sentence or a phrase. "Please," she said, beckoning me to the piano, "*mmn*, play something for me."

Being extremely shy, and also in awe of Madame, I could only manage a "thank you," or a "yes" or a "no" for the first ten minutes or so. In fact, I looked forward to playing as a means of finding a refuge from my own shyness. Two Steinways sat side by side. Madame ushered me to the one on the right, while she took her place to my left. I adjusted the bench, took several deep breaths, and tore into the *Wanderer* Fantasy. Madame allowed me to play the entire first section, but she stopped me after a few measures of the Adagio: "Very good. *Mmn*, please play something slow for me — perhaps a Nocturne by Chopin?" I played her the one in *C* sharp minor, a piece that I felt particularly close to. She actually heard it all the way through. "You are very talented," she told me. "You phrase naturally, and you are very relaxed." Hardly able to believe this, I broke into smiles and answered quite simply, "Thank you." She then continued: "Tell me, *mmn*, how did your teachers relax you so well? I have a great deal of difficulty relaxing my own pupils." My shyness instantly gave way to temporary confidence: "How wonderful of me to be so relaxed," I thought. "Even she hasn't discovered my technical inadequacies. I have deceived her, just as I have deceived everyone else!"

Subsequently, there ensued an amicable discussion during which Madame asked me all sorts of personal questions — the names of my teachers, where I lived, my father's occupation, my parents' nationality, how many brothers and sisters I had — and so on. She was particularly interested in the fact that Aunt Clara had studied with Leschetizky. Leopold Mannes had mentioned Vengerova's own connection with the Viennese master, and I questioned her about this. "*Mmn*, I did not study with the professor directly, but rather with his assistant, Annette Essipoff. You know, *mmn*, she was the second of his four wives." Madame seemed charmed by my interest in her own student days, and a certain warmth broke through her austere manner. Encouraged by this, I spoke to her more freely — like a friend. Soon the hour was up. Madame suddenly became remote and rose imperiously from her piano bench: "I will telephone Mr. Mannes to say that I have accepted you as a pupil. *Mmn*, if you will telephone me in September (it was then May), I will inform you when to come for your first lesson."

Joy was written all over my face as I stepped into the elevator. It must have been infectious, for the elevator operator smiled at me all the way down to the first floor. Unable to wait until I got home, I rushed to the nearest telephone booth to call my mother: "She accepted me! She accepted me!" I cried. It was one of the happiest moments in my life.

Acceptance and Rejection

Few things can be more of a boost to one's confidence than the open arms of acceptance. In the competitive world, rejection lies sinisterly around every corner, waiting to snuff out our dreams and expectations. Acceptance, then, keeps rejection at bay — at least for the time being. In the case of my audition for Madame Vengerova, I fully expected her to see at once that I was, as I believed, a fraud. Even though Leopold Mannes told me in advance that the audition was a mere formality, Madame's acceptance of me meant only one thing — I got away with it one more time!

I have auditioned many young musicians in their teens and twenties who have already been battered by rejection. Having lost more contests than they have won, having become inured to hearing the same words over and over again, "Sorry, we're all booked up for the next two seasons," and knowing the pain of reading dreadful reviews, which are forms of rejection also, such young musicians are grateful for every positive word or action thrown their way. While they are gifted enough to be among the treasures of any teacher's class, they will express unbounded joy simply to know that I have accepted them as a pupil.

Later, I accumulated my own files of rejections. But at nineteen, I had a fairly good record of successes save in one area: I was my own worst enemy. In other words, if anyone rejected my playing, it was I! Curiously, I had not the faintest notion of the one important gift which I *did* possess, that very thing which accounted for everyone else's positive response to my playing — and that was my natural gift for projecting musical feeling. If only one of my teachers had made me aware of this all-important asset, I would have latched onto it as a primary source of confidence. I was not, by any means, totally devoid of confidence. That is, I knew that in time I would overcome my faults. Yet, had I known that I possessed the most important gift of all, this in itself would have served as a wellspring from which I would have garnered even greater courage and determination.

The ability to say something musically is the *goldene* ingredient which makes one performer the artist, and another a mere mechanical reproducer. Knowing this now, I never fail to point out that pure gold whenever I hear it in my own pupils. Regarding those who sound unmusical, I assume that the *goldene* ingredient is lying somewhere within them, barricaded by physical problems or emotional blocks. It is my responsibility, then, to help them technically and to remove the obstacles to their emotional worlds, those psychological obstructions which prevent them from being moved by the music they are playing.

I had always been an inveterate practicer. But during the summer preceding my first lesson with Madame Vengerova, I practiced harder than ever. In early September, I telephoned her to arrange my first lesson, and was told to come the first week in October. In the meantime, I registered at the Mannes School and familiarized myself with the building. In the process I met several students who were studying with other teachers in the school. I felt proud to tell them that I had been accepted by Madame Vengerova. Instead of being impressed, they related ominous tales about Madame — how sadistic and pedantic she was, and how many of her students stopped playing the piano altogether. But having already had a pleasurable encounter with her, I theorized that it must have been the pupils themselves who were at fault; they were untalented, stupid, or both. I of course would bring out the best in Madame as I had done with most of my other teachers. Thus, I turned a deaf ear to all the negative stories I heard about her.

Sweet, innocent youth. It is a time of unconditional trust — especially in your teacher. Soon, however, I was to suffer the disillusionment of discovering that my own piano teacher was the incarnation of evil.

Madame Plays Her Hand

The day of my first lesson arrived. More than merely a piano lesson, it was for me the beginning of a whole new phase in my life, one in which I would be exposed to the very best in teaching. I awakened on that day full of enthusiasm and filled with love for Madame. For days in advance I had fantasies of rushing into her studio and kissing her affectionately on the cheek. She would then know that I was open to a personal as well as a musical association.

I rang the bell to Madame's apartment and was greeted by her servant, who asked me to wait in the foyer. I had settled in a chair for some five minutes when I heard muffled voices issuing from the studio. Then, suddenly, the door burst open, and a tall, attractive young woman came rushing out with tears streaming down her cheeks. As she passed me, she glanced sideways in utter embarrassment and was out the front door in a flash. Before this incident had fully registered upon me, I heard Madame's voice emanating from the studio: "*Mmn*, please come in!" It was more of a command than an invitation. Considering the stern tone of her voice and the sight of her pupil rushing past me in tears, I was, understandably, apprehensive of Madame's mood. Least of all was I inclined to plant a kiss on her cheek. Madame extended her hand and asked, "Did you have a good summer?" "Yes, I did. Thank you." Clearly, there was a tempest brewing beneath her affected charm. She lost no time in beginning the lesson. "What repertoire did you work on since I last saw you?" I mentioned the *Chromatic Fantasy and Fugue* by Bach and the "Emperor" Concerto by Beethoven. I was about to mention some five other works which I had prepared for her, but she cut me off abruptly with, "*Mmn*, play the Bach for me."

By that time in my life, I was no stranger to various degrees of nervousness, ranging from mild anxiety to utter panic. But the contained cyclone within Madame, plus the scene I had just witnessed, conspired to induce the worst anxiety I had ever experienced. As I began the Bach, I had the distinct impression that my fingers were encased in a block of cement. It took all of my determination to articulate the opening passage. I was much relieved when Madame stopped me almost at once: "Now the Beethoven!" I barely finished the introduction of the Concerto when she stopped me again: "Good. Now we will begin the lesson." With this, she looked at me so menacingly that I felt my shoulders rise towards my ears: "*Mmn*, tell me, how do you practice?" Perplexed by a question that no one had ever asked me before, I paused for a few seconds to collect my thoughts: "Well," I began hesitatingly, "it all depends upon what I am practicing." Frankly speaking, I was pleased with my answer, and I fully intended to explain this further when Madame fired another question at me: "Did you go to grammar school?" To my ears, this sounded like a non sequitur, but I responded all the same: "Yes." "Did you graduate?" "Yes." "Did you go to high school?" "Yes, of course," I answered. "Did you graduate from high school?" Once again I answered in the affirmative. This, I thought, is the strangest interrogation I have ever had. Suddenly, Madame's voice rose in anger: "Were you never asked questions in school? Why can't you answer me properly when I ask you such a simple question!" With this, I felt the blood leave my face and I stopped talking entirely.

Pulling herself upright with an imperious air, she went right on in her brusque manner: "Now, *mmn*, I am going to show you something. Pay careful attention, for I expect you to do it the first time. Do you understand me? Not the second time, but the first time!" At this point, I could only nod my head. Seated at her piano with much of her spilling over the sides of her chair, she demonstrated and also explained the first stage of a technical approach for which she was well-known — the down-up wrist motions on each successive tone of a five-finger pattern beginning on middle *C*, the "ones," as the Vengerova students derisively referred to them. According to what I gleaned from Madame, the wrist was supposed to undulate up and down while the fingers and the elbow remained fixed. But as I reasoned many years later, the wrist undulates more naturally and effectively by means of the forward-backward movements of the upper arm. Madame's approach was not only physiologically unsound, but it also led to injuries. Had I been in the presence of anyone else, I would have confessed to feeling uncomfortable while making these movements. But it was clear from the start that Madame would brook no discussion whatsoever. As Ela Brailowsky told me — one never asks questions of a Russian.

At nineteen, I knew nothing about controlled wrist motions at the piano. "At last," I thought, "an authority is supplying me with real answers on how to acquire a sound technique." I was, therefore, not only willing, but also desperate enough to follow Madame's advice, however awkward it felt. Yet all of my attempts to simulate her demonstration of the "ones" proved futile. The whole time, Madame appeared utterly bored, as though all of this, including my confusion, was a routine affair. Apart from pausing now and then to have me write down some inconsequential direction or concept which she dictated, she offered no personal communication to me whatsoever. Finally, and not too soon for me, the hour was up.

Stepping onto the elevator was like being rescued from a life-threatening experience. One look at me, and the elevator operator lowered his eyes and continued to avoid my glance until we reached the ground floor. I wasn't the only broken spirit he had confronted in that elevator. There was the young woman before me, for instance, and heaven knows how many others. And the only thing we ever wanted was to improve our playing and to love our teacher in the process.

Once outside, the full horror of my first lesson seeped into my consciousness like acid being drawn into a syringe. Morose and disillusioned, I must have walked along Riverside Drive for hours trying to sort out the significance of this first encounter with Madame. "There must be a logical explanation for all of this," I reasoned. "She must have something important to pass on to me; otherwise, how could she have become so famous? And here I am, judging her after only one lesson."

By the time I returned home, I had made a good case for blaming myself. Resolution upon resolution followed: I'll give the down-ups my best effort; I'll show her what I'm made of; I'll convert this whole nightmare into a constructive attitude that will benefit my playing.

Early the following morning, I set to work on the ones. In spite of all of my resolutions, I had to fight off boredom almost at once. And before I knew it I found myself reading through whatever music happened to be lying around the piano. It was not long, though, before guilt overtook me. I imagined Leopold Mannes' voice: "She's the greatest teacher in the United States." That I could not apply myself to her method, even at stage one, was certainly my fault, and not hers. Back to the down-ups, even if it kills me!

While I was battling with myself, the telephone rang. To my surprise, it was that mysterious figure who had rushed out of Madame's studio in tears moments before my first lesson. She introduced herself as Irene Rosenberg.* "I hope you don't mind my calling you. I got your telephone number from the registrar at the Mannes School," she said. "I feel that I must apologize to you for having put Madame Vengerova in such a foul mood before your lesson." She went on to explain that she was scheduled to perform Beethoven's Concerto in *C* minor the following week. Madame had expressed a desire to attend the first rehearsal. There was a last minute change, no fault of Irene's, which necessitated a complicated re-arrangement of Madame's schedule. "She flew into a rage," Irene told me, "and scolded me for not letting her know sooner. And you, poor Seymour, happened to arrive for your first lesson right at that moment! Knowing her as I do, I am sure she punished you for my having inconvenienced her."

When I reported to Irene all that had transpired at my first lesson, she was filled with remorse. And we spent the rest of our telephone conversation commiserating. It all spelled the beginning of a long and deep friendship, one that has lasted to this day.

The Assistant

Madame Vengerova had a large class of pupils — so large, in fact, that it was virtually impossible for her to give weekly lessons to each pupil individually. Most of her pupils, then, and especially the new ones, had alternate lessons with assistants. After a so-called initiation period, a few pupils studied with Madame exclusively, while others continued to work with assistants. There were, of course, the stars among her pupils who were Madame's private property from the beginning. Since all of her pupils were highly gifted, it seemed impossible to predict which ones would be so favored. Secretly, I always wondered if Madame's decisions

---

* Dr. Irene Rosenberg Grau is Professor Emeritus of Converse College, in Spartanburg, South Carolina, where she was for ten years the director of the Pre-College Department. Later she was an Adjunct Associate Professor at the Blair School of Music at Vanderbilt University, Nashville, Tennessee. She is now retired and lives in Florida.

in this regard were influenced by lesson fees. Madame, for instance, had a large contingent of private pupils in addition to those who were enrolled at the Mannes School and the Curtis Institute. While conservatories of music are notorious for underpaying their faculty, they stretch their pockets for teachers with big reputations. This is one reason why so many eminent musicians have settled in New York City, where fees for teaching are the highest. Yet, no school could match the high fees that a figure such as Madame Vengerova commanded from her private pupils. The question is, did the temptation of higher fees from private pupils influence Madame in deciding who, in fact, received weekly lessons? If this was so, Vengerova was certainly not the only eminent teacher whose artistic idealism wavered in the face of money. Even Nadia Boulanger, teacher of practically every renowned composer of the twentieth century, was known to be mercenary with some American pupils — all of whom she assumed were rich. Once, in her dealings with me, she exhibited a crassness unbecoming an artist of her caliber. As it happened, I had written to her from London asking if I might attend Sir Clifford Curzon's master classes at Fontainebleau. I was studying with Sir Clifford at the time, and, as a matter of fact, he wanted me to accompany him there. Boulanger promptly answered my letter. She sent me warm greetings and added some remarks about her remembrance of my having won the first prize in the Fontainebleau competition five years earlier, and what a privilege it would be for me to return, etc. Then in closing, she specified how much it would cost me to attend the master classes merely as an auditor. Sir Clifford, in reading this letter, was so outraged that he threatened not to give the master classes at all unless I received an invitation from her. She then sent back another letter, begging me to be her guest at Fontainebleau.

Back to Madame Vengerova, I did not stay long enough with her to discover whether or not I would have been singled out to have weekly lessons. Being a novice in the Vengerova method, I was sent to Mildred Jones, one of the six assistants, a clone, albeit a somewhat gentler version, of Madame Vengerova.

Of the six assistants, all but one were women, and all were, or had been, disciples of Madame. Some were brilliant performers; others, like Miss Jones, taught exclusively. While most disciples emulate something of their masters' personalities, in this particular case it would be unfair to ascribe full monster status to all of Madame's assistants, although Olga Stroumillo, also a Russian, was a high contender for monsterdom. As for Miss Jones, an American, she, like Madame, seemed quite human at first. But by the second lesson, I discovered that she had imbibed more from Madame than merely the knowledge of how to move the wrist. At my first lesson, Miss Jones asked me to sight-read the first of Mendelssohn's *Songs Without Words*. She might have asked me to play something from my repertory, so as to gauge what sort of pianist I was. But quite obviously, that would have been counter to her convoluted plan. Being sick to death of the down-ups, I threw myself into the Mendelssohn with unbridled passion. Considering the fact that I was merely sight-reading, I thought that I did an acceptable job. Miss Jones, however, thought otherwise. Stopping me half way through the first page, she summed up my playing as follows: "You don't know how to phrase, you have no legato, you don't know how to pedal, and you are stiff!" I looked at her aghast, more angry than offended. In light of this appraisal of my playing, I sincerely wondered why Madame Vengerova had accepted me in the first place. I kept this to myself, of course, and waited obediently for Miss Jones to begin the process of rectifying all of these faults. Instead, she went directly into the subject of the down-ups — but with one exception: whereas Madame did not specify whether I should play these exercises *forte* or *piano*, Miss Jones insisted that I play each tone as *forte* as possible. This would get me "deep into the keys" and rectify my "surface-like approach to the keyboard!"

Practicing the down-ups *forte* produced an unwelcome effect: several days later I sprained my right wrist. Madame, at the next lesson, was quick to diagnose its cause: "*Mmn*, it is because you carry a heavy briefcase!" Then, contradicting what Miss Jones had demanded, she instructed me to practice my down-ups *piano*, and not *forte*.

Several weeks went by (they seemed more like years) and I was graduated to the "twos," and even to the "threes." That is, my wrist would go down on *C* and glide up on *D*; then beginning again on *C*, I glided up on one impulse to *D* and *E*. "Gosh," I thought, "if I continue at this pace, I might even reach the 'fives' by Christmas!"

It was during my third lesson with Madame (I had three alternate ones with Miss Jones) that she rose from her chair and walked over to me. Standing to my right, she took hold of my wrist to maneuver it into the correct position for the threes. The warmth of her pudgy fingers against my cold hand, frozen with nerves, embarrassed me greatly. Never one to lose the opportunity to express her sadistic nature, Madame uttered a malicious whine which froze my spirit as well: "*Mmn*, why are your hands so cold?" Having good manners at least, if not sufficiently flexible wrists, I replied, "It's very cold outside, Madame." Still bending over me, she released my hand, lowered her eyelids and responded sneeringly, "But you have been in this room long enough to be warm!" I could only sit there in silence and cringe in embarrassment. She stood her ground, and continued to stare down at me, while I receded ever more deeply into an abyss of despair.

Returning to her piano, Madame suddenly looked at me with unmistakable compassion. And with what appeared to be genuine concern, she inquired "Why do you look so unhappy?" Taken off guard by this least expected show of human kindness, I lost no time in unburdening myself: "Oh Madame," I replied, "I *am* unhappy. I have tried my best to do the exercises which you have prescribed, and I know they are good for me." I hated myself for lying! "But I miss playing pieces. In fact I have lost my motivation for practicing altogether. Please, may I have one piece to practice along with the exercises?"

Madame, who had remained silent throughout my confession, gave no visible evidence whatsoever of the fury which was gathering inside her. But no sooner did I reach the end of my last sentence, than fire shot out of her eyes. In the next moment, she unleashed her-pent up rage: "You fresh American upstart!" she screamed. "You never speak a loud word to me, but your thoughts are fresh! How dare you tell me how to teach! Why don't you study with Frank Sheridan (he was a distinguished pianist and a member of the faculty at the Mannes School); he will give you nothing but repertoire. (She then went down the list of other faculty members at the school — all of whom she criticized in a similar fashion.) You don't deserve to study with me. I do not know why I ever accepted you as my pupil!"

The barrage against me lasted for so long, and was so violent, that some protective device within me blocked out her words. In fact, most of what Madame said, like many of the painful experiences of my childhood relating to my father, faded instantly from consciousness. It is merciful that the mind can filter out pain.

After five minutes or so, the fury subsided, and I remember coming back to consciousness simply because she asked me a question: "Have you studied the first Bach Partita?" I swallowed hard and managed a weak, "No." "Write that down!" she commanded. "Have you studied the first Chopin Impromptu?" "No," I answered again. "Write that down! And don't you dare return for your next lesson unless every note is memorized!" It was a negotiated settlement. "You want repertoire, then you had better memorize it!"

Even as I wrote down the assignment, I wondered what price I would have to pay for the fact that Madame had given in to my request. Being by this time numb with anxiety, I gathered my belongings and slunk out of the studio without so much as a word of goodbye.

I received my first therapy from the elevator operator. Seeing my deathly pale complexion, he exclaimed, "Take it easy, kid; everything will be okay!" He actually cared, this complete stranger. Yet I was too battered emotionally to "take it easy," nor did I think that everything would be okay ever again. As I walked away from that building, I knew for certain that I would never again return.

Would I have been able to pass over this traumatic scene had I been older and more experienced? Many adult students who had had similar traumatic experiences with Vengerova and other irascible teachers seemed to possess an endless capacity for forgiveness and forbearance, presumably because they learned something at their lessons, or hoped to. In my case, there was nothing to recommend Vengerova. My youthfulness notwithstanding, I knew that her technical approach was not only limited, but also faulty. My instincts told me that this, coupled with her sadistic nature, would make it impossible for me to continue my lessons. I feel certain that I would have arrived at this conclusion, whatever my age or experience.

Whether I looked suicidal as I left Madame's studio, or whether she had misgivings about her conduct, I cannot say. Whatever the reason, she lost no time in telephoning the school to ask the secretary to deliver the following message to my mother: "Tell him when he returns home not to worry. Everything will be all right." It proved that there was, after all, something human within her.

Understandably, my mother was worried and perplexed to have received a message like that. When I arrived home, I explained to her what had happened. As far as I was concerned it was not "all right," and would never be so. I could never continue to study with a person who not only misunderstood me musically, but who also thought I was "fresh!"

On the following day, I went to see Leopold Mannes and reported the entire incident to him. He, of course, had heard all about it from Madame herself. I asked him to assign me to another teacher. Having my best interests at heart, however, he begged me to reconsider: "You don't simply walk out on a figure such as Madame Vengerova." As Leopold Mannes continued to talk, it became clear that his priorities were antithetical to mine: He was more impressed with her reputation than her teaching abilities. And I simply wanted to learn to play the piano — but not under the guidance of a sadistic monster! The more I discussed the affair with Leopold Mannes, the more determined I was to leave Madame. Before we parted, I told him that she should be forbidden to teach altogether, and that under no circumstances would I ever go back to her.

All three of us were placed in an awkward position: Vengerova, knowing that I intended to leave her, saw this as a blow to her pride; Leopold Mannes, in assigning me to another teacher, risked offending Madame; and I had to prove to the Manneses that I was worth all of the trouble.

Proving myself was more difficult than I had first realized. To begin with, my confidence was severely shaken. But if anyone helped me over this hurdle, it was my new teacher, Dr. Herman DeGrab. Sensitive, aristocratic, he took time out of each lesson to draw me out on whatever anxieties remained after that traumatic experience. After several months of his wise counseling, and hard work on my part, I was able to dismiss the whole Vengerova incident as one of those unfortunate experiences in life.

Waiting in the Wings

The first inkling I had of just how deeply I had wounded Madame Vengerova's pride was revealed to me four months later. I had attended the New York City debut recital of Polish pianist Jan Gorbaty, with whom I subsequently studied. "Janicktovitch," as I fondly called him (he addressed me as "Seymourkeyavich" and sometimes "Seymoursky"), coached his debut program with none other than Madame. After the concert, my friends and I joined a long line of well-wishers wending its way slowly across the impressive stage of Town Hall. From a distance I could see Gorbaty standing by the piano and greeting people amiably. Some twenty feet beyond him, standing like some royal dignitary about to hold an audience, was Madame Vengerova herself. She was surrounded by a retinue of young people, presumably her students. Needless to say, my heart skipped a beat. I lost no time in whispering to my friends, "You always wanted to know what Madame Vengerova looks like...well, there she is!" While they cast surreptitious glances in Madame's direction, I tried my best to hide behind the person in front of me so as to avoid eye contact with her. Yet I knew that eventually I would have to pass her. She stood like some terrifying gargoyle alongside the only exit from the stage. There was no question about it: I was on a collision course!

After reaching "Janicktovitch" and showering him with well-deserved compliments, I turned away from him to face my ordeal. How long those dark, piercing eyes had been upon me, I could not tell. As I trudged the remaining distance to where Madame stood, I felt myself grow pale. Now I was opposite her, and my eyes were pulled into her cold stare. Whether it was wishful thinking on my part, or simply a self-protective instinct, I falsely assumed that she could not place me. I broke the awkward silence and said to her in a matter of fact tone, "Hello, Madame Vengerova, don't you remember me? I'm Seymour Bernstein." All at once there was a dramatic moment of recognition on everyone's part: my friends who had suffered vicariously through all of my ordeals with Madame were now open-mouthed to be standing before her. The Vengerova pupils, who no doubt had heard of the scandal, were seeing the "fresh American upstart" for the first time. All eyes fell upon Madame, who immediately responded to my question. "Of course I remember you," she said loudly enough for the entire auditorium to hear. Then gesturing towards Gorbaty, who was still in the process of greeting his admirers, she added, "*Mmn,* I wanted to teach *you* to make that tone. But you could not stand me!" "That tone," to which she referred, was, of course, part of Gorbaty's playing and admired by distinguished figures such as Heinrich Neuhaus and Wilhelm Backhaus long before he met Vengerova. According to Jan Gorbaty, he played for Vengerova for only one reason: his well-meaning friends told him that American pianists played differently from European pianists. As it turned out, Vengerova not only corroborated everything Gorbaty did, but she also became his friend and staunch supporter. Did he actually learn something from her? When pressed, Gorbaty told me "No."

The truth is, Vengerova had a double standard in her approach to her students. On the one hand, she, like many European pedagogues who immigrated to the United States, used terroristic tactics in order to dominate her young, inexperienced pupils. On the other hand, it seems that toward older, more experienced artists who came to her for advice, she behaved like a warm, supportive colleague.

Returning to my own experiences with Vengerova, I soon discovered that it really is therapeutic to return to the scene of the crime. Being once again in the presence of Madame, and hearing her petty remark, made me realize in a flash just how fortunate I was to have escaped her clutches. Things were different now. I had rejected her for the very reason she stated: I could not stand her! From a stronger and hard-earned vantage point, I calmly met her gaze and simply walked away from her, leaving her to seethe in the poison of her own making.

For me, everything pertaining to Madame Vengerova soon took on the aspect of a bad dream, while she, evidently, kept the flame of vengeance alive. Although she held seniority in "monsterdom," no one, least of all I, could have predicted what sort of reprisal she had in store for me. She was waiting in the wings — waiting for the opportune moment to deliver a death blow.

In the meantime, the school year proceeded far more productively and happily than it had begun: I accompanied the finest instrumentalists and singers enrolled in the school, and I had the privilege of playing with David Mannes himself for a group of pre-college students and faculty members. His performance of the Dvorak Sonatine for Violin and Piano was touching beyond words. Knowing that the patriarch of the school was near eighty made the occasion especially moving. I also had classes in solfège, chamber music (my teacher, while he was certainly not a monster, was no angel, either!), and counterpoint with Felix Salzer. The latter was one of the musical inspirations of my life. Yet, years later, when I was writing my book *With Your Own Two Hands*, his comments to me on the telephone temporarily reawakened the depression I had associated with the Mannes School. As it happened, I wanted his permission to quote him as the author of an experience which changed my musical life. It had to do with the way he introduced us to three-part counterpoint. Specifically, we had been concentrating on the horizontal autonomy of voices, and had, up until this time, dealt only with two-part counterpoint. Standing by a blackboard, and introducing us to the addition of a third autonomous voice, he suddenly stood back and stared at us in amazement: "Look at what we have here!" he cried. "Behold! We have a chord!" For all of us, the revelation concerned the fact that a chord, as none of us had ever realized before, was a meeting place of three or more voices! Reminding Felix Salzer of this incident, I then asked his permission to use his name in conjunction with it: "What are you talking about?" he responded, angrily. "Why, everyone knows that a chord is a meeting place of voices. You'll be the laughing stock of the music world if you ever write such a thing in your book. No! Under no circumstances can you use my name!" I made a feeble attempt to explain that not all musicians know this fact, and that at nineteen, I, personally, had always thought of chords as being vertical entities alone. But he was not to waver from his stance. I regretfully removed his name from the manuscript, and with it, a good measure of my admiration for him.

Success

With only one month left before the end of the school term, the Manneses decided to climax the school year with a gala concerto concert. I was one of the four students chosen to perform. In spite of the fact that I was in fine spirits and working productively, Dr. DeGrab, ever mindful of my past troubled days, did not want to tax my energies to the fullest. He suggested, therefore, that I program the Bach Concerto in *F* minor, a work which he thought I could learn and perform with a minimum of strain. In a show of confidence, Leopold Mannes wrote a short cadenza for the third movement, and dedicated it to me.

The evening of the performance arrived. There was a capacity audience in the small auditorium, and the one box hovering over the stage was filled with distinguished guests. Nervously pacing backstage, I heard the Mendelssohn Piano Concerto in *G* minor, brilliantly played by another student of Dr. DeGrab, Lillian Kallir, and a fairly good performance of Beethoven's Violin Concerto. The second half of the program was to include the Bach concerto followed by Chopin's Concerto in *E* minor.

The intermission was now over, and it was my turn to perform. Filled with a passion for the Bach, and not intending for a moment to disappoint Dr. DeGrab, the Manneses, and all of the faculty and students, I walked out onto the stage with great resolve. As I adjusted the bench with my head tilted slightly upward and towards the right, my eyes caught two bright daggers — the eyes of Madame Vengerova. There she was, sitting in the front center seat of the only box in the small auditorium. If ever a performer wanted to be anywhere else but on that stage, it certainly was I! My panic lasted for only a few seconds, though, for the next glance I encountered came from the conductor awaiting my cue. I nodded to him, and was instantly swept away by the *F* minor introductory chord. Then there was no turning back. Only occasionally did my thoughts wander to that box. By the time I arrived at the sublime second movement, I abandoned myself entirely to the music. This, I thought, was the best part of my performance. Armed with confidence at being able to concentrate so successfully, I burst into the final movement with more verve than I was accustomed to. But then, as I came closer to Leopold Mannes' cadenza, anxiety suddenly gripped me. I had learned the cadenza only a few days earlier. But now, with the end of the concerto in view, it occurred to me that it was too new to survive the performance. And the fact that Leopold Mannes was sitting in the audience did not help matters any. As any performer will tell you, nothing is more unnerving than anticipating a memory slip. No sooner had I entertained the thought of my own insecurity, than I did, in fact, suffer a slight memory slip in the few measures preceding the cadenza. Undaunted, I improvised according to the harmonic sequence and somehow I recovered without marring the flow of the movement. Everything after that, the cadenza included, went without mishap. As a matter of fact, Felix Salzer, during my counterpoint class on the following day, seemed more impressed with my improvisation than with my otherwise faithful adherence to the printed score.

At the risk of sounding immodest, I must say that I had a handsome success that evening. This was no small victory considering the giant concerti which opened and closed the program. For me, of course, the victory over myself was more important than the enthusiastic response to my playing. I had survived! And I learned from this that no person could harm me unless I, myself, allowed him or her to do so. From that moment on, I learned, too, to ward off all the monsters who subsequently entered my life. Paradoxically, I have Madame Vengerova to thank for this. It was the only thing I learned from her.

Part 2: Monsters and Angels

Reprisal Extreme

Unbeknownst to me, my success at the concerto concert was, to Vengerova, the last straw. The very next day she telephoned Leopold Mannes and delivered the following ultimatum: "I will no longer tolerate the gossip being circulated about me — that I am not good enough to teach Bernstein. So, either he leaves the school, or I do!"

Leopold Mannes was now, himself, a victim of the monster. Justice, as he well knew, was on my side. No one, least of all he, considered my dissatisfaction with Vengerova to be a crime punishable by expulsion. Yet to oppose her would result in Vengerova's resignation from the Mannes School, and the loss to the school of its greatest asset.

When Leopold Mannes sent for me on the following day, I had no notion whatsoever of Vengerova's ultimatum. I was all smiles as I entered his office. He greeted me warmly, but with a constraint unnatural to him. He spoke first of my performance of the Bach Concerto, and he showered me with compliments. But suddenly, he lowered his eyes and looked grave. I had a forewarning of doom. "There is something painful that I must tell you," he began with a quivering voice. "I must ask you to leave the school." As he explained the reason for this, tears began rolling down my cheeks. I felt bereft. We were, both of us, victims of Madame Vengerova's evil intent. Mixed with my own sense of loss was a feeling of compassion for Leopold Mannes. That circumstances had forced him to expel one of his favorite students must surely have caused him as much pain as it did me. I wept as much for him as I did for my own loss. Nothing more needed to be said; nothing more *could* be said. I arose from my chair, shook his hand dejectedly, and slowly walked out of the office.

I was devastated! In fact, my whole world seemed to collapse all at once. I had come to love everything about the school — the Manneses, the faculty and the students, and the many opportunities to perform. I saw the latter as a proving ground to help me get over my stagefright. Moreover I loved the building itself, its old-world charm and the intimacy of its rooms. One great advantage in going to a small school is the size of the classes. My counterpoint class, for example, had no more than seven students. Now it was all gone. Expulsion! The very word connoted delinquent behavior. How could I explain this to my parents, Aunt Clara, Louise, and my friends? What would they think of me now?

Delirium

By the time I arrived back in Newark, I was in a delirium of depression. My mother was the first to hear the news. Predictably, she damned Vengerova and the school as well: "You'll be a great man without them,"

174

she said. In spite of my mother's and everyone else's support, I, and I alone, had to face the fact of my expulsion. I felt isolated, like being on the stage. I had thought all along that surviving not only those lessons with Vengerova, but also the performance while she stared down at me, would have made me strong enough to endure anything at all. Now, the realization of just how vulnerable and insecure I was made me even more depressed.

Weeks went by during which I did not so much as touch the keyboard. Little by little, though, I began to play through my favorite works. It was the only thing that helped me to overcome that heaviness of spirit which all of us suffer from time to time. Music itself proved to be my best friend. It comforted me, inspired me, and actually renewed my purpose in living.

As I look back upon that experience, I am struck by the fact that Madame, then at the peak of her fame, actually felt threatened by a young unknown pianist from Newark, New Jersey. Surely this tells us more about her than anything else. And so does another incident concerning Irene Rosenberg.

Irene had been a pupil of Madame's for six years. Accumulated outrage at the way Vengerova treated her, plus my own stand against Vengerova after only six lessons, encouraged Irene to discontinue her lessons with Madame shortly after I did. The circumstances surrounding her case, however, were quite different from mine. Whereas I had been in the school for only one year, Irene was scheduled to graduate the following month. Nothing could have whetted the monster's appetite for destruction more than this one fact. Madame got to Leopold Mannes, of course, and he in turn sent for Irene. When they were together, he delivered an ultimatum that Madame had insisted upon: "Either continue your lessons for one more month, or else you will be forbidden to graduate." Irene's decision summed up six years of being victimized by Madame's special brand of sadism: she chose liberty and forfeited her diploma. As for Leopold Mannes, had he turned a deaf ear to Madame's ultimatum and allowed Irene to graduate, then Vengerova would have resigned from the faculty.

Predictably, Madame handled Irene's rejection of her with the same sort of pettiness she had shown me. One day, a week after Irene had escaped from Madame, the doorbell rang at the Rosenberg residence in

Brooklyn. Irene happened to open the door herself. There, unannounced, stood one of Madame's pupils with a package. Opening it, Irene found two ceramic angels that she had given to Madame for Christmas, plus a photograph of herself which previously had hung on the wall in the Vengerova studio. Such was a teacher's response after six years of teaching a pupil.

One wonders what tragedies or disappointments in Madame's life caused or contributed to such abhorrent behavior. As I reconstruct these events, I imagine that all of her musical gifts, all the professional acclaim that was hers, must only have afforded her fleeting moments of satisfaction. Whatever was the source of her problem, be it life's betrayals, or self-betrayal, it had warped her mind and turned her into a musical dictator. Far from leading out the best within her pupils, she suffocated their talents and their aspirations as well. All dictators, I believe, have a common weakness: not being able to command themselves, they end up commanding others. It is an oft-repeated story of power falling into the hands of unworthy and psychologically unhealthy people.

To have been expelled from a school for being a model student was, to be sure, a paradoxical situation. I felt grief, at first. But in time, I turned the whole thing around to my advantage: it was *my* victory, and a defeat both for Madame and for the school as well. The real tragedy, of course, was Madame herself. Talented, and knowledgeable to a certain extent, she cheated herself and her pupils of that special bond that can exist between teachers and pupils. Pedagogical success, love, and respect were hers for the asking. Instead, she left behind a smoking pyre of resentful and disillusioned young pianists, some of whom left music altogether. She died more scorned than admired.

JUILLIARD SOJOURN

In 1947, a year after my expulsion from the Mannes School, I decided to enroll in the extension division of Juilliard. By all rights, I should have auditioned for the regular school, for I no doubt would have benefited greatly had I studied with a figure such as Rosina Lhévinne. But my unpleasant associations with the Mannes School made me wary of all institutions and well-known teachers. By simply electing a few courses, therefore, I would have one foot out the door, so to speak, just in case things did not work out to my expectations.

There was a course offered at Juilliard entitled History and Materials of Music. It met twice per week and covered absolutely everything, from the history of music to exercises in music theory, including dictation of melodies and chord progressions. But if ever a course could be called a farce, that was one. Our teacher, Walter Hendl, a well-known conductor, was not exactly organized. As a matter of fact, he gave the impression of improvising everything right on the spot. And with a disparate group of students, all at different levels of achievement, nothing of any consequence was accomplished from lesson to lesson. For example, only a few of us were sufficiently advanced to write down dictations, while all of the other students simply sat there, utterly defeated and left behind. In the final analysis, the course was embarrassing for all concerned, and a total waste of time and money.

Something, however, was accomplished that had nothing to do with the course itself. Because Walter Hendl invariably came late to class, I always went to the small Steinway grand piano in our classroom and spontaneously performed for the students whatever pieces happened to be in my fingers at the time. I am sure that some of the students thought me a show-off. But the truth was that I could not resist using the class to test my concentration. During one such performance, our teacher suddenly burst into the room while I was playing Mendelssohn's *Variations sérieuses*. I stopped instantly, but he insisted that I continue playing to the end of it. He was so impressed that several weeks later he took the entire class all the way to Newark to attend my second concert at the Mutual Benefit Life Insurance Company auditorium. On the face of it, this seemed like a most unusual show of support on the part of the teacher and the students as well. But secretly I suspected that our teacher would do anything at all to skip a class.

I also took a two-piano course, and at least had the opportunity to perform some of this repertory in a recital held at the end of the semester. Apart from this, I learned very little during the two years I spent at Juilliard.

It has been said that there is no such thing as a bad orchestra, but only a bad conductor. Similarly, discontent among a majority of students derives not from *what* is being taught, but rather *who* teaches it. My one year at the Mannes School was extremely beneficial because I was fortunate enough to be assigned to artist faculty members who knew how to teach — except for Madame Vengerova. It is a pity that my studies there were abruptly interrupted because of her histrionics. In the long run, though, I see music education as a private affair — as a one-to-one exchange between a teacher and a pupil. Besides, not all young people fresh out of high school are candidates for higher education. I certainly was not. I find it curious that more students do not opt to take a year or more off before going on to college or to a conservatory of music.

DEGREES — YES OR NO?

If the process of practicing can influence our lives, then certainly the reverse is true: Life, and especially the study of non-musical subjects, adds to the resources of the mind and thus enhances a musician's ability to understand and to perform music. But the fact is, some performers, like certain athletes, have built major careers on physical prowess alone. This calls forth the image of a tenor I once knew who, although he could sing anything, had no interpretive understanding of music whatsoever. A friend of mine once referred to him as "the Empire State Building without elevators." These physical freaks often win contests or are awarded full scholarships to college. And why? There are always the thrill-seekers who enjoy pyrotechnical display for its own sake. The danger is that the success of these "thoroughbreds," as one of my pupils liked to refer to them, can create a false model for success in the minds of young hopefuls. For the greater the market for "mindless" and "soulless" virtuosic display, the more young musicians are inclined to lessen the importance of emotional and intellectual growth.

A Hierarchical Order

Virtuosity is, of course, a necessary component in a commanding performance. But when it is achieved at the expense of musical feeling, the results are as meaningless as a poem fashioned by computer chips alone. If we are to become the music we practice and perform, then our chief priority must be the development of our emotional and intellectual worlds. Virtuosity, then, is a means to a successful performance, but must not be an end in itself. There is an end, however, which dedicated musicians do achieve. It is a status that defies all academic descriptions: they become true philosophers.

All practicing musicians confront one major challenge — to achieve that delicate balance existing between spontaneity and conscious control. In order for spontaneity to function at its best, it is necessary to place various functions in a hierarchical order. In my opinion, all musicians ought to adhere to the following rule: first, respond emotionally; second, discover the physical connection to musical feeling. As to the first, *respond emotionally*, the question arises, "What are we responding to?" By way of answering this difficult question, I have listed what I believe are requisites for defining and heightening our responses:

A sensitive ear. If you don't have perfect pitch, do everything possible to develop relative pitch: Practice solfège, improvise, and force yourself to play by ear.

An awareness of the period in which the piece was written.

An understanding of each and every notational indication on the printed page.

An auditory response to rhythmic, melodic, and harmonic stresses and relaxations.

An ability to convert all of these elements into living experiences through the feeling function.

As to the second step, *making a physical connection to musical feeling*, this requires a thorough understanding of the human and instrumental mechanisms. It is imperative, therefore, to study with one or more good teachers.

Following these steps, you have the feeling that music is playing *you*.

Being Prepared

Since few people, if any, would deny the benefits to be derived from studying non-musical subjects, the question is: Should students who aspire to careers in music enroll in a liberal arts course or enter a music conservatory immediately after graduating from high school? I can think of two reasons why some students ought to wait a year or more before doing either. One reason concerns the level of their playing. Whether they are late starters, or whether they are suffering the deleterious effects of poor teaching, the fact is that their performing skills may not be commensurate with what is expected of music majors in colleges or conservatories. The second and more important reason concerns the ability to confront practicing for what it really is — a stringent exercise in concentration during which feeling, thinking, sensory perceptions, and physical coordination are examined independently and then synthesized in the performance of a whole musical composition. As I have observed in my years of teaching, few high school graduates and, for that matter, few people in general have the capacity for such discipline. This may explain why there are now, and have always been, relatively few profound performers.

I have often been asked to coach students in preparation for their college or conservatory auditions. I have listened to enough of them to know that most high school seniors are ill-equipped, both musically and technically, to meet the demands of degree programs. In the course of discussions with them and their teachers, I believe that I have discovered the major cause for their shortcomings: most of them had been concentrating exclusively on two or three audition pieces for an entire year. As a result, they bypassed the very thing which would have promoted their musical and technical growth — accepting the challenge of practicing new and ever more demanding works. Doing the opposite, circling around the same repertory for a year or more, stunts a musician's growth and, moreover, leads to boredom.

With good teaching and diligent practicing, such students learn to play their three or four pieces so persuasively that they are accepted in first rate schools. They not only pass their auditions, but are actually assigned to the finest teachers on the faculty. For all but exceptional students, this is what I regard as a dangerous state of affairs. For once such ill-equipped students begin their formal education, they realize all too late that their basic weaknesses can hardly be rectified amidst the demands of academia.

Some faculty members of conservatories and colleges tell of their utter disillusionment with some of their freshman pupils. They assign new pieces to them, and at the next lesson, they are shocked to discover the weak fibers of poor training in some of the pupils whose auditions impressed them the most: they cannot sight-read, they are technically deficient, and they cannot process even the simplest musical notation. Were such students allowed to devote an entire year to learning a few pieces, they might conceivably pass their jury examinations. But most schools' repertory requirements pose challenges even to students who are far more advanced. Besides, the majority of teachers in colleges and music conservatories are not interested in teaching the basics of technique, musicality, and memorizing. Moreover, the time that it takes to attend classes, study, write papers, and prepare for exams leaves little enough time even for advanced students to practice sufficiently. But when students are deficient to begin with, they can never keep up with what is required of them. Being unable to fulfill their teachers' expectations, some of these students shift to another major, while others leave music altogether.

As I have discovered, most college students who aspire to careers in music cram in one or two hours of practice time per day. Often, when papers are due or exams are imminent, they cannot find the time to practice at all. Conservatory students, however, practice an average of three to four hours per day. Some do more than that. But even here, the demands of course work and the poor facilities for practicing in most schools do not exactly promote the kind of concentration necessary for students to make progress. Thus, in my opinion, conservatories of music and music departments in colleges are suitable only for those young musicians who can prepare the works they are expected to perform with, let us say, two hours of practicing per day. For all other students who aspire to careers in music performance, higher education can be frustrating and often a counter-productive experience.

I believe that the directors of music departments do their schools, their students, and music itself a great disservice by admitting inadequately trained students into their performing arts programs. Part of the fault lies with jury members who make the mistake of judging a student's abilities on the basis of a ten minute audition alone. Paradoxically, students with no foundation to speak of may somehow pass their auditions, while knowledgeable and more fully developed students who have temporarily fallen prey to nervousness may be categorically rejected.

Some school administrators have no scruples whatsoever. With their schools always in the throes of an economic crisis, they apparently never intend to be selective during so-called auditions. Shamefully, then, all paying students, regardless of their levels of performance and preparedness, are admitted into their programs.

Stay Home and Practice

When I hear serious deficiencies in the playing of potentially gifted students, I strongly advise them to devote a year or two to serious study and practicing before auditioning for a music school. Curiously, few students act upon this option. And rarely have I met parents who would sanction an interruption in their child's formal education. As they see it, taking a year or more off after high school in order to develop a particular talent, or merely to reflect upon life, delays what they believe to be a far more important gain: acquiring degrees in some professional field.

Students who do take time off to catch up on neglected skills ought to have a master plan for practicing and performing certain works within a specific time frame — a time frame that is compatible with their level of achievement. Unless one has specific goals in mind, practicing tends to be aimless and unproductive. It is best to devise such a plan with the help of a teacher.

Some of my private pupils study with me at their own pace while majoring in non-musical subjects. Without pressure, they benefit from music's harmonizing effects. During exam time, I do not expect them to practice at all. They appear at their lessons, nevertheless, and at these times, I supervise their practicing and sight-read four-hand works with them. Invariably, such students end up being happy, fulfilled people.

Meting out advice is, to my way of thinking, merely presenting options, for I cannot assume that I know what is best for anyone. Besides, as with all people and in all fields, there are exceptions to what we think are the rules. Perseverance, for example, can make a musician with modest gifts sound prodigious. Similarly, people with the capacity for hard and consistent work can earn Ph.D.'s and still fulfill performing engagements. I have witnessed accomplishments from modestly gifted musicians that were nothing short of miraculous. In one case, a musically and technically deficient student entered college against my, and everyone else's, better judgment. Surprisingly, he transcended his limitations. In another area, I have, on occasion, discouraged some of my own pupils from appearing in major concert halls in New York City for much the same reason. A few of them have insisted upon performing, and predictably, not all of them were successful. But occasionally, some outdid themselves, and, moreover, elicited favorable reviews from critics with *The New York Times*. It comes down to this: the mind has unlimited potential, and we have the power to decide how far we wish to expand it.

Why do would-be performers want degrees to begin with? Some students whom I have interviewed on this subject came up with varied and very frank answers:

1) "I feel deficient in theory and music history, so I've decided to enroll in a music conservatory."

2) "I hope to get a college teaching post. But without a doctoral degree, I don't stand a chance of being considered for a job."

3) "I realize I ought to stay home and practice all day. But I know myself. If I have the whole day free, I'll just while away the time. Schools have built-in structures. And since I can't structure my life myself, school is where I belong."

4) "I really want to go to school so I can meet people, maybe even find someone to date."

Let us hope that after sowing his wild oats for four, six, or eight years, student number four will have learned to strike a balance between practicing and socializing. Regarding the other students, although they prided themselves on being honest in their replies, I sensed that many of them fell into the third category — students who lack the discipline to practice properly. Whatever reason a musician might have for wanting to major in music, he or she must at least be able to learn and to perform new pieces within a reasonable time span.

Concerning pupil number three, a total dependency on an imposed structure in order to work properly is, in effect, an admission of an inability to discipline oneself. Nor will such a pupil necessarily learn self-discipline even after years of schooling. Once formal education comes to an end, pupils may well be faced with the original question: "How can I motivate myself to practice?" This inability to create an internal disciplinary structure has frequently prompted people to abandon themselves to anything at all that seems to supply what they themselves lack. All too often, this can lead them to make unfortunate choices, whether it be in selecting a school or entering into matrimony. In short, we all need valid reasons for doing what we do.

But what is the *right* reason for going to college? Quite obviously, a desire to learn. Some students are blessed with a thirst for knowledge from the beginning. Others, who formerly showed no interest in reading whatsoever, might suddenly be awakened after reading one assigned book in a college course. I know of a case in which a student in his late teens who had fallen prey to drugs, gangs, and the worst sort of delinquent behavior became a disciplined and devoted college student majoring in music, after one teacher showed a genuine interest in him. When such students are finally inspired with a true desire to learn, they can benefit enormously from a structured environment such as colleges offer them. The assignments alone can motivate them to learn for the rest of their lives.

Doctoral Candidates Speak Their Woes

Being a composer myself, I have always been interested in meeting aspiring young composers. To hear their complaints about their college and conservatory teachers, one might conclude that all schools are bad. But as we know, schools, like all institutions, have good and bad elements. Yet it takes only one destructive and domineering teacher to damage the reputation of an entire department, or even an entire school.

Some college students complain about their teachers much as they do about their parents. It seems that rebellion is part of the growing up process. But many adults, knowing how quick students are to criticize everything and everyone, tend to discredit *all* of their complaints. This is just as unfair as always siding with students against their teachers. As a teacher myself, I have tried to maintain an objectivity when hearing complaints from pupils. When they are directed against a teacher, I try, whenever possible, to hear that particular teacher's point of view. It is often difficult to filter out the truth from so many accusations on both sides. Often, though, students have good grounds for their complaints.

One doctoral student in composition recently expressed to me his grave concern about the future of composing in general: "How can there ever be another Beethoven so long as self-centered and short-sighted composition teachers limit their pupils' output to atonal works only?" Another young composer was more specific in her complaints. She related how her teacher summed up the orchestral work which was to serve as her doctoral thesis: "This measure sounds like Shostakovich, and that one reminds me of Copland. It's all clichés!" She continued on with a litany of grievances: "Every sincere effort I made at saying something of my own was not only discouraged by my teacher, but categorically forbidden. And why? My teacher told me that I had to say something that was never said before. 'You have to be original,' which to him meant restricting myself exclusively to atonality. It seems to me that if anything is a cliché, it is atonality."

History presents many examples of composers who have tried to impose their own compositional styles upon their students. Imagine what the world would have lost had Haydn, for instance, confined his pupil, Beethoven, to a Mozartian classical purity, and if Beethoven had followed his advice? As a matter of fact, Haydn, who had been invited to Prince Karl Lichnowsky's palace to hear the première of Beethoven's Opus 1 piano trios, with the composer himself at the piano, advised Beethoven not to publish the third one, in *C* minor. In contrast to the above teacher's objection, he thought that the trio was too original for public tastes. Beethoven suspected Haydn of being jealous of his "originality." Besides, the third piano trio happened to be Beethoven's favorite. And so, fortunately for us, he did not follow Haydn's advice.

Doctoral candidates, however, are required to follow the advice of their teachers and advisers. I have observed that dictatorial advice such as "compose atonally or don't compose at all" often comes from composition teachers who cannot write a simple melody. I once studied composition with Ben Weber, who wrote a great deal of atonal music. I chose him in particular because it troubled me that I had no musical response to, or understanding of, atonal writing. "If I learn to compose atonally myself," I thought, "then I will come to appreciate this style of composing."

Ben Weber was extremely encouraging and patient. He taught me various contemporary techniques and asked me to incorporate them in compositional exercises. One day when I arrived for my lesson, I noticed one of his own orchestral works sprawled out across his writing easel. While I certainly do not have the best ears in the world, I can at least peruse a musical score with a certain degree of aural comprehension. As I studied Ben Weber's score, I could not honestly make any musical sense out of it. As far as I was concerned, the horizontal and vertical intervallic relationships might as well have been ink spots strewn randomly upon the manuscript paper. I could not resist asking him, "Can you actually hear this music in your mind's ear?" He was more amused than insulted by my question. "What do you mean, hear it? If it's logical, then it *must* sound musical." His response spelled the end of my foray into atonality, for to me, that kind of writing divorced feeling from thinking. The following day, I trumped up an excuse to discontinue my lessons with him. In acknowledging my aversion for atonal composing, I felt at one with the composer George Rochberg, who said, "You can't fool the central nervous system." Yet I would not presume to criticize anyone who has a genuine affinity with atonality. When Arnold Schoenberg created a language without tonal centers, he did so out of an aesthetic need. What for me validates his extreme break from tradition is the fact that he had successfully composed tonal music, the melodies and harmonies of which might well have come from a mature Schumann. Similarly, Pablo Picasso's abstract style emerged from a representational one akin to the old masters'. He knew how to draw eyes and noses with anatomical precision long before he decided to displace them all over his canvases.

A teacher's style is, of course, his or her own affair. But when a teacher rules out a pupil's preferences, then I consider this to be the worst sort of teaching. What prompts teachers to be so closed-minded? In some cases, the teacher may possibly be jealous of his pupil, as Haydn reportedly was of Beethoven.

When carried to an extreme, jealousy and competitiveness can actually lead a teacher to wish his pupils ill. This was dramatically revealed one evening in 1972 during a string section rehearsal of the National Youth Orchestra of Canada conducted by the late Thomas Monohan, a prominent double-bass player. The rehearsal was held in the auditorium of the music building at the University of British Columbia, with approximately sixty of Canada's most gifted young string players, of age 14 to 24, and four faculty members in attendance. According to the brilliant cellist Myles Jordan, who played in the orchestra for three years, Monohan interrupted the rehearsal and commented on the new crop of music majors who had been accepted into his class at the University of Toronto: "When I get talented students, the first thing I want to do is break their fingers. Because it's not long before they become your learned colleagues and competitors." That some of his "talented students" were playing in the orchestra did not seem to faze Monohan in the slightest. But far worse than that, the other faculty members present laughed at his comment. Tragically enough

185

for his students, I suspect that there was real hostility underlying his attempt at sardonic humor.

Returning to college programs, course work is one thing, but most instrumentalists and composers look to their private teacher as the most important person in their lives. Were I to decide to get a degree, my choice of school would be predicated upon one criterion only — the teacher with whom I wished to study. Had the composition teacher and his student mentioned above been musically and personally compatible, the dilemma they experienced might never have arisen. The first lesson to learn, then, is to choose your teacher as you would choose a friend and enroll in the school where that teacher is on the faculty. If music study serves as a barometer for all the other areas of a musician's life, then it is reasonable to assume that a harmonious relationship with such a teacher can have a positive effect on all the course work — musical and otherwise. The other lesson is that the composition student might conceivably have turned the difficult situation into a learning experience. By restricting herself to atonal techniques, purely as an experiment, she might eventually have chosen to adopt something or even all of this language as a natural means of aesthetic expression. In other words, she may eventually have come to like what she formerly had disliked so much.

When all is said and done, nothing can tarnish the principles upon which schools of higher learning are built — not even the large number of questionable administrators, teachers, and students who befoul the very word "education." In all areas of society, there are undesirable as well as exemplary people. Quite obviously, this applies also to school faculties. Thus, along with incompetent faculty members are those whose positive influences are felt by students long after they have earned their degrees. And along with disillusioned students, there are enlightened ones — those who see their education as having been indispensable to everything that they have subsequently achieved.

PROFESSIONAL-AMATEUR

The desire to become a so-called professional musician, someone who makes a living in music and perhaps achieves fame, can cause more unhappiness among musicians than anything else. Ask career-minded students what their goals are in their study of music and you receive responses such as "I want to win a big contest!" or "I want to perform with a major symphony orchestra!" or "I want to concertize all over the world!" Rarely do I hear from such students what almost all amateur musicians would say — that they study music for the sheer love of it. I admire amateur musicians more than I do some professionals because most amateurs study and perform music for the right reason — out of an unconditional love for music. This and this alone motivates them to practice their art.

On the negative side, because most amateur musicians do not perform publicly, they tend to neglect their practicing. In this respect, they differ from the professionals, those who make a career of their playing. But there are a few amateurs who reach those Olympian heights that we have come to recognize in the finest professional performances, heights that define the other meaning of the word "professional," namely, the attainment of a high standard of competence.

I should like to propose, therefore, the creation of a new category of musician, one that combines the characteristic virtues of the two categories, amateur and professional. Such a musician practices music for the love of it, as the word "amateur" implies, and he or she is as serious about practicing music as is the professional. In other words, the ideal musician, whom I here envisage, does not separate a love of music from the serious practicing of it, any more than a performer would separate interpretation from technique. Combining the merits of these two categories, we arrive at a third category, what — with full awareness of the oxymoronic overtones — we might call the "professional-amateur."

My pupils Michael Kimmelman, the chief art critic of *The New York Times*, Donald Shaw, an interior designer, and Steven Ryan, a computer consultant, fit perfectly into this category. Professional-amateurs may occasionally receive small fees or honorariums for their performances, but they make their living in non-musical professions. They earn sufficient money to buy the finest instruments and to study with the finest teachers. Their playing is on the highest level, and they perform whatever and whenever they wish. They are in competition with no one but themselves. They serve their art with a zeal akin to religious devotion. In my estimation, they embody the ideal in the study and performance of music. For them, music is a way of life, and not just a business. As these devotees of music will tell you, a Schubert melody will always beguile them, whether they have a career or not. Just to be able to sound music on an instrument or to sing is, to them, the very essence of life itself. They see music not as an anaesthetizing agent or a means through which they can achieve stardom, but as an expression of all that is good and noble in people.

Not that professional musicians cannot achieve this same status, this same pure and single-minded attitude towards their art. In fact, the greatest compliment I can pay to a professional musician is to compare his or her attitude with that of an amateur.

The following incident confirmed my belief that a professional-amateur may possess qualities not shared by all professional musicians. One of my pupils, Jeffrey Middleton, a brilliant and sensitive artist, was on the stage of Weill Hall reaching the end of a two-hour rehearsal for his debut recital the following day. During the finale of Schumann's Sonata in *F* sharp minor, Ludwig Tomescu— one of the finest piano technicians in New York City — arrived to tune the piano. Slipping into a seat next to me in the center parquet, he listened for a few moments in rapt attention, and then whispered, "What does he do for a living?" Knowing as I did that my pupil was a highly-respected professional musician, I was somewhat puzzled by the question. Later, at the end of the rehearsal, I asked Ludwig what he had meant. "Few professionals play with that kind of sensitivity," was his insightful and highly telling reply. During a brief exchange that followed, he affirmed all that I have been discussing, that is, that many professionals, caught up as they are in career frustrations, have lost their initial love of music and end up playing with routine proficiency, producing performances that lack the magic ingredient of feeling. Inadvertently, the tuner had given my pupil the supreme compliment: he had taken him for a professional-amateur.

DRAFTED

By September of 1949, I had rejected the notion of enrolling in any school whatsoever. I was determined not to allow anything to interfere with my need to practice the entire day. Thus I returned to my cloistered life in Newark, where I could practice uninterruptedly and earn some money through private teaching. I continued to study with Brailowsky once or twice a month, I played for Aunt Clara and other musicians, and I performed a great deal of chamber music. I read books on non-musical subjects and took some courses in philosophy and psychology.

It was all cut short, though, one day in early November, when a letter arrived from the United States Army Conscription Center. I was ordered to appear for a physical examination for induction into the army. I had received a similar letter four years earlier, in 1945, the year that the second world war ended. I remember coming before the very last doctor, who noticed on my records that I had had rheumatic fever as a boy of twelve. Placing his stethoscope on my chest, he asked me to take six deep breaths. As I did so, I felt a dull pain in the vicinity of my heart. After listening for quite a long time to my heart beat, he turned to his colleague and exclaimed, "Do you want to hear something interesting?" The second doctor placed his stethoscope over my heart, listened for some fifteen seconds, and said to the first doctor, "I don't hear anything!" "It's in this area," the first doctor retorted as he pointed to a specific spot on my chest. The second doctor listened again: "I still don't hear anything." To this, the first doctor replied, "It was so obvious, that I didn't even think I needed a second opinion." "Well, do what you think is best," said the second doctor. Whether the first doctor misdiagnosed what he heard through his stethoscope, or whether the anxiety I experienced did, in fact, cause a momentary irregularity in my heartbeat, I will never know. The end result was that I was diagnosed as having valvular heart disease, and was therefore rejected.

When my application was stamped 4F, I was partly relieved, and partly ashamed — ashamed because I would not be able to do my share for the war effort. Many of my former classmates were already serving in some capacity. My conscience was eased somewhat, however, when the armistice was declared several months later.

Valvular heart disease? ...it sounded ominous! My mother lost no time in taking me to a heart specialist recommended by the army doctor — coincidentally a Doctor Bernstein. He gave me a stringent examination and declared me perfectly healthy.

Now, in 1949, before my second physical, the army orders specified a preliminary examination by Dr. Bernstein. Once again, I was declared fit to serve in the armed forces. Later, the general physical examination given at the army center confirmed this. And on December 7th, 1949, I boarded an army bus amidst many tears on the part of my parents, sisters, and brothers-in-law.

As the bus headed towards Fort Dix, New Jersey, I had the feeling that I was living through a dream sequence. To begin with, I had never been away from home before. And at twenty-three, I looked, and also felt, like a teenager. The truth was, I was no more able to identify with becoming a soldier than I had been with becoming a man at thirteen at my *bar mitzvah*. I looked around the bus filled with young inductees. No one exchanged glances, and no one spoke during the entire trip. They no doubt were all terrified of the unknown, exactly as I was. I imagined all sorts of nightmarish situations at the final destination — unpleasant living conditions, sergeants and officers pushing me around, and the possibility of injuries to my hands. It was even more nerve-wracking than being backstage before a concert. Two hours later, the bus drove into the Fort Dix compound. And thus began one of the most dramatic experiences of my life.

At twenty-four, flanked by my parents, after my recital at Mount St. Mary's Academy, New Jersey, just before my induction into the army.

PART 3:
THE ARMY

I used to view myself as being two different people: one person sat at the piano; the other related to his family and friends. But which person was the real me? This identity crisis was so acute that I thought my popularity in school and with people in general derived solely from the fact that I played the piano. I deduced from this that I, the musician, must be the real person, and this explained, at least to my satisfaction, why I used to feel so awkward in social situations: "Just let me get to a piano," I reasoned, "and then I'll earn everyone's attention."

This duality in my personality caused me such distress that when war broke out in Korea I secretly looked forward to being drafted. For if I were detached from my musical life, I thought, I would then have the opportunity to discover if I could be liked for the person I was. I would put my personality to the test once and for all.

As the bus entered the Fort Dix compound, I suddenly had second thoughts: going into the army was, after all, an extreme measure to take in order to solve an identity crisis. It was December 7, 1950, and a war was raging in Korea. On June 25th of that year, President Truman had announced it as "police action," a term designed to camouflage one of the bloodiest wars in history. Willing or not, I was now a part of it.

The bus stopped in front of a large building that resembled a warehouse. There, we were issued army clothing and bedding supplies which we stuffed into a duffel bag. It was like being a prisoner: we all dressed the same and we were told what to do. I was now part of a military machine, and my freedom was long past recovering. Just how much I missed that freedom became more apparent during that first week of indoctrination. I realized another thing, too: I had become spoiled in civilian life because of all the fuss made over me. Whenever I performed, my photograph appeared in newspapers and magazines. Clearly, I was a hometown celebrity, and I am not ashamed to admit that I had enjoyed that status considerably. Now I was a non-entity — just another soldier being ordered about.

RED

Shortly, though, my non-entity status was to became a thing of the past. As it happened, Fort Dix had a newspaper in which articles appeared from time to time about inductees and their former civilian activities. On the third day after our arrival, the chief sergeant of our company passed out questionnaires to us in which we were to specify our professions, our interests, and any other personal data that might be deemed newsworthy. Shortly before I pulled K.P., an article, plus a photograph of me sitting at the piano, appeared in the *Fort Dix News*. My civilian identity was now known to everyone, including Red, the mess hall sergeant.

Being assigned to K.P., or kitchen police, was a fact of Army life. Because such assignments were made alphabetically, I was always among the first on the roster. The duties included washing dishes, mopping the kitchen and dining room floors, serving food, and attending to garbage.

It was quite a crew that lined up in the mess hall at dawn. The swift adjustment to army life and the first hectic days of basic training had left their mark on all of us. Gaunt, exhausted, and apprehensive, we stood at attention in front of Red to await our orders. Red was a heavyset and gruff-sounding man, his large round head crowned with a crewcut of red, bristly hair. He barked rather than spoke as he pointed to the men: "You two guys, get to the mops! The three of you, serve the food — and no double portions! You and you — dishwashing detail!" It was soon to become clear why Red had reserved my orders for last. Looking straight at me with no change of expression in his face, he exclaimed in the same barking voice, "You, *Paderooski*, ain't gonna ruin your hands in no dishwater. Get outside on garbage detail!" hat this seemingly insensitive character recognized me from the newspaper article and was intent on protecting my hands moved me more than I can say. Of all the K.P. duties I pulled at home, tending to garbage had always been a detestable chore to me. My mother used to tease me about it. Now, ironically, garbage duties had followed me into the army. That same evening, I telephoned my mother to tell her the whole story. She was deeply touched to learn of Red's concern for Paderooski's hands.

BASIC TRAINING

In 1950, Walter Winchell, perhaps the most celebrated news commentator of his day, issued the following statement during one of his radio broadcasts: "If you have sons in Korea, write to them; if you have sons at Fort Dix, pray for them!" His dramatic reference to Fort Dix stemmed from the fact that the camp had become notorious for implementing the most stringent basic training program in the country, especially during the winter months. In fact, the simulated battle conditions to which all inductees were exposed were thought to be far worse than those on the Korean front lines. In fourteen weeks, we were trained to fire and dismantle every weapon being used in Korea, from pistols to heavy machine guns, and from hand grenades to mortars. My own basic training took place during the frigid months of December through February, when temperatures often dipped below zero. The hazard associated with this was a constant source of worry to me: having to remove my gloves during weapons firing drills on the target field might easily have resulted in frostbite, with the possibility of permanent damage to my hands. And there was another worry, too — that of crushing my thumb in the chamber of my M-1 rifle.

The M-1 Thumb

Apart from a toy pistol I possessed as a little boy, I had never held a weapon in my hands before — not even those simulated rifles that one sees in target booths at circuses or carnivals. Imagine, then, how I felt when an M-1 rifle was handed to me for the very first time. As I think back to my basic training and those fourteen weeks of systematized terror, few things were more frightful to me than the moment I cradled that fearsome weapon in my hands. Though I felt certain that I would never be able to fire it at anyone, I knew that the army would try its best to make me into an instrument of destruction.

During our indoctrination, we were told two things about the M-1 rifle: one was that it fired ball ammunition that could penetrate six inches of steel; the other was the ever-present danger of incurring an M-1 thumb. This was because the rifle had a chamber on its top side with a visible spring fixed an inch or so below its surface. To close the door of this chamber, which in turn armed the rifle, it was necessary to insert your thumb into the chamber, trigger the spring and then quickly retrieve your thumb before the chamber door snapped shut. A fraction of a delay had obvious consequences. It was not uncommon to see inductees walking around Fort Dix with bandaged thumbs swollen to twice their normal size — the M-1 thumb.

The awesome recoil of this fearsome weapon had yet another danger — that of causing a dislocated shoulder. The only precaution against this was the proper cradling of the rifle's base into the crook of the shoulder. Understandably, then, I was extremely apprehensive when the M-1 was issued to me. It was, as we were told, to be our constant companion during our two-year stint in the army. The officer in charge instructed us to "make it your friend, take it apart, oil it, keep it clean, and take it to bed with you!"

I vividly remember sitting on my bunk in the barracks with my new friend, the M-1, resting on my lap. "One wrong move," I thought, "and Paderooski will have to seek another profession." The first order of the day was to practice retrieving my thumb. Curiously, my training as a pianist made this easier than I thought. I began by resting my thumb on the closed door of the chamber and, in a flash, flipping my hand back and toward the right from my wrist — exactly as I would do when playing an octave or a chord *staccatissimo*. In pianistic jargon, the rotational movement of the forearm towards the fifth finger is called "supination," and no pianist ever supinated with such lightning speed as I did then. I next opened the chamber door and peered at the ominous spring which, eventually, I would have to trigger. The first ten tries made me so tense that I thought I would never breathe normally again. But to my surprise the quick supination of my forearm whipped my thumb clear of the chamber in ample time before that metal door slammed shut.

Next, I practiced cradling the base of the rifle until it actually felt comfortable. While I made considerable progress in allaying my fears of incurring an M-1 thumb or a dislocated shoulder, my efforts could not simulate what it would be like to have a bullet in the chamber. For just as playing the piano at home cannot in any way be compared to the profound responsibility of performing on a stage, so, too, was all of my diligent practicing with the M-1 merely a prelude to the experience of actually firing the weapon.

The Marksman

The day had come. I suddenly found myself lying in a prone position on the target field with my rifle tucked securely in that special cushioned area which I had carefully staked out days in advance. But this time, there were real bullets loaded in the magazine of the rifle. The sheer panic I experienced at that moment made pre-performance anxiety seem minor by comparison. There was one difference, however: performers find themselves alone on the stage with only their preparation and their resolve to carry them through the ordeal. For this performance, there were inductees to my right and to my left, and the lieutenant standing behind me the whole time served, in my mind at least, as the finest therapist an anxiety-ridden soldier ever had. He issued the final instructions: "Aim, take a deep breath, let half of it out, which will steady you considerably, and, finally, pull the trigger." I followed his instructions explicitly, although I did so with a sense of impending doom, like a man being led to his execution. To tell the truth, hitting the target at the far end of the field was the very last thing on my mind. My chief concern was to keep from fracturing my shoulder. I closed my eyes, took a deep breath, and let half of it out. Then, slowly, and with the greatest trepidation, I squeezed the trigger. In a fraction of a second, I heard the loud report. But to my astonishment, and to my great relief, I felt nothing at all. With sweat pouring down my face and with a smile like a person who has just been rescued from death, I reported this to the lieutenant. "Of course you felt nothing," he said with an amused air. "The sound you just heard came from the weapon on your right. You haven't even fired yet!" Crestfallen, I began again, and as a matter of fact, my shoulder absorbed the recoil as it would the opening chords of the Tchaikovsky Concerto in *B* flat minor. A few more tries at it and I actually braved opening my eyes. With all the reluctance I have been describing, it seems absurd now to say that I soon began to enjoy the challenge of hitting the target. Then one day, when I hit fifteen out of sixteen bull's-eyes, the surprised lieutenant warned, "Better cool it, Bernstein. If you keep firing like that, they'll send you to the Korean front." It was a prophetic comment, for some sixteen months later I was, in fact, sent to Korea as a fully trained infantryman.

Bivouac

Twice during those nightmarish fourteen weeks of basic training — once during the mid-point, and again around the twelfth week — we were required to live out in the field for two weeks. Bivouac, as it was called, was an attempt to expose and condition soldiers to everything they might encounter on a real battlefield. It began by intermittently marching and jogging twenty miles to the bivouac area. Our heavy winter gear made this difficult enough. But in addition, we had to carry our tent equipment and disassembled parts of heavy weapons the entire distance. I noticed at the start that two ambulances were trailing the long line of soldiers marching in double columns along the frozen dirt paths. The reason for their presence soon became clear: within five miles, two men fainted from sheer exhaustion; and in the course of the next few days, others succumbed to pneumonia and to other severe respiratory problems caused by the extreme cold and damp conditions within our flimsy pup tents. One cannot determine what factors enable certain people to survive under such conditions. But I felt sure that my own survival was a result of the discipline and determination that I had learned at the piano and on that other battlefield, the stage.

The officers in charge used all possible means to prepare us for real battle conditions. For instance we had to crawl across a 100-yard obstacle course, once during the day and again at night. The ordeal consisted of scrambling under barbed wire while dragging our M-1 rifles. To make matters worse, buried explosive charges were detonated all around us. Simultaneously, live machine gun bullets whizzed inches above our heads. It was drummed into us time and time again that ultimate survival under battle conditions depended upon one crucial thing — protecting our M-1 rifle. For dirt in the barrel could result in misfire, and, possibly, death. As we emerged one by one from that hellish ordeal, officers examined our rifles scrupulously. If even a few grains of dirt were found in the barrel of any weapon, the unfortunate soldier was then ordered to traverse the obstacle course again, and to keep on traversing it until he emerged with a clean weapon. It was a consequence so terrifying that we would rather have torn our own flesh on the barbed wire than place our rifles down on the ground for easier maneuvering.

It was during the evening and my final ordeal across that simulated battlefield that I heard a terrifying scream from a soldier only a few feet behind me: "Oh my God! I've been shot!" Hugging the ground to avoid being hit by machine gun bullets, I managed to turn my head far enough around to see several of my buddies pounce on a soldier who seemed intent on standing up and running in panic. Shouts of "Cease fire! Someone's been shot!" were heard over the din of explosions and the insistent rattling of the machine guns. Mercifully, floodlights illuminated the scene of horror, the firing ceased, and officers came rushing onto the obstacle course. They went directly to the screaming soldier and huddled around him. As it turned out, his crawling and twisting under the barbed wire caused such a severe cramp in his leg that he thought he had been shot. This having been determined, the officers left the obstacle course, the lights were turned off, and all of us, the panic-stricken soldier included, resumed our ordeal as though nothing had happened.

Immediately upon emerging from the obstacle course, we were instructed to fix our bayonets and charge dummies strung up and dangling from tree limbs. "Scream, damn you! Scream as you go in for the kill!" one officer shouted. "That's the way you scare the hell out of the enemy!" This was tantamount to an order. Yet I would have risked being taken to the stockade rather than stab that dummy. And certainly I would not scream. In the melee of screaming soldiers and flashing bayonets, my refusal to obey orders was, fortunately, unobserved. The ordeal now over, I collapsed on the frozen ground along with my buddies, utterly exhausted but with a sense of exquisite relief.

Rebellion

I seemed to have sufficient determination and discipline to survive everything that was required of me. Twice, though, during those fourteen weeks of basic training, my physical condition made it impossible for me to obey orders. Once when I was battling the worst bout of bronchitis imaginable, we were taken on a forced march over a terrain of mud. As my combat boots, weighed down by heavy, mud-clogged galoshes, sank ankle deep into the sludge, the sergeant in charge kept shouting "Faster! Faster!" Each step that I took brought on violent spasms of coughing. Finally, it appeared to me that it was a question of either choking to death or refusing to take one more step. No sooner had I thought this than my feet seemed to develop a mind of their own. They reversed their steps, and I found myself walking slowly in the direction of my barracks. Nor did I respond to the shouts of the sergeant: "Hey, Bernstein! Where the hell do you think you're going?!" I knew that my insubordination would not be taken lightly, yet I continued to walk at my own pace away from the company. Once inside the warmth and protection of the barracks, I went directly to bed.

As one might imagine, the sergeant sent for me a few hours later. Ironically, he was the very person who had placed publicity about me in the Fort Dix newspaper. My apprehension mounted as I stood before him. I noticed at once a placard sitting prominently on his desk: "Your story has touched my heart. Go see the chaplain!" Reading this, I felt squeamish about unburdening my woes to the sergeant. Besides, my hacking cough, I thought, would speak for itself. Fortunately for me, I escaped with only a tongue lashing and a harsh warning. "Get off the stage, Bernstein!" he shouted. "You're in the army now. One more stunt like that and I'll see to it that you spend the rest of your two years in the stockade!"

Another time, during the final bivouac of basic training, I developed an agonizing pain on the left side of my right ankle. The pressure of my combat boot against what seemed to be an exposed nerve sent me into spasms of pain. I solved the problem in the only way I could devise: I wore a regular shoe on my right foot and a combat boot on the left. This, of course, did not escape the captain's eagle eye. Knowing for years that inductees used various ploys to avoid stressful activities, the captain viewed my explanation with great suspicion. To my good fortune, however, he observed me limping during the final week of bivouac, and when it came time to reverse our twenty mile trek and march back to the Fort Dix compound, he ordered me to ride on a weapons carrier. I shall never forget him for extending this kindness to me. Nor will I ever forget the scene that ensued in the shower room shortly after my arrival at the barracks.

Part 3: The Army

Attack in the Shower and in a Foxhole

Because I was driven back to company quarters, I arrived at my barracks hours before everyone else did. Two weeks of living out in the field certainly takes its toll on a person. For one thing, I had the feeling that the cold, damp weather to which I had been exposed for fourteen days had penetrated to my bones, and that I would never be warm again. The other thing was that I was grimy from head to toe. Still shivering, I tore off my fatigues and headed for the shower room. Whatever Fort Dix may have lacked in physical comforts, the showers, at least, functioned ideally. While I was luxuriating under the comforting stream of warm water, a sergeant assigned to our company suddenly appeared as though from nowhere and positioned himself under the shower head next to mine. With a choice of some eight showers, I wondered why he had chosen the one next to me. I did not have to wait long for the answer, though. In seconds, and with not a single word exchanged between us, he became wildly aroused. As his hands came up in an obvious attempt to grab me, I rushed from the shower room pausing only long enough to swoop my towel off the hook. At that very moment, and much to my relief, I heard the loud conversation of two soldiers who had just entered the barracks proper. Had it not been for them, I am sure the sergeant would have pursued me to my bunk. A towering, bear-like man, he easily could have held me in a vise from which I would not have been able to escape. Considering the lustful look in his eye, it is more than probable that he would have raped me.

A week later, I had a similar experience in a foxhole, of all places. Learning to dig foxholes was part of basic training for all soldiers during the Korean war. I remember vividly being in one, far from other members of my company, with a sexually aroused soldier who seemed not even to care whether I was a willing party or not. He knew I was a pianist, and perhaps he assumed that all concert performers were gay. Whatever was in his mind, I had to use physical force to fend him off. Had it not been for the sudden appearance of a lieutenant who came to check on the effectiveness of our foxhole, I am not sure who would have won that battle!

The subject of homosexuality seems to come up wherever men live in proximity, such as in boys' camps, the armed forces, and prisons. While even today there remain those bigots who view homosexuality as abhorrent, abnormal, and downright sinful, general opinion today has changed considerably from what it was in the 1950s. At the time that I was a soldier, being "queer" carried with it a stigma. It was frowned upon and harshly dealt with — especially in the armed forces. Dishonorable discharges for homosexuality were as common as witch hunts in Massachusetts. Because of the climate of the day, it was unthinkable for

198

me to discuss the shower and foxhole scenes with anyone at all, especially my buddies. Like actual rape victims, I was afraid that the mere mention of these experiences would be, in effect, an admission of complicity.

Trained to Kill

Being inducted into the army during the Korean war was truly a life and death situation. For more often than not, the completion of basic training meant only one thing: you were now sent to FECOM, the Far East Command, as a qualified killer. But as an intelligence officer once confessed to me, "It is foolhardy to assume that we can undo a lifetime of moral and ethical training in fourteen weeks and actually train men to kill. This, of course, explains our biggest problem in the war effort — and that is that eighty percent of our men freeze on the firing line!"

As far as I was concerned, basic training was far too short a course to be effective in training men to fight a war. For one thing, most of us were so exhausted that we fell asleep during key lectures, so that we lacked information which, under real battle conditions, would have spelled the difference between life and death. Dozing off during one lecture in particular had serious consequences for me.

Once during the first week of bivouac we were awakened in the middle of the night and herded into jeeps. We were then driven miles from the campsite, individually deposited at what seemed to be arbitrary points in a wilderness, and handed a map, a compass, and a book of matches. The gravity of the situation soon became apparent to me: I was hopelessly lost, and I had to find my way back to the camp with the help of these three objects. The fact was, I had slept throughout the entire lecture on map reading, and how to use a compass. What was I to do? To make matters worse, it was sub-zero weather, and I seriously thought that I would be found frozen to death. Fortunately, there was a bright moon, and this at least enabled me to see the pines and the underbrush as I made my way across the frozen terrain. After approximately thirty minutes of aimless wandering, and with panic mounting with each step, I heard a voice — like the proverbial voice in the wilderness. It belonged to one of several corporals who had been stationed at key points to rescue lost soldiers. When I came face to face with my rescuer, I had all I could do to keep from hugging him. Stragglers like me were rounded up and driven back to camp. No doubt thinking that the incident spoke for itself, the officers in charge felt no need to reprimand us.

There were moments of levity, too, when basic training seemed more like playing cops and robbers. One time, for example, we were taken into a field to learn judo — how to disarm an enemy by fracturing his arm, and how eventually to kill him. The lieutenant in charge was a charming man, articulate in speech and particularly adept at throwing men over his shoulder. After his demonstration, we were instructed to pair off in order to practice these judo skills on our own. "Now," I thought, "my performing career is over. For surely I will not emerge from this exercise without a broken arm, or worse!" With self-protection the only thing on my mind, I frantically looked around the company and focused on a bruiser, if ever I saw one. He was well over six feet tall and sported a physique like one of those menacing wrestlers one sees on television. In a flash, I rushed up to him and asked him to be my partner. He took one look at my thin, unmuscular frame and broke out into a knowing smile. The physical maneuvers between us which then followed would no doubt have made us strong contenders for the first prize in a slapstick comedy competition. From my perspective, trying to lift his hulk even an inch off the ground was like trying to uproot a Sequoia. And because he could have shattered me with the slightest movement of one of his fingers, he became a pussycat, lifting and placing me down again as though I were made of Dresden china. At the end of an hour or so, I knew nothing about judo technique, but we had provided some much needed laughter.

Fun and games were rare, though. For basic training was, as I said before, a life and death struggle from beginning to end. Accidents and even fatalities, though rare, were unavoidable. Once I witnessed a hair-raising incident which, had it not been for the quick thinking of a corporal on duty, might have had dire consequences. Around the seventh or eighth week of basic training, we were taught to de-pin hand grenades, count several seconds, throw them over an embankment, and fling ourselves to the ground. One member of our company standing very close to me was so traumatized by the whole business that he pulled the pin and literally froze, the armed grenade locked in the grip of his right hand. I, and several other soldiers nearby, began shouting for help. An alert corporal darted onto the scene as though from nowhere. He wrenched the live grenade out of the poor fellow's hand and hurled it over the embankment, while simultaneously shouting to all of us at the top of his lungs, "Hit the dirt!" This we did, just in time to hear the grenade explode. Fortunately, it spewed its shrapnel harmlessly against the stone wall.

Whether my psyche refused to absorb the seriousness of these war games, or whether some self-protective mechanism kept assuring me that basic training was, after all, only a simulation of war, I cannot say. But curiously enough, much of what I have been describing took on the aspect of those toy pistol games that I used to play as a child with other little boys. Even later, on the front lines in Korea, when an enemy shell landed some 100 yards away from where I was bathing in a stream, this, too, took on a fictitious aspect as if I were watching a movie of myself. It is merciful, I believe, how the mind refuses to absorb the full impact of reality. Interestingly, some performers who suffer extreme stage fright have similar responses: they speak about their performances in hindsight as though they were dream sequences. My former dentist, Dr. Julius Stern, a passionately devoted amateur violist, once described to me his own departure from reality after his first public performance: "I haven't the slightest idea how I played. The only thing I remember is that someone had to lead me off of the stage when it was over!"

The Service Club

Every camp had one or more Service Clubs, and every Service Club had at least one piano. Soldiers gathered there in the evening to dance with local girls, to have a snack in the canteen, to enjoy a game of ping pong, or simply to socialize. There was a jukebox to supply music for dancing and, occasionally, USO troupes provided live entertainment. For me, however, the Service Club meant only one thing: I had a captive audience for whom I could perform. Practically every evening, then, when most of my buddies were near dead from one more grueling day of basic training, I wolfed down my dinner and went directly to the Service Club, where I played some of my repertory for whoever happened to be there. One evening, while I was going at one of my warhorses with unbridled passion, a captain from Special Services happened to visit the club. He approached me afterwards and introduced himself as Captain Sumner. He was a short, dark-haired man who spoke in a soft, almost sinister voice. I could tell at once that he was highly intelligent and knowledgeable about music. He complimented me on my playing and then asked many questions about my background. He vowed to use his influence to have me assigned to Special Services once I finished my basic training. In the meantime, he urged me to continue playing in the various Service Clubs around Fort Dix. "You can count on me," he said, "to speak about you to Major Conte, the officer in charge of Special Services. But other officers from the Special Services office frequent these Service Clubs as I do, and I'm sure they'll speak about you, too. So perform as often as you can." Even without Captain Sumner's advice, I would have continued to perform anyway. It was reassuring to think that that I might be assigned to Special Services once my basic training ended.

Before long, I discovered that I was not the only musician at Fort Dix. One evening while I was dashing through Chopin's twenty-fourth prelude, an inductee approached me and introduced himself as Kenneth Gordon.

First portrait as a soldier.
(Photo by J. Abresch)

He had a fiddle case tucked under his arm. In 1951, I knew relatively little about the professional music world, so I neither recognized his name nor did I have the slightest notion of the fact that he had been enjoying a brilliant career at the time of his induction into the army. He was a protégé of the well-known violinist Michel Piastro, the concertmaster of the NBC Symphony Orchestra under Arturo Toscanini. Kenneth was for years the assistant concertmaster of the New York Philharmonic. At any rate, when I had finished my Chopin prelude, he asked me if I would like to read through the Sonata in *D* minor by Brahms with him. The chamber music repertory had always been my first love, and I remember sight-reading this work as though I had known it all of my life. During the following weeks, Kenneth and I played through the staples of the violin and piano repertory — Sonatas by Beethoven, Brahms, and Franck, plus countless other works including *Tzigane* by Ravel, *Suite Populaire* by Manuel de Falla, and that great violin warhorse, *Zigeunerweisen* (Gypsy Airs) by Sarasate. Thus began my association with an artist of the first calibre, one that was to bring me untold rewards throughout my two-year stint in the army. We had no idea, of course, what adventures lay in store for us. In fact, the year and nine months that followed would prove to be the most significant period of my life.

SPECIAL SERVICES

I survived basic training without incurring an M-1 thumb, a dislocated shoulder, or frostbite. In fact, I seemed all the better for it; I was stronger and in much better health than I had been as a civilian. Even though the obstacle course gave me nightmares for months afterwards, I was proud of myself for having endured all of those hardships. Though the worst seemed to be behind me, the possibility of being sent to FECOM hung over me like some ominous storm cloud. Kenneth, who had still to endure another month of basic training, was no less apprehensive. Imagine my relief, then, when orders came down from the high command requesting me for Special Services. Kenneth's orders followed quickly upon mine. It seemed to us a reprieve from a death sentence. I telephoned home immediately with the good news. My mother, filled with her own apprehensiveness about the possibility of losing her *zeenala* to the war, wept with relief.

The Movie Janitor

Captain Sumner was now my immediate superior. He hatched a scheme by which I could satisfy the army's work requirements and, at the same time, have a piano at my disposal. There were two kinds of installations at Fort Dix in which there were pianos — Service Clubs and movie

203

theaters. We decided upon one of the theaters, mainly because it would afford me complete privacy during the day. Every morning I had to sweep out the entire theater and clean two latrines — one for men and one for women. It was, in fact, the first time I had ever entered a ladies' room. Not that I expected anything other than a series of stalls. But it was a curious feeling, nevertheless, to invade the private domain of the opposite sex.

Years later, while on a trio tour in Kansas, I was to have another experience involving a ladies' room. As it happened on that occasion, the closest restroom to the backstage area was the one for ladies. With concert time some ten minutes away, I gave in to the urging of my colleague, the cellist Ruth Alsop, who offered to stand guard by the ladies' room while I answered nature's call. She turned her back only momentarily to speak with someone. But it was long enough for a woman to slip by her unnoticed. What I then experienced when I heard the restroom door open and then heard the click of heels coming to rest in the stall to my right can only be imagined. I quickly assumed a lotus position to hide my pants legs from my next-door neighbor. And I remained that way, perfectly still and hardly breathing, like a yogi, until the unsuspecting woman left the restroom. It was a new sort of panic for me, and one that was the subject of much laughter throughout the rest of the tour.

To return to the army theater, though I loathed my janitorial duties, I knew each day that a reward awaited: I would have the entire afternoon in which to practice. There was an old upright piano in the theater office that was in surprisingly good condition. I cannot possibly express what it meant to me to practice regularly again. I revived my repertory in no time at all, and I also learned new works to play with Kenneth. Captain Sumner visited from time to time just to see how I was faring. Occasionally, he lingered to listen to me play. It would be difficult to say whose joy was greater in this arrangement, his or mine.

Alas, the following week Captain Sumner was assigned to another post. But good fortune smiled upon me again, for I came under the protection of another officer from Special Services, Lieutenant Harold Gilmore, who had been a composer-pianist in civilian life. When the theater to which I had been assigned closed down, he put me in charge of a Service Club: "You will not only have a grand piano at your disposal, but there is also a hi-fi unit there and a fairly good collection of classical recordings." My duties were more or less the same: every morning I cleaned the entire club and the two latrines, and had also to wax the dance floor. While Lieutenant Gilmore thought that this assignment would be an improvement over the first, it soon proved to be the worst possible place for serious practicing: the telephone rang constantly, a veritable army of men arrived throughout the day to service the vending machines or to deliver supplies to the canteen, and a parade of soldiers wandered in and out for a break from their routines or simply to chat with me. When informed of all this, Lieutenant Gilmore lost no time in assigning me to another theater that closely approximated my original assignment.

Debut as a Tap Dancer

Fort Dix was teeming with a wide variety of talented soldiers and WACs, some of whom were of professional stature. Besides traditional instrumentalists, singers, and dancers, there were two specialty acts: Billie Dodson, a fire-eater and sword-swallower, and Rolando Johansson, an acrobat who climaxed his act by standing straight up on his index finger on top of a lighted crystal globe. *The Great Rolando!* was in constant demand even while he was stationed at Fort Dix.

Outclassing us all was the pop singer Vic Damone, a superstar if there ever was one. He was inducted into the army shortly after I was. Like me, he was assigned to Special Services. Coincidentally, he occupied the bunk directly to my right. Some stars who spend the greater part of each day dealing with agents, photographers, and reporters and signing autographs become unbearably snobbish. Vic Damone, however, was totally unas-suming and as congenial a fellow as one could ever meet. When, for example, he was not able to attend a recital that Kenneth Gordon and I gave at Fort Dix — "I have to sign checks all evening!" — he was merely stating a fact. He did catch one of my informal performances at a Service Club, though. Thereafter, there grew between us a strong bond of mutual respect for one another's gifts.

One day, he produced the sheet music of a new song he wanted to learn. Whether he found it difficult to sight-sing music without a piano, or whether he could not read music at all (which is sometimes the case even among classical singers), I cannot say. The fact is, he asked me to sing the piece for him. I managed the pitches all right, but the foghorn quality of my voice was more than his professionalism could take. After a few bars or so, we both broke into uncontrolled laughter.

Stepping out of character and singing for Vic Damone in private was one thing. But that I would soon be called upon to perform a tap dance routine, and in public no less, was something I could hardly have predicted.

As I said earlier, there were some very gifted soldiers and WACS at Fort Dix. With all of this talent at his disposal, Lieutenant Gilmore decided to create a variety show called *Sound Off!* Just as there is rank in the armed forces, so, too, does it exist in the performing world.

205

Major Conte (center), officer in charge of Special Services in Fort Dix, New Jersey, flanked by Kenneth Gordon (right) and me.

Accordingly, Vic Damone was cast in the starring role. My own partici-
pation in *Sound Off!* included a variety of functions: playing *The Ritual
Fire Dance* by Manuel de Falla while Billy Dodson, our fire eater, went
through his routine, accompanying Kenneth Gordon in *Gypsy Airs* by
Sarasate, and, finally, taking part in the chorus line, which required
singing and marching routines. During the latter, we "sounded off" in
marching cadence as soldiers are taught to do during their basic training.
Rehearsals were held almost every evening. With the exception of Vic
Damone, the entire cast was required to attend all of them.

Apart from learning the song "There's No Business Like Show
Business" and rehearsing the various chorus line maneuvers, I remained
uninvolved during the long and arduous rehearsals. To fight off boredom,
I surreptitiously practiced a soft-shoe routine in the back of the room
while three WACS rehearsed it as part of the show. Unknown to me, my
antics did not escape the watchful eye of Lieutenant Gilmore. One day,
several weeks later, we took our show to Camp Kilmer, New Jersey. One
of the WACs suddenly became ill moments before the show began.
Lieutenant Gilmore handled the emergency with one phrase: "Okay,
Bernstein, you're on!" At first, I took this to mean that I was to play
another solo to replace the tap dance routine. But as I soon discovered, it
was not my playing that he wanted, but rather my dancing! "Oh, no sir!"
I cried frantically. "You wouldn't make me do a thing like that!" "Get out
there," he insisted. "That's an order!"

The first thing an inductee learns in the army is to obey orders from his
superiors. While Lieutenant Gilmore was exceedingly friendly towards
me, and a fellow musician at that, he was, nonetheless, an officer. Without
another word, then, I took a center position between the two WACs, joined
arms with them and shuffled out onto the stage to the piped-in music of
"Tea for Two." All of this was greeted with taunting jeers and whistles
from a thousand or more soldiers and civilians in attendance. While I am
sure I cut an awkward figure, I did at least execute the steps with
automatic precision. One other positive thing emerged from what was for
me a very embarrassing situation: performing my piano solo later in the
program was easy by comparison. At the end of the show, the howls of
laughter from family members helped me to view the whole thing light-
heartedly. It took approximately a year, though, before my brothers-in-law
stopped addressing me as Fred Astaire.

To this day, more than fifty years later, I can still perform some of the
key steps of that soft shoe routine. As a matter of fact, those steps became
the nucleus of my own choreography when I tap danced on the stage of
the 92nd Street Y at the première of *American Pictures*.

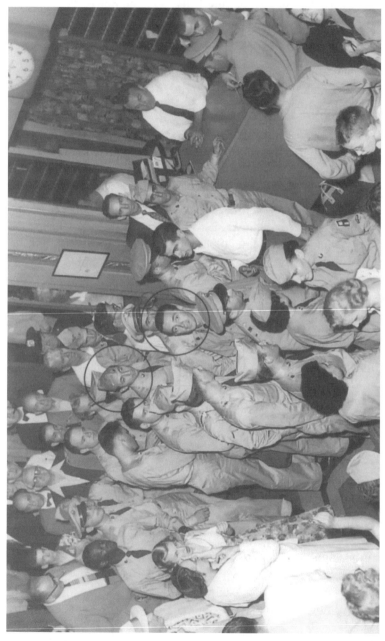

The Fort Dix soldier show *Sound Off!* checks into a hotel in New York City. Circled faces, Vic Damone (foreground) and myself.

With all of the hullabaloo made over Vic Damone, the potential for booking the show was limitless. During the summer of 1951, we performed at the Center Theater in New York City, that erstwhile showplace which stood opposite Radio City Music Hall. What a theater it was! Once used for mammoth productions such as Ice-Capades, it had a seating capacity of over 2500. Our show was a sell-out, with hundreds of people being turned away at the door. All of the proceeds went to the Veterans Hospital Program and an organization called Entertainment Service Associates. As one might imagine, the facilities at the Center Theater were beyond anything we had experienced thus far. For one thing, I had a bona fide concert grand piano at my disposal — a far cry from the deplorable instruments at government installations. The stage crew rolled out the piano and placed it on the theater's left apron, which extended approximately halfway along the side of the parquet. No sooner did I begin the long chain of trills at the beginning of the *Ritual Fire Dance* than crimson lights crisscrossed their beams around me and the piano. Simultaneously, Billie Dodson, standing center stage under his own spotlight, went through his act of swallowing swords and flaming torches. It was not exactly my idea of good taste. But I was in the army, and being a lowly private, I had no clout whatsoever — not even when it came to performing. It would not be long, though, before I would prove that serious music can hold its own without any such props, and that it can be enthusiastically received even by servicemen who have never heard classical music before.

"The Kate Smith TV Show"

After several other performances of *Sound Off!* at army and air force installations, life at Fort Dix returned to normal. By this time, Kenneth and I were assigned to secretarial duties in the Special Services office. It was one more protective maneuver on the part of Major Conte to keep us stateside for as long as possible. One day while sitting at my desk I opened a letter from Ted Collins, a producer at NBC and Kate Smith's personal manager. It seemed that "The Kate Smith TV Show," one of the most popular programs on TV at that time, was about to inaugurate a new segment highlighting gifted servicemen. According to the letter, a group of talent scouts from NBC planned to tour Service camps around the country in search of these talents. They proposed a date a few weeks hence when they would come to Fort Dix. Major Conte instructed me to write back and confirm the date. Kenneth Gordon and I were to be among those who auditioned for the talent scouts. At the appointed time, I played Chopin's Polonaise in *A* flat and was chosen to be the first serviceman to appear on that new series. Kenneth and I were chosen to appear as a duo the following week.

In early January, 1952, I received a three-day pass to return home in order to do some constructive practicing. All of the distractions of the recent show and my ever-increasing duties at Fort Dix had taken a heavy toll on my technique. In three days, however, and after a strict regimen of scales, arpeggios, octaves, and other various technical exercises, my fingers regained some of their former flexibility. Armed with a far greater sense of security about my playing than I had felt for months, I set off for the Hudson Theater on West 44th Street in New York City. I found myself amidst a maze of TV cameras, technicians, and orchestral musicians. Ted Collins and his staff greeted me warmly. Almost immediately someone escorted me to a room backstage where a makeup artist gave my pale complexion that suntanned appearance one associates with movie stars. As I emerged from the makeup room, I happened to walk onto the set where Kate Smith was rehearsing her songs. "Let's start from the B^7," she said to the conductor in that deep, penetrating voice that had stolen the hearts of Americans for as long as I could remember. "A B^7?" I wondered. "How does she know it's a B^7 without having any music to refer to?" As I subsequently discovered, Kate Smith was endowed with one of nature's miracles — perfect pitch. The rehearsal continued with more such cues: "Give me that E minor again, please." "Let's do the section one more time from the F^7." I was so impressed by her adeptness at naming pitches and chords that I temporarily forgot the reason for my being there.

At the end of Kate Smith's rehearsal, the stage manager ushered me to a piano for some sound and video tests. A background had been constructed of various armed forces insignia. According to what I gathered from the discussion, my face and hands would be superimposed upon the army insignia when I began my performance of the Polonaise. One might think that all of this activity would disrupt my concentration moments before such an important performance. On the contrary! The truth was that it served as a welcome distraction from those waves of anxiety that swept over me at the thought of making my TV debut.

Suddenly, I found myself alone in the stillness backstage. Just at the moment when my nervousness reached a new height of intensity, a door opened a flight above where I was standing. The great star emerged from her dressing room looking positively regal in a glittering blue sequined gown. I watched in fascination as she descended the stairs with the slow, measured gait of royalty. She came directly over to me as though she had known me for a long time. Taking my moist, clammy hands in her own cold ones, she inquired, "Are you nervous, Seymour?" "Nervous?" I answered. "I'm ready to die!" "It's all to be expected," she responded in a low, soothing voice. "But if you think you're nervous now, wait and see how you'll feel when you become famous!" And with a warm, gracious smile, she added, "Don't you worry, honey; you'll be fine."

Kate Smith's comment did not actually come as a surprise to me. I had long suspected that world class performers, having always to live up to their reputations, suffer an even greater degree of pre-performance anxiety than do novices. What *was* surprising, however, was Kate Smith's openness about her own anxiety. Her warmth and concern for me made me feel close to her — like kindred spirits in mutual suffering.

The stage manager approached us: "Two minutes, Miss Smith." With this, Kate Smith squeezed my hands, released them, and added, "Good luck, Seymour." I caught a final glimpse of her standing by the stage entrance. She held her head high like that of a proud and determined warrior about to go into battle. The strains of "When the Moon Comes over the Mountain" filled the theater, and Kate Smith walked briskly out in front of the cameras to tumultuous applause.

It is an old and familiar story — that of drawing upon hidden resources when having to cope with critical situations. On that occasion, I remember being carried along by a do-or-die attitude. To be sure, three days of intense practicing had its positive effects upon my playing. Beyond this, however, no sooner had I sounded the opening E flat octaves, than I was instantly taken over by a profound sense of responsibility — responsibility to the music, to my own self-esteem, and to countless individuals at Fort Dix and at home, all of whom I had no intention of disappointing. Then, of course, there was Kate Smith herself. I would have to survive, I thought, for her sake especially. It was not only my own sense of responsibility that prodded me on, but also an unshakable conviction that everyone else wanted me to succeed. It was indeed a vast support system that took me under the arms, so to speak, and carried me through that performance.

It is astonishing how quickly seven minutes can go by under such circumstances. Almost before I knew it, I was bowing to an ovation so intense and so long that there was no time to play my scheduled encore. A decision had to be made on the spur of the moment. While the cameras focused upon the audience, one of the stage crew grabbed my arm and literally pulled me to a desk where Kate Smith was sitting. In another instant, someone produced a chair and placed it to her right. When the cameras switched back to the desk, Kate Smith was holding both of my hands and beaming with delight. When the applause died down, she expressed her admiration for my playing, all in her inimitable homespun manner, and made me promise to return soon again. Finally, after a brief commercial, Kate Smith broke into a rousing rendition of "God Bless America," as she did at the end of all of her programs. Thus ended my TV debut.

My appearance on "The Kate Smith TV Show" created a furor. It would be impossible to estimate just how many people across the United States heard me play that Chopin Polonaise. Thousands watched the show at Fort Dix alone, and with advance publicity in the New Jersey papers, it seemed that the residents of the entire state were tuned in to Kate Smith that day. Or at least it appeared to be so, for when I returned home on occasional weekend passes, strangers stopped me in the street and congratulated me. Such was the impact of just one TV appearance. Nor did Kate Smith forget me. She seemed to have developed a special affection for me. According to my mother, who watched her show faithfully each day, Kate Smith spoke of me for days after my appearance, and mentioned the fan mail that poured in. Imagine, then, how enthusiastic she was when I returned to her program the following week to accompany Kenneth Gordon. Later, while I was in Korea, the appearance of other servicemen who appeared on her program sparked remembrances of me. "I wonder how Seymour is doing," She would say. "We all pray for his protection."

From TV to Truck Driving

While the officers in charge of Special Services were thrilled with my success, they had no intention of pampering me more than they had already done. Playing the piano was one thing, but performing army duties was quite another. So one day, the entire Special Services staff was given a drivers' manual to study in advance of taking a written test. "Memorize it," I said to myself, "exactly as you would a piece of music." And memorize it I did — so thoroughly, in fact, that I scored the highest mark in the company. Had I known what the consequences of that high score would be, I would never have been so conscientious. For as it turned out, I was assigned to driving a truck. Each day, I walked a mile or so to the Fort Dix garage, hosed down the truck, gassed it up, and delivered supplies for various Special Services activities. And when visiting dignitaries and high ranking generals visited the post, I often supervised the moving of the very pianos on which I later performed for them. When such occasions arose, I was allowed several hours of practice time in between my chores. For the greater part of the day, though, I continued to work at my desk at the Special Services office.

Barbershop Quartet

One day while I was busily typing out some documents, Major Conte called me into his office. He asked me to read a letter he had just received from a David Weisburger, the president of the men's club of Temple Israel on West 91st Street in New York City. It seemed that the Temple officials had chosen to honor Kate Smith during Brotherhood Week with their Annual Award for Humanitarian Ideals. The letter went on to inquire whether Fort Dix could send a barbershop quartet to sing during the presentation ceremonies: "And if possible, could the quartet include an arrangement of Kate Smith's theme song, 'God Bless America'?"

The fact that the very soldier who had recently appeared on "The Kate Smith TV Show" was now reading a letter about a plan to honor her was purely coincidental. Moreover, I am sure that his choice of Fort Dix was predicated solely upon geographical convenience to New York City. At any rate, I ought not to have been surprised by what followed, considering Major Conte's tongue-in-cheek expression. "Answer him, Bernstein," he commanded with his typically officious air. "Tell him that we will be happy to send a barbershop quartet." "But sir," I responded, "we don't have a barbershop quartet." "Oh yes we do, Bernstein," he said with a gleeful expression. "You're going to organize it, and you'll sing in it, too."

By this time, I knew better than to argue a point with an officer — and a major at that. I lost no time in gathering together three men who seemed eager to be a part of the quartet. Charles House, the finest tenor on the post, was my first choice. And to my surprise, Lieutenant Gilmore was eager to be a part of the enterprise. The fourth member was Lieutenant Robert McCallion, who had participated in our show *Sound Off!* We met evenings and worked out one of the staples in the barbershop quartet repertory, "While Strolling in the Park One Day." The foghorn quality of my voice notwithstanding, we blended together surprisingly well. When, however, it came to whistling after singing the line, "A kiss was all she gave to me," we all doubled up with laughter. As everyone knows, one cannot whistle with even the slightest hint of a smile, not to mention laughing. It took the greatest discipline, therefore, to maintain our poise until the end of the song. Finally, I made a four-part arrangement of "God Bless America," giving the solo part to Charles House.

In just a few weeks, the Fort Dix Barbershop Quartet was primed for action. We set out in a requisitioned army sedan for Temple Israel. As the car pulled up at the Temple entrance, we were amazed to see a large crowd spilling over into the street. Everyone, of course, wanted to see Kate Smith in person. But with the seating capacity in the Temple limited to some fifteen hundred, scores of people had to be turned away at the door.

The Fort Dix Barbershop Quartet. Clockwise from top left:
1st Lieutenant Harold Gilmore, 1st Lieutenant Robert McCallion,
Private Charles House, and myself.

As the quartet stood in a long hallway near the door leading to the synagogue proper, we suddenly saw Kate Smith, Ted Collins, and a large entourage of NBC officials walking towards us. As she passed me, Kate Smith stopped in her tracks. "Seymour," she said in a loud, surprised voice, "What are you doing here? Are you going to play?" "No, Miss Smith," I replied rather sheepishly. "I'm going to sing — in a barbershop quartet." With this, she let out a roar of laughter so loud, and so infectious, that everyone standing around began to laugh along with her — myself included. She literally slapped her sides and had finally to mop her eyes with a handkerchief. When Kate Smith had regained her poise, she and the distinguished group walked into the synagogue amidst a rousing ovation. They took their seats on the bema (the platform from which religious services are conducted in a synagogue) facing the overflowing audience. The quartet sat in the front pews and awaited its turn to perform.

There were speeches, and a variety of musical and comedic acts. Then finally, it was the quartet's turn. I am happy to say that we did a creditable job. During our two songs, I sneaked glances at Kate Smith, who sat on the edge of her chair seemingly enraptured at our performance. We took our bows and returned to our seats in the front row. The ceremony ended with Mr. Weisburger presenting the award to Kate Smith. This was followed by a brief acceptance speech on her part. Then the most unexpected thing occurred. In a voice charged with emotion, Kate Smith went on with, "Before I go, may I say one more thing? One of the members of the barbershop quartet appeared on my TV show a few weeks ago. In all of my years of radio and TV appearances, I have never received so many letters requesting a repeat performance." Then, gesturing towards me, she added, "So, if it would not be an imposition upon you, Seymour, would you mind playing that Chopin Polonaise you played on my program?"

With this, I froze in my seat. The applause which followed was, as far as I was concerned, for someone else. In another moment, two members of the quartet sitting on either side of me literally lifted me to my feet. My first concern was that I had not been able to practice for weeks. Then, too, where was the piano? I awkwardly looked around and spotted a spinet piano standing below the platform. I approached it with great trepidation and took my place on the piano bench. As fate would have it, the bench was miles too high. But matters being as they were, I decided to make the best of it. According to the way the piano was situated, I found myself sitting at the keyboard with my back towards the audience and looking directly into the faces of Kate Smith and the NBC staff. The hushed silence which followed simply increased my self-consciousness. I was on the spot, all right; there was no way out of that situation. I placed my hands on the

A civilian again. The first of eight appearances
on the Kate Smith TV Show.

opening *E* flat octaves, took several deep breaths and tore into the Polonaise. I knew in advance, of course, not to expect a big sound from a mere spinet piano. But the volume was even less than I had anticipated. I ought to have known better, but I began to force the sound — something that is a no-win situation when performing. The result was that I made even more mistakes than were to be expected in my unpracticed state. In spite of this, I received a standing ovation. In my estimation, it was not because of *how* I played, but, rather, because Kate Smith had shifted the spotlight away from herself and onto a soldier who had just sung in a barbershop quartet. On her way out of the Temple, Kate Smith embraced me warmly and proceeded to introduce me to each member of her staff. Out on the sidewalk, it seemed that there were just as many people surrounding me as there were around Kate Smith. Through the ensuing bedlam, she managed to wave goodbye to me as she stepped into her limousine. Curiously, I remember nothing after that — not even the ride back to Fort Dix. It all seemed unreal, like living in a novel. Even while writing about these incidents, I can hardly believe that they actually took place.

After our success in singing for Kate Smith, Major Conte had no intention of disbanding the quartet. In fact, he decided that we should enter a national barbershop quartet competition. We were to compete with army, navy, and marine corps quartets sent from camps throughout the United States. Since the contest was restricted to enlisted men alone, I had to replace Lieutenants Gilmore and McCallion with two privates. We had a smashing success and actually won first prize. After that, the quartet disbanded, and my singing career ended once and for all.

Several weeks later, a new order was issued at Fort Dix requiring all servicemen with more than six months left to serve in the armed forces to be sent to FECOM (I myself had eight months to go). Predictably, Kate Smith spoke of my departure for Korea on one of her TV programs with great solemnity: "Let's pray for Seymour's safe return," she said. "And let's pray for the safety of all of our boys." Her comments continued during my eight month ordeal in Korea: "We wonder if Seymour is safe, and playing the piano." Later, after I returned to civilian life, I appeared eight times on her evening show. And when I made my New York City debut on January 3, 1954, a sleek black limousine bearing the license plate *KS* pulled up in front of Town Hall. As I was told later, everyone was open-mouthed to see Kate Smith herself step out of that car and enter the hall. Her presence in the center box was clearly the chief focus of attention during the entire concert. I spotted her at once as soon as I walked out onto the stage. Her exuberant expression and her enthusiastic applause after each piece did much to spur me on during that important occasion.

Years later, in 1986, Kate Smith, ill and confined to a wheelchair, received a presidential citation. A newspaper article about the award also mentioned that she had retired to Raleigh, North Carolina. Coincidentally I had just been engaged by a college in Raleigh to give masterclasses and lectures. "Would she remember me after thirty-four years?" I wondered. Some two months before my scheduled engagement, I wrote to the great star at the address given in the article. To my delight, I received a warm letter from her sister, who also lived in Raleigh. Indeed, Kate Smith remembered me with great affection and invited me to visit her. Sadly, though, she died on June 17th — only ten days before I came to Raleigh. When I arrived in Raleigh, her sister, out of courtesy, and also for sentimental reasons, was kind enough to escort me through Kate Smith's home. Wandering through the modestly furnished rooms, we came to her bedroom, where she had spent her last moments. There, in a large walk-in closet, I saw her vast collection of gowns, the last vestiges of her stardom. Among them was one made of blue sequins. I wondered if that possibly could have been the same gown she was wearing when I first met her. One glimpse of it, and waves of nostalgia spread through me. In a flash I relived all of the dramatic incidents just described. I left the house deeply saddened, and with a feeling of having been cheated out of seeing that great woman one more time. To this day I can still recall her warm smile and sparkling eyes. Her generosity, her naturalness, and her vibrancy will remain with me always.

FECOM

The dreaded day arrived — the day that my FECOM orders went into effect. I set out from Newark, New Jersey, for LaGuardia Airport with my parents, my sister Lillian, and my brother-in-law Frank, who did the driving. My poor mother was beside herself with worry. Her *zeenala*, after all, was not only flying far away from home for the first time, but he was actually going to fight a war in Korea. She did not believe for one moment the story I had made up — namely, that the Special Services office in Tokyo had requested Kenneth and me to tour Japan. During the trip to the airport, there was no discussion at all, save an occasional question from my mother. "What time is it?" she would say with an unnatural calm. It was the way that my mother always handled difficult situations — by asking what time it was. Whenever she did this, I always had the feeling that she had temporarily lapsed into a state of semi-amnesia. It was her way of keeping at bay the emotional impact of some painful experience.

As for me, I experienced a general numbness in facing the unknown. To begin with, I was, according to the army at least, a full-fledged infantryman. For all I knew I might end up on the front lines in Korea. Then, too, I was about to take my first airplane trip, and a cross-country one at that, to Seattle, Washington. There were no jets in those days, and a trip to the West Coast took twelve hours, with a stopover in Minneapolis for refueling. It is not unusual to experience a certain degree of anxiety when you have never been on an airplane before. And I was no exception. In my case, it was not the anticipation of the flight itself that caused the anxiety, but rather the possibility of getting airsick. Having always been subject to motion sickness, even in a car, I had visions of being a hospital case for twelve hours or more. Just in case of such an eventuality, I had a bottle of Dramamine tablets tucked into my jacket pocket: I would take one pill when I arrived at the airport, and another one if need be. As one can see, the members of my family were not the only ones concerned about me; I was concerned about myself!

DIARY

After fastening my seat belt, I made the first entry into my diary. Receiving frequent mention were my two buddies from Fort Dix who had also received FECOM orders. They happened to be sitting on either side of me on the plane. Kenneth Gordon had checked his duffel bag but refused to part with his precious Vuillaume violin. After much discussion with the airline officials, he was allowed to take the instrument on board, but only if he promised to hold it securely between his legs at all times. On my other side was Jerry Jacobs, with whom I was very friendly at Fort Dix. He had been a reporter in civilian life. I saw him for the last time in Korea. Since then, I have lost track of him.

As far as I was concerned, the airplane looked like a large and crowded hotel lobby. In fact, I wondered how it could ever take off. Reading the entries in my diary now, I am struck not only by my innocence and my wide-eyed wonder at absolutely everything that took place, but also by the lack of advanced technology in the airplanes of those days:

March 18th, Tuesday, 11:30 PM
We are sitting in the second row on the right side of the DC4. The pilot has gone into his compartment and I don't think it will be long before takeoff. As I look out, I see two tremendous propellers. One appears to be almost touching the window. It's strange to be locked inside a plane — like being submerged beneath the ocean in an airtight submarine. The sparks of anxiety course through me like the tiny bubbles shooting upwards as water is about to boil. The droning of the fan has now ceased and the suspense is mounting. If only I

219

could make contact with my family and assure them that everything is all right. The hostess has just completed checking the tickets. There go the propellers. It seems no more exciting than a toy airplane. We're moving! The take off was so smooth that I didn't realize we were already in the air. High above New York City, I see a vision I shall never forget. Looking down, it seems that we are moving at a snail's pace. The altitude is making my pen leak. [At that point in the diary, I switched to a pencil.] I see the labyrinth of highways and streets far below. We are moving at 220 miles per hour! How graceful are the gentle sloping wings holding the propellers — the heartbeat that will bring us to safety. It's strange, but I don't even entertain the thought of an accident. Perhaps it's the closeness to God that brings this calm. Now it's impossible to distinguish the props from the wing. All is enveloped in darkness save for the polkadot lights somewhere below. Our cruising altitude is 6000 feet.

The Dramamine pill went into effect almost immediately, and I slept deeply for most of the trip. Soon, though, the pilot's voice coming over the airplane speakers awakened me. We were over the Rocky Mountains:

The Rocky Mountain ranges are fantastically beautiful. They soar 9200 feet into the sky. We are making our way between the peaks at a height of 9000 feet.

Considering today's jets that cruise at altitudes of 35,000 feet or more, it is disquieting to think that we wended our way *between* the mountain peaks.

Debut in a Bar

Everything was a novelty to me, even the fact that we gained three hours on our trip to the west coast. It was early morning when we arrived in Seattle. We checked into the Hotel Hungerford and then spent the entire day walking around Seattle. It was all like a grand vacation, and temporarily, at least, we forgot that we were on our way to a war. After attending a movie, Kenneth, Jerry, and I, and three other soldiers who were on the airplane with us, wandered into a bar for a drink. Innocence of innocents. This was the first time I had set foot in a bar since Aunt Clara took me into that "dive" in Newark, New Jersey. There was a platform at the far end of it where a scrawny elderly man was going at a spinet piano, a cigarette dangling from his mouth. He was surrounded by men and women who sang along with him while waving their drinks back and forth in rhythm to the songs. The smoke-filled air and the crimson lights reminded me of those familiar Lautrec posters depicting the Moulin Rouge. Suddenly, my buddies decided that I was to play the piano. In spite of my loud protests, they surrounded me and literally pushed me onto the platform. The piano player got up at once and hung over the keyboard as I launched into *Malagueña* by Lecuona. To my utter surprise, everyone in the bar fell instantly silent. When I had finished, there were cheers and applause. One piece led to another, and before I knew it a half hour had gone by. The whole time the piano player stood to my left looking very much rejected. Somewhere in the middle of Chopin's Polonaise in *A* flat, he bent over and whispered into my ear, "Look, buddy, any tips you get are mine!"

FORT LAWTON

Upon returning to Fort Lawton for our processing, we first went to the USO building where we had checked our duffel bags. It was no small thing to lug a sixty-pound duffel bag and a twenty-five-pound briefcase filled with music up the mountainous paths of Fort Lawton to the barracks where we were assigned. The following entry in my diary describes the barracks and my state of mind as well:

March 20th, Thursday

At 12 AM we drew scanty bedding. After laughing away our tensions and despair, I lay down in my bunk and braced myself for the horror of the personnel center the following morning. The last embers of the crude coal stove cast dying shadows on the ceiling. There is a hole in the wall of the barracks directly above my head, a full three inches in diameter. An icy finger pierces the air and makes sleep impossible. Loud voices bespeaking a variety of accents and diverse backgrounds echo all around me: "It's colder than a Minnesota well-digger's ass in here!" one soldier blurts out. It certainly is, although I would not have phrased it exactly like that. Occasionally, a GI wracked by fatigue, and no doubt filled with dread of the unknown, cries out in his sleep or convulses in his bunk — like flailing out in resentment against the evil forces responsible for wars. After 15 months in the army, I sure have learned patience and have acquired a great deal of endurance. There is a curious calm within me that brings with it assurance and optimism for the future. Jerry always asked me how I could remain so optimistic as a soldier in light of my former life and all the promise which it held for me. It's music, I told him, that sustains me through everything. It even enables me to convert the cold into a sedative that brings luxurious sleep.

221

Like Rome, Seattle is built on seven hills. After trudging for miles around Fort Lawton during our processing, I was convinced that the camp occupied all seven of them! It was a grueling day, including orientations of all sorts and inoculations against what seemed to be every disease known to humans. In one instance, we waited in line for three hours to receive our official orders.

It was a relief to return to the barracks around 4 PM, although I had to trudge up the highest of all the hills at Fort Lawton to get there. The view from the barracks, however, was spectacular. From every window one could see Puget Sound and Mount Rainier rising majestically in the distance. Each glimpse of its snow-capped peak brought with it waves of contrasting feelings — awe and inspiration on the one hand, and dread of the unknown on the other. More than once, visions of being killed on the battlefield superimposed themselves upon the scene before me. This morbid preoccupation with the possibility of death found its way into my diary:

> March 21st, Friday
> The military airplane has landed at Newark Airport. A grief-stricken crowd composed of my family and friends watches in utter devastation as a military escort carries my remains off of the airplane and into a hearse. They bring the flag-draped coffin to my home and place it in front of my Steinway. My poor mother is beyond comfort. As I followed all these visions in my mind's eye, tears trickled down my cheeks. As one might imagine, such musings dissipate whatever pleasure I might otherwise have gained while looking out upon that magnificent vista.

Thoughts of death were common among the men. We were, after all, on our way to FECOM. Like Kenneth and me, most of the men were trained as infantrymen. Curiously, though, once I got to the fighting front in Korea itself, I never entertained such macabre thoughts again. For during those months I had only one thought in mind — how to stay alive.

We remained a little more than one week at Fort Lawton. It was a week of continuous performances in the Service Club, in the officers' club (we were treated to gourmet food, there), and a performance on the American Armed Forces Radio station. We also made some recordings for a Colonel Willoughby, a high-ranking officer at Fort Lawton. His wife was present, and extended all sorts of courtesies to us — coffee, sweet rolls, and, later, an invitation to dinner at the officers' club. It was no easy task to maintain a high standard of performance during that week: a combination of fatigue, walking for miles in the pouring rain, and the side effects of the inoculations brought on a violent case of bronchitis. In spite of a hacking cough and a raging fever I fulfilled all of my performing commitments. Why? Not because I felt compelled to uphold the performer's credo, "the show must go on." Besides, I felt too sick and miserable to play the hero. The real reason was that our survival depended upon performing as often as we could. There were powerful officers at Fort Lawton whose influence, I thought, would assure us a safe assignment in Tokyo. Colonel Willoughby, especially, tried his best to intervene for us with other high-ranking officers in Japan. But as it turned out, letters and telephone calls were to no avail. Kenneth and I, it seemed, were slated for Korea from the moment we left Fort Dix. We were, however, treated with the greatest respect during our brief stay at Fort Lawton and afforded luxuries unheard of among enlisted men. On March 29th, for example, the day we boarded the troop ship, Colonel Willoughby, knowing of all the extra things Kenneth and I had to carry, placed his private car and chauffeur at our disposal. As we drove to the pier, I actually felt exhilarated at the thought of my first ocean voyage. Little did I know then that it would turn into a fourteen-day nightmare, one that almost resulted in my death.

THE *GENERAL W. M. BLACK*

It was 8:40 AM when we arrived at the pier. Having retained a romantic image of the *Queen Mary* and the *Queen Elizabeth* standing majestically at their piers on the Hudson River in New York City, I was gravely disappointed to walk up the gangway of a small freighter with only one smokestack. One look at her, and it seemed impossible for me to believe that she could hold three thousand men, plus a staff and crew. Formerly, the *General Black* had been used to ferry troops between Japan and Korea. This would be her maiden voyage as a troop carrier across the Pacific. Being 522 feet long, she was by no means a small craft. Yet she was unusually narrow for her length, which resulted in our having to live in abominably cramped quarters. We were led down into the bowels of the ship and into a small compartment approximately half the size of an average barracks. There were more than two hundred men crowded into this one area. The bunks — two abreast and four rows high — were suspended from two posts which ran from floor to ceiling. The air, whatever there was of it, was dank and foul-smelling. The dim light simply added to the dismal atmosphere. This would be our bedroom for fourteen days. As to the mess hall, this consisted of another cramped and dismal room containing row upon row of waist-high counters. On these we would place our trays and eat standing up. This would be our dining room for fourteen days.

Filled with a sense of foreboding, I eagerly rushed up on deck where the fresh air made me forget temporarily, at least, all that I had seen below. The deck was swarming with soldiers and air force personnel, including a thousand French-Canadian troops with their red berets. Kenneth, Jerry, and I took our places at the starboard rail and watched as a group of sailors untied the gangplanks. It all seemed like a newsreel, complete with cheering crowds waving goodbye and a band playing farewell music. Even though I knew that my family and friends were three thousand miles away, still, I found myself searching the pier for one familiar face. As I did so, a wave of loneliness swept through me, a sensation such as I had never known before. It lasted only a moment, however, for I was suddenly brought back to reality by a low, organ-like whistle so intense that I had to press my hands over my ears. It echoed through the hills of Seattle for some ten seconds afterwards. At exactly 6 PM, the *General Black* slipped away from her pier. It took a long time for the tugs to nudge her into the center of Puget Sound. A storm was brewing as the *General Black*, now under her own power, aimed her bow towards the setting sun and the Far East:

> March 29th, Saturday
> The ship is rocking precariously, and it's a feat just to walk on the deck. There was a Bob Hope film shown this evening. It was clear, visually, but the soundtrack was so weak that I couldn't hear a thing. It was freezing on deck, but I was lucky enough to find a little nook that was heated by the exhaust fan of the kitchen. It's 9:00 PM, now, and I'm going to attempt to maneuver my way to my bunk. Fortunately, I was assigned to a lower berth, so I won't have to climb over bodies to get in and out of bed. The bunks are nothing but slabs of green canvas fastened to a metal frame with cord. There are no mattresses. When I'm lying down, my nose is no more than eight inches from the bunk directly above me. I can hear the sea churning against the sides of the ship. I took two Dramamine pills — just in case! If anything, they'll put me to sleep almost immediately.

The Voyage

And so they did — at least until 12:30 AM when the nightmare began. I remember being temporarily awakened by severe rocking. The Dramamine, however, acted as a sedative, and I fell back to sleep again. At 5:30 AM, I attempted to get out of my bunk to go to the latrine.

Suddenly, the ceiling changed places with the floor. It did not take more than that for me to know that I was in the throes of the worst motion sickness I had ever experienced. As I half staggered, half crawled along the floor of the ship on the way to the latrine, I stumbled over groaning men and puddles of vomit, all of which merely increased my nausea. More than once, I left my own puddles behind. The distance to the latrine seemed interminable. I had to trudge down two flights of stairs and go through the mess hall and a chain of other compartments. Approximately eighteen hundred men used that one latrine. Since every stall was occupied, I leaned over a sink and heaved so violently that I thought surely my end had come.

After the spasms subsided, I attempted to make my way back to compartment 505. But I was far weaker than I thought. After taking a few steps, I collapsed onto a row of duffel bags. Then almost at once, another wave of nausea sent me back to the latrine. Nor did the tempest within my head and stomach subside in the slightest when I made a second attempt at the long journey back to my compartment. Along the way, I stepped over an even greater number of heaving, writhing bodies. Seeing misery all around me merely intensified my distress. It was truly a modern-day purgatory, like a scene out of Dante. A sense of despair overcame me as I thought of the long voyage ahead.

No sooner did I reach my bunk than the fire alarm went off. It was merely a routine drill to practice evacuation procedures in case of an emergency. "I'll never make it," I thought. "I can't even stand, much less walk up the stairwell to the deck." While everyone fled my compartment, I continued to lie on my bunk, moaning audibly. Suddenly I was aware of someone standing to my right. Since I was as near to the floor as possible, I saw nothing but two legs and a pair of shoes. With what felt like my last glimmer of strength, I rolled onto my right side and somehow managed to focus my eyes upward. It was the captain of the ship: "Son, you'll have to go up on deck," he said in a gentle, soothing voice. "There's a fire drill, you know." "Sir," I answered weakly, "I'm very sick, and I simply can't move." "Well," he replied in the same therapeutic voice, "would you rather burn to death?" "Oh, yes," I replied without hesitation. "Frankly speaking, I don't care what happens to me!" The captain chuckled at this, but insisted that I had to go up on deck. "Let me help you," he said; "I know you'll feel better once you breathe some fresh air."

Resigned to the fact that enlisted men simply had to obey orders, I slowly rose out of my bunk, being sure not to move my head any more than was necessary. Without daring to look down, I worked my toes into my shoes. Then, with the captain's support, I dragged my feet across the compartment to the stairwell and slowly mounted one step at a time. When I finally reached the deck, I discovered that I had no legs at all. I simply slumped into a heap, feeling more like an amoeba than a man. The captain gave me a bit of valuable advice: "Even though you think it's impossible, stare straight out to the horizon. You'll find that seeing the fixed horizontal line will help to stabilize you." I followed his advice with what seemed to be my last flicker of energy. At first, the swells of the sea merely increased my distress. But soon I was able to focus beyond the swells to the horizon. And to my utter relief, my nausea subsided slightly — but not enough to prevent me from being sick over the rail of the ship.

Later that afternoon, I managed to get down some spaghetti and dry bread. For supper, I stood in line for one hour to get a small piece of meat and a boiled potato. Eating in a standing position was totally unthinkable to me, so I slumped to the floor, slid underneath the counter and propped myself up against the wall of the ship. With my eyes focused straight ahead, I lowered my fork to the plate and raised it to my mouth, as though the fork had eyes all of its own. Somehow I was able to swallow at least a portion of the meager ration. Early in the evening, I took two more Dramamine pills and snuggled under my warm blankets. The sea churned mercilessly against the walls of compartment 505. Kenneth and Jerry were nearby in their own bunks, seemingly unaffected by the sea voyage. I fell into a deep sleep almost at once. As I have always experienced after taking Dramamine, I was treated to an ecstatic sequence of dreams that made going to sleep an adventure in itself.

Debut at Sea

Jerry lost no time in establishing himself as assistant editor of *The Black Sails*, the ship's newspaper, while Kenneth and I were quickly snatched up by the ship's chaplain, Father Karniesewicz, who also acted as the Special Services director. He was a cheery sort of man with a high-pitched voice and effeminate gestures. He radiated goodness and spent his days trying to ease our lives as best as he could. We were, to be sure, on a death mission, and one had the feeling that the Father silently prayed for us each time we came into his presence. He took an instant liking to me, and he succeeded in freeing Kenneth and me of all duties so that we could practice again. We rehearsed in the officers' mess, where we quickly made friends with the kitchen crew. This meant first class meals, which we ate while sitting at a real table. Considering the scanty fare offered in our mess hall, the variety of food now at our disposal was, as far as we were concerned, equivalent to a five star restaurant.

Within one day, the Father rounded up all the talented servicemen on board and organized a show. It was given in the recreation room, a large, dank, and airless area in the bow of the ship. The audience sat on the floor. Since the room could only hold approximately one hundred men, we had to give three performances each night, for ten days, in order to accommodate all of the troops. There was a spinet piano in the room, chained to the wall of the ship for obvious reasons. As I played, the piano bench kept pace with the rolling of the bow, and the keyboard seemed to swim before my eyes. If I was not nauseated before I began to play, I certainly became so within a few measures. Each night, then, after the final note of Liszt's 6th Hungarian Rhapsody, I paused only long enough to acknowledge the wild cheers and applause and then rushed up onto the deck where I heaved over the rail of the ship. Moments later, I returned to accompany Kenneth in a state that can best be described as a stupor. Though the violin accompaniments were before me, I did not dare focus my eyes upon them for fear of inducing another wave of seasickness. Had it not been for a lifetime of practicing during which I learned to rely on my "automatic pilot," I do not think that I would have been able to play at all.

From time to time, I experienced an hour or two of equilibrium — especially at twilight. One evening, I sat on the deck with my diary in a deeply reflective state:

April 2nd, Wednesday

I'm sitting on the upper deck facing west, sixty-five feet above the water. According to the ship's captain, you can see for fourteen miles from this point on the ship. The sea is a deeper blue now, which means that we are entering tropical waters. It's all so peaceful and breathtakingly beautiful. We spotted a school of porpoises, and, a few minutes later, a school of flying fish. The expanse thrills me more than I can say. Certainly this is the largest uninterrupted vista I have ever seen. Do I actually see the curve of the earth? Or is it an illusion?

There are few experiences more awe-inspiring than following the sun until it sinks over the horizon. In its wake, the sky and clouds reflect a thousand shades of crimson, like a ceiling of glowing embers. The clouds cast dark shadows upon the sea. There in the east, the stars have begun to blink; and in the west, the old day is whispering its farewell to tomorrow. The temperature has risen considerably, making our field jackets unnecessary.

There are Americans and Canadians sitting on the deck all around me, and people from all ethnic groups. No one speaks.

Everyone is deep in his own thoughts — waiting and wondering A nagging question mars the beauty all around us: Will we ever see home again? Why does God allow us to pass on this mission of death? When can man look to the sea again with calm humility and say, "God made this passageway for me so that I might travel in peace."

My indisposition notwithstanding, I played surprisingly well at those evening concerts. Kenneth always played well. Having been a child prodigy, he has retained to this day a stability and an ease of execution that make him the envy of his colleagues. The Wilhelmj transcription of Schubert's *Ave Maria* affected our audiences perhaps more than any other piece on our programs. Apart from the fact that the theme was familiar to practically everyone, the octaves on the violin and the cascading harp-like arpeggios in the piano accompaniment seemed to "wow" our audiences.

S. O. P.

On April 5th, I awakened to find myself as nauseated as I had been on the first morning of our voyage. During the hours which followed, I experienced first hand all that I had heard as a civilian concerning the army's *S.O.P.* — Standard Operating Procedure. As the following anecdote shows, the enforcement of it, like the army machine itself, could be cruel, inflexible, and totally inhuman:

April 5th, Saturday

I awakened on the verge of regurgitating. I ran to the latrine only to find that the door was locked: it was being cleaned. I dragged myself back to my bunk. But within five minutes, a sergeant told me to get out of the compartment as officers were coming around for an inspection. I told him that I was too sick to move, to which he replied that I needed a note from the doctor giving me permission to lie in bed. "But the doctor won't be in until nine," I moaned. "And it's only eight now." "Well isn't that too bad," he sneered. "Wait on the stairwell." So out of bed I went and slumped down on the stairs. Within a few seconds, however, another sergeant rushed down the stairs and came to an abrupt halt by my side. No one could have been more obnoxious; "Get off these stairs," he bellowed. "We're about to wash them down!" I told him that I was waiting for the doctor. "Tough," was his response to this. "Wait out on deck." By this time, I was near collapse. But I did manage to half walk, half crawl up the stairwell and onto the deck, only to discover that this, too, was in the process of being washed down. The whole damn ship, it seemed, was being sterilized! And there I was, desperately ill, with no one to help me and nowhere to go. I realized in a flash how desperation can lead a fellow to do drastic things. And believe it or not, I actually entertained the thought of slipping over the rail and ending my misery. But since I had a performance to give that night, I staggered to the sickbay door and simply leaned against it until the doctor arrived.

The doctor was an army lieutenant and a prince of a man. He was a music lover and had heard me play often. He asked me all sorts of questions: Did I have a history of seasickness? Do I get anxious before a performance? Have I taken medication? He was trying his best to be helpful. Having concluded that my indisposition was not, in fact, caused by pre-performance anxiety, he gave me more Dramamine and sent me out onto the deck. "Lying in your bunk," he explained, "will merely worsen your condition. Get out into the fresh air and look out to the horizon." It was the same advice which the captain of the ship had given me on that first nightmarish morning.

I followed his advice, and in a few hours I began to feel better. Later, I even downed some lunch. By 3 PM, though, the Dramamine that the doctor had given me had its predictable effect: I became sufficiently drowsy to return to my bunk, where I fell into a deep sleep — so deep, in fact, that Kenneth had to shake me for a full minute to awaken me for the first performance. Once up, I experienced a sense of health and well-being that made me almost tipsy with happiness. Perhaps this explains why I played exceptionally well that evening. The octaves in the Liszt Rhapsody went at a lightning fast tempo, and without mishaps, too, and the arpeggiated accompaniment in the Wilhelmj transcription of Schubert's *Ave Maria* fairly rippled up and down the keyboard. The effect was more like a harp than a piano. The men sat in silence at the end of it for ten seconds or so before applauding. The atmosphere was like that of a religious service, and I noticed many moist eyes as we took our bows.

Church Services at Sea
On Sunday morning, April 6th, I played hymns for the Catholic and Protestant services. There was a harmonium in the recreation room with a keyboard span of approximately five octaves. That innocent looking mechanism had two foot pedals which activated bellows, making it capable of producing a wide range of dynamics. The faster I pumped, the louder the sound.

I have already spoken about my predilection for the organ, and how as a boy I used to thrill to its sound at religious services. Imagine, then, how elated I was at the prospect of creating those reed-like sounds myself. With the first plagal cadence, waves of inspiration coursed through me. I pumped away on that minuscule instrument with a religious fervor that surprised me and everyone present.

There was an excellent singer among the troops by the name of Bob Reim. He and I joined forces to provide hymns and religious arias chosen from the finest repertory. It is difficult to say who was more inspired, the chaplains or we. Not surprisingly, then, I looked forward to the final services to be held on Good Friday and Easter Sunday. It was not just for religious reasons that Easter Sunday would hold a special significance for everyone on board. On that very day we were slated to arrive in Japan.

"There's No Tomorrow"

For passengers on a ship, crossing the international date line is a major event. People who have never crossed the meridian before are called polliwogs, and are singled out for initiations, such as hair-shaving, dunking, and pranks of all sorts. Many of the officers on board who had taken this trip before advised Kenneth and me to avoid those initiations at all costs. They suggested that we pretend to have crossed the Pacific several times previously. It was good advice, for many servicemen got severely roughed up during the next day. And the very last thing I needed was to add any sort of physical stress to my already precarious state of health.

It was April 6th, the day before the great event was to take place. Crossing the international date line, one loses a day. Fittingly, then, at 6 PM the ship's intercom carried Bob Reim's voice singing a well-known song of the day, "There's No Tomorrow." I had no way of knowing then just how ironic the title of that song really was. For had it not been for the quick action of a doctor, there may not, in fact, have been a tomorrow for me.

Escape from Death

We hit turbulent waters during the evening of April 6th, so turbulent that the captain had to reduce our speed to 12 knots. I remember being tossed about in my bunk throughout the entire night, which I knew would result in severe illness in the morning.

We sailed over the meridian during the night, so that it was April 8th when I awakened. No sooner did I attempt to get out of my bunk than I was instantly seized with spasms of nausea. In fact my malaise matched, or even exceeded, what I had experienced on the first morning of the voyage. One does not have to be a medical expert to know the consequences of constant nausea lasting nine days. I needed help. At the moment I could only think of one person who would be compassionate enough to help me — Father Karniesewicz. Fortunately he was in his cabin when I knocked at the door. One look at me and his face registered alarm. "Father," I said to him in a barely audible voice, "I can't take this much longer." He took me by the arm at once and led me to his sofa. He then placed a pillow under my head and spread a blanket over me. After many assurances and words of support, he flew out of the stateroom and returned in a few minutes with the doctor. To my surprise it was the lieutenant who had conducted the Protestant Service the day before. "We'll have to take you to the ship's hospital," he said at once. "You're severely dehydrated and we have to feed you intravenously."

The three of us traipsed through the ship's corridors, the doctor in the lead, I in the middle, and the Father trailing behind. From time to time the doctor looked over his shoulder to be sure that I was still following him. This extreme show of compassion from those two men charged me with a strength born of perfect trust. As I followed in the doctor's footsteps, I could not help thinking of those well-known lines from the Christmas carol "Good King Wenceslas," in which the King urges his page on as they trudge through a wild winter storm on a mission of mercy:

> Mark my footsteps my good page,
> Tread thou in them boldly;
> Thou shalt find the winter's rage,
> Freeze thy blood less coldly.*

We arrived at the off-limits passageway that led to the ship's hospital. We continued on through the ward into a private room containing two beds. Under ordinary circumstances there would have been nothing exceptional about seeing mattresses and sheets on beds. But considering the slab of green canvas on which I had been sleeping for nine days, the mere sight of those beds seemed to induce the healing process at once. I noticed a captain dressing in an adjoining bathroom, which led me to conclude that I had been brought to a private room reserved for officers. It was one thing to eat in the officers' dining room. But being allowed to occupy an officer's bed seemed beyond the realm of possibility. I knew that these privileges resulted from my being a musician, and the doctor a music-lover. I felt a wave of gratitude for him that went beyond words. At

---

* The melody of this Christmas carol dates back to the 1500s. The text is by John Mason Neale (1818-1866), English poet and linguist, who wrote hymns and translated many more of them from Latin and Greek.

the doctor's orders I went into the bathroom, removed my fatigues, and slipped into a set of white hospital pajamas. I then took possession of one of those beds, and as I snuggled between the clean white sheets, I gave such a loud sigh of relief that the doctor and Father K. chuckled with delight. The sheer comfort of that bed produced its own therapeutic effect: my head stopped spinning and my nausea subsided considerably.

Father K. kept his vigil at the foot of my bed even as an intern inserted the I.V. needle into my left arm. No sooner was it taped into place than, to my surprise, the doctor appeared with Kenneth, whose face was avocado green. "I thought you'd be lonely," he said good naturedly, "and so I brought you one of the finest violinists I've ever heard!" Poor Kenneth, who until that day had been a paragon of good health, had now, too, succumbed to seasickness. Being a Christian Scientist, he had often sermonized to me in the face of my own repeated bouts of nausea: "How can you be sick when you're God's perfect being?" He was not the sermonizer on this occasion, however. Like me, he could not wait to enjoy the therapeutic comfort of the one remaining bed. Once he settled down into it, I couldn't resist chiding him by quoting his own words: "How can you be sick when you're God's perfect being?" He was too miserable, though, to find any humor in this, and he merely shot me a glance of utter despair.

Thus it was that the concert duo was reduced to abject helplessness in the ship's hospital. Kenneth did not need intravenous feeding. As it happened, he regained his equilibrium much sooner than I did. Some five minutes or so after the I.V. needle had been inserted into my arm, the doctor appeared once again and assured me that I would be feeling better in a matter of minutes: "I'll return in a quarter of an hour or so just to see how you're doing." At that point, Father K., who was now convinced that I was in good hands, gave me his blessing and went off to perform his customary duties.

Kenneth and I were now left alone. He fell fast asleep almost at once, and I, feeling convinced that my indisposition would soon come to an end, closed my eyes and fully anticipated that I, too, would fall asleep. Suddenly, though, I became aware of a dull headache at the top of my head. After ten minutes, the pain increased to an agonizing intensity. To make matters worse, my bouts of nausea grew more violent by the minute. One might have thought that the sounds of those eruptions and the loud moaning which accompanied them would have awakened Kenneth. But he continued to sleep, oblivious to the fact that I was in serious trouble. Finally, when I went into convulsions and began screaming for help, he awakened with a start. Alarmed at my condition, he pressed the emergency button fastened to his bed. The doctor happened to walk into the room at that very moment. Seeing me trembling from head to toe and vomiting without pause, he was at my side in a flash. He pulled the needle from my arm and administered a sedative. During my last moments of consciousness, I felt someone poking at my eyelids and taking my pulse. I then had the sensation of spinning down through a long spiral. It was not an unpleasant sensation, and I was not in the least frightened. The last thing I remembered was a pleasurable warmth which began in my head and spread downward through my entire body. I then fell into a sleep so satisfying and so deep that I did not awaken for six hours or more.

I believe I would have slept even longer had someone not turned on the light in the room. I opened my eyes and looked around in that state of bewilderment that often follows a prolonged sleep. The doctor was taking my pulse, Father K. was actually sitting at the foot of my bed, and Kenneth was propped up on one elbow looking deeply concerned. The doctor was the first to speak: "We've been terribly worried about you," he said with a grave look on his face. "The intravenous solution that we gave you was contaminated! The odds are a million to one that such a thing should have occurred." According to the doctor, he had never before encountered a contaminated intravenous bottle, nor had he ever heard of such. "You might actually have died," he said, "had I not come into the room when I did. And for heaven's sake, tell your manager to limit your means of trans-portation on tours to walking or horseback riding!" Everyone in the room had a good laugh over this, and I, having slept off the worst of my setback, felt well enough to laugh along with everyone else.

It was now 6 PM, and neither Kenneth nor I had eaten a mouthful of food the entire day. An orderly brought us trays of plain crackers and orange juice, which I was barely able to swallow. By the next evening, however, things had changed considerably: we were both ravenously hungry. Father K., who had visited six times during the day, insisted that he would take care of everything. He disappeared for some thirty minutes and returned with a thermos of whiskey and pineapple juice, and three cocktail glasses. I had never been attracted to alcohol, and considering my condition, a cocktail was the very last thing to tempt me at that moment. But not being one to dampen the Father's good intentions, I joined in the ritual and raised my glass for the toast. "This is to celebrate your escape from death," he said, as he clicked his glass to mine and then promptly swallowed half of its contents in one gulp. There followed trays of food which Father K. had ordered from the officers' kitchen. As was his custom, he said grace before we ate. All was well again. Thinking about my brush with death just the day before, I silently offered my own prayer of thanksgiving for my deliverance.

Passover at Sea

The following morning I felt well enough to leave my bed in order to secure some fresh clothing and some personal effects from compartment 505. Along the way, I realized just how weak I was, and immediately returned to my bed in the ship's hospital. Later that afternoon, though, I was determined to make another stab at it. The ship's captain was to take the entire cast of "The Black Sails Variety Show" on a tour of the ship, something I did not want to miss. At the appointed time, I put on my fatigues and joined the others on the bridge. It was more than worth my effort, for I discovered some fascinating facts about the *General Black*, which I noted in my diary. She certainly was more impressive than I had imagined. The tour began on the bridge, where the captain explained something of the complex mechanisms at the heart of the ship. The *General Black* had cost $5,000,000, and was propelled by fuel oil combustion. She used one and a half barrels of oil per mile, each barrel costing over two dollars. A complete revolution of the propellers moved the ship twenty-six feet. She was fitted with an automatic pilot that kept her on a perfect course. Moreover, she boasted a state-of-the-art device which, when activated, neutralized the magnetism of the ship's steel. Thus, as the ship cut her way through hostile waters, her hull would not trigger magnetically activated mines. Needless to say, we all felt comforted by this last bit of information.

At the end of the tour, I was amazed to hear the following announcement: "Now hear this: Passover services will be held in the officers' lounge at 7 PM." With so much of my time taken up with Christian services, I had all but forgotten the Jewish holidays that always occur around Easter time. After all, the last supper at which Jesus sanctified the bread (his body) and the wine (his blood) and passed them on to his disciples, was actually a Passover ceremony. Living in a predominantly Christian society, Kenneth and I were surprised to find thirty-five Jewish enlisted men and officers gathered together for the Passover observance. We improvised the various symbols required for the Service as best we could: there was a whole roasted egg to serve as a burnt offering and horseradish to symbolize bitter herbs. Father K., who seemed prepared for all occasions, supplied us with *Hagadas*, the prayer books for the Passover Service, *matzos*, the unleavened bread which the Jews ate in the desert during their exodus, and, of course, a bottle of wine. A captain offered to officiate at the Service, and I volunteered to ask the *fir kashes* (Yiddish for the four questions), just as I had always done at home.

Up to this point in my life, I had gone to Jewish religious services only because of my father's insistence. Why, then, did I attend this one on my own? Was I seeking divine intervention to help me through this ordeal, as the Christian soldiers did? One question haunted me, as it did everyone else: Will this be the last service of my life? There is nothing like a religious service to stir up the whole question of mortality.

My desire to attend that service was paradoxical: for on the one hand, I have always preferred not to seek answers to these profound mysteries, any more than I ever hope to discover a rational explanation as to why and how music affects us the way it does; on the other hand, I envied all those soldiers whose faith assured them of immortality. Is it possible that the hours I spent in the company of those devout ministers and soldiers triggered some unconscious desire for a religious identity that overrode the skeptic in me? Perhaps the unanswered question really could have an answer. At any rate, I was too vulnerable to take any chances.

Filled with nostalgic remembrances of home, which the Passover service induced within me, and still feeling weak from my ordeal in the ship's hospital, I was not exactly my buoyant self as I headed for the recreation room and the final performances of the show. This would be the last of fifteen performances that we had given since we set sail. I was not at all sorry to see it come to an end. For to tell the truth, it was tedious and frustrating to have to play serious repertory on that terrible piano. Besides, it would be a relief to place the Liszt Rhapsody in dry dock for a while.

Happily, though, nature's gyroscope was functioning normally again. And while I still felt weak from my brush with death, I no longer felt nauseous. I was able to read the prayers at the Passover service earlier that evening and to focus my eyes upon music once again. The following morning, Bob Reim and I read through arias by Handel, Haydn, Mendelssohn, and Dubois. We lost ourselves in the wonder of these musical masterpieces. I was certainly no stranger to the transporting properties of music, nor was this by any means the first time I played song accompaniments for a singer. Yet something occurred during that session with Bob Reim — something that went beyond inspiration. From that time on, the human voice became for me the epitome of musical expression. Even today, place before me a Schubert or Schumann *Lied*, and I have the feeling that my fingers are vocalizing along with the singer. Is it not ironic that I should have become aware of this predilection for vocal repertory on a troop ship, of all places? And that was not the only revelation I had on the *General Black*. The various comments passed on to me by those men on board who had never heard a single measure of classical music before led me to comprehend for the first time the true power of music: how its message can be intelligible to inexperienced listeners and even to those rough and ready types whose natures one might think to be antithetical to music's subtleties. Soon I would have further evidence of this on the battle front itself. It is enough to say now, that by the end of our tour of duty, Kenneth and I had made thousands of converts to classical music.

The Misuse of Power

After that uplifting session with Bob Reim, I made my way out of the officers' dining room, where we had been rehearsing, and headed towards the stairwell which led to the deck. As I passed the kitchen, I came upon a scene so disturbing in its utter lack of humanity that I was compelled to write about it in my diary:

April 10th, Friday

The stark reality of being a soldier intrudes itself upon me when I least expect it to. One example of this occurred directly after that inspirational session with Bob Reim. Outside the kitchen entrance, I came upon a sergeant chewing out a private. There seemed to be no justification for the sergeant's aggression other than his need to pull rank. The sergeant, barbarian-looking and disgustingly loud-mouthed, insisted that the private remove a garbage can, even though he, the private, was not even assigned to K.P. At the height of the argument, a warrant officer happened to walk by. The private, mistaking the warrant officer's insignia for that of a lieutenant, must have seen in him the hand of justice. For he immediately began to plead his case. There was nothing unusual about this; if that man really had been a lieutenant, he certainly could have told that sergeant where to go! What was unusual, though, was that the private began to tremble from head to toe as soon as the warrant officer came onto the scene. Whether he had an authority problem, or whether the poor guy suddenly suffered an anxiety attack, I cannot say. At any rate, the warrant officer was just as pained in seeing the trembling as I was. "Don't shake, soldier," he said to the private sympathetically, "I'm only a warrant officer. I have no rank over this sergeant." He then walked away, leaving the private at the mercy of the sergeant. I, too, slunk away, feeling dejected at the inhumanity of people. I can just imagine what went on in that sergeant's distorted mind when the private made a futile attempt to appeal to a higher authority. I am sure he put that private through hell once the warrant officer walked off of the scene.

It is a relief to sit out on the lower deck and clear my head of that awful scene. Words fail to describe the magnificence of the sea. The sheer vastness of it overwhelms me. Everything is magical. The moon illuminates a trail of white churning foam as far as the eye can see. It sparkles like a silver sequined veil fluttering in the breeze. Directly ahead, all is enveloped in a mysterious darkness. You get the feeling that the ship is pulling us inexorably towards the unknown. I'm at once enthralled by this scene and frightened when I contemplate the future.

The captain tells us that the sea is actually five miles deep at this point. Our course has taken us south to the 28th parallel (on a line with California), then west to the meridian. Now we're heading north towards Japan. We were forced to veer off of our course and take a southerly route due to storms over the northern waters. Moreover, the sheer weight of 3000 troops required that we reduce our speed to 17.5 knots, a rather slow pace as voyages go. We cover an average of 400 miles per day. The change in course and the reduction in speed have added two and a half days to our journey.

The weather is cooler now and I am huddled in a blanket while making these entries. Nothing is more satisfying to me than seclusion. I like to be with people up to a point. But if I had my way, I would prefer to be alone with my thoughts.

In reflecting upon this incident of bullying, I was moved by compassion for that poor private. As I stated in my diary, I was also dejected, thinking of just how inhuman some people can be. What I did not mention in my diary, however, was my feeling of utter helplessness and frustration at my inability to come to the private's defense. The army had stripped me of my courage, it had forced me to cower, and I hated myself for it.

In civilian life, I would not have hesitated for a moment to intercede in a situation such as that. In fact, I have always been a maverick in the face of injustice. Once, for instance, while waiting in a courtroom to protest an unfair parking ticket, I witnessed a no less painful miscarriage of justice on the part of a judge. A lovely young nurse was called to the stand to plead her case. In between fits of uncontrolled sobbing, she told of having driven her desperately ill child to the emergency entrance of her local hospital. Unable to find a legal parking space, she was forced to park in an illegal zone. As she explained to the judge in very emotional terms, it came down to having to choose between saving her child or risking a parking violation. Quite obviously she was now in court for having chosen in favor of her child. "My husband has abandoned us," she added. "And I don't have $75 to pay the fine!" "You should have thought of that before you parked where you did," the judge snapped back at her. And then with a business-as-usual air and without so much as looking in her direction, he lowered the penalty to $50, brought his gavel down with a crash and summarily said, "Next case."

Now it was my turn to stand before the judge. The Dickens line "The law is a ass!" resounded in my ear. To my mind, it was not only the law that was an ass, but also the judge himself. I was furious with him. Before giving my testimony about my own ticket, I looked at him with fire in my eyes and asked him, "In all decency, how can you penalize that poor woman for wanting to save her own child?" With this, the judge's mouth fell open. But before he could say a word in his defense, I launched into a rather lengthy oration on justice: how the law ought to be tempered with compassion; and if laws are designed to protect people as well as censure them, should not the law bend according to unusual circumstances such as those in the previous case? I then accused the judge of being guilty of "inhuman treatment." My closing lines concerned myself: I told the judge that I was not in the least concerned whether he punished me for my insubordination, but that I could not sit there idly and watch the miscarriage of justice.

The courtroom was filled with people. At the end of my outburst, the room grew deathly silent; the people all froze in their seats fully anticipating, as I did, the judge's reprisal in the form of a harsh judgment against me. He stared at me for a few seconds, obviously stunned by this unexpected show of support for a total stranger. Suddenly, though, his expression changed from amazement to that of a benevolent magistrate. And with a voice of quiet authority, he exclaimed, "You're a fine young man." Although he could no longer reverse his decision against that young woman (she had fled the courtroom immediately after his pronouncement), he did dismiss my ticket while adding further words of praise for my character.

Speaking out in civilian life is one thing. But in the army, any defiance of authority is met with harsh reprisals: privileges are taken away, unreasonable duties are assigned to you, or you may even be thrown into the brig. In other words, a lowly private in the army may champion the cause of justice all he wants to, but he does not have the slightest chance of getting away with it. Besides, I had only eight months left to serve in the army, and I certainly was not about to say or do anything that might delay my discharge even by a single day.

Good Friday

On the morning of April 11th, I fulfilled a lifetime ambition: I performed an organ solo for the first time in public. The occasion was Good Friday and the recreation room overflowed with worshippers at each service.

Before my induction into the army, I had made my own piano transcription of the Organ Toccata and Fugue in D minor by J. S. Bach. Audacious as it seems to me now, I could not resist seizing the opportunity to play an authentic organ work at those services. I had only Thursday evening to do all of my practicing. I centered my attention on the Toccata. Although I did not have the music with me, my memory and my ear were intact, which is more than I can say for the rest of me. Given the reduced keyboard of the harmonium, I had to eliminate octaves and transpose certain registers so as not to over-shoot the runway, so to speak. The result was ironic, for in rearranging my own transcription to suit the confines of the harmonium, I reverted to the original version for organ. In my desire to capture the grandeur of that Toccata I pumped so fast and furiously that my leg muscles gave way in a matter of minutes. I might as well have been running a marathon for the painful "charley horse" cramps that gripped my legs. Suddenly, I thought of a perfect solution, one that I subsequently employed whenever I had to perform on thin-sounding upright or spinet pianos: I simply placed a floor microphone behind the instrument. Having relegated the responsibility for playing *forte* and *fortissimo* to an amplifying system, and not to my legs, I was able to simulate the full resonance of an authentic pipe organ. Thus, when I launched into that defiant mordant on *A*, the recreation room seemed transformed into a cathedral. The sheer volume of sound swept me away in an ecstasy of musical expression. I had the distinct feeling that I was not doing the playing at all; the Toccata was playing me! I then modified the amplification system to play the hymns and the accompaniment to Dubois' "Oh, My Father," which Bob Reim sang magnificently.

I spent the remainder of the afternoon in the doctor's cabin listening to his surprisingly large collection of LP records. Breathtaking performances by Horowitz, Heifetz, Eileen Farrell, and various symphony orchestras transported me to other places and times. Fittingly, the doctor chose Debussy's *La Mer* to round out this private concert. The experience of listening to the ebb and flow of that masterpiece while gliding over the most expansive sea on earth was unforgettable. I actually forgot that I was on a troop ship, and when the piece ended, I floated out of that stateroom feeling insignificant in the face of those overwhelming performances.

I have not mentioned Jerry Jacobs for some time now. The fact is, once his writing skills were known, he was made editor in chief of the ship's newspaper, a job that occupied all of his time from morning until night. I saw him only briefly, therefore, before we went to sleep and occasionally at breakfast. Jerry was now hard at work preparing a souvenir edition of *The Black Sails*. Knowing that he would not stop his work to eat properly,

I went into the officers' kitchen, where Kenneth and I were regulars by this time, and persuaded one of the cooks to prepare a tray for Jerry. I experienced great satisfaction in bringing him a steak large enough for two, a slab of cheese, and four slices of bread. As far as Jerry was concerned, this was one of the finest meals he had ever had.

Why did I have all of these privileges? I was a musician. And as that voyage continued, I became ever more aware of music's power — a power that had been transmitted to me by means of some genetic miracle. The fact that I was talented placed me among the privileged members of society. I had evidence of this even at the beginning of basic training when Red, the cook in the Fort Dix mess hall, would not allow "Paderooski" to ruin his hands washing dishes. It is one thing to receive preferential treatment as a civilian. But in the army, rank and S.O.P. usually override all personal considerations. Not that all of my superiors were sympathetic to me. There were some officers on board that ship, for instance, who were disgruntled at having to share their food with mere enlisted men. Later at Camp Drake in Japan, Ken and I were to meet strong opposition from army hard-liners when various requests for concerts conflicted with army details, such as K.P. or guard duty. But on the whole, I was blessed. In fact, I have always secretly thanked music for the protection it has afforded me, and for the many bounties that have come my way. Certainly it is not just for material comforts that I express my gratitude, but more especially for the love and the care shown to me by special people throughout my life — people like Father Karniesewicz and the doctor, who not only eased my life, but actually prolonged it.

Preferential Treatment

Being singled out for preferential treatment can easily spoil a person. We often see examples of this among world-renowned performers — those who use their status as a justification for temperamental behavior. Worse, still, are the patronizing attitudes of certain family members, pupils, and managers who surround these prima donnas: "He's an artist! What do you expect?" It is as though irrational behavior is looked upon as a concomitant of genius. If a person is born with the latter, then everyone must put up with the former. In my opinion, nothing sanctions tempera-mental or boorish behavior. Try, however, to get this point across to managers, publicists, and producers — those who make their living off the talents of others, and the chances are you will get a response such as, "So, if it's a question of importing Dover sole for his lunch or having him cancel his concert, then by all means let's get the Dover sole!"

Fortunately, not all geniuses behave like that. I have always thought that if normalcy really exists, then certain geniuses are more normal than anyone else. Of course you don't have to be a genius in order to inspire respect and special treatment from others. If I, not being a genius, may speak for myself, I have never taken advantage of whatever status I have gained as a result of being a musician — although occasionally prima donna status has been literally thrust upon me. And why? Certain people seem to enjoy exercising their romantic fantasies in this regard; others who suffer feelings of inferiority may have a neurotic need to place me in a false position of power which they can then maliciously tear down.

Exceptionally gifted people are put to a severe test when they are the recipient of someone's generosity: either they are inspired to make themselves worthy of unexpected benefits, or else they may use generous people and their God-given talents as weapons to serve their own selfish ends.

The Heavens Part

To continue the saga of my voyage on the *General Black*, I last mentioned the sumptuous steak dinner that I wangled out of the kitchen staff for Jerry. At twilight, I persuaded him to suspend his work temporarily and walk with me on the deck. He did not regret his decision to do so. For of all the seascapes we saw on that voyage, the one which enveloped us that night was by far the most extraordinary. I tried to capture the sheer magic of it in my diary:

> April 12th, Saturday
>
> Jerry took a few moments off from his work on the ship's newspaper to walk with me on the deck. Surely, everything that I saw was a dream. Had I color film with me, I would have tried to capture that scene so that I could share it with everyone back home. I feel so inadequate, now, trying to find words to describe it. Yet I must give it a try, so that I, at least, can recall this moment years from now — that is, if I ever make it back home again.
>
> For the want of a better description, I would call it a study in black. It was nighttime, and one would expect to see the sky darker than everything else. Yet the sea was actually blacker than the sky, so that I could barely see the horizon. As I leaned against the rail looking out at this foreboding scene, spurts of white foam stood out in contrast to the black ink of the sea. Beyond the foam, patches of turquoise phosphorus glowed like so many elves dancing in the darkness. As Jerry and I watched all of this in silent wonderment, something occurred that made us gasp simultaneously. For suddenly

the black curtain of sky parted, and the next moment, the heavens were alive with millions of brilliant stars. It happened in a flash, the way a stage set changes abruptly from scene to scene. Everything, then, turned topsy-turvy: the sky which, formerly, had been a lighter shade of black, now turned jet black; and the sea revealed her true color of rich aquamarine.

The whole experience was so overwhelmingly beautiful that I lapsed into a sort of reverie that lasted until I went to bed. I got a sense of some supreme intelligence at work, an intelligence that not only created all of this, but also imbued me with the capacity to experience it. I don't know what that intelligence is; nor would I be so presumptuous as to give it a name or to suggest anything more specific about it. It is enough that I am privileged to have witnessed this miracle of nature and to know that there is something out there so profound and so vast that my ego diminishes at the mere thought of it.

Ave Verum

Johann Sebastian Bach was one of numerous great masters of vocal works inspired by the Bible. One has only to observe the frequent insertions in his manuscripts of *S. D. G. (Soli Deo Gloria*, "God alone be praised") and *J. J. (Jesu juva*, "Help me, Jesus") to know that God inspired everything he wrote, everything he did, and everything he taught. As Albert Schweitzer put it:

> Music is an act of worship with Bach. His artistic activity and his personality are both based on his piety. If he is to be understood from any standpoint at all, it is from this. For him, art was religion and so he had no concern for the world or with worldly success. Bach includes religion in the definition of art in general. All great art, even secular, is in itself religious in his eyes. For him the tones do not perish, but ascend to God like praise too deep for utterance![*]

The word "God," and the profound mystery associated with it, has always stirred up a tempest of existential complexities and questions within me. Equally mysterious is a composer's ability to encapsulate within music his or her own concept of God and the essence of religious experience. The question is, does the music, once it has issued from the

---

[*] Albert Schweitzer, *J. S. Bach,* Vol. 1 (New York: Dover, 1966) p. 167.

mind of the composer, become autonomous? In other words, does it free itself from the text which inspired it? I believe it does. To take a case in point, while the biblical text of Bach's *Saint Matthew Passion* describes specific happenings according to the New Testament, the music becomes a universal testament of pure spiritual feeling. As I see it, the music transcends not only the text, but even religion itself. Though I am not Christian, I want to fall on my knees when I hear the *Saint Matthew Passion*. For me, then, the words are mere reminders of music's dominion over them, as though the musical tones are, as Schweitzer suggested, "praise too deep for utterance."

I experienced this very thing with a work by another of music's titans, Wolfgang Amadeus Mozart. It was the eve of Easter Sunday, and Bob Reim and I met with three chaplains to rehearse the musical portion of the services. As I sat at the harmonium sight-reading through a dozen or more hymns and vocal accompaniments, one of the chaplains placed before me a keyboard arrangement of a work I did not know at that time— Mozart's *Ave Verum*, K. 618. One would have thought that it was the Bible itself, so reverently did he place it on the music desk of the harmonium. Even by the second measure I had the impression that the dank and dismal recreation room was being transformed into hallowed ground. It was not that I made an ecumenical association with the spiritual feeling emanating from those wondrous harmonies, for the feeling went beyond names and categories, as love itself does. It was that the whole aura of *Ave Verum* was unequivocally religious in the true meaning of that word. I was playing only a keyboard reduction of this work. In its original form, *Ave Verum* is a motet scored for four voices, strings, and organ. It had, as the chaplain explained to me, a Latin text that wove specific meanings throughout its contrapuntal tapestry. But I, having no text to refer to, clung to the music itself as the sole means of guiding my senses. Thus did the keyboard arrangement alone carry its wordless message to me, in the way that a tree, reaching its limbs towards the sky in mute majesty, declares in deafening overtones the miracle of all creation.

Easter Sunday

One thing that distinguishes slow ocean crossings from jet flights is the sense you get of having traversed a vast distance. You can actually see the bow of the ship laboriously cutting its way through time and space. By April 13th, having been at sea for fifteen days, I was keenly aware of just how far away from home I really was. I recalled those days of nausea that had made me wonder how I could possibly make it to the next day. Just thinking about it exhausted me. I thought, too, of the *General Black*.

Curiously, she had begun to take on human aspects. It occurred to me that she must also be exhausted. Certainly her fuel supply and food rations were all but depleted. In a matter of hours, all of us, the ship included, would finally come to rest in Yokohama Harbor.

From early morning on, the troops stood shoulder to shoulder against the rail of the ship straining for a first glimpse of Japan — that is, everyone except the men who attended the Easter Sunday Services in the recreation room. Except for a few breaks, I remained down there the entire morning, pumping away at the harmonium. I had awakened at 5:30 AM and had quickly thrown off a minor bout of nausea. For the next five hours I had my responsibility cut out for me. There were so many Catholic men on board that it was necessary to hold three successive masses: two of them were conducted by Father K., and a third by a Canadian padre. The padre, who knew me only as a pianist, was moved almost to tears when he heard me play his favorite modal hymns on the harmonium. "One feels very soft during a religious service," he said to me afterwards, taking both of my hands into his. A fourth service was conducted by the Protestant minister, the doctor who had been so kind to me. I slipped in a performance of *Ave Verum* at each service, whatever the religious implication might have been. No amount of repetitions of this sacred work could satisfy me. Had there been a Jewish service, I would have performed it there, too, without telling anyone its title.

Playing the harmonium and discovering *Ave Verum* were not the only gratifying aspects of those services. Religious faith, on the rare occasions when I have sensed its pure intent, has always inspired me deeply. Speaking about hallowed ground — the deep emotional scenes that I witnessed during the services affected me more deeply than I can say. Seeing all of those men in the prime of their lives kneeling in supplication on the cement floor of that recreation room nearly broke my heart. For them, taking the sacrament not only symbolized eternal life, but also protection from the war. This would be a one-way passage for many of them. As the chaplains sanctified the wafers and placed them on the tongues of those kneeling men, I could not help thinking that the chaplains were actually administering the last rites. This was no ordinary ritual; some of those soldiers were being sent to their eternal rest.

As I think about those services now, I realize that there were two things that ought to have separated me from those men: I was Jewish; and, in a purely logistic sense, I was seated at the harmonium, apart from everyone else. One might think that I would have felt alienated — like an intruder, or even an infidel who has dared to violate sacred ground. Yet the opposite occurred. As I sat at the harmonium, caught up in the beauty and pathos of those services, I was struck by the realization that faith, in its truest sense, transcends religious sects in the same way that music transcends words. It became clear to me that this idealized faith of which I am speaking was locked into the music that I performed at those Services. Through the music, then, and especially when I played *Ave Verum*, I felt connected to the whole idea of one God, one faith, and an all-encompassing spiritual love that binds people together. Though a Jew, I was being sanctified along with the Catholics. Although the chaplains bypassed me as they meted out the sacrament, I felt the spiritual nourishment of it nonetheless. The music established a common bond between us so deep, and so strong, that words such as Catholic, Protestant, and Jewish seemed insignificant.

One other thing bound me to those men: I was in uniform, exactly as they were, and I, too, faced the uncertainty of my future. The possibility of being a war casualty was something that I, and everyone else on that ship, had to live with every day. It was by no means an easy task for us to face the prospect of premature death. This time, however, no sooner did that gloomy subject intrude itself upon my consciousness than a spiritual arm, if I may call it that, wrapped itself around me like a protective shield. It was so strong and so all-pervasive that it went beyond rituals and beyond words. For me, it took the form of a belief in some divine intelligence that did not differentiate between people and their religious preferences. Whatever it was, I felt certain that it had guided the hand of Mozart when he composed *Ave Verum*. It lifted me up and beyond the dark images of war and prejudice. In fact, as I sat at that harmonium and experienced all that I have been describing, I had the feeling that nothing negative could penetrate the aura of holiness which pervaded that room.

Many people are repelled by everything and anything that contradicts their own views on religion and faith. I am reminded of a discussion that took place many years ago around a dinner table in the home of a former pupil of mine. His mother, the hostess of the occasion, taught a class of children in the Hebrew school associated with their Temple. It was not unusual, therefore, that the rabbi of the Temple had also been invited to the dinner.

It was the Christmas, Hanukkah season, and in the course of conversation I expressed my delight in seeing the festive decorations in the village square on the way to their home. Just the evening before, I had attended what I thought was a definitive and inspiring performance of Handel's *Messiah*. This I discussed also. With the very mention of the word *Messiah*, my hostess launched into a diatribe: "It is blasphemy for a Jewish person to love Christmas decorations and to listen to Christian music. And the

Messiah, of all things! Have you ever stopped to think of what those words mean? Why it's nothing but an affront to the Jewish people!"

Speaking about feeling alienated, her words and the tone of her voice caused a revulsion within me so intense that I felt like a foreigner in a hostile land. Moreover, I blushed in embarrassment for her son, my pupil. Needless to say, the very last thing I wanted to do was to finish my dinner. I, as well as everyone else seated at that table, fell into shocked silence. During the moments which followed, the rabbi and my pupil continued to stare at their plates. Least of all did they dare to glance in my direction. For it was obvious to everyone that the attack was directed not only at everything Christian, but at me. My pupil, who already knew my own views concerning religiously inspired works of art, braced himself for what he knew would be my harsh counter-attack against his own mother. Indeed, when I had gathered my thoughts, I answered her with a firmness that caused her to lose her own appetite: I told her that her deep-seated prejudice had deprived her of experiencing the profundity and inspiration of Handel's *Messiah* and other works like it; that her views were actually antithetical to the very humanity which the Jewish religion and, for that matter, all religions teach. Finally, I told her that I felt sorry for her pupils, who no doubt were being adversely influenced by the poison of her own limited understanding.

Curiously, the rabbi, who one might think would have contributed something of his own understanding to this subject, continued to stare at his plate. Perhaps he thought it more prudent to remain silent rather than to counter the views of his hostess, who also happened to be one of his own teachers and parishioners. Whatever the reason, he gave the impression of being more interested in his chicken than he was in whether Christmas decorations and Handel's *Messiah* were anti-Semitic.

To return to the *General Black* and the Easter Sunday Services, after the second mass, I rushed up onto the deck to get a glimpse of Japan. At 8:30 AM, a shout of excitement went up among the troops. For suddenly a thin, chalky-gray line appeared on the horizon. One sight of it and my heart seemed to double its pace. By the time the third mass had ended and I had the opportunity to go up on deck again, we were passing by a small island, rich in vegetation. The mainland, too, came into sharper focus. I could now detect shades of tan and green and an occasional structure here and there.

JAPAN

Considering that in all of my twenty-five years I had not ventured farther than some fifty miles from Newark, New Jersey, one can imagine how my romantic nature responded to the first sight of Japan. To begin with, I had preconceived notions about the country from having done a school report on it when I was eleven or twelve years old. More than a report, it was a scrapbook containing various photographs of city and village life that I had obtained from the Japanese Embassy in New York City. From my recollection of those photographs, I thought myself to be a few miles away from the most exotic and alluring country on earth. I felt intoxicated, and in my euphoric state I transformed a simple hut into a Shinto shrine, and a dark curved line, which might have been a road or the side of a hill, became, in my mind, a gracefully arched Japanese bridge. I imagined exotic-looking women walking to and fro across the bridge, dressed in long, floral brocade kimonos, twirling bamboo parasols covered with parchment, and wearing clogs on their feet. Such images flashed through my mind as we drew closer to Yokohama harbor.

By the time the fourth service ended, we had dropped anchor and lowered a lifeboat in order to bring a pilot on board. He subsequently steered the *General Black* towards the pier. All the romantic visions of an hour ago were now replaced by warships and freighters anchored all around us in the harbor, and factories and smokestacks clearly visible on the land. At 2:30 PM, tugboats completed the task of gently nudging the *General Black* against her pier. There were scores of people standing on the pier waving handkerchiefs and scarves, and there was the customary military band blaring out the marine and air force anthems.

During the full hour it took to turn the ship and secure her to the pier, I stood at the top of stairwell number five loaded down with my combat gear. We had all drawn numbers for systematic disembarking. Mine was 229, which meant that I would be among the first three hundred men to walk down that gangway. Not that it mattered in the long run. But after fifteen days at sea, I could hardly wait to be on land again.

As the lines were cast ashore to fasten the *General Black* to her berth, the band broke into a rousing performance of "Hold That Tiger!" At that moment, Father K. rushed up to me. He had with him a WAC major who had come aboard with a group of officers before anyone on the ship had disembarked. It seemed that she was attached to Special Services in the Yokohama area. In my presence, the padre asked her to use her influence to get Kenneth, Bob Reim, and me assigned to Japan. To the very end, then, Father K. tried his best to protect us. I thanked the major in advance for whatever she could do for us. Suddenly, the line began to move. Hurriedly, then, I turned to Father K. for what amounted to an emotional farewell. Then, with the Father's blessings still ringing in my ears, I walked down the gangway. Thus began the greatest adventure of my life.

I cannot begin to say how overjoyed I was to find myself on solid ground again. One would think that my status as a soldier and the possibility of my being sent to Korea would have over-shadowed everything else. But at that moment, I could only think of one thing — the sheer luxury and security of terra firma. I had a strong inclination to kneel down and kiss the ground. Had I been alone, I would actually have done this. As it was, we were immediately herded onto trains waiting about a block from the pier.

My first impression of Japan was that everyone and everything was diminutive. The laborers with their black unruly hair tied with brightly colored head bands might have been characters out of *Gulliver's Travels*. Even the train was small; I had actually to duck my head when entering the dining car. And freight cars standing on neighboring tracks looked like a toy train display.

The excitement I felt at my first glimpse of Japan faded in comparison to my heightened responses to all that I saw during the three-hour train ride to Camp Drake. The remembered photographs, and whatever I had imagined Japan to look like, all materialized as I looked through the window of that train. I actually saw the arched bridges and traditionally dressed women walking across them twirling their parasols. Quaint villages flashed by, crowded with tiny huts. They looked like so many fragile boxes covered with rice paper and strips of bamboo. Lanterns hung across dirt roads, and market places bustled with swarms of people in their clogs and Asian dress. Their smiling faces and waving hands won me over immediately, so that I found myself smiling and waving back at them. Rice fields abounded, and temples with up-curving roofs dotted the hillsides. It was, in short, a living scrapbook that unfolded before my eyes.

Camp Drake

It was 7 PM when the train came to a halt. Buses were waiting nearby to drive us to our final destination — Camp Drake. In a few minutes we found ourselves in an immense building resembling an airport hangar. There, we were issued bedding and received our bunk assignments. To everyone's surprise, we were given the privilege of sending cablegrams to our families. Considering the prohibitive expense of sending cablegrams and making telephone calls between Japan and the United States in 1952, this was, indeed, a magnanimous gesture on the part of the army. There was, however, one problem: it was virtually impossible for the overseas communication center to handle personal messages from so many men. Accordingly, we were allowed to choose from two or three pre-composed messages. The one I chose went something like this:

248

Arrived safely in Japan. Health is excellent. Spirits high.
Best wishes from _____.

The insertion of our names at the end of those messages was the only personal touch allowed to us.

No gesture, however, was more welcome than the distribution of mail. When mail call was announced, the loud cheers continued for a full minute. I have already mentioned feeling the enormous distance separating me from home. To me, then, and I am sure to many others, it was something of a miracle that mail had actually reached us. I received two letters — one from my family and one from Nikki. Reading them was like having comforting arms around me.

Finally, at midnight, we all slipped into our bunks. For obvious reasons, there was a loud chorus of sighs and grunts of delight as our weary bodies luxuriated in clean white sheets and warm blankets. In my diary, I speak of strange phantoms inhabiting my dreams. And small wonder, for when you stop to think about it, that one day seemed like a lifetime: it began with the Easter Sunday Services on the *General Black* and ended with my introduction into a new world.

Cosmoline and Ice Cream

The following day, April 14th, was earmarked for processing, exactly as the first day at Fort Lawton in Seattle had been. This meant a repeat of slow-moving lines, indoctrinations, and disbursement of special equipment. But there was one basic difference which came as no surprise to us: we were issued carbines, a smaller version of the M-1 rifle. I had not so much as seen a weapon since basic training at Fort Dix. The issuance of one now had a far different significance: it suddenly made the war seem real.

When the carbines were handed out to us, the company emitted a collective groan that must have echoed over the Pacific Ocean, not because of the symbolism which I have just mentioned, but because those weapons were completely covered with Cosmoline, a thick, greasy substance having the consistency of Vaseline. One would have to be a soldier to know how utterly miserable and frustrating it can be to clean a weapon covered with Cosmoline. Two things added to our frustration: one was that we were forbidden to clean our weapons in the barracks. On the face of it, there seemed nothing wrong with this restriction. In fact, it ought to have been more pleasant cleaning our carbines outside than in the barracks. The problem was, there was a slow, steady drizzle that made everything damp and clammy, and trying to clean off Cosmoline in the rain was like using water to clean a paint brush laced with oil-based paint. The second thing was that there were no supplies available to us, such as turpentine or rags. As though to teach us self-reliance and ingenuity, the army shifted the burden of responsibility to us. We had to scrounge around the camp to find our own cleaning agents and rags. Even as I write this, I can still feel that slimy, gooey stuff on my hands, which stubbornly kept re-infecting the weapon itself. Somehow, though, we managed to get the job done. In the end, it did not escape us that our carbines were now capable of delivering their death blows.

Kenneth and I spent the rest of the afternoon in the Service Club performing informally for whoever happened to wander in. It was my first experience playing a Yamaha piano. Although the action was extremely even and responsive, the tone was thin and nasal sounding. As a result, I found myself using undue muscular force and getting stiff in the process.

I knew that our music-making carried a powerful message to our audiences. It did not come as a surprise to me, therefore, when Lee, the Service Club hostess, took it upon herself to arrange performances for us in military installations in and around Tokyo. As I have already mentioned, we felt that each contact and each performance could play a vital role in assuring us a safe assignment in Japan. With this in mind, we returned to the barracks somewhat more optimistic about the future.

Dinner that night in the mess hall featured the sort of unappetizing fare that GIs always complain about. It consisted of watery soup, spam, and overcooked vegetables. The meal ended, however, on a more positive note, albeit a comical one. It took the form of an exchange with one of the workers in the mess hall — an exchange that presaged the all-too-frequent fiascos I experienced whenever I attempted to speak Japanese, and later, Korean.

As it happened, we were all treated to ice cream for dessert. It was with no small degree of enthusiasm that I stood at the ice cream counter waiting eagerly for my share. The dispenser on that occasion was a young Japanese man who seemed delighted with the job assigned to him. With merriment flashing in his eyes, he thrust the scoop into the tub with a passion born of generosity. The result was a scoop large enough to satisfy even a person as hopelessly addicted to ice cream as I was — and still am. With my own enthusiasm now exceeding his, I wanted to express my gratitude to the young man. We had been given small dictionaries during our processing which contained useful words and phrases in Japanese. Now, I thought, is a perfect opportunity to try out at least one of words. "*Ari-ga-to*," I uttered shyly, in what I believed was a respectable pronunciation of the Japanese word for "thank you." I did not know then that the correct Japanese pronunciation of the last syllable "to" lies somewhere between the sounds of the English words "toe" and "two." To begin with, the ice cream server, who happened to speak perfect English, hardly expected a newly arrived GI to speak any Japanese at all. While I may have pronounced the first syllables of that word correctly, I no doubt must have opted more for the sound of "two" than "toe" on the final syllable. Hearing this, and also seeing the voracious look in my eye, the boy concluded that I wanted a second helping of ice cream. His merriment instantly gave way to annoyance bordering on anger. And in very articulate English, he snapped back, "No! Not two, only one!"

A group of soldiers standing next to me in line could not help overhearing this comedy of errors. They laughed so hard and so long that the ice cream line came to a complete halt. When I explained the misunderstanding to the ice cream server, he laughed harder than anyone else. And I walked away from that counter with a second scoop of ice cream.

The Death List

Early the following morning, the entire Company marched to the target practice area in the pouring rain with our cleaned carbines. We had, after all, to keep in trim for that destination which would be the lot of the majority of us. That we would discover within two hours the names on the death list, as we called it, was something none of us could have predicted.

Suddenly, we were ordered to gather around a platform and line up in three columns. A stern-looking sergeant mounted the platform holding a stack of papers in his hands. It was the dreaded list itself. We all turned to stone. To us, the sergeant was an executioner; he would seal our fate, and we would have no recourse whatsoever. It was one of those tense moments when anxiety causes people to avoid sharing glances. There was only one person whom we did look at — the sergeant himself. It was as though our fixed stares alone might influence his decision. No one spoke. We all stood there in dumb silence while the rain spattered loudly on our helmets and ponchos. In fact, it rained so loudly that the sergeant had to shout in order to be heard: "The following seventy men will be assigned to Japan." Neither I nor anyone else I knew was on that list. As the sergeant turned the page, my heart skipped a beat. "The following three hundred and twenty men will be assigned to Korea." At this point, a gloom descended upon me so thick and so devastating that I found it difficult to concentrate on what the sergeant was saying. While all of the names were announced in alphabetical order, it was not a continuous list. In other words, the sergeant read off some twenty names from one page, all alphabetized, turned the page, and then began from the A's again. To us, this meant

251

living and dying anew each time he turned a page. Suddenly, one of the names triggered a surge of adrenaline within me: "Jerome Jacobs, 7th Infantry Division, Korea." In another moment, Bob Reim's name was called out; he was given the same assignment. Bob had lost a brother during the Second World War. I could only think of his parents and the devastation they would feel when they learned of Bob's assignment. To me, hearing those two names called was like having knives thrust into me. Being on the verge of tears, I did not dare to look at Jerry or Bob. There was one final announcement before we were all dismissed: "Fifty men have not received their assignments as yet. This group will be notified shortly. Fall out!"

A wave of ambivalent feelings overcame me. On the one hand, I grieved for Jerry and for Bob; on the other, I was grateful for my own deliverance, however temporary it might be. This in turn brought on feelings of guilt for experiencing relief while my friends had received those dreaded orders, the real name of which we whispered among ourselves: death sentences.

We all had known, of course, that orders for Korea awaited the majority of us. Yet, like people who are told that they have a terminal illness, the men so assigned were, at first, in denial. My own feelings of compassion for my two friends, and my anguish at the thought of losing them, found their way into my diary:

> April 15th, Tuesday
> I have never felt so alone. I have a strong compulsion to telephone home. I haven't turned coward, and I don't want to whine or complain. I simply have a need to share the burden of my grief with my mother. I desperately need a sympathetic ear, but there is no one to offer it to me.

It is clear to me now that the life and death issues raised by the reading of that list caused me, as of that moment, to begin making the long and arduous transition from adolescence to maturity. I was forced to abandon the naivete of my youth, and to adopt a new and more mature format for coping with that trauma and the ones which I knew would inevitably follow. Would I have made a similar transition in civilian life had I not been drafted? While any answer to this question would merely amount to conjecture on my part, I can say with certainty that such a transition would have required an experience no less powerful than the one I have just described. And powerful is not even the proper word. The fact is, by the time the sergeant finished reading that list, I felt as though every cell in my body had gone through a radical transformation.

Through the years, I have had similar experiences. One of them occurred two years after my discharge from the army. The occasion was my New York City debut in Town Hall. For all aspiring performers, a debut, in that city especially, is symbolic of having arrived at a level of professional acceptability. In short, it is a major turning point in a musician's life. I remember awakening the following morning with the realization that I was no longer the same person. As I explained to my family and friends, I went to bed one person, and awakened another.

Another experience of this kind, and a devastating one, occurred when my mother died. With her final breath, I felt as though some vital organ within me had died along with her. I was then left with a profound sense of loss and emptiness — a feeling which, I expect, will never go away.

Back to Camp Drake — as we soon discovered, the reading of the death list was only the first phase of this waking nightmare. The second phase consisted of facing the reality of it, of following all of the detailed instructions issued by an emotionless voice that blared out orders over the intercom system in our barracks. To everyone's astonishment, it was announced that departure would begin at 1:30 AM and continue at half-hour intervals. Names were called out again. Jerry and Bob were slated to leave at 2:30 AM. "There is no time to lose," the voice said. Within a few minutes, all the men assigned to Korea were in a frenzy of preparation. The cloud of despondency which had fallen upon everyone by this time was now replaced by a sense of urgency on the part of all those men assigned to Korea. Paradoxically, there was one positive aspect to the hustle and bustle which then ensued: the men had no time to reflect upon their swift and cruel sentences.

My bunk was on the second floor of the barracks, while Kenneth, Jerry, and Bob lived on the first floor. Within one hour, every square inch of floor space on both floors was covered with the contents of duffel bags and field packs. I stayed up half of the night helping as many men as I could to organize their field packs and tie their bedding into horseshoe rolls.

At the appointed time, I joined Jerry and Bob outside of the barracks for a final farewell. Jerry, who, as I said earlier, was short and squatty, looked like a comic strip character loaded down with his combat gear. We both managed to laugh over this. The hurry-up-and-wait syndrome which has always been associated with army procedures was true to form even now. The men assigned to Korea waited in line outside the barracks for a full hour beyond the designated time of their departure. We were all too overcome with emotion and fatigue to engage in anything other than small talk. Finally, at 3:30 AM, a sergeant called the line to attention. I had only time to grab Jerry's and Bob's hands before they marched away in a maze of rifles and helmets.

When I returned to the barracks, I was too exhausted to do or to feel anything at all. I simply pulled off my boots and slipped into my bunk fully clothed. I fell into a deep sleep almost at once. When I opened my eyes in the morning, the events of the previous day took on all of the aspects of a bad dream. Yet, no sooner did I leave my bunk than the reality of the situation fell upon me like an unbearable weight. The sight of the scores of empty bunks on both floors of the barracks was enough to inflict new wounds upon the old. I was devastated. It was only the strong instinct for self-preservation that helped me shake off my lethargy and concentrate on what was now important to me — how to survive the ordeals that awaited me.

Tokyo

After Jerry and Bob left, a pall descended over me. It was as though they had died. At twenty-five, I was fortunate in that I had never lost anyone close to me. Some relatives had died, but since I had seen them only infrequently, their deaths had only a mild effect upon me. Losing my pets, however, was extremely traumatic. When I was ten or eleven, I watched in horror as a car ran over my dear Persian cat, Fuzzy. My world came to an end and I grieved as though a member of my family had died. Years later, when my beloved dog Scottie died (he was poisoned by an irate neighbor), I thought that I, too, would die. Since then, I have suffered the deaths of my parents and various relatives, friends, teachers, and pupils. I have also lost other beloved pets, the last of which were my two Siamese cats, Köchel and Sheila. I am no stranger, therefore, to the crushing symptoms of bereavement. As far as I can ascertain, Jerry's and Bob's departure caused me to suffer symptoms no less severe.

Leave it to the army, though, to uphold the adage "life must go on." The following morning was no different from any other morning: reveille sounded, we all fell in, and details were assigned for the day. No one around me seemed any the worse for all of the empty bunks in the barracks.

Life, indeed, did go on. And now Kenneth and I had to bend our efforts to try to save ourselves. We had been given letters of introduction to important people in Tokyo, both in the military and otherwise. Kenneth, for example, had already telephoned ahead and made an appointment to see a news reporter on the staff of *The New York Times*. In order to justify our taking a trip into Tokyo, Lee arranged a concert for us in an officers' club on the evening of April 17th. We were given a pass and left for Tokyo early in the morning so as to have enough time to make the rounds of our contacts. We felt sure that at least one of the people whose names appeared on our list would be influential enough to countermand our shipment to Korea.

During our first trip to Tokyo, we were fortunate in having with us a guide and interpreter named Johnny Yakamura. He had been an English literature major at Tokyo University, and his English was excellent. Since the occupation, he had worked at the Service Club at Camp Drake. It was our good fortune that Lee allowed him to spend the day with us. No American ever had a better guide than Johnny. He pointed out everything of importance, and provided long and detailed information about subjects that he thought would be of interest to us. Around noon, he took us for a *sukiyaki* dinner in a traditional Japanese restaurant, complete with geisha girls who served and entertained us while we sat on tatami mats. I had my first experience using *hashi*, chopsticks, to the constant giggling of an exotic looking girl who sat attentively at my side during the entire meal. She spent the better part of an hour taking the chopsticks from me, wiping the upper portion of them clean, and patiently reinserting them in their proper positions. As any *hashi*-phile will tell you, near paralysis of the hand can be the consequence of improper handling of chopsticks. In my own case, I had the feeling that I would never be able to use my thumb in scales again! I persisted, however, although most of the food had turned cold before I got the hang of it. But poor Kenneth, who was starving by degrees, not being able to guide so much as a grain of rice into his mouth, had finally to resort to a fork.

Some high-ranking officers introduced us to distinguished musicians, including the American cellist Robert Lamarchina. Highly nervous and fidgety, he was a chain smoker, and his hand trembled visibly each time he maneuvered his cigarette to his lips. In conversation, his dark eyes hardly ever focused upon yours. When they did, frenzy, coupled with mischief, shone in them. Bob had been inducted into the army like us and was assigned to Tokyo. Speaking about preferential treatment, he might as well have been a civilian, considering the benefits he enjoyed while stationed in Tokyo. For one thing, he lived with a Japanese family. Moreover, he concertized extensively, and he also taught at the Royal Academy, the most celebrated school of music in all of Japan.

Bob was a virtuoso on his instrument. At seventeen, he had been appointed first cellist of the NBC Symphony Orchestra under the direction of Arturo Toscanini. Needless to say, it was a thrill for me to play César Franck's Sonata with him, a work originally written for the violin but also arranged for the cello. With Kenneth, we performed trios from the standard repertory. We also included some "cheapies," as we called them, arrangements of light classical pieces, just to satisfy the less sophisticated tastes of some of our superiors. The plan was for the American Trio, as we called ourselves, to make its debut in the Ernie Pyle Theater, which was, at that time, one of Tokyo's most prestigious auditoriums. The top brass, who made all of the arrangements, and who were genuinely interested in us, were convinced that a concert of this calibre would do the trick: "Everyone will be proud to be associated with such brilliant musicians," one officer suggested, "and the Trio's assignment in Tokyo will be assured."

Bob had his own car. On the day of our rehearsal at the Ernie Pyle Theater, we decided to meet him at his home and drive to the rehearsal together. There I saw an incident that showed me why so many GIs decided to remain in Japan after their discharges rather than to return to the United States. As the three of us were leaving Bob's home, the young and beautiful daughter of the family escorted him to his car, which was the custom in Japanese households. She then spoke some words to him in Japanese. Kenneth and I were amazed to discover that Bob spoke the language fluently. While I understood nothing of the conversation, I felt the great emotion with which the girl spoke. As we drove off, I could not resist asking Bob what she had said to him. "Oh," he responded quite nonchalantly, "it was a typical scene of farewell. She told me to please hurry back, and that she will not live until I return."

When we walked out onto the stage of the Ernie Pyle Theater for our rehearsal, I could hardly believe my eyes. There stood a nine-foot Yamaha. It was the first concert grand I had seen since leaving home. Without waiting for Kenneth and Bob to unpack their instruments, I rushed to the piano, eager to make contact with it. With the first tones I produced, however, I knew that I was in for trouble. Like all of the other Yamahas I had played, this piano, for all of its length, sounded like a much smaller grand. I should add that since that time, the Yamaha piano has been improved considerably. In fact, it can now hold its own with some of the finest instruments in the world.

During the rehearsal at the Ernie Pyle Theater, I began to experience pains in the muscles on the underside of my forearms. This was to pose a serious threat to me over the next few months. My penchant for programming technically challenging pieces with insufficient practice time, along with my tendency to force the tone out of those thin-sounding pianos, led to an occupational hazard that often plagues pianists — tendinitis.

The concert went on as scheduled. It drew a large and enthusiastic audience and inspired rave reviews from Japanese and American critics. Yet nothing, not even our success, could influence the orders which, as it seemed, had already been issued to us by the high command. As a matter of fact, Robert Lamarchina with all his connections was himself sent to Korea a few months after we had arrived there. As it happened, we found him waiting on a chow line somewhere near the front. By reciting code language to various military telephone operators, I finally succeeded in contacting the Special Services office in Taegu, where Kenneth and I were stationed at the time. As a result of my efforts, Bob, from that moment on, joined Kenneth and me on a tour of the front lines. But more about that later.

There was a general feeling of defiance among the remaining men at Camp Drake: if we were going to be sent to Korea, then at least we should enjoy whatever time we had left in Japan. Thus, "goofing off" was the order of the day. Whenever we could slip out of assigned detail, we did so. Over the next few days, for example, I returned to Tokyo several times ostensibly to play concerts. The fact that I sometimes had commitments to perform there made my scheme easier. On one occasion, I decided to go it alone and explore the city on my own. Signs of the occupation were everywhere: street and building signs appeared in Japanese and English, and there were swarms of young boys who wanted to make arrangements to satisfy every conceivable sexual fantasy for whatever you wanted to pay — even for a pack of American cigarettes. The black market, too, was flourishing. I was repeatedly enticed to sell whatever I happened to have in my possession — cigarettes, chocolate, my watch. Moreover, a tempting rate of exchange was offered to me for changing greenbacks into yen.

On one street corner, I saw a middle-aged woman dressed in rags. "Boot shine?" she asked in a sweet voice and with a gentle tilt of her head. I could not resist — not because my boots needed shining, but because I knew she needed money. While she rubbed the brown polish into the leather directly with her fingers, I was amazed to hear her whistling themes from Beethoven symphonies. I discovered that she spoke English, and I lost no time in asking her where she had learned the Beethoven symphonies. "You like music?" she asked me, much astonished. I told her that I was a pianist. At this, her eyes lit up. To her, I was, as of that moment, no longer just another GI walking up and down the Ginza: I was a musician! With this kinship established between us, she related the following story: Before the war she studied piano with her sister, who was an accomplished pianist. Later, she entered a university in Tokyo where she earned a degree, the specifics of which I could not determine because of her English. Then the war came, and sadly, her sister and all the other members of her family were killed in a bombing raid. She was all alone now, and eked out a living by polishing shoes. My heart broke for this woman. When she had finished her work, having smeared some four or

257

five layers of polish onto my boots, I gave her the equivalent of ten American dollars. She bowed almost to the ground, while making guttural sounds of delight and gratitude. I heard her *arigato*'s fading in the distance as I walked away from her.

The Ugly American

I had occasion to meet other soldiers in Tokyo and to observe them in their dealings with the Japanese people. On the whole, I found them rude, arrogant, and vulgar. There was no question about it: the phrase "ugly American" had an element of truth to it, judging from the outlandish behavior of certain officers and GIs that I witnessed. Nowhere during my tour of duty did I experience greater evidence of this than at a concert which Kenneth and I gave at the officers' club associated with the Veterans Hospital.

All of the officers' clubs in Tokyo were luxuriously appointed, and this one was no exception: crystal chandeliers, exquisite table settings, and new Yamaha grand pianos were the order of the day. Although the piano at this particular club was the best one I had encountered thus far, I continued to feel frustrated at the sheer lack of resonance from these instruments.

I remember that club in particular because of the association it evoked — the rowdy court of Caligula in ancient Roman times. To begin with, the officers were much more interested in drinking and smooching with their wives or a host of beautiful Japanese girls than they were in appreciating the entertainment. An excellent Japanese band, together with a variety show, was lost on them entirely. Nor did the boorish behavior of the captain who acted as emcee help matters any. Drunk and ill-mannered, he sounded like one of those barking announcers at a freak show, so vulgar were his choice of words and his delivery of them.

When we were announced, there was barely any applause at all as we walked out onto the stage. During our performance, which lasted the better part of an hour, most of the officers and their escorts continued to behave as they had before we began to play: they talked and laughed uproariously, they clicked their wine glasses loudly, and they went right on eating. One group of people in that room, however, proved to be the exception — the Japanese musicians and entertainers who performed at the club each night of the week. There being no extra chairs available, they sat on the floor directly in front of the stage. Deep interest and admiration shone from their faces. In fact, they seemed so absorbed in the music that Kenneth and I found ourselves projecting our playing to them alone. Afterwards, their enthusiastic comments, coupled with deep bows of respect, warmed our hearts considerably.

After our recital, Kenneth and I were invited to one of the tables for dinner. From the superficial conversation it became obvious to us that few of those present had paid the slightest attention to our playing. The general feeling of apathy was such that I had no desire whatsoever to eat the gourmet food spread out before me. The personal insult was one thing; but far worse to deal with was my feeling of shame before the Japanese musicians. In fact, it was the first time in my life that I actually felt ashamed to be an American. I was, after all, a soldier, like all the other men in the room. As such, I felt guilty by association. While I knew from experience that civilized behavior is rare, whatever one's nationality, still, the unruly behavior of my compatriots overrode my reason. At that moment, I knew what the phrase "ugly American" really meant.

When it was time to leave, the Japanese entertainers came to the door to bid us goodbye. Their expressions of admiration told us that they didn't think all Americans were ugly. After the experience in that officers' club, and having observed the behavior of a host of spoiled and obnoxious Army personnel whom I met in and around the Tokyo area, I was not sure that I wanted to remain in Japan. Moreover, I became the victim of harassment at Camp Drake which made even Korea seem desirable by comparison.

The Bully

There were two sergeants who seemed to run things at Camp Drake; one was human, the other was a monster. The monster sported a crew cut through which you could see his scalp and all of its contours. And contours there were, with hills and valleys and ugly sores along the way. Obese and loud-mouthed, he had a look in his eye and a curl to his lips that spoke of malevolent intent. Just the sight of him was enough to make my blood run cold. He seemed to be the sort of person who hated everyone and everything. It seemed to me that he singled me out for the full measure of his sadism. I made up my mind that he either hated Jews, or else thought that all classical musicians were "queers." Perhaps it was both. Whatever was the cause, he seemed intent on ruining my life. For example, when telephone calls came into his office requesting Kenneth and me for concerts, he simply doubled our chores during the night. I would, for example, be assigned to guard duty from 12 AM to 4 AM. Because of lack of sleep, I could hardly function at the piano during our evening recitals. The more fuss that was made over Kenneth and me, the more he inflicted work assignments on us.

On the very evening of the recital at the officers' club in Tokyo, we returned to the barracks around 1 AM ready to turn in, completely exhausted. There was the sergeant, glowering with an invidious sneer that sent shivers through me. "You both goofed off today," he shouted threatcningly. Without a word, I produced the pass given to us by the captain of the officers' club who had engaged us for the recital. "No one told me about it," he answered, gruffly. "And how do I know that you didn't forge that pass!" That was the last straw. My patience, and my better judgment as well, gave way like a dam collapsing under the pressure of a turbulent river. I accused him of stupidity and bigotry, and I actually threatened him with reprisals from the top brass with whom I had contact. All of this, of course, was exactly the wrong thing to say to such a brute. His fury got the better of him, and with eyes blazing with anger, he actually raised his fists. I believe that he would have used them, had not a lieutenant who was on duty in the office come running over at that exact moment to see what all the disturbance was about. The lieutenant was too sleepy, however, to want to be involved in what seemed a clear-cut case of insubordination. He simply walked away and left me at the mercy of the sergeant.

While the lieutenant's approach seemed to have defused the sergeant's temper considerably, my own temper remained at high pitch. My sense of pride compelled me to prove that I could take whatever the sergeant could dish out. So I demanded to be placed on guard duty for the rest of the evening. The sergeant, who by this time had flared up again, exploded with a large repertory of familiar and unfamiliar curse words. Having guard duty until dawn was, he thought, a good idea. But as of the morning, I would also be put on garbage duty throughout the day. He placed a corporal in charge of me for each hour of my assignments. I subsequently made several attempts to have the sergeant censured, but everyone at Camp Drake was busy with his own problems. Besides, I had the feeling that my superiors would chalk up my complaints to artistic temperament. Finally, when Kenneth and I did not show up for a performance at the Service Club, Lee thought it time to intervene. The following entry in my diary describes what ensued:

April 19th, Saturday

Guard duty was no problem. What was a problem was dealing with my own anger. I paced through the barracks in the middle of the night like a maniac on the brink of going berserk. My rage knew no bounds. I only wanted to bash the sergeant's head in. I am certainly no stranger to rage; after all, I directed it often enough against my father. Now, however, it has taken on a larger meaning. I see clearly how men can be turned into killers, how human beings can commit atrocities, and why there are wars to begin with. We were told of actual murders committed on the front lines by GIs who had an axe to grind with some officer, and how such murders were attributed to casualties of war. I can see myself aiming my carbine at that sergeant's skull. I can't believe that I'm writing all of this! God knows I never thought of myself as a killer. Yet I can now see how certain extreme circumstances could turn me into one.

When Kenneth and I did not show up for a scheduled performance, Lee and various officers went to the CQ (a sergeant in charge of quarters) to find out why we had to pull so much detail. They sent for me, and, of course, I told them exactly what was happening. So they sent for the sergeant in question. He, of course, tried to justify his actions on the grounds that I went AWOL (absent without leave), that I goofed off, and that I was just plain spoiled. The officers present did not swallow his defense one bit, and they reprimanded him right in my presence. I knew what would happen once he got chewed out by his superiors. He would find ways of making life even more intolerable for me. Therefore, I insisted on going through with everything he assigned to me. I also made a little speech — how such bigotry starts wars, and how it is responsible for all the evil in the world. It was my victory and not the sergeant's. My message was, "You dish it out and I'll do it!"

Smart Seymour! Now I have to satisfy everyone — not only the sergeant, but also Lee and a host of officers as well, all of whom want Kenneth and me to perform. So, in between my chores, off with my fatigues and on with my class *A* uniform. Exhaustion, though, is making it nearly impossible for me to play with any degree of control. Just last evening, I began the Black Key Etude by Chopin three times before I could get into it. I am so tired, and so depressed, that I seriously wonder if it would not be better to be assigned to Korea after all. There's a war raging there. With life and death as the real issues, I imagine that no one tries to push privates around — especially when weapons are always at hand.

The harassment continued, and so did the performances. The final performance took place at the Camp Drake officers' club on April 21st. When we returned to the barracks late that evening, a corporal from the orderly room informed Kenneth and me that our orders had arrived. In spite of our having entertained the idea that anything might be better than remaining in Camp Drake, Kenneth and I grew pale when he told us what those orders contained — assignments to Korea.

Part 3: The Army

Orders for Korea

Early in the morning of April 22nd, Kenneth and I officially received our assignments. The document read, "Special Services, Company 10, Korea." Immediately there arose a storm of ambivalent feelings within me — fear of the unknown on the one hand, and relief at leaving Camp Drake on the other. At one moment, anything was better than seeing that sergeant's face one more time; but the next moment, I knew that going to Korea, in whatever capacity, was potentially life-threatening.

There followed then what the army calls a "shakedown," a thorough perusal of everything that had been issued to us. One very impatient sergeant, for example, went through every stitch of my clothing: "You won't need this class A uniform any more where you're going!" he said to me derisively. Off we went to the commissary to turn in practically everything we possessed. In its place we were issued steel helmets, fatigues, heavy boots, mosquito netting, a canteen, and a poncho. Even the sight of a steel helmet did not dampen my desire to be rid of Camp Drake once and for all. But when another sergeant at the commissary placed an M-1 rifle in my hands, fear took the upper hand. This was no longer a charade of cops and robbers, as I had felt it to be during my basic training at Fort Dix. I had been issued combat gear; I was being sent off to war. "Oh God," I thought, "how will I ever survive this?"

Now it was I who had to make a horseshoe roll, exactly as my buddies had done a few days earlier. This accomplished, I decided to spend the remainder of the evening browsing through the PX. There my eyes focused upon the most beautiful camera I had ever seen — a Mamiyaflex with its own flash attachment. It was quite a contrast to the box camera that my brother-in-law Saul Armm had given me when I was twelve. Though it cost sixty-four dollars, my desire to own this extravagant object was more than my sense of frugality could resist. I bought it, rushed back to the barracks, and familiarized myself with all of its functions. There was something about owning that camera that helped me to stave off the reality of my situation. I fell asleep while reading the manual.

Birthday at Sea

Kenneth Gordon and I were to remain an inseparable team for the next eight months, until my discharge from the army the following November. On April 23rd, we gathered outside of the barracks loaded down with field packs, duffel bags (my own included thirty pounds of music), and rifles strapped over our shoulders. I remember the discomfort of the straps cutting into my shoulders and the utter misery that invariably accompanies troop movements. We were loaded onto a bus and then a train that retraced the route by which we had reached Camp Drake.

At Yokohama harbor, we boarded a large ship, ironically called the *General Gordon*. It had three smoke stacks, and in comparison to the *General Black*, it seemed like a hotel. While the bunk arrangements were the same, the compartment to which we were assigned was twice the size. The best improvement was that each compartment had its own latrine. The ship was crowded with dependents of servicemen and married couples. Many of them were GIs returning to the United States with their Japanese wives via Sasebo, a port on the western coast of Kyushu.

The scene at the pier was even more dramatic than the one I remembered in Seattle. Crowds of GIs and Japanese civilians threw rolls of brightly colored confetti up onto the deck and into the hands of their friends and loved ones. It was a beautiful scene, with the varicolored streamers tracing arched patterns from the pier to the deck. A large military band played all the routine anthems amid shouts of "Goodbye" and "Sayonara." Finally, there were tears from both onlookers and passengers as the ship drifted slowly away from the pier, snapping the streamers as it went.

It was April 24th, my 25th birthday. My diary paints a picture of a person who had already been through too much to feel anything at all. I did everything routinely, like a robot. Even performing became a routine affair. I had, of course, enjoyed the responses of my audiences on the *General Black*. But to be truthful about it, Kenneth and I had a purpose beyond music making each time we performed on that ship: we wanted a decent meal, and playing for the officers always assured us of one. No sooner did the *General Gordon* free herself of the tugs than Kenneth and I made a beeline for the officers' mess where we volunteered to give a concert that evening. It worked like a charm: the officers and their wives were wildly enthusiastic, and Kenneth and I feasted on the finest food. Once again, we played for our supper.

After docking in Sasebo at ten o'clock the following morning, we boarded another ship, the *Private Sadao Munemori*, which looked like a rowboat next to the *General Gordon*. It was loaded down with soldiers who had just come from Korea. As we went down one gangplank to the *Munemori*, those troops went up another one to the *General Gordon*. They had completed their tour of duty and were now rotating back to the United States. Seeing their combat equipment and the grim look on their faces sent chills through me. It was then that I recalled what a sergeant at Camp Drake had told me: "Whatever you do, don't go to Korea! Life there is the cheapest commodity." To me, then, the *Munemori* took on the aspect of a death vessel. And the association I made between *Munemori* and *memento mori* (remember that you must die) certainly did not help matters any.

Death, in fact, seemed to be the chief motif during that brief voyage across the Sea of Japan — not only for me, but for many other men on board. We lifted anchor at 6 PM and were scheduled to arrive at Pusan Harbor the following morning. Dramamine helped me to sleep for a few hours, at least. The waters were so turbulent, and the ship so flimsy in construction, that I was literally tossed from one side of my bunk to the other. Thoughts of death invaded my dreams, as the following entry in my diary reveals:

April 25th, Friday

I have had a recurring dream for three nights running. In it, my father has died, and I see myself viewing his body in the coffin. I am prostrated with grief. Later in the dream I leave the room in the funeral parlor for only a brief period of time. When I return, the doctors and the members of my family are helping my father out of the coffin. He is actually alive! According to what they tell me, the embalming fluid dissolved the blood clot which had been the cause of his death.

Coincidentally, Kenneth told me that he, too, dreamed of death. This prompted me to draw out some of the other guys around my bunk. My hunch was correct: two of them reported similar dreams. Under the circumstances, it is not so surprising; for after all, death is stalking us. There is a haunted look in everyone's eye, even among the "gung-ho" soldiers. Let's face it: this is a one way passage for many of us. And I feel sure that I am not the only one grappling with one gnawing question: who among us will return in coffins?

I can now read a great deal of symbolism into the dream about my father's death. On the one hand, I often wished him dead, and the dream may have symbolized the fulfillment of that wish. But that in the dream he came back to life leads me to conclude that I did not really want him to die.

On the other hand, my guilt in wishing my father dead may have resulted in role reversal. In other words, perhaps in my dream, I received the ultimate punishment for my sin: it was I who was lying in the coffin, and not my father. To carry this even further, the embalming fluid may very well have symbolized the contaminated intravenous injection that had almost killed me.

CHOSUN (KOREA) — LAND OF THE MORNING CALM

At 5:30 AM we all filed out onto the deck. A deathlike silence fell over the troops as we saw the ghostly shadow of Korea rising out of the mist. One glimpse of it and my anxiety reached an all-time peak. In fact I was so traumatized that I made a silent vow right there and then: "If I come out of this alive, nothing will ever frighten me to this extent again — not even playing in public." I have held to that vow, even to this day. On many occasions, for example, when the torment of pre-performance anxiety makes me rue the day that I ever decided to be a performer, I recall those moments on the deck of the *Munemori*. And suddenly I gain a clear perspective on real life and death issues, and not just imagined ones.

By 7 AM, the *Munemori* was tied up at her pier in Pusan Harbor. I shuddered when I remembered that our troops had been ambushed and trapped at that very port only a short time earlier. It all looked so peaceful, now, and the customary band blaring out its welcome with brass, winds, and percussion lent a festive air to the occasion. For the next few hours, at least, this was no longer a war scene, but rather another segment of a travelogue in which I was a player.

In 1951, Korea was, by American standards, a primitive country. The arrival of United Nations troops, however, brought with it both good and bad influences, as is usually the case during wars. My diary best describes my first reactions to Korea, a country that was to play a vital role in my life:

April 26th, Saturday

We were hustled off of the *Munemori* and into a tremendous warehouse where we dumped our gear. It was a relief to rid myself of that impossible weight. My shoulders felt as though they had been cut with knives. The warehouse was actually a huge mess hall. Ken and I took our place on a chow line that seemed to be a mile long. Looking around me, I noticed something most unusual: officers and EMs (enlisted men) actually stood side by side on the chow line and then ate together at the same tables. We're all dressed in fatigues; so apart from our insignia, you can't distinguish an officer from an EM. There is no question about it: a barrier has been broken, and I get the feeling that rank is merely a word now.

After chow, we gathered our gear and boarded a train. The scenes of village life that flashed by my window made me feel grateful to be living in the United States. Never in my wildest imagination could I have envisioned such poverty and such primitive conditions. To begin with, the air was permeated with the stench of human excrement. It is collected in what GIs call "honey buckets," and spread onto fields for fertilizer. Do Koreans, then, eat vegetables which have been fertilized with human excrement? This is something I can't handle.

I am fascinated by the way people dress. The women wear long skirts, fastened above the waist, and short blouses. Most of them have crude rags or towels tied around their foreheads on which they balance tremendous baskets filled with laundry, food, or anything that they wish to transport. Many of the women go right about their work with babies strapped to their backs. It's a curious thing to see these infants nestled in their blanket sacks fast asleep while their bald-topped heads bob this way and that.

Concerning the men, we passed many "Papa-sans" — elderly men, with long beards. They were dressed in flowing white robes and sported tall black hats made of lacquered horse hair. Both men and women sit around squatting on their haunches, with their knees far apart. We're told that they sit this way for hours on end, chatting away. In the long run, it must be good for their posture, for I saw elderly people walking briskly with their backs as straight as rulers.

Along the way, we passed narrow canals filled with muddy water. These canals run right through the center of every village. Scores of children line the shores and fill their buckets with this foul water. They probably cook with it, wash their dishes in it, and they may even drink it! It's too gruesome to contemplate. The huts look as though they have been improvised with whatever material happened to be available — wood, cloth, metal, and even pieces of cardboard cartons. All in all, the poverty is appalling.

From time to time during our journey, we passed young men walking arm in arm. As one might imagine, this invited all sorts of disgusting comments from the men, plus a symphony of whistles and hoots so loud that the young Koreans turned their heads towards the train. According to Americans, men are not supposed to show any outward sign of affection towards one another. You're "queer" if you do.

When you add it all together, it's not difficult to understand why so many Americans are hated in foreign countries. I am resolved to do something about this, to dispel the false notion that all Americans are interested only in sex and materialism. I'll use my music as a means of establishing the highest form of communication with these people.

After two hours or so, the train stopped at a depot where trucks were waiting to take us to our quarters. We were driven up the side of a mountain, and when we got to the crest, we looked down and saw our camp nestled in the valley below. At first glance, it seemed luxurious in comparison to what I had seen in the center of Pusan. There were stretches of Quonset huts and tents, all laid out in an orderly fashion. By good luck, Kenneth and I were assigned to a Quonset hut — not that it really mattered: this was only a temporary camp, where men would receive their final assignments. We were to remain there for only one day. Most of the men had received infantry assignments. Kenneth and I were among the lucky ones in having been assigned to EUSAK (Eighth United States Army, Korea), Special Services, in Taegu.

For the time being, I began to learn what life is really like for a soldier in a war-torn country. For one thing, we had C-rations for dinner, a first experience for me. It consisted of a can of spam, with noodles, biscuits, jam, chocolate, and cookies. Although this made many of us angry and resentful, it was not the worst problem. Far more serious was danger everywhere due to the infiltration of North Korean guerrillas. Attacks would occur without warning. For instance, we were told that two weeks earlier, one GI had been killed and another seriously wounded just four miles up the road. Korean and American guards stood side by side at each entrance to the camp, and no one was allowed past those gates at night. "Land of the Morning Calm" indeed! This was a country racked with the pain of a death struggle. And I was now a part of it.

The Caress of a Deer

It was not just the cold that caused me to shiver during the entire night. To tell the truth, I was just plain scared. I had visions of the camp being attacked while we slept. Whereas I had formerly viewed my M-1 rifle as a toy weapon, I now huddled close to it as the only means of protection I had. At dawn, an hour or so before reveille, I was the only one in the shower room. I stood under the comforting stream of hot water for fifteen minutes or so. It was a clear-cut demonstration of just how effective hydrotherapy can be. For my nerves untangled within minutes, and I felt considerably better. Afterwards, I went to the day room, where there were plentiful supplies of peanuts, candy, and other items, just for the taking. It was the first time that I ate peanuts and candy for breakfast.

Once outside, I found myself enveloped in a mist so thick that I could not see more than a few feet in front of me. Suddenly, the faces of two baby deer appeared through the mist. At first, I thought I was dreaming. Surely I would awaken and find myself back in my bunk. No sooner did I think this than one of the deer walked straight up to me. I extended my hand, and to my utter amazement it nuzzled its cool, moist nose into my palm. My heart leapt with joy. It was as though some spiritual force had sent an angel in disguise to comfort me in my anguish. I knelt down, emptied an entire bag of peanuts into the palm of my hand, and offered it to the deer. I felt only the cool velvet surface of its nose as the sweet creature gratefully ingested the peanuts. Having finished the peanuts, the deer licked every grain of salt off of my hand with its little pink tongue. Perhaps to show its gratitude, or as a gesture of trust, the deer came even closer and gently sniffed at my face. This alone would have sufficed to enrich me for a lifetime. But when those almond-shaped eyes filled with love and gratitude met mine, I was transported out of myself. While I was stroking the deer's head in an ecstasy of delight, the bugle sounded reveille. Startled by the sound, the deer took a few steps back and disappeared into the mist.

The mere thought of that experience rekindles the intense love I feel for all animals. Even today, when I look into the eyes of chipmunks and raccoons during the blissful summer months I spend in Maine, I often think of that deer, and I bless it for the comfort it brought to me during that trying time.

TAEGU

The next day, Kenneth and I boarded a train for Taegu, one of the few places as yet untouched by the ravages of the war. Taegu was the headquarters of EUSAK. To our great relief we found ourselves in one of the most luxurious camps in all of South Korea. Occupying the former campus of Taegu University, Company 10 was sprawled over a valley surrounded by green hills. The officers lived in what was the former administration building of the University, while the enlisted men were housed in Quonset huts. A few fortunate men, like Steve Fischer, for instance, whose family owned chains of stores such as Lord & Taylor and Haynes, actually had private rooms. Steve, a congenial and highly intelligent fellow, had, perhaps, the most desirable room on the entire compound. In it were luxuries unheard of by army standards — cases of Napoleon brandy and Canadian Club whiskey, cocktail glasses, some thirty sets of Class A uniforms, an oriental lamp, and silk hangings on the walls. A group of us met there practically every night for long discussions and lots of drinking. I have never been able to tolerate hard liquor. It was quite an occasion, therefore, when I was introduced to my first martini. I had to be helped back to my bunk. But it was when I drank two "Pineapple Surprises" before a performance, a drink which Steve had invented, that disaster struck. I remember playing my old standby piece — Liszt's Hungarian Rhapsody No. 6 — in front of a large audience at the officers' club, and finding myself on the second page almost before I had begun! It is not very likely that anyone in the audience so much as suspected my memory slip. But I was mortified by it. This one experience drove home the lesson once and for all: never drink "Pineapple Surprises" or any alcoholic beverages whatsoever before playing in public.

Auditioning for Our Lives

Lieutenant Sporup was the officer in charge of Special Services in Taegu. From the very beginning, he thought that classical music would simply not go over among the troops in Korea. The USO troupes that entertained a great deal near the front lines comprised exclusively pop singers and comedians. I suggested that Kenneth and I give a tryout concert right there on the compound. If the GIs liked us, he could then send us on a tour of the front lines. After all, we were trained infantrymen. As such, we could perform in areas where USO entertainers were forbidden to go. If our concert was not received favorably, however, he could do with us what he wished. Both he and I knew what that meant — reassignments to the war front as regular infantrymen. He accepted my proposal and temporarily assigned us jobs in the Special Services office until we could make proper arrangements for our tryout concert.

First we chose the setting for the concert, the Company's movie theater housed in one of the Quonset huts. It had a stage and three hundred seats. Next, I searched around for a decent piano and discovered a six-foot Yamaha grand in a Korean Military Police school just a few miles from our camp. The Korean officer in charge, who, to my great relief, spoke English, graciously agreed to allow me to borrow the piano — but with one condition: Kenneth and I would have to repeat our recital for the men in his military school. Quite naturally I agreed to this. I then set my mind on the most difficult task of all — moving the piano.

With the help of Lieutenant Sporup, I requisitioned a truck and six Korean laborers. Never having moved a grand piano before, and, in addition, having to deal with six Koreans who could not speak a single word of English, I hardly knew what to do first. Necessity being the mother of invention, I gesticulated with my hands and grunted sounds which I am sure had never been heard before, and somehow my helpers and I managed to turn the piano on its side and get it onto a dolly. We removed the legs and the pedal shaft and rolled the piano onto the truck. Re-assembling the piano on the stage of the theater posed a new set of problems. Using sheer logic, however, plus a whole new vocabulary of grunts, I accomplished this, too — and all without a single scratch to the high-gloss finish of that Yamaha grand.

269

Part 3: The Army

It was now a question of planning the program and getting into pianistic shape. Needless to say, my technique was in a deplorable condition due to a lack of consistent practicing. Nor did the constant repetition of those demanding warhorses that I programmed over and over again help matters any. The stiffness and pains in my arms from which I had been suffering ever since that voyage on the *General Black* had worsened. Lieutenant Sporup sized up the situation and did everything possible to help us. He of course had to justify our stay in Company 10 in accordance with army requirements. First, he assigned Kenneth and me to desk jobs in the Special Services office. Our duties were kept to a minimum so that we could practice during the afternoons. Next, he thought that a few days away from the piano would ease my tendinitis. So he sent me on a secret mission with Corporal Bill Groover, the entertainment coordinator, and a key figure in the Special Services office.

Sy, the Spy

Bill Groover called me Sy, as some people have done throughout my life. I suppose that the very sound of my name, Seymour, connotes an English formality which some people want to avoid. I am the sort of a person who bends over backward to break down the barriers of formality, so I don't mind being called Sy in the slightest. Curiously enough, I have never identified with my first name, not for the reasons stated above, but simply because to my ears, Seymour and Bernstein sound as antithetical as the music of Mozart and Scriabin. As far as Bill Groover was concerned, he called me Sy, I believe, more out of his desire to Americanize an English-sounding name than to avoid formality. As a matter of fact, he was unusually formal, even straight-laced at times. This may have been due to the influence of his father, who had been a major in World War I. Whatever the reason, there was something decidedly militaristic in Bill's manner.

While working at his desk and when communicating with other people in the office, Bill showed himself to be a leader-type in the full sense of the word. Hard-working, clear-thinking, and aristocratic in a masculine sort of way, he was the kind of person one thought would run for President one day. One could just picture him campaigning and winning people over with his deep and authoritative voice. His appearance was no less impressive than his personality: he was tall, good-looking, and one of those people who looked extremely good in glasses.

There was a no-nonsense air about Bill, such that a person might not at first be inclined to discuss anything of a personal nature with him. But as I subsequently discovered, this was merely a veneer, which he no doubt adopted to keep personal issues from infringing upon his army duties. This veneer served another purpose as well, one of which he had no notion: it inspired all of us to work with the same sort of integrity and single-mindedness that he himself demonstrated in everything he did.

At heart, though, Bill was deeply sensitive and unusually respectful of anyone with talent. While I thought of my own emotional makeup as being opposite to his, he, on the other hand, easily adapted himself to my overly exuberant nature and my sometimes irrepressible need for simple fun. I would, for example, make teasing comments to all of the personnel working around me in the office — Bill included. In fact, I took special delight in directing cutting remarks at him, all designed to break down his formality.

One morning I was speaking on the telephone to a Captain Carver who was to deliver a dolly to the office in order to facilitate the moving of the piano for our recital. He was to telephone me that afternoon as to the time of the delivery. Knowing that I would be practicing during the latter part of the day, I said loudly enough for Bill and Lieutenant Sporup to hear, "I probably won't be in the office when you call. But I'll see to it that Corporal Groover will remain on duty to take all of my messages." At this, Lieutenant Sporup broke into convulsions of laughter. As for Bill, while I am sure he was secretly amused, he pretended to be otherwise. He pounded his fists on his desk and tightened his lips in a mock rage. He then flashed me a disdainful look with only a trace of mirth in his eyes, and went right on working. But no one was more devoted than Bill in championing Kenneth's and my talent wherever and however he was able to. I had great respect and affection for him. And I felt flattered, therefore, when he asked me to accompany him on a secret mission — one that earned me the title, "Sy, the spy!"

As it happened, there were various dance clubs in operation throughout Korea where GIs would gather for some evening diversion. These clubs were managed by a Korean man who tallied the expenses entailed in running them and then billed our Special Services office. Bill Groover suspected that he was guilty of fraud — that he inflated the expenses and pocketed the profits. Unfortunately for that manager, Bill had been on to him for some time. Now he and I would go together on a spy mission to one of the clubs in Pusan. We would examine their indigenous talent files, and see with our own eyes the exact expenses involved in running the club. Spying, of course, is a dangerous occupation. It was with some degree of anxiety, therefore, that I went with Bill to the weapons room, where we each drew a carbine and two clips of ammunition. We then stuffed our personal effects into a light cargo field pack and set out for the airport. It was one of those hot, sultry days. The sky was overcast and the airport terminal felt like a blazing furnace.

Our airplane, a C-47, looked hardly strong enough to hold us, much less thirteen other soldiers. Canvas strips subdivided into mesh-like pockets — bucket seats, they were called — stretched along both sides of the cabin. This flimsy means of support was unsettling enough. But when Bill slipped easily into a parachute and then handed me one, I lost whatever confidence I had in surviving that flight. Never having maneuvered into a parachute before, I was at a total loss in dealing with the complex array of straps. A lieutenant sitting next to me was the first to offer assistance; we both laughed as he undid the hopeless entanglement that resulted from my futile endeavor. Finally, the parachute was properly secured, and the C-47 taxied down the runway and laboriously rattled off the ground.

The intense heat and the lack of oxygen in that crude aircraft set off my motion sickness almost at once. While Bill sat there completely engrossed in a magazine, appearing to be as complacent as though he were sitting at his desk, I had all I could do to keep my breakfast down. I did such a convincing job of masking my airsickness that Bill had no notion that there was anything wrong with me. Or else he pretended not to notice. Once we landed and had coffee and doughnuts in the Red Cross canteen, my nausea subsided considerably. We then boarded a bus for Hialeah Compound, which was even more luxurious than our compound in Taegu. It was used to house important military figures and visiting dignitaries. Bill and I were shown to a western-style cottage, complete with real beds. One look at the mattresses and I thought immediately of the beds in the officers' ward on the *General Black*. My first inclination was to climb into one of those beds and go fast asleep. But we had serious work to do, spy work, which frightened me to death.

We attended the club that evening ostensibly to socialize along with the other servicemen. There we found a Korean band going at it and dozens of soldiers and sailors dancing with Korean girls. We drank Cokes and, rather awkwardly, asked two girls to dance with us. Later that evening, when we were sure that no one was watching, we slipped into the club's office and quickly shut the door behind us. Bill went directly to the file cabinet. The whole time, I felt sure that the manager would suddenly appear and that shots would ring out. "So that's why Bill requisitioned carbines," I thought to myself. "I will have to fight the war in a Korean dance club!" Such thoughts coursed through my mind as Bill and I jotted down the hard facts which, eventually, incriminated the manager in question. Our mission completed, we returned to Hialeah Compound and the security of those luxurious beds.

Upon returning to Taegu the following morning (and that trip was no easier on my stomach than the first one had been), Bill turned in his report to the Military Police headquarters. They in turn contacted the proper Korean authorities, and the manager was arrested, tried, and imprisoned. At that point I abandoned my role of "Sy, the spy," never to return to it again.

A Pianist Again

It was May 3rd when I returned to Taegu. After a few days of systematic and productive practicing, my tendinitis subsided considerably. It merely proved what therapists know today — that a healthy physical approach to the piano is the best remedy for this disability. Between then and June 18th, life for me was a series of adventures that would fill a book in themselves. In quick succession, Kenneth and I were discovered not only by high-ranking Americans who worked or were stationed in Taegu, but also by the whole Korean cultural community. For one thing, the American Embassy staff adopted us, in a manner of speaking. Whatever the occasion, such as a visiting dignitary, a member of the top brass returning to the States, or a celebration of a holiday, we were there, not only performing, but also benefiting from meals as elegantly served as they were prepared.

The Embassy occupied several buildings which, formerly, had been a Protestant Mission. The compound stood on the crest of a hill from where one could see green carpeted mountains in every direction. Social functions were held in a modest cottage comfortably furnished in what we called a "stateside" manner. There were two large rooms on the first floor: one of them served as a dining room; the other housed a magnificent six-foot mahogany Steinway. The first time I ran my fingers over the genuine ivory keys, my eyes grew misty. It was out of tune, to be sure, but it had, nonetheless, the warm, resonant tone so characteristic of good Steinways. Besides the thirty pounds of music which I had carried with me since I left the United States, I also had a tuning hammer and dampers for all such eventualities. While I could not by any means do a thorough job of tuning a piano, I was at least able to tune unisons. Within an hour, that Steinway sounded much better. The cultural attachés, Bob Wenck and Art Bunn, were delighted to discover a pianist and tuner all in the same person. They arranged musical evenings for us that were reminiscent of another century. And Art, being the director of the United States Information Service, arranged a concert for Kenneth and me in the USIS library several weeks later.

I have already discussed how rare are the occasions when I felt that I performed my best. On the evening of May 10th, I enjoyed just such an experience. The occasion was an informal recital that Kenneth and I gave at the Embassy to an audience of American music-lovers and Korean musicians. The rich sound of that Steinway piano must have inspired Kenneth as much as it did me, for he, too, outdid himself. I found myself daring to play works such as the *Chromatic Fantasy and Fugue* by Bach and the *Mephisto* Waltz by Liszt with a minimum of practicing. By that time, the pains and stiffness in my arms had vanished entirely, so I felt as though I could play anything at all with the least amount of effort.

Later that evening, a Korean soprano by the name of Kim Bohki (in Korean, last names appear first) asked me to accompany her in some operatic arias. Although she was a lyric soprano with dramatic intensity (the technical name for this particular quality of voice is *lirico spinto*), she actually reached a high *E* flat at the end of one of her arias, a pitch usually out of the range of a lyric soprano. Her vocal technique and her musical interpretations, however, left a great deal to be desired. I concluded that these faults were mostly due to a lack of proper teaching, so I took it upon myself to coach her privately. Although I was not then, nor am I now, an authority on vocal technique, I was able to help her considerably. As all performers soon discover, having a clear musical concept is the first step in controlling technique, whether you are a singer or an instrumentalist. In other words, musicians ought first to respond emotionally to music's language and then make a physical connection to those responses. Not all performers, of course, can do this successfully. And this is where a good teacher can be extremely helpful — merely by observing the physical counterpart to musical feeling. In Kim Bohki's case, I observed that she had no center of support for her vocal production, and that her mouth was moving "all over the place." But before I discussed her physical problems, I addressed myself to interpretive matters. By employing musical logic, I helped her not only to sculpt the individual phrases of her arias, but, more importantly, to create large musical ideas by relating one phrase to another. Having educated her musical responses, I then made suggestions of a purely physical nature, such as the following: "Allow the floor to hold you up; support your upper torso by gently contracting the muscles in your buttocks (this, as one might imagine, brought wary looks on her part!); keep your shoulders down at all times; hold your head erect and do not lower and raise your chin for low and high tones, respectively." After a few more coaching sessions, Kim Bohki sang like a true professional.

To return to the Embassy, one of the guests that evening was Major Hue, the aide to the commander-in-chief of the Korean army, General Lee. He was so impressed with our performances that he decided right then and there to arrange a recital for Kenneth, Kim Bohki, and me in the Munwha

Kok Chung, a large theater in Taegu. By the following morning, the date had been set for June 16th. Since the auditorium served as a movie theater throughout the day and into the night, the concert had to take place at 9 AM. It would be a free concert and open to Koreans and Americans alike.

Debut at EUSAK

Kenneth and I made our debut at the EUSAK theater on June 14th. Performers who enter major competitions often speak about them as being life and death situations. They mean, of course, their ability to survive the superhuman challenge of performing difficult works under the most stringent circumstances. With the EUSAK concert, Kenneth and I would, in fact, be auditioning for our lives. For accordingly to our agreement, if the soldiers did not take to our presentation, Lieutenant Sporup would have no justification for keeping us in Special Services. One can imagine, then, the anxiety we experienced both before the concert and during the playing itself.

The concert had all of the trappings of a major debut; posters were circulated throughout the camp, and Bill Groover prepared beautifully printed programs which he personally handed out as the soldiers filed into the theater. I even found an excellent Korean tuner, a Mr. Chai Moon Ho, who made that piano sound like a Steinway. After working for hours on the instrument, he refused to take money from me. I secretly stuffed some American currency into his pocket, anyway. I also bought him an entire box of Nestle's chocolate bars from the local PX for his three children. He was moved almost to tears by these gifts. Mr. Chai subsequently became an invaluable aid to me, not only in tuning the pianos on which I had to perform, but also in supervising the moving of them. In planning the format of the program itself, we decided to include Captain Ben Denton, a baritone, who worked in Special Services at EUSAK. He had a beautiful voice and sang with the deepest expression.

I began the program with the *Wanderer* Fantasy by Schubert, a twenty minute piece consisting of four continuous movements. Because of its episodic nature and relentless technical demands, the Fantasy is considered one of the most challenging pieces in the repertory. Unless the performer infuses each and every measure of the piece with the greatest intensity of feeling, the work can tax the concentration of the most sophisticated audience. For all of these reasons, my decision to play this work to soldiers who were mostly uninitiated in music was downright chancy. My very life depended upon their favorable response. Yet I had faith in my ability to win over the soldiers. Moreover, I was tired of always playing the pieces I have mentioned which assured immediate success. Now with the advantage of a grand piano, properly tuned and regulated, I felt the need to challenge myself, and at the same time to elevate my audience, by programming one of the major works of the piano repertory. Besides, having had afternoons off for practicing, I felt in excellent shape, both musically and pianistically. This gave me the confidence to tackle such a warhorse.

Fortunately, I had made the right decision. For some two hundred soldiers in attendance sat transfixed throughout the Fantasy. After the final *C* major chords, they applauded so loud, and so long, that I had finally to refrain from bowing for fear of delaying the rest of the program. Kenneth and Captain Denton performed magnificently. I became aware, though, that playing solos and accompanying other musicians on the same program can be extremely fatiguing. When Kenneth came onstage to perform his final piece, I felt more inclined to crawl into my bunk than to play the introduction to a violin solo.

At the end of the concert, which had lasted approximately an hour and a half, the soldiers gave us a standing ovation. The applause continued until each one of us had performed two encores. Both Lieutenant Sporup and Bill Groover were ecstatic over our success. Indeed, we had passed the audition. According to the terms of the wager I had made with Lieutenant Sporup, Kenneth and I would now be sent on a concert tour. We would perform for all of the United Nations troops in areas where civilian entertainers were forbidden to go — namely, on the front lines.

Near Tragedy

Two days after our EUSAK concert, we were to perform at the Munwha Kok Chung. There was always a question of a suitable piano, and here, Major Hue used his influence to my good advantage: I received permission to move the borrowed piano from EUSAK to the Munwha Kok Chung before returning it to the Korean MP school. Having already encountered the difficulties involved in moving a grand piano, I asked for twelve men this time in order to ease my task as much as possible.

Post-concert fatigue found me utterly spent the following morning when the truck pulled up to the EUSAK theater. As I greeted the men in the back of the truck, my heart sank: I counted only six short and weak-looking laborers whose combined strength would not be equal to the task. Once again, I would have to bear the brunt of the piano's weight. Getting the piano onto the truck posed no problem whatsoever. But when we arrived at the Munwha Kok Chung, we discovered that the scheduled movie had already begun, and that the theater was filled with people. The only entrance available to us was a veritable obstacle course. The piano would have to be maneuvered up several steps and down a narrow, circuitous passageway along the left side of the auditorium. To make matters worse, the dolly, which formerly had been so helpful, was simply not available on that morning. Instead, we had to settle for a series of pipes on which we rolled the piano forward, inch by inch. Every few feet we held the piano stationary while some of the laborers moved the rear pipes to the front, thereby making a continuous platform of rolling pipes.

We encountered mishaps almost at once: while we were rolling the piano off of the truck, the pedal shaft split to smithereens. Faithful Mr. Chai, who met me at the theater, assured me not to worry. He would repair the damage. Later, in the passageway itself, the rear of the piano suddenly slipped off of the pipes, and the piano fell onto my right toe. Fortunately, the helpers were alert enough to lift the piano up before its full weight caused me serious injury. But now disaster struck. We had one more narrow doorway to negotiate before we reached the backstage area. Whether one of the pipes became dislodged, or whether the floor was uneven, I cannot say for sure. I only know that the piano suddenly teetered over to one side and pinned my left wrist against the wall of the corridor. I screamed so loudly that some theater-goers came rushing out of a side door to see what the disturbance was all about. Instinctively, I pushed against the piano with my right arm while my helpers did everything that they could to right the piano again. But the damage had been done. I feared that my wrist had been broken, as it was already beginning to swell. Fortunately, though, it proved only to be bruised, and with the help of ice packs and a sling, both of which I used until the moment I walked out onto stage the following morning, I regained the use of my hand in time for our concert in Taegu.

In spite of the early morning hour, the theater was overflowing with Korean music lovers. People stood three and four abreast in the aisles. Some mothers had brought their infants and even nursed them during the playing and singing. Nerves were running high that morning. Kenneth and I were exhausted from the concert at EUSAK, and Kim Bohki was not exactly a seasoned performer. Besides all of this, everyone was on tenterhooks because of my injury. And well they might have been. For my left wrist was noticeably swollen, and the pain persisted throughout the performance. This made the left-hand passages of Liszt's *Mephisto* Waltz feel like one more obstacle course.

"No rest for the weary," as they say. At 8:45 AM the following morning, a two-and-a-half ton truck and ten Korean laborers, this time, pulled up to the backstage door of the Munwha Kok Chung. With the help of the dolly, it was now a relatively easy task to load the piano onto the

277

Clasping hands with Lee Eneh outside of her home
in Taegu, with her children nearby.

truck. We then picked up Mr. Chai and drove to the MP school to return the piano to its home — much to my relief.

Lee Eneh

There were now three days left before Kenneth and I were to begin our tour of Korea. During that time, we gave our promised concert for the Korean soldiers at the MP school. On the following day, I had the honor of meeting and playing for one of Korea's most distinguished pianists, Lee Eneh. The meeting took place at the American Embassy. She was a tiny woman and had the hunched-over look of a person suffering from osteoporosis. Her hair was jet black and she wore horn-rimmed glasses. She spoke with a deep, authoritative voice, so that even before I played for her, I had the feeling that I was in the presence of a very knowledgeable and experienced pianist. Indeed, she proved herself to be all of these things. I played the *Wanderer* Fantasy for her from the beginning to the end. The whole time, she sat to my right, poring over the score. Her comments afterwards were deeply perceptive. In fact, she put me to shame by pointing out some details of interpretation and pedaling which I had overlooked. When our musical session was over, a Colonel Anderson drove us back to Lee Eneh's home. Immediately upon opening the front door, she called out some orders to the occupants. I glimpsed several people hastily removing babies and mattresses from the floors of two small rooms. She then graciously beckoned to me to enter her humble home. I was wide-eyed at what I saw. There were two rooms, each approximately nine by twelve feet in dimension. In one of them stood two large grand pianos and an upright. As she told me, she had bought them in Germany when she was a student there. Later, she had them shipped to Seoul. During the invasion, she moved from Seoul to her present address in Taegu, the pianos being the only things she was able to salvage. This latest move, however, had taken a heavy toll on the instruments: the Hamburg Steinway had broken strings, and the Bechstein had a broken pedal shaft. To make matters worse, five years of poor health had interrupted her performing and teaching careers. As a result, she could not afford to repair her beloved instruments. She wept as she related this story; and it pained me to hear her apologize for the poor condition of her pianos.

The following day, I knew exactly what I had to do. I went directly to Lieutenant Sporup with all the details of Lee Eneh's sad story. I knew, of course, that he would help me carry out my plan. He arranged for a jeep to drive me to Mr. Chai's home. Mr. Chai and I then went to Mrs. Lee's studio where Mr. Chai spent all of that day and part of the next restoring her pianos. I told him that I would pay whatever it cost, my sole concern being that Lee Eneh should have workable pianos again. As Mr. Chai went about his magic, replacing strings, repairing the pedal shaft, tuning the strings over and over again, and regulating the actions of those two pianos, Lee Eneh wept quietly. The results were gratifying beyond measure: the pianos functioned perfectly and Lee Eneh began to perform and to teach again.

THE TOUR

On June 17th, Kenneth and I met with Lieutenant Sporup and Bill Groover to discuss the final details of our tour. Lieutenant Sporup: "I don't intend to overbook you. After all, I don't want to deplete your energies altogether." Bill Groover: "I will insist on a grand piano wherever you play, or an upright with a microphone if a grand isn't available. And if they don't provide you with a page turner when you accompany Kenneth, then I'll tell them, 'no concert!'" But as the tour progressed, none of these well-intentioned stipulations were, or could be, enforced. As far as overbooking was concerned, this, at least, Kenneth and I could control. For we were instructed not to accept a single engagement without contacting Bill first.

Generally speaking, we were prepared to perform two complete programs containing mostly "crowd pleasers," but with a few more esoteric compositions thrown in to raise the level of appreciation among soldier audiences. For publicity purposes, the Special Services office asked a Korean artist who worked for our department to design posters which were then circulated throughout the United Nations forces. Our "Soldier Show," as it was referred to, was entitled *An Hour of Classical Music*. We all agreed that the average soldier could not be expected to sit quietly and listen to serious music for more than an hour. We were to look the part, too. A Korean tailor measured us for gabardine uniforms which were subsequently made in Tokyo and then returned to EUSAK by a special messenger. They arrived a day before we embarked on our tour.

Everyone, it seemed, wished us well and participated in our departure: the quartermaster in the supply warehouse gave us cases of orange and pineapple juice, six cans of tuna, two jars of mayonnaise, four bottles of fruit salad, packages of crackers, soap, gum, and even tooth powder. The Embassy staff made us a farewell roast beef dinner with all of the trimmings. Bob Wenck then drove us to the 25th Evacuation Hospital where a Dr. Purdee supplied us with vitamins, Dramamine, and even sleeping pills. The doctor also gave us six hospital sheets which, we were soon to discover, offered us more comfort and protection than we might ever have anticipated. And so with our duffel bags loaded down, we boarded a train for Pusan at 8:15 AM on June 18th.

On June 30th, in the midst of the tour, we received a communication from Lieutenant Sporup informing us that Walt Thompson, bass-baritone, would now be a part of our soldier show. As we soon discovered, he sang only semi-classical songs. At first, Kenneth and I resented the fact that a third party had been added to our duo. Nor were we eager to compromise the strictly classical format of our programs. But as the tour progressed, it became evident that the mixture of styles appealed to all tastes. And Walt, besides being an amiable fellow, had a beautiful voice and made a strong impression wherever he performed.

I, like most touring pianists, have a large repertory of stories concerning problematic pianos. Pedals falling off in the middle of a performance, black keys snapping off leaving a cavernous hole in the keyboard — such are the calamities that have befallen me on the stage. Once, on a State Department tour, I encountered an upright piano in Brunei Town, Borneo, that had, among other problems, a faulty spring on a treble key. As a result, the key remained depressed, resting, as it were, in its key bed. Absurd as it may seem, that one faulty key loomed up as the most important one of the eighty-eight. To a pianist playing a full recital, one sticking key can become so maddening that you find yourself anticipating the problem long before you even come to it. I took the piano apart and transplanted the spring from the highest key in the treble — a key that I did not have to use in that recital — to the faulty key in question. This operation, complex for me, necessitated my having to stay up half of the night. But whatever problems I encountered on those tours were paltry in comparison with the ones I met in Korea. With all of Lieutenant Sporup's and Bill Groover's good intentions, the piano situation, especially, was deplorable: pianos so out of tune that the depression of a single key would produce a chord that defied analysis; pianos with broken keys and pedals; miniature spinets with reduced keyboards; and, occasionally, *no piano at all*, so that anything faintly resembling a piano would be moved to the site of a concert at the last moment, leaving me no time to tune a sea of discords or to adjust multitudinous action malfunctions.

On a more positive note, I improved my performing skills considerably by having to perform as many as three concerts a day, and always in different situations — in concert halls and schools for Korean audiences, in Service Clubs, in officers' clubs, on the backs of trucks, on a hospital ship, and in open fields on the front line. In fact, I soon achieved what I had thought was impossible — namely, that "at home" feeling in front of audiences. There was one other thing from which I benefited — another sort of basic training, so to speak: I learned to speak in public for the first time. For I had taken it upon myself to make some introductory remarks to our audiences, and to give a running commentary about each piece on the program. As a civilian, I had always shied away from public speaking. But on tour as a soldier, it was not long before I discovered that I not only spoke quite well in public, but more surprisingly, I even enjoyed it.

On the Front Lines

Touring the front lines had its risks, as well as its hardships. To begin with, Kenneth, Walt, and I were flown into various areas on three separate L-19's, single-engine airplanes, these being the only size airplanes that could land on the short, improvised airstrips near the front lines. To my eyes, the names of all of those units on our itinerary sheet looked more like a military code than a list of concert engagements. Included among them were the 45th Division at Kwandae-ri, the 180th Regiment at Hwanchon, the 700th Ordinance, IX Corps, "A" Battery-92nd Armored Field Artillery, also called "The Red Devils." Although I always fortified myself with Dramamine before the flights, the bumpy rides over the endless stretches of Korean hills at low altitudes invariably left me more of a candidate for a hospital bed than a concert stage. Occasionally, there were terrifying moments during landings when the pilots would miscalculate the short runways and have to pull up at the last moment. Such maneuvers played havoc with our stomachs, not to mention our nerves.

All of our flights were arranged by Air Force Sergeant Johnny Simpson, who happened to be at Service Club #1 in Pusan when we performed there. He looked more like a Hollywood movie star than an Air Force Sergeant. His manner was all warmth and cheer, so that when he spoke to you, you had the feeling of having always been his friend. I remember that he was smoking a pipe at the time that he introduced himself. When I casually mentioned that I too had smoked a pipe as a teenage boy, he immediately gave me his pipe as a present. That was the beginning of a long and cherished friendship which extended into civilian life. A music-lover and an intelligent, sensitive person, Johnny had our itinerary in hand at all times and would surprise us by appearing at airplane strips and even at train stations when we would arrive. He simply could not get enough of our music-making.

Some ten years later, we met in Houlton, Maine, where Johnny was living at the time and where I was scheduled to give a concert. Then some years after that, when I thought that I had lost track of him, I happened to wander into an antique shop in Freeport, Maine, a town about an hour away from my home in South Bristol. The young woman in charge of the shop suddenly approached me and asked if I was Seymour Bernstein. She introduced herself as Beth, and told me that she and Johnny had been married for several years. She recognized me from a photograph which Johnny had in his possession, a reproduction of which appears in this book. The following day, Johnny was at my door in South Bristol. It was a reunion noisy enough to echo from one cove to another. But alas, only a year later, his wife telephoned me in New York City to say that Johnny, who worked as a salesman, had been killed in an automobile accident. I have never recovered from the shock of losing my dear friend, who was not even forty at the time of his death. Seeing his photograph now reawakens the joyous moments we shared, and a host of other memories associated with Korea.

To return to those harrowing flights into units on the front lines — once on the ground, we were met by a half ton truck with a canvas top. Each corps* had one spinet piano assigned to it which we used for all of our concerts within that area. We loaded the piano onto the back of the truck and strapped it to the steel side supports. Kenneth, Walt, and I sat on a bench attached along one side of the truck and pressed our feet against the piano to keep it from careening over. Off the truck went over the potholed and dusty roads. Our drivers seemed not to make the slightest attempt to avoid the shell holes that made the roads a veritable obstacle course. For us, it was like riding a bucking bronco. Once we arrived at our destination, it took hours to regain our equilibrium. Kenneth and Walt, however, always recovered sooner than I did. For they, at least, were not prone to motion sickness. I, on the other hand, was always hopelessly airsick from those harrowing airplane rides, and the added gyrations of those trucks invariably left me in a state that can hardly be described. It is enough to say that the pianos were not the only things that got shaken out of kilter.

The dust in Korea posed a serious problem to all of the troops. It seemed to seep into one's very pores, and it played havoc with the respiratory system. Our sinuses were congested most of the time, and we all walked around with red, swollen eyes. When we climbed down from those trucks, we looked like old men, with gray, stiff hair. Our eyelashes, too, were so thickly coated with dust that we could not fully blink our eyes. Nor did the piano escape a dust bath; the keys and the action became so caked with the thick, grayish stuff that I had to brush them down for an hour or so before tuning the piano.

Everyone who has ever been in Korea knows just how hot and humid

---

* A large tactical unit of combat forces composed of two or more divisions and auxiliary service troops.

In IX Corps, after a sleepless night battling insects.

With Air Force Sergeant Johnny Simpson, right,
who arranged all of our flights in Korea.

the months of July and August can be. Imagine, then, what it was like to perform three concerts a day in open fields with temperatures that often soared well above 100 degrees Fahrenheit. Hours of exposure to the broiling sun without any protection whatsoever seemed to turn our skin into scorched parchment. And the reflection of the sun upon the white keys gave me a perpetual headache. As there was always the danger of enemy shells landing on us, we placed the piano at the foot of a hill as a precautionary measure. The soldiers sat along the slope of the hill giving the impression of an amphitheater. Needless to say, attendance at those concerts was not obligatory. Those men sat and listened to us merely because they wanted to. It was here that we made countless converts to the classics among men who had never heard a single note of serious music before. Once, for example, a soldier who was perhaps from the hill country approached Kenneth after one of our performances and blurted out the following in the thickest drawl imaginable: "If ah evah heah y'all play that junk music stuff, ah'll break yaw fiddle ovah yaw head!"

Danger stalked us everywhere. But I, having an insatiable appetite for adventure, simply refused to recognize just how precarious matters were. My bold and rather foolish excursion around the Hwanchon reservoir during our stay with the 180th Regiment illustrates just how reckless I was. The unit was some ten miles away from the MLR (the main line of resistance), and the scars of the war were everywhere — burned out buildings, demolished bridges, and craters in the roads where shells had landed. These things ought to have been sufficient warning that the area was dangerous. Yet, one afternoon, I decided to take a walk into the mountains and photograph the reservoir from a high vantage point. Along the way, I passed a tombstone engraved with Korean symbols. It seemed to make the perfect composition for my photograph — the tombstone in the foreground, and the reservoir beyond. I must have spent a half hour or so walking around the tombstone and photographing the scene from every angle. When I later returned to the unit and related my adventure to one of the officers, he blanched: "Don't you know that this entire area is mined? The North Koreans know of our curiosity, and before they retreated from this area they rigged up booby traps around every landmark which they thought would attract us." He knew about that tombstone, and he told me that there were live grenades buried in the earth all around it. Fortunately for me, the rains had washed layers of sand over them. But according to that officer, I was lucky to have escaped with my life. After that incident, I never gave into my curiosity again — at least not while I was in the army.

Funereal Explosions

There were dramatic moments, too, moments which are indelibly etched in my memory. When we arrived at the 10th F.A. Battalion, for instance, six eight-inch howitzers were firing alternately. As soon as the sixth one went off, the first began the sequence all over again. It seemed that all hell had broken loose. The noise was deafening, and the earth trembled as though we were in the midst of an earthquake. Today, of course, missiles have replaced those big guns. But in those days, the statistics associated with eight-inch howitzers boggled the imagination. To begin with, they had a firing range of 10.8 miles. They were, in fact, the largest weapons used in the Korean war. Each gun weighed eighteen tons, and the shells that they fired weighed two hundred pounds apiece. The firing ceased only long enough for our performance, and commenced again immediately afterwards. One did not have to be a war expert to know that a bombardment of such intensity was not an ordinary occurrence. Kenneth and I concluded from this that the unit would soon be under attack, and that the firing was intended to destroy as many of the enemy and as much of their supplies as possible in advance of the assault. But as we soon discovered, this was not the case at all. The colonel in charge of the unit had ordered the firing in retaliation for the recent deaths of a lieutenant and a sergeant. Functioning as forward observers, they had been killed that very morning by a direct hit from a mortar shell. The lieutenant had been particularly loved and respected by the men in that unit. While Walt sang Albert Hay Malotte's setting of "The Lord's Prayer" (I have always enjoyed playing the expressive piano accompaniment to that song), and Kenneth and I performed Schubert's *Ave Maria*, many men wept openly. After the concert, we wept along with them — not only for the lieutenant and the sergeant, but for the misery of war and for the longing we all felt to be united again with our families and loved ones.

The fact was, Kenneth, Walt, and I were always potentially in danger of having to fight along with everyone else. Our safety, then, was merely a question of our being in the right place at the right time. Being targeted or overrun by the enemy was a constant worry, especially when we were at the First Marine Division. There, while I sat on an improvised stage in the middle of an open field playing Chopin's Polonaise in A flat, shells were screaming over my head continually. The situation was, I believe, similar to that in which the great English pianist Dame Myra Hess found herself, performing concerts in London during the Blitz. Perhaps for me, as for Dame Myra, the only thing that mattered was surviving the performance. My concentration was such that it actually blocked out my fear and even the screeching sounds of those shells. Later, however, when

I reflected upon just how dangerous that situation really had been, I wondered how I was able to perform at all.

Our living quarters ranged from luxurious to almost subhuman. When we performed in embassies, we were put up in beautiful homes. But on the front lines, we lived in crude tents. During July, those tents, like everything else, were covered with dust. During the rainy season, which lasted for the greater part of August, all of that dust turned to mud, and the roads became almost impassable. I remember, in particular, one truck ride to the 120th Engineer Battalion. The truck had to climb mountains of mud at a fifty-five degree angle with a fifty foot drop on one side. Kenneth, Walt, and I, sitting in the back of the truck, had one foot on the piano and the other ready to jump out at a moment's notice. When our driver had finally maneuvered the truck over the mountains, he had to face yet another obstacle — that of crossing over several dangerously swollen streams. We could feel the truck inching its way against the fierce currents, and we surely expected to be swept away at every turn in the road. It was evening by the time we arrived at our destination. Although the ordeal of that trip left me totally spent, I had still to requisition some soldiers to help me unload the piano. I then set about tuning and regulating it as best as I could. Nothing else but my conditioned reflexes (the automatic pilot) enabled me to play the concert that evening. I was so numb with fatigue that I could not consciously control any aspect of my playing whatsoever. Instead, I simply allowed my fingers to activate the keys, seemingly by themselves.

The floor of our tent that night was, like the roads we had traversed, a sea of mud. We took off our shoes and socks at the door, and with the aid of a dim flashlight waded barefoot through the deep, squelching mud to our bunks. Then, sitting on the edge of our bunks, we cleaned the mud off our feet with rags. Ordinarily, we would have draped mosquito netting over our bunks, but on that occasion, there was none available. This is where Dr. Purdee's hospital sheets showed their worth. We improvised frames of wire and then draped the sheets over them. Although we could hardly breathe, we at least did not suffer the bites and buzzings of the hordes of ravenous insects which flew and crawled all around us.

I had another valuable object in my possession — a tiny gasoline stove that my brother-in-law, Saul Armm, had sent me from home. As he wrote to me, that stove had been indispensable to him during his own stint in the army during World War II. The stove, approximately six inches square and four inches high, served a double function: we used it to heat water in our helmets for washing, and we also used it for cooking. For it seemed that we never got enough to eat. By bedtime, especially, Kenneth, Walt, and I were always starving. Thanks to the care packages my mother and sisters sent, my buddies and I were never without food. It was quite common, for instance, for me to sauté canned lobster meat in margarine and then throw in a can of cream of mushroom soup — my own version of lobster thermidor. When we had devoured the last of my mother's canned offerings, an extra concert for the officers would result in some leftover chicken, or a dozen eggs and a loaf of bread from the cook. I would then fill my helmet with water, light my stove, and wait an hour or so till the water was hot enough to boil the eggs. To hungry soldiers in a battle zone, sliced hard boiled egg sandwiches could be just as delectable a meal as a dinner at Lutèce.

Laundry and clothing maintenance posed no problem whatsoever. There were always *boy-sans*, as we called them, living around each camp — young boys whose parents had either been killed or were missing in the war. For the equivalent of ten cents, these *boy-sans* did our laundry, mended our clothes, and straightened out our bunk areas. A few boys endeared themselves to us to such an extent that we had to exercise the greatest restraint to keep from adopting them. I had a particularly close relationship with one such *boy-san*, Tony, who worked at EUSAK in Taegu. When our Special Services unit moved to another location, Tony was sent to an orphanage. Near the time of my discharge, I visited him at the orphanage to say goodbye. Even today, I am filled with profound sadness when I remember our farewell hug and that forlorn and desperate look in his eyes as I walked away from him for the last time.

The POW Compounds at Koje-Do

The tour afforded us the unique opportunity of traveling from one end of Korea to the other — from the 38th parallel to the island of Koje-do situated off of the southern tip of Korea. Seeing the white sandy beaches and the tropical growths, one might have thought that this was a South Sea island paradise. Yet Koje-do held all the prisoner-of-war compounds, and the problems facing the UN troops in controlling the prisoners made the island as far from being a paradise as any place could be. During the second week of July, we performed here at an officers' club and for the personnel of a counter-intelligence unit.

On the day of our arrival at Koje-do, one of the counter-intelligence officers took us to a building called "the Black Shack." There we were shown slides depicting life in the prison compounds as it existed once our so-called "Police Action" began. We learned of the major problem facing General Boatner and his staff — that of persuading the POWs to leave the buildings where they were housed and submit to being interviewed. Because their leaders had convinced them that they would be killed after being interviewed, they were terrified of the Americans. In a desperate attempt to protect themselves, the prisoners improvised weapons out of whatever they could find, such as bunk frames, and were prepared to defend themselves to the end. Finally, the Americans had to resort to using tanks in order to break up their resistance. Faced with the real threat of death, the POWs came pouring out of their billets screaming, "Please don't cut our heads off!" Only when their leaders were taken into custody and placed in billets away from their men could our MPs finally win the confidence of those prisoners. In time, they did submit to interrogation, and peace returned to the compounds.

Strange Illness and Miraculous Cure

On July 18th, we left Koje-do for Masan, a city approximately one hundred and fifty miles west of Pusan. At the Koje-do pier, we boarded a small freighter that shuttled between Koje-do and Pusan harbor. The freighter was so old and in such poor condition that we marveled at its ability to move at all. Every turn of the propellers sent groans and convulsions throughout the entire ship. "She's coming apart at the seams," one soldier commented as he looked over the rail and gazed at the ship's rusty sides. The freighter had no seats at all. All of the passengers, civilians and soldiers alike, stood elbow-to-elbow against the rails for three hours. As it turned out, we would have stood there anyway, even if there had been seats. For the scenery on the Sea of Japan bordering the eastern coast of Korea was breathtakingly beautiful. The water, looking like a sheet of aquamarine marble, was extremely calm, so that I did not experience even a second of seasickness. I remember a similar voyage across the Inland Sea of Japan during my tour of Japan in 1960.

Once in Pusan, we were literally stuffed into the back of a mail truck along with four other soldiers and approximately two dozen mail bags. Off the truck zoomed, making the two-and-a-half hour trip to Masan in less than an hour and a half. The way the driver careened around the mountain passes, we wondered if we would arrive at all. To make matters worse, the truck had only one door in the back and a tightly fitted canvas top. The stifling heat and humidity and the complete lack of air soon began to take its toll on us. I fell so violently ill that poor Kenneth was ready to stop the driver at one word from me. As on all of my other trips, however, I somehow managed to survive, and by six that evening, I felt well enough to perform. The concert went extremely well, and we were quite prepared to follow it up with a second program on the following evening. But this was not to be. My diary explains why:

July 19th, Saturday

I didn't sleep a wink last night. This was most unusual because I was totally exhausted after that harrowing ride to Masan. I got out of my bunk at around 7 AM with a splitting headache and sore eyes. I forced myself to walk to the mess hall where I drank a cup of coffee and downed a half of a bowl of cereal. But eating only made me feel worse, and I couldn't wait to get back to bed. I waited it out for an hour or so, and when I did not feel any better, I went to the dispensary. The orderly on duty there didn't so much as take my temperature. He simply gave me two APCs (something equivalent to aspirin) and sent me back to the Quonset. By 1 PM, my head felt like a blazing inferno, and I knew I was in trouble. I went back to the dispensary, and this time, the orderly handed me a codeine pill and a cup of water. He told me to come back at 1:30 to see the doctor. In spite of the codeine, my headache persisted. So back to the dispensary I went — trip number three. The doctor on duty was not much better than the orderly. He made no attempt whatsoever to examine me. He simply stuck a thermometer in my mouth which registered 100 degrees. The remedy? — two more APCs and the assurance that I would be all right for the concert that evening.

But I was not all right. In fact, my headache got so bad that I had to cancel the concert. Ken knew, of course, that I would never cancel a concert unless I was at death's door. So he rushed to the dispensary intent on persuading the doctor to come to me. The doctor, however, could not leave his post, so I dragged myself back to the dispensary for the fourth time, thinking surely that the doctor would examine me more thoroughly. Yet the only thing he did was to take my temperature again. That it had risen to 101 degrees seemed not to disturb him in the slightest: "Go back to bed," he said, rather perfunctorily. "If you're not better in the morning, come back." As I stood up to leave, I felt extremely dizzy and had to grab the nearest chair to stabilize myself. The doctor came rushing over to me and helped me onto a cot in his office. Considering my condition anew, he suggested that I had better spend the night there. And then it started. As I lay on the cot, I felt a strange tingling in my arms and legs — the kind of feeling you get when a limb falls asleep. Then my arm muscles drew up until my fingers were locked against my shoulders. Next, my legs stiffened and turned inward, and finally, my stomach muscles contracted to such an extent that I could hardly breathe at all. Needless to say, I panicked. "So this is it," I thought. "I have polio, and I'm going to die in Korea far away from home."

291

Seeing my entire body contort in this way, the doctor had his own panic attack. He rushed to the telephone, dialed a special number, and fairly shouted at whoever was on the other end: "Emergency! Emergency! I have a very sick man, here. I need a truck, a stretcher, and three MP guards immediately. We have to get him to the 21st Evacuation Hospital in Pusan." Ken rushed back to the Quonset to pack up all of our gear. There was no need for two people to accompany me, so Walt remained behind. The truck and the MPs were on the scene in minutes. They put me on a stretcher and carried me out to the truck. In around fifteen minutes, my paralysis began to wear off. One of the MPs noticed my fingers moving and placed a cigarette in my hand. I don't smoke, of course, but I did so on that occasion. In all truth, I was convinced that I was going to die. Moreover, the trip to Pusan took two and a half hours over guerilla infested roads, which is why the MPs were riding along with me. "If the paralysis doesn't do me in," I thought, "then certainly we'll all be killed in an ambush."

What a relief it was to arrive safely in Pusan! By the time I was brought to the hospital, the paralysis had left completely. The doctor on duty there explained to me that my muscle spasms were due to exhaustion from the severe headache. He sent me to Ward 15 and joined me there shortly afterwards. Being severely dehydrated by that time, I was given an I.V. feeding, which took two hours to complete. I assumed that it was supposed to make me feel better. But if anything, my headache merely increased. And once again, I did not sleep the entire night.

The following morning, my eyes were so sore that the electric bulb directly above my bed felt like a dagger piercing my brain. Even the voices of the nurses felt like arrows shooting into my head. Someone brought me a tray of food. But eating was totally unthinkable. Just the thought of it made me nauseated. I simply lay in my bed groaning and with my eyes closed until the doctor came over to my cot. He diagnosed me as having mononucleosis. In fact, he told me that all of the men on Ward 15 were laid up with the same thing. Later, however, another doctor told me that we all had a strange blood disease that defied analysis — some virus, perhaps, that was indigenous to Korea.

What I am now going to describe seems far-fetched, and yet it actually occurred. At approximately 1 PM, I fell into a deep sleep — the first sleep I had had in two days. When I awakened at 2:30 PM, my headache was completely gone and I was ravenously hungry. The nurses gaped at me in disbelief as I gulped down every morsel of food on my tray. Shortly afterwards, Kenneth came to visit me. He seemed not the least surprised that I had recovered. "I prayed this afternoon with a Christian Science healer," he told me. "So of course you're all right!" I was astonished at this. Was I living proof that miracles can occur? I like to think so. For I know from the doctors that it ought to have taken approximately three weeks to recover from whatever it was that I had. Johnny, who faithfully stood by my bed throughout most of the day, returned for another visit that evening. He gave me a beautiful pen and pencil set, "to celebrate your miraculous recovery." He's simply a great guy.

By the following morning, I was out of bed, to the utter amazement of the doctors. They went over me with a fine toothcomb and could not find a thing wrong with me. So by noon, I was discharged from the hospital. A few hours later, and thanks to Johnny's skill in arranging flights, Kenneth, Johnny, and I were on our way to Taegu. Back at the Special Services office, Lieutenant Sporup, secretly happy to see me alive, scolded me, nonetheless, for what he assumed was the cause of my illness: "How many times have I told you not to eat Korean food!" Fortunately, I had two witnesses with me to verify the fact that Spam, and only Spam in all of its forms, had been my staple for at least a week before my illness.

Only recently, while reminiscing with Kenneth Gordon about our adventures, I discovered the truth about that strange illness. It seems that the seriousness of it had been hidden from me. I did not have mononucleosis at all, but rather "Korean" hemorrhagic fever (later dubbed Hanta virus after a river in Korea), a viral infection passed on by the saliva and urine of rodents. According to a medical journal, recovery is usual, but fatal cases can occur. The disease became known to American medicine when it struck United Nations troops serving in Korea in 1951, hence the term "Korean." The doctor on duty told Kenneth that my temperature had soared above 105 degrees, that I had slipped into a coma, and not a deep sleep as I had recorded in my diary, and that he was not sure I would make it. Knowing all of this now makes it seem all the more miraculous that I recovered so quickly.

I have often searched for a rational explanation for my cure. There have, in fact, been many times throughout my life when I was violently ill one moment, and then completely recovered the next. As I often explain to my family and friends, I have no time to be sick. So instead of drawing out the symptoms, I seem to concentrate them in a brief span of time, and

The Hindu festival *Thaipusan*, in Kuala Lumpur, Malaya, in 1960.
This young man has just driven a skewer through his tongue.
(Photo by Seymour Bernstein)

then exorcise them from my body. But the paralysis and blood disease mentioned above were far more serious than anything else I have ever experienced. Did the prayers said on my behalf actually effect a miracle?

Speaking about miracles — in 1961, while on a State Department tour in Kuala Lumpur, Malaysia, I attended a Hindu religious festival called *Thaipusan*. It is a day similar to Yom Kippur, the Jewish day of atonement. The *Thaipusan* ritual took place along the banks of a river which was sacred according to Hindu belief. Nearby were some two hundred stone steps leading up the side of a mountain to the holy *Batu* caves. Inside these caves sat the chief Hindu priests, who performed the religious rites.

When I arrived at the scene, camera in hand, small groups of young Hindu men clad in loincloths had already gathered in a clearing alongside the river. They held long silver skewers in their hands. Led by older priests, they chanted for some fifteen minutes while breathing in the rising fumes of burning incense. They paused now and then to smear the white ash of the incense over their faces and bodies. First one and then another of the young men fell into a trance. Their bodies became rigid, and their friends, fully clothed, had to hold them up to keep them from falling. As I continued to watch with a mixture of horror and fascination, the young men, now in a deeper trance, drove skewers into one cheek and out the other, and then directly through their tongues. Finally, after having driven many other skewers through the pinched skin of their torsos, they rushed up hundreds of stone steps and into the *Batu* caves where high priests removed the skewers. That not a drop of blood was shed during these gruesome enactments was astonishing enough. But even more astonishing was the fact that there were no discernible holes in the cheeks of these young men after they emerged from the caves.

Seeing this, I was prepared to believe anything at all — even the miracles I read about in the Bible. I was, after all, no stranger to the extraordinary powers of the mind. For is not the Sonata Op. 111 by Beethoven a true miracle of the human mind? And is it not also a miracle that a pianist can assimilate and then perform it? My amazing recovery in that hospital in Pusan made me a firm believer in ESP and everything else related to parapsychology. It all left me convinced that a particular kind of concentration can have curative powers.

Thousands of people ascend the steps to the Batu caves
during *Thaipusan* in Kuala Lumpur, Malaya.
(Photo by Seymour Bernstein)

Giggles in the Chapel

Whenever we were in Taegu, I offered to play the organ for the Sunday morning services held in the EUSAK chapel. Formerly, Captain Denton had conducted a choir of six soldiers and also sang in it. But now that he had been rotated back to the United States, the chaplain's assistant took over his responsibilities. That he was a poor and inexperienced musician was unfortunate enough. But that he refused to allow the choir members (and I had volunteered to be one of them) to point out a wrong pitch or a wrong rhythm, or to make any constructive suggestions at all, inflamed tempers to the breaking point.

One Sunday morning, I began the service with a Prelude and Fugue by Bach. There was a Wurlitzer electric organ in the chapel complete with pedals and stops — a far cry from that small harmonium on the troop ship. With a little practice and a great deal of deductive reasoning, I was able to draw out of that Wurlitzer organ a fairly acceptable balance of registers, although the poor instrument had no volume to speak of due to an electrical malfunction that no one seemed able to fix. At the end of the service, I joined the choir in the singing of a hymn while the collection was being made. Corwin Gordon, a fine baritone assigned to EUSAK, stood to my left — too close to me, it seemed, for him to maintain his poise as I scooped up to a high *G*. The quality of my hooting falsetto voice might best be described as a foghorn transposed an octave higher. The altogether unearthly sound emanating from my throat was too much for Corwin. He snorted once or twice, and then stopped singing altogether. And I, seeing him convulse out of the corner of my eye, lost my poise as well. I simply lowered my head into my chest and giggled until the hymn's final *Amen*.

As fate would have it, a general and two chaplains, both of them colonels, happened to have chosen that particular Sunday to attend the service. Moreover, they sat in the front row directly in front of the choir — at our feet, as it were. Seeing those officers glaring at us made us giggle all the harder. We took measures to contain ourselves, such as clenching our teeth, holding our breath, and even thinking of tragic circumstances. But nothing helped in the slightest. The giggles persisted while our faces turned beet red. It was one of those situations in which humor and utter shame battled for supremacy. When the service finally ended, everyone filed out without saying a word to us, those high-ranking officers included. Corwin and I were sure that the general would issue a D.R. (delinquency report) against us. For certainly our behavior was unbecoming under any circumstances, but especially in the army. Fortunately, however, the incident passed without repercussions, and Corwin and I had another go at it on the following Sunday. I am happy to say that we behaved quite properly on that occasion. But then, there were no high *G's* for me to negotiate.

Reunions Near the Front

On August 15th, while Kenneth and I were standing in a chow line in the 40th Division, we suddenly came face to face with Robert Lamarchina, the extraordinary cellist with whom we had performed in Tokyo. His name had been placed on the "surplus personnel" list, of all things. (Judging from this army terminology, one might think that he was a piece of baggage!) The next thing he knew, he was assigned to the 40th Division in Korea, where he played the French horn and the glockenspiel in the band, drove a truck, and worked as a projectionist in the company theater. I immediately contacted the Special Services office in Taegu and requested that Bob join us on the tour. My request was granted, and Bob performed with us for the time remaining before his discharge.

On August 18th, I met another person from the past — that monster sergeant from Camp Drake who had made life so miserable for me. Our eyes met across the tables in the mess hall of the 115th Medical Battalion. The tent where we were billeted happened to be near the general's tent. Ironically, this sergeant was assigned to walk guard duty that evening while Kenneth and I slept soundly in our bunks. He knew we were there, of course, and I'm not ashamed to say that I experienced just how sweet revenge can be. The next evening, I saw him standing at attention while the general complimented us after our recital. He had that whipped dog look, which, believe it or not, made me feel sorry for him.

Finally, on September 19th, while I was on R & R (rest and recreation) in Seoul, I met Jerry Jacobs. It was a reunion I shall long remember, for I had last seen him marching away when he received orders for Korea at Camp Drake. He was a civilian, now, and was working as a war correspondent. To see him again, and to know that he had escaped the horrors of combat, lifted my spirits considerably.

Dr. Helen Kim

We also performed at Korean civilian and military schools in Taegu, Pusan, and Seoul. One performance at Ewha University had a special significance to us, for there we had the privilege of meeting Dr. Helen Kim (1899-1970), the school's president and the most prominent woman in Korea. An educator, stateswoman, evangelist, and writer, Dr. Kim received undergraduate degrees in philosophy and education from Wesleyan University in Ohio in 1924, earned a master's degree in literature from Boston University in 1930, and was the first Korean woman to earn a Ph.D.

— from Columbia University in 1931. Her dissertation subject was "Rural Education for the Regeneration of Korea." Subsequently, Dr. Kim was awarded five honorary doctorates. Through her connection to Ewha University as professor, dean, president, and chairman of the board, the school became the largest women's university in the world. A devout Christian and possessed of a missionary zeal, Dr. Kim devoted her entire life to liberating Korean women and converting all Koreans.

Upon meeting Dr. Kim, I was struck by her aristocratic bearing and her dynamic personality. She was short in stature with round, sturdy shoulders, and her expression was one of dignified composure. But her eyes revealed a vibrancy, warmth, and an inner smile which made us feel immediately welcomed and comfortable in her presence. She had straight black hair, the strands of which were fastened neatly at the back of her head with pins. She dressed in the traditional Korean fashion with a flowing floor-length dress and a loose blouse fastened above the waistline. She greeted us in perfect English and immediately led us to the auditorium where the students were already seated and awaiting our performance. Although the school was closed for the summer months, the school girls and some other invited guests had made a special trip to hear us play. To my delight, the school owned an old Mason & Hamlin grand in excellent condition. We began the recital with the Sonata in *D* minor, by Brahms, in what turned out to be our best performance up to that time. The high level of that performance seemed to set the scene for the rest of the recital. On my part, this was partly due to the excellent piano. But generally speaking, Kenneth and I performed our best for Korean audiences.

After the concert, Dr. Kim invited Kenneth and me to her home for dinner. She occupied one wing of an old Korean palace; the rest of the palace had been converted into a museum of Korean art. While she attended to the arrangements for our dinner, she left us in the care of a charming young woman who took us on a tour of the museum. There was an impressive collection of artifacts from the various Korean dynasties: the Shilla (7th to 10th centuries), the Koreyo (10th to 14th centuries), and the Li (14th to 19th centuries). I saw for the first time celadon porcelain with its indescribably beautiful glaze of pale grayish green, the secret of which was lost with the Koreyo dynasty at the end of the fourteenth century. I myself purchased an exquisite celadon water vessel in 1955 while on my first State Department tour in Korea. It is one of my treasures, and now rests majestically on a Japanese black lacquered table in front of the sofa in my New York City studio.

Dr. Kim's home was of a splendor which almost defies description. In fact, it was the most beautiful Asian home I have ever seen. The living room and dining room were combined into one vast area. As she explained to us, half of it was decorated in the Korean style, while the other half was typically Japanese. The former seemed to be more ornate than the latter. As we sat on the floor and engaged in a stimulating discussion about music and politics, a host of servants served us seven Korean specialties — all prepared in our honor. Afterwards, we sat in comfortable chairs and were served coffee and delectable nut cake, which Dr. Kim had baked for us. She then gave Kenneth and me beautiful Korean fans which we treasure to this day.

I have observed that true greatness in people is not usually confined to one talent or to one discipline alone. In the case of Dr. Helen Kim, there seemed to be an aura of greatness about her which showed itself in everything she said and everything she did. It is possible, of course, to glorify important figures to the extent of reading into them qualities which they do not actually possess. But undoubtedly Dr. Helen Kim was one of the truly great figures of our time, and certainly she was one of the most impressive people I have ever met.

The *Repose*

I have as yet barely mentioned the worst aspect of that war — the casualties. Out-and-out attacks, ambushes, and accidents resulted in a huge number of dead and wounded men on both sides of the conflict. A case in point was the area near the Hwanchon reservoir where the 1st, 2nd, and 3rd Battalions were "dug in." This was the area where I foolishly set out on a photographic spree unaware of the live mines and grenades buried in the sand. A battle raged nearby for control of a mountain called "Old Baldy," a strategic location from which one could see for a distance of ten uninterrupted miles. The mountain exchanged hands between the UN forces and the North Koreans more times than I can remember, and reports of those protracted battles made world-wide news daily. The UN forces had suffered as many as three hundred casualties by the time we arrived there. Our three concerts drew an audience of twelve hundred soldiers, most of whom had come from "Old Baldy" itself. They were grimy and fatigued. And while I delivered my introductory remarks, I could see that glazed look of fear and hopelessness in their eyes. Many of those men told us that our concerts offered them the only pleasurable distraction from the anxiety with which they lived from day to day.

Some of the wounded men were flown by helicopter to the United States hospital ship, the *Repose*. This was only one of three hospital ships in service in 1952, the others being the *Haven* and the *Consolation*. The ships rotated on their missions of mercy, docking either in Pusan or

Inchon Harbor and remaining there for several months before sailing on to Japan or to the United States. The depth of the water in Pusan Harbor allowed the ships to pull up directly to the pier. But Inchon Harbor, being more shallow, required them to dock several miles off of the coast.

On September 5th, after playing for the 1st Marine Division, we were driven to "Charlie Dock" at Inchon Harbor in an honest-to-goodness station wagon, the luxury of which we could hardly believe. The leather seats, the suspension system which enabled the vehicle to traverse the bumpy roads with a minimum of discomfort to us, and our facing in the direction of our ride for a change (this meant no motion sickness for me) — all of these things transported us back to civilian life, if only for three hours. After arriving at the dock, we loaded the PA system onto a motor launch and climbed aboard. In approximately ten minutes we saw the great white ship with the huge red cross painted on its side. It looked like a white cloud resting peacefully upon the water.

Once on board, we found ourselves on a luxury liner of the most extravagant sort. Most of the ship was air conditioned — certainly a novelty to us after those stifling months near the front. There were other luxuries, too, luxuries that we had all but forgotten: fresh water instead of that chlorinated "poison" which had been our everyday fare, real butter instead of margarine, and fresh meat instead of Spam. For one of our meals, we were given hot dogs and all of the trimmings. Having been brought up in a kosher home, I was not used to eating dairy products with meat. But on this occasion I actually spread thick butter on my hot dog roll and wolfed it down without the slightest compunction. After that meal, we went to the ship's PX and bought chocolate sundaes topped with real whipped cream, which we ate while sitting out on the deck and watching a spectacular sunset.

All of these luxuries, however, scarcely veiled the sheer horror of what lay below the main deck — namely, the wounded men on that ship. Those who were ambulatory or in wheel chairs managed to attend our concert on the vast upper deck where three hundred folding chairs were lined up row-upon-row. Others in respirators or too wounded to leave their beds listened to us through the PA system. Still others were beyond listening. They would never see home again. Even now, forty years later, the thought of what I saw when the ship's commander took us on a tour of the hospital wards fills me with indescribable grief.

General W. H. Harrison and the Peace Conference

On Saturday, September 6th, we performed at the peace conference at Munsan. Its exact location, on the 38th parallel, the demarcation line between North and South Korea, received a special name which had not existed before — Panmunjom. Lieutenant General W. H. Harrison, the United States representative at the conference, had personally requested us to appear there. Kenneth and I had once performed for the general at Fort Dix during our basic training. At that time, he was a major general, a rank designated by two stars. But on the very day of our appearance at the base camp, the general celebrated his promotion to lieutenant general — a rank designated by three stars. And that was not all. Coincidentally, it was also the general's birthday, and so our concert served as a double celebration for him.

The base camp was constructed in the center of a large apple orchard containing acre upon acre of symmetrically planted trees. Tents were set up in clearings along the way. Each path leading to the tents was named for a military figure. Harrison Lane, for instance, led to the general's tent. Beyond this was a long circus-like tent where our concert took place. It was an ideal setting for a concert. Some seventy-five feet long, the tent had a platform on one end and rows of benches fixed to a wooden floor, divided by a center aisle. The entire structure was built on an incline, as are most concert halls, so that the last row of benches was level with the platform. There were more top brass at the base camp than at any other unit in South Korea. In fact, all the men below the rank of major were considered to be junior officers. It was not surprising, therefore, to be met by a Major Goerke, who introduced himself as the coordinator of the concert. First on our agenda was a meeting with General Harrison himself. But as protocol dictated, Major Goerke had first to introduce us to his superior, a colonel, who, in turn, would make the final introduction to the general. "Oh, you can come along, too, Major Goerke," the colonel said, much to our amusement. The major had a red mustache that seemed to wilt as we approached General Harrison's tent. The colonel went into the tent alone.

To our surprise, General Harrison came out in a T-shirt, of all things. We all snapped to attention, of course, and sported our finest military salutes. At the sight of the general, Major Goerke blanched so noticeably that his red mustache seemed to stand out in relief against his white complexion. The general, however, was all informality and did not even bother to return our salutes. I immediately recognized his friendly smile and the mischievous look in his eyes from my first meeting with him at Fort Dix. He seemed much thinner now, however, and he had the harassed look of someone who was grappling with severe problems. The colonel gave the introductions, and General Harrison shook our hands in the most welcoming fashion. He told Kenneth and me how happy he was to see us

Walt Thompson, Kenneth Gordon, and I pose for a publicity photograph in the 1st Marine Division.

again. Then, looking directly at me, he asked, "What have you all been doing since you left Fort Dix?" "Oh," I replied, "we've already performed approximately one hundred concerts. And we're about to tour the front lines again." "Well," the general said, looking first at the colonel and then at Major Goerke, "we certainly don't have an opportunity to hear this sort of thing very often." Then, fixing his eyes upon Major Goerke, he inquired in a more official voice, "Are all arrangements made for this evening's concert?" With this, the major froze so stiffly at attention that his whole torso seemed to list backwards. "Yes, sir," he answered in a tremulous voice. "The piano is on the stage, sir, and the PA system is all set up." "Fine," the general replied. "I'll see you all this evening." And without so much as giving us the opportunity to salute him, he turned on his heel and retreated into his tent.

While Kenneth and Walt went to the MP tent where we were billeted, I went directly to the improvised concert hall to begin work on the badly out of tune upright piano. I then connected the PA system and set one microphone behind the piano and the other at center stage for my announcements. I then settled down at the piano for an hour of concentrated practicing.

After chow, which consisted of veal roast and cherry pie, one of the finest meals we had on that tour, we went to the tailor shop on the compound to have our uniforms pressed. At 6:40 PM, I went to the tent to check on last minute details. By that time, dusk had settled over the base camp, and I suddenly realized that I had overlooked one very important requirement: lights on the platform. Major Goerke, the epitome of efficiency, rectified the problem immediately. He rushed to the officers' club and requisitioned two floor lamps which we placed at strategic positions on the platform. At exactly 6:50 PM, General Harrison, sporting his three stars for the first time, took his place on one of the wooden benches. He was surrounded by an array of United Nations generals and other high-ranking officers who, like him, had been assigned to the peace conference. At 7 PM sharp, I walked out to the microphone and greeted the audience in my customary fashion.

General Harrison was the first person to reach us after the concert: "I don't have to tell you how enthusiastically your program has been received here. Certainly you could tell this by the applause. Speaking for myself, this was the best birthday present I ever had."

As one might imagine, all of this left Kenneth, Walt, and me in a state of euphoria. We felt privileged to have been a part of the peace conference, and to have shared in General Harrison's double celebration. Later that evening, we were privy to a military secret of major importance. It seemed that a North Korean MP officer, assigned to guarding the northern borders of Panmunjom, had decided to defect to South Korea. He trumped up a story of a spy who had infiltrated the North Korean units. After he ordered his men to fan out in all directions in order to apprehend the spy, the officer calmly walked down the road to the United Nations base camp and gave himself up to the American MPs. It was not long before news of his defection had spread around the world.

On the following day, General Harrison, as a token of his appreciation, asked Major Goerke to escort us around the base camp before our departure from Panmunjom. Among other things, we were shown the general's personal helicopter. A photographer assigned to us shot photographs which subsequently appeared in newspapers distributed throughout the UN forces.

In between these two engagements, and afterwards, as well, life for the concert trio was a constant series of adventures of all sorts — from inspiring moments to situations of unimaginable hardship and danger. The experience of performing for the large contingent of United Nations troops gave me a taste of what audience reactions might be like in other countries. Once, for example, we performed for a thousand Philippine troops in an open field. Each time those men heard a beautiful melody, or an exciting technical passage, they would show their delight by applauding and cheering right in the middle of a piece — exactly as audiences do when they see a gymnast perform impressive feats. As a result, I found myself having to play *forte* in certain *piano* passages just to be heard over their spontaneous but rather noisy show of enthusiasm.

General James A. Van Fleet

The thrill of performing for General Harrison at the site of the peace conference was surpassed only by the concert we gave for General James A. Van Fleet, the commander-in-chief of the Eighth United States Army, Korea — EUSAK. My diary best describes all that transpired on Thursday, September 11, 1952:

> Captain Calvert drove us to General Van Fleet's compound at 6:45 PM. A guard stood watch in front of the door leading to the general's private office. The room was darkened. At first, the guard would not allow us to enter the office even though I told him that we were going to give a concert there, and that I had to tune the piano. "Give a concert? Tune a piano?" he retorted incredulously. "Look soldier, no one goes into this office without a written order!" Captain Calvert then sought out the general's secretary, a master sergeant. He

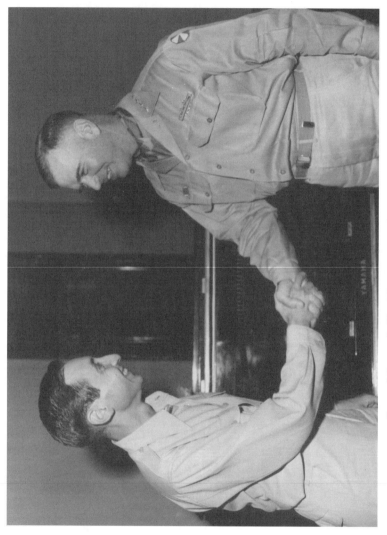

General James A. Van Fleet congratulates us after our concert in his private office in Seoul.

in turn told the guard of our mission. The guard then softened up considerably, turned on the light inside the general's office, and ushered us into the room.

We were bowled over by what we saw. The room was huge, at least by army standards. The general's desk stood at the northwest corner of the room. Directly behind it hung the American flag, the United Nations Flag, and a red flag with four white stars. A black lacquered nameplate inlaid with mother of pearl rested on the edge of the desk. It was a real eye-stopper if I ever saw one. The general's name was emblazoned on it in large gothic letters. A table stood at the northeast corner of the room holding a variety of antique objects and souvenirs, no doubt gifts to the general from the Koreans. There were red taffeta drapes on the windows, and the floor was covered with a large beige rug with two beautifully designed eagles woven into the center of it. The map of Korea in bas-relief hung on the south wall. Photographs of Presidents Truman and Rhee Sungman hung on the north wall. The piano stood directly in front of the map of Korea, where crucial military decisions were made.

After I touched up a few notes on the piano, Ken, Walt, and I (Bob was, for a change, not available) were escorted into an anteroom to await the general's arrival. At exactly 7:40 PM, General Van Fleet, together with approximately ten other high-ranking UN generals, including a three-star Korean general, plus various colonels and lieutenant colonels, walked by the room where we were standing and took their seats on folding chairs set up in the office. A few seconds later the great man himself came into our room. To begin with, Walt was a corporal when he joined our tour. Kenneth and I had by that time been promoted to the rank of Private 1st Class. Perhaps we might even have made corporal were it not for the fact that the army had issued an order freezing all promotions. At any rate, considering our rank, imagine how we felt in the presence of a four-star general! One sight of those four stars and we all froze to attention. Perhaps because musicians have a certain rank of their own, General Van Fleet, like General Harrison before him, would have none of this formality. He ignored our salutes and instead, extended his hand to each one of us in turn. I shall never forget his warm, intense eyes, his equally warm handshake, and his towering figure. He expressed his appreciation to us for coming to his office. Before he joined his guests, he added, "I'm really looking forward to your concert."

Captain Calvert introduced us to the distinguished audience with some general remarks about our past activities in Korea. Quite spontaneously, then, General Van Fleet made his own introduction, one which bespoke his regard for the arts: "These men," he said, "are the best weapons Americans have to offer!" This was greeted by a rousing ovation which, curiously enough, brought me out alone. For as we had planned, I began the program with the 6th Rhapsody by Liszt. Walt sang *Invictus*, and Ken and I then performed *Gypsy Airs* by Sarasate. Then, at that point, I decided to say something to the audience. Imagine me, a Private 1st Class, standing up in front of all of those high-ranking officers. One look at them, and I had all but forgotten the English language. This was certainly no time for the sort of remarks I made to average soldiers. So quite spontaneously, I began to relate some of the experiences we had on tour — among them, my having seen a grand piano being moved down the main street in Pusan. I especially wanted to relate my surprise in seeing the legs of the piano strapped to wooden A-frames on the backs of Korean laborers. But no sooner did I begin the story than I caught sight of the Korean general sitting directly in front of me. "Oh no!" I said to myself, "I'm about to insult the commander in chief of the Korean army — and in the presence of General Van Fleet, no less!" But there was no turning back. I was too far into the story to change its direction. When I got to the part about the A-frames, I mentioned this as diplomatically as I could, adding how remarkable and inventive it was for the Koreans to improvise such means of moving a grand piano. I will always wonder what that Korean general was thinking and if the other men in that room realized my predicament. When I finished the story, there was a moment of silence that implied all too well: "What was that all about?!" At that point, I just wanted to die. Fortunately, however, General Van Fleet saved the day. His eyes suddenly lit up and he emitted the loudest laugh imaginable. Hearing this, all of the other officers burst out laughing. I wanted to crawl under the rug and disappear entirely. But there was still the rest of the concert to perform. I was red with embarrassment when I took my place at the piano again. I played *The Engulfed Cathedral* by Debussy and the all-time favorite — the Polonaise in *A* flat by Chopin. Walt sang "When I Have Sung My Songs" and "Some Enchanted Evening" from *South Pacific*. The latter happened to be General Van Fleet's favorite song. Ken and I then ended the program with *Ave Maria* and "The Hot Canary."

At the end of concert, everyone followed General Van Fleet's example. When he shouted "Bravo!" everyone else joined in. And when he gave us a standing ovation, all of the other officers stood up. The general then introduced us to each officer in the room. He then summoned a photographer who was waiting outside. As he posed with each one of us, I had the feeling that he knew we would treasure those photographs one day. He promised to send them to us together with letters of appreciation. Before he left, he told us how honored he was to have hosted our concert. His humility and his warmth overwhelmed us.

Flowers for the Mama-sans

We were billeted in a lovely house on a residential street of Seoul — a home which the army had requisitioned for visiting USO shows. Servants tended to our every need — young, beautiful women, and older women whom we called *Mama-sans*. And how they took care of us! One would have thought that they were mothers and sisters tending their sons and brothers. Beyond their natural goodness, they, like most Koreans, were particularly grateful to the American GI for supporting the South Korean cause. These women also knew from reading Korean newspapers that we were musicians. Considering all that we represented to them, it was not unusual, therefore, that they treated us with a mixture of awe, gratitude, and affection.

On September 13th we were scheduled to give a concert for the students of a Korean Middle School. To the *Mama-sans* and the younger women, this was a major event — one which demanded extra care and responsibilities. At 7:00 AM, after we had showered and dressed in our freshly laundered fatigues, we went downstairs to the dining room, where we were served a lavish American-style breakfast, complete with bacon and eggs, toast, and griddle cakes. While we ate to our hearts' content, a host of giggling and excited women swooped upon our personal belongings. They pressed our gabardine uniforms, polished our shoes and our belt buckles, and laundered and ironed all the rest of our clothing. When it was time for us to leave, they stood side by side outside of the front door bowing and uttering phrases of good luck in Korean as we passed by.

As at all our other performances for Korean audiences, we were showered with bouquets of flowers afterwards. It took an extra car to carry them and us back to our quarters. All of the women greeted us as though we were conquering heroes returning from battle. The first thing we did was to break off a few choice flowers and insert them into their hair. Next, we presented each one of them with a particularly beautiful bouquet. As

309

one might imagine, all of this elicited *oohs* and *ahs* and embarrassed giggles. They bowed to us in gratitude and promptly rushed about the house gathering vases, bowls, and whatever receptacles they could find to hold the flowers. In an instant, our home was transformed into a magnificent botanical garden.

The ROK Navy Symphony and Chorus

The most rewarding aspect of that tour was our performances for Korean audiences. Especially inspiring was the rapport we established with the members of the ROK (Republic of Korea) Navy Symphony Orchestra and Chorus, all of whom had been drafted into the Korean Navy as a protective measure. The orchestra's conductor, Kim Sang Ryu, who was more commonly known as John S. Kim, was to play a vital role in bringing Kenneth and me back to Korea in 1955 on my first State Department-sponsored tour.

The orchestra rehearsed in a large room in Pusan, dismal and dank, with cracked cement walls and rows of crude wooden chairs. For our concert, John S. Kim had borrowed an old Weber grand piano from a friend of his, a piano that proved to be in good condition. This was the piano I saw being moved down the main street in Pusan, in the bizarre procession I described for General Van Fleet and the others. Four laborers rolled the body of the piano on a dolly, while several other men walked behind carrying the legs and the pedal lyre on A-frames strapped to their backs. It was the strangest procession I ever saw. The men assembled the piano on an improvised platform at one end of the rehearsal room. Some two hundred musicians and students gathered there to hear the "honorable musicians from the United States."

Kenneth and I gave two full recitals, in which I played the following solos: the *Chromatic Fantasy and Fugue* by Bach, the Sonata in *D* minor, Op. 31, No. 2, by Beethoven, the Rhapsody in *E* flat by Brahms, *Feux d'artifice* by Debussy, the "Revolutionary" Etude, the posthumous Nocturne in *E* minor, and the Polonaise in *A* flat, by Chopin, and the *Mephisto* Waltz by Liszt. Kenneth performed the Chaconne for unaccompanied violin by J. S. Bach, and I joined with him in performances of the Sonata in *D* minor by Brahms, the Sonata by César Franck, *Tzigane* by Ravel, and other shorter works. Given just a few days of concentrated practicing at a Swedish hospital, I was able to get into excellent shape for those recitals. Our audience's response was beyond anything we might have expected. At the end of the second recital, the musicians and students swarmed around us presenting flowers and pleading for our autographs. When it was time for us to leave, a group of them carried our music and all of our personal belongings to a waiting car. As we drove away, they thrust their hands through the open window of the car for a final handshake. Kenneth and I, drained of energy by that time, could hardly believe this extreme show of enthusiasm and warmth. Interestingly, we both made the same association: we felt as though we were being given the sort of reception accorded rock and roll stars in the United States. As we looked back, it seemed as though the entire audience had assembled in the street to wave goodbye. Nor did they cease waving until our car turned a corner several blocks later.

Several months later, John S. Kim arranged two orchestral concerts in Pusan in an auditorium nearly the size of Carnegie Hall. We were the featured soloists. It was an endlessly long program, reminding me of the type commonly given around the turn of the century. The first half included the *Meistersinger* Overture by Wagner, the Violin Concerto in *D* by Brahms, and the Piano Concerto in *E* flat by Liszt. After intermission the chorus and orchestra performed *Beautiful Ellen* by Max Bruch, a work which calls for soprano and baritone solos. These were sung respectively by Lee Guan Ok and Walt Thompson. Bob Lamarchina, playing first chair in the cello section throughout the concert, more or less supported the entire orchestra with his dynamic temperament and penetrating tone. There was such an enthusiastic demand for tickets that we had to perform twice — once at 10 AM, and again at 7 PM. Although both concerts were sold out as soon as they were announced, hundreds of eager music-lovers surrounded the ticket office before the evening performance. Advance ticketing was, I am sure, haphazardly organized, with certain seats having been reserved twice, or perhaps even three times. This caused a near riot outside of the hall. In fact, standing in the corridor along the right side of the hall while Kenneth played the Brahms Concerto, I saw at least a dozen irate Koreans frantically waving their tickets outside of the locked entrance way to the auditorium. At one point, the surging crowd literally pushed through the doors and tore them off of their hinges. Finally, it was necessary to call in the MPs to restore order.

The Nightingale Tearoom

During my eight-month stay in Korea, I met many exceptionally gifted Korean instrumentalists and singers, among them Han Pyung Sook, a dramatic soprano. Peggy, as we called her, owned and was hostess of the Nightingale Tearoom in Pusan, a favorite meeting place among GIs. We were introduced to the tearoom around the time of our rehearsals with the ROK Navy Symphony Orchestra. All four of us, Kenneth, Walt, Robert Lamarchina, and I, went there frequently while we were in Pusan. It was not the tearoom that attracted us, but rather Peggy herself. She had an overflowing beauty about her, reminiscent of Anna Magnani. Her bright, luminous eyes and her effervescent personality made you feel as though you had been friends with her for years. We never discovered how old Peggy actually was, for her taut facial skin and her jet black hair made her look about thirty. But judging from all that she told us about her past, I am sure that she must have been in her forties.

Peggy's singing reflected her outgoing and dynamic personality. She had a large voice, capable of a wide range. Although her interpretations were sometimes questionable, still, she sang with an unusual degree of warmth and expressiveness. A fairly decent baby grand stood on an improvised platform at one end of the tearoom, and I, of course, always accompanied her on it whenever I visited. At her request, I invariably played some solos afterwards. Then, when her clientele had thinned out, I often coached her musically and vocally, as I had done previously with Kim Bokhi in Taegu. It was the first coaching she had received in years, and the results were nothing short of spectacular.

Considering all of the publicity associated with the four American musicians, Peggy was thrilled each time she saw us walk through the door of her tearoom. Fruit, pastries, and drinks of all sorts were brought to us routinely, and gratis. As she repeatedly told us, "The honor of having such distinguished guests in my tearoom is payment enough." Quite predictably, news of the American musicians visiting the Nightingale Tearoom spread quickly around the cultural community of Pusan. Her business increased considerably. And no one was prouder than she at seeing so many Koreans of all ages clustered around the tables and staring in our direction with expressions of awe and delight. Later, when she and I performed for them, she became positively euphoric. Because of this, it was natural that she singled me out as her favorite. For my part, I found Peggy utterly captivating.

Peggy had an American boyfriend, a colonel, who was completely devoted to her. Being fully aware that singing was life itself to her, and seeing how happy she was in our company, he decided to give her the ultimate gift — a debut recital, with the four of us as guest artists. At the very mention of this, Peggy squealed with delight and burst into tears. Her happiness knew no bounds. Whereas she had worked diligently to improve her singing after the first coaching session I gave her, she now redoubled her efforts and soon began to sound like a professional. Since we were scheduled to leave Pusan on October 9th, time was of the essence. The colonel went to work immediately and booked the Special Services Auditorium in Pusan for October 8th, only four days after our performance with the ROK Navy Symphony Orchestra.

To the colonel, we were celebrities. Quite naturally, then, he took enormous pride in the fact that his very own Peggy was in such august company. When plans were firmed up for Peggy's debut, he hosted a party at his cottage in the Hialeah Compound to which he invited the highest ranking officers in the vicinity. Needless to say, our hectic schedule, which included as many as three concerts a day, plus the recent gala concert with the ROK Navy Symphony Orchestra, had left us in a state of utter exhaustion. Kenneth, therefore, left his violin in the barracks, while Walt arrived without his accompaniments. As for Bob, he always managed to have his own plans. That left me, of course, to bear the brunt of the playing that evening. The colonel owned an upright piano whose keys, at least, went down and sprang back up again. But it had the worst sound imaginable. By then, however, having performed on so many wrecks of pianos, I did not expect anything better. From the moment we arrived, it was obvious that I was to spend the greater part of the evening accompanying Peggy and performing solos for the guests. How the colonel and his friends fussed over us, and me in particular, can hardly be imagined. He was so proud of Peggy's and his own connection to us that at one point during the evening, while Peggy and I were going at it, he telephoned an officer friend and held the telephone in our direction to show us off. Finally, when the party broke up, he presented us with three bottles of very expensive Napoleon brandy, and also promised to use his influence to fly us home once our tour of duty in Korea had ended.

Brandy in the Gutter

Kenneth, Walt, and I had been billeted at the 409th Infantry Unit in Pusan since late September, when rehearsals began for the concerto performances with the ROK Navy Symphony Orchestra. Concerning Bob, he almost always lived apart from us. He must have replaced his Japanese sweetheart with a Korean one. If not this, he must certainly have been up to mischief of some sort. At any rate, immediately upon returning to the barracks after the colonel's party, Kenneth and I slipped our bottles of brandy into our duffel bags. Walt, however, made the fatal mistake of leaving his bottle on a table alongside of his bunk. He and Kenneth had gone to the latrine, and I was undressing, when an officer happened to walk through the barracks for a bed check. That the lights were burning after 11:00 PM was a violation in itself. But when that officer saw the bottle of brandy on Walt's table, hell's fury was, at that moment, not confined to scorned women alone! He grabbed the bottle, untwisted the cork as though it were a pin in a live grenade, rushed with it outside, and poured every drop of the expensive brandy into the street. Returning to the table whence

313

he had snatched it, he slammed the empty bottle down with such force that all of the men in our room, and in an adjacent one as well, sat up in bed with a start. Since I alone of the three musicians was the only one visible to him, he fixed his blazing eyes upon me and shouted, "This is one fucking thing we don't allow here. The first thing in the morning, all three of you are moving out!"

Most of the other soldiers billeted with us were awaiting infantry assignments. They were no less anxious about their future than Kenneth and I had been seven months earlier. They knew who we were from the huge painting of Peggy and the four of us which had been strung up over the main street in Pusan, and they had read articles about us in various army newspapers. Moreover, they had seen us getting in and out of fancy army limousines chauffeured by MPs. As far as they were concerned, we were, for reasons unknown to them, enjoying unheard-of privileges, while they were going off to fight a war, and perhaps die in the process.

Reprisals

Considering all of this, it is not difficult to imagine how those soldiers felt, not only to have witnessed all of the preferential treatment lavished upon us, but also to have been awakened from a deep sleep by that irate officer. They were wild with indignation, and they were determined to get back at us. At 6:00 AM, while the three of us were sleeping off the effects of the previous night, derisive shouts arose all around us, such as: "Are those goddamn musicians still in the next room?" "Get out of bed. Who do you think you are, sleeping until the middle of the morning?" "Leave the poor little darlings alone. After all, they're going to the officers' mess for dinner tonight, and they need their beauty rest!" An hour later, when we returned from breakfast, we found ping pong tables positioned over our bunks.

As I think about it now, I can hardly blame those soldiers for resenting us. But at that time, this occurrence, and others like it, hurt us deeply. It seemed futile to explain to our buddies that apart from exploiting the possibilities of getting decent meals, we neither courted nor expected special privileges. Brandy, limousines, and the like were all forthcoming, nonetheless, simply because our musical gifts inspired certain officers in power to become our self-appointed protectors. We were grateful for this beyond measure. To us, it all showed just how powerful music and talent really are. In truth though, we felt no different from the average soldier. We had had our own share of basic training. We pulled KP and guard duty, and, in short, we fulfilled all of the responsibilities expected of soldiers during a war. It saddened us, therefore, to know that the privileges we received as a result of our performances often alienated the men with whom we lived on a daily basis.

My telephone call to the colonel later that morning sufficed to put to rest the brandy bottle incident. The colonel's aide came personally to the unit where we were billeted and pacified the officer in charge, who was in the process of having us arrested for the possession of alcoholic beverages. Poor Walt, however, was now left staring at an empty bottle of the most expensive brandy money could buy. But since I had no use for the stuff, I gave him my bottle, much to his delight.

Will the Curtain Go Up?

On October 8th, a group of Korean laborers descended upon the Tearoom, dismantled Peggy's piano, and moved it to the stage of the Special Services Theater. It was now two hours before our concert, and I was busily practicing a mountain of music, when a Corporal Parr, attached to counter-intelligence, suddenly appeared out of the theater wings. He walked directly over to the piano, took me under the arm, and said calmly: "Just follow me, and don't say anything. I want to show you something." There was an urgency in his voice. While I sorely needed every precious minute of practicing before the concert, I followed. The corporal led me out of the theater to a music store directly across the street. Upon entering, I saw the owner of the store hand over a program of our concert to a young Korean man in exchange for a large bundle of *won* (Korean money). The corporal and I exchanged glances, I looking more shocked than he did, and we walked out of the music store without exchanging a word. As we returned to the theater, the corporal told me that a counter-intelligence officer dressed as a civilian had purchased one of these programs himself. At the exact moment that the corporal was discussing this incident with me, a group of counter-intelligence officers was deliberating whether to allow the concert to go on. The point was, Kenneth, Walt, Bob, and I had been ordered from the start of our tour never to receive payment from Koreans for our performances. Quite obviously this rule did not apply to our sponsors, for others — Koreans, Americans, perhaps both — were capitalizing on our talents. It suddenly occurred to me that someone might think that we ourselves were getting extra fees for our performances. Later, much to my relief, I learned from the corporal that we were not suspected of being involved in this scam. But the fact was, our perform-ance was now in jeopardy. It was a very disillusioned and anxious pianist, therefore, who returned to the theater stage to continue practicing for a concert that stood a good chance of being canceled. As it turned out, however, the concert was allowed to take place without further incident.

My colleagues arrived at the theater totally unaware of the emergency. I decided not to tell them about it until the concert was over. For heaven knows, we all had enough to think about without having to worry about MPs closing down the theater and perhaps arresting us.

There is a special aura of excitement surrounding debut recitals, and this one was no exception. The colonel, proud as anyone could be, stood nervously in the theater lobby greeting his friends as they walked in. He then sat in the center seat of the first row beaming throughout the entire concert. Peggy was in her element. Dressed in a beautiful white gown and with bright red flowers in her black hair, she sang her Mozart and Brahms magnificently. But as often happens to performers, she became more and more nervous as the program wore on. Her other solos, therefore, did not fare as well. On the following page is the program in its entirety.

As one can see, I bore the lion's share of responsibility that evening. To this day, I do not know how I survived the Mendelssohn Trio. For the truth is, I had only read it through informally many years earlier. Moreover, with the Liszt Concerto occupying whatever time I had for practicing, plus all of the other accompaniments, I had very little time to learn what amounted to another piano concerto. I would say that I crammed in the Trio in approximately five hours of intense practicing during the few days preceding that concert. I have always been a good sight-reader, however, and this, especially, helped me to absorb the piece quickly. While the performance may not have been a model of accuracy, I am certain that it had a good deal of passion.

"I've got condoms for ya!"

After the concert, the colonel hosted an extravagant Chinese banquet in the Nightingale Tearoom. Peggy, who by this time radiated a happiness that can hardly be described, presented the four of us with brass candle-sticks as a token of her appreciation. She was teary-eyed when expressing her gratitude to us. Bob, who was never one for social occasions, left in the middle of the banquet; and Walt, having been invited to spend the evening with a friend, excused himself shortly afterwards. This left Kenneth and me alone with Peggy, the colonel, and two women who had been introduced to us earlier as Peggy's friends. Although they were beautifully dressed and very sociable, there was something grotesque about them. They sat opposite us during the dinner staring at us flirtatiously and intermittently whispering and giggling to one another. This was not in the least surprising to us, for many Korean women and men openly declared their attraction to "the famous American musicians."

Allelujah   MOZART
  (from the Motet, *Exultate Jubilate*)

Three Lieder   BRAHMS
  Wiegenlied (Lullaby)
  Die Mainacht (May Night)
  Von Ewiger Liebe (Eternal Love)

Un bel di vedremo   PUCCINI
  (from *Madama Butterfly*)
                    Han Pyung Sook
                    Seymour Bernstein

                         II
Trio in D minor   MENDELSSOHN
                    Kenneth Gordon
                    Robert Lamarchina
                    Seymour Bernstein

                    INTERMISSION

Song of the Open Road   MALOTTE
Thine Alone (from *Eileen*)   VICTOR HERBERT
On the Road to Mandalay   OLEY SPEAKS
                    Walter Thompson
                    Seymour Bernstein

                         IV
Ritorna vicitor (from *Aida*)   VERDI
Villanelle   EVA DELLAQUA
If I Loved You   HAMMERSTEIN
                    Han Pyung Sook
                    Walter Thompson
                    Seymour Bernstein

Soon, however, we discovered that these women had been invited to the banquet for reasons other than their admiration for us. For no sooner did we finish eating than the colonel, showing the signs of too much alcohol, initiated the first stage of his own plan for rewarding us. Suddenly, he shouted at Peggy across the table in a boisterous voice loud enough to be heard on the enemy line: "How about fixing Seymour and Kenneth up with your friends, here?" At this, Peggy's eyes flashed daggers at the colonel. It took just that one sentence to change her expression from elation to utter outrage and dejection. Seething with anger, she got up from her chair, rushed over to the colonel, and pulled him aside. The colonel whispered something in Peggy's ear, and she soon quieted down. We knew, of course, that Peggy would do anything for us, and from all that followed, it seemed quite obvious that the colonel had persuaded Peggy to give the two hot-blooded American soldiers what they really wanted — an evening alone with her two friends. At least something of the sort took place, for Peggy went over to her friends and conversed with them in soft tones. At the same time, the colonel took Kenneth and me by the arm and led us into a corner: "See Mrs. Lee there sitting to Peggy's right? A major assigned to my office had her. And according to him, she's great. Now, they can fix two beds for you guys out of those upholstered chairs. I've got condoms for ya, just in case you've run out of 'em. So spend the whole night here if ya want, and don't worry about a thing. I'll send my car for ya at 6 AM." With this, he walked over to join Peggy and her friends.

Kenneth and I looked at one another with an expression of disbelief. To begin with, nothing was more repugnant to us than the thought of sleeping with those two women. While the colonel was sincere in wanting to please us, we thought him to be outrageously boorish for including Peggy in his sexual scheme, and on the very day of her debut, no less. Then suddenly it occurred to me that the Nightingale Tearoom might be a house of prostitution, and Peggy and her friends prostitutes. If this were so, it would explain why Dr. Helen Kim (I had visited with her a few weeks after I had performed in her school) and others of our Korean acquaintance looked askance at the very mention of Peggy's name.

All of these thoughts went through my mind in a flash. I was careful, though, to guard my expression so as not to make my feelings known to the colonel and to Peggy, who were staring at us from the other end of the room. Finally, when I had regained my poise, I explained to the colonel that we were totally worn out from the concert, and that we would leave as planned at 11:15 PM.

The colonel looked very disappointed. He wanted to please us in the only way he knew how, and we had rejected his good intentions. The next half hour was uncomfortable for all of us. When it was time for us to leave, Peggy, whose expression by this time was one of shame and despair, broke down into heartbreaking sobs. She and the colonel followed us outside and waved goodbye as the car sped away. I never saw them again.

Farewells and New Friends
We left Pusan for the last time on October 9th. Little did I know then that I would return to that city in 1955 and again in 1960 as a civilian on State Department tours. Back at our headquarters in Taegu, I discovered that orders had been issued for me to begin the rotation process back to the United States on October 24th. In the meantime, the Special Services office had booked us for a dozen or more performances — at military installations, for Korean audiences, and tapings for future broadcasts. It was a time, too, to say farewell to all of the people who had helped and supported us during those eight months. Dinners and parties, therefore, commingled and often conflicted with a hectic schedule of practicing and performing. The result was that my energy was all but depleted. Quite predictably, the people to whom we said farewell were promptly replaced with other engaging personalities who were associated with our performances — one of them being Dr. Hyun Bong Hak, a pathologist who was assigned to the Presbyterian Hospital in Taegu.

Bong Hak introduced us to a tearoom in Taegu, the Renaissance Taban ("taban" meaning tearoom). A cultural meeting place for Korean music-lovers, it boasted the largest collection of recordings in all of Korea. In fact, I have never seen so many recordings in one place. The owner, Sam Lee, a tall, lanky man with warm sensitive eyes, was just as honored to have us visit his tearoom as Peggy was when we visited hers. His business increased to such an extent that people waited in line outside for a seat at one of the tables. Their patience was well-rewarded, for Kenneth frequently played along with the recordings of notable violinists such as Fritz Kreisler and Jascha Heifetz. I remember in particular the evening he played the Brahms Concerto along with Kreisler. Kenneth was magnificent, and I had the feeling that everyone there would never have an experience like that again. Often the electricity would go out, and the young girl serving tea and coffee would light kerosene lamps. At such times, Kenneth would play unaccompanied works, and the flames of the lamps cast eerie shadows of his bow arm dancing across the walls and the ceiling. There being no piano in the tearoom, I spent many relaxing hours there in utter bliss sipping tea or coffee, thrilling to Kenneth's brilliant playing or listening to rare recordings of legendary instrumentalists and singers. Occasionally, students would come up to us and ask for our autographs. And Sam Lee, overjoyed by the fact that his tearoom had become the "in" place in Taegu, gave us lavish gifts — mine being a 24 carat gold key and ring. The key alone, some two inches long, must have been prohibitively expensive. I was overwhelmed at receiving it. Not being able to show my appreciation by playing for Sam Lee in his tearoom, I invited him to all of our subsequent performances. He and I exchanged letters for years afterwards.

The New Testament Comes to Korea

Bong Hak asked us if we would give a concert for the staff and patients of his hospital. Needless to say, we were happy to do this for him. He called for us in a beautiful station wagon owned by an American, Dr. Lyons, who was attached to the Presbyterian Mission. Although the hospital had an upright piano, one of the doctors there thought it would be a disgrace for me to play on it. So he arranged to have a Steinberg upright (this name was totally unfamiliar to me) moved into the chapel where we performed. Alas, the piano was half a step flat in pitch, and poor Kenneth and Bob were beside themselves trying to stay in tune with me.

After the concert, Dr. Lyons invited us for coffee and cookies. He lived in a beautiful American-style house near the American Embassy with his wife and another American woman of middle age. Having been missionaries in Korea for twelve years, they all spoke Korean fluently. Towards the end of the evening, Dr. Lyons told us a dramatic account of how the New Testament found its way to Korea.

As the story went, in the 1870s, a ship called the *General Sherman* crossed over from China and anchored in a river near the shores of Pyongjong, now the capital of North Korea. At the time of this incident, Korea was a hermit nation and barred all foreigners from her shores. The few foreigners who managed to infiltrate Korea were either murdered outright or disappeared mysteriously.

While the *General Sherman* was anchored in the harbor, the tide went out, leaving the ship stranded on a reef. Among the passengers was a missionary carrying the first Korean translation of the New Testament. The Koreans, hostile to the intruders, saw the ship as a threat to their security. They gathered small boats, piled them high with driftwood, set the wood on fire, and then floated the boats down the river towards the *General Sherman*. According to Dr. Lyons, all eye-witness accounts concur as to what then followed: the ship was totally destroyed, and everyone on board perished in the flames. Several who tried to make it ashore were killed before they reached land. One man, however, a missionary, managed to wade ashore where he threw pamphlets towards the enraged crowds. After he was killed, some of the Koreans gathered up the pamphlets and papered the walls of their homes with what turned out to be the New Testament. During Dr. Lyons' assignment in Korea, enough pages were found in various Korean homes to form one complete book which has since become an historical relic in a museum in Taegu.

By the time Dr. Lyons finished his story, we were all spellbound. I, for one, wanted to stay the entire night, for I was sure that Dr. Lyons had many other stories to tell of historical significance. But stifled yawns and heavy eyelids on the part of our hosts signaled that it was time for us to leave

How Deep the Roots!

Around this time, I was suffering from a severe irritation caused by an upper wisdom tooth that was trying in vain to cut through my gum. I went to the EUSAK dispensary, only to find that the dentists working there were all booked up for several weeks. Bong Hak examined my gum and thought that I needed immediate attention. He therefore made an appointment for me with his own dentist.

My colleagues, being extremely wary about my going to a Korean dentist, decided to accompany me to the appointment. I myself was apprehensive. Yet my gum was seriously inflamed and I felt that I had to take a chance.

The dentist appeared to be very professional and very pleasant. He explained to me that wisdom teeth present more problems than they are worth. He then asked my permission to remove the one in question. I agreed, of course, and the dentist proceeded to numb the area with Novocain. Two shots had no effect upon me. Even after three more shots, I still felt the point of his needle as he tested the area. Thinking that the area would, in time, become numb, the doctor proceeded with what he thought was a routine affair. Not having taken an X-ray of the area, he did not know that the roots of my wisdom tooth were twisted into the bone. In short, the tooth was impacted. What ensued then can only be described as a living nightmare. He cut a larger and larger patch in my gum, he yanked, he tugged, and still the stubborn tooth would not budge from the bone in which it was embedded. I moaned, I cried, and I prayed that I might faint so as to relieve my agony. But I remained conscious throughout the ordeal. My colleagues and Bong Hak suffered along with me. Finally, the tooth yielded to extreme pressure, and out it came, gnarled roots and all. Feeling utterly relieved and exhausted, I had a rather bizarre thought: "I wonder if women feel like this after giving birth." As any dentist will tell you, trauma of that sort to the bone often leads to what is known as a dry socket — a blood clot on the bone that causes excruciating pain. And that is exactly what happened to me. For the next few weeks, and even on the way back to the United States, I suffered spasms of pain that often made me cry aloud. I took aspirin and even stronger pain killers which Bong Hak gave me. But nothing seemed to help. Finally, the clot dissolved. And by the time I returned to my family I was free of pain.

Dear Aunt Clara Is Dead

It was October, and the fall season seemed to chill me to the bone. Strangely enough, no matter how many blankets I piled over my cot when I went to bed, I continued to feel cold and clammy. In fact, I wrote several times in my diary the words, "I wonder if something is wrong at home." On October 17th, I received a pile of mail which included letters from Louise Curcio and Nikki. Since I looked forward to the latter more than the former, I opened Louise's letter first. After reading it, I began to sob so uncontrollably that Kenneth came rushing over to me in great alarm. No one could have been sweeter or more concerned than he was, seeing his friend, his colleague, in such a state of distress. When I was able to speak again, I explained to Kenneth what there was in the letter that devastated me to such an extent. I recorded it in my diary later that evening

> I just took a pill to help deaden the excruciating pain in my gum. If I'm lucky, perhaps it will help me sleep. As I sit on the edge of my bunk sipping hot Nescafe and huddled over my gasoline burner, I begin to recover from the shocking news of Aunt Clara's death. It grieves me to think that on the very day I last wrote to her, that dry, rasping laughter I loved so dearly, a laughter that seemed to mock the cares of the world, had already been silenced forever. "You'd better get a good supply of tea," I warned her in that letter, "because I have lots and lots to tell you when I return." And all the time she lay dead, dead! What wouldn't I give to feel her firm hand and hear that vital, loving voice just one more time. Here I am, thousands of miles away from home and feeling tormented, helpless, and utterly alone. Kenneth is so caring, and so understanding. But finally, what comfort can there be now that my dear friend is gone? Those magical hands on the keyboard holding within them musical secrets of the sort that I could never hope to attain; that silly, towering hat, years out of style, that dusty velvet coat, and her regal figure turning those antiquated garments into royal attire; the awed silence when she spoke in the presence of others; her naughtiness in making inferior colleagues cower by holding forth in a way that

brooked no rebuttal whatsoever; her child-like nature that enabled her to take me into bars simply because she wanted her Sonny to enjoy one of her secret passions — beer on tap; her lack of tolerance of anything that was ugly or in poor taste and her audaciousness in speaking out against it; her enthusiasm, and her generous expressions when she really liked someone or something; the abrupt, no nonsense voice on the telephone and her rude way of hanging up when she thought that everything necessary had been said. She is gone now. My dear Aunt Clara is no more.

I shall never forgive Louise for the cold, matter-of-fact way in which she wrote to me about Aunt Clara's death. How ironic that I should have read the news for the first time from someone who despised her. In contrast to this, it was balm to find Nikki's letter, full of sympathy and warmth, as though she were here weeping along with me. I will sleep now. But in the morning, my beloved teacher will still be dead. The living are close to the dead, for in a sense, they die along with those whom they love.

Earlier, I confessed to believing in ESP, especially because I have had a few striking experiences along these lines. I have retained, for instance, a vivid memory of an incident that occurred when I was sixteen. I was a student in high school at the time, and I was baby-sitting one evening with my niece Lisa, my sister Lillian's first child. It was something I looked forward to. For one thing, I adored her; for another, it afforded me time to do my homework.

I had a special friend in high school named Harriet, with whom I walked to school each morning. At one point during the evening in question, I distinctly heard Harriet's voice calling from the driveway along the right side of the two-story building where my sister lived: "Sonny, Sonny!" The voice rang out so clearly that I went outside to greet Harriet who, I assumed, had walked over on an impulse to keep me company. But when I went outside and looked in all directions, there was no one there. As I stood in the darkness, a chill ran up and down my spine. I remember looking at my watch and noting that it was a few minutes after 8 PM. It then occurred to me that some passing young people may have shouted a word or name that sounded like Sonny. As the evening wore on, I went on with my homework and thought no more about it.

The following morning, I related this entire incident to Harriet during our walk to school. On hearing the story, she suddenly blanched and stopped walking abruptly. When she finally found her voice, she told me that at exactly 8 PM on that previous evening, her aunt, with whom she was living, precipitated a violent altercation on the subject of Harriet's relationship with me. Later, in a fit of depression, she went into the bathroom and swallowed an entire bottle of iodine. Fortunately, it was a fresh bottle, and, therefore, not as potent as it might have been. As Harriet told me, the unpleasant sensation to her taste buds made her vomit immediately. The sounds of heaving brought her aunt rushing into the bathroom. Upon seeing the telltale empty bottle of iodine, she immediately made Harriet drink several glasses of milk, which evidently ameliorated the effects of whatever portion of the iodine might have remained in her stomach.

Having had that experience, and others like it, I was prepared to believe that the coldness I experienced the week before I received those letters announcing Aunt Clara's death was a telecommunication from Aunt Clara herself, a message of alarm which she sent to me over that vast distance.

Final Concert in Korea

I went into deep mourning after I heard the news of Aunt Clara's death. Each time I thought about her, I began to sob. There were enough distractions over the next few weeks, however, to help me over this trauma, and in time I was able to control my emotions.

Robert Lamarchina left for the United States on October 18th. He was not at all happy at the prospect of returning home. He had a wife whom he did not love and who refused to give him a divorce. Apart from his mother, who lived in South America, he had no family to speak of. He would have preferred, instead, to return to Japan where he was revered as an artist and where he had lived with a family whom he loved and who loved him in return. At 4 PM Kenneth, Walt, and I went to see him off. It was a farewell charged with emotion. Before Bob's jeep sped away, he promised to keep in touch with us. Considering the dramatic adventures we had had together, one might have thought that staying in touch would be a matter of course. Yet, after returning to civilian life, Kenneth and I alone of the four musicians continued to contact one another, albeit sporadically. This, I believe, was primarily because we both lived in New York City. Concerning the others, even if we had wanted to exchange letters, it would not have been possible to do so. For the truth was, none of us remembered to exchange addresses when we parted for the last time. Perhaps this was an indication that we secretly never intended to stay in touch. Being in the army, after all, was an unwelcome hiatus in our lives. Perhaps we all wanted to bury the whole experience as quickly as possible and get on with our careers. Many years after my discharge, however, I heard through Kenneth that Bob had been appointed principal conductor of the Honolulu Symphony. He has since been replaced, however, and at this writing, neither Kenneth nor I know what has happened to him or to Walt Thompson.

I shall never forget Bob's magnificent phrasing and his extraordinary bow technique. I remember hearing a contest between him and Kenneth in a tent somewhere near the front line. They dared each other to play *The Flight of the Bumblebee* by Rimsky Korsakoff on one bow. The result was a draw, for they both succeeded in doing what seemed to be the impossible.

Kenneth, Walt, and I gave our last concert on October 20th in the Moonwha Kok Chong, the site of our first concert for a Korean audience. It was also the theater where the grand piano fell over, pinning my wrist against the wall. This time, however, the piano was moved for me. The posters in front of the hall announced a farewell concert. As a result, people were queued up for blocks. High-ranking American and Korean officers were in the audience, among them General Heron, a leading military figure in Taegu. As part of my solo group, I played the theme from the *Warsaw* Concerto by Richard Adinsell, a piece that I learned for the occasion. Never having performed it in public before, I was unusually nervous, and this precipitated a memory slip right in the middle of the piece. But I managed to bring it to a dramatic close. Bob Wenck and other Embassy officials were there. In fact, Bob brought me the adjustable artist's bench from the Embassy — a luxury, indeed. For as every pianist knows, the success of a performance depends to a great extent upon sitting at an accustomed height. Heretofore, I had had to scrounge about in order to find a suitable chair or bench.

Later that evening, the Embassy hosted a final farewell dinner for us. After a sumptuous dessert and delicious coffee, Kenneth, Walt, and I sat in front of a roaring fire and reflected upon all of our adventures. Suddenly, Bob Wenck stood up in the center of the room and delivered a speech. He told us that we were the most famous musicians in all of Korea, and that the enthusiasm of GIs, who he thought were the most discriminating audience of all, was, perhaps, the greatest measure of our success. With this, everyone applauded. When it was time to leave, Bob shook our hands for the last time. As he came up to me, he looked deeply into my eyes and said, "You are the best thing that happened to me in Korea."

On the face of it, I ought to have accepted this as an extreme compliment without thinking more about it. But the truth is, that one statement affected me more than I can possibly say. For in those days, I thought that most people, Bob included, liked me specifically for my musical gifts, and not for my personal attributes. Even though he and his staff were exceedingly friendly and generous to all of us, still, I secretly thought that this was because we functioned as did court musicians of another era. After all, we provided the Embassy staff and their guests with performances of a caliber that was not likely to be equaled during those war years. They in return reciprocated with dinners and kindnesses of all sorts. But now after Bob's touching pronouncement, I suddenly realized that I was more than just a status symbol to him, more than someone whom he could show off to his friends and to distinguished visitors. In other words, he liked me, the person, and not just me, the musician. For me not to have known and accepted this led me to two other conclusions. One was that I had been ungenerous to Bob, and heaven knows how many other people, by dismissing the idea that he liked me just as much as he liked my playing. The other conclusion concerned the root of the problem: I must not have liked or respected myself very much. I left the Embassy, therefore, with a sinking feeling of having unwittingly wronged Bob and his staff. That experience and others like it led eventually to the thesis of my book *With Your Own Two Hands* — a thesis which holds to the conviction that the person and the musician ought to be one and the same.

HOMECOMING

Like most giant institutions, the army was entangled in red tape and hard, inflexible rules. To change or reverse an order, for example, necessitated a chain of commands that filtered down from the highest echelons and usually took an interminable amount of time. With my rotation back to the United States now imminent, I could think of only one thing: another trip across the Pacific such as the one I had endured would surely kill me. Or at least, I would become so debilitated that my family would be alarmed when they saw me. No one knew better than Kenneth what fourteen days of seasickness had done to me on the *General Black*. He urged me, therefore, to contact General Van Fleet's office and remind them of the general's offer to fly us home. On October 23rd, I flew to Seoul and managed somehow to see General Van Fleet's aide, Colonel Edwards. He had been a member of the audience on the evening we performed for the general. No one could have been more understanding of my situation. He told me that he would speak to the general. When I returned to Taegu later that day, the company clerk rushed up to me with a telephone message from "the old man himself." "You're flying home," he said with great excitement. And you're to leave tomorrow!" It seemed too good to be true. I had Kenneth to thank for this. For as much as I had wanted to pull strings to secure a flight, I hesitated to bother General Van Fleet's staff with what I assumed would be a trivial matter.

Making It on One Propeller

Everything happened so fast, that I was numb when I said goodbye to Kenneth and to Walt. Besides, I knew that they would follow in my path within a matter of weeks, weeks which lent more of a festive air to my departure than the sort of sentimentality I had anticipated. It took only one hour to receive my official orders and to clear Seoul. Before I knew it, I found myself on a K-16 airplane en route to Japan. I knew by this time how to strap myself into a parachute. I then fastened the seat belt on the bucket seat and read my orders for the first time. There it was: VO (verbal order) "Army Commander General James A. Van Fleet: Re: PFC Seymour Bernstein, US51026493 (my army serial number); Request immediate flight to Tachikawa Air Base, Japan." Speaking about high level orders, one could not get any higher than that.

I happened to be sitting next to a PIO (Public Information Officer) who introduced himself as John Smith. Working for the Red Cross, he had visited a MASH hospital in Korea for the purpose of interviewing a number of patients there. His assignment was to write a letter in the guise of a patient in order to inform "Mr. & Mrs. America" about the conditions on the battle front in Korea. We were in the air some two hours when I happened to look outside one of the few windows of the airplane for a glimpse of the Sea of Japan. To my horror, I noticed that the propeller on that side of the airplane was not spinning. We were being kept aloft by only one of the two propellers. Panic overtook me, and I quickly shifted my glance to the men sitting in the cabin. They were all reading or talking to one another seemingly unaware of what I considered to be an out and out emergency. "Am I the only passenger on this airplane who knows of this calamity?" I wondered. My first instinct was to keep the whole thing to myself so as not to alarm the other men on board. But in a few moments, I could not contain myself any longer. I poked John Smith sitting next to me and whispered to him to look outside the window at the propeller. "Oh," he said in a very matter of fact tone, "propeller number one went out after we were airborne for ten minutes or so. Don't worry about it. We can easily make it on one propeller." While I felt slightly relieved at his optimism, it gave me a queasy feeling to know that half of the airplane's power was now defunct. We landed safely, however, and none too soon for me.

I had thought that my orders from General Van Fleet were the army equivalent of the voice of God! Yet, according to the processing office at Camp Drake, Japan, those orders were good only from Korea to Japan. Nothing about them assured my flight over the Pacific. With the remembrance of the *General Black* and those fourteen days of seasickness ever before me, I tried to telephone Colonel Edwards from the International Telephone Office in Camp Drake. But there was no way that I could get through to Korea without knowing the military code numbers. So I had to start the whole process of pulling strings all over again in order to secure a flight to California. How I was tossed about from one office to another, I cannot begin to say. One might have thought that General Van Fleet's name on my orders would carry sufficient weight, but it seemed to have exactly the opposite effect upon a few hard-core army officers. They looked at the orders and then viewed me as some sort of prima donna who expected preferential treatment just because I played the piano. Hostile and demeaning language greeted me everywhere. In desperation, I went to the Service Club where Kenneth and I had performed so frequently when we first came through Camp Drake. The hostess there, Jessie Elliot, remembered me from months earlier. No one could have been more understanding or more helpful. She immediately introduced me to a Captain Avery, who in no time at all issued me orders to fly home. It was now a question of waiting for the first available seat on an overseas flight. The rest was routine procedure: I turned in the bulk of my equipment — my rifle and various articles of clothing such as my combat shoes and several sets of well-used fatigues. I then drew from the commissary a class "A" uniform, one which I had not worn since I left Fort Dix.

In the meantime, I discovered how deplorably Korean veterans were treated on their way home to the States. I was assigned to Company 535, which housed returning veterans. Despite all we had been through, we were treated no better than inductees. We were all assigned to KP, to guard duty, to fire guard, which meant walking the halls all night, and to policing the grounds for hours on end during the day. Men who had fought on the front lines, some of whom had even been wounded, were walking beside me picking up cigarette butts and trash of all sorts. I wanted to shout out my anger and my resentment to all of the hard-line army personnel responsible for this. But I had already experienced the consequences of voicing my indignation to my superiors. I would be home soon, I thought, and any counter-aggression on my part would result in harsh retaliations that might delay my departure.

On October 27th, my name was called out over the loudspeakers: "Private First Class Bernstein, report to the orderly room immediately." And there they were — my official flight orders. I rushed to the telephone center and put in a call to my parents. "I'm coming home," I cried. "The flight will take some thirty-six hours. I'll call again when I land in the United States." My mother was choked up with emotion and hardly said a word. It was all like a dream. Within minutes I was put on a bus and driven to Haneda Air Base. It took only ten minutes to be processed. At 12:30 PM, I boarded a California Eastern Airlines airplane, a commercial airplane with four propellers, which was, in those days, the most luxurious means of travel available. The long awaited moment had come. I was on my way home.

From that point on, the entries in my diary reflect a young man in a delirium of expectation:

> My eyelids refuse to blink. I just stare straight ahead as though I am living through a dream. But as I see the islands of Japan disappearing far below, I know for sure that I am headed for home. My joy is unbounded.
>
> The airplane is luxurious. The soft, blue reclining seat enfolds me in a comfort that I have long since forgotten. Little by little it quells the sparks of anxiety rushing through my body. The stewardesses are all kindness and warmth. They serve whatever beverage you want. And they have even brought me a delicious box lunch containing cold chicken and my favorite — tuna sandwiches. We hit a few rough spots over the Pacific. Other than that, this has been a very smooth flight, and there is no need for Dramamine this time. I have a window seat, and I can see a blanket of clouds below me like one vast sheet of cotton candy. Towards evening, the clouds parted, and the moon made visible the sparkling sea below me and the star-studded heavens.

The trip to Travis Air Force Base in California took thirty-six hours, with two stops along the way — Wake Island and Honolulu. They were hours spent in reflection and musings of all sorts:

> On the one hand, I am relieved to have left Korea. But on the other hand, I already miss certain friends, especially Dr. Helen Kim, Lee Eneh, and Hyun Bong Hak. Army life and my wild performing schedule cheated me out of spending as much time with them as I wanted to. I yearn, now, to live with Asians one day and absorb their culture and their beautiful way of life. In return, I have a strong need to share with them all that I have gained from practicing and performing — not only information of a technical and musical nature, but, more importantly, how the study and practice of music can influence one's whole life. This will have to wait, though, for some future time.

Am I excited about returning home? Excited isn't the word. I'm positively numb! I've waited two years for this moment. Now that it has come, I simply don't know how to react. Anticipation, of course, is always greater than realization. Nevertheless, I do know one thing: I long for the moment when I can wrap my arms around my dear mom and dad again and see my sisters, brothers-in-law, and their children, all of whom I love dearly. And I can't wait to see Nikki and my other friends. While I think about this, the thought of Aunt Clara's death opens a deep wound within me. Speaking about incompleteness — for eight months I looked forward to telling her about my performing experiences. Now, I feel cheated and bereft. How will I ever get used to living without her?

If I was airsick on the way to San Francisco, I certainly was not aware of it. In fact I spent most of the trip staring straight ahead — unaware, even, when a tray of food was placed before me. As every nuance of those eight and a half months flashed through my mind, I sensed that I had undergone a profound change — one that would take a lifetime to assimilate. Yet certain aspects of that change were clear to me even then: I knew, for example, that surviving the ordeals of being a soldier, knowing that I could perform with a minimum of practicing and under the worst possible conditions, and learning to speak in public for the first time — all of these things increased my self-confidence to a degree that I had never experienced before. I was filled with gratitude, too, for having been allowed to function as a musician. And I was especially grateful that my family had been spared the heartache of my possible injury or death.

And there was another change that is far more difficult to describe. It concerned music itself and my alignment with it. Throughout those eight and a half months, music served as my protective shield against the war and the misery all around me. To be as music is — harmonious, noble, and honest — was, from that moment on, the only goal worth attaining. While the war taught me just how fragile we really are, music revealed a far greater truth: that there is a beauty in the world that is stronger than death itself.

As the airplane neared the west coast of the United States, I lived out in my mind's eye the reunion with my family and friends. The sight of the Golden Gate Bridge caused me to sob so intensely that a woman sitting next to me felt obliged to place her arm around me in a gesture of comfort. I wept for my survival, for all that I had gained, and for the sheer joy of returning home:

Tuesday, October 28th, 1 PM

    Once we had landed at Travis Air Force Base, I and the other GIs on the plane were immediately processed and sent to a comfortable lounge in the terminal where we waited for a bus to take us to Camp Stoneman. The place is swarming with strange-looking people called civilians. At first, their stares made me feel self-conscious. I suppose they're wondering if the battle ribbons on my uniform mean that I was wounded in action. Curiously, as I walked around the terminal, I felt uncomfortably conspicuous. Soon, though, my self-consciousness gave way to a sense of pride. I'm proud of my uniform, and proud of all I have been through.

Other entries in my diary describe me at twenty-five as a different person from what I am today. I saw myself as the center of the universe. "I am a missionary type," I wrote. "And a person like me ought not to belong to one person or to one place." Apparently, all of the adulation I had received from the Japanese and Koreans had caused me to adopt a "savior" image of myself. Considering the responses to my teaching and the praise I received for my playing from such a vast number of people, it was quite natural for me to feel both needed and respected. But as my diary reveals, this bigger-than-life image which I had of myself was getting out of hand. In the airport terminal in California, I imagined that I was "standing taller than anyone else. Look at me, everyone! I'm one of those returning GIs whom you see in newsreels. I have survived it all. The conquering hero has come home."

    What causes a person to see himself as the center of the universe? In my case, I believe it was my insecurity — an insecurity that made me a bundle of contradictions. One part of me did not think that I had what it takes to have a career in music. I was, therefore, humble about my place in the profession. When, to my surprise, people admired me for my playing or teaching, I secretly thought that somehow I was "getting away with it." Another part of me intended to stick with it, no matter what — to do whatever was necessary to survive performances. Add to this the life and death struggle in which I had found myself, and you have a general picture of a frightened, insecure young man. Perhaps in order to survive, I had sublimated my fears and insecurities and replaced them with fantasies. Some of those fantasies had a basis in fact — that is, I was told repeatedly how good I was — while others bordered on delusions of grandeur. By the time I returned to the United States, I was not only glad to be alive, but proud of the way I had survived all of the ordeals, both as a soldier and as a performer. Perhaps I was too proud, too ego-inflated, with the result that I blew up out of all proportion my importance to everyone and to everything.

Continuing now with my diary:

> The bus arrived at 4 PM and a group of us set out for Camp Stoneman, an hour's drive from the airport. The highway was unusually narrow, but it was smooth, without shell holes. We passed peaceful lakes along the way, and I could actually smell the pungent odor of fish. And oh, the broad fields, brown with the harvest, and free of the stench of human fertilizer. "America, the Beautiful." The anthem began playing in my head as though it was accompanying a travelogue and I was in the audience looking at a movie. The hour seemed to slip away in no time at all. Suddenly, I was awakened out of my reverie as the bus turned into the entrance way of Camp Stoneman.

> We all drew bedding and were taken to our barracks. I threw everything onto my bunk and went directly to the mess hall. There I saw a huge banner affixed to the wall over the serving counter: "Welcome," it said. One sight of it provoked tears of happiness. It all seemed too good to be true.

> After dinner, at which there was real milk and not the powdered kind which was the only thing available in Korea, I shaved, made up my bunk, and practically ran to the Service Club. I had one thing in mind: to use music as a way to get home as fast as possible. This was the most beautiful Service Club I had seen in all of my army experience. I sought out the hostess there, a Miss Helt, and told her that I played the piano. The next thing I knew I was seated at a grand piano reading through a stack of popular and semi-classical songs. A huge crowd of soldiers gathered around and sang along with me. Before I knew it, two hours had slipped by. It was now 10 PM, and the time change had now taken its toll. I was utterly exhausted. Before I left the Service Club, Miss Helt told me that she would use her influence to help me get on a flight to New York City. I thanked her and fairly staggered back to the barracks, where I fell into my bunk totally exhausted. The luxurious feeling of an honest-to-goodness box-spring and mattress lulled me to sleep almost at once. But in a few hours, I was wide awake again and unable to sleep for the rest of the night.

October 29th, Wednesday

It has started all over again — processing, and more processing. Nothing can be more demeaning to a Korean veteran than standing for hours in long lines carrying heavy gear and wondering if you can actually make it to the next building, which is a mile or more away from where you are at the moment. And then the details: more K.P. starting at 3:30 AM, more policing of the area, more papers to read and to sign, and the worst of all — the humiliating short arm inspection.* After that disgusting groping of my privates, I sought out the Special Services officers, Captains Baggerly and Davies, and begged them to help me get on a flight home. According to them, this has already been arranged; I am scheduled to leave tomorrow. What a relief! My anxieties subsided immediately. My orders from General Van Fleet always drew raised eyebrows. Of course everyone inquired about the circumstances surrounding my meeting him. No sooner did those officers discover that I had performed for him as a pianist, than they asked me to record an eleven minute tape for a radio station called KECC, Eastern Contra Coastal, whatever that means.

Serious performing is the very last thing I feel like doing on this last leg of my journey. To begin with, I haven't practiced for the longest time. But somehow I managed to record a fairly decent program. After that, I spent the rest of the afternoon in the music room of the Service Club, which had a phonograph and a piano. I found a recording of the Liszt E flat Concerto with Rubinstein as soloist. I actually played along with him, although I could not keep up with his tempi. God, my technique has all but disappeared. But then, what can I expect without having practiced for so long now? The day has slipped away. I have exactly eight cents left after buying a snack in the Service Club. But tomorrow is pay day and I'll be rich again.

---

* "Short arm" is Army slang for penis. The inspection, a perfunctory examination for the purpose of spotting tell-tale signs of venereal disease, is carried out by a group of Army doctors. Soldiers are ordered to strip off their clothing and line up in front of their bunks. The doctors then go from soldier to soldier examining their rectums (each soldier is asked to "bend over and spread your cheeks") and their penises.

October 30th, Thursday

I have a story to tell of the most vicious, the most sadistic army savages that I have ever encountered — a lieutenant and a sergeant. They were attached to the 6212 Company in this Separation Center in Camp Stoneman and were placed in charge of Korean vets. Some of my buddies sported purple hearts and battle ribbons on their uniforms. One look into their eyes, and you knew that they had been through a living nightmare. This didn't faze the savages in the slightest. We were all ordered to police a four-block area. Needless to say, with the Korean experience behind us and our return to civilian life only a few days away, none of us felt particularly enthusiastic about picking up trash around Camp Stoneman. The savages in charge of us didn't like our attitude, and so they ordered us to drill for one and a quarter hours in the broiling sun without a break and then police the same area three times in succession. I am absolutely sure that there would have been two murders had we not turned in our weapons. And I would have been among the first to do the shooting. That lieutenant and sergeant typified the worst aspect of the brutal, inhuman army machine. It was a frightening example of what happens when power falls into the hands of twisted men, social misfits who end up punishing others because of their own failures in life.

I never did get my flight orders. Instead, I was given a train ticket for a three-day trip across the United States. At least I got a first class reservation, which included a berth in a Pullman car. So at the moment, I'm sitting on my comfortable lower berth in complete privacy. And I'm now ready for a good night's sleep.

November 3rd, Monday

The train pulled into the Trenton station at 5:30 AM. We had only to cross over to the other side of the platform to board a local train to New Brunswick. There, we got on an army bus which took us to our final destination, Camp Kilmer. We were told to report to building 1000, where all incoming soldiers had to be processed. Some of the men there told us that they had been waiting for weeks to be discharged, when it ought to have taken only a few hours. There were thousands of troops ready to be discharged and relatively few men to process them. In fact I met a few guys who had already exceeded their twenty-four month induction time.

Predictably, all of us were put to work immediately, pulling all sorts of details. I have Captains Morgan and Kimberly to thank for putting me on the roster to be formally discharged on November 8th.

After accomplishing this, I asked for a two-day pass, since I knew that it would take a few days before my papers were processed. I telephoned home, and Frank was standing by ready to pick me up. I then rushed into the latrine to shave and to shower. The water was ice cold, and it made me feel miserable.

When I had telephoned home, I had given Frank instructions to pick me up at the Camp Kilmer information booth. I waited outside for two hours and concluded that he must have driven to Fort Dix by mistake. The fact was, he and my father had taken a wrong turn and went twenty-five miles out of their way. It was getting dark, and I had all but given up on them, when I saw the headlights of my father's black Buick slowly coming towards me. My heart quickened. The car stopped directly in front of me. The driver's window rolled down, and a frantic sounding man, looking directly at me, asked, "Can you tell me where the information . . ." "Dad!" I cried, interrupting him. "Dad, it's me, Sonny!" My father was so upset at being late that he didn't even recognize his own son. Besides, I had grown very thin, and I must have looked haggard. Hearing my voice, and taking another look, he rushed out of the car without engaging the emergency brake. So the car continued to roll forward as he ran towards me shouting, "Sonny, Sonny, Sonny!" He repeated my name over and over again. Frank slid hurriedly behind the wheel and stopped the car. My father was sobbing when he flew into my open arms. For that brief moment, all of my past conflicts with him seemed to vanish. We embraced for a minute or two and I then hugged Frank, who by this time had come out of the car to greet me.

It took only forty minutes to drive home. There, across the pillars at the head of the stone steps was a sign, WELCOME HOME SONNY. My mom and my sisters were standing on the landing beneath the sign. I think I flew up four steps at a time and into my mother's arms. She kissed and caressed me and covered me with tears. Lil, Sylvia, and Evy were laughing and crying all at the same time. Saul was there, and I embraced him and thanked him for the kerosene burner. I then rushed up the stairs to our second floor apartment and flung off my coat. When Mom walked into the living room, I held her for minutes on end while she shed the rest of her tears. Finally, she dried her eyes. I was so overcome with emotion and fatigue that I found myself acting everything out without feeling anything at all. It embarrassed me that I did not cry along with everyone else.

My eyes scanned the living room. The piano had been moved to a different spot, and the sofa was now covered in scarlet red. On the piano were two photographs which I had sent home — one taken of me and General Van Fleet, and another one of me bowing on the stage of the Moonwha Kok Chong. After a few minutes, my mother flashed a broad smile and told me to go into my bedroom. I knew that a surprise awaited me there. I felt that same tingle of anticipation such as I remember experiencing as a little boy when awakening on Christmas morning. When I opened the door of my bedroom, my mouth fell open. It had been transformed into a dream world. I was too stunned to utter a sound. Never, never in my wildest imagination could I have envisioned such a room. It was all done in shades of brown, one of my favorite colors. The walls were covered with beige grass cloth with a bamboo motif, and chocolate brown drawstring curtains hung on the three windows. There was a new studio bed against the side wall covered in a heavy beige-colored fabric. There were bolsters and pillows on it covered with the same chocolate brown curtain material. My nieces flocked all around me wondering where their uncle had been all of this time, and wondering, too, why everyone was crying. I am sure that they felt self-conscious in trying to pick up the pieces of our relationship again.

The evening went by with high emotions expressed on everyone's part — everyone, that is, but me. My mother fed me a huge rib steak and my favorite potatoes mashed with chicken fat. Every few minutes I left the table to peek at my bedroom. I simply could not believe it. Finally, all of the family members went home, and I took a long shower. It seems silly to say so, but just being able to lock the door of the bathroom and turn on faucets that spewed forth hot and cold water seemed miraculous to me. I donned my favorite pajamas and kissed Mom and Dad good night and thanked them for everything. What it was to roll back the quilt of my new studio bed and slip in between the fresh sheets, I cannot begin to say. I fell into a deep, peaceful sleep almost at once — my first in a long time. My ordeal was over. Oh God, I was home again.

Policing of Another Sort

I was actually discharged from Camp Kilmer on the date that was promised — November 8, 1952. According to my discharge papers, I had spent one year, eleven months, and two days in the army. I had been awarded a Korean Service Medal with a Bronze Service Star, a United Nations Service Medal, and something called a Merit Unit Commander

Company 508 Headquarters EUSAK. On the appointed day of my separation from the army, I collected $296.74, turned in my duffel bag containing all of my clothing and bedding, and left Camp Kilmer with only the uniform I was wearing. It still hangs in my closet as a reminder of an experience whose impact upon my life can never really be adequately described in words.

Curiously, I had not read so much as a page of my diaries when I began this section of the book. It was September of 1992, almost forty years since I was discharged. I have mentioned that everyone in my family cried upon my return from Korea — everyone except me. But when I read my two diaries one Sunday in my New York City studio, I wept for hours on end, tears that had taken me forty years to shed. To use army jargon, one might say that I policed my unconscious and rooted out buried memories associated with that intermission in Korea. I faced it all for the first time — my youthful innocence, the dangers, the hardships, and the vital relationships that coursed through my life like those ever-changing patterns in a kaleidoscope. As I turned the pages, I realized what a privilege it was to rehearse and to perform as often as I did with artists like Kenneth Gordon and Robert Lamarchina, and what an adventure it was, performing under conditions such as few musicians experience. And I wept for other reasons, too. For at various points in those diaries, tragic scenes too intense for me to absorb at the time of their occurrence flashed into my consciousness with an agony that seemed more intense for all those years of sublimation: the sight of body bags, dying soldiers covered with bandages, the look of impending death in the eyes of my fellow soldiers on and near the front lines, and, in short, all of the horrors of war which words alone could not express. It is now clear to me that I had to repress certain things in order to survive. They have been haunting me all of these years. Only now can I face the full impact of them. The process has been, to be sure, a catharsis in the full meaning of the word.

The Korean War has gone down in history as being the first unpopular war this country fought, the Vietnam conflagration being the second. Generally speaking, the support system of governmental and private agencies seemed rather low-keyed, so that certain supplies which might have made our lives safer and more bearable never reached their destination. Americans continued to live their lives with little, if any, sacrifice on anyone's part, while military personnel in charge of supply units hotly complained about not receiving the supplies and rations which were promised them. Nor was there even enough money allocated to promote us from one rank to the next, promotions which would have meant an increase in our meager salaries. To cite my own case, I was promoted to

Part 3: The Army

Private First Class on July 27, 1951, and never exceeded that rank for the remainder of my induction period — and this after I had performed on the front lines and for practically every important military and civilian person in Korea. Because of all these things, many Korean veterans were embittered long before they returned to civilian life, not to mention the severe psychological problems they suffered once they experienced the apathetic climate at home. I remember the ho-hum attitude on the part of many Americans. With the exception of close relatives and friends, no one fussed over returning Korean veterans as they had over the veterans of World War II, for instance. Nor is there even today anything resembling the Vietnam Memorial recently erected in Washington, D.C., to which grieving families and friends could go for some small measure of comfort.

The first thing I did on the morning after my discharge was to go directly to Aunt Clara's home on Clinton Avenue, where her sister still lived. I was so grief-stricken when I arrived at the front door that I could hardly ring the bell. Once inside, the reality of losing my beloved teacher and friend merely intensified my bottled up emotions. I could neither openly grieve nor even communicate my feelings intelligibly. I heard myself saying rather perfunctory things to Aunt Clara's sister. She, on her part, hardly knew how to bring me out of myself, or what to say to comfort me. Much of Aunt Clara's music and other possessions had already been given away. But a drawing of me made by my friend Maxine Giannini, the wife of Ugo Giannini, with whom I had studied art while in my twenties, had my name on the back of it. I had given it to Aunt Clara, and she had hung it proudly in her music room on the wall to the right of her piano, where it had remained for almost ten years. I was sixteen when I posed for it, but Maxine, whom we all called Mikki, sketched me as a much older person. "You'll look like that when you're fifty," Aunt Clara said when she first saw it. Indeed, she has been proven right.

Thanks to my family, and especially to my mother, life at home could best be described as a protective cocoon in which I luxuriated in love and comforts too numerous to mention. My favorite foods, new clothing, and repeated hugs and kisses were all heaped upon me in almost embarrassing proportions. Little by little, I started to play the piano again and to explore various means of building up a class of pupils. My father wouldn't hear of my going back to work so soon. "Don't worry about teaching for a year or more," he told me. "Just stay home and practice and get back to yourself. I'll support you." Earlier, I mentioned that I viewed my father as a raven flying around outside of my protective dome. During the time I spent in Korea, however, I created a fantasy father who fulfilled all of my expectations. His offer, then, to support me during that transitional period

338

did much to fortify that fantasy. But in a month or so, the ghosts of the past and the ever-present awareness of a lack of communication between us intruded upon my everyday life. His generosity to me, which I ought to have appreciated, was one more confirmation of what I had always known: financial support and material things were poor, if not pitiful, substitutes for that precious bond between father and son, a bond which, I am sad to say, never did and never could exist for us.

Soon after my return to civilian life, I felt a strong need to separate from my father entirely and to strike out on my own. I had dreams of having my own apartment in New York City. But then there was my mother to consider. She had lived for nine months in constant fear that a telegram might arrive one day announcing the worst — that her son had been killed in action. She had decorated my room and had done every-thing possible to create the ideal environment for me. Certainly she deserved to have me home for at least a year. I planned to do just that — to remain at home for one more year before making the final break.

I, like so many other returning veterans, found it extremely difficult to adjust to civilian life. I never thought about what those difficulties were until years later. For one thing, I felt numb to the realities of civilian life. All the pleasures which I had taken for granted two years earlier — my mother's delectable cooking, the security and comfort of my room, and even the luxury of a long shower — now seemed temporal and unreal. I had the feeling that these simple pleasures would vanish again, leaving me bereft. It also occurred to me that I could not possibly convey to my family and friends the overwhelming experiences I had had, experiences that changed me considerably. This not only frustrated me, but it also caused me to think that those close to me would have preferred the person I used to be. The changes in me were more subtle than basic, the way a musician will alter a fingering, a nuance, or a rubato without changing the compo-sition itself. Similarly, although certain tastes, attitudes, and tolerances had gone through transformations, my personality remained the same. For one thing, after living through a life and death struggle, I had no patience with complaints or even innocent remarks about things which suddenly seemed petty to me: "I have to get a refund; the dress simply doesn't fit properly." "The steak was much better last week." "It's supposed to rain tomorrow." My intolerance of these things was totally unfair; after all, my family members had merely continued on familiar paths during my two year absence. But I had been wrenched from the course of my life and my relationships as well and thrust onto a new path, a life-altering one. It was up to me to readjust to old habits and attitudes. Now, two years later, I had to pick up the pieces and continue from where I had left off. But while the pieces seemed to be the same, the person who had left them behind had changed.

I am sure many servicemen who returned to civilian life must have battled with similar problems. Unlike most of them, I, at least, had my music to turn to. The thing that helped me more than anything else was adopting goals that would require a wholehearted dedication to practicing. Nothing, of course, makes a musician practice more diligently than a commitment to a performance. I had not been home more than a month when I did two things that shook me out of my lethargy: I enrolled in the summer music program at Fontainebleau, France, in 1953, and I booked Town Hall in New York City for January, 1954, in order to make my formal debut. At the time that I did this, I could not have been more ill-prepared to meet the standard of performance expected of me either at Fontainebleau or, least of all, in Town Hall. Simply taking on these commitments, however, returned me to that productive and satisfying life which I had been forced to leave two years earlier; my technique came back by leaps and bounds and I began to learn new pieces again. Just the latter, learning new pieces, gave me a sense of rebirth, and the courage to face the inevitable battles lying ahead.

PART 4:
THE BATTLE CONTINUES

And battles they were. Few activities in life are more difficult, more frustrating, and, at their worst, more ruinous to one's whole nervous system than striving for a performing career in music. Nevertheless, when I was in my twenties, my desire to overcome stage fright and my star-struck view of a career masked the reality of life on the stage.

While there is no set formula for achieving a career in music, certain requirements must be met, such as acquiring a virtuoso technique, expanding one's repertory, and playing frequently for conductors and managers. Above all, you must perform wherever you can find an audience. For no matter how well a piece may go during your practicing, nothing can supplant performing experiences.

The intense demands of practicing may result in neglecting everything else that makes for a well-rounded person. Creative activities like composing, writing, or painting get short shrift. Books are left unread, no matter how interested one may be in the subject. In short, one can shut out the world to the detriment of one's own humanity. This may result ulti-mately in a loss of self-esteem, a general feeling of dissatisfaction, and, ironically, an inability to probe to the heart of the music, which is our primary concern to begin with. All of us, I think, know secretly what we *ought* to do to become well-integrated people. What we may not fully appreciate, however, is that there is no justification for neglecting our total development, not even world-wide acclaim as musicians.

One might think that music teachers would be more qualified than other people to guide their students along the difficult path that leads toward a career in music. Curiously, though, the majority of music teachers are either ill-equipped for this task, or else they are too involved in their own careers to be concerned with their students' problems. In my own case, Clara Husserl and Louise Curcio knew absolutely nothing about careers, even though Aunt Clara's daughter, Hortense Monath, was one of the most respected performers in the profession. Regarding Alexander

Brailowsky, as I have already recounted, the only interest he showed in the status of my career was to suggest that I telephone his manager. He did so after the first lesson I had with him, and then for the next twenty years he never brought the subject up again. To be sure, his wife Ela made a superficial attempt to put me in touch with his manager in Spain after my recital in Alice Tully Hall — and this only because Donal Henahan, former music critic of *The New York Times*, who was known and feared for his acid reviews, happened to give me a rave review. As for Sir Clifford Curzon, he had all he could do to handle his own neuroses, let alone promote anyone else's career.

Can performing musicians turn to managers for help and guidance? Hardly. For one thing, the artist listings of big managers resemble the Manhattan telephone directory, a fact which prompted one manager for whom I once auditioned to exclaim, "I need another pianist like a hole in the head!" And considering the disparity between the supply of and demand for artists, most managers are the very last people to dispense help and guidance to performing musicians.

One can see, therefore, why so many young musicians with degrees from colleges and music conservatories feel utterly helpless and hopeless once they face the professional world. Having formerly drawn their audiences from faculty members and classmates, they now find it nearly impossible to assemble an audience on those rare occasions when they *do* play in public. A lack of engagements is bad enough. But the prospect of always having to play to empty halls can be most discouraging.

In point of fact, there *are* numerous and enthusiastic audiences everywhere. The trouble is, most of them have already been monopolized by concert representatives who prey upon key members of concert committees and promote their artists with the highest price tags. And why shouldn't they? The higher an artist's fee, the bigger a manager's commission, and commissions can range from ten to twenty-five percent of an artist's fee. Big fees, far from discouraging the members of concert committees, actually entice them. For if an item is more expensive, isn't it supposed to be better? This faulty way of thinking results in re-engagements of the same performers — those with high price tags. Not that the majority of them are undeserving of their popularity and their high fees. The point is, the public often rejects performers whose fees are more modest, in spite of the fact that some lesser-known musicians may perform as well as, if not better than, their well-known and high-priced counterparts.

WARNINGS

During their quest for performing careers, young aspiring musicians today face the same dangers as I did forty years ago. But knowing in advance what the career market is really like, they will, at least, be wary of overtures from those managers who demand retainer fees and have no intention of augmenting the careers of their artists. Besides, foreknowledge can cushion the blows of disillusionment should one's career go awry.

It is important to remember one thing: Performers who are marketable are in no less danger than those who are not. For paradoxically, they are often played to death by money-crazed managers who are more interested in commissions than they are in their artists' well-being.

Concerning musicians who are not marketable, managers simply drop them from their rosters with cold-hearted indifference. This is more likely to happen to international contest winners than to anyone else, and with devastating results. For what can be more defeating to a young performer than to emerge a winner, taste the "big time" for a year or two, and then suffer the shame and despair of being replaced by the next winner — especially if that person is better looking and has a wealthy backer? It would not be an exaggeration to suggest that exploitative managers use the same criteria for signing up an artist that they would for buying a car: both have to be totally efficient, nice to look at, and the latest model. And should a newly acquired artist prove not to be the money maker that had been anticipated, then managers, like all good businessmen, know exactly how to deal with a "white elephant": If a product doesn't sell, then get rid of it and find one that will.

Even if the former winner is retained by management, the number of his or her concerts may soon dwindle to a piddling few. Rejection, for whatever reason, can daunt the staunchest heart. But being dropped from a manager's roster is, to a performer, like the death of one's career, and a grave personal failure as well.

So long as money-crazed managers stalk the career jungle, younger performers can never, never, never be free to grow naturally and productively. An organization like Pro Musicis teaches us what can be accomplished when a concert agency is privately endowed and when the promotion of musicians is entrusted to saner people. We learn, too, from this organization the far-reaching benefits to be derived from extending sponsorship to musicians over the age of thirty-three, the upper age limit of most competitions.

I mourn the fact that State Department-sponsored tours, such as I enjoyed for over ten years, no longer exist. Recipients of such grants signaled to the world that the United States considered the arts and humanities to be a requisite of a civilized society. Without such sponsorship, there is little hope for the treasures of our society, those gifted musicians who have it within their power to spread harmony to a world sorely in need of it. Fortunately, not all of them will be plowed under like so many cornstalks. Functioning as though music itself dictates their actions and choices in life, a few musicians will find ways to sustain themselves and contribute beauty to the world. But the extent to which they get battered along the way was best expressed by one young performer who recently said to me, "I seriously wonder if society deserves what I'm trying to do." Considering what performing musicians must endure, one can understand how a person can be provoked into making a statement like that.

Musicians, of course, are not alone in reacting to the cruelty of the world. The fact is, most people question their motives and have compunctions about doing anything of a truly challenging nature, even in the unlikely event that society rewards them for their efforts. If the ego is, as Jung suggested, "the gatekeeper to consciousness," then it seems that all manner of real and imagined phantoms constantly crash through that gate. Some musicians build up their defenses against such phantoms and become aggressive and arrogant. Others, being gentler by nature, pursue an idealistic course, only to be slapped down repeatedly by more aggressive people and by one rejection after another. Still others, mercilessly invaded by the most destructive phantom of all — low self-esteem and its consequence, self-destructiveness — whimper into submission and fade away: "I have no engagements, which means that no one likes my playing." A kin feeling to: "I have no lover, which means that I'm not lovable." And needless to say, there are gifted people with harmonious natures whom society has just plain neglected.

SIR CLIFFORD CURZON — INSPIRATION AND CONFLICT

Sir Clifford Curzon, more than any of my other teachers, was in a position to help me gain a foothold in the performing field. Unfortunately, however, he had a problem related to his own career. While he was undeniably one of the most revered artists in the world, he nevertheless used to joke far too often about his not being a household name, as Rubinstein and Horowitz were, for instance. I always took this to mean that he felt slighted by the public and not appreciated as fully as he thought he deserved to be. Yet, complain though he did, Sir Clifford once told me that he never felt more unhappy than when he was on the stage. I would even go as far as to say that he hated to perform in public, mostly because he suffered from

Sir Clifford Curzon trying out pianos in Steinway's basement.
(Photo by Seymour Bernstein)

performance anxiety — an anxiety that often gained in momentum as he continued to play. He did his best playing during the last years of his life. (He died in 1982 at the age of seventy-five.) When I expressed my awe at the beauty of his playing when he was in his seventies, he exclaimed, "It's because I no longer care. I have let go of my defenses." But earlier in his career, I rarely heard him play as beautifully in public as he did in the Steinway basement, during those memorable hours when he and I were either going over concerti or trying out pianos for his New York City appearances. But even at such times, he would often be seized by some internal agony, and without warning, he would vent his rage on me.

What most disturbed me about Sir Clifford was his inner conflict. This took the form of his openly expressing ambivalence about the stage and being hyper-critical of himself and suspicious of me and everyone else. Early on in our relationship he showed clearly that he would do nothing to promote my career. When, for example, my manager tried to get me a date at the Metropolitan Museum of Art in New York City, he was told by the director of the concert series that a letter of recommendation from Sir Clifford would carry great weight. Without informing me, my manager wrote to Sir Clifford. Back came a flat refusal. The reason? "If Seymour cannot get the date on his own merits, I don't believe he should be engaged at all!" I would never have known about this had not Sir Clifford himself brought up the subject during his next tour to the United States. It would be difficult to say who angered me more — my manager, for writing to Sir Clifford without first consulting me, or Sir Clifford, for his refusal to write a letter of recommendation for his own pupil, something most teachers do as a matter of course.

Sir Clifford's sanctimonious stance — make it on your own, or don't make it at all — was inconsistent with the facts surrounding the early stages of his own career. For he had had the support of such notable figures as Nadia Boulanger and Sir Henry Wood. Why, then, did Sir Clifford take this position when it came to helping me and other musicians? Being unduly critical of my own playing, I concluded, at first, that he didn't think me capable of measuring up to the high calibre of performance expected of those who appear on such a series. I later ruled this out, however, primarily because he openly admired my playing and even once confessed to being envious of certain qualities I had. Being taken aback by what was obviously a supreme compliment from someone of his stature, I was too modest to pursue the subject. I therefore never discovered what those qualities were.

I have several theories about Sir Clifford's refusal to recommend me, one being that he was highly competitive, even with a person like me, though I at the time of this incident had no career to speak of. Moreover, he did not trust anyone's ability to survive a performance, no matter how gifted he or she might be, simply because he felt such insecurity himself. Possibly he thought that were I to succumb to nerves at a performance which had come about through his recommendation, my failure would certainly reflect upon him. And so he was reluctant to extend a helping hand to a student. I believe that his never-ending struggle against stage fright and the fragility of his nervous system required him to marshal all of his energy toward surviving from day to day. He simply had no energy to spare and was too insecure about his own reputation to extend himself in altruistic endeavors. Quite obviously, I had ambivalent feelings towards Sir Clifford. For though he was my hero, musically, he fell far short of that status, personally.

Sir Clifford performed in the United States every two years. Each time that something displeased him — "The hotel desk clerks are rude!" "I can't get a decent pot of tea in this country!" — he swore never to return to America again. But he continued to come, nevertheless, until he died. On one of his tours, he was scheduled to perform two concerti at the Metropolitan Museum of Art in New York City. I brought with me to that concert a large contingent of my pupils. Afterwards, we tagged onto the end of a long line of well-wishers. In fact, we were the very last ones to enter the green room. My intention was to introduce my pupils to Sir Clifford, while my pupils, on their part, wanted only to express their admiration for his artistry.

Sir Clifford, like most performers, suffered intense anguish when he felt that he had not performed his best. Here, too, artists are put to the test: some learn to suffer in silence and allow well-wishers to express their own opinions; other artists will attack you with the venom of their own discontent. Sir Clifford belonged to the second group.

Proud of my long and intimate relationship with Sir Clifford, and proud, too, in being the teacher of the gifted students who were now standing before him — his grandchildren, as I referred to them — I proceeded to introduce each one to the master. They, however, became awestruck in his presence and simply lost their tongues. They filed past him more like mourners viewing a body than inspired members of his audience. Unable to bear the silence one more moment, Sir Clifford screamed out to them, "Say something! Don't just stand there and gape at me. I have no patience for this. Besides, I have to leave for a reception."

There was another matter between him and me, a matter which my pupils knew nothing about. As it happened, Sir Clifford had mentioned to me on the previous day how desperately he needed to have a sport jacket cleaned: "But I don't like to send it to the cleaners," he said. "The fabric is too fine to be submitted to harsh chemicals." Having a neighbor who happened to be a well-known fashion designer, I consulted with her about this matter. She graciously consented to hand-clean the jacket herself. This being accomplished, I then personally delivered the jacket to the hotel and gave it to the head concierge. "Do not under any circumstances disturb Sir Clifford today," I warned the man. "He has a concert to perform this evening, and he will either be practicing or resting. Please wait until the morning to deliver it."

After Sir Clifford had shot his hostile barbs at my pupils, he then turned upon me with a rage that sent shivers through everyone present. "And where's my jacket?" he screamed. "If it's lost, there will be hell to pay!" This was the last straw. I turned on my heel and stormed out of the green room without so much as a word about the jacket or anything else. My fledglings, all pale and much perturbed by this attack upon their teacher, followed me obediently, and, I am sure, with a sense of relief.

The following evening, Sir Clifford invited me to dinner. He was amiable and typically generous in his insistence on my ordering whatever I wanted from the menu. He had, by that time, received his jacket, meticulously hand-cleaned and pressed, which brought on garlands of thank-you's and apologies for doubting my responsibilities to it. Sir Clifford could not know, of course, that I had gathered from my pupils written declarations of praise, the very sentiments they would have expressed to him directly had he been civil and patient enough to help them break through their reticence. After the order had been given to the waiter, I produced these notes and waited until he had read each one of them. Then my own temper got the better of me: "All of this," I said to him, "would have been told to you directly after you played. But your own discontent cheated you out of enjoying it, and cheated my pupils, too, out of expressing their admiration for your playing. And in regard to the way you treated me, it would be impossible for my pupils to know that I was anything other than a lackey to you — and an irresponsible one, at that. So from now on, I will simply admire you as a member of your audience. You will never see me backstage again."

Sir Clifford was mortified by all of this. He apologized profusely, and begged me to extend his apologies to my pupils: "And thank them, please, for their touching notes," he added. Although he was fully aware of his irascible behavior, he seemed unable to control it. He was guilty of similar behavior on many other occasions. I noticed that he seemed to lash out most viciously at the people who were closest to him. He and I were very close — close enough to have seen one another almost every day during his stays in New York City. His attacks upon me flared up now and then over a period of some twenty years. They would come when I least expected them to. In a flash, he would all but destroy me with some unwarranted criticism that was not even related to what we were doing at the moment. I would, for example, be sitting at a second piano playing the orchestra part of a concerto with him in the Steinway basement, or we would be discussing some fine musical point after a rehearsal he had had with the New York Philharmonic, when suddenly a demon would possess him. "Why do you comb your hair that way," he once snarled at me in the lobby of Avery Fischer Hall. "You look like a parrot!" The fact was that it was very windy outside, and the wind had blown my hair into a sort of cockscomb. Since I wanted to be on time for Sir Clifford's rehearsal in that hall, I did not stop for any reason whatsoever, and least of all to comb my hair.

Unquestionably, Sir Clifford suffered from some deep-seated psychological disorder. On the one hand, I had deep compassion for him just thinking of the suffering this must have caused him; on the other hand, my concern for him did not lessen in the slightest the impact of his cruel attacks upon me. At one point, I became so distressed that I began to wonder whether the musical benefits I derived from him were worth the pain he inflicted upon me. I finally decided that it was, in fact, worth it, and that I could not forfeit the musical nourishment I received from him. While I always had the deepest musical respect for Sir Clifford, a respect which bordered on hero-worship, I countered his attacks upon me with harsh reprimands. It was the only way I could find to continue our inspirational and highly productive musical relationship, and at the same time maintain my sense of dignity in the face of his irrational behavior.

It saddens me to say that Sir Clifford, his great artistry notwithstanding, showed nothing in his person that in any way resembled the integrity, the devotion, and the humanity which informed his playing. Some terrible weakness within him, some insecurity which, I believe, was exacerbated by the demands of a major career, often caused him to make unwarranted attacks on others and even to self-destruct on the stage. For although he was unquestionably one of the great artists of our time, he was, nonetheless, capable of falling far below the high standard which one expects of an artist of that calibre. A demon resided within him, and I, for one, was repeatedly exposed to it.

In this book and elsewhere, I have often expressed the view that music can integrate the personality and thus unite the musician with the person. This profoundly unifying property of music can only be activated under two conditions: the practicers of music must believe in it wholeheartedly, and they must consciously work towards its promotion. To be sure, artistic gifts are often incommensurate with moral and philosophical principles, as is exemplified by the repugnant social views of figures such as Richard Wagner, Pablo Picasso, Ezra Pound, and T. S. Elliot. Their magnificent works seemed not to have harmonized the person in the slightest. If the truth be told, Sir Clifford, being an example of how the musician can be divided from the person, spurred me on to suggest that the opposite can obtain.

I responded to Sir Clifford's death with ambivalent feelings: one part of me was relieved never to have to suffer at his hands again; the other part of me, the musical part, was bereft. No musician I have ever heard understood and projected the language of music more poetically and more convincingly than he did. It saddens me to think that his genius could not ameliorate the confusion of his inner world, that the artist could not create within the person the grace and harmony with which he sculpted those inimitable Mozartian phrases.

Now that Sir Clifford is gone, I can disclose something that I have kept secret all of these years: In 1976, I wrote a letter to Queen Elizabeth. Never having written to royalty before, I had no idea of how to address a Queen. So my salutation read quite simply, "Your Majesty." I told the Queen that we in America revered Clifford Curzon's artistry and we wondered why he had not been knighted, as had been Dame Myra Hess and other notable English musicians. I addressed the letter to Buckingham Palace, London, and thought no more about it. Then one day, during the Christmas season of 1976, I received an envelope with a beautiful red seal on the back flap. "What good taste for a Christmas card," I thought. I opened it and gasped at its content:

BUCKINGHAM PALACE
The Private Secretary is
commanded by Her Majesty The Queen
to acknowledge the receipt of
Mr. Seymour Bernstein's
letter and to state that it has been
transmitted to the Prime Minister.
15th December, 1976

Two months later, Clifford wrote to me that he had been knighted. Was this mere coincidence, or did my letter achieve this end? I will never know. But I do know that had Sir Clifford been aware of what I had done, he would have erected a guillotine in the plaza of Lincoln Center and gleefully beheaded me.

ON MY OWN

The long and short of it was that I was left to fend for myself. I sought the advice of my colleagues as to how to promote my career; I read accounts by well-known performers on how they made it to the top; and I met various managers along the way who had their own pet formulae for success. Arthur Judson on the subject: "You've got to have a gimmick!" A "gimmick," I reasoned, must be anything from specializing in one composer to assuming eccentric poses, such as crossing one leg over the other during a piano recital in Carnegie Hall or placing a glass of water on the music desk and sipping it while the New York Philharmonic plays the introductory *tutti* to Beethoven's Concerto No. 3. These were only two of Glenn Gould's premeditated and, in my opinion, outrageous eccentricities, to which audiences were drawn with a sort of morbid fascination. With all due respect for Gould's magnificent performances and recordings of Bach, I found his interpretations of almost every other composer to be an affront to the art of music. Once, for example, while listening to him play the Beethoven's Sonata Op. 110 in Carnegie Hall, I had the distinct feeling that I was being slapped in the face, such were the aberrant interpretations presented by this arrogant cult figure. One has only to hear his recordings of Mozart and Beethoven sonatas to understand just how far an artist can go in duping the public. But what else can one expect from a person who expressed contempt for masters such as Mozart and Beethoven?

Back to making it as a performer — apart from specializations and bizarre devices, there were then, and still are, other more legitimate means of making it to the top. Winning an international contest, getting a rave review in *The New York Times*, attracting the enthusiastic support of a major conductor, or having a rich sponsor who *buys* your career can all be eminently effective. Concerning the latter, it is possible to buy the services of big time managers and artist representatives and even to buy engage-ments with major symphony orchestras. I have already told the story of my own manager who offered me a debut with the London Symphony Orchestra for $750, an offer which I categorically rejected. Needless to say, neither money nor even being the daughter of the President of the United States (I am thinking of the soprano Margaret Truman) will launch a career, unless the person in question can deliver the goods. Moreover, the unpredictable factors associated with careers are such that even though a musician delivers the goods, he or she may still not make it to the top. But it must also be said that true genius carves out its own destiny, with or without awards, money, or the influence of people in high places.

For the fifteen years following my discharge from the army, I tried my hand at most of the means mentioned above. It was specifically to

A moment in musical history, during a chamber music class at Fontainebleau, France, 1954. Georges Enesco, bent over with tuberculosis of the spine, is playing from memory the openings of each movement of the Beethoven string quartets, in order to demonstrate what he believed to be convincing tempi. Violist Pierre Pasquier, leaning against the organ, is sketching Enesco. And Nadia Boulanger, overcome with emotion, is wiping away a tear. (Photo by Seymour Bernstein)

promote my career that I attended the Conservatoire de Fontainebleau during the summer of 1953, less than a year after my return from Korea. There I met Sir Clifford Curzon, who gave three days of master classes. Since only one other student and I adhered to the syllabus chosen by Sir Clifford, we were the only ones allowed to perform for him. And what sessions they were! The phrases that Sir Clifford demonstrated while sitting at a second piano and each comment he made were genuine revelations to me. Memorable, too, were classes with Nadia Boulanger and chamber music master classes with Georges Enesco, who was pitifully hunched over due to tuberculosis of the spine. Yet his memory, for which he had always been famous, was as keen as it had always been. As Nadia Boulanger said when she introduced Enesco to us, "He can play every instrumental piece from memory, including all chamber music works." Enesco, as though to prove her point, hobbled to the piano and played the openings of each movement of the Beethoven String Quartets in order to demonstrate what he believed to be convincing tempi. None of us had ever witnessed such an astonishing feat. During the second day of his classes, the violinist Bill Bruni and I performed the Sonata by César Franck, only to learn that Enesco had actually performed it for Franck himself. He then proceeded to demonstrate the tempi which Franck had requested of him, tempi which were decidedly slower than ours.

At the end of the summer session, I won the Fontainebleau competition, which carried with it the Prix Jacques Durand, a cash award of 200,000 francs. According to the rate of exchange in those days, it came out to $560.00, a sum which I considered to be a fortune of money. The Fontainebleau award caused only a moderate stir in musical circles.

As for international competitions, I never entered them. Nor was I able to engage the support of a major conductor, even though I once performed for Eugene Ormandy on the stage of the Academy of Music in Philadelphia, albeit badly, and for Leopold Stokowski in his Fifth Avenue apartment in New York City. That audition went very well, but he retired from conducting shortly afterwards. I also auditioned for Stanislaw Skrowaczewski, who was very enthusiastic about my playing, but admitted that he could not engage me with his orchestra because I did not have a big enough name. Only big names, he told me, could attract subscribers to his concert series. I did, however, accumulate some rave reviews in *The New York Times* and elsewhere. And, what is more, I had a rich patroness.

I was only moderately disheartened by these rejections because, as I have already stated, I never wanted to make it to the top. The thought of it frightened me. Besides, after performing in Korea and discovering firsthand just how gratifying it could be to perform for people who really wanted to listen to me play, I saw the commercial aspects of careers — scrounging to obtain performing dates and, especially, dealing with managers — as being unwholesome, anti-musical, and altogether repugnant. Rich sponsors can be exceedingly helpful to young artists by subsidizing them so that they can practice without worrying about how to pay the rent. But many of them exact a price for their support, such as openly or tacitly demanding your time, your gratitude, or even your body. Few, if any, support young musicians unconditionally. Why then, I asked myself repeatedly, should I, or anyone else, for that matter, want a major performing career? Why was I grooming myself for one by making telephone calls, arranging auditions, and sending off my publicity materials to concert agents and directors of concert series — things I resented doing? I always came up with the same answer: "I am doing this because I love music. I want to serve music by performing it." A love of music, then, was my chief motivation. Beyond this, I knew that performing regularly would eventually enable me to overcome my fears and weaknesses.

If I were now asked to give advice to young aspirants, I would say that playing as often as you can and wherever possible — school auditoriums, places of worship, or simply at a friend's studio where two or three people may gather to serve as your audience — is the surest way of overcoming stage fright. It is a way of establishing a belief in your own ability to survive, of building your self-esteem, and, in short, of learning respect for yourself and trust in others. Survivors learn the true meaning of self-respect, so that even when critics or judges deride them, they are left, nonetheless, with a sense of victory within themselves.

THE MOVE TO NEW YORK CITY

After Fontainebleau, and after my New York City debut, I combed the streets of New York City looking for an apartment. My father hotly opposed my desire to move away from home: "You'll spend all of your time trying to support yourself, and you won't have enough time to practice." On the face of it, his warning sounded convincing. Yet he had other reasons for wanting me to stay at home, reasons that were not altogether in my best interests. For one thing, my three sisters had married by that time, and I was the last child remaining at home. It is not unusual, of course, for parents to miss their children when they go off to college or leave home permanently. But when a relationship is fraught with difficulties, a child's move away from home can cause a

354

parent to experience real or imagined associations — from rejection to an awareness of advancing age. Beyond this, it is never easy to abdicate the role of parental protector and adviser. In my father's case, I believe that losing me meant facing the emptiness of his own personal life. He was also a man consumed with fears, and my presence at home, however odd I must have appeared to him, somehow served to ameliorate his fears. In short, I felt that his warning to me stemmed more from his own selfish needs than from consideration for my well-being.

My mother, on the other hand, hotly argued against my father's point of view: "Let him go, Max. What can we offer him here? He's an artist, and he belongs in New York City, where he can pursue his career. Besides, he's a man, and he ought to be on his own." Quite obviously, my living at home enabled my mother to exercise her best maternal instincts. Yet she proved her love for me over and over again by wanting what was best for me. In this instance, she urged me to find a suitable apartment where I could begin to lay the foundations for achieving a goal that is even more difficult to attain than a career in music — that of becoming an adult.

My Haven

In 1955, the real estate market in New York City enjoyed a period of prosperity that has not been equaled since. It was a buyer's market for enterprising investors, especially those who bought up those grand old brownstones on the Upper West Side for the purpose of converting them into separate apartments. For prospective tenants like me, the choices were endless and the rents reasonable. I could not have chosen a more opportune time to move to the Big Apple. One ad in the Apartments for Rent section of *The New York Times* looked particularly attractive: an entire brownstone was being renovated, and interested parties would have a wide choice of apartments and even a voice in the final decoration of them.

Arriving at the address the following day, I was immediately greeted by the owner, Minnie Small, who was as petite as her two names implied. No sooner had I seen apartment 1A than I made up my mind to rent it. It had an old-world look and epitomized my fantasy of the sort of apartment I had always wanted. What attracted me most were the high ceilings, the wood-burning fireplace, sculptured cupids above the mantelpiece, and one wall composed of bevel-edged granite blocks typical of the architecture around the turn of the century. Twenty-five feet long and fifteen feet wide, the room had an interesting shape. There was an alcove carved out at the far end of the room which looked very much like a stage. I imagined my Steinway standing there, and I felt strongly that its sound in that strategic location at the front of the house would hardly disturb anyone living above or below me. Mrs. Small escorted me to all five floors of the brownstone to see the other apartments. Some of them were exceedingly beautiful. But in the end, my first impression was the strongest, and I decided upon apartment 1A. When I told her that I was a pianist, that I practiced a great deal and also gave lessons, she was not fazed in the slightest. As she told me, the rent for that one-and-a-half room apartment would have been $110 a month. But with a semi-professional lease — and this was exactly what I needed — it would be $115. In spite of settling all of these particulars, Mrs. Small was in no hurry to have me sign a lease. She may have looked innocent, but she was shrewd and cautious. To her, I was a young, struggling musician and, therefore, a poor security risk. She would not offer me a lease until she met my mother. This was totally acceptable to me, for I would not have taken the apartment anyway before showing it to my mother.

On the following morning, I returned to the building with my mother. Seeing the facade of the brownstone, she was just as excited as I was. Rushing into the main room from the hallway, I noticed the contractor standing in the middle of the floor with a sullen expression on his face. In the next moment, my eyes scanned the right wall of the apartment. To my horror, I noticed that not only were the magnificent granite blocks covered over with plaster, but worse than that, the cupids above the fireplace had been chopped off of the wall and were lying in pieces on the floor. "What have you done?" I asked the contractor incredulously. "You have destroyed a work of art!" He looked at me with a woeful expression. "I argued with the old lady all morning," he cried. "But she forced me to do it. She was convinced that your mother would think that the sculpture and the granite blocks were old fashioned. Then she would never let you sign the lease."

Needless to say, my mother and I were devastated. To us, it was an unforgivable act of barbarism. But with or without the sculpture and the granite blocks, the layout of the apartment suited my needs ideally, and I was intent upon renting it. Suddenly Mrs. Small appeared. One look at my mother, who, as always, was exquisitely dressed, and a few minutes of conversation with her, and the deal was consummated.

The Portable Supermarket

I was euphoric on the day that I moved to New York City, but my mother was positively shattered. At first, she seemed to be in control of herself. But when the movers arrived and rolled my Steinway out of the house, she broke down in sobs. And when they emptied my bedroom, the room that my mother had fussed over in anticipation of my return to civilian life, she seemed disconsolate. She was still wiping away her tears as I hugged her goodbye and went with the movers to my new home.

In time, my mother got over the shock of losing me. Several months later, when my father was more solvent than he had been in the past, they moved away from Newark and into a smaller apartment in Millburn, New Jersey, an elegant community with lots of good shopping nearby. There were other conveniences too. For one thing, they were now living closer to my three sisters. But the best convenience of all, as far as my mother was concerned, was the bus stop directly in front of her apartment. She not only had access to a local bus, but, more importantly, to an express bus, one every hour, to New York City!

And into the Big Apple my mother came, every other week. That she was able to walk with the three or four heavy shopping bags she always brought merely proves that earth mothers can accomplish anything. The bags contained a veritable supermarket — meat, chicken, eggs, butter, cheese, bread, toilet paper, soap, paper towels — everything that she thought I needed. That I was able to buy my own paper towels, for instance, just around the corner did not dissuade my mother in the slightest. "Paper toweling is the greatest convenience in the world," she told me. "You can never have enough paper toweling." So she always managed to stuff two giant-size rolls into those shopping bags along with everything else.

Gefilte Fish, Chicken Soup, and Turmoil

The first day in my new apartment, I realized that I had never been alone before. Those one and a half rooms symbolized to me then, as they do now, a self-contained universe over which I had complete control. I loved my privacy. Even to this day, nothing makes me happier than spending hours alone in the seclusion of my apartment.

I was determined to live as disciplined a life as possible, which meant, first of all, no television. In fact, I lived in that apartment for ten years before I weakened and allowed my mother to give me her old black and white portable TV set. But by that time, I had learned that practicing and reading came before everything else.

The winter months were especially appealing to me. For then, the slightest chill in the air was reason enough to light the fire. I often spent hours sitting cross-legged on the floor in front of my fireplace luxuriating in my new-found independence. When friends visited, we all sat on the floor and tackled the world's problems, as the fire cast flickering shadows upon our faces.

Part 4: The Battle Continues

Mrs. Small lived with her two daughters in a duplex basement apartment, the top entrance of which was down the hall from my apartment. In time, she replaced "Mr. Boinstein" with "Seymour," which she managed to pronounce very decently. Usually on a Friday, my bell would ring, and Mrs. Small would appear with samples of her Jewish Sabbath cooking — a portion of gefilte fish, a container of chicken noodle soup, or some other specialty which she was sure a nice Jewish boy would enjoy. Although I was merely her tenant, she treated me as though I were her grandson.

After I had been living there for five years, Mrs. Small's elder daughter, Ann, began to show signs of mental deterioration. She died within a year. Then shortly after that, Mrs. Small herself began to show the same symptoms. One Friday afternoon while I was teaching, I smelled acrid smoke. Opening my apartment door, I peered out into the hall and saw smoke rising from the basement area where Mrs. Small lived. Fortunately, I had been given the key to her apartment, just in case of an emergency. I rushed downstairs, followed by my pupil, and knew enough to unlock the door to the Small apartment cautiously. For had there been a fire in the apartment, I and the entire building would have been in danger. The scene that greeted me was appalling. The apartment was filled with the smoke of burnt cooking, and there, sprawled on the living room floor, was poor Mrs. Small alternately moaning and crying for help. I don't know whether she had fainted or simply tripped. But the fact was, she was lying there with a broken hip. First, I rushed over to her to assure her that she would be safe. Next, I ran into the kitchen to close the burners on her gas range. The kitchen light activated a ventilator fan in the ceiling, and instantly, the smoke was pulled up and out through a vent. At the same time, my pupil opened all of the windows. I then dialed 911 for an ambulance. Finally, I telephoned Lillian, Mrs. Small's younger daughter, at the office where she worked.

And now I directed my attention to Mrs. Small herself. When I knelt down and cradled her head in my arm, the poor woman was almost delirious with gratitude. She told me that she had been lying on the floor for a full hour calling for help. The policemen who arrived on the scene told me that entering the kitchen with thick smoke billowing out of two pots might have been life-threatening to me. All agreed that had I not found Mrs. Small when I did, she would have died from asphyxiation. Lillian and the ambulance arrived almost simultaneously. Shocked and tearful at the same time, she thanked me for saving her mother's life. Mrs. Small was taken to the hospital and then to a nursing home. I never saw her again. She died some nine years later.

The Noise Maker in Apartment 1A

In the meantime, Lillian, who had been living on the top floor of the building, moved into her mother's basement apartment. Around 1968, she married a dentist named Henry Littman, a man whom her mother despised. Together, they managed, or, as we tenants used to whisper to one another, haunted, the brownstone. Lillian used to prowl from floor to floor with a chain of keys dangling from her hand. More than one tenant remarked that she looked, and also behaved, like the warden of a prison. She always knew when her tenants were out, and she had the habit of letting herself into their apartments and snooping around. As to her speaking voice, when I mimic the nasal twangs and inflections of New Yorkese, I sound in jest exactly as Lillian sounded in fact.

Henry haunted the brownstone in his own inimical way. If anything needed fixing, he was on the spot with his tool chest. Whether he was qualified or not, he would attempt to fix anything at all rather than pay a professional. More than once, a problem that could have been rectified easily ended up costing much more money, not to mention aggravation and wasted time.

I found something frightening about the man. The mere sound of his sinister voice, which emanated from rigid jaws and lips whose corners alternately lifted in sneers, was enough to send shivers through the bravest of souls. His eyes were no less sinister than his voice; they constantly shifted and rarely met yours. When they did, they fixed you with the menacing look of a criminal who might be hatching some ungodly scheme against you.

Around the time of this delightful couple's reign, our building, along with many others in New York City, came under the aegis of the Rent Stabilization Bureau, a city-run agency that regulated the percentage at which landlords might raise their tenants' rent from year to year. When, however, tenants moved out of rent-stabilized apartments, it was common for landlords to make minor renovations and then jack up the rent for the next tenant. The same practice exists today.

Back to the newlyweds — at first, they behaved rather civilly towards me and the other tenants. But soon, higher taxes and out-and-out greed on their part overrode common decency and turned them into miserly, Dickensian landlords. Fabricating reasons such as "I need your apartment for a relative of mine," Lillian systematically evicted a few of the low-paying tenants who, like me, had lived in the house for many years. Having met with no resistance whatsoever on the part of the tenants in question, she then fixed her attention on the lowest-paying tenant in the building — me. That I had been the building's first tenant, and that I had rescued her mother from certain death, seemed not to matter to Lillian in the slightest. Besides, words such as allegiance, devotion, or gratitude are not usually found in the vocabularies of people who are ruled by money. Speaking about gratitude, more than one friend suggested to me that Lillian was perhaps secretly furious with me for having saved her mother's life. For as I said earlier, Mrs. Small loathed Henry. Moreover, she had grown senile and was a constant source of worry to Lillian. From Lillian's standpoint, it may have been more convenient had her mother died of smoke inhalation.

Before recounting the details of the protracted war which my landlords were soon to wage against me, I should mention that until that time I had lived in almost total harmony with the Small family and with all of the tenants in the building. This is saying a great deal when one considers the sheer number of hours I practiced and taught daily. My neighbors were almost exclusively music-lovers. One of them, a woman who lived on the third floor, used to slip her favorite compositions under my door in the hope that I would add them to my repertory. Moreover, before 1977, there were some five different tenants in the basement apartment below mine. All but one of them complimented me repeatedly on my and my pupils' playing. One neighbor, a physicist, loved my playing to such an extent that he rang my bell one morning and asked if he could come into my apartment and listen to me practice the *Eroica* Variations by Beethoven. While I was extremely flattered by this, I had to turn him down. For I did not think that I could concentrate properly were he to sit in the room and stare at me during my practicing.

In July of 1977, Lillian rented the apartment to one Ms. L., who seemed quite amiable at first. All previous tenants living there had been informed in advance that a pianist practiced and taught on the floor above. Whether my landlords purposely withheld this information from Ms. L., or subsequently used her to achieve their own end, I cannot be sure. The fact is, she began to complain about my piano playing almost immediately. "I've got a splitting headache," she would squeal over the telephone, "and the piano is driving me crazy!" Yet she thought nothing of blasting her hi-fi late into the night and on Sundays as well. The rumble and the vibrations disturbed not only me, but also the tenants on the second floor.

I have always been aware of how disturbing intense and prolonged piano playing can be, so I did not think it unreasonable when Lillian asked me to carpet the area under my piano to protect Ms. L. from the intense sound. I went to Macy's department store, consulted with an acoustician there, and ordered a double acoustical pad, plus the thickest carpet that one could buy — all at a considerable expense to me. Beyond this, I respected Ms. L.'s need for silence as far as I was able to, especially during evenings and on weekends when I knew she was home. At such times, I either played *pianissimo*, or else I restricted my practicing to a silent keyboard, as I was already in the habit of doing. I also moved all of my performing classes to my pupils' own apartments. But when the time drew closer for my own performances, I had to practice full throttle and simulate the dynamics that I would use for the performance itself.

In spite of all these measures, Ms. L. continued to telephone the police, once as early as 8 PM. I remember that evening in particular, for I was practicing the "Trout" Quintet by Schubert, *pianississimo*, for a forthcoming performance. Whatever one might say about the policemen in New York City, the ones who rang my bell could not have been more polite or considerate. They told me, quite frankly, that I had a right to practice. With a smile and a wink, they then went downstairs to try to placate Ms. L. The policemen were no more successful, however, than I had been. The squealing on the telephone increased, policemen continued to ring my bell, and heaven knows how often and how intensely she must have squealed to Lillian and Henry.

Then one morning in early January, Lillian slipped a note under my door. It was, in effect, a schedule of practicing which she insisted I adhere to. Evenings were restricted entirely and I was forbidden to begin my practicing before 10 AM. Having to prepare for various auditions and performances, I simply ignored this new schedule and went on with my practicing. Lillian's response to my insubordination was swift and firm. On the morning of January 22, 1978, I received a registered letter from "Lams Realty" ("Small" spelled backwards), signed by Lillian, to the effect that my hours of practicing must be limited and my teaching curtailed. Lillian knew that I derived my income chiefly from teaching. What she did not know, however, was that some of my gifted pupils were simply too poor to pay my full fee, while a few others, who did not even have enough money to eat properly, were on full scholarships. Considering the fact that I barely eked out a living in those days and that apartment rentals elsewhere were almost three times higher than what I was paying, I had to fight to stay in my apartment.

At the time that Lillian and Henry hatched this scheme to get rid of me, I had been practicing, teaching, and rehearsing with other musicians for twenty-three years. I had done so thinking that I was still under the protection of my original semi-professional lease. But as I subsequently discovered, the clause which had originally given me permission to practice and to teach had been left out of all of my leases for the past fifteen years. What still protected me, however, was a real estate law called "squatter's rights," a wordless contract which gives a tenant of long standing the right to continue his tenancy and his activities. To be sure, twenty-three years of practicing and teaching certainly qualified me for squatter's status! I explained all of this to Lillian in a letter which I wrote a week later. In it, I rejected the contents of her letter as being "arbitrary, capricious, and an invasion of my rights as a tenant in this building." The last phrase, containing pure legal jargon, was only one of many that I learned from the lawyer husbands and fathers of several of my pupils. In fact, all of my pupils rallied to my defense.

Three weeks later, Lillian's attorney informed me that I was in violation of the law and would be forced to move. My initial response to his letter was one of sheer panic. Without knowing my rights as a tenant, I seriously thought that I would be evicted from my apartment. But when I consulted with the directors of the West Side Tenants Union, I was advised to do absolutely nothing and to allow my landlords to try me in court. For they were convinced that the law was on my side. So I ignored the attorney's letter and went right on practicing and teaching.

HARASSMENT

On Sunday, March 5th, 1978, at exactly 6 PM, I was trying out a few pieces for my pupil Christopher Lewis, when, suddenly, all of the lights in my apartment went out. I first checked the fuses in my apartment and found them in good working order. The problem, I thought, must surely be with the main fuse in the cellar. The cellar door, one flight down, happened to be directly opposite my landlord's front door. When I reached that area, Lillian was standing by the door of her apartment, while Henry was standing at the entrance to the cellar which was yet another flight down. Both had a vacant look of disguised innocence. I to Lillian: "My lights have gone out." Lillian to Henry in a falsely nonchalant voice: "Henry, Seymour says that his lights have gone out." "Oh, is that so?" said Henry with the kind of a sneer that a snake might sport before he strikes. When I went down the stairs into the cellar and directly to the wall holding the electrical meters, I discovered that someone had unscrewed the main fuse to my apartment. I rang my landlords' bell, and, in a not too gentle voice, reported this to them. Henry screamed something at me, and Lillian, who had answered the door, simply slammed it in my face.

The next day, a lock appeared on the fuse box. It seemed obvious to me, and to everyone else, that the landlords had done this in a feeble attempt to shift guilt away from themselves.

The Criminal Pianist

Poor Ms. L. — she had a real problem on her hands. She lived directly below a practicing concert pianist. The landlords seemed powerless to silence me, and even her constant complaints to policemen proved ineffectual. Intent on evicting me, Lillian and Henry provided Ms. L. with their attorney, who lost no time in filing a suit against me. One morning in early September, a policeman rang my bell and presented me with a summons to appear in Criminal Court on September 20, 1978. The charge: "Harassment/Ex Noise" — a criminal offense.

Ordinarily, a case of this sort would have been assigned to the Landlord and Tenant Court. But that I had been charged with willfully harassing Ms. L. with "noise," a word which did not exactly speak well of my piano playing, categorized me as a criminal. Thus, on the appointed day, I found myself in a large courtroom with other defendants who had been charged with having committed a variety of crimes, including murder.

When our case was announced — "The People of the State of New York on the complaint of [Ms. L.] versus S. Bernstein" — my heart quickened. In fact, I felt as nervous as I would for a performance — and not just nervous, but also guilty, as a criminal might feel. Of course, in the best sense of the law, a person is innocent until proven guilty. But at that moment, I felt that the opposite was true: In the judge's eyes, I was guilty until proven innocent.

The three of us stood before the judge — Ms. L. to the right, and I to the left of her attorney. He was the first to speak. He stated the complaint against me quite convincingly, I thought, and asked the judge to direct me to stop practicing after 6 PM on weekdays and altogether on the weekends. Concerning teaching, he insisted that I had no right to do this in a residential building. The judge looked at Ms. L. and then back at the attorney, and asked: "How long has she been there?" Ms. L. answered: "A year in July." The judge then looked directly at me: "How long have *you* been living there, Mr. Bernstein?" "Twenty-four years, Your Honor," I answered in a rather tremulous voice. With this, his dark eyes opened wide, and he flashed an unmistakable look of disbelief at the attorney and Ms. L. — a look that seemed to say, "Are you both kidding — bringing this man into criminal court?" Seeing the judge's expression as an encouraging sign, I immediately launched into the story of my recent ordeals with the Smalls: the threatening letters from her and her attorney, the collusion between her and Ms. L., the unscrewing of the main fuse to my apartment, and Ms. L.'s three complaints to the police. I made a point of saying that I had practiced and taught in my apartment for twenty-four years without any complaints from my landlords. By the time I had stated my defense and answered some questions, I had the feeling that the judge had come to the conclusion that I, not Ms. L., was the victim of harassment. Moreover, when I informed the judge that I had moved all of my performing classes to my pupils' apartments and that I had laid a double acoustical pad and a carpet underneath my piano, he looked at my adversaries and exclaimed, "It sounds like Mr. Bernstein is doing whatever he can to try to cooperate." Later, he made clear to the attorney the squatter's rights mentioned earlier: "The man has developed professional and personal habits over a lifetime, a span of twenty-four years," and he placed a great deal of stress on "twenty-four." The judge asked Ms. L. why she took the apartment knowing that a pianist lived above her. "I moved into the apartment in July of 1977," she explained in her usual high-pitched voice. "At that time he was away. The landlady informed me that the gentleman upstairs had a piano. That was it. I did not know that he was a professional pianist!" To this, the judge replied, "This is something you should try to resolve between yourself and the landlady." Ms. L. squealed something else to the judge, and he suddenly had had quite enough of her complaints. Fixing his angry eyes upon her, he exclaimed, "Why do you have to say anything right now? Just be still. You were given notice that there was a piano that was going to be played above you and you took the apartment because you wanted the apartment. Now I am trying to resolve your dispute."

Try as the attorney did, he could neither persuade the judge to curtail my hours of practicing, nor keep me from teaching. The only point of contention now remaining was Sunday: Should I refrain entirely from practicing, even if I had a concert scheduled for that day? The following was the judge's solution, quoted directly from the court's transcript:

> If you are preparing for a concert, why can't you rent a few hours in a concert hall when you have to do your heavy playing for a concert on that particular Sunday? Why don't you do that? Wouldn't that sound fair and reasonable? Let the woman know that come Sunday, no matter what, she is going to be deafened by the silence. Wouldn't that be fair and reasonable? Try to work it out — unless it's an emergency. Then, will you go down to her apartment and tell her, "[Ms. L.], there is an emergency. I couldn't get a particular practice hall for a particular Sunday because the building burned down. Here is five bucks. Go to a movie or go see a matinee." Do something like that, but you have to make an attempt to give her peace. You have to.

I had to stifle a smile, not only because of the judge's caustic comments, but also because he had a mirthful look in his eyes when he suggested that I offer Ms. L. "five bucks" to go to the movies.

When it became clear that the judge was on my side, and that he had rebuffed all of the attorney's attempts to curtail my practicing and teaching, Ms. L. lost her cool. She covered her face with her hands and emitted one of the loudest squeals I ever heard from her: "Well, what about me?" This seemed to be more than the judge could tolerate. He glowered at her and raised his voice to a threatening intensity: "Why are you covering your face? This is not a church. It's a court of law. Uncover your face and stand with dignity. Nobody has to hide from anybody. I am trying to be a friend to both of you. The lawyer is caught in the middle and he is a lawyer, not a member of the clergy. There is just so much he can do."

The judge's reprimand of Ms. L. actually triggered a wave of compassion within me. In the next moment, then, I felt a need to interject a bit of levity into the proceedings. I told the judge that the attorney was not only a lawyer, but also a pianist. "That makes his role even more difficult," the judge retorted in a calmer voice. To sum up the trial, we discussed a schedule for Saturdays. "Okay," the judge said. "So, let's play until 5:30 PM on Saturdays if you have students. But be reasonable. If you can give her an opportunity for reverie and silence, even on a Saturday, do it. Next case."

One can imagine how Lillian and Henry took this defeat. Any semblance of civility and politeness towards me vanished completely. For example, my hello's when passing them on the sidewalk were always greeted with pursed lips and a decided snub on the part of Lillian, and dagger eyes from Henry. They were seething with hostility. Little did I know, however, the extent to which their hostility would go. And little did they know what sort of an opponent they had taken on — one who had already served in one war and was now prepared to fight another one on the home front.

The Slamming Vestibule Door

During the next few years, my landlords hatched one sadistic scheme after another, all designed to break down my defenses. Their maliciousness centered on the building's entrance door, a door which happened to be adjacent to my apartment. Lillian and Henry hired a door specialist and instructed him to remove the hand-operated control knob on the door-check and replace it with a key-operated one. Having copies of this key, the charming couple took turns adjusting the door-check counterclockwise. The result was that the door banged shut with a crash that not only made me jump, but also disturbed other tenants as well.

Part 4: The Battle Continues

Sleep now became impossible. During the daytime, I would find myself almost falling asleep during my practicing and teaching. Moreover, this was the very period during which I was writing my book *With Your Own Two Hands*. How often I almost fell asleep from sheer exhaustion, and how generally debilitated I became, would be hard to describe. Lillian and Henry had succeeded in undermining my health and my ability to function as a musician and a writer. The more desperate I became, the more my landlords reveled in their victory.

In the meantime, Ms. L. moved out of the basement apartment, and thus her constant telephone calls and whining complaints ceased. But the noise of the slamming vestibule door continued to exact a heavy toll on my nervous system. At one point when my temper got the better of me, I called them monsters and threatened to sue them for harassment. At this, Henry charged up the stairs like a bull bent on the kill. I had just enough time to seek the protection of my apartment. Henry's rage knew no bounds, and in another second he began banging with fists and feet upon my door, all accompanied by a spew of vulgarity. My fear was that he would run back down to his apartment and return with his pass key. I thus had one hand firmly positioned on my door knob, and the other on the telephone, ready to dial 911. The whole time, I heard Lillian trying to soothe her husband in the way that a serpent might hiss comfort to her mate. Finally, the tempest subsided, and the wild beast returned to his lair in the basement. Even to this day, I am convinced that Henry would have injured or even killed me had I not barricaded myself inside of my apartment.

For the next two years, the war between my landlords and me intensified. Desperate situations require desperate actions, so I withheld my rent and was taken to court. The judge on that occasion ordered my landlords to allow me to buy a new door check. Within a few days, however, Henry removed it and replaced it with the former one. I withheld my rent a second time, and the pattern repeated itself — another court appearance, further reprimands to my landlords from the judge, and more hostility from Henry. To make matters worse, someone poured super glue into both locks on my apartment door one night. A few days later, my apartment was burglarized. Whether my landlords were implicated in these crimes, I cannot be sure. But it seemed more than mere coincidence that all three incidents occurred within the space of a month.

Final Ploy

When, after all these incidents, I continued to hold my ground, Lillian and Henry hired a new attorney and sent the following petition to all the tenants in the building:

> In light of recent muggings and robberies in the neighborhood, WE, THE UNDERSIGNED TENANTS OF _____, MAKE KNOWN that in the absence of its owners a full time superintendent, living on these premises, would greatly enhance the security and\or protection of tenants in this building.

Thinking it a good idea to have a superintendent on the premises, all of the tenants were only too eager to sign the petition. That the proposed superintendent was to occupy my apartment never so much as occurred to them, for that information was conspicuously missing from the petition. It must now have appeared to my landlords and to their lawyer that my eviction was a foregone conclusion. They filed an eviction claim with the New York City Conciliation and Appeals Board, known as the CAB, an organization established specifically to mediate such problems.

I was by this time primed to take whatever defensive measures were available to me. I hired a lawyer to represent me at the eviction hearing. That Lillian and Henry actually produced the superintendent, a man in his thirties, who claimed to be willing to move into my apartment with his wife and children, seemed threatening to my case indeed. But further questioning of this rather embarrassed and phlegmatic man showed that he would be going to school while his wife posed as the building's superintendent and "gate keeper." Moreover, that two adults and two children would be living in a one and a half room apartment did not, of course, escape the notice of the arbitrator in charge.

In the meantime, in a letter to the chairman of the CAB, my lawyer, Arthur Kanter, established convincingly that Lillian "detested" me and would stop at nothing to evict me, primarily because I, unlike the other tenants whom she had so easily evicted, challenged her authority.

A final hearing held in October 1982 confirmed beyond a shadow of a doubt that something was "rotten" in Ms. Small's building. Subsequently, the Appeals Board sent me a copy of a six page document which unequivocally censured my landlords. The document listed chronologically each attempt on the part of Lillian and Henry to evict me. I quote here the final paragraphs of that document, entitled "Determination":

> The events leading up to the owner's application, partly listed above, indicate that it is the owner's intent to obtain the vacancy of the tenant and not the installation of a superintendent. Accordingly, the Board holds that the owner is not acting in good faith as required by Section 54D (2) of the Code. The owner is cautioned to refrain from any further actions which may result in a finding of retaliatory eviction.

The document instructed Lillian and Henry to furnish me with a new lease. They failed to do this and were fined for a lack of compliance with the CAB's order. Beaten in all of their schemes, they sold the building in July of 1984 and moved out, "in the middle of the night," as one of my neighbors observed. None of the tenants had so much as a hint that the building had been sold and that Lillian and Henry had decided to move out. Suddenly, one morning, their apartment was empty. The following day, the new owner introduced himself to me and to the other tenants with a warmth and graciousness that I, for one, had all but forgotten could exist in a landlord. For me, it meant that five years of living in a hostile environment with people who wished me ill had now come to an end. As for Lillian and Henry, they took up residence in New Jersey, where, I hope, they have abandoned their status as landlords.

I did not think that five years of unrelenting maliciousness should go unpunished. The following year, therefore, I sought out a lawyer and sued Lams Realty for a million dollars. With hearings, counter-suits, interminable delays, and overcrowded court schedules, it took six years before I was given a firm date in court. Before we went to trial, however, I settled for $10,000, a third of which went to my lawyer.

Harassment can be more frightful than one imagines. In one case that I know of, neighbors living close to a flutist hated her practicing to such an extent that they put pesticide around the entrance to her apartment. The result was that the flutist, her husband, and their dog became violently ill. In my case, beyond the actual events, which wore down my nervous system, I had to battle constantly with mounting anger and resentment towards Lillian and Henry. As I remembered the peaceful years I had previously enjoyed with the Small family, I saw Lillian as a traitor to the memory of her mother. How, in fact, would dear Mrs. Small have felt had she known just how wickedly her own daughter had treated the man to whom she had brought her Sabbath specials?

People close to me questioned why I continued to live in such a hostile environment, and some of my friends actually took it upon themselves to look for another apartment for me. All of these good intentions notwithstanding, I decided to fight to the end on principle alone rather than give in to the sadistic intent of my landlords. Besides, my low rent enabled me to pursue a lifestyle that was beneficial to me and to my pupils. So in spite of the deplorable situation, I decided to hold my ground. I would slay the dragons or be slain.

Was it only my "insubordination," as Lillian called it, in not vacating my apartment at her whim, and her greed in wanting a higher rent for my apartment, that caused Lillian and Henry to wage a war against me for so long and with such vehemence? I will never learn the truth. What I did learn, however, is that evil really does exist in people, and that one can win out over evil as long as one holds one's ground. While I emerged the victor in that protracted war, I did so at the expense of my emotional world. It took me almost a year to regain that inner calm which I had enjoyed when I first moved to New York City.

FILLING IN THE GAP

Returning now to an earlier time, my move to New York City in 1955 brought out the best and the worst in me. On the plus side, I learned to perform life's menial tasks, such as cleaning my apartment, shopping, preparing meals, and doing laundry, tasks that my mother had performed uncomplainingly when I lived at home. Now that I had to manage all of these things myself, I appreciated her all the more for her virtuosic handling of the overwhelming responsibilities that fell upon her.

On the debit side, I fell prey to distractions of all sorts which, though stimulating, absorbed a great deal of my time: long telephone conversations, visits with friends into the wee hours of the morning, and, to be sure, love affairs. I could no sooner resist being with an interesting or attractive person than I could abstain from eating hot fudge sundaes with whipped cream. In short, I found myself on a social merry-go-round, spending most of my time gratifying all of those human desires that can easily surface when one is on one's own. I paid a price for this, however: fatigue, a lack of concentration, guilt for being self-indulgent at the expense of practicing — all of these things diminished my energies and took a heavy toll on my musical progress. And once I stopped developing musically, I lost my sense of well-being.

ARTHUR JUDSON AND CAMI

Fortunately, this phase did not last too long. I had signed a contract in 1952, three years before I moved to New York City, with CAMI — Columbia Artists Management, Inc. I was to be a part of a newly formed trio called the Gotham Concert Trio. There were tours to fulfill, and I had to pull myself together. Interestingly, all of this came about through Louise Curcio, my former teacher with whom I had had so stormy a relationship. Early on, however, she introduced me to her friend Major M. C. Migel, a patron of the arts. He knew Arthur Judson, then the president of CAMI, and it took only a telephone call to arrange an audition for me.

To this day, I remember each moment of my audition for Arthur Judson, and I can say with certainty that I did not play well for him. I have often wondered, therefore, what he saw in me. I was twenty-six at the time, and it is possible that he recognized a strong potential in me. Or perhaps he simply decided to stretch a point so as to extend a favor to his friend Major Migel, who attended the audition. As I played, I thought of only one thing: I was in the presence of a person who was known in the profession as the "lion." And as everyone told me, his "roar" could either make you, or break you. Considering how poorly I had played, it came as a total surprise to me when he asked me to return in a month to play some Brahms for him. What my Brahms would show him that my Beethoven, Chopin, and Liszt had not was certainly beyond me. Nevertheless, I returned to Judson Hall on West 57th Street and played a Capriccio, an Intermezzo, and a Rhapsody. My playing, though far from perfect, was somewhat better than it had been at the first audition. Still, having to make music while paralyzed with nervousness left me spent and utterly depressed. When I came to the end of the Rhapsody, Judson, a tall, imposing figure with a noble bearing, rose from his seat midway back in the auditorium, stepped into the aisle, and began talking as he walked towards me. His voice was loud and resonant, indeed like a lion's: "You have a big tone, and big tones sell. You have as much technique as you will ever need. You play with a great deal of expression." Thus did he assess me like a product on the open market. Feeling miserable for not having played my best, I secretly discounted his complimentary appraisal of my playing. "He's only a manager," I reasoned. "What does he know about anyone's playing?" It was merely another example of the manner in which compliments can fall upon the open wounds of self-criticism. I had enough good sense, however, to hide my feelings, and I simply thanked him.

At that point, I fully expected Judson to return to his duties as president of CAMI. But to my surprise, he came closer to the stage, stared directly into my eyes for a few seconds, and then inquired, "Do you play chamber music?" Yes," I replied, "a great deal of it." "Good," he snapped back. "Come with me." First he shook hands with Major Migel and Louise Curcio, who had also attended the audition. He then turned on his heel and walked briskly out of the auditorium and into an elevator. I hurriedly said goodbye to Major Migel and Louise and trailed behind Judson, my heart quickening with each step. Whether the elevator went up or down, I cannot say. When it stopped, Judson led me down a corridor and came to a halt in front of an office door. Without even knocking, he barged into the office of Horace J. Parmelee, one of CAMI's chief representatives. Parmelee, with a cigarette dangling from the right side of his mouth, was a short, rotund man in his sixties. He had thin, gray hair with that tell-tale yellowish cast which hair dyes often produce. The strands were plastered down to his scalp. His physique seemed like a series of different sized circles — a large one for the head, two smaller ones for the pudgy shoulders, and an extremely large, bulging one for the vest-covered torso. Strangely, though, the circles seemed to be bolted together, so that when he stood up, his movements appeared to be all of a piece.

Parmelee was positively awestruck at Judson's unannounced arrival in his office. He rose from behind his desk with a military rigidity, and half whispered, half grunted: "Why, Mr. Judson!" It was a rasping voice that made one think of coarse sandpaper. The "s" in Judson revealed the most pronounced lisp I had ever heard. Judson, looking like a tall, poised athlete in comparison to his short, cowering employee, seemed to enjoy his dominant role. He barked at Parmelee in a business-like tone: "Have you found the pianist for your new trio?" "Not yet, Mr. Judson," Parmelee replied. It was pitiful to see and to hear how nervous he was. "Good," said Judson. "Here he is." And with an air of having already spent more time than he had bargained for, he turned abruptly and strutted out of Parmelee's office without so much as glancing in my direction. Parmelee emitted an audible "whew," picked up his cigarette, which he had temporarily placed in a huge ashtray on his desk (the ashtray was already overflowing with smoldering cigarette butts), relit it, and slumped down into his swivel chair.

Thus the stage was set for my first contract with what was then, and still is, one of the world's most important concert agencies. Parmelee was a major force in Arthur Judson's creation, Community Concerts, Inc., an affiliate of CAMI. Their large staff of representatives strung across the United States, and their slogan, "A Carnegie Hall in Every Town," resulted in the implementation of more concert series in small-town America, and more opportunities for newcomers to perform, than any other management in existence. As I quickly learned from Parmelee, CAMI was in the process of forming a trio comprising three soloists — a pianist, a violinist, and a cellist. As Parmelee explained, "Your programs will begin and end with movements of Trios. In between, you will each play a segment of solos lasting fifteen to twenty minutes. You, of course (and he pointed to me), will have the lion's share of responsibility, for you will accompany the other two soloists." He and his staff were in the process of auditioning violinists and cellists, and he would contact me when the final decisions were made. Throughout our discussion, a cigarette never left the corner of his mouth. When one had burned down to the filter, he lit a new one from its dying embers. His appearance, his pronounced lisp, and the spasms of coughing which interrupted his sentences gave me the feeling that I was in the presence of a comic-strip character. Parmelee then stood up, awkwardly to be sure, shook my hand, and congratulated me on making such a strong impression on Judson. "Welcome to CAMI," he said, as I walked out of his office.

In view of the limited performing experience I had had up until that time, it is not difficult to imagine what an impact all of this had upon me. Suffice it to say that I arrived home in Newark in such a state of euphoria that I could hardly find the proper words to describe the whole adventure to my family.

"We want to see how you look together"

A few weeks later, a letter arrived from Parmelee. The other members of the trio had been chosen: Diana Steiner, violinist, and Ruth Condell (later Alsop), cellist. We were instructed to meet in a room that CAMI had reserved for us at The Juilliard School on Claremont Avenue in New York City (the building now occupied by the Manhattan School of Music). We were told to practice the slow movement and the finale of the Trio in *D minor* by Mendelssohn. One week later, we were to perform these movements in addition to groups of solos for Judson, Parmelee, and other CAMI representatives in Judson Hall. "Wear formal attire," the letter went on to say. "We already know how you play, but we now want to see how you look together."

The three of us met at the appointed time and place. Having been chosen independently, we were much relieved to find ourselves compatible, both musically and personally. We were all so excited at the prospect of signing up with CAMI that we could hardly concentrate on the fine points of interpretation during our rehearsal. As I think about it now, it was quite a feat to cram the Trio movements, plus the solos that I had to accompany, into a period of only two hours. Youthful verve and daring, however, compensated for all that more rehearsal time might have achieved.

The day of the audition arrived. Inquisitive eyes turned in my direction as I boarded the Hudson Tube train in Newark at 9 AM dressed in tails. Arriving at Judson Hall, I found my colleagues resplendent in beautiful evening gowns, but with tell-tale signs of anxiety peering through their radiant smiles. Under the circumstances, I was no less anxious, for there sat Judson and Parmelee, plus a large contingent of CAMI representatives and their secretaries.

The Gotham Concert Trio

Something about being dressed in tails always makes me feel professional. On that occasion, my awareness of how I looked had a positive effect upon me — so much so that I actually outdid myself. I cannot, however, comment upon the level of my colleagues' performances; I was too caught up in my own playing to listen to them objectively. We first performed our solos and then came together to perform the fragmented Mendelssohn Trio. With the final note of the rousing coda, Judson rose from his seat, turned to Parmelee with an imperious air, and spoke three words: "Sign them up." And as of that moment, the Gotham Concert Trio was born.

By the second season, 1954–1955, the period in which I moved to New York City, the Trio had become one of CAMI's star attractions. Benefiting from an extravagant sales pitch, at which big agencies are unusually adept, we would have to have played pretty poorly to escape the attention of prospective buyers. Not only were we purported to offer FOUR CONCERTS IN ONE! — that is, solos and trios — but also, according to another blurb on the publicity sheet, we were said to be A FEAST FOR THE EYES, AS WELL AS FOR THE EARS! Seeing the latter, it dawned on us that it was not mere coincidence that I was taller than Diana and Ruth, and that we were all single. Talent and performing ability aside, we had unquestionably been hand-picked to fit extra-musical requirements.

Shortly after I signed my first contract with CAMI, I made my New York City debut at Town Hall. Parmelee was there, beaming with pride. After reading my reviews, some of which were excellent, he telephoned me and asked me to come to his office on the following day: "If there had been a screen in front of you while you played Prokofiev's Seventh Sonata, no one could have been able to tell you from Horowitz. [I beamed with gratitude at this.] A few years of touring experience with the Trio (cough! cough!), and I'll personally book you for solo recitals." In my heart of hearts, that is exactly what I had hoped for when Judson first introduced me to Parmelee. Diana and Ruth confessed to having the same aspirations — namely, to have solo careers. But as a novice in the concert

The Gotham Concert Trio: Diana Steiner, left; Ruth Condell Alsop, right;
Seymour Bernstein, center.
(Photo by J. Abresch)

field, I thought it would have been presumptuous on my part to discuss this either with Judson or Parmelee. Parmelee brushed off the cigarette ashes from his vest, lit another one, and continued: "And don't think for one moment (cough! cough!) that the Trio will play in small communities indefinitely. Just give us a few years, and we'll book some major dates for you."

In truth, my colleagues and I felt so fortunate in having a contract with CAMI that we barely gave the future a thought. The present was all that mattered to us. But now that Parmelee spoke of a solo tour for me and major dates for the Trio, the future glowed brighter than ever. Perhaps I would make it to the top after all.

The Vicissitudes of Touring

The Gotham Trio's first season was a modest one, with approximately fifteen engagements, beginning in New England and extending to the southeastern states. My frequent performances while in the army had already taught me that it is actually possible to achieve that "at home" feeling on the stage. To my mind, however, the army experience was one thing, but performing as a CAMI artist was quite another. The thought of having to live up to the trust placed in me by Judson and Parmelee filled me with more apprehension than I can possibly describe. I shall never forget my feelings of despair after the first engagement, in Great Barrington, Massachusetts. I was so nervous during that concert, and felt so inept as a pianist, that I was ready to telephone Parmelee and cancel my contract with CAMI. In addition to my own sense of insecurity, the piano had no sound to speak of, and the action was so stiff that all of my technical passages fell apart. Drawing upon some inner reserve, I "hung in there," as they say. And by the fourth concert on that tour, I was actually able to maintain on the stage that sense of objectivity and control which characterized my practicing at home. Inferior pianos notwithstanding, I began to feel more optimistic about my playing, and, therefore, better about myself. It was not a question of completely overcoming my fear of performing. For like most performers, I felt then, as I do now, some degree of nervousness on the stage. Rather, frequent exposure to audiences that did not exclusively comprise family members and friends, plus the adjust-ment one makes to a variety of performing conditions, eventually taught me to focus upon my responsibility as an interpreter of music to the exclusion of everything else. Nervousness takes the upper hand when performers suffer extra-musical distractions, such as worrying about what this one or that one thinks about your playing. Being single-minded, then, and accepting the fact that the music you are performing is far more

important than your precious ego, can enable you to play convincingly —
despite cold hands and all the rest.

Once I achieved what someone once called an "acceptable worst" on
the stage, I, like most performers, learned firsthand just how grueling
touring can be: nightmarishly poor pianos, dry acoustics, inferior lighting,
overheated hotel rooms, and the vicissitudes of traveling in general —
these things eventually made touring anything but glamorous. We drove to
most of our engagements. By the third year, when violinist Sylvia
Rosenberg replaced Diana Steiner, this included wending our way clear
across the United States. I remember steering Ruth's Ford through
blizzards and floods and careening over frozen mountain passes in
California where a skid of only a few inches would have spelled disaster
for all of us.

Receptions

Then there was the endless stream of post-concert receptions, many of
which were pleasurable occasions. But as I soon discovered, the majority
of them were tiresome events at which concert committee members
swarmed around us and spoke of everything under the sun except their
responses to our playing. In most cases, we were taken directly to the
receptions after our concerts without any prior invitation whatsoever.
Occasionally, though, telegrams would arrive from Parmelee, often long
ones for which the Gotham Trio had to pay. As a matter of expediency, I
was appointed the Trio's representative. So all of the telegrams were
addressed to me:

> Dear Seymour: [Mrs. Cattlegut], the concert chairperson
> from Larned, Kansas, has extended an invitation to the Trio
> for a reception after your concert (stop) She will arrange
> transportation to her home and back to your hotel (stop)
> Please inform me whether the Trio accepts or not (stop)

The answer, of course, was always, "Yes." After our performances,
then, local committee members ushered us into waiting cars and drove us
to where the reception was held. This could be anything from a palatial
mansion to a modest apartment where dozens of people were crammed
into a small room like sardines in a can. Exhausted and ravenously hungry,
we were occasionally treated to full dinners of the most extravagant kind.
But all too frequently, we had to stand in the middle of a room making
small talk with people who balanced a plate of tempting food in one hand
and a drink in the other. Curiously, it never occurred to them that

musicians could be hungry, too. So while we attempted to bite into a cucumber sandwich which the hostess brought us (the tuna fish sandwiches having been already snatched up by the guests), we had to respond to all manner of questions. I used to be too shy to confess that I was about to faint with hunger. By the time I was finally left alone, the banquet table was all but depleted. On many occasions, therefore, I returned to the hotel and went to bed with visions of barbecued chicken and potato salad dancing around me.

The stories told by musicians about post-performance conversations could fill a book in themselves. Alexander Brailowsky once told me a particularly funny one of a Texas oil magnate who escorted him to a reception in his chauffeur-driven silver Rolls Royce. He suddenly blurted out, "Tell me, Mr. Brailowsky, what do you do for a living?" When he related this story, Brailowsky and I laughed so much that he simply forgot to tell me his response to the question, a response which must have been as humorous as the question was. A world-famous violinist, however, had an immediate reply to the same question asked of him at a reception. Looking directly into the eyes of his inquisitor, a prominent Chicago socialite, he replied, "I fuck pigs!" I was not told what the socialite's response was to such vulgarity, but I like to think that she had the courage to slap his face.

While our audiences, for the most part, comprised genuine music lovers, there was also an abundance of people who went to cultural events only to be seen. Many of them were socialite types with fixed grins and pat expressions. One shouldn't complain, because such culturally illiterate people support concert series and therefore make it possible for artists to have careers. But I shall never forget one woman in particular. Sporting a floor-length mink and bedecked in more jewels than I had ever seen on one person before, she had missed the performance altogether, as soon became embarrassingly evident. Yet she had to make her appearance. No doubt confusing me with the next artist scheduled on the series, she rushed up to me, gushing with false enthusiasm, and exclaimed, "Oh, Mr. Bernstein, I simply adored your singing!" Taken aback, but at least polite, I thanked her in my best baritone voice, while slowly but resolutely slipping my hand from her clutching grasp. This incident, and many more like it, added to my general disillusionment with the whole structure of performing careers and with the people who support and run them. On the positive side, I learned to appreciate genuine people all the more.

Then, of course, there are the professional reception-goers who flit around from one room to another, being sure to attach themselves to whoever is important. I learned to recognize them at once. Speaking about being a victim of one's environment, there we were, performers in a strange city and in a strange home, with no means of escape from obnoxious people who made sure that we could neither eat nor converse with people who really interested us. Boring conversationalists, never without drinks in their hands (they never seem to want to eat and must wonder why musicians have such healthy appetites), they have perfected the technique of rattling on about sheer nonsense. Somehow, all of this fascinates me. That is, I am amazed that someone can stretch out a simple comment to five sentences or so, when one sentence would easily have sufficed. Professional hangers-on, they are primarily interested in introducing all of their friends to you, as though they had some special claim on your private world. Attracting attention by any means whatsoever, such as talking loudly, laughing uproariously, or putting their arms around you, they vicariously live out their fantasies and find their place in the sun by associating with important people — fame by association, as one might call it. The presence of such people in positions of power on concert committees, despite the fact that they have little or no knowledge either of music or those who perform it, is one reason why touring can often exact a heavy price from musicians.

I shall never forget a woman somewhere in Illinois who escorted me to the hall in order to try the piano. From the moment I met her, I had the feeling that she had not done her job properly and that she resented me for reminding her of her lack of responsibility. "Try the house piano," she said in an offhand manner. "If you don't like it, there is still time to rent another one." Imagine her having waited until the afternoon before the concert to make such a decision. After all, I was certainly not the first pianist to appear on the Community Concert Series in that city. Some local pianist could easily have tried that piano well in advance of the concert, and I could have used that precious time for practicing. As it turned out, the piano in question was totally inadequate. Visibly annoyed, the woman went to a telephone and ordered a rental piano from the local dealer. Having done this, she eyed me with an unmistakable air of contempt, and exclaimed, "Now you won't have any excuse for not playing your best!"

As I later discovered, the Baldwin concert grand that was moved into the hall at the last moment had been rented as a matter of course for all of the previous concerts in that town. I deduced from all of this that I, being a newcomer to the musical scene, did not warrant the expense of renting that piano unless, of course, I demanded it at the last moment.

That I did not counter that woman's disdainful comment indicates just how insecure I felt at that phase of my life. For as touring musicians soon discover, one word of discontent, or even a hint of insult on the part of a musician to a local representative, is immediately reported to your manager. I know of two cases in which young musicians were dropped from a major management firm simply because they refused to tolerate the brutish behavior of certain people in charge of the local concert series.

Fred R. Emerson, Barrister and Amateur Pianist

To be sure, not everyone I met on tour was guilty of brutish behavior. I met certain individuals along the way — most of them were in fields other than music — with whom I established an immediate and lasting friendship. Fred R. Emerson, a barrister from St. Johns, Newfoundland, is a vivid example. He hosted a reception for us after the first of two concerts that we performed in St. Johns in November of 1955. A passionate lover of music, an amateur pianist, and as warm and communicative a person as one is ever likely to meet, Mr. Emerson was especially fond of Chopin's Polonaise in *F* sharp minor, the very Polonaise which I happened to have included in my solo group that season. My interpretation of this work pleased him to such an extent that he spent almost the entire reception discussing it with me. I have already confessed to having a special regard for amateur musicians. But Mr. Emerson's keen understanding of every nuance of that Polonaise was certainly beyond anything I had ever encountered from any other musician, amateur or otherwise. The result was that we were immediately drawn into that special sort of alliance of which deep friendships are made. During our discussion, I learned from him some facts about Chopin which were revelatory to me at that time: how Chopin, for instance, who was not an avid reader, was drawn, nonetheless, to the works of his compatriot, the Polish poet Adam Mickiewicz. Several weeks later, when I returned home from that tour, I found a small package waiting for me. It contained a copy of Mickiewicz's epic poem, *Pan Tadeusz*, together with a letter from Mr. Emerson. There then ensued a correspondence which I treasure to this day. His letters were filled with a romantic verve. Reading the following brief quotation from his first letter, one might think that Mr. Emerson was a musicologist as well as a barrister:

19th November, 1955

If I remember correctly, *Pan Tadeusz* appeared a few years before Chopin began writing his Polonaises and I have always been interested in the idea as to how far Mickiewicz influenced him. Although the two did not "click," Chopin never lost his profound admiration for

379

Mickiewicz. Chopin used to attend his lectures on Slavonic literature at the University in Paris. Chopin was Polish "plus," and Mickiewicz was too much of a patriot to appreciate the "plus," which probably accounts for their not being closer than they were.

At any rate, I have always felt that *Pan Tadeusz* is the stuff of which the Polonaises are made, and if you ever come across anyone with enough Polish erudition to substantiate my theory I shall be interested. I associate many melodies with quotations from the poem, for example: "Oczyzna moja ty jestes` jak zdrowie" (Fatherland mine thou art as health itself).

Many musicians and musicologists have substantiated Mr. Emerson's theory.

Subsequent letters were filled with references to various writers on Chopin, few of whom I recognized in those days. I was astonished that Mr. Emerson knew so much more about music than I did, not to mention his vast knowledge of literature and languages. In his second letter he wrote, "Your playing haunts me. Even the atrocious piano couldn't hide the lovely qualities of those pianissimo notes." I felt that my talent alone was sufficient to establish a bond between us, a bond that enabled him to forgive my literary and linguistic ignorance. I was, of course, deeply flattered by his compliment. But more than that, I felt privileged to know such a sensitive and erudite man.

Maintaining your status in the performing world requires something that I mentioned earlier — the ability to play the game. Knowing that re-engagements, more than anything else, inspire a manager's best efforts, some musicians go to great lengths in order to remain on the good side of concert committee members. I knew of one musician who kept a special book containing all manner of personal data about the people she met on tour. She could always be counted on to send birthday and anniversary cards, even including a personal note to the family cat: "Special regards to Felix." Though she was not the greatest pianist in the world, her efforts earned her a large number of re-engagements.

Returning to the Gotham Trio tour — in Phoenix, Arizona, Ruth, who had by that time married the violinist, violist, and clarinetist LaMar Alsop, suspected that she was pregnant. She made an appointment with a local doctor to learn the truth. "If I am pregnant," she told us, "I'll whistle as I come out of the doctor's office." Sylvia and I sat expectantly in the waiting room for some thirty minutes. Finally, the door of the doctor's office opened and Ruth came waltzing through it rolling her eyes and whistling some improvised tune. From that moment on, I propped her up in the rear seat of her car and did all of the driving myself. Ruth's pregnancy was not an easy one; she even hemorrhaged several times during the remainder of that tour. Fortunately, she returned home in good health and in ample time for the birth of her child. And it was thus that Marin Alsop, the distinguished conductor and violinist, came into this world.

Glamour Turns to Disillusionment

During our second year with CAMI, our engagements doubled; by the third year, they had almost tripled. Even then, when we had as many as forty concerts, we could hardly support ourselves for the remainder of the year. And why? When more photos and publicity fliers were needed, and they were strewn by CAMI across the United States and Canada, we had to pay for them; when lengthy telegrams were sent to us for any reason whatsoever, we had to pay for them; every postage stamp, every telephone call — in short, all expenses incurred in promoting the Trio were automatically charged to us.

Then there was the issue of our fee. It is known in the profession that managers, contractual agreements notwithstanding, can sell their artists for whatever they can get and pocket the difference. In our case, the Trio shared a fee of no more than $500 with a minimum of $350 for each concert, from which CAMI deducted a 20% commission. With living costs being what they were in those days, such fees ought to have been sufficient to carry us through the year with a modicum of comfort. Yet in one instance, our tour began in Newfoundland, with the result that the airplane fare and hotel expenses far exceeded our fees for the two concerts we gave there. In another instance, one concert in a small town outside of Detroit was followed by an interim of two weeks during which we did not play a single concert. Once again, our living expenses ate up all of our profits.

At other times, one night stands left us completely spent. Memories of trying to stay awake during long and arduous drives, arriving in a town totally exhausted and ravenously hungry with time only to change into our concert gear, careening over ice-covered mountain passes, and escaping rising rivers in the wee hours of the morning (I shall never forget Lakeland, California, where we awakened to find water lapping at our motel rooms) — many such unpleasant memories haunt me to this day. The whole time, the CAMI staff sat safely behind their desks, earned fortunes of money, and enjoyed luxurious apartments and lavish meals. We, on the other hand, endangered our lives, requested the least expensive hotel accommodations, and avoided expensive restaurants.

Would it ever have occurred to me or to my colleagues to complain about the sort of scheduling that swelled the pockets of CAMI and left us in the red? Of course not. We were afraid to do anything that might jeopardize our good standing with them. Besides, CAMI raised our fee during the third season to $600 with a minimum of $400 a concert. But while we were on tour somewhere in Idaho, a lengthy telegram arrived from Parmelee that to me, at least, made one thing clear: CAMI would continue to exploit us indefinitely, while we continued to play only in small towns and barely eke out a living. The telegram informed us that the Beaux Arts Trio, well-known even as far back as 1957, had signed an exclusive contract with CAMI. In fact, they were so well-known that their fee, according to Parmelee, would have to begin at $600, the same fee now offered to the Gotham Concert Trio. Being in competition with musicians whose reputations far exceeded ours (and indeed, they deserved those reputations), the Gotham Concert Trio would, quite obviously, be forced out of business. From CAMI's vantage point, there was only one thing to do: reduce our fee to an even lower amount than what we had previously earned — from $400 to $250.

Reading all of this in that lengthy telegram, a telegram for which we had to pay, cast us all into the worst depression imaginable. I remember having with me the complete works of Shakespeare, my reading project on that tour. That same evening, I happened to read the fourteenth Sonnet and was struck by its last line: "Lilies that fester smell far worse than weeds." I underlined it and read it to Ruth and Sylvia over breakfast on the following morning. We all agreed that it summed up the situation perfectly, and that it expressed our disillusionment with what had formerly seemed the promise of a flowering career. CAMI's intentions smelled of exploitation at the expense of our very future as performing musicians.

To be sure, Parmelee was not the sole author of that telegram. One could just imagine the conversation that must have taken place between him and Judson once the Beaux Arts Trio signed their contract with CAMI:

PARMELEE:
By all rights, Mr. Judson (cough! cough!), the Gotham's
fee ought to be raised, and not lowered.

JUDSON:
True, true. But the Gotham's reputation can't begin to
compete with that of the Beaux Arts Trio. If we sell both
groups for $600, the Gotham will be forced out of business.
And there go our profits.

PARMELEE:
You're right, Mr. Judson (cough! cough!).

JUDSON:
Now let's face it, Parmelee. Those kids are thrilled to be under our management. I'm sure they will agree to anything we propose. Let's lower their fee to $400 with a minimum of $250 and sell the Beaux Arts for $600 to $400. The Gotham is already in great demand. And we'll make up the difference in the number of concerts we will book for them. They may have to work harder, but they'll probably end up making the same amount of money.

PARMELEE:
I couldn't agree with you more, Mr. Judson. I'll send them a telegram to that effect (cough! cough! cough!).

The telegram I mentioned arrived near the end of our tour. During the long drive back to New York City following our last performance, Ruth, Sylvia, and I discussed the pros and cons of continuing to tour under CAMI's management. To be sure, the news from Parmelee about the cut in our fee infuriated us. But we had also our own artistic aspirations to consider. Sylvia had already decided to go it on her own. So with or without the cut in our fees, we were faced with the prospect of having to replace her. Considering what an extraordinary artist she was, this would have been difficult to do. Ruth, on the other hand, loved touring, and she wanted to negotiate with Parmelee in the hope of restoring our fee. I, personally, felt ambivalent about touring for many reasons. To begin with, I felt trapped in a scheme that made CAMI richer and cheated us out of a decent living. Beyond this, something else weighed heavily upon me. For after three seasons of performing one program each year, programs which included only movements of trios, I began to feel artistically bankrupt. I valued the experience of frequent performances under real concert conditions. But it meant compromising my desire to expand my repertory and to perform solo recitals in more important places than towns which, in some cases, we could not even find on the map. Moreover, I began to see that Parmelee's promise to arrange tours for me as a soloist had been nothing more than a bit of bait designed to lure me into a lesser role as a member of a trio, a role which spelled big bucks for CAMI.

While the Gotham Concert Trio was not of the calibre of the Beaux Arts Trio, we nevertheless fell into the category of saleable attractions. Should

Horace Parmelee have actually succeeded in his intent to get us five or more dates per week, then the Gotham Trio would probably have been played to death. For apart from the benefits of frequent performances, which enabled all three of us to achieve that "acceptable worst" on the stage, the constant traveling between dates, the limiting effects of playing only one program for the entire season, and the fact that we literally had no opportunity to practice and to learn new repertory would, I believe, have soon devitalized us musically and ruined our health in the process.

Immediately upon my return to New York City, I made an appointment to see Parmelee so as to give him my final decision. There was, as he told me on the telephone, a new contract lying on his desk waiting to be signed. Whether it was artistic purpose, self-preservation, or just plain pride, I cannot say. But the fact is, I found myself sitting calmly opposite Parmelee in his CAMI office and looking directly into his eyes through the now familiar cloud of cigarette smoke which surrounded him. In my own mind, at least, the master-slave roles were now reversed, and I delivered what amounted to an oration which had been forming in my mind for a long time prior to this meeting. When I told him that I not only refused to sign the contract, but that I also intended to resign from the Trio, the poor man instantly had a coughing fit that almost did him in. I have already described Parmelee's speech impediment — the lisp and the stuttering which increased whenever he was under pressure. Hearing my pronouncement, Parmelee recoiled against the back of his swivel chair and removed the cigarette dangling from his mouth. For him to remove a cigarette was the gravest indication of discontent. His speech impediment and his smoke-filled lungs conspired to do violence to him and to the English language as well. With anger flashing from his eyes, he began with, "How dare you *flit*, how dare you *flaunt*, how dare you (at last he found the correct word) flout a CAMI contract! Why, dozens of pianists would give anything to be under our management." "Fine," I replied with an indifferent voice. "Then sign them up. I, personally, want nothing more to do with your management. Let's face it, Mr. Parmelee: You have me slated to be a member of a trio for the rest of my life. In three seasons, we have not played one date in a major city. Now, after three years of accumulating rave reviews and re-engagements, you dare to ask me to sign a contract for a lower fee. I am grateful for the performing experience. But quite frankly, playing the same program forty times in a season, a program which doesn't even include a complete trio, repeatedly endangering my life on the road, and battling with rotten pianos night after night is not exactly my idea of a productive musical life. Now, if you can give me one good reason for signing your contract, then I will reconsider."

When I had finished, Parmelee, sat in his chair and stared at me for a few seconds. He seemed utterly dumbfounded. I had the feeling that no one had ever spoken to him like that before. His managerial arrogance notwithstanding, it must have been the possibility of CAMI's losing hard cash that suddenly converted his anger into a more conciliatory approach. For after all, his files were already bulging with trio dates for the forthcoming season. While he otherwise would have had no compunction about replacing me, it was certainly not to his advantage to do so at that time. His voice now became saccharine sweet: "Now Seymour," he lisped, while re-lighting the half-smoked cigarette and restoring it to its accustomed spot between his lips, "don't be hasty about your decision. You should speak to Mr. Judson about this. He thinks the world of you, and he would not want you to do anything for which you will be sorry later."

And that is exactly what I did. I went directly to Judson's office and made an appointment with his secretary. When, on the following day, Judson heard me out, he looked at me more like an understanding friend than the ruthless lion of his reputation. He then replied quite sincerely, "You know, I agree with you." Even though he headed the agency which stood to earn a great deal of money from our trio, still, something within him applauded my decision. While he and I parted on the best of terms, Parmelee, on the other hand, was far from giving up on me. In a letter dated March 19, 1957, he asked me to reconsider my intention of resigning from the Trio. He outlined a prospective tour covering eighteen states and lasting nine weeks. The fee would be restored to $500-$350, "at which price we are reasonably sure that the Trio should have forty to forty-five dates. We aim at booking five dates a week with the possibility of a sixth date in some weeks." The letter ended with lofty projections into the future in which the Trio's fees would increase to $750-$400.

Even if Parmelee had doubled our fee, I would not have changed my resolve to quit the Trio. On the very day I received the above letter, I wrote to Horace Parmelee and tendered my resignation from the Trio. I never heard from him again. A few years later, I read of his death in *The New York Times*.

One can see something good in everything, negative experiences included. In my case, I not only learned what to avoid in the future, but I was also in a better position to advise my career-oriented pupils who, themselves, might have been tempted to sign contracts based upon false promises. To be sure, I derived self-confidence from frequent performances. For as I have already stated, nothing is more important to a performer than performing itself. Along the way, however, I learned firsthand just how unprincipled and deceitful managers can be.

Part 4: The Battle Continues

BERNSTEIN AND BERNSTEIN

During that last visit with Judson, I somehow found the courage to tell him about John Ortez's attempt years earlier to contact Leonard Bernstein on my behalf. To my utter surprise, Judson volunteered to reopen the contact and wrote the following letter to Lenny:

> November 22, 1957
> Dear Lenny:
>   It seems too bad that two people of the same name, as you and Seymour Bernstein, the pianist, can't have a chance to appear together. If you are free of monopoly proceedings, perhaps you will do something about this.
>   I am glad to give Seymour Bernstein this letter because he is a good pianist and a fine fellow.
>   Regards,
>   Yours Sincerely,
>   Arthur Judson

Judson sent me a copy of this letter together with the following note:

> Dear Mr. Bernstein:
>   Here is your letter. Present it, and God help you!

Was there ever a more pointed prophecy of all the anguish, frustration, and unpredictability associated with careers in music? "God help you!" indeed. No one knew more about the difficulties of getting one's career going than did Arthur Judson. He must have known that my chances of securing a concerto date were practically nil. In addition, perhaps he knew something about Lenny from which only God could protect me. In any case, that letter from Judson achieved its purpose. A week or so later, Helen Coates telephoned me to arrange an audition. By this time, Lenny had taken his post as permanent conductor of the New York Philharmonic.

I arrived at the appointed time at the Osborne Apartments on West 57th Street and Seventh Avenue, an elegantly designed pre-war apartment building that stands diagonally opposite Carnegie Hall. I am sure I am not alone when I say that being in the presence of a famous person can induce anxiety. Whatever feelings of insecurity, inferiority, or just plain shyness one may have become accentuated. I have seen some business men, for example, shrink into a state of painful ineffectiveness when introduced to an extremely wealthy person. Though I have never been in awe of wealth, standing before a world-renowned musician was quite another matter.

386

Lenny was all charm, however, and his warm greeting disarmed me. He ushered me into a rather small studio which seemed completely taken up by a grand piano. To my surprise, I noticed that it was a Baldwin, which explained Lenny's connection to John Ortez and the Baldwin Piano Company. In those days, the South American owners of the Baldwin Piano Company had unlimited funds earmarked for promotional purposes. Thus well-known musical figures were provided with good pianos, not only in their homes, but also wherever they performed. As a point of fact, it troubled me that a musician of Lenny's stature would choose the Baldwin over a Steinway, especially in his own studio.

"Start with the fugue!"

At any rate, I had more to think about at the time of my audition than the make of the piano. Lenny spoke first "What are you prepared to play for me?" he asked in a very business-like voice. My heart beat *prestissimo* as I handed him a piece of paper. "Here is my repertory list," I answered. "Please choose whatever you like." The list contained three concerti, and a complete solo program. I fully expected, however, that he would allow me to choose my own warm-up piece. This is a common courtesy which had always been extended to me at previous auditions. But to my utter surprise, his voice suddenly took on a dictatorial tone: "Start with the fugue of the *Wanderer* Fantasy." Hearing this, I was instantly seized with panic. As any pianist will tell you, that fugue is one of the most unpianistic pieces in the whole repertory. In sheer desperation I asked him, "Would it be all right to start at the beginning of the Fantasy, just to warm up?" "No, no," he snapped back, "I want to hear the fugue!"

Many stories have been circulated about Leonard Bernstein. Some of them paint him as having been a generous, considerate person, while others tell of a cruel, competitive streak underneath a veneer of charm. Nothing, as far as I am concerned, is more sadistic than one pianist asking another to begin with the fugue of Schubert's *Wanderer* Fantasy. Assuming that I played it to Lenny's satisfaction, what would this prove? I suspected that he granted me an audition only in deference to Judson, and that he never intended to go along with the Bernstein and Bernstein gimmick. If he challenged me to the breaking point, he would then be justified in rejecting me.

The panic I at first experienced was instantly replaced by a storm of anger. Without another word, I tore into the fugue with a fury compatible with the music itself. He stopped me half way through and made some comments, such as "It needs more rhythmic propulsion — *"Daa-da-da Daa-da-da."* I played the opening of it again while he sang and conducted me: "That's better," he cried. "Much better!" The truth was that it was faster, but not very much better, and I grew more and more angry with him. I cannot remember what else he chose from my repertory list. It seems to me that the audition lasted some twenty minutes. Finally, he gave me some half-hearted compliments, extended his hand, and showed me to the door. Once I emerged onto West 57th Street, my anger knew no bounds: "He can go to hell, as far as I'm concerned!" I muttered. "Another audition, and another rejection; that's what careers are all about!"

Little did I know that Lenny had no intention of rejecting me. In fact, Helen Coates telephoned me one month later to arrange another audition: "Mr. Bernstein wants to hear how you sound on the stage of Carnegie Hall," she told me. "And he wants you to bring your manager." Nothing could have surprised me more. I did not think that I had played well for Lenny, and I still resented him for making my first audition so difficult. But after Helen Coates' telephone call, it suddenly occurred to me that Lenny may have had a hidden purpose underlying his behavior. Perhaps he reasoned that playing a concerto with the New York Philharmonic is far more challenging than beginning an audition with the fugue of the *Wanderer* Fantasy. If you cannot survive the latter, then let us not even speak of the former. All speculating aside, I was extremely fired up by Helen Coates' telephone call. Perhaps I would fulfill my ambition after all and play a concerto with the New York Philharmonic.

Carnegie Hall

I suppose that every aspiring pianist dreams of playing on the stage of Carnegie Hall. In my opinion, it is the grandest hall in the world — the Mecca for the highest standard of music-making. When I sat at the concert grand and looked out into the vast expanse of the hall, my hair stood straight up on end out of sheer thrill. Looking back on my performing career, there were three other times when I experienced this: in 1954 as I walked across the stage of Town Hall for my New York City debut; in 1955 when I performed with the New Jersey Symphony Orchestra and began the glorious theme of the fifteenth variation of Rachmaninoff's *Rhapsody on a Theme of Paganini*; and in 1967 in Orchestra Hall when I made my debut with the Chicago Symphony Orchestra and premiered Villa Lobos' 2nd Piano Concerto. In all four instances, the thrill of these occasions transcended my nervousness.

Lenny sat in the fifth or sixth row of the parquet. David Rubin, who had recently replaced John Ortez as the new public relations director of Baldwin, sat to his left, and Lenny's secretary, a young, good-looking man, was to his right. Lenny's commanding voice, now familiar to me,

Seymour Bernstein performing the world première of Villa Lobos' Concerto No. 2 with the Chicago Symphony Orchestra, Irwin Hoffman conducting. Orchestra Hall, Chicago, 1969. (Photo by Baylis Thomas)

boomed up from the audience: "Play the *Mazurka*!" (I had given him the same list of repertory, which included the Chopin *Mazurka*, Op. 24, No. 2.) No sooner had I started than I felt an aversion towards the Baldwin piano. I found it was voiced too brightly and I could not, therefore, play softly enough. Accordingly, I was not able to play the *Mazurka* with the control I would have desired. Lenny heard it all the way through and then said, "Now play the third and fourth movements of the Barber *Sonata*." A lump formed in my throat. "Another fugue," I thought. "This man must be preoccupied with fugues!"

It is embarrassing to speak positively of my own playing. Yet I have often played so poorly in public that I feel I have a right to speak about the successful performances I have given. Suffice it to say that I played the *Adagio Mesto* and the *Fugue* of the Barber *Sonata* so well that Lenny shouted from the audience, "*Gut gespielt!*" Still reeling from the emotional turmoil of the Barber *Fugue*, I was not at all prepared to hear Lenny speaking to me in German. "Excuse me...?" I responded, hardly able to speak at all. Lenny cupped his hands around his mouth and shouted the phrase more slowly: "I said, *gut gespielt!*" He got through to me that time. "Thank you," was all I could answer. What I really wanted to do was to get off that stage and to seek the protection of the wings. I got up from the piano and walked off the stage with a false appearance of composure. By the time I arrived in the wings, Lenny's secretary rushed up to me with open arms. Still dazed from the whole experience, I could hardly respond to his effusive compliments and added hugs. But through it all, I knew that I had made a strong impression upon everyone present. My heart was singing.

When Helen Coates telephoned me about the audition in Carnegie Hall, she had mentioned that Lenny wanted me to bring my manager along. I was under contract at the time with Berenice Kazounoff, whom I'll speak of shortly. She seemed thrilled to have been invited to the audition. From my vantage point on the stage I saw her grotesque form sitting in the last row of the parquet. As I left the hall, I came face to face with her outside: "I never thought you could play like that," she said loudly enough for all of West 57th Street to hear. "It was terrific!" As though she knew anything at all about good or bad piano playing. By all rights, she ought to have gone directly to Lenny after my performance. Yet she made no effort whatsoever to contact him — then or afterwards. She had been given an open invitation to negotiate a date for me with the New York Philharmonic, and she allowed the opportunity to slip right through her fingers.

Being Lured

The following morning, the telephone rang: "Seymour, this is David Rubin from the Baldwin Piano Company. I want you to come down to my office and talk about how to get your career going!" I could hardly believe what I had just heard. I was still tipsy with happiness after my audition with Lenny. But now, I was absolutely euphoric. Surely, this must be a dream, I thought, and I will soon awaken.

I met with David Rubin three days later and was excited by the first part of his conversation: "Lenny listened to instrumentalists and singers throughout that afternoon. Of all the people he heard, he liked only three, and you were one of them! Now let's talk about getting your career off the ground." As I soon discovered, getting my career "off of the ground" had one condition: I would have to sign up with the Baldwin Piano Company. In other words, I would become a Baldwin artist. As such, I would enjoy the associative privileges — namely, having a Baldwin piano in my home, a concert grand delivered wherever I performed, and my name included on the so-called Baldwin Artists list, which included such notable figures as Claudio Arrau, Georges Bolet, and Leonard Bernstein himself. High company! "Can you get me performing dates?" I inquired. "Well, Seymour, we're not exactly a management," David Rubin answered sardonically. "But we will publicize your name along with all of our other artists."

The fact is, my name was included on the Steinway artist list, similar to the Baldwin listing which David Rubin had mentioned. I also had a congenial relationship with certain members of the Steinway family and the technicians as well. How, then, could I betray the piano I loved best and the institution associated with it? I turned down David Rubin's offer, and, in the process, forfeited a potentially strong ally — one who might have intervened on my behalf with Lenny. I never did fulfill my ambition to play with the New York Philharmonic. Yet I have never regretted rejecting David Rubin's offer. Nor have I ever been able to shed my ambivalent feelings concerning Leonard Bernstein. It would have been so simple for him to engage me on his own. He put me to the test, and by his and David Rubin's responses to my playing I was led to assume that I passed with flying colors.

What went wrong? Did David Rubin tell me the truth? Even if he did, perhaps Lenny chose only one new soloist, and I may not have been the favorite of the three he liked. Was it my refusal to sign up with the Baldwin Piano Company? Lenny was easily swayed by powerful individuals. If the Baldwin Piano Company had sanctioned my engagement, Lenny may have gone along with it. It is also reasonable to assume that

Berenice Kazounoff might have succeeded in getting me an engagement with Lenny had she made the slightest effort to contact him. Finally, why didn't I pursue Lenny on my own?

All these questions aside, there was a fundamental truth about myself which I couldn't face then, but I can now: I believe I suffered from what psychologists call "a fear of success" syndrome. It worked this way: If Lenny had engaged me, and if he was sufficiently impressed with my performance to engage me again, I felt that I could not live up to the responsibilities associated with such a success. While it was unforgivable of Berenice Kazounoff not to follow up on such an important lead, I was secretly happy that she hadn't. I may have gone through the motions of pretending that I wanted to perform with Lenny, but the coward in me hoped it would never come about. But what would I have done if everything had worked out as it should have? The chances are I would have plucked up my courage and made my debut with Lenny — syndrome and all. Perhaps I would then have conquered my neurosis. But even if I had, I believe that the tensions associated with a major career would most assuredly have shortened my life.

In the final analysis, I believe that Lenny would have found a way to contact me had he really liked my playing. At any rate, the opportunity to play with him never presented itself again. In fact, all of my subsequent dealings with him and Helen Coates have proved unpleasant and futile. For example, I sent Helen Coates the manuscript of my book *With Your Own Two Hands*, a few months before its publication. During a telephone conversation with her, I told her how much it would help the book's promotion if Lenny would write a favorable sentence or two. Helen Coates was as negative about the book as anyone could be. "Seymour," she said during a telephone conversation several weeks later, "I read the manuscript. I'm sorry to say that I was not impressed. Everyone knows that practicing the piano integrates the personality. How naive can one be, Seymour? Imagine how the teachers at Juilliard would respond! I could not possibly show a book like that to Lenny." I found Helen Coates' remarks to be both insulting and infuriating. To begin with, I have discovered that few people suspect that productive practicing can integrate the personality. Convinced of the book's thesis, and in a defiant tone of voice that must have surprised Helen Coates, I reminded her that some well-known teachers on the faculties of prestigious music schools are among the world's most *disintegrated* musicians. Predictably, my opposition to her assessment of my book annoyed her considerably, and we parted on an unpleasant note.

As I reflect upon this now, I cannot help thinking that Helen Coates overstepped her authority, as many secretaries of well-known figures do.

For I find it difficult to believe that Lenny would have given her the license to go so far as to filter out what he should or should not read.

My final contact with Lenny occurred before the presidential inauguration of Jimmy Carter. I had written a song called "One World" which, I felt, would have been an ideal contribution to the inaugural concert that Lenny himself was organizing. Lenny's dentist, whom I met through a mutual friend, offered to deliver the manuscript to him personally. I attached a note to it, of course, which included my New York City telephone number, and that of my mother in Millburn, New Jersey, where I taught twice a week.

One Tuesday afternoon, while I was teaching in Millburn, the telephone rang. In a moment my mother was in the studio: "Sonny, someone on the phone is pretending to be Leonard Bernstein. I think you ought to handle this." "Mother," I cried, "it *is* Leonard Bernstein!" My poor mother grasped her cheeks with her palms and wailed, "Oh, my God!" My pupil and I burst into laughter as I ran to the telephone to speak with Lenny. "It's a beautiful song," he told me, "but unfortunately, I have already chosen the material for the inaugural concert. I'm sorry to turn you down."

That was the very last contact I had with Lenny. It was very considerate of him to telephone me, but I nevertheless suffered the familiar pangs of rejection — something which career-oriented people must learn to live with. I had to face the fact that he may not have considered me sufficiently gifted to promote my career as a performer or composer.

MONSTERDOM REVISITED: THE MANAGERIAL SCENE

Of all the people associated with careers in music, certain private concert managers, agents, representatives — whatever name they go by — must certainly be among the lowest and most unprincipled individuals in all of society. They have existed for a long time now — ever since performing became big business. They are so immoral that they make big agencies like CAMI seem altruistic by comparison. If I repeat myself in speaking about these charlatans, it is because I feel obliged to protect young hopefuls from the damage, both professional and psychological, which some managers can cause. So I wish to say emphatically that the managerial profession is peopled with more frustrated musicians and human wrecks than one is likely to find in any other profession. The worst ones are those who once aspired, or continue to aspire, to performing careers. In dealing with the few distinguished artists whom they represent, however, they are the epitome of honesty and decorum, proving that they at least have good business sense. After all, well-known artists, being in great demand and commanding large fees, attract engagements with little or no effort on the part of such managers. Like the line from Gershwin's "Summertime," "the livin' is easy," and commissions are high. But as I know from personal experience, younger, less experienced musicians, in plentiful supply, make for the kind of prey that these managers relish.

Most managers, like music critics, are not qualified to judge the fine points of anyone's performance. Yet, since their job is to sell musicians, the keen ones, like Arthur Judson and Sol Hurok, for instance, learn to "sniff out" that special something in a performer, be it his or her particular kind of musical and personal projection, general appearance (it never hurts to be good-looking), or something as superfluous to artistry as the way one walks across the stage. In short, when a performer has charisma, managers know that they may have a saleable item on their hands. Should a performer have these qualities but lack certain credentials, such as a first prize in an international competition, a recording contract, or a rave review, then certain managers demand a retainer fee. They do this knowing the obvious — that whatever engagements are available almost always go to well-known performers. The fact that such managers hold out the promise of performing careers to young, unknown musicians demotes them to criminal status.

Berenice Kazounoff

I was completely innocent of this when I met one such charlatan, Berenice Kazounoff, the first manager I had after I broke with CAMI. Heavyset, eccentrically masculine in manner, and loud-mouthed, she operated like many others in her profession: she demanded retainer fees from her unwary clients. In other words, for a monthly salary, which varied according to how much money she sensed was available to her, she deigned to take a young artist under her management. There were conditions, however. Foremost, she offered no guarantee of securing performing dates. Moreover, she demanded a twenty percent commission for whatever dates she did get for her artists. The retainer fee went, ostensibly, for the expenses entailed in trying to secure dates — telephone calls, letters, and various office expenses. Would any one of her artists ever ask her for an accounting of how the retainer fee was spent — to see her telephone statements, for example? Of course not. To cross her was to risk being scratched from her list and left without a manager altogether. At all costs, one must have a manager — at least, that is what most young artists are taught to think.

In the two years during which Berenice Kazounoff managed me, she secured only two dates for me — one at Goucher College in Baltimore and the other at the Gardner Museum in Boston, a date for which I had to audition. Later, I discovered that anyone could arrange an audition for the Gardner Museum series — with or without a manager. At any rate, I found myself competing with scores of other instrumentalists and singers. Luckily, I passed the audition and was chosen to be part of the forthcoming concert series. Even here, Berenice Kazounoff retained 20% of $75.00, the honorarium which the museum sent to her office.

Not that any manager could have augmented my career at that point, simply because most concert dates are available only to musicians with big reputations. And those musicians never have to pay a retainer fee. It is a "Catch-22" situation, not unlike that which exists in other professions. Even if someone had explained to me that being asked for a retainer fee by a manager is tantamount to an admission that you are not a saleable item, still, I would have gone along with the arrangement. And why? For ego gratification alone. It felt professional, and also secure, to be able to say, "I have a manager!" The Duchess, my patroness at that time, generously paid Berenice Kazounoff her monthly fee of $600, for two years. When I think of it, that $14,000 could have been invested in making several recordings and performing a number of concerts in major cities. As it was, however, my career remained stagnant, while Berenice Kazounoff paid her rent, ate in expensive restaurants, and went on cruises.

"I have five dates for you!"

Around the time that I met this stunning creature, she had ensnared another innocent victim, a young English cellist who had come to the United States to compete in an international competition. Having failed to make it to the finals, he extended his stay in New York City to audition for managers, Kazounoff among them. She was particularly effusive in her praises of his talent: "I'd like to add your name to my roster of artists," she told him. "But you are unknown to the public, so in order to work for you, I will need a monthly retainer fee of $1000." Thrilled at the prospect of having a manager, he thanked her profusely, borrowed the money from his parents, and signed a contract binding him to her management for two years. A year and a half later, Kazounoff finally contacted him: "Book your flight," she said. "I have five dates for you." It never occurred to him to ask her where he was booked, or what his fees would be. This, he thought, was out of keeping with artistry for its own sake. Overjoyed at the prospect of playing in the United States, the young man went further into debt by purchasing two roundtrip airplane tickets, one for himself and one at half fare for his cello.

Part 4: The Battle Continues

Arriving in New York City, the cellist could hardly wait to learn the details of his itinerary. What he subsequently discovered, however, so discouraged him, that he was ready to take the next flight back to England. To begin with, the scheduling could not have been more disadvantageous, both to his time and to his pocket. The five concerts, the first being for a group of wine merchants in California, required him to crisscross between the west and east coasts five times within one month. He had also an hour's recital for a women's club, an appearance at a small museum that no one had ever heard of, a youth concert scheduled in a high school auditorium, and a library concert in a small town in Iowa. His total remuneration for the five concerts — $2000. From this, he had to pay his own expenses plus a 20 percent commission to Kazounoff.

The scattered dates left him with two options: either return to New York City in between concerts, where he could stay with a friend, or remain on the road and incur hotel and food expenses. Having already borrowed a great deal of money to promote his career, and being in fine shape, performing-wise, he decided to go through with the tour and live on the road. When his tour was over, he did not even have one review to show for his efforts. Never daring to complain to his manager for fear of being dropped from her roster, he went back to England dejected and very much in the red.

When his two year contract was about to expire, he telephoned Kazounoff from England and asked her if she would continue to represent him without a retainer fee. To this she replied, "We will see, dear; we will see." A few weeks later, he telephoned her again. She did all of the talking, at his expense, of course: "My dear," she told him with a syrupy voice that made him cringe, "I would really like to help you. But with inflation being what it is, I could not possibly work for you for nothing. If you wish to continue under my management, you will need to sign another two year contract. And by the way, I have raised my fee to $1500 a month."

With his hopes now shattered, and with no means of paying back his debt to his parents, the young cellist broke with her entirely. Kazounoff, on the other hand, could find plenty of other young instrumentalists and singers who would agree to anything in order to say, "I'm under management."

What emerges from this story is that a young artist's musical and personal well-being seems to be the very last thing certain managers consider. Such managers can discourage their artists to such an extent that many young aspirants leave music altogether.

Winners May Be Losers

Whereas the young cellist suffered from a lack of engagements, international contest winners experience just the opposite. Suddenly within one season they are booked for more concerts than most performers play in five seasons. In fact, certain orchestras and managers of concert series reserve dates on their rosters for first prize winners whoever they may turn out to be. After all, big contest winners *have* to be good. Everybody likes a winner, and tickets for the victor can easily be sold in advance.

Some young artists fit into the "big time" quite naturally. Others, however, are unaccustomed to major concert appearances. Being young and lacking performance experience, and not as yet having amassed a sufficient number of important works in their repertory, some contest winners crumble under the strain of a major career. In one such case, a brilliant young prize winner successfully fulfilled twenty dates within one season. She was somewhere in the Midwest when her newly acquired manager telephoned her about the possibility of substituting for a prominent pianist who had suddenly become ill: "It's a major date, honey. You have one week to get the Grieg Concerto in shape." "But I have never played the Grieg Concerto," the poor girl declared. "And I could never get it ready within a week." None of this sat well with the manager: "You mean to tell me that you're willing to forfeit a date with a major orchestra and a world-renowned conductor?" What he did not tell her was that the date would have netted him an unusually large commission. He would, therefore, neither forget nor forgive her refusal to accept the date, however plausible her reason. That she might have crammed and performed badly, and ruined her health in the process, was of no concern to him. Retribution followed swiftly and ruthlessly. The following year, with engagements still coming in for her, the manager dropped her from his roster and signed up a new contest winner who did not play as well as she did, but who had a larger repertory.

Paul Winchell and Breakfast at the Plaza

Earlier, I made a brief reference to my second manager. He was the one who urged me to pay $750 for the privilege of making my debut in Carnegie Hall with a major orchestra from Europe. He then got furious with me when I refused to go along with this scam. Yet, as managers go, he showed that he had, at least, a high degree of imagination, when in 1958 he organized my debut in Paris, the city where I had first met him. By asking Jean Cocteau to create a drawing for my posters (Cocteau did this for him gratis), and speaking in fractured French about my debut to Parisian college students as they milled around between their classes, he

A few days before my debut in the Salle Gaveau in Paris. My manager points to the poster designed by Jean Cocteau. I am pointing to a poster announcing Brailowsky's concert scheduled a week after mine.

(Photo by Seymour Bernstein)

actually succeeded in filling the Salle Gaveau. This was no small feat, considering that I was unknown to Parisian audiences. The concert was a smashing success.

After our return to the United States, my manager, his wife, and I were very close. There were dinners and concerts, and a concerted effort on my manager's part to promote my career. At one point he teamed me up with the well-known ventriloquist Paul Winchell for the purpose of giving youth concerts. One of them took place at Town Hall. As Paul Winchell's script writers conceived it, Knucklehead Smiff and Jerry Mahoney were attending their first concert. By means of verbal interplay among the four of us, and my performing and discussing around a dozen contrasting pieces, the dummies' abhorrence of serious music was soon replaced by acceptance and enthusiasm. The ultimate idea was to win over the young people in the audience to the classics. And since the children identified with the dummies, that is exactly what happened. The program was a huge success, and everyone, including the critics, predicted a brilliant future for all of us. The Winchell managers even spoke of a TV series. With education a top priority in my life, this was one project that truly interested me. But like Berenice Kazounoff, who never took advantage of Leonard Bernstein's enthusiasm over my playing, this manager let the potential for future engagements with Paul Winchell slip through his fingers.

Shortly after this, my manager fell upon hard times. High ideals and personal devotion are often compromised in the face of financial difficulties. Whatever the reason, he soon began to take on all of the negative aspects of the West 57th Street managerial underworld. Once, for example, he asked me to meet him for breakfast at the Plaza, a very expensive invitation indeed for someone who found it difficult to pay the rent. The magnificent ambience of the Elizabethan Room and one of the Plaza's special breakfasts — what perfect accompaniments, I thought, to a discussion on how to further my career. Yet furthering my career was the very last thing on his mind. No sooner was the coffee served than he launched into a tirade of complaints against me, the subject being my lack of development as an artist. Knowing in my heart of hearts that the opposite was true, that I had, in fact, made significant strides as a performing pianist, I asked him pointedly, "On what basis are you making such an unfair judgment? The fact is, you haven't heard me play since the Paul Winchell productions." He simply ignored my question, or perhaps he could not bring himself to answer it honestly. For him, the easier course was to go right on deriding me.

The old adage about giving a person enough rope certainly proved true in this case. We were nearly finished with our breakfast when my manager finally confessed to the thing that had precipitated his crisis of conscience: he had signed up another pianist whose parents were willing to pay him a retainer fee each month. Whatever engagements were available now had to go to this pianist. Breakfast at the Plaza, then, was my manager's way of relieving his guilt for having to deprive me of performing dates.

On the one hand, I understood my manager's plight: he had a wife and a child to support and he was desperate to earn money. On the other hand, he need not have unjustly attacked my competence as a pianist simply to justify a decision born of desperation. His unwarranted criticism not only compromised our friendship but also destroyed his credibility with me. Needless to say, I could never trust him again.

Few things are more insensitive, even sadistic, than choosing meals as a suitable occasion for deriding others. Once a pupil invited me to her home for lunch. "I've got something very important to discuss with you," she said. Thinking that she might be ill, or in the throes of some emergency, I made a special effort to make an appointment with her. Even as she removed two salads from her refrigerator, she began berating me for placing her in a performing class with pianists who were inferior to her. Through all of this, I was expected to swallow my tuna fish, overly chilled as it was. After that vitriolic lunch, as similarly after my breakfast at the Plaza, I was left fighting a fine case of indigestion for the rest of the day.

The Seed Catalogue

Shortly after Ruth Alsop and I resigned from CAMI, she, her husband LaMar, and I formed the Alsop-Bernstein Trio. The hard reality of having only a few concerts a year, instead of fifty, as we had with CAMI, made us face the fact that self-promotion can only go so far. We thus invited a well-known manager to hear us perform at the Alsops' home in Dobbs Ferry, New York.

It was one of those fortunate auditions in which we all played extremely well. On the following morning, I took it upon myself to telephone the manager, eager to hear his response to our playing. To my surprise, he expressed a desire to manage me alone. I was flattered, of course, but also taken aback at his dismissal of our Trio. While the Alsops were understandably disappointed, they urged me, nevertheless, to take advantage of this opportunity. Management was hard to come by; if a manager expressed a desire to promote my career without a retainer fee, then I would be foolish to turn down his offer. To add to my good fortune, the manager's assistant and secretary subsequently became my pupil. With my own pupil working at the core of the management, my career, I thought, was assured. I would soon get solo engagements and earn substantial fees. Filled with visions of stardom, I began to practice harder than I had ever done before.

This manager was actually a performer himself. He played in a chamber ensemble that enjoyed wide popularity. Yet no musician I have ever met exemplified more clearly how a person can remain untouched by the harmonizing effects of music. Even though I knew some of the artists under his management, not one of them so much as hinted as to the sort of person he was. But then, it is not unusual for professional musicians to protect their managers and their teachers, the people to whom they entrust their careers and their musical development. I have confessed to doing this very thing. During the brief time I studied with Madame Vengerova, for example, I spoke of her in glowing terms. And why? I wanted to love and respect all of my teachers and managers, as I did my parents.

My new manager had a secret plan for me. Because he did not have a piano duo on his roster, he intended to team me up with a fine pianist who was a member of his own chamber ensemble. Unbeknownst to me, he had signed me up for this purpose alone. Imagine my surprise when one Sunday, while perusing the Arts and Leisure section of *The New York Times*, I suddenly came upon an announcement of an orchestral concert to be held in the Grace Rainey Rogers Auditorium at the Metropolitan Museum of Art. One of the works listed was *Carnival of the Animals* by Saint-Saëns, a work scored for orchestra, narrator, and two pianos. The soloists were announced in bold print — the woman pianist in my manager's ensemble and myself. I telephoned him immediately and questioned him about this. He thought that his assistant, my pupil, had informed me about the date; she, as I subsequently learned, had assumed that this was the province of her boss. My manager was very cavalier about the whole thing and seemed not to be concerned in the slightest when I informed him that I refused to make my debut at the Metropolitan Museum as part of a two-piano team. "Don't worry about it," he said in a matter of fact tone. "I'll get someone else to fill in for you." If nothing more was gained from that conversation, I at least had the satisfaction of making clear to my manager exactly what my intentions were — namely, to perform solo recitals. While I had the highest regard for the pianist with whom I had been paired and would ordinarily have been priv- ileged to perform with her, I now wanted to perform solo repertory — and that was that!

As it turned out, I did perform with the pianist in question several years later in two all-Mozart recitals. The first one featured the Concerto for Two Pianos, the second, four-hand works. At another time, we performed the *Liebeslieder* Waltzes by Brahms at a distinguished choral concert at

Avery Fisher Hall. There is no finer artist, nor any person more loved and admired, than Harriet Wingreen.

In the meantime, my pupil, who handled the bookings for my manager, managed to steer a few choice dates my way. The first one was at the University of Missouri. One thousand students and faculty members attended that concert. Acutely aware that this was the first concert under my new management, I was resolved to make a favorable impression. As it turned out, I played my best, and the audience response was truly explosive. I attributed the latter to several factors: I spoke to the audience and shared with them my own feelings about the works on the program; I premiered a work of my own, *Birds*, Book 1, which, if I can be trusted to be purely objective, seemed to generate the greatest enthusiasm. Finally, it did not hurt that I closed my program with one of the all-time crowd pleasers — Mussorgsky's *Pictures at an Exhibition*. To my good fortune, the entire concert was recorded, including the audience response. On t he way back to New York City, I thought only of one thing: "When my manager hears those hoots and screams, his interest in me will be justified."

Feeling proud of my accomplishment, I could hardly wait to play that tape for my manager. On the appointed evening, I went to his apartment not only with the tape of my recital in hand, but also with a rave review that had come out on the morning following my concert. He glanced at the review perfunctorily, inserted the cassette into his tape machine, and we settled in chairs at the far end of his living room.

I was looking off into the distance listening to the first piece on my program, Beethoven's Sonata Op. 110, when suddenly my manager's voice created a discordant counterpoint to the entrance of the great fugue subject: "Are you interested in gardening?" Startled by a question which under the circumstances was a blatant non sequitur, I turned my head to the left where he was sitting. And unbelievable as it seems, I saw him poring over a seed catalogue. Had my sense of dignity been greater than my desire to protect my precious career at all costs, I would have removed the tape from the machine and walked out of that apartment. But did I, in fact, exhibit so much as a hint of indignation for this total indifference to me and to Beethoven as well? Of course not. I simply sat there like a whipped dog, trying my best to maintain some semblance of poise. In a barely audible voice, I answered his question: "No, I know nothing about gardening." When Op. 110 had finally come to an end, its considerable length having afforded my manager ample time to absorb a great deal of information about flowers and shrubs, I quietly removed the tape from the machine, thanked him for his time, and prepared to leave the apartment.

"Good job," he said, in a bored tone of voice. "Make some copies of the tape so that we can send them to other schools."

To say that I was downcast when I left that apartment hardly describes the low state to which my emotions sank. My manager's indifference to my playing was, to be sure, both crushing and insulting. But the greater issue, as I saw it, was whether artistic gain or even a flourishing career could justify my having anything to do with such a person. His behavior on that occasion was certainly bad enough. But soon he was "to cover shame with shame," as Milton put it. And like a modern day Judas, he was to betray me in such a way that even now, I can hardly believe it was possible.

Thirty Telephone Calls

Any performer under management, or any published composer or writer, must learn one thing from the start: never expect your manager or your publisher to do everything for you. In other words, it is incumbent upon performers, composers, and writers to continue playing an active role either in securing performing engagements for themselves or promoting their own works. I have always done this as a matter of course, not only because I believe that I am my own best salesperson, but also because I have learned from bitter experience just how irresponsible and even deceitful some managers and publishers can be. Whether they feel that there is no profit to be gained, or whether they are acting upon a neurotic need to enjoy a false sense of dominance over another person, certain managers and publishers cannot be trusted to promote anyone other than well-known clients. There seems, also, to be an element of jealousy among certain managers and publicists who are themselves gifted. Guilt for never having been properly disciplined, or the nagging awareness of unfulfilled aspirations, can result in conscious or unconscious feelings of resentment towards the very people they promote. For instance, I instinctively felt that it was not just a professional oversight when a high executive working at one of my former publishers actually allowed my book *With Your Own Two Hands* to go out of print, even though the marketing people told me it was selling well. Nor could his refusal to return my telephone messages be attributed to a busy schedule alone.

Having heard far too often "Don't call us, we'll call you," I learned through the years to play a more active role in promoting my career. So when, in the 1970s, the 92nd Street Y was fast becoming the Mecca of cultural life in New York City, I was determined to get a booking on their concert series. The director of the concert department knew me by reputation, and it was not difficult, therefore, to secure an appointment to speak with him.

Sitting across from him at his desk, I lost no time in stating the purpose of my visit: I wanted to give another recital in New York City, but I was tired of always having to rent halls. Would it be possible to be a part of the Y concert series? The director, known for his outward charm and his predilection for flattery, "deared" and "darlinged" me almost from the start. To my surprise, he reached above his head to a shelf and pulled down a massive date book in which he recorded all of the concert bookings for the year. As I looked on in utter disbelief, he assigned me a firm date for my debut at the Y in late September — a perfect date, I thought, for a fresh beginning to the concert season. As he recorded my name in a box under the date in question, I thought to myself, "I did it! I have actually secured a date on a major concert series in New York City!"

Imagine the sense of triumph I experienced after that highly success-ful meeting. I rushed out onto the street, all aglow with excitement, and stopped at the nearest telephone booth to make two calls — one to my mother and one to my pupil in my manager's office. "It's a coup," I said jubilantly to them. "I can hardly believe that I pulled it off so easily." Although the date I secured was nine months hence, I spread the news about it to everyone I knew.

As it happened, my manager visited the director shortly after I had been there, his purpose being to firm up two dates for his ensemble. As I remember, the ensemble had been reengaged to perform all six Brandenburg Concerti by Bach. As fate would have it, my date, being a choice one, was the first to come under consideration. "Take it," the director suggested. "I'll give Seymour another date." Although my manager saw my name inscribed on the calendar of events, he had not the slightest compunction about booking that date for himself. Without my knowledge, then, my debut at the 92nd Street Y was scratched.

My poor pupil, having been informed by my manager of his recently assigned dates, was horrified to see that one of them was the one that had been assigned to me. She quietly but firmly reminded him of this fact. "Don't worry about it. I'll see to it that he gets another date," he said. But he never did see to it. Balancing her need to maintain a modicum of discretion where her boss was concerned and her allegiance to me, my pupil was hard put to know what to do. She decided to shield this news from me in the hope that someone, my manager or the Y concert director, would, in fact, re-schedule my concert. Four months went by, months during which my pupil brought up the subject repeatedly to her boss. When it seemed apparent that no action would be taken, my pupil felt obliged to break the news to me as gently as she could.

It would be impossible to describe the mixture of heartache and anger which welled up within me when I was informed of this double treachery. And one can imagine the state of my pupil who had to deal with her own frustrations at being powerless to help me. Apart from my personal anguish, I could not help thinking of all the people I had told about my debut at the Y. At the end of my telephone conversation with my pupil, I put down the receiver and sat on my sofa in a state of numbness and disbelief.

When I had finally regained my composure, I telephoned the director at the Y. "He's busy at the moment," his secretary told me. "But he'll get back to you as soon as he's free." The day passed and the director did not return my call. The next day I tried again, and of course he was at a meeting. As I made my daily telephone calls to the Y during the better part of a month, I knew even then that I would be writing this story one day. I therefore kept track of the number of calls I made. And astonishing as it seems, they numbered thirty in all! It was on my thirtieth try that the secretary happened to have left the office and the director picked up the telephone. "Now I've got you!" I said to him derisively. He recognized my voice at once. "Oh, Seymour," he exclaimed, with false sincerity, "I'm going to kill myself! Now, what are you doing this moment, dear? Can you taxi over to the Y to negotiate a new date for your concert? Let's do it right now — that is, if you're free."

I *was* free, and I taxied across Central Park immediately. Down came the book again and another date was recorded for my recital. This time, the date remained firm, and I did perform at the Y — not merely once, but three times over the next few years, in both solo and chamber music recitals. But there was something unpleasant associated with each performance; either the publicity was not out in time or stage arrangements went afoul. At one point, when publicity for the Alsop-Bernstein Trio's debut at the Y was unforgivably delayed, I left a dozen or more messages for the director. Once again I received the cold shoulder treatment. Finally, in desperation, I dictated the following message to his secretary: "Inform your boss that unless the publicity is in my hands within three days, I will contact certain friends I have at *The New York Times* and tell them how he demeans his artists." One can well imagine with what trepidation the poor secretary placed this message on her boss's desk. But I did have the publicity in hand within three days. Nor was there so much as a hint of resentment towards me when I met the director many times afterwards. For the truth is, his behavior to others has inspired even harsher responses than the irate message he received from me.

The question is, why did I continue to court that director for future engagements once I discovered how treacherous he was? Were the same situation to occur today, I would use every means at my disposal, legal and otherwise, to get him fired. But twenty years ago, my desire to be engaged on a major concert series in New York City was greater than my pride. Whatever it took and whatever the consequences, I was determined to make my debut at the Y. As I explained to a friend, "It was I who won out in the end. I walked out on that stage and did my thing." Were I now asked by young aspirants for advice about managers, I would unhesitatingly begin by telling them, "You don't have human relationships with most managers and directors of concert series, you *deal* with them."

As for my manager, the third and very last one I had, I was bound by a contract to stay under his management for two more years after my debut at the Y. Immediately thereafter I broke with him. Not long after that, my pupil struck out on her own also.

A Managerial Oath?

If one might envision the ideal manager, what would one suppose his or her qualifications to be? And if an oath were to exist for music managers, as the Hippocratic oath does for doctors, how would it be worded?

In fantasizing about these questions, I would say, foremost, that the ideal manager would love music, as much as performers supposedly do. I say "supposedly" because some performers, in their frenzied craze to achieve success, sadly enough often lose the very thing that sparked their interest in music to begin with — a love of it. If managers loved music, they would quite naturally bend their efforts towards promoting music's chief protagonists — performers. For as managers know all too well, without performers, music's voice would be silenced forever.

I believe that concert managers ought to have studied voice or an instrument, just as art critics ought to have tried their own hand at painting. For as I see it, the more concert managers develop and refine their own talents, the more sensitive and discriminating they would be to the artists whom they manage.

I cannot imagine, however, that managers would be able to nurture their artists properly without financial backing. A manager might be independently wealthy or else draw support from agencies or individuals. Economic solvency would mean two things: managers would not have to depend upon commissions for their own livelihood, and their artists would not feel obliged to perform concerts just to support their managers. This would enable performing artists to grow at their own pace. It takes time and patience, after all, to amass repertory and to develop that "at home" feeling on the stage. And since the time span for an artist's maturation differs as widely as does anything else that grows in nature, then no arbitrary time limit ought to be placed upon a performer's development.

Whatever the source of financial backing, managers and performers alike would, in my utopian vision, draw yearly salaries, with the performers' salaries based upon a sliding scale. In other words, as performers gained in proficiency and popularity, their fees would rise proportionately. As I continue to dream about such ideal conditions, I imagine how beneficial all of this would be to young aspiring artists. For once relieved of financial pressures, they would be able to concentrate more fully on studying, practicing, and refining all of the performing skills which, eventually, they would bring to the stage. The fulfillment of their gifts, then, would enhance society and afford joy and satisfaction to their benefactors.

Returning to the real world, the perpetuation of noble endeavors quite obviously requires economic solvency. But where are the agencies or the individuals who would invest in music and performers? And where are the managers who would place music and their artists above their voracious appetites for money and power? At this writing, the future looks bleak, indeed. The managerial profession is infested with people who, for a quick buck, will compromise not only their artists' musical and personal well-being, but even music itself.

Regarding a managerial oath — it is, of course, easier to conceive of one than it would be to imagine its being implemented. For predictably, far too many managers would betray their oath, as doctors have been known to betray theirs. Nevertheless, simply as an exercise in wishful thinking, I offer the following:

> I embrace the managerial profession for the sole purpose of promoting, protecting, and defending the noble art of music and music's chief protagonists — composers and performers.

Considering the music profession as it exists today, it is not very likely that managers, as I know them to be, would sanction such an oath, or least of all, swear allegiance to it. In fact, I would go so far as to say that the very idea of an oath would be as inimical to most managers as praying would be to an atheist.

OUTLINE FOR SELF-EXAMINATION

If, as Socrates said, the unexamined life is not worth living, why is it that so many people rarely, if ever, examine their true feelings and their motives in doing things — and, as the case may be, the reasons for their failure to fulfill their aspirations? All of us have our own opinions as to whether we are successful or not in whatever we do in life — successful in our own eyes and in accordance with society's definition of success. Let us suppose that a musician reaches the age of forty and faces the following realities: He can neither get performing engagements nor amass a sufficient number of pupils to pay the rent. Had he both — performing engagements and a large enough class of pupils — then these two things would be, in his eyes, symbolic of having made it. One might think, however, that having failed to achieve these symbols of success, such a musician would ask himself, "Why? Why haven't I made it?"

One or more points in my Outline for Self-Examination may provide some of the answers, not just for the musician I envisioned above, but for all musicians who aspire to careers in music. It is not an easy task, however, to face the truth about ourselves — which is of course the reason why so few people ever examine their true feelings. Yet, when one stops to think about it, what is more difficult than facing the stage? If anyone epitomizes determination, sharpness of mind, and the bravery of a warrior, it is the performing musician. But in spite of their heroic status, musicians are often fearful and reluctant to face the person behind the performer and, in the process, to come to grips with the psychology behind performing careers. One cause of this anxiety is the secret fear that there may be no resolution to a problem once it is defined and faced squarely. But just as flowing water circumvents obstacles, so too can people discover their own solutions to problems which, at first, might seem to be insoluble.

It is even possible that self-examination might cause musicians to abandon a career in music altogether. Suppose, for example, that musicians face up to the fact that they practice, perform, and teach only because they are not equipped to make a living in any other field? Drastic as it may seem, I believe it would be far better to abandon a musical career and get any job at all, rather than to be dishonest to themselves and to music.

The following outline may serve as a guide for self-confrontation for all musicians, whether they have successful careers or not. For the sake of our development and for our general sense of well-being, we ought to face these points courageously and honestly. And needless to say, it will require no less courage to take whatever remedial measures are necessary once certain truths are revealed:

Outline for Self-Examination
1. I am not talented enough.
2. I am very talented, but extremely lazy.
3. I have what it takes, but I lack confidence.
4. In my opinion, I have what it takes, but no one else seems to agree with me.
5. I am one of those successful performers whom everyone admires. But the truth is, I am afraid of success. For success means that I have to be responsible. And in that area, I have no talent at all!
6. I am a retiring type who recedes from all that is expected of me once I am on the stage.
7. I lack the initiative to make contacts.
8. I cannot function in competitive situations.
9. I am aggressive to the point of repelling the very people who are in a position to help me. I invariably set up situations which lead to rejection and failure. This is because I secretly loathe myself, and, therefore, feel unworthy, either of achieving success or even of being loved.
10. Someone close to me does not want me to succeed. I act out failure because preserving that relationship is more important to me than my personal success.
11. I was forced to practice from early childhood on. Now, as an adult, I not only practice with nothing more than a dutiful obedience, but I also feel ill-equipped to do anything else.
12. Someone else has implanted the image of failure in my mind by projecting their own sense of failure onto me, or by harping on my inadequacies to the exclusion of my positive traits.
13. The world doesn't deserve me.

Most musicians will identify with one or more points in the above outline. In subjecting themselves to self-examination, musicians might be faced with the overwhelmingly difficult task of separating truth from fantasy: "Are my responses real or imagined? If they are real, can I change for the better? But if my responses have no basis in fact, why do I imagine them to be true?" Thus musicians must ponder, probe, and examine themselves, even as they would each and every note of a musical composition they wish to perform.

Considering how difficult it is to be honest with and objective about ourselves, it might be to our advantage, therefore, to consult with a friend, or even to seek professional counseling. It is also difficult to be honest and objective about the music we are practicing, which is why we seek out teachers. Yet I have taught pupils who were reluctant to analyze the emotional and physical requirements of music for fear of inhibiting their spontaneity. It is true that too much analyzing can impede spontaneity. But in the right proportion, asking "why" should no more impede spontaneity in performing music than in relating to people. The reason is that knowing *why* provides a foundation from which confidence, love, and, indeed, spontaneity spring forth in even greater abundance. My own self-examination and my observations of my colleagues and pupils have taught me an important fact: Although musicians invest unlimited time and energy in preparing each note of music for a performance, they may, in the process, neglect something far more important, something which ultimately will spell the success or failure of their performance — and that is self-examination.

I have often spoken about how productive practicing can lead towards the integration of the personality by fusing together the musician and the person. Careers, however, because they are so demanding and, at times, so frustrating, often militate against this fusion of the musician and the person. Should this be the case, then several points in the above outline might enable a musician to discover the causes of the disintegration.

One word of caution: Musicians beset with conflicts may draw the wrong conclusions from this outline. For example, a musician might see herself or himself in point No. 2 as being the incurably lazy type. But a closer examination may reveal that laziness is merely a symptom of a far more serious problem — a fear of success. I have on many occasions pointed out to pupils that their fear of success stems from their reluctance to make that difficult transition from the irresponsible child, whom everyone takes care of, to the responsible adult, who is self-sufficient. Only the latter, the adult, has the capacity to walk out onto the stage and perform with control and conviction.

SEX AND CONTRACTS

I have often mentioned my vision of the ideal musician — one whose musical self and personal self interact in harmony. Yet we have seen that working at music, the paradigm of harmony and order, does not necessarily create this interaction. In fact some musicians are among the world's most *unharmonious* people. They are at war with themselves and with others, and many of them exhibit abusive sexual behavior. In gathering information for this book, I interviewed some music students who were victims of outrageous sexual abuse on the part of teachers, managers, and other people in authority. While I was saddened to hear their stories, I was not by any means shocked, for I have had my own experiences with sexual abuse.

As I said earlier, though I was not altogether innocent as a young man, I was not worldly, either. As a result, I became embroiled in situations that more experienced people would have avoided. That I, for example, chose my room in the former Imperial Hotel in Tokyo as a place to say goodbye to Japan's chief music critic was, perhaps, something which a more worldly person would not have done. For it should have occurred to me that he might read into my invitation a desire for intimacy. And that is exactly what happened. No sooner did I close the door of my room than this distinguished gentleman rushed up to me, wrapped his arms around me, and pressed his lips against mine. It all happened before I was able to fend him off. Even after I collected myself and pushed him away, he continued on with verbal expressions of passion, which ended with, "You and I understand one another." I can only speculate as to what he meant by that statement. He was, I had learned, the grandson of Thomas Mann, a fact which had made me awestruck on the few occasions when I met him socially. Moreover, his reviews of my playing were complimentary beyond anything that I had encountered up until that time. It is possible that he read into my glazed look something more than admiration. The invitation to my hotel room, then, would have confirmed this in his eyes. Whatever the cause of his effusive and unwelcome show of emotion, I felt more furious with myself for not anticipating his attentions.

I must confess to something else — something which sheds light on one aspect of the situation. And that is, that in spite of everything, in spite of my revulsion at being forcibly kissed on the mouth, something within me was flattered to know that such a distinguished figure was attracted to me. Nor did it escape my attention that someone else in a similar position might use his or her own power of attraction for exploitative purposes: "I'll give the critic what he wants, and he, in return, will use his influence to augment my career."

Some authority figures, knowing this tendency in aspiring young musicians, use their clout or their hero status as a means of extracting favors. Sheer arrogance leads them to think that a hero worshipper will concede to a hero's every whim. So it was that one of my teachers used my awestruck admiration of him as a means of trying to ensnare me in a sexual liaison. The result was that everything from which I had benefited musically and personally was suddenly placed in serious jeopardy. My musical admiration for him was one thing, but going to bed with him was quite another. How much this hurt and infuriated him, I cannot begin to say. When at a calmer moment I said to him in all sincerity, "You would no longer respect me if I complied with something which I honestly felt I did not want to do," his indignation knew no bounds. "Do you know whom you are turning down? Why, I could have anyone I want, simply by snapping my fingers!" "Well, bully for you," I answered, being quite angry with him by this time. "I'm happy that there are so many people who will grant you sexual favors. But I'm not one of them."

My rejection of my master caused a breech in our relationship which lasted until his death. I believe that he was too self-centered and proud to suffer remorse. But he did suffer in another way: He was perpetually frustrated and resentful of me whenever we were together. It saddens me to say that I was never able to feel comfortable with him again. Although I sorely miss the artistic stimulation which somehow filtered through this psychological quagmire, I cannot say, in all honesty, that I grieved at his passing, as I did for my other teachers.

"Maybe you like me to touch your shoulder?"

Sexual harassment in the music world is so widespread today, that music students have come to expect it everywhere — at private lessons, in the classroom, and at auditions. The following statement by one young violinist is typical of what many young musicians have confessed to me:

> My generation lives with sexual harassment all the time. For example, when I hear a young violinist play a concerto with a major symphony orchestra, I find myself wondering if she slept with someone to get that date — the conductor, the manager, or even both! And the same goes for international contest winners: I automatically think that they slept with the head of the jury. It's all very unfair of me to think this way, because I know quite logically that most of those performers deserve these honors.

This same violinist had her own experiences with a lecherous teacher who wanted to exercise a master's prerogative over his disciple. At the first lesson, he walked over to her and put his hand on her shoulder:

> I dropped my shoulder, and he immediately got defensive: "Oh, you don't like me to touch your shoulder? Or maybe you *do* like me to touch your shoulder." Then, there was something in the way he looked at me that was extremely distressing. When speaking about my bow arm, for

instance, he looked me up and down until I squirmed under his glance. And when he wasn't doing this or commenting about my playing, he would light a cigarette and just look out of the window, apparently bored to death.

After each lesson, I went back to my room and simply wept. I didn't want to discuss this with my parents. For after all, I was a college student, and I was determined to handle this on my own. I did, however, confide in my friends, only to discover that some of them were also victims of harassment from their own teachers.

Victims of harassment often experience reverse psychological reactions. As this young violinist confessed to me, she thought that in some unconscious way she had brought these experiences upon herself:

> This may sound irrational, but somehow, I felt guilty for having caused this teacher to behave that way. I used to think to myself — perhaps there's something suggestive in the way I dress; maybe it would be better for me to wear pants; or perhaps there is something in my look that encourages his worst behavior.

She went on to describe what she had always expected of a teacher-pupil relationship, and how utterly disillusioned she became at what actually occurred:

> A pupil expects honest criticism with a constructive bent from a teacher — criticism for the sake of improvement. I fully expected to love that teacher, and I therefore laid myself open to him, waiting for and wanting musical and technical advice. To tell you the truth, I even dressed for each lesson out of respect for him. And when I received that kind of treatment, my whole world fell apart.

Her friend, a student of poetry, shed a great deal of light on the problem, as only a real friend could:

> There's nothing to feel guilty about. You, like all serious students, have a sincere desire to please your teacher in all ways — musically, psychologically, and even in the way you dress. Quite simply, you wanted to make a good

impression on him, not only violinistically, but even in the way you looked. There's nothing wrong with that.

Hearing this astute analysis from her friend, the violinist felt instantly better. She then recounted the pleasurable experiences she had had with her former teachers, all of whom happened to be women. It was unfortunate enough that her first male teacher treated her so outrageously. But later, she had to fend off another male teacher, who employed a different technique of harassment:

> During the first few lessons I had with my next teacher, his comments to me got completely out of control. I would flash him looks which said, "Don't you dare start this with me!" I never verbalized my indignation, but he got my message anyway. And he behaved himself during subsequent lessons.
>
> The following year, I switched schools and played an audition which happened to go very well. Afterwards, I happened to meet this teacher in the hallway. At first I thought that he was a member of the jury. But as I discovered, he had been assigned to the faculty of that school, and ours was simply a chance meeting. "Let's have a drink across the street," he said, which I interpreted as pedagogical interest on his part — a desire to discuss the audition. No sooner had we sat down than he began to make overtures to me. It all ended up with an invitation to his home that evening: "Let's have a cognac to celebrate the successful audition." I was very polite about it and told him that I had another engagement. Then the telephone calls started: "When are we going to have that cognac? How about 11 PM?" I began to wonder if he was just plain lonely and wanted to socialize with someone. At any rate, I always refused his invitations. Then I would occasionally meet him in school. He would sidle up to me and begin pressuring me all over again to have a cognac with him.

Most people who take advantage of others eventually do or say the wrong thing to the wrong person. So it was that this teacher's hour of reckoning was close at hand. As it happened, a pupil of his brought an accompanist with her to one of her lessons, a diminutive, attractive-looking

Korean girl. She looked demure and utterly defenseless — a pushover for a lecherous teacher. What that teacher did not know, however, was that she had already spent four years at Juilliard fending off her own teacher. While she may have looked demure, she was a tough cookie!

No doubt delighted at the prospect of a new victim, the teacher lost no time in trying to impress her with his smutty street knowledge of Korean society: "I hear a lot of stories about how Korean men control their wives; how they beat them, and...." But before he could utter another word, the Korean pianist shot him a scathing look and veritably exploded with "Cut that shit!" According to the violin student, who witnessed the entire scene, her teacher's mouth literally fell open. As she reasoned, it was unimaginable in itself that an Asian student would dare to defy an authority figure. But that she had such words in her verbal repertory simply shocked the teacher into silence. At any rate, he had finally met his match, and he never attempted to harass that student or her accompanists again.

The stories I have heard concerning sexual abuse and public embarrassment in the music world could easily fill a book in themselves — how teachers seduce their pupils, how managers produce contracts in return for special favors, and how conductors wield extra-musical authority over their orchestra members and soloists. An oboist who used to play in the NBC Symphony Orchestra told me of one incident. The occasion was a rehearsal conducted by Arturo Toscanini, with the extraordinary dramatic soprano Zinka Milanov as soloist. At one point during an aria, Milanov stopped the rehearsal, turned to Toscanini, and said in a rather seductive tone of voice, "Tony, it's too slow." Whereupon "Tony," eyeing her with daggers, bellowed out for all to hear: "In bed, you call me Tony; but on the stage, you address me as Maestro!" According to my friend, this outburst was followed by a frozen silence on everyone's part. Milanov grew pale and sank into submission. It never occurred to me to ask whether the Maestro did, in fact, move the tempo faster. But considering Toscanini's petulant nature, it is just as likely that he conducted the aria even slower, to punish Milanov for her insolence.

Some people believe that since the study of music requires a deep emotional identification and projection, musicians may be more demonstrative with their libidinal feelings than non-musicians. I hardly think that there is any validity to this theory. As I see it, the answer is more "positional" than libidinal, in that certain authority figures, intoxicated with their high positions, are arrogant enough to abuse their power. Moreover, it is not beyond the ability of some authority figures actually to delude themselves into believing that they are irresistible in the eyes of their potential victims — like my former teacher who claimed that he could have anyone he wanted, simply by snapping his fingers

The Tables Are Turned

The tables are turned, though, when certain young, attractive students use their charms for something beyond the acquisition of knowledge. As I myself have experienced, seductive looks and body language, for instance, or a student's inclination to press his or her body against my shoulder while I am sitting at the piano demonstrating a passage, are signals announcing a potential for establishing what the pupil sees as a mutually rewarding relationship: "You give me free and extra lessons and use your clout to augment my career. In return, you may enjoy my charms!" Teachers travel a dangerous road when they are dealing with such a manipulative and exploitative pupil. For even the strongest moral fiber might crumble in the face of premeditated wiles. I, myself, have known such manipulative pupils. And I can say from personal experience that had their musical skills been as advanced as their seductive ones, then they most assuredly would have been candidates for a major career.

In all truth, I am no less attracted to "pretty young things" than anyone else might be, and I have often had to exercise great restraint to pursue an ethical course. In one case that I remember, a pupil used her attractiveness as a license to shirk the assignments I gave her. As her progress decreased, her flirtations increased. When frank and open discussions and even warnings about her lack of preparation proved to be of no avail, I felt obliged to deliver an ultimatum to her: "Either memorize those three pages for your next lesson, or find another teacher!" Firmly believing that my pedagogical principles would dissolve in the face of her charms, she ignored my ultimatum and did *not* memorize those three pages. To her utter astonishment, I discontinued her lessons. It was a decision that caused both of us great suffering. But at least I had the satisfaction of having upheld my principles.

Did I discontinue my pupil's lessons to prove how self-righteous I am — that my pedagogical principles are stronger than my inclinations? A music critic, for example, reviewing the concert of someone he or she knows personally, might be so conscientious about remaining objective that the review could end up being unfairly negative. Similarly, the possibility exists that I, too, might have been overzealous in upholding my principle, and that I would have given any other pupil many more chances to memorize those three pages. I can only say that I believed then, as I still do, that my actions were both honest and justified.

Should a teacher and pupil fall in love, such intimacy does not necessarily have an adverse effect upon the teaching-learning process, as some people might think. On the contrary. I, myself, have enjoyed the deepest relationships with certain pupils. From all that I have experienced, the musical exchange between us has not only kept pace with the personal one, but has even accelerated in an never-ending interaction of musical fulfillment and personal pleasure. But as everyone knows, when a musical relationship, or any relationship for that matter, is based primarily on lust, then it is doomed from the start.

Platonic Relationships

Many people associate the word "love" with sexual attraction. In fact, certain psychologists hold to the Freudian theory that sees the libido consciously or unconsciously present in all relationships, from the parental to the interpersonal. Quite naturally, two people, whatever their relationship, can be sexually attracted to one another. But there is nothing like that rare exchange between a teacher and a pupil to prove that platonic relationships really exist. The love I feel for most of my pupils, for example, is totally devoid of sexual attraction. Their unfailing devotion to music, their constant strivings to overcome whatever weaknesses they might have, and their respect for me — all of these things inspire certain feelings within me which only the word "love" can adequately define. I express that love by a musical and personal interaction with my pupils from the moment they come into my studio until they leave. Some of my pupils, however, interpret my love for them as being anything but platonic, and I have had to make my feelings clear.

Authority Figures

An authority figure might be defined as a person who is a specialist in a certain field and who has real or imagined influence over us. In most cases, authority figures are older than we are. But in light of the above definition, we might assign authority status to a person of any age. Because authority figures command our trust and respect, and because people are, generally speaking, unpredictable, relationships with authority figures can range from love, both sexual and platonic, to destructiveness of the worst sort.

Perhaps the most important authority figure in a musician's life is his or her teacher. Yet not many teachers fully understand and accept the overwhelming influence that they have over their pupils. I believe that teachers and pupils ought to have open discussions about the roles they play in each other's lives. One important subject to discuss is the part which pupils play in upholding the relationship. Pupils, for example, may lean upon their teachers and relegate too much responsibility to them: "This passage is impossible! I just won't practice it until my teacher assigns me a good fingering at my next lesson." Or, "I would love to play the highest note of this phrase softer. But I'd better not do that until I get my teacher's permission!"

On the one hand, some pupils are simply too insecure and inexperienced to make decisions on their own. On the other hand, certain adult pupils who *are* perfectly capable of making decisions are too lazy and undisciplined to do so. This being the case, it is not so much a question of, "I don't *know* what to do," but rather, "I don't *want* to do it!" All responsibility, then, is shifted to the teacher, who, like a parent, is expected to make all final decisions. The problem is further exacerbated when a pupil with little or no sense of responsibility falls into the hands of a domineering teacher. The teacher, then, enjoys a false sense of power by making all decisions for such a pupil. If anything, this diminishes the pupil's sense of responsibility even more.

Oddly enough, many adult pupils behave like children when faced with solving musical and technical problems. Some of them will even go so far as to blame their teachers for their own lack of motivation for practicing: "You're not interested in me the way you used to be, so I've lost my motivation to practice." And some pupils will either praise or condemn their teachers according to how their performance went. If the performance went well, then "my teacher is great." But a bad performance means "I'm not getting the best training."

Audience members, too, often judge a teacher by the level of a pupil's performance. This was strikingly brought home to me one evening during one of the performing classes which I hold regularly in my New York City studio. Because I teach amateurs as well as artist pupils, the level of performances in those classes may range from poor to extraordinary. One such amateur, a businessman, was simply not capable of performing on a professional level. Yet his devotion to music inspired love and respect from me and my other pupils. While his technique was not on a par with my other pupils', we all admired him, nevertheless, for his beautiful tone, his sensitivity to music's language, and above all, for the decided improvement he made from lesson to lesson. He had recently memorized a Schubert Impromptu and wanted to perform it in one of my classes. Like most of my pupils, he was always terrified whenever he performed in my studio. For one thing, my pupils do not like to disappoint me; for another, they do not want to embarrass themselves in front of the other pupils. For obvious reasons, then, I instruct my pupils to have tryouts prior to performing in my classes. But this pupil was simply too busy to find the time to play for anyone prior to that class. Predictably, then, the Impromptu fell apart almost from the beginning.

Occasionally, I invite auditors to these performing classes, provided that they understand the purpose behind them — that they are not formal recitals, but merely opportunities for my pupils to try out new pieces. On the evening in question, I asked a close friend of mine to attend the class and to make constructive comments about everyone's playing. She had formerly studied with me and was now a highly respected teacher. Moreover, she was friendly with the pupil who was suffering agonies trying to control that Schubert Impromptu. Given my friend's experience as a performer and a teacher, one might have thought that she would know exactly why that performance fell apart — that my pupil was only moderately gifted, that he was racked with nerves, and that he had no performing experience to speak of. Yet, at one point in the performance, when his trembling hand inadvertently accented the final note of a tender phrase, my friend flashed me a look of utter disbelief, leaned over to me, and whispered in my ear, "Did you teach him to do that?" To begin with, that accent was inconsequential in the light of much more serious deficiencies which were clearly in evidence throughout the performance. That she made such a fuss over the miscalculation of a single tone, and moreover imputed the unmusical results to my teaching, caused me almost to explode with anger. Suffice it to say that I had to exercise the strongest control to keep from socking her. In fact, I was so angry and disillusioned with her that I never trusted her opinions about anyone's playing again. As I subsequently observed, she repeatedly hurled barbs at other teachers after hearing their pupils have similar difficulties in performances. I finally concluded that she was, at heart, a hostile and competitive colleague.

Returning to authority figures — age has not diminished my own need for having authority figures in my life. They include people younger as well as older than I, whose expertise in certain areas I admire greatly. At the time that I bought my first computer, for instance, I assigned teacher status to my own supremely gifted pupils, David Rissenberg and Francisco Nuñez. They were authorities or experts in a field which I knew nothing about. Although I was more than twice their age, I might as well have been six years old during the teaching process. My pupils were, at first, both delighted and embarrassed to be teaching their own teacher. But I yielded gratefully, and, I must say, *helplessly*, to everything they taught me. I was such a good pupil, in fact, that I soon learned from David something that Francisco did not know. That being the case, Francisco telephoned me some six months later and asked quite sincerely, "Can you teach me how to make a macro?" We both had a good laugh over the fact that a pupil had actually surpassed his own teacher in something.

Another pupil, Donald Shaw, who, among other things, performs the *Goldberg* Variations as though Bach himself had whispered their secrets in his ears, is a decorator by profession. He functioned for me as yet another authority figure when he undertook to redecorate my New York City studio. He also helped me edit this book. As for Flora Levin, I could not possibly describe with words alone the overwhelming influence she has had, and continues to have, over me. In editing and advising me on everything that I write, she has harmonized my brain, so to speak. And then there is my pupil Michael Kimmelman, a world-class figure, whose astute comments after reading this manuscript resulted in a change in my entire outlook on writing. In all these cases, it is one of the most rewarding aspects of my life that my pupils and I can function as both teacher and pupil.

As my pupils and I relate to one another in our teacher-pupil roles, no money is exchanged between us. For the spirit in which we help one another has no price tag. Of course Don Shaw had to buy supplies and hire people to implement the decorating of my apartment, but even here he kept costs down to a minimum.

In thinking about this exchange of roles, I am convinced that all pupils have something special to teach their teachers. It remains, then, for teachers to encourage, and to be open to, such exchanges. The desire always to remain a pupil was something which Sir Clifford Curzon taught me when he would stop after a phrase and ask me what I thought of it. Now, I do the same thing with my own pupils. They have taught me a great deal, musically and otherwise. Beyond the acquisition of knowledge, being a pupil humbles me in the face of my position of authority. But in the final analysis, nothing has inspired my gratitude more than two non-corporeal forces that I look upon as ultimate authorities in themselves — music and the creative process. I bow to them with the reverence due a deity. They are constant and predictable, like the tides surging outside my window. They nourish me in proportion to the effort I expend on their behalf.

STATE DEPARTMENT SPONSORED TOURS

To return to the story of my performing life, I must confess to something: In the past, I invariably performed better whenever I was *not* given a fee. For in my mind, a fee represented a handout, or something I would earn only if I played well — like "singing for one's supper." If there was anything I wanted to earn, it was the reward of living up to my own standards of performing and gaining the acceptance of my colleagues. Payment for services rendered, therefore, symbolized to me the wrong reason for performing or teaching. It would, indeed, be a utopian situation were I to be independently wealthy so that I would not have to charge a fee for any activity related to music.

Considering all of this, one can understand how privileged I felt in going on non-commercial tours sponsored by the State Department in Washington, D.C. — "non-commercial" in that the Office of Cultural Affairs paid my fees and all of my expenses. There was one condition laid down, however: I was not to receive payment in foreign countries for any purpose whatsoever. Needless to say, I was more than happy to agree to this condition.

I participated in four such tours in all. In 1955, I toured Japan and Korea for two months with four other musicians. In 1960, I went on a solo tour to the Far East and Southeast Asia for four months. In 1961, the violinist Sylvia Rosenberg and I formed a duo. We began our tour in Japan and played our last performance on the BBC in London — seven and a half months later. For my final tour in 1965, I was a guest artist with the Claremont Quartet. It lasted over two months and consisted of some 60 concerts throughout South and Central America. One highlight of this tour was meeting Alberto Ginastera at his School for Contemporary Music in Buenos Aires. There we gave the world premiere of a newly composed piano quintet by one of the school's faculty members.

Our mission in all of these tours was to give concerts, to lecture on various musical and pedagogical subjects, to conduct master classes, and to exchange ideas with teachers and students. Since the State Department paid our traveling expenses and gave us a monthly honorarium, plus a per diem that varied from country to country, we did not have to haggle about fees. Nor did we have to cram in as many concerts as possible just to satisfy a manager's greed. This gave us time to interact with teachers and students. Local sponsors incurred no expenses whatsoever in presenting us, and attendance at our performances was by invitation only. All of this enabled us to perform and teach for the sheer love of our art. One might say that our cultural presentations were gifts from the United States to other countries. They dignified the status of the American musician by eliminating commercialism entirely, thus exemplifying the ideal artist-manager relationship about which I fantasized earlier.

Beyond the contributions we made to musicians and to music lovers as well, we experienced firsthand how music could transcend political differences and the arms race as well. Mildred Dilling, the harpist, who went on many State Department sponsored tours, had no compunctions about speaking out on this subject. Knowing full well the power of music, a

Having sake with Sylvia Rosenberg in Tokyo, 1961.
(Photo by Seymour Bernstein)

power which, in its own inimitable way, is stronger and more persuasive than the war machine, she ended her report to the State Department with, "I am worth more than a thousand missiles!"

I found those four State Department tours reminiscent of my experiences as a soldier in Korea. For one thing, they were full of the adventures and misadventures of travel in remote places. And on my return home, I had the feeling that I had left something of myself behind as a result of all the teaching I had done.

The Cultural Affairs officers within each country always consulted us in regard to repertory choices and the number of concerts, master classes, and lectures we felt we could reasonably handle within a given period of time. Because the itinerary included out-of-the-way areas where commercially sponsored musicians rarely went, we became, as it were, musical pioneers. On my solo tour in 1960, for instance, I was the first pianist to give concerts in East Pakistan (now Bangladesh), Borneo, and in more cities throughout the Far East and Southeast Asia than I can now recall. The means of traveling to certain cities proved, occasionally, to be actually life-threatening. I shall never forget an airplane ride with the members of the former Claremont Quartet to Oruro, Bolivia, a small town nestled in the Andes at an altitude of 15,000 feet. During the trip, which necessitated having to soar over mountain peaks more than 20,000 feet high, the air pressure mechanism on the rather primitive two-propeller airplane suddenly malfunctioned. Nor did the oxygen masks, which we had to pull out by hand from the compartments above our seats, offer us more than minimal relief. I would hesitate to recount yet another anecdote concerning motion sickness, but for one thing: the wave of airsickness which suddenly swept over me on that flight was accompanied by an intense pressure in my chest. I thought I was having a heart attack. A stewardess assured me, however, that it was nothing more than altitude sickness, a diagnosis which, I am happy to say, proved to be correct. For once we had landed in Oruro, and not too soon for me, the tightness in my chest disappeared entirely. My colleagues told me that it was a sweaty, green-complexioned creature who slumped into a chair in the airport lounge. Almost at once, a stray dog jumped into my lap, and with wagging tail proceeded to lick the perspiration off of my face. He was so adorable that I temporarily forgot my indisposition.

Once in our hotel, we began to experience other symptoms. At 15,000 feet, we could hardly walk a flight of stairs without panting and becoming light-headed, and when we went to bed, we were all instructed to keep the windows open, the cold temperature notwithstanding. For at such an altitude, it was necessary to compensate for a lack of oxygen while sleeping. Insufficient oxygen was something that the inhabitants of Oruro had learned to live with over time. But we, newly arrived, found the slightest exertion difficult. Imagine, then, what it was like, trying to achieve pyrotechnics on our instruments! I recall having the sensation of living through one of those slow-motion dream sequences in which the simple act of walking is like pushing through an invisible barrier. Our sponsors provided oxygen units for us backstage. But even with that, wind players found it nearly impossible to play at all. In fact the clarinetist who was part of our troupe, and who ordinarily would have performed on our programs in Oruro, developed respiratory complications and had to spend four days in bed under a doctor's supervision.

Apart from these small hops within countries, Specialists, as we were called, traveled in a style befitting dignitaries. On two occasions, I proudly sported a first class airplane ticket, literally around-the-world. In addition to this luxurious means of traveling, I was given an extra stipend of $500, a sizeable sum of money in those days, "to enhance the effectiveness" of my solo tour. I used the entire amount to purchase music and books as gifts for musicians who I knew would have no access to certain material. I felt like a patron of the arts, dispensing to teachers and to deserving students Urtext editions, technical treatises, teaching material, and works by American composers, many of which were donated by various publishers. As one might imagine, the weight of my suitcases seemed more befitting an ocean voyage than an airplane flight. But the State Department anticipated this, too: they issued me vouchers for two hundred and fifty pounds of excess baggage beyond the sixty pounds allotted to first class passengers.

While our concerts were enthusiastically received, nothing was more appreciated than the private lessons and master classes we gave in practically every city we visited. These tours proved to me that ideas implanted in the minds of teachers and students remain long after the remembrance of even the most stimulating performance. It would not be possible to describe the overwhelming gratitude that greeted all of our interpretive and technical suggestions. And as though this was not reward enough, those generous people showered us with gifts of all sorts. My New York City apartment and my home in Maine are adorned with rare and magnificent objects, testimonials to the most rewarding phase of my life as a touring musician.

Dripping Mayonnaise

My first State Department tour, in 1955, was organized by John S. Kim, the conductor who in 1952 had played such a vital role in my army experiences. He had no intention of forgetting about Kenneth Gordon and me. The effort it took to arrange the second tour, however, was yet another example of the veritable tug of war that I have had to wage throughout most of my professional life. As it happened, in 1959, with the remembrance of my first tour still fresh in my memory, I thought how challenging it would be to go on a solo tour. The first step was to contact the USIS (United States Information Service) officers who arranged cultural events in the countries in which they were stationed. (Subsequently, this agency changed its name to USIA — United States Information Agency.) I wrote to the State Department and requested a directory containing the names and addresses of these USIS directors. I was amazed at how quickly the State Department responded to my request. And what a directory it was! Almost every country in the world was represented in it. Focusing upon the Far East and Southeast Asia, I typed (there being no personal computers in those days) fifty-five individual letters to USIS directors containing a proposal to give concerts and to conduct master classes within each country. I had, of course, to specify a time frame for such a tour, for otherwise, possible engagements might be strewn haphazardly throughout the year. I then painstakingly made fifty-five copies of a tape recording of my playing. Finally, I addressed fifty-five envelopes, inserted within each one of them a letter, a cassette tape, and publicity and sent them out into the world. The postage alone resulted in belt-tightening for weeks afterwards.

Months went by, during which I anxiously perused my daily batches of mail. But not one USIS director so much as responded with a "yes" or "no" to my proposal. Finally, after more than six months, I did actually receive one letter, from the USIS director in Iran: "I'm sorry to turn you down," the letter said, "but the time when you are available to tour coincides with the mourning season in Iran." That was it: one response to fifty-five letters! I was crestfallen, and I resigned myself to continue performing solo concerts in people's living rooms and for local organizations.

One afternoon during the winter of 1960, I made a bacon, lettuce, and tomato sandwich for myself — heavy on the mayonnaise, of course. I had just taken my first bite when the telephone rang. "Whoever it is," I thought, "will just have to wait until I swallow my first mouthful of sandwich." I therefore allowed the telephone to ring some six or seven times before I was able to say "hello" with something more refined than garbled speech. Fortunately, the caller was not discouraged by the time lapse. What followed caused my heart to skip a beat: "Is that Seymour Bernstein?" a woman's voice asked. "This is Martha Geesa from the cultural exchange program in Washington, D.C. The cultural affairs officer in Tokyo has contacted us about the possibility of your touring Japan under our auspices. On the basis of this one request, we would like to offer you a four month tour of the Far East and Southeast Asia."

All the while, I was holding the telephone in one hand and my sandwich in the other. I was so dumbfounded by what I was hearing that I unconsciously squeezed the sandwich, causing the mayonnaise to ooze out all over everything — the telephone line, the table and myself. Though my heart was beating fast, I tried to remain calm. I remember speaking with Mrs. Geesa with the air of someone for whom all such proposed tours were mere routine affairs. When I hung up the telephone, however, I remained in a trance for minutes on end. Regarding that sandwich, I have no recollection whatsoever as to whether I ate the rest of it.

The U-2 Incident

One might think that American artists touring under the aegis of the American government would be required to include at least one American work on each program. Yet, this was only suggested, not demanded of us. We alone decided whether an American work suited a particular program or not. Since Japanese music-lovers were particularly interested in contemporary music, I decided to perform an all-American program in Tokyo in 1960. That an American pianist playing an all-American program should incite a protest was something that neither I nor the State Department could have foreseen. As it happened, the concert coincided with an event of world-wide significance: An American U-2 jet, flying a spying mission over Russia, was shot down. The pilot, the airplane, and top-level secret equipment were all captured by the Russians. Quite predictably, this became a *cause célèbre* for anti-American extremists in Japan and throughout the world. On the evening of my concert, some one hundred protesters formed a human chain across the entrance to the audi-torium. It took the skillful management of scores of Japanese policemen to escort me and the audience through that unruly mob and into the audi-torium. The protesters held their ground throughout the concert, and their shouts could be heard even over the *fortissimos* of the Samuel Barber Sonata.

A political protest was not the only dramatic occurrence on those tours. In fact, my experiences ranged from humorous to life-threatening. This was to be expected, not only because political unrest can suddenly flare up anywhere in the world, but also because traveling, performing, and living conditions in remote parts of the world were, in those days, unimag-inably primitive. Battling these conditions during the 1961 tour, which lasted for seven and a half months, left me so exhausted that I resolved never again to tour longer than two months.

Musicians must have nerves of steel, for one, and resourcefulness in the face of emergency situations, for another, if they expect to survive the rigors of touring. Indeed, concert touring is not the glamorous activity which most people imagine it to be. In spite of the hardships, though, I would not have wanted to miss a single experience, harrowing though some of them were. For those tours belonged to a period in my life when I was ripe for all such adventures. Besides, even if I had known that the streets of Agra, India, were dangerous for tourists at night, I would have traveled them a thousand times over rather than to have missed seeing the Taj Mahal glowing in the moonlight. Everything about those tours, the dangers included, enriched me, strengthened me, and added to my general growth.

Seoul, Korea — 1955

During the summer of 1954, John Kim came to the United States, consulted with the directors of the Cultural Exchange Program in Washington, D.C., and solicited their help in organizing the first summer music festival ever to be held in Korea, during July and August of 1955. So it was that Kenneth and I returned to Korea exactly three years after our stint in the army. We were joined by Richard Kay, cellist, Michel Nazzi, oboist, and Peter Altobeli, who, at that time, played principal horn in the Pittsburgh Symphony.

Being the only pianist of the group, I had the lion's share of responsibility. When I now think about the vast amount of repertory I had to learn, I am quite frankly amazed that I was able to function at all. We began to rehearse months before our departure for Seoul. I remember working throughout each day and late into the evening in order to get a firm hold on the mountain of instrumental works, not to mention my own solo repertory.

Our arrival in Seoul was perhaps the most dramatic part of the tour, for Kenneth and I were greeted like returning heroes by a host of Korean musicians and students who had attended our performances when we were soldiers. The flowers, the enthusiastic welcome, and a horde of reporters flashing their cameras — all of this was, of course, heart-warming. But through all of the hullabaloo, I had only one thought in mind — getting to a piano as soon as possible. For suddenly, the vast repertory to which I had committed myself caused my stomach to twist into a knot. We were driven directly to the Bando Hotel, which was, at that time, the only first-class hotel in Seoul. Only nine stories high, it was

427

My first State Department tour in Korea, 1955. Standing left to right: conductor John S. Kim; the Korean Minister of Education; oboist Michel Nazzi; cellist Richard Kay; violinist Kenneth Gordon. I am in the foreground.

nevertheless the tallest building in the city. Our rooms, while not luxurious, were clean and adequate. To my good fortune, I was given the key to the Presidential Suite on the ninth floor, where I had the use of a beautiful Steinway grand piano, with a walnut case, whenever I wished to practice. And practice I did at every available moment.

During the month of July, our ensemble set out on a tour of various Korean cities. We performed combination programs, which included chamber music works and groups of solos. Returning to Seoul in August, we began intensive rehearsals among ourselves and with the Seoul Philharmonic, as it was now again called, in preparation for the summer music festival. Within a two week period, I performed two different solo recitals and two concerti with the orchestra — the first performances in Korea of Brahms' Concerto in D minor and Gershwin's *Rhapsody in Blue*. In addition, I collaborated with my colleagues in a violin recital, a cello recital, and two chamber music recitals. Apart from these performances, I conducted daily master classes from 9 AM to 12 noon. It is not difficult to imagine, then, how carefully I had to conserve my energies and with what concentration I had to practice in the few hours remaining in between my professional responsibilities.

Interrupted Practice

It was on the very day that I had to perform the Brahms Concerto that I heard a faint knocking at the door, cutting through one of the gentler sections of the Concerto's first movement. Reluctantly leaving the piano, I opened the door and discovered a lovely young Korean woman standing there. She was as thin as a willow, and her expression bespoke a mixture of terror and urgency. She clutched a volume of music tightly to her chest. "Oh no," I thought to myself. "Not a student at a time like this!" Exhaustion and annoyance must have been written all over my face, for suddenly, this young woman seemed to have second thoughts about disturbing me. But a few seconds later, she pulled herself up to her full height and exclaimed in broken English, "Please, sir, I need piano lesson." "A piano lesson?" I responded in disbelief. "Don't you know that I am scheduled to perform with the orchestra in a matter of hours?" With this, she seemed to grow taller by inches. And with her eyes fixed resolutely upon mine, she retorted, "God gave me this opportunity, and I will not leave without piano lesson!"

Both of us were desperate, for different reasons. My reason was obvious: I had to première the Brahms Concerto that very evening. It was a "first" for me, as well, for I had never performed it in public before. As for that Korean pianist, the opportunity to consult with a foreign musician was so rare in 1955 that she actually looked upon it as a "God-given opportunity." The anguished look on her face, combined with her desperate plea, conspired to break down my resolve. Without another word, I ushered her into the Presidential Suite, and within moments we were hard at work on Beethoven's *Waldstein* Sonata.

There is no substitute, of course, for those precious hours of concentrated work before an important concert — especially when practice time is limited to begin with. In this case, however, I spent that time teaching instead of practicing. Whether my preparation was more adequate than I had thought, or whether the lesson I gave to that student served to distract me from pre-performance anxiety, I cannot say. Perhaps it was both. For I performed far better that evening than I expected.

"Someone slept in the President's bed!"

Before leaving this second adventure in Korea, I cannot resist relating a non-musical incident which caused an unprecedented scandal in the Bando Hotel. In fact, had this incident not been discreetly hushed up, news of it might very well have spelled the end of our tour and of our affiliation with the State Department as well.

The Presidential suite where I practiced was a luxuriously appointed apartment consisting of a large living room, which held the Steinway grand piano, a dining room, a bedroom, and a full kitchen. It was, in fact, the apartment where President Rhee Syngman, and other heads of state, stayed on special occasions. The hotel manager, an American by the name of Mr. Dugan, had entrusted the key to the suite to me alone, with the understanding that I was to use it for practicing purposes only.

One day, our cellist, Richard Kay, a roué if ever there was one, wanted to entertain a love-stricken Korean girl. I should have known better than to lend him my key to the Presidential suite. But thinking that he wished only to impress this girl with having access to the place where Korea's President stayed, I weakened and gave in to his pleadings. Early the following morning, Kenneth, Richard, and I were summoned to Mr. Dugan's office for what we were told was a meeting of "grave importance." We found him sitting at his desk with a look of contained rage. As we stood before him, like three soldiers at attention, he began by speaking slowly and deliberately. But by the time he had finished delivering his message to us, his voice had risen to explosive intensity: "One of you occupied the Presidential Suite last evening." And then, flashing accusing eyes at me, he added, "And what's more, someone slept with a girl in his Excellency's bed!" The seriousness of this charge notwithstanding, I had to bite my lower lip to keep from laughing out loud. I was, of course, furious with Richard for having taken advantage of the favor I had granted him. Nor was it by any means pleasant to have suspicion cast upon me, the person to whom Mr. Dugan had entrusted the key. But somehow, the image of Richard and his sweetheart being discovered in President Rhee's bed by a chambermaid at 6 AM struck me so humorously, that I could hardly contain myself. There followed a confession and humble apologies on Richard's part, which at least exonerated me. But evidently, neither apologies nor anything else, for that matter, would placate Mr. Dugan. He was intent on exposing Richard's "crime" to every newspaper in Korea. It was fortunate for all concerned that John Kim and an official from the United States Embassy interceded and were finally able to reason with Mr. Dugan. They made him see that the whole import of our musical mission in Korea would be lost if word of this got out to the press. Why punish all the musicians for the indiscretion of one of them? After more apologies from Richard and assurances on my part that the key would never leave my hands again, Mr. Dugan finally agreed not to pursue this incident further. And he restored my practicing privileges in the Presidential suite. Thereafter, Richard confined all of his extra-musical activities to his own room.

An Earthquake and Beethoven

The very presence of a microphone can cause even the most seasoned performer to fall prey to uncontrollable nerves. One reason for this is that performers find it unsettling to project feeling to a mechanism instead of a live audience. Another reason is that playbacks, like an x-ray or CAT-Scan, may tell us what we secretly suspect but do not want to know. And few things are more frustrating than knowing that every note has been frozen for posterity — even when one plays one's best. For at anytime thereafter, an artist may change his or her mind about the interpretation of a particular phrase or, for that matter, of an entire piece.

Broadcasting studios are, perhaps, even more unpleasant than recording studios. Claustrophobic cells, dry acoustics, temperature controls which never seem to work properly (it is either too cold or too warm), and the fact that you have only one chance at it — all these things conspire to intensify a performer's inevitable nervousness. Worst of all are the microphones, a constant reminder of an unseen audience. It is not exactly the kind of environment that inspires one's best playing.

But recording studios can produce their own brand of apprehensions. For one thing, making mistakes in front of the producer and recording engineers is both frustrating and embarrassing. As it often happens, mistakes beget more mistakes during retakes. For there is nothing like the slightest miscalculation to remind a performer of his or her own vulnerability. At such times, the face of self doubt seems to hover in front of the microphone, grimacing and daring performers to do their best under the least favorable circumstances.

Beyond the level of one's own playing, acoustics play a major role in determining the success or failure of the final product. For this reason, many recordings are made in acoustically excellent concert halls or churches. If ever a pianist can feel lonely, it is while sitting at a concert grand on the stage of a vast auditorium and seeing row upon row of empty seats. So intense is the stillness (which, of course, is a requisite for all recordings) that every sound is conspicuous — even a musical one!

Such were the conditions in Tokyo as I prepared to record Beethoven's Sonata Op. 101 for a cultural radio program. The auditorium, chosen for its excellent acoustics, was the size of Carnegie Hall. The producer and the recording engineers sat in a glass-enclosed booth high up towards the ceiling on stage left. They communicated with me by means of a speaker placed on the stage to the right of the piano. Suddenly, the speaker came alive: "Are you ready, Mr. Bernstein?" "Yes," I replied, although at that moment, I wished that I were anywhere else but on that stage. "Fine," the voice answered back. "When you see the green light, please begin to play." With this, an all too familiar wave of anxiety swept over me. The speaker hummed one last time, "Take one," and the green light flashed on.

This was it. I poised my fingers over the keys for the gentle opening of Op. 101. But in that brief moment before I depressed the first chord, the most curious thing occurred: the stage began to rotate! "This is ridiculous," I thought. "Someone in the control booth has accidentally pressed the wrong button and I'm going to end up backstage!" No sooner did I entertain this rather bizarre thought than I became aware of a groaning, creaking sound coming from the dimly lit auditorium. At that point, the truth of the situation fell upon me with a terror that transcended my nervousness: an earthquake had struck! The flow of adrenaline which had mounted once that green light went on now seemed to increase to dangerous proportions. I sat there frozen with terror, wondering whether I should run off of the stage or dive for cover under the concert grand. Even as I entertained these thoughts, the stage began to pitch from side to side, like the heaving deck of that dreadful troop ship, the *General Black*. When the tremor finally subsided (it lasted only seconds, but to me it seemed like many minutes), my hands, formerly poised over the *E* major chord, were now clutching the piano for support. Being a novice with earthquakes, I must have looked quite a sight to the more experienced men in that control booth. For as I shot them a desperate look, I saw what I could not actually hear — the antics of uproarious laughter.

Earthquakes, of course, occur quite frequently in Japan, but the degree to which they are felt depends upon where one happens to be at the moment of their occurrence. For example, this tremor (it measured 5.2 on the Richter scale) might actually have gone unnoticed to someone walking on the noisy Ginza. But in that vast and silent auditorium, it seemed far worse than it actually was.

I finally did record Op. 101, and not too well, either. In subsequent performances of it, I could never play the serene opening measures without anticipating external tremors to mix with my internal ones.

Concert by the Light of a Lantern

The city of Niigata, situated on the west coast of Japan, had received ample warning: One of the worst typhoons in Japan's history would pass through the city at the very time that Sylvia Rosenberg and I were scheduled to give a concert. All public functions were canceled, save for our concert — the reason being that the auditorium in which the concert would take place was constructed of reinforced concrete. As the USIS director explained to us, "You will be far safer there than in your hotel." He also thought that the auditorium would provide protection for the members of our audience, most of whom lived in fragile homes. As events proved, his assessment was wholly accurate.

Strong gusts of wind whistled around our car as we drove through the now deserted streets of Niigata. When we arrived at the auditorium, we discovered that approximately one hundred people had taken their seats hours before concert time. Under ordinary circumstances, this would have been considered a comparatively small show of support for a concert given by foreign musicians. But taking into account the ominous storm warnings, it was surprising to us that anyone at all had come. The over-whelming ovation which greeted us as we walked across the stage made one thing clear from the start: the small audience intended to make up with enthusiasm what they lacked in numbers.

Nothing unusual occurred during the opening work, Beethoven's Sonata for Piano and Violin Op. 96. Sylvia then played an unaccompanied sonata by J. S. Bach, while I repaired to my dressing room. Suddenly, in the middle of her performance, I heard a wailing sound emanating from the backstage area. As she continued to play, it grew louder and louder until it almost drowned out the sound of the violin. One did not have to be an expert in typhoons to know that the full fury of the storm was now upon us. It seemed to be venting its rage against the back wall of the auditorium.

Seeing glass windows all around me, I left my dressing room and sought the protection of the backstage area. By that time, the wall directly behind the stage was literally vibrating as it stood in defiance against the increasing fury of the wind. Suddenly, I heard the shattering of glass. The windows in our dressing room had blown through, moments after I left it. At the next moment, the entire auditorium was plunged into darkness.

The flashlight which escorted Sylvia Rosenberg off the stage at the end of her Bach brought me onto it for my solo presentation — Mussorgsky's *Pictures at an Exhibition*. The fact that it lasts thirty minutes was not a particularly tempting prospect at that moment. For as soon as the stage manager had ushered me to the piano with his flashlight, he disappeared again, leaving me in total darkness.

Performers make every attempt to prepare themselves for unforeseen eventualities. Yet performing in a blackout seems beyond the realm of possibility. Fortunately, though, I had developed a certain skill during my practicing which proved to be of invaluable assistance during this emergency — and that was, that I often practiced either with my eyes closed or looking straight ahead, past the keyboard. I had done this specifically to develop a secure sense of distances on the keyboard. Some pianists actually practice in a darkened room, which certainly would have simulated the situation more exactly. For the present, however, my own method of preparation would now be put to the test. Using the groups of two and three black keys as reference points, I located the opening note — the *G* above middle *C*. Having sounded the first tone, I then listened in retrospect, so to speak. In other words, I immersed myself in the sounds *after* they emanated from the piano, instead of anticipating them. I allowed my automatic pilot to guide my fingers onto the correct keys while I listened to the results as though I were a member of the audience. To my surprise, I hardly missed a note. Soon, though, I began to wonder whether I would be able to maintain this accuracy in the more difficult sections which were soon to follow. At the exact moment when this rather worrisome thought threatened to disrupt my otherwise successful performance, a soft, orange-colored light fell upon the keyboard. It grew brighter and brighter until the entire keyboard was clearly illuminated. The stage manager had walked across the stage with a lighted lantern and placed it on a chair to the left of the keyboard. He then carried out a second lantern, and a third, until the entire stage glowed with a soft, flickering light.

With the wailing noise growing louder by the moment, I wondered whether the audience had, by that time, sought shelter in the lobby. A quick glance to my right provided the answer: a hundred pairs of eyes sparkled in the eerie glow of those lanterns. Seeing this, and feeling the rapt attention of my audience, I was inspired beyond myself. More befitting a *Noh* play than a concert, the lighting and the storm actually worked to my advantage: for by the time I reached *Baba Yaga*, the Russian witch, the silhouette of my hands on the backdrop, plus the howling wind, made this piece a visual as well as an aural dance of terror.

All of this drama notwithstanding, Sylvia Rosenberg and I were truly frightened. While we kept our poise throughout the concert, we breathed a sigh of relief when it was over. Later, we went to the lobby of the auditorium to greet the members of our audience. Considering the intensity of that storm, we were not in the least surprised to see that entire families had gathered there. Many people had brought sleeping bags with them just in case the storm lasted throughout the night. As comments were passed on to us through an interpreter, I noticed a woman making her way towards us through the crowd. She cradled a sleeping child in her arms. Upon reaching us, she exclaimed, "While I was listening to you play, I felt a bond with you that calmed my fears." "It was the bond of music," I explained to her. "While we played, we, too, felt a bond with you."

After another hour or so, the typhoon had spent its fury. What we saw on the way back to our hotel made us realize how fortunate we all were to have had the protection of that auditorium. Roofs of homes and other buildings had been shorn off, store windows were blown in, and trees and wires were down everywhere. On the following day, we learned that thirty-four people had been killed in Niigata alone. Through all of the horror of that storm, there remained one comforting thought: perhaps our audience had been spared a similar fate by attending our concert.

Barks for Mozart

The scene was a modest sized auditorium in Brunei Town, Borneo, a city that sits on the equator. It was one of those torrid afternoons when the intense heat slowed everything down — my tempi included. Although the windows and doors on both sides of the auditorium were open, nothing brought relief from the searing temperature.

I was in the middle of the first piece, Mozart's Fantasy in *C* minor, K. 475, when I noticed a dog enter the auditorium through one of the open doors. Since my hands were the only moving things in the entire auditorium, he must have seen in this a potential for a pat on the head. He slowly mounted the steps leading to the stage, sauntered over to me, and simply stood there, panting and wagging his tail. The sheer delight of a dog suddenly appearing on the stage in the middle of one of Mozart's most profound works did not exactly promote my best concentration. I could

Visiting the headhunters in Borneo, 1960.

not help casting him an affectionate glance from time to time, which only caused his tail to wag all the faster. The curious thing was that no one except me seemed to be the slightest bit surprised by the dog's appearance. I concluded that audiences in Borneo were quite accustomed to having all sorts of creatures wander into public places at unpredictable moments. At any rate, when the dog was finally convinced that I would not reciprocate his show of affection, he started to bark. The faster and more forcefully I played, the louder he barked, which raised the question: At whom was he barking, me or Mozart? Being an animal lover, I felt frustrated at not being able to give him what he wanted — a loving scratch behind the ear. Nor would I have been able to do so for quite some time, considering the length of the Fantasy. The poor creature must have thought that Mozart was a poor substitute for affection. For with a look of utter dejection, he stopped barking, lowered his eyes, and slunk away just as slowly as he had arrived.

Mothballs in the Piano

Sylvia Rosenberg and I motored from Hué, the ancient former capital of South Vietnam, to Torane, a lovely resort nestled on the coast of the South China Sea. We were to be the first American musicians to give a concert there, the invitation having come from the Mayor.

The rainy season was in full swing, and it had poured steadily for four days. To musicians, extreme dampness means two things in particular: instruments are adversely affected, and there is nothing like pouring rain to discourage audience attendance. But I had much more important matters on my mind than worrying about the effects of rain upon our performance. For I had been told in advance that I would not only have to search throughout Torane for a suitable piano, but also supervise the moving of it into the hall. Quite naturally, this called forth memories of my army days in Korea.

After depositing Sylvia at our hotel, I set out with John Rhodes, the director of the USIS in Torane, to check out the hall. It was most fortunate that we did so, for at the moment we arrived, a group of laborers was putting the finishing touches on a specially constructed platform. It consisted of three rows of cinder blocks, haphazardly placed on the floor and covered with cracked, moldy boards. Since the workers seemed quite pleased with the results, I thought it would insult them to voice my disapproval. Instead, I decided to demonstrate graphically what I knew would be the consequence of such a construction. As everyone watched, I gingerly mounted the platform, and quite predictably, the weight of my body splintered the first board I stepped on. After a brief discussion, they all agreed that Sylvia and I would have to perform on floor level with the audience. And so the platform was removed entirely.

For the next three hours, Mr. Rhodes drove me around Torane in search of a suitable piano. After playing on one wreck of an instrument after another, I finally discovered a fairly decent grand piano in a private home. Its owner was extremely flattered to know that a visiting pianist thought highly enough of his instrument to use it for a public concert. I telephoned the Mayor's secretary, who was to make all of the arrangements for moving the piano. Just as our host had finished serving us tea and sandwiches, the secretary and the movers arrived.

It seems that each country has its own method of moving pianos. The experience of seeing laborers rolling the body of a grand piano down the main street in Pusan, Korea, on a dolly, while others carried the legs and pedal shaft on A-frames, was quite enough to teach me restraint in dictating to others how pianos ought to be moved. In this case, however, I could not resist sounding a note of warning, for, as I soon discovered, the men intended to wrap up the piano and carry it in one piece. It was five blocks to the hall, and the rain was pouring down. "Don't you intend to remove the legs and the pedal shaft?" I inquired as diplomatically as I could. "Oh no," the Mayor's secretary was quick to respond. "The piano is very heavy. The legs must remain on so that the men can put the piano down and rest along the way." I tried to explain that this was no way to move a piano. But a smile here, and a chuckle there made it clear that pianists ought to tend to their business, and piano movers to theirs. I remained silent, therefore, and watched the proceedings with a sense of foreboding. And indeed, my worst fears were realized from the start. For no sooner did the men roll the piano away from the wall than the right leg began to buckle. My shouts of alarm instantly brought all bodies to where they were needed, and fortunately, the piano was spared an untimely end. Seeing "I told you so" written all over my face, the secretary finally agreed to turn the entire operation over to me.

Needless to say, the owner of the piano, who had by this time grown pale with anxiety, must certainly have had second thoughts about lending me his piano. I assured him, however, that, I, personally, would protect his piano at all costs. Having to save face, the poor man simply sat in a corner of his living room, resigned to whatever fate lay in store for his precious instrument.

First, I sent for a truck and some tools. With the secretary acting as my interpreter, I had the men support the piano while I removed the left leg and the pedal lyre. Then all hands turned the piano over on its side and gently rested it on a bench covered with pillows. Next, I hammered off the two remaining legs — all to the accompaniment of "oohs" and "ahs." In fifteen minutes, the body of the piano and its legs and pedal shaft were safely on the truck. So impressed were the men by how simply this was done that I am sure they would have followed me into battle had I asked them to. But more importantly, as I left that home, my host flashed me a smile of relief.

The Mayor arrived in the hall just as I was re-fastening the pedal shaft. Filthy, and wet with perspiration, I must have looked like anything but a concert pianist. As Mr. Rhodes made the introductions, the Mayor tried his best to hide an expression of utter bewilderment. Nevertheless, he went through the motions, at least, of shaking my hand warmly. When I had to excuse myself to get on with my work, the Mayor's expression told me that there must be some mistake. I could not possibly be the man whom he had invited to Torane to give a concert!

With the piano fully assembled, the men helped me to position it properly for the evening's concert. Then, with a look of mutual triumph on their faces, they formed a half circle in front of the piano and waited expectantly for me to demonstrate exactly why we had gone through so much trial and effort. I lifted the lid, pulled up a chair, and poised my hands over the keyboard. My favorite line of music for trying out pianos is the opening of Beethoven's Fourth Concerto. It was Sir Clifford Curzon who taught me that few passages in the whole piano repertory reveal more of a piano's potential than does this profound statement. I depressed the first G major chord, and my heart sank: all the keys stuck down in their key beds. I tried another chord, and the same thing happened. What had gone wrong? The piano had played perfectly before it was moved. Seeing my despair, the men rushed to the piano and peered inside. Knowing, of course, that the situation called for more aggressive measures, I unscrewed the blocks on either side of the keyboard, removed the fall board and carefully slid out the action. This elicited a chorus of gasps from the men such as one might hear at the enactment of a miracle. And there they were — dozens of mothballs, scattered seemingly between every moving part of the action! A sack of them had been placed in the piano to deter insects, and they had become dislodged when the piano was turned over on its side. Had the piano remained on its legs, as was originally intended, the mothballs, no doubt, would have remained in their sack. Everyone, it seemed, arrived at the same conclusion, for suddenly all their eyes met mine and we simultaneously burst into laughter. After we regained our composure, dozens of fingers reached into the action to retrieve the mothballs, while the Mayor, who had, by this time, concluded that pianists have to do more than merely play the piano, good-naturedly held out his hat to collect them. The last mothballs, being too deeply embedded to be reached with fingers alone, finally yielded to tweezers.

I mentioned before that "mistakes beget mistakes." And one might say the same thing about calamities. As it happened, one of the hammers in the middle register of the piano was slightly raised due to the extreme dampness. In my haste to slide back the action, that one hammer snapped off with a sickening "crunch." Just as I was about to give in to despair, the tuner arrived. He urged me to leave all repairs and adjustments to him, which I was more than happy to do. Besides, it was now 6:30 PM, and with the concert scheduled to begin at 7:30, I had only time to go to my hotel, shower and change into my concert clothes.

What enables a musician to survive a performance after such a day? Experience, of course. Sylvia Rosenberg and I had already performed the works scheduled for that concert some fifty times before we arrived in Torane. Surviving the actual performance, therefore, was the very least of my worries on that day.

Scanning the faces of the audience that night, I noticed a group of young men smiling and applauding louder than anyone else. They were the movers, who in a very real way had played an active role in that concert. Little did they know, however, that they would soon witness another bizarre incident.

I had reached my solo group, and was cascading up and down the entire length of the keyboard in *Feux d'artifice* (Fireworks) by Debussy, when one of the legs of the piano chair suddenly collapsed. I was left half standing, my right foot still on the pedal and my left foot far back for support. To keep from toppling over, I grabbed at the keyboard desperately, creating some chords unknown to Debussy. A collective gasp arose from the audience. The Mayor, who happened to be sitting in a place of honor directly opposite the keyboard, shot up out of his chair as if jet-propelled. In a flash, he pushed the broken chair away, and slid his own chair under me. And there he stood, breathing over my shoulder, while I brought *Feux d'artifice* to its dramatic conclusion.

The loud cheers that continued for minutes afterwards seemed more befitting a stunt man in a circus than a pianist. The Mayor's arms were instantly around me in a show of great admiration. As for the movers, they simply sat there, open-mouthed, hardly believing what they had just witnessed.

I have often wondered whether the Mayor ever extended an invitation to another pianist. But one thing I do know: our performances there will be long remembered, and least of all for musical reasons.

Caught in a Revolution

It was April 19, 1960, and I was halfway through a month of engagements in Korea. I had been scheduled to give a piano recital and a master class at Yeon Sei University in Seoul at 12 noon, a rather odd time for a concert. "Wait in the wings," Dr. Park, the head of the music department, told me. "When the audience is assembled, I will come backstage and tell you when to begin your recital."

I believe that those were his very words. In fact, all conversations and everything that occurred on that day in particular are indelibly etched in my memory. And why? I was soon to witness and to play a part in a living nightmare, one which was unprecedented even in Korea's stormy and often violent history. But not having the slightest forewarning of the events that were soon to follow, I paced the backstage area with only one thought in mind — surviving the performance.

It was now 12:15 PM, and I remember thinking, "How quiet the audience is." While I knew that Korean audiences sat in utter stillness before a concert out of sheer respect for the performer, the hall was too quiet. As the minutes ticked by, I suddenly had a strong presentiment that there was not a single person sitting in that hall. Finally, my curiosity got the better of me and I stealthily peeked out between the edge of the curtain and the proscenium arch. Indeed, my hunch was correct: the hall was completely empty. At that very moment, I heard shouting outside the auditorium. "Some calamity must have occurred," I thought. I grabbed my briefcase, walked the length of the center aisle, and emerged at the front entrance of the auditorium. There, I found myself at the top of a large flight of granite steps, looking down upon hundreds of students who had massed together in a marching contingent. Most of them wore headbands and some held placards with writing on them which, of course, I could not understand. Leaders shouted, and the marchers responded in a chorus with wild, waving fists. It was all perplexing to me.

As I stood there, somewhat frightened by the mounting rage of the crowd, a jeep carrying three American military policemen appeared out of nowhere and came to a halt at the base of the steps. An army sergeant jumped out, ran up the steps to where I was standing, and shouted above the din of the crowd, "Are you Seymour Bernstein?" "Yes," I replied, not having the slightest notion as to what this was all about. "Quick," he barked at me. "We've come to evacuate you. The revolution has started!" The sight of that man's uniform and the very sound of the word "revolution" instantly transported me back to my army days. For all intents and purposes, I was a soldier again, automatically responding to a military order. Without another thought, I followed the sergeant down the steps and into the jeep. By this time, Dr. Park had joined me and somehow managed to squeeze into the jeep himself. I noticed at once that the other MPs had M-1 rifles poised in their hands. In an instant, the jeep shot forward at breakneck speed. As we careened through the narrow streets of downtown Seoul, I heard shots ringing out. "My God," I thought, "I'm in the middle of another war!" As Dr. Park explained to me (and he later translated everything we heard along the way), the uprising had been precipitated by an incident a day earlier. It seems that an organized band of hoodlums, allegedly sponsored by the government, had attacked a group of peaceful student demonstrators with lead pipes. One student was killed and many others were critically injured. Incensed by this act of violence, tens of thousands of students mobilized all over Seoul. Even as I waited backstage at Yeon Sei University, several students had been shot down in cold blood directly in front of President Rhee's palace.

On the way to the Bando Hotel, we passed the home of Lee Ki Bung, the speaker of the assembly. Only a week earlier, he and his wife had invited me to dinner. Imagine, then, how astonished I was to hear him described as among the most corrupt of government officials. Now his home was surrounded by armed policemen, and a carpet of stones covering the street in front of it spoke chillingly of the violence that was raging all around me. Nearby, swarms of students rushed out of a high school. They stampeded around our jeep like a herd of wild cattle and shouted threats to their classmates who remained behind: "If you don't join us, we'll return and kill you!" Needless to say, the remaining students rushed from their classrooms and swelled the existing ranks to overflowing. Somehow, though, the jeep managed to weave its way through the wild throngs. In approximately fifteen minutes we reached the Chosun Hotel, which was around the corner from the Bando Hotel. To go any further would be courting danger. At that point, therefore, I jumped down from the jeep and thanked the MPs and Dr. Park. I took a back path to the Bando Hotel on Taipyung Ro (Taipyung Street) and reached the safety of the hotel lobby with a sigh of relief. As soon as I was safely inside, a steel grating rolled down over the front door, sealing us in and protecting us from the outside world.

Many Koreans had already spoken to me of governmental corruption. It was commonly known, for instance, that President Rhee Syngman and his appointed officials were guilty of criminal acts. They diverted American funds for personal gain, they were guilty of graft, and worst of all, they hired secret policemen — "the President's henchmen," as they were called — who were considered the Korean counterpart of the German Gestapo. Dressed as ordinary civilians, they infiltrated tea rooms and nightclubs and eavesdropped on innocent conversations. A student, for example, who might voice opposition to government policy, just as any student might do, would be arrested on the spot. "Your son (or your daughter, as the case may be) is being detained for questioning," the parents would be told. The truth was, all such students were imprisoned. Some of them were tortured and others disappeared, never to be found again. To most Koreans, then, the so-called democratic republic of Korea had now become a fascist state, robbing its citizens of their rights. Considering this background, one can well imagine how the majority of Koreans responded to the latest show of violence on the part of those pipe-wielding hoodlums. Enough was enough! Students throughout the country had chosen that day to begin their organized revolt. A full-fledged uprising was in progress.

The first three or four floors of the Bando Hotel contained offices occupied by international businessmen. Many of these businessmen, along with a number of hotel guests, took elevators to the hotel roof in order to watch the proceedings. I was among them. From that vantage point, we could see City Hall Square, the center of the uprising. What I witnessed filled me with a sense of horror. A line of armed Korean policemen stood shoulder to shoulder blocking off Taipyung Ro. As wave upon wave of students marched against them, the policemen fired directly into the surging crowds, killing some of the students and wounding scores of others. Their weapons? — M-1 rifles, no doubt part of American military surplus from the Korean war. Above the din of screams and rifle shots, I heard one businessman shout to another, "Hey, come over to my side, there's much more action here!" — meaning, of course, that he could see more murders from his vantage point. From his cavalier attitude and the gleeful tone in his voice one might have thought that he was watching a sports attraction and not the cold-blooded murder of Korcan students. His comment, coupled with the sardonic grin on his face, incensed me to the point of wanting to commit murder myself. No sooner did I think this, than it appeared as though the "God of retribution" was meting out a punishment. For suddenly, the businessman clutched his chest and screamed, "They got me!" "Stop horsing around," his friend told him. But he was not horsing around. A stray bullet from an M-1 rifle had careened upward from the street, gone through the iron railing against which he was standing, and lodged in his chest. In another instant, he fell into the arms of his associates.

I have already mentioned that the M-1 rifle used ball ammunition that could penetrate steel. It was not surprising, therefore, that the bullet had lost none of its power during its nine story flight, and had left in its wake a hole in the iron railing the circumference of a quarter. Now that the revolution had escalated to include the roof of the Bando Hotel, all of us panicked. For quite obviously, if one bullet had found its way to the roof, then others might follow. Instantly, then, all of us dropped flat on the roof and lay there without moving.

But what about the wounded man? For all we knew, he was dying. And considering the violence directly outside of the hotel, how, in fact, could we get help for him? Least of all could his associates be counted upon to take any constructive measures whatsoever. Frozen with terror, they crouched beside their wounded friend, and covered their own heads with their arms.

The Bando Hotel was, as I have said, directly across the street from the American Embassy. The Embassy's roof, lower than ours by several stories, was swarming with American officials and Embassy workers who, like us, were watching the horror on the street below. They did not know, of course, that someone lay wounded and perhaps dying a stone's throw away from where they were standing. While I, and most of the bystanders on the roof, had been furious with that critically wounded man, we certainly had no intention of standing idly by and watching him die. One woman, a Mrs. Clark, who was a reporter on the former New York City newspaper *The Herald Tribune*, had enough presence of mind to shout across to the Embassy, "Someone's been shot! Send for an ambulance!" One man came to the edge of the Embassy roof, cupped his hands around his mouth and shouted back, "What's his name?" His question suggested that there was a condition for calling an ambulance: If the wounded man were American, "most certainly," but if he were Korean, well, then, "let's not meddle in this affair." We were all outraged. Several of us, then, screamed back to that man, "What the hell difference does it make what his name is! He's been shot. Stop with the questions and call an ambulance!" No doubt the anger in our voices shocked that man into understanding the real issue at hand — that saving a human life was more important at that moment than abiding by protocol or playing politics. He rushed across the Embassy roof and disappeared through a door.

In the meantime, several of us ran down to our rooms to fetch blankets for the wounded man. We covered him with some of them and improvised a stretcher out of the others. Four of us gently carried him onto the elevator and down to the coffee lounge. There we were met by medics from the 8th United States Army headquarters. Fortunately, they came supplied with morphine, plasma, and intravenous fluids. After tending to the wounded man as best they could, they placed him on a stretcher and carried him to a waiting Red Cross station wagon. He was then taken to

Severance Hospital, which was already bulging with wounded students. As I learned afterwards, an operation disclosed not only fragments of the bullet, but also a piece of the iron railing. The surgeons removed whatever they could. But unfortunately, a fragment of the bullet had lodged near the man's spine. Removing it might have resulted in paralysis or permanent damage of some kind. The surgeons decided, therefore, that it was safer to leave the fragment exactly where it was. Although I inquired about the wounded man for days afterwards, no one seemed to know whether he had lived or died.

Needless to say, none of us returned to the roof. I, for one, went to my room on the eighth floor, from where I continued to hear rifle shots until 10:30 that evening. My window afforded me a panoramic view of downtown Seoul and the suburbs beyond. Numb with horror, I watched students torching the homes of government officials and other buildings as well. The twilight was now punctuated with flames and billowing clouds of smoke rising from different points of the city. This posed a new emergency which, ironically enough, firemen were powerless to control. For no sooner did fire engines arrive at burning buildings, than hordes of irate students commandeered them. With several students sitting in the front cabs and dozens of others perched on ladders and hoses, they drove those fire engines crazily through the streets of downtown Seoul, screaming slogans and sporting the bloodied jackets and shirts of their fallen comrades.

Seeing the gruesome evidence of the massacre, thousands of adults joined forces with their younger compatriots. Among them were university professors, doctors, and well-known figures from all walks of life. When it finally became clear that Korean policemen, even with their M-1 rifles, were no match for tens of thousands of demonstrators, the Korean Army reserves were called in for support. I could see the army trucks roll onto the grounds of the Duk Soo Palace. Soldiers poured out of them and set up tents on the Palace grounds. Tanks rolled into the center of Seoul and armed soldiers with steel helmets stood guard at every corner. There followed what invariably occurs after an uprising of such magnitude: martial law was declared. No one was allowed out on the streets at night and all public functions were canceled.

I cannot say whether I slept or not. I only remember rushing from the hotel at six o'clock the following morning intent on telephoning home. There were no satellite communications in those days, and a long distance telephone call was not only difficult to make, but also exceedingly expensive. In fact, one had to go to a communications building and actually reserve time for the complex procedure. After several hours, I finally did get through to my mother. Fortunately, she had not yet heard about the uprising, for she would have panicked to think of my being caught in yet another sort of war.

What was I to do now? The State Department had scheduled me to spend an entire month in Korea, and I was only midway through my itinerary. With all of my concerts canceled and transportation in and out of Korea banned, I was faced with two weeks of inactivity. And what about the wounded students? How would they know that Americans were on their side? I knew exactly what I had to do: I would go to the hospital and perform for the wounded students who had participated in the revolt. This plan would, of course, require the approval of the American Ambassador, Walter P. McConaughy.

The Ambassador was an excellent clarinetist — so gifted, that at one point in his life he faced a choice between a musical and a political career. Choosing the latter, however, did not diminish his passion for music, nor did it discourage him from continuing to practice diligently. He personified the professional-amateur, that ideal musician of whom I spoke earlier. I had already discovered how musically proficient the Ambassador was. Only a week earlier, he and his wife had invited me to dinner at the Embassy residence and informal music making afterwards. Music, as he once told me, was the only thing that could restore his spirits whenever he faced a crisis.

The political situation was a tricky one. Whatever the Ambassador felt personally about the Korean government, he was the envoy of American policy. As such, he had to voice support for President Rhee so long as Rhee was in power. The fact was, America and Korea enjoyed a favorable diplomatic relationship before, during, and after the Korean war. Almost all Koreans loved the American people and wholeheartedly supported our policies. Certainly no one blamed America for the hardships which undermined every sector of Korean life. As far as the Koreans were concerned, the blame lay squarely with President Rhee and his corrupt administration.

The Ambassador was overwhelmed with responsibilities: His battery of telephones never stopped ringing; he made several trips to the Presidential Palace urging President Rhee to resign; and through all of this, he had constantly to keep international reporters and photographers apprised of each new development. It was only when he put everything aside in order to have a private meeting with me that I first realized the true significance of my project. As I had anticipated, the Ambassador could not officially side with the militant students. But as he explained to me, I, being on a non-political mission, could take any stand that I wished.

Surprisingly, he not only gave me permission to perform for the wounded Korean students, but also assigned key people on his staff to help me with all of the arrangements, the chief one being to rent a piano and have it moved to the hospital. He then did something which truly amazed me: he called a host of international reporters into his office and told them what I planned to do.

I am convinced that the Ambassador alerted all of those reporters for one reason: he was proud of the fact that an American wanted to express support and sympathy for the students through a language which transcended politics. In fact, had he not been the American Ambassador to Korea, I am sure he would have joined me in performing for the wounded students. Small wonder, then, that he risked political backlash to see to it that the entire affair received international coverage.

Not everyone was enthusiastic about my plan to perform for the wounded students. One Korean musician, whose name I now feel obliged to withhold, was furious with me: "My government invited you here," he said to me heatedly on the telephone. "And now you want to perform for anti-government demonstrators! What will happen to me when government officials discover that it was I who wrote you a letter of recommendation?" He knew, of course, that I came to Korea because of his invitation and not the government's. And secretly, he disapproved of the government's policies as much as everyone else did. His outburst, therefore, had nothing whatsoever to do with whether it was ethical for me to perform for so-called anti-government demonstrators. The truth was, this musician was fearful of reprisals against himself and his family. In order to protect him, I avoided mentioning his name in all subsequent interviews with the press.

The following morning, a spinet piano was delivered to the hospital, where the beds holding wounded students spilled out into the corridors. At the entrance, I was greeted by a swarm of international reporters and TV crews, who were prepared to follow me from ward to ward. One look at them, and it suddenly occurred to me that they, and everyone else, must have thought that I had staged the entire thing as a publicity ploy for myself. Besides, I had wanted to play informally for those students. Now with the TV cameras pointing at me, I felt self-conscious. There was a brief moment when I wanted to cancel the entire project and return to the Bando Hotel. But in the next moment, I thought of Ambassador McConaughy and his vested interest in this project. Clearly, he wanted the world to know of my gesture. Considering all of this, I decided to go through with it, more for the Ambassador's sake than my own. Ignoring the reporters and TV crews, I plucked up my courage, settled myself at the spinet piano, and began to play. And so it happened that my parents,

447

The hero of the day, American Ambassador Walter P. McConaughy, after asking President Rhee Syngman to resign. The Bando Hotel is in the background. (Photo by Seymour Bernstein)

watching the Huntley-Brinkley news report that evening in their Newark, New Jersey, apartment, simultaneously gasped. For there was their son on the TV monitor, playing Schumann's *Träumerei* in a hospital ward full of wounded Korean students.

After my performance in each ward, I dispensed bars of chocolate which I had purchased in the army PX. I also had brought with me a Korean instrument called a *kayagum*, a plucked zither with twelve strings, related to the Japanese *koto*. While I was not by any means adept at playing the *kayagum*, I had taught myself to strum out a recognizable rendering of a well-known Korean folk song entitled "The Bluebird." Hearing this familiar and beloved song, many of the students wept openly. With the help of an interpreter, they expressed their deepest gratitude and sentiments to me. Above all, they were heartened to know that an American sided with them in their mission and sympathized with them in their suffering. As I left the hospital, my former doubts were replaced with the knowledge that I had lifted the spirits of those students. My own spirits were lifted as well.

As I subsequently learned, news of my appearance at the hospital was distributed worldwide. The fervor of the Korean reporters produced articles and photographs of the incident that filled an entire page in one of Korea's leading newspapers. The headline read, "American pianist demonstrates to Korean students that he is on their side!" As a result, people stopped me on the street for days afterwards and thanked me for what I had done. It was exactly the sort of response for which the Ambassador had hoped.

I received much more than I gave to those students. Yet that morning brought with it one of the most painful experiences of my life. To begin with, the doctors pointed to certain students who were not expected to survive their wounds. But even more heartbreaking was the gathering of family members outside the hospital's morgue. I can still hear the wails of grief-stricken mothers, "Aigoo, aigoo! (My God, my God!)," they cried, as they identified their dead sons and daughters. Their agony haunts me to this day.

The struggle for independence, however, was not to be won so easily. On April 25th, at 9:15 PM, while I was having dinner with a Korean family in the suburbs of Seoul, the telephone rang. It was an urgent message from the American Embassy alerting me to the fact that the uprising had started all over again. Martial law had been declared, and it was imperative that I leave immediately and seek the protection of my hotel. As I taxied to the Bando Hotel, I came face to face with lines of troops blocking the main thoroughfare. Shots crackled through the darkness. Panic-stricken, I left the taxi and ran the several remaining blocks to my hotel. By the time I reached the safety of the hotel lobby, I was literally gasping for air.

These new waves of protest eclipsed anything that had occurred six days earlier. The demonstrations defied martial law and lasted throughout the night and into the following day. The entire city seemed to be up in arms. Even grade school children marched along with their parents and teachers. Ambassador McConaughy left the Embassy the following afternoon amidst applause and shouts of "bravo" from thousands of Korean demonstrators massed in front of the American Embassy. As his car slowly wove its way towards the Presidential Palace, loud cheers rose up from the crowds. Demonstrators of all ages pressed their hands against the windows of his car, chanting, "Thank you! Thank you!"

At the very moment that the ambassador was on his peace mission, an irate crowd was ransacking Lee Ki Bung's home. They piled his furniture and his personal belongings in the street and set them on fire. I myself could see the pillar of smoke rising from behind the Duk Soo Palace. One of the students found an American flag in the rubble. According to an eye witness account, the student folded the flag with an air of solemnity and presented it to an American newsman who was there on the scene. The newsman was overcome with emotion at this touching gesture.

Another incident reflected the high esteem in which Koreans held Americans. The details of it were told to me by a reporter who had followed the demonstrations on the final day of the uprising: There was, formerly, a bigger-than-life bronze statue of General Douglas MacArthur standing majestically on Sejong Ro, the main street in Seoul. Ironically, the statue had been placed directly in front of the Anti-Communist Building, a building which had served as the headquarters for the hated secret police. The students had burned the building down to the ground six days earlier. To the accompaniment of a cheering crowd that numbered some five thousand demonstrators, one of the students climbed the statue and placed a wreath of flowers around the General's neck.

The most heart-warming stories, however, were told of the Korean soldiers. Although many of them were wounded by irate students who tried forcibly to break through their ranks, not a single soldier fired into the crowds, nor were there any reports of soldiers injuring students in any way whatsoever. Clearly, the military was on the side of the people. It was specifically the hated policemen who were responsible for all the killings and injuries, which numbered into the thousands.

And now the events of six days of turmoil reached a dramatic conclusion. As Ambassador McConaughy was on his way to the Presidential

Palace, the highest ranking general of the Korean Army invited one university student, one high school student, and two civilians to accompany him to President Rhee. The general felt that the President ought to know exactly what his own people thought of his administration. Later that evening, the ambassador himself told me the following story: Having finally arrived at the Presidential Palace after maneuvering his car through a sea of demonstrators, he waited in an anteroom while the general and his guests met with President Rhee. As the ambassador was ushered into the room, he saw President Rhee, the general, and the civilians all weeping and embracing one another. After they left, the ambassador's plea was the final bit of persuasion that turned the tide: President Rhee agreed to resign.

It was now 7 PM, and I sat dazed on the edge of my bed in my hotel room. Visions of the dead and wounded students and their grieving parents immobilized me and left me numb with my own grief. When my telephone rang, therefore, I jumped up with a start. To my surprise, it was Ambassador McConaughy: "Seymour," he said in a voice burdened with the strain of his responsibilities, "I need your help. It has been a terrible day and only music can comfort me. If I send my car for you with a military escort, would you meet me at my residence at 7:30 and play the two Brahms Sonatas with me?"

Within thirty minutes or so, sirens announced the arrival of the ambassador's car. Korean guards, seeing the official insignia, stood at attention as I stepped inside. We sped through the now deserted streets of Seoul where the events of only a short time ago would provide history with yet another story of heroism. The ambassador arrived a few moments later, paused only long enough to greet his wife, and then went directly to the music room, his clarinet in hand. As we played the two Brahms Sonatas Op. 120, for Clarinet and Piano, and discussed various questions of interpretation, something in our communication dispelled all the horrors of the day — something "more restorative than food or rest," the Ambassador said. We were suspended in time, lifted beyond tragedy, and drawn together in music's bond. Two hours later, we had our first disagreement: we argued, good naturedly, of course, about who, in fact, had benefited more from that music session. The truth was, we had both received the only kind of therapy that could ease our anguished spirits. As I left the residence, we embraced in mutual gratitude.

The following day, airplanes dropped leaflets all over the city containing a message from the President: "If the people wish me to resign, I will." Yet, in the light of past governmental betrayals, the majority of Koreans read into the word "if" a continuation of deception. As they saw it, the scores of dead and wounded students ought to have provided the President with reasons enough to resign outright. If anything, Rhee's obsequious message inflamed the demonstrators to new heights of violence. As the riots and killing continued to escalate, the President and his advisers must have concluded that the resistance could not and would not be contained. By late afternoon, the news spread throughout Korea and the world that President Rhee had resigned unconditionally. Justice, as the demonstrators saw it, had prevailed, and all hostilities ceased within an hour.

Now that the Koreans had rid themselves of their corrupt leaders, one would have expected victory marches and various signs of exultation. But this was not the case. The nightmarish events of almost a week had cast a pall over the entire country. Wounded and dying students filled every available space in hospitals all over Seoul, and reports of suicides among corrupt government officials merely added to the horror. Among them was Lee Ki Bung, the speaker of the assembly. He, his wife, and his son, a high-ranking military figure, were all found dead in the family home. To this day, no one is quite sure what occurred. But it is assumed that the family made a suicide pact to save face, and that the son first shot his parents and then himself.

During the writing of this book, I have told of various times throughout my life when my emotions got the better of me. Curiously though, I did not shed a single tear from the moment the uprising started until my departure from Korea. But at the airport, where a host of musicians and students had gathered to bid me farewell, the floodgates opened wide, and we all sobbed until we thought that our hearts would break. The recent events seemed too difficult to bear. Moreover, it hurt me to leave so many of my friends behind.

Among the students at the airport was a young Korean pianist, Lee Kong Ju, whose tape recording I brought home with me. I subsequently played it for Hans Neumann, who was my teacher at that time and a faculty member of the Mannes College of Music. He was so impressed with Kong Ju's playing that he used his influence to arrange a full scholarship for him to study at the Mannes School. It then took two years of letter writing on my part to various Korean and American officials before he was granted permission to come to the United States.

Having miraculous ears, Lee Kong Ju later wrote down all of Vladimir Horowitz's transcriptions, simply by listening to Horowitz's recordings of them — the *Stars and Stripes*, the three versions of the *Carmen* Fantasy, and many others. It was an arduous task that took twenty-five years to complete. After Horowitz's death, I met with Mrs. Horowitz along with Kong Ju and Thomas Frost, the producer of Horowitz's recordings, to discuss the possibility of having these transcriptions published. Despite the enthusiasm of Mrs. Horowitz and everyone else, the project never materialized.

In May of 1993, I returned to Korea after thirty-three years. The occasion was the publication of my book *With Your Own Two Hands*, translated into Korean by my pupil Paik Nakcheung. Gone was the old city of Seoul that I had retained in my memory. In its place was a thriving, modern city complete with luxury hotels, restaurants, apartment buildings, cultural complexes, and American-style supermarkets. None of these modern advances, though, had diminished in the slightest the sheer passion for music and music education which has always played a vital role in Korean life.

During my three week visit, I met several people who actually remembered my performances as far back as my army days in 1952. One of them, a violinist who had played in the ROK Naval Symphony Orchestra, both in 1952 and 1960, was one of the guests at a dinner party to which I was invited. His name is Won Kyungsoo, and he is now the principal conductor of the Stockton Symphony Orchestra in California. Coincidentally, he happened to be in Seoul as a visiting teacher at the same time I was there. I knew, of course, that Kenneth Gordon and I had made a deep impression on the Korean people. But I never knew how far that impression extended until Won Kyungsoo told me the following: "The Korean musical community had heard recordings of the finest artists, but we had never heard live performances of such a high calibre before. Your solo recitals and concerto performances raised the standard of music making in Korea from that time on. I am not exaggerating when I say that your appearances were of historic significance."

I was deeply humbled to hear this moving testimony from one of Korea's most respected musicians. Needless to say, it is a privilege to know that we made such a significant contribution to the Korean musical scene. It was the realization of what I had in mind almost from the beginning of my music studies — to use music for something more than mere fame, applause, and money.

Conclusions

Alas, with economic woes having plagued the federal government for years now, State Department-sponsored tours of the type which I have described no longer exist. A poisoned cloud of commercialism and competitiveness has now settled upon all artistic endeavors. It has polluted the artistic community and has discouraged young potential artists from fulfilling their missions — missions from which the world would have benefited. I have already discussed how some money-crazed managers, representatives, and recording company directors have swooped down upon the geniuses in the field of music, not to protect or to encourage them, and certainly not for music's sake, but only because genius talent earns them fortunes. As though to prove how the lure of money can undermine the noblest intentions, many of these very geniuses, caught up in a craze to maintain their star status at all costs, have become as mercenary as their managers. There are, of course, artists who serve music for reasons apart from economic gain. But most of them are too engrossed in their own careers to show more than a superficial concern for their less fortunate colleagues. Moreover, no virtuoso today that I know of composes as did the masters of the past.

Managers and advertising people are chiefly responsible for foisting upon the public false criteria for success. Thus, dedicated musicians who are not geniuses are made to feel that there is no place for them in the performing world. Family members and friends tell them, "Why continue to practice all day when you haven't made it to the top?" In their eyes, some of those drug-crazed rock stars who earn millions with little or no talent have, in fact, "made it to the top." Such people undervalue the accomplishments of the inner person and see the external evidence of success as being the only justifiable cause for the pursuit of anything.

Around the time that I toured for the State Department, I was simply a struggling young musician who had not even made a significant mark for himself in the professional world. Yet the directors of the cultural exchange program in Washington, D.C., seemed just as interested in me, the person, as they were in my credentials. They were looking for potential emissaries of good will — emissaries who would raise the image of America in foreign countries by means of their own specialty, be it music, language, or science. It did not matter to them whether the musicians among them had sold a million records or had performed with major symphony orchestras. If our level of performing met with their standards and we had even a modest degree of performing experience — modest compared to performers who have major careers — and if we had teaching experience and were personable and articulate in speech, these were the only criteria necessary to qualify us for our mission. To think that such opportunities, from which I so greatly benefited artistically and personally, are no longer available to young aspiring artists fills me with profound sadness for my own pupils and for all other young musicians.

What, then, does the future hold for young artists? In my opinion, performing careers as they exist today are, in the long run, musically counter-productive and often ruinous to a musician's emotional and physical health. More specifically, the relatively few concert artists who have indeed made it to the top are over-worked and over-played by their managers to the point of exhaustion and burnout. Few, if any, have the time to heed their creative calling, and all too few take the time to teach young hopefuls and counsel them on ways in which they might promote their own performing careers. I am not suggesting, of course, that such artists abandon their own careers and cheat the world out of the inspiration of hearing them in live concerts. But I would settle for their appearing in public less frequently, were I to know that, 1) they were in seclusion composing or writing something that is infused with their own genius, and that, 2) they were taking the time to share their knowledge and their experience with others.

GETTING ENGAGEMENTS AND GETTING PUBLISHED

From time to time people ask me, "How can I get performing engagements and eventually go on concert tours?" and, "How can I get published?"

To answer the first question — some musicians believe that it was easier to have a performing career in the 1950's than it is today. If this was true, it certainly didn't seem so to me. I struggled to get engagements then exactly as my own pupils do today. In fact few musicians in any generation have been able to devote their lives to their art and pay the rent at the same time. As far back as 1932, *New York Journal, Inc.* published an article entitled "Our Starving Musicians — First to Suffer, Last to Seek Aid:"

> No people have suffered more and complained less in recent months than the professional musicians.
>
> They were the first to be affected by "hard times," for their services as performers and teachers were regarded as luxuries rather than necessities.
>
> The great majority of them are untrained to make their living in other fields, even if opportunities for employment were open to them, yet they have been more backward than any other class in applying for relief. The hardships that these cultured and sensitive artists have endured make one of the most tragic chapters in the unwritten annals of the city.

A few musicians inherit success, such as the gifted children of famous people. Some affluent musicians, or those supported by sponsors, buy success. Finally, there are a few musicians with phenomenal gifts who seem destined for stardom on the strength of their playing alone. One might say that success is thrust upon them, and deservedly so. With everyone else, however, it is a question of playing an active role in promoting one's own career. This entails making telephone calls, writing letters, playing auditions, and doing whatever is necessary to secure even one performing engagement. Hearing this advice, young hopefuls invariably respond with "I am embarrassed to act as my own manager." "Embarrassed or not," I tell them, "either act as your own manager or else be prepared to perform exclusively for your family and friends."

It all comes down to two questions: How much do you want to perform in public? And why do you want to perform? I have repeatedly stated what motivated me to perform. I reasoned that the more frequently I performed, the more likely I was to develop confidence and control. And in the process, I would deepen my love for and understanding of music. In this respect, any performance whatsoever constituted a proving ground for me, whether it was an informal run-through for two people, or playing a fifteen minute program for an organization, for example. Since I made my living through teaching and taking photographs of musicians, I said "yes" to all engagements, whether I received fees for them or not.

As far as actually going on tour is concerned, I have already recounted how my teacher's friend Major Migel arranged my audition for Arthur Judson, and how this eventually led to a contract with CAMI. But even the audition for Arthur Judson would not have come about had I not asked Major Migel outright for his help in promoting my career.

Let's face the facts squarely: concert tours can only be arranged by major concert agencies. All of the performers on their rosters are either well-known figures or else international contest winners. In other words, managers sign them up only because they are thought to be saleable items. The days of impresarios like Sol Hurok, who actually invested his own money in building careers, are over. So if you are not a genius, are not well-known, and if you have not won an international competition, then you cannot expect to be signed up by a big manager and go on concert tours. These are the indisputable facts. The sooner young hopefuls accept them, the more logical and also practical they will be in trying to augment their performing careers.

Nine Rejections

If anything, getting published is more difficult than getting performing engagements. Some people, however, are supplied with two necessary ingredients which may help them to defy the odds: one is a belief in themselves; the other is a belief in their work in the face of constant rejections. Self-belief may be natural or acquired. In my own case, it was a little of both. For one thing, I always had a strong conviction that I had something to say. But in addition, my mother instilled self-confidence in me from childhood on. All of this supplied me with enough courage to charge headlong into life's battles. In defiance of my fears and shyness, I forced myself to perform and speak in front of audiences. After years of painstaking preparation, I gradually learned to survive. Even to this day the remembrance of past survivals is like a pair of supporting arms carrying me across the platform, quelling my fears and assuring me of yet another survival. I also knew instinctively that I could integrate my personality through the process of practicing, performing, composing, and writing. I was well into my thirties, however, before I became aware of this. My desire to harmonize the musician with the person, and thus feel good about myself, was always stronger than my desire to be published or to get engagements. This integration theory, my credo, continues to guide me in everything I do. Moreover, it has served as an effective buffer against the pain of rejection.

Over the years, my mother, who was my strongest ally, quietly observed my trials in getting published and getting engagements. No one was prouder or more supportive of me than she was. Even when she was in her late eighties, it would have taken an act of God to keep her from attending my local performances and workshops. Afterwards, at formal receptions or at get-togethers in private homes, her warm and outgoing personality, plus her homespun philosophy, would invariably make her the center of attraction. She was the mother of the performer, after all, and she played her role with the panache of a full-fledged actress — especially when she was asked personal questions about her son: "Did you have to force him to practice?" or, "Was he a well-behaved child at home?" Such questions brought out the performer in my mother. She would then regale her listeners with all sorts of stories about me, often to my embarrassment. But her favorite theme was my tenacity: "He never gave up," she would say, with a proud air about her. "When they threw him out of the front door, he came in through the back!" My mother did, in fact, sum up the truth about her *zeenala* in her own inimitable way. For in almost all instances, I did not take "no" for an answer. I shamelessly and repeatedly telephoned and wrote letters to people in high places who, for whatever reason, had rejected me. In many instances, I believe that it was my very show of determination that achieved its purpose: I did get engagements and I finally did get published.

When I was in my twenties, I may have fantasized about being a modern-day Beethoven, but it never occurred to me to send my little pieces to publishers. It was only when the late Mark Nevin, the well-known composer of student material, expressed enthusiasm for my compositions and then handed me a list of ten publishers, that I began to think seriously about the possibility of being published. "Be prepared for rejections," he advised me, "and don't get discouraged. If all ten publishers reject you, simply start from the top of the list again."

In 1964, I had no notion whatsoever as to why I practiced or composed. I only knew one thing: it was unthinkable for me *not* to do these things. At any rate, I followed Mark Nevin's advice. Although I tried to be brave about it, I always experienced a sinking feeling of hopelessness with each letter of rejection — all nine of them! Perhaps this made my eventual success seem all the sweeter by comparison. For the tenth and last publisher on the list, G. Schirmer, actually sent me a contract for my piece called *Forgotten Waltz*, my first published composition. Being published spurred me on to compose other works. But it was not until 1972 that I received my second contract from G. Schirmer for my suite of *Birds*, which is perhaps my most popular work. On the heels of that success, Ron Herder, who was at that time the editor-in-chief of G. Schirmer, telephoned me and asked for Book 2 of *Birds*. Not since I was fourteen and studying with Herman Holzman, my high school teacher, had anyone asked me to compose something. My inspiration knew no bounds. Other published works followed in quick succession. Then Ron Herder asked me to write a concerto for teenage students, which is how my *Concerto (for our time)* came to be written. For seventeen years I enjoyed a relationship with G. Schirmer and its distributor, the Hal Leonard Publishing Corporation, such as few creative people have ever experienced with their publishers.

In 1978, I completed the first draft of a book which I first called *Beyond Practicing*, but which later became *With Your Own Two Hands*. Two and a half years later, and after inestimable input on the part of Flora Levin, the manuscript was completed. Having established by that time a modest reputation as a pianist, teacher, and composer of mostly student teaching material, I assumed that it would be far easier to find a publisher for my book than it had been for my compositions. Yet my manuscript was rejected by every major publisher in the United States, including two rejections from Schirmer Books-Macmillan, the very publisher that eventually signed up the book. While readers gave it rave reviews, and, in one case, even predicted that it would become a "best seller," the publishers' surveys always arrived at the same conclusion: "There is no market for a book on practicing." Hearing this, I was convinced that the marketing people, whoever they were, had not read my manuscript thoroughly. For if they had, they would have known that my book is not a methodological one, but rather a philosophical and psychological treatment of practicing, which, in a larger sense, could be applied to practicing anything. *With Your Own Two Hands* is, in marketing jargon, a self-help book.

Ultimatum and Success

We are all put to severe tests in the face of rejections, bad reviews, and, the cruelest of them all, indifference to our best efforts. Call it blind faith, an inflated ego, or anything else other than humility — something within me knew that my book had to get out to the world. After two years of being rejected by so many publishers, I was desperate enough to take a drastic step. I made an appointment to speak with Kenneth Stuart, the music editor of Schirmer Books. (Schirmer Books is a subsidiary of Macmillan and is often confused with G. Schirmer, the music publisher.) Sitting opposite him in his office, I delivered the following ultimatum: "Random House is interested in publishing my book. Because you were my first choice, I'm giving you one last chance. If I don't hear from you within two weeks, I'm giving the manuscript to Random House." This was not true, of course. There was no expression of interest on the part of any publisher. But at that moment, I was not above inventing such a story. Without a word, Kenneth Stuart ushered me into another office and sat me down in front of a typewriter: "Compose a letter and state exactly what you have just told me. When you finish, bring it back to me."

During those moments when I was alone in front of that typewriter, I could only think of one thing: I have lied, and I will no doubt be caught in my own net. I felt like a common criminal, and it took a great effort not to allow my feelings of guilt adversely to affect my grammar and spelling. At any rate, I typed the letter, handed it and my manuscript to Kenneth Stuart, and left the office. The above incident took place on a Monday in 1980.

At that period of my life, I used to drive Tuesdays and Thursdays from New York City to Millburn, New Jersey, in order to teach in my mother's apartment. Going to Millburn served two functions: it afforded me an opportunity to visit with my mother twice a week, and it served as a convenience for my New Jersey pupils. How my mother looked forward to those two days, I cannot begin to say. Quite simply, my visits enabled her to act out her motherhood as only an earth mother could. While I was teaching, aromas from her Jewish-style cooking wafted into the music room. On many occasions, when temptation got the better of us, my pupils and I would leave the piano and line up in the kitchen with a ravenous look in our eyes. My mother, who secretly looked forward to this ritual, would then dip her spoon into whatever she happened to be cooking and give us each a taste of the gravy. One taste led to another, and it was not unusual for a pupil to spend the rest of the lesson time writing down the recipes. So it was that my mother established a heart warming relationship with all of my pupils which lasted until her death. I think that my visits to Millburn and everything associated with them actually prolonged my mother's life, as well as enriching my own.

It was now Tuesday, only one day after I had met with Kenneth Stuart. Thinking that it would take Macmillan at least two weeks to respond, I thought nothing more about it during the drive to New Jersey. My mother lived in a garden apartment facing the main street in Millburn. As I parked my car in front of the apartment complex, I noticed her standing at the main entrance awaiting my arrival. Since she had never done this before, I thought surely that there was an emergency of some sort. As I was climbing out of my car, my mother cried out to me, "Kenneth Stuart just called! They signed up your book!" My bluff had worked. Kenneth Stuart had presented my letter at a board meeting only twenty-four hours after the discussion I had with him. It all proved the power of positive thinking, with a slightly dishonest twist.

But my trials, and those of the book itself, were far from over. As it happened, two copies of the book had been mailed to me, and Flora Levin and I met in my studio to celebrate its publication. First I opened a bottle of champagne and we drank toasts to one another. Now it was time to open the envelope and see the result of so much effort. And what an over-powering experience it was! Just seeing the cover and holding my first published book was a thrill beyond description. Flora and I then sat on the sofa and began leafing though the book. I happened to open my copy to a musical example. What I saw caused an instant panic attack. Before I spoke about it to Flora, I turned to other musical examples just to be sure that my eyes were not playing tricks on me. More panic. Then I revealed the horror to Flora: the uncorrected musical examples, over sixty of them, had been mistakenly printed throughout the book. Our spirits which a moment ago had been soaring, now fell in disbelief and despair. "It's a nightmare," I cried. "Surely I'll awaken." But it was all true, and those errors gnawed at me like a pain that would not go away. When on the following morning I apprised Kenneth Stuart of the error, he and the entire staff of Schirmer Books were shocked beyond belief. The printers had to destroy the entire existing stock — five thousand copies — and reprint the edition. When the corrected publication was finally released, the book generated a great deal of interest: fan letters poured in, reviews were enthusiastic, and I received invitations to lecture and to conduct master-classes on the book's thesis.

Shortly before publication, the director of publicity had assured me that Macmillan would defray my expenses for all book tours. But in the end, I received no help whatsoever. Whatever engagements I accepted were at my own expense. Thinking that this was what all writers must do, I fulfilled my engagements anyway and at least had the pleasure of seeing great numbers of my book being sold. One might have thought that the publicity staff would have taken advantage of the enthusiastic response to my book and exerted more than a routine effort in promoting it. Yet the opposite occurred. Soon, computer messages in book stores announced that the book was no longer in print. This was either an unintentional blunder on the part of Macmillan, or else an indication of their intent to allow the book to die. My telephone messages and my letters to the director of marketing were ignored. "Enough of this," I thought. "I'm going to the top." And so I made an appointment to speak to the president of Macmillan.

Presidents and directors of big companies have constantly to deal with complaints of all sorts. Indeed, as I shook hands with Macmillan's president, his ho-hum attitude and bored expression told me that he was prepared to placate yet another disgruntled writer with routine assurances. With an air of "here we go again," he gestured me to sit opposite him in his large and luxuriously appointed office. I then delivered my opening line, which, I am not ashamed to admit, I had rehearsed: "I thought it best to talk to you first before consulting with my lawyer." Hearing this, he immediately sat upright in his chair with a look that seemed to say, "I had better take this guy seriously!" I then told him of the complete lack of interest shown to me and to my book on the part of his staff, and that I had the feeling that they were actually snuffing out the life of my book. I reminded him that a failure to do a second printing was, quite obviously, a breach of contract. I even suggested that Schirmer Books must be func-tioning at a loss and was, therefore, a tax write-off for Macmillan. While the president hotly denied my bold assertion, he seemed to view me as a tough opponent and not simply another complaining writer. He quickly assured me that he personally would see to it that my book be given the treatment it deserved. "You are talking to a professional now," he said in a sincere tone, the inference being that the people handling my book were *not* professionals. Immediately, then, he began making telephone calls to key people. By the time the meeting was over, I had every reason to feel assured that the marketing staff would henceforth treat my book seriously.

My book did go into its second printing. But later the same thing occurred again: computer monitors in book stores once again flashed the ominous message — "Out of print." My patience had run out by that time.

As far as I was concerned, the publisher and I were now in a state of war. In fact, I protested so hotly to the president and to everyone else that a high level decision was made to get rid of me and my book at all costs. To my great satisfaction, Macmillan transferred the book to my music publisher, G. Schirmer — free of charge. It has been flourishing ever since — not by any means due to G. Schirmer's efforts, but because I single-handedly have promoted it through my workshops in the United States, Europe, and Asia. It has now been published in German, Japanese, and Korean.

My creative energies were not only directed towards my book. During the years after my farewell concert at the 92nd Street Y I composed many piano works and wrote books and articles on technical and pedagogical subjects. In the case of my technique books, *20 Lessons in Keyboard Choreography* and *Musi-Physi-Cality* — when publishers would not take them, I published them myself. Once teachers and students discovered my music and my book *With Your Own Two Hands*, my career took off in a new direction. I became one of the most sought-after clinicians in this country and abroad, giving lecture-demonstrations, including performances of my own works, and conducting masterclasses. Beyond the satisfaction I derive from making a contribution to teachers and students, I enjoy the fact that I no longer have to deal with managers. Program directors contact me directly, and my fees are contingent upon the solvency of the organization in question. Occasionally, I give my presentations without a fee in order to contribute something to the educational field. No manager would tolerate this. As I experienced in the past, my managers often turned down organizations who could not meet my specified fee. Thus I not only lost whatever money might have been available, but I was also deprived of performing experience.

The Magic Ingredient — Self-Belief

All of us deserve a chance to fulfill ourselves, whatever our degree of talent and whatever others say about our work. In the process of pursuing our calling, we may find support and encouragement from family members, teachers, and colleagues. The trustworthy people in our lives will steer us away from self-deception. But in the final analysis, self-belief is the ultimate key to success. No matter how much others may help and influence us, it is only self-belief that supplies us with the courage to do our work properly and to walk across the stage in the face of overwhelming challenges. And it regenerates our motivation to begin again when we fail to live up to our standards.

Beyond this, people so richly endowed with self-belief have a desire to benefit others through teaching. If I were to single out the most important function of a teacher, I would unhesitatingly say that it is the ability to help pupils believe in themselves. Few joys are comparable to what a music teacher experiences when his or her own pupil is able to perform a time-honored masterpiece with control and expression. The circle of giving and receiving is then complete. More reason why eminent artists whose self-support system is proportionate to the magnitude of their gifts ought to enrich talented students by infusing them with their own hard-earned knowledge and security.

As I have discovered, the building up of a self-support system begins with a passionate interest in some worthwhile pursuit and a capacity for hard and consistent work. No one needs to be told that the learning process itself is a struggle from the beginning to the end, a struggle which not everyone can or is willing to endure. But people who are sufficiently courageous and who persist, even in the face of hardships and rejections, eventually find strength and belief in themselves once they experience the joy of their hard-earned accomplishments — more control of a technical passage, a musical insight, or an improved compositional or writing skill, for instance. As often happens, the successes of non-geniuses — the many who are called — prove that they, too, can be among the few who are chosen. Geniuses or not, resolute people can carve out impressive careers for themselves in whatever way and on whatever level is compatible with their gifts.

Each manifestation of nature, human and otherwise, has its own unique genetic programming. Musicians, therefore, vary from one another even as do trees of the same species. It should follow, then, that a pupil might excel his or her teacher in one or more areas, and vice versa. The sheer technical ability of some of my own pupils, for example, far exceeds mine. I not only admire their virtuosity, but I also improve my own technique just by watching them maneuver on the keyboard. My responsibility as a teacher is to encourage my pupils' assets and to help them acquire whatever qualities I have which they might lack. But then, all relationships flourish in reciprocity. One of the chief impediments to personal development and to love itself is being jealous of what someone else has that you do not. I have always thought that jealousy indicates a dangerously low degree of self-esteem, coupled with a sense of hopelessness in overcoming one's own weaknesses.

Let jealous and power-hungry teachers, managers, and colleagues say and do what they wish. They will never kill music's fire, which in spite of everything will always burn brightly in the hearts and minds of devoted musicians. It is indeed unfortunate that people who are engaged in noble pursuits today have to wage such a battle against forces which would undervalue their efforts. Yet it is possible that the absence of music and art programs in our schools and the dwindling number of solo engagements and college teaching posts might end up having a positive effect:

> Should children continue to be deprived of music in grade school, and should conservatories of music and music departments in colleges not educate their students properly and humanely, then students of all ages must restrict their music education to the private sector alone. And should a private teacher, no matter how famous, prove to be one of those monsters such as I have described, then the student must search for another teacher, one who is both knowledgeable and humane. Should one fail to find such a teacher, it is far better to work alone. The finest and most ambitious musicians will seek each other out for advice and stimulation.

> Should mediocrity and the present day criteria for success continue to be foisted upon serious musicians and the public, then musicians will have no other recourse but to reject everyone and everything responsible for this — dishonest managers and artist representatives, and incompetent teachers and critics. Musicians will then have to manage themselves. They may perform less frequently, and their audiences may be limited, but at least performers and audiences will gather together in a rite of artistic giving and receiving, one that is free of commercialism and competitiveness. Like professional-amateurs, some musicians may have to make their living in non-musical fields. But they will be free agents. Without managers dictating to them, they can study and perform only those works dear to their hearts and share them with audiences of their own choosing. They and their art are will flourish more than in earlier years when they tried in vain to make music into a business.

In spite of everything, I am not at all pessimistic about the future of music. On the contrary! I predict that music and its protagonists will ultimately prevail, while music's detractors will fade into oblivion.

EPILOGUE:
THE DOUBLE BAR

Our lives are, in a sense, themes with variations — the themes being our own distinctive selves. Just as musical themes contain the seeds of their development, so, too, are we endowed with potentials which presage our fulfillment.

When writing music, composers signify the ends of movements and whole compositions with a double bar. Occasionally, when a composition struggles against its own leave-taking, the composer inserts a *da capo* sign, meaning that it goes back to the beginning again — a sort of last embrace before the final farewell. Inevitably, we, too, reach that double bar. But there are no *da capos* for us, as there are in music, and no opportunity to begin again — at least, not here on earth. We have only one chance at it, which is exactly why each day deserves our best effort.

I have a boundless gratitude towards music. It has nourished and inspired me. And it has accompanied me through each phase of my life, like a friend who takes my hand and prods me on in spite of human frailties. During that journey, music has afforded me the opportunity to repeat over and over again phrases of fathomless beauty. With each repetition, I have tried to sharpen my perceptions, and to clarify my feelings. For this, after all, is what music requires of us.

Whenever I hear the oft-quoted phrase and its variations, "Music does not merely influence my life, it *is* my life," I think of the composers without whom such a phrase would never have come into being. I revere composers not only because they gave us the *St. Matthew Passion, Don Giovanni, Winterreise*, and the Ninth Symphony, but even more because they transcended their human limitations. Through their own Herculean efforts and perseverance, they tapped into that reservoir that has no double bar. Noble thoughts, profound feelings — all this they were able to extricate from themselves despite the impediments of everyday life. See the treasures they have left us! They are monuments to the finest attributes of the human mind, each one a pillar of civilization, as my friend Flora Levin described Mozart's K. 595. Music, then, can be seen as a notational representation of all that is good and noble in people. And in the process of playing or singing our favorite works, we, too, can call forth what is best within ourselves.

The benefits to be derived from the practice of music can enrich us for several lifetimes. Beyond this, serious students of music can reap a reward that transcends music itself. For when we go far enough in tapping into those internal currents which the ultimate composer has implanted in our minds, we ourselves may experience intimations of immortality. In other words, it at least becomes thinkable that we may not come to an end after all. To know that we, like music, can be self-regenerating, and perhaps continue on in some other sphere, enables us to place abuse, rejections, and disappointment, for instance, in proper perspective. We see ourselves in the presence of something far greater than these things, and greater, too, than we are. To be so humbled in the presence of music inspires us to serve it for its own sake, and not merely for petty, self-seeking reasons.

Above all, I have learned just how important it is for all people to express their thoughts and feelings through purely creative acts, whether the medium be music, words, or brush strokes. I trust that I may continue to tap those stirrings deep within myself even in the face of infirmity, as did my dear friend, the artist Erna Friedlander. In her mid-eighties, when the curtain of blindness darkened her canvases, she picked up a mound of clay for the very first time in her life, and with feeble hands, molded an objective representation of her inner world. It was a crude form, to be sure, and hardly destined to be handed down to posterity. But its creation symbolized her indomitable spirit, one that insisted upon regenerating itself until the final curtain descended.

As I have frequently told my pupils, especially the undisciplined ones, no one is too young to understand that all of life is a preparation for meeting that double bar. Euripides was prophetic on the subject:

> Whoso neglects learning in his youth
> loses the past and is unprepared for the future.[*]

Finally, we alone are responsible for how we define each measure of that grand composition called life. We choose, or else reject, the angels and monsters who drift in and out of our lives. We, and we alone, allow people either to enrich us with the gifts of their own self-discoveries, or to

---

[*]A fragment from the lost play *Phrixus*.

wreak havoc upon us. Without a clear understanding of what music means to us, however, we cannot make the right choices of teachers, career goals, or anything else, for that matter. Earlier in this book, I stated that creating a world apart from my family helped me to survive the personal difficulties that I encountered in my youth. In my mature years, however, I can point to two things in particular that helped me to survive in that jungle called a career in music: the first concerns my attitude; the second pertains to two people who influenced me greatly.

As to the first, I aimed my practicing towards the high standards of human achievement that were all around me. Somehow, I instinctively knew that the process of practicing could lead towards an integration of the person, as well as the improvement of the musician. And, rather late in life, I discovered that the composers whose music I practiced and performed were, by their own example, urging me to make my own statements. As to the second, I had enough good sense to know that I needed help if I were to untangle the emotional and intellectual knots that impeded my development. My dear friend Flora Levin, classicist and musician, who first sought me out as her piano teacher, later became the best teacher I ever had. As it happened, I showed her the early manuscript of my book *With Your Own Two Hands*. Seeing in its thesis an extension of ancient Greek thought, she undertook to teach me the skills of writing so as more convincingly to express the book's message. I am hardly exaggerating when I say that her instruction changed the atoms of my brain.

The other influence was Sir Clifford Curzon. Sitting at his side in the Steinway basement so many times during the twenty years I knew and worked with him, and watching those quiet, expressive hands coax out of inanimate keys living phrases of transcendent beauty, was more beneficial to me than all the words of my other piano teachers. It saddened me that the harmony of his playing could not penetrate the dissonance of his personal world.

I have tried to be a good student and to be worthy of the gifts of time and interest which these two figures lavished upon me. That with all of my efforts I cannot write as Flora Levin does, or play as Sir Clifford did, is a fact that I humbly accept. My joy, my satisfaction derives solely from striving towards the ideals exemplified by these models. Just to be a little better each day is more important to me than winning prizes or getting published.

In the past, I have sometimes acted out frivolous vignettes and played games with people and with myself. I am happy and also relieved to say that at this period of my life I have stopped playing all such games. Age and experience have taught me to assess my place in the scheme of things.

Flora Levin, my dear friend and guide.
(Photo by Seymour Bernstein)

Considering the extraordinary achievements of geniuses, both past and present, I am, by comparison, a person of modest talents. I realize now, and I teach my pupils, that joy comes from making the most of whatever talent we possess, and by establishing an inviolate relationship with one's work and with the personal attachments one is privileged to enjoy.

The career war that I continue to fight has often seemed far worse than the actual war in which I participated as a soldier. If most of the career battles were not actually life-threatening, they certainly took their toll on me emotionally and psychologically. But my desire to improve myself, and, in the process, to make a contribution to others, has supplied me with the energy, passion, and resolve to surmount life's obstacle course.

Now that I have reached my seventies, everyday choices of even simple things have gone through radical changes. When having a meal or a snack, for example, I now choose a plate and a glass which, formerly, I would have reserved for special occasions. Each day, each hour has become that special occasion. As choices present themselves, the word *now* reverberates in my mind's ear: "Use it, do it, *now*." Recently, I applied this credo when I performed the Brahms Quintet with the DaPonte Quartet in a lovely church in South Bristol, Maine. Performing infrequently can be very trying, whatever one's past experiences. During my practicing, I wondered how I would survive so many difficult passages while under pressure. For after all, music's demands can undermine the confidence even of those who have considerable knowledge and experience. At such times, and at the performance itself, I said to myself, "*Now*, it has to be *now*, because there will be few, if any, chances left," and as if by magic, determination cast out self-doubt. Ideally, doing one's best *now* ought to be a credo at any age. But it takes on a greater urgency in later life. For whereas youth can safely postpone concentrated effort for a future time, age whispers at twilight that there may not be another sunrise.

While I may not have had a spectacular career, I have, nonetheless, learned to practice conscientiously and to shape musical phrases with control. I have also learned to recognize a split infinitive, a dangling participle, and subject-verb disagreements. Above all, I have tapped the creative centers of my brain. This thought alone — being able to express my true self through purely creative activities — sustains me during the coda of my life. It gives me confidence to go on working even harder. And I feel certain that it will afford me comfort and a sense of accomplishment when I reach the double bar.

ESSAY:
THE MUSIC CRITIC

If you want to elicit a volcanic response from even the most "laid-back" performer, simply bring up the subject of music critics. For if we interpret correctly the content and tone of some reviews today, we must arrive at one conclusion: Certain music critics seem to hate music and those who perform it. It's no wonder then why no group of people associated with the music profession is looked upon more contemptuously and, at the same time, is more feared than music critics.

No one knows better than music critics just how bleak the performing scene today really is. Because few things are more powerful than the written word, critics, more than anyone else, can sway public thinking for or against performers and music itself. Yet, certain music critics, far from alleviating the performer's plight, actually augment it. It is deplorable enough that many performers have appeared in New York City for three or more consecutive years without having a single review to show for their efforts. But far worse is the tone of reviews when they *do* appear. Reading them, one might think that music critics are hunters bent upon thinning out a herd of deer. And how do performers respond? Victims of insult, indifference, and base ignorance, they mutter to themselves or to their colleagues, and then go right on practicing.

Many musicians find it difficult to communicate in any other language save their own wordless one; so even if they wanted to protest to critics, their lack of writing skills prevents them from doing so. Some musicians are also eminent scholars and highly skilled writers. Occasionally, a letter of protest from one of these figures finds its way into a newspaper or a magazine. Beyond arousing a momentary flurry of responses from the public, nothing more comes of it; the derisive tone of reviews and articles continues much as before, and the gulf already existing between critics and performers continues to widen so much that some artists do not even read their own reviews.

Other musicians who can write are far too busy promoting and protecting their own careers to worry about anyone or anything else. Yet, for a person not to be his brother's keeper is to invite plagues upon himself. For if the injustices which appear frequently in the pages of *The New York Times* (to cite only one publication) are allowed to go unchallenged, then all musicians are in danger.

471

Essay: The Music Critic

The musicians I know personally, and others whom I have interviewed, have voiced similar complaints about music critics. To begin with, they feel that music criticism as practiced today is archaic and in need of drastic reforms. They are incensed by the lack of compassion and the outrageous snideness evident in far too many reviews. This is more hurtful to musicians than the rejection they face everywhere. In fact, the musicians I have spoken to feel that the way critics write about performers and the time-honored masterpieces they perform not only contributes to but actually creates some of the problems which beset musicians today.

Criticizing Critics

Do musicians wish to eliminate critics altogether? Some actually do, but the majority of musicians are convinced that critics can be their staunchest allies, that the power of the written word can help their cause more than anything else. Towards this end, critics ought to be as open to constructive criticisms as musicians are. For if they continue to express hostility and indifference to music and musicians, then they will be guilty on two counts: worsening the plight of performing musicians and turning the public away from serious music.

Because performers function in much the same way as critics do — they criticize themselves endlessly in preparing performances, they criticize their pupils and their colleagues, and they too have deadlines to meet — they are eminently qualified to criticize critics. At 8 PM, for example, out they go onto the stage, whether they are in the mood or not. Moreover, certain music teachers can be just as cruel as some of the more acerbic music critics when criticizing their pupils and colleagues. None of this would happen, I believe, if teachers and critics would focus upon one thing: they are criticizing *people*, and not just their performances. Even the harshest criticism can be beneficial provided that its tone is humane and its message constructive. In short, performers, being all too human, should inspire within teachers and music critics the deepest, most humane concerns. Without a sense of humanity, teachers and critics are as much a menace to performers, to music, and to society as callous and case-hardened physicians are to their patients.

While the majority of my reviews have been fairly good, I have, on occasion, been as much a victim of indifference and distortion of facts as anyone else. Once, for example, when I participated in an all-Schumann chamber music concert in Alice Tully Hall, my favorite hall in New York City, I performed in all of the works on the program. Yet, to read the review, I might as well have been a plant decorating the stage. For the only mention of my playing occurred when the critic discussed the Trio in *D* minor, Op. 63, and faulted the balance between the strings and the piano, "which was played by Seymour Bernstein." That was all. After hearing me maneuver through some of the most difficult works in the chamber music repertory, including the great Quintet, the critic, Allen Hughes, could find nothing whatsoever to say about *how* I played the piano or what I projected, or did not project, musically.

Another time, and coincidentally with the same ensemble and in the same hall, I hobbled across the stage with the help of a cane: I had broken my right foot. The accident had occurred only four days earlier, while I was jogging in Central Park. Looking pale and shuffling *molto adagio* on the heel of my right foot, I must have cut quite a pathetic figure to the large audience in attendance. For as soon as I emerged from the wings, a collective gasp, mixed with a subdued applause, accompanied what must have been the longest trek ever made across a concert platform. Fortunately, the break did not hamper in the slightest my ability to pedal, nor did I experience any pain once I sat down at the piano. Yet Donal Henahan, the critic on that occasion, had his own opinion about the matter. Sending out his journalistic probe, he simply concluded that a pianist with a broken right foot could not possibly pedal correctly, and on that account he wasted precious space in his review complaining about my "blurred pedaling." Curiously enough, my pedaling was the one thing I was especially pleased with on that occasion.

Nothing exasperates a performer more than having only one review after a major concert, something that happens routinely these days. In contrast to this sorry state of affairs, I had five reviews after my New York City debut in 1954. For the most part, they were favorable. Later, in 1958, my debut in Amsterdam elicited six reviews, all of which appeared on the very next day. Reading them, one might have thought that they were about six different pianists! One headline read "GREAT PIANISTIC TALENT," which made me blush with delight when my host translated it for me. The headline of the very next review, however, had two words only: "LOST EVENING." I was instantly cast into a pit of dejection. While the contrasting opinions were confusing, and even humorous, they at least pointed out a truth concerning music criticisms: they are mainly subjective responses reflecting diverse opinions similar to those of the audience. In light of this, it is revelatory and also educational for both the performer and the audience to have this fact confirmed in the form of several reviews. It is far better to have six varied opinions than just one.

On the whole, I have been treated more generously by critics than I felt my playing warranted. In fact, one morning, after reading the kind of headline and review which performers dream about, and this after a performance which I thought was far from my best, I actually telephoned the critic, Donal Henahan, to thank him, "for all the reasons you know about." Taken completely by surprise, he remarked that it was, indeed, refreshing to be thanked rather than berated. For critics receive their share of vitriolic letters, threatening telephone calls, and icy stares.

My own good fortune notwithstanding, I am obliged to say that Donal Henahan has been exceedingly cruel to performers. From the tone of his reviews and articles, one might have thought that he was intent on turning the public against musicians and music. In one article entitled "The Trouble With Irony, Frivolity and Such"[*] he spoke about those rare times when a critic's mind wanders:

> A voice inside the head will begin posing such peripheral philo-sophical questions such [sic] as "why, since no one eats it, is purple cabbage put in salads?"

But that was only the beginning. In the next paragraph, he expressed himself as follows about Beethoven and Brahms, apparently barely able to stifle a yawn:

> That is why at a performance consisting of nothing but the most familiar Beethoven sonatas and Brahms symphonies, you will sometimes see a grizzled music critic hunched over a score: reading along with the musicians helps focus attention and makes the intrusion of purple cabbage less likely.

Later, he assured his readers that this was all in good fun:

> I have slipped a certain amount of irony into the above paragraphs.

So he claimed. But to a large public, and to every serious musician who read that article, Mr. Henahan's treatment of the concert scene dese-crated the sacred art of music. His message was clear: music and musicians bored him. Understandably, then, musicians shudder to think that people like him sit in judgment of them while they project their innermost feelings on the stage.

People aren't all bad, though. Mr. Henahan has displayed some redeeming characteristics during his tenure on *The New York Times*. In one illuminating article, for example, he showed how music can influence

---

[*] Donal Henahan, *The New York Times*, November 14, 1982.

politics; in another, he gave performers some good advice concerning pre-concert publicity:

> Selective quotation from reviews for publicity purposes is an annoyance to both critics and musicians.

I could not agree with him more. Critics and audiences alike want to make up their own minds about a performer's abilities. Besides, performing is difficult enough, so why make it more difficult by having to live up to extravagant quotations? If the truth be known, many quotations used on fliers and posters are hodgepodges of chiseled off words and phrases from sentences which were actually damning in their original context. Thus a harshly critical sentence such as, "The final movement of the Beethoven sonata, while played with a daring virtuosic flair, was, nevertheless, rushed, lacking in subtleties and altogether unmusical," is pared down to become "...played with a daring virtuosic flair."

Of course if critics would write one whole positive sentence in their reviews, performers would not have to resort to such deceitful practices. An intact quotation of a critic's well-considered opinion can be a very useful addition to a performer's biographical notes.

I should like to clarify one point: We all have a right to express positive and negative opinions and even to be bored by repetitions of a Beethoven sonata or a Shakespeare play. But I believe that it is unconscionable for critics to express their boredom for the whole world to see. Certainly all works of art and people who perform in public deserve more than that. In my opinion, the critics who waste precious space in their reviews expressing their boredom tell me only about themselves and nothing about what they are supposed to be writing about.

Chopin, Liszt, and Coca-Cola

The following review epitomizes the utter contempt with which some critics hold music itself:[*]

> Pianist in Chopin and Liszt
>   Krystian Zimerman is a pianist with so much to give that one longs for him to choose his gifts more carefully. His program at Avery Fisher Hall Sunday afternoon settled into the deep ruts of familiar repertory — the Ballades and Fantasy in F minor of Chopin and the Liszt Sonata. It is territory crossed and recrossed so many

---

[*] Bernard Holland, *The New York Times*, May 26, 1988.

thousands of times in this city and elsewhere that its beautiful prospects and startling promontories no longer startle. Through constant repetition, they have been neutralized in our sensibilities — numbing the thoughtful, soothing the short-sighted. Playing these pieces once again — no matter how forcefully — simply told us what we already know and have been reminded of too often.

The review goes on to praise Mr. Zimerman's "elegant dotted rhythms" in the Fantasy, and his "sound that is both wide and rich and still transparent." And then:

Yet, beautiful as these Chopin performances were, they reinforced the suspicion that one of music's most original composers becomes more and more a consumer item every day. One listens to the Chopin Ballades for the same reason one buys Coca-Cola; no surprises — we know just what we are going to get. Mr. Zimerman has the powers to surprise us — to stimulate and to excite rather than simply placate. We wish he would start doing it.

Mr. Holland is clearly suffering from "burnout." That he expends two of the three paragraphs of his review denouncing Chopin and Liszt and, moreover, casts aspersions upon Krystian Zimerman's and the public's musical taste — "One listens to the Chopin Ballades for the same reason one buys Coca-Cola" — categorizes him, in my estimation, at least, as boorish, insolent, and cruel. I should like to think that Krystian Zimerman, who can easily take a place among the great artists of the twentieth century, was untouched by such folderol, and that he saw this review for what it really was — an egregious example of criticism gone sour and the critical ear gone awry.

The New York Times is, of course, one of the most highly respected newspapers in the world. But when its music critics allow themselves to associate purple cabbage and Coca-Cola with Beethoven, Brahms, and Chopin, they dishonor the great paper for which they write.

The Claudia Cassidy Story

Sarcasm and cruelty, like horror films, can actually be marketed and turned into hard cash. For there is something within human nature that delights in hearing or reading about someone else's defeat. Claudia Cassidy, one of the cruelest music critics who ever haunted musical circles, loved to cater to that unwholesome craving in people. As one of her long-time colleagues ironically suggested, "Cassidy's astrological sign is Scorpio. And somehow, she has always to get her stinger into people." Some owners of big newspapers condone and encourage the "stinger" approach for one obvious reason: there is nothing like cruelty and the controversy which inevitably follows it to sell newspapers. In fact, when Cassidy joined the *Chicago Sun* in 1941 at the invitation of Marshall Field, it was her acerbic style that accounted for a great increase in readership. Duly impressed by the magnetism of her "multi-colored fireworks with a stick of dynamite thrown in" (which is how Bernard Asbell described her style in a scathing article entitled "Claudia Cassidy, the Queen of Culture and Her Reign of Terror," *Chicago Magazine*, June, 1956), Colonel Robert R. McCormick, owner of the *Chicago Tribune*, outbid Marshall Field for her. Cassidy's big chance had come. Lured by a tempting salary, she accepted the post of chief music, drama, and dance critic on one of the nation's most prestigious newspapers. There she continued her "reign of terror" until the *Chicago Tribune* retired her in 1965. With that appointment, she found her potential readership doubled, even tripled on Sundays. Her first review, that of a ballet production, was so outrageously malicious that she received over a hundred letters of protest. Worried that the backlash would reach the ears of Colonel McCormick, Cassidy took all of the letters to him and offered to resign. Far from being perturbed, Colonel McCormick thought that any critic who could incite the public to the point of generating so many letters must be an asset to his paper. Thus he not only refused Cassidy's offer to resign, but actually raised her salary. Spurred on by her boss' show of enthusiasm, Cassidy spent the rest of her tenure at the *Tribune* criticizing performers so maliciously that many big name artists flatly refused to accept engagements in Chicago. Robert Emmett Keane, an actor in the road cast of South Pacific, fired back at her one day, saying "One vitriolic woman...pours sulfuric acid over every new show which comes here." Her power was such that managers and conductors of the Chicago Symphony, including such eminent figures as Desire Defauw and Rafael Kubelik, were fired at her bidding. And it was not uncommon for one of her acid reviews to result in the cancellation of a soloist's projected dates in and around Chicago.

Though certainly possessed of journalistic skills, Claudia Cassidy was basically ignorant of music, drama, and the dance. This may explain why she shunned all meetings and interviews with knowledgeable critics and performers. Socially, however, Cassidy, according to those who knew her, could be charming. Moreover, she was always helpful to people who telephoned her for information.

Burnout

Over-exposure to something even as elevating as music can cause burnout not only in critics, but in musicians and the public as well. Burnout poses a major threat to those whose professions require spontaneity and the ability to generate fresh enthusiasm for that which is all too familiar. "I refuse to teach *Für Elise* and the first movement of the 'Moonlight' Sonata to one more pupil!" one piano teacher shamelessly exclaimed before a large audience at a seminar for piano teachers. She and I were among nine panelists. Her statement revealed her increasing alienation from these time-honored masterpieces. My indignation at hearing what I thought to be a disgraceful admission of boredom on the part of a teacher made me deliver a veritable oration even before the moderator could invite the audience's response. "Do you remember how you felt as a child when you first played those two pieces?" I asked her pointedly. "I remember my own experience vividly, and I can tell you that my life was changed forever. Although I was a just little boy, I was transported out of myself with the very first measures of the 'Moonlight' Sonata and *Für Elise*. If you refuse to teach these pieces to your pupils, you will certainly be depriving them of two of the most profound utterances in the whole range of human expression." There ensued a discussion on how teachers can best be of help to their pupils, during which I pointed out that teachers ought to *become* their pupils and empathize with their positive and negative responses to music during each lesson.

At this point, I would like to say something of my own experience in teaching. When I take into myself my pupils' responses to music, I enjoy a benefit beyond personal satisfaction. For as I have discovered, the process of identifying with what my pupils are expressing reaffirms music's special power to teach as well as to "move the soul." Over the years, it has taught me to find my own niche in the scheme of things. One indication of this is that I have learned to place my pupils' needs before my own. Their enrichment is my chief priority. Beyond the joy derived from their pupils' development, teachers often receive yet another reward: as they empathize with their pupils' musical responses, they may find that the embers of long-ago inspirations flickering under layers of life's disillusionments and frustrations are rekindled and renewed. This can happen even a thousand times over in the course of a teacher's lifetime. What can be boring about that? Nonetheless, some teachers place their own tastes and selfish needs above those of their pupils, just as some performers elevate themselves above the music they perform.

It is not uncommon for some well-known performers who have played to death certain pieces in their repertories to feel, and also project, boredom in each and every note they play. Critics, too, hearing over and over again performances of certain works, are inclined to resent performers for programming them. I remember a chance meeting with a former critic on *The New York Times* who had married a pupil of mine. He was on his way to Town Hall to review an all-Ravel concert. Suddenly, he blurted out, "If I hear *Gaspard de la nuit* one more time, I'll lose my mind!" Understandably, I hardly believed that the pianist on that occasion deserved the dreadful review that appeared the following morning.

Victims of burnout get bored not only with their work and with themselves, but also with everyone and everything else around them — friends, pets, even the wonders of nature— all the things they used to love. This happened to the mother of my late dear friend, Sheila Aldendorff. At one time the two lived in that sun-bathed paradise, St. Thomas, in the Virgin Islands. Sheila was sipping coffee one morning when her mother sauntered into the sun-drenched kitchen, went to a window, and looked out at what must have been a scene of indescribable beauty. And with a deep sigh she exclaimed, "Oh God, another beautiful day!" It struck my friend that her mother's boredom with her life turned everything else into routine — even a beautiful day. Boredom, like negativity, has a way of feeding upon itself, with the result that beautiful things can actually intensify a person's ennui and even increase his or her feelings of guilt and self-contempt:

> He that has light within his own clear breast
> May sit in the center, and enjoy bright day,
> But he that hides a dark soul and foul thoughts,
> Benighted walks under the mid-day sun;
> Himself is his own dungeon.*

I am convinced that the miraculous faculty with which nature has endowed us — a conscience — whispers to us what we ought to do with our lives. If we heed that inner voice, or super-ego, we will discover our own best self, whether it be in music or art or any equally rewarding endeavor.

Returning to the "Moonlight" Sonata, I should like to say that no matter how often I have performed this piece, and how frequently I have taught it, I feel deep gratitude to Beethoven for having bequeathed it to the world. It grieves me to think that some piano students may never know the indescribable loneliness intimated by that endless stream of broken chords

---

* Milton, *Comus*.

and the repetitive *G* sharp that throbs like a beating heart — *dum-de-dum*. Not to know it is to be deprived of one of life's profound experiences.

Is it not tragic, then, that some people become disenchanted with the beautiful things in life, and speak so perfunctorily about unsurpassed masterpieces? Such disenchantment is really a kind of death, precipitated by an atrophy of the mind that can begin at a comparatively early age. Performers and teachers who suffer from severe burnout of this sort might try some or all of the following remedies:

1) Learn new repertory, which will enable you to see old repertory in a new light.
2) Take lessons with stimulating teachers.
3) Play often for colleagues.
4) Engage in something purely creative, such as composing, painting, or writing.

I say "purely creative" in point four because I feel strongly that for music teachers, especially, creative activities, more than leisure-time hobbies, tend to rejuvenate the brain.

For critics suffering from burnout, I suggest that they take instrumental or singing lessons from the finest teachers. Learning to synthesize feeling, thinking, and physical coordination will make them more understanding and appreciative of the efforts of musicians whom they write about.

There is nothing like a commitment to a performance to make the probability of burnout so remote as not to exist at all. And why? A performance reveals the truth about ourselves, perhaps more so than anything else we do in life. For when we perform, we want to project our own best selves to others. If we do not succeed in doing so, we suffer unspeakable shame. This stimulates us to search deep within ourselves in order to find the means of doing our best. The process is so time-consuming and so all-encompassing that burnout finds no way to intrude upon our intense concentration.

Critics, performers, and teachers are not, of course, the only people whose ho-hum attitudes have negative effects upon others. A bored director of a music school, for instance, may invent a reason for undervaluing a student's love for music: "If solo careers are no longer available, then why study Beethoven sonatas?" In another light, we are all too familiar with the advice given by those who have never known anything comparable to a musician's devotion to his or her art: "If you can't support yourself by what you do, then why do it?"

Burnout can not only lead critics to censure everything performers do, but it also may dampen their enthusiasm for a performance which they may actually have liked. For example, a critic might rave about a performance, but then take it all back by suggesting that it might have been "...one of those freakishly great days that good pianists sometimes enjoy..." — this from the very first sentence of Donal Henahan's review of my Tully Hall recital. I do not suggest that the chief criterion for good musical criticism is unconditional praise. Rather, I am suggesting that critics ought to be unconditionally enthusiastic when they like something, and more humane when expressing disapproval. Just as a performance reveals the truth about a performer, so, too, does the tone of a review tell us a great deal about its author. I always think that a snide review speaks more about a critic's own feelings of anger and resentment than it does about the performer who is being victimized. It is even possible that such critics might consciously be appealing to those sadistic readers who secretly revel in another person's failure. Whatever lies behind unjustifiably mean reviews, performers learn absolutely nothing from them.

To return to burnout, perhaps no group of musicians is more prone to this condition than orchestra members. After abandoning their status as solo performers, some orchestral players find it demeaning to be subservient to a conductor. As one instrumentalist put it, "Following a conductor is like studying with those tyrannical teachers who assign all of your pieces and then insist that you use their fingering and imitate their interpretations." When orchestra players suffer from authority problems, then an overly domineering conductor can pose a double threat to them: a loss of their independence and a veritable collapse of their feelings of self-worth.

Ideally, it ought to be a privilege to be one of a hundred expert musicians all bending their efforts to recreate a musical masterpiece. But for those who have no musical life apart from the orchestra, no position in the music world can be more boring and self-defeating.

The utter contempt with which some orchestral players view their jobs was shockingly expressed by the first oboist of the Chicago Symphony during a rehearsal in Philadelphia. His repeated lack of attention during one particular rehearsal did not escape the notice of Kurt Masur, the guest conductor from Germany. What should a conductor do when his oboist's eyes are constantly focused on the floor instead of his baton? Enough was enough. With his temper rising to the boiling point, Masur left the podium and walked over to where the oboist was sitting. What he saw caused a musical scandal that was reported around the globe: the oboist was watching a baseball game on a portable TV set! As one might imagine,

Masur's rage knew no bounds. Suffice it to say that it took the most diplomatic handling on the part of the orchestra's administrative staff to keep him from taking the very next flight back to Germany. As for the oboist, one wonders why he was not fired.

Finally, not everyone can overcome burnout. The truth is, when boredom continues to intrude despite all reasonable and practical measures, it may then be necessary to take the final and admittedly drastic measure of changing to another profession. How do we know whether we are reading the signs correctly or not? Are struggle and unhappiness always symptoms that indicate the necessity for a change of direction in life? Happiness and satisfaction do not always accompany that agonizing struggle which worthwhile endeavors demand. And unhappiness is not always final proof that we are engaged in wrong pursuits.

Because emotional responses can deceive us, we can all too easily make wrong decisions. For example, we might be convinced that we have made the right decision about something and even feel elated about it. Then suddenly, and much to our dismay, we discover that we have mistakenly chosen the line of least resistance in order to avoid a painful confrontation with the truth.

For obvious reasons, most people shun struggle and conflict. Yet few things of value have been accomplished without them. Performance anxiety, for instance, as hateful a condition as there ever was, creates an internal crisis which requires a superhuman harnessing of oneself. As a result, performers usually end up being prepared even more thoroughly than would seem necessary, and therefore they may achieve a performance that is beyond their wildest expectations.

But what if we have learned to cope with severe anxiety and harsh demands on us, but still end up choosing the wrong path in life? I, for example, in renouncing my performing career, might have discovered in time that I had followed my creative calling in order to avoid the demands of performing. If such a thing had occurred, I certainly could have changed my mind and gone back to performing. The option of changing our minds as often as is necessary in order to discover the truth about ourselves or about things was graphically demonstrated by Beethoven in his *Sketch Book*. For as Beethoven struggled to find the exact means through which to express his cosmic stirrings, he would re-write a musical example as often as thirty times. Having traversed a whole labyrinth of changes, and perhaps *because* of the struggle he endured, he finally achieved that inner and outer rightness in his music which is now our legacy.

Who are we in comparison to Beethoven that we should expect ourselves to perform and to create without struggle, without paying a price for our seriousness? Pain, suffering, conflict, or whatever names one assigns to struggle, are all part of the creative and re-creative process. On a positive note, struggle and self-doubt humble us in the face of challenges. And they indicate something else as well — how alone we ultimately are.

The ability to renew ourselves is sometimes instinctive. Yet more frequently it is the result of disciplined working habits which ideally begin in early childhood, but can be learned at any age. Alas, not everyone's home environment is conducive to structured learning, nor can schools always compensate for this lack. Certainly the enormous percentage of illiterate people in the United States alone, and the fact that many students cannot do simple addition or multiplication exercises without the aid of calculators and computers, says a great deal about the inherent weaknesses in our homes and in our schools. While some educators are now making a concerted effort to rectify these problems, still the effects of undisciplined working habits and permissiveness in and out of the classroom have crept into practically every area of human endeavor. Undisciplined minds can lead to undisciplined behavior, which may explain the enormous crime rate throughout the world. And it may explain, too, why irresponsibility, rudeness, and a general lack of humanity have eaten away at the foundation of our social structure. When educators and music critics become insensitive to the finer things in life, then quite naturally they view music, the paradigm of humanity, as being a nonessential subject. One ominous sign of this is the fact that music itself is gradually disappearing from our public schools. Vanishing are glee clubs, sing-ins, school orchestras, and bands where average students were able to *make* music, and not just listen to it.

Ancient Heritage

Nowhere, perhaps, were music and musicians held in greater esteem than in ancient Greece. In antiquity, students were not considered to be properly educated unless they had a thorough foundation in music. All students were taught music, whether they had the potential to become performers or not. Imagine, then, the calibre of audiences which attended concerts in ancient Greece. Average concert-goers knew enough about music to listen to it with understanding, respect, and reverence. They had discovered empirically how music nourishes the soul and expands the mind. With music playing such a vital role in education, it is no wonder that practically everything that has come down to us from ancient Greece is imbued with order, harmony, and passion.

Music, as some people theorize, is feeling converted into sound. Ideally, our responses to music, whether we perform it, listen to it, or even just talk about it, ought to have some of that spontaneous fire that is at the core of music itself — a fire tempered with intellectual control and refinement. I once witnessed such a passionate verbal response to music from my dear friend Flora Levin, the classicist, writer, and musician. One evening, she and I heard Sir Clifford Curzon in a never-to-be-forgotten performance of Mozart's Concerto in B flat, K. 595. Immediately afterwards at a private meeting, Sir Clifford asked Flora for her impressions of this work. Without hesitation, she replied, "It is one of the pillars of civilization." Sir Clifford was temporarily stunned into silence at hearing such an eloquent statement about a work that remained so close to his heart even after over a hundred performances of it. And I think that Sir Clifford could be described as another of civilization's pillars for his magnificent performance of the work.

In Defense of My Master

Speaking of Sir Clifford, I once attended a performance in Carnegie Hall of another work with which he and the conductor on that occasion, George Szell, were identified — Beethoven's "Emperor" Concerto. Sir Clifford was in rare form that evening. And being someone who was close to him during his biannual visits to New York City, I can testify to the fact that this was not always the case. At any rate, the Szell-Curzon combination attracted the crème de la crème of musicians. As a matter of fact, I met and spoke to no less than five well-known pianists after the concert, and they all agreed that the performance of the "Emperor" that night was of historic proportions.

But Harold Schonberg, who was at that time the senior music critic of *The New York Times*, was not of this opinion. In fact, nothing about that performance met with his approval. He even went so far as to fault Sir Clifford for not always being together with the orchestra, a criticism perhaps more dim-witted than any of the others he expressed. One might have thought that Sir Clifford, who had been alternately lauded and crucified by the press a thousand times over, would have become inured to the likes of a Harold Schonberg. On the contrary! What Sir Clifford said to me on the telephone revealed that time and experience had done nothing to lessen his vulnerability. "Imagine all of the people who will read that review," he said, in an atypically dejected voice. "And now they will never, never know the truth about the performance."

Hearing the lifeless tone in my master's voice was enough to spark the fire of rebellion within me. As soon as I hung up the phone, I mapped out a plan that I hoped would topple the whole festering apparatus of *The New York Times* music critic staff. This, I thought, would not only vindicate my master, but also the other performers whose playing and reputations had been trampled upon by the Harold Schonbergs of the world. With the support of sponsors whom I rounded up within the hour, I intended to procure an entire page in *The New York Times*. The headline was to read INSULT TO ARTISTRY. The infamous review would be reprinted, followed by statements from eminent musicians who had attended the performance. Our plan was to demand a public hearing with Harold Schonberg.

Now everything was in readiness, and there remained only a discussion about it with Sir Clifford himself. "How happy he will be," I thought, "when he learns all the details of my plan — that a host of his followers would openly decry the affront to his artistry, and that rich sponsors with a musical conscience would underwrite the enormous expense of buying a full page in *The New York Times*. Above all, won't he be proud of his disciple for being the author of this plan?" With all of this in mind, I telephoned Sir Clifford.

Far from being happy about the plan and proud of me, he flew into a rage: "You are using this incident as a means of gaining publicity for yourself!" he screamed at the top of his voice. "Has it escaped your notice that everyone will think that I put you up to this? My career will be the thing that will suffer in the end. If you insist upon carrying out this plan, I will have no other recourse but to sue you!"

While I was crushed and also disillusioned by what I thought was my master's self-centered viewpoint and his obvious show of weakness, I could not, in good conscience, add to the hurt which the review had already caused him. Rather than argue the point with him, I abandoned the plan entirely.

I thought at the time that had Sir Clifford sanctioned my plan, it would have laid the groundwork for what I had always envisioned — an out and out protest by world-renowned figures against certain ignorant and incompetent music critics. I strongly believed that Sir Clifford would have been heralded as a hero, and that his career, far from being harmed, would have been augmented. He would have gone on record in the eyes of the world as being a staunch opponent of injustices against *all* performers. Now, however, I see my actions as having been totally misguided. Such publicity would no doubt have threatened Sir Clifford's integrity and elevated Schonberg's importance.

Performers First, Composers Second

There is one curious thing about critics who admit to being bored after hearing repeated performances of certain works: rarely will they call time-honored masterpieces "threadbare" when they are played by superstars. Did any critic, for instance, dare to associate Coca-Cola with Vladimir Horowitz' thousandth performance of Chopin's Ballade in G minor? Or would critics have dared to express their utter boredom with yet another performance of the "Moonlight" Sonata when it was played by Artur Rubinstein? Hardly! Each comment in those reviews seems to have centered on the superstars themselves. Are we to conclude, then, that a performer's status takes precedence over music?

I believe that it now does. For since appreciation of the composer-pianist has been replaced by the cult of the virtuoso performer, the superstar and not the composer is now the center of attention. In fact, so star-conscious have some people become that one wonders if music touches them at all. The very layouts on concert posters and programs would seem to indicate the performer's supremacy over composers. With few exceptions, soloists' names are emblazoned in large letters, while the names of composers appear to be dutifully added in smaller print, as in the past "BERNSTEIN/ Beethoven" programs.

Compassion

Most people have been victims of injustice at one time or another at the hands of family members, a friend, or, in fact, a critic. To be sure, anyone may suddenly say something or do something that temporarily riles us up. For humans err, and the least we can do is try to forgive them. But there is one thing that most people consider to be unforgivable, and that is a lack of compassion.

To begin with, compassion stems from the capacity of one person to be sympathetic to the needs of another. Certain people seem to have a natural sensitivity for others, just as certain musicians have a natural sensitivity for the language of music. All of this gives rise to the following question: Can compassion, or musicality, be taught to those who seem to lack these traits?

As to musicality, teachers can demonstrate and verbally explain the ingredients contained in a genuinely musical performance. Instead of giving up on students who appear to be unmusical, good teachers will indicate to them the proper dynamics for each and every note, demonstrate the rhythmic pacing and rubato, and guide them through the course of the piece. By following their teacher's instructions to the letter, such students can learn to sound musical even when they do not instinctively feel the music they are playing.

One of the most rewarding aspects of teaching is to discover hidden reservoirs within a pupil. A teacher may even be privileged to lead out the capacity for genuine musical expression in a pupil who formerly seemed to be unmusical. It may seem paradoxical, but this is often accomplished by stressing the physical aspects of playing over the interpretive ones. More specifically, when pupils are taught to make the exact choreographic motions which correspond to musical feeling, some deep emotional response within them may suddenly surface into consciousness. One deduces from this that an earlier lack of musical projection was simply due to a physical block, or a lack of understanding of how to make a physical connection to musical feeling. But even when genuine musicality is not revealed, simulated feeling is better than no feeling at all. In the same way, simulated courtesy and civility are far superior to rude and coarse behavior.

As recently as ten years ago, the subject of compassion and the lack of it was brought to the attention of instructors in medical schools. They learned about compassion what good music teachers know about musicality — that such intangibles can be simulated, or, what is better, inculcated through direct instruction. Thus, according to a report in *The New York Times*:

> Leading medical professors and physicians are moving to correct what they regard as a serious problem in their professions: a lack of compassion in the treatment of patients. Educational programs stressing humane values and ethics have recently been adopted in most of the nation's medical schools.[*]

We learn from the same article that doctors themselves have been victims of inhumane treatment at the hands of their own colleagues:

> In all the years [that Dr. DeWitt Stetson, Jr.] was losing his vision, none of his technically talented ophthalmologists ever suggested any of the numerous devices and programs that would have made his life more tolerable.

Few people, if any, have been spared the pain of other people's indifference. But when it comes from one's colleagues — comrades in battle, so to speak — then its effects are particularly devastating.

Around the time that I broke my foot, I had an engagement in upstate New York as a member of a large ensemble. In spite of having to use crutches, I was able to drive my own car. I took for granted that one of the

---

[*] Bryce Nelson, *The New York Times*, September 13, 1983.

ensemble members would help me with my briefcase once we arrived at our destination. To everyone's good fortune, all three cars were able to park just in front of the stage entrance. While I was positioning my crutches in order to get out of my car, I watched my colleagues go directly into the auditorium. They all knew of my affliction, and all of them had seen me on crutches. Yet not one of them offered me a helping hand. Finally, the stage manager, who had been observing the whole scene, rushed to my aid. By that time, I had another affliction to deal with: a depressed spirit. For it pained me to think that my need escaped the notice of so many of my colleagues.

Once on the stage, however, everything changed. With music overriding everything else, our hearts and minds were linked together in a common bond. Yet, a short time earlier, my colleagues had proved that a sensitivity for music does not necessarily indicate a compassion for human afflictions.

Curiously, non-musicians are always surprised when they learn that musicians, of all people, can behave insensitively or inhumanely towards their colleagues. As many of them have told me, they find it difficult to dissociate musicians from music itself, an art which, to their way of thinking, is a paradigm of sensitivity and compassion. Quite obviously, there is nothing within music itself that can be faulted in this respect. For music, like religion, ought to enrich its practitioners with its own spiritual powers. But the fact that religious leaders have been guilty of the worst crimes against humanity, including conspiratorial murder, and that eminent musicians have been known to act with gross inhumanity towards others, sadly suggests one thing: the real significance of religion and music can elude certain practitioners so utterly as to leave them totally unaffected. Perhaps it is time for institutions that teach religion and music to follow the example of medical schools, namely, to institute courses in compassion. Regarding my colleagues, I would have welcomed a simulated show of compassion in the absence of the genuine thing.

Critics who are imbued with compassion, or who have learned to simulate it, are more likely to approach musicians humanely. For just as experienced performers place music above and beyond all other considerations during performances, so, too, will critics focus upon music and its makers to the exclusion of their own petty feelings: "I secretly hate the *Waldstein* Sonata. But my responsibility is to listen to the performer's interpretation of it with understanding and objectivity. If the performer fails to make his point, I will know how to treat his efforts with compassion. And if space permits, I might state my own views about the work."

Music, the Integrator

Compassion, like music itself, has restorative powers. It is so powerful, in fact, that when doctors treat patients with compassion, even in small doses, they show marked improvement when all other measures have failed. Music, too, can make people well. An appreciation of its properties, achieved through practicing, can lead to personal health as well as musical understanding. Heinrich Neuhaus, the eminent Soviet pedagogue, was convinced of this peculiar property in music to affect human nature:

> I confess that in the many years I worked with very indifferent pupils (of my own free will, incidentally) and suffered a great deal from it, I comforted myself with the thought that though I would never teach them to play well, that I would never make pianists of them, I would still, by means of music, by injecting into them the bacillus of art, drag them some way up into the realms of spiritual culture and would help them to develop their best spiritual qualities. This is not quixotic: with very few exceptions, I did manage to achieve something.[*]

My fundamental faith in the power of education leads me to believe that even the "purple cabbage" critic is not beyond redemption. I feel sure that if critics knew something of music's integrating powers — and this would require that they study music seriously — they would be armed with the full knowledge of what the practice and performance of music really entails. It would be clear to them, for instance, that every performance represents the highest form of dedication and discipline, even when performers are not at their best. With this in mind, critics would salvage something positive from practically every performance, without, of course, resorting to false praise. For nothing insults a performer more than insincere compliments. I know certain musicians who compliment performers and later deride them to their friends and colleagues. Let someone do this to them, and they become incensed to the point of murder!

A critic's skill should lie in criticizing performers in such a way, that they, the performers, are revealed to themselves. This holds true for teaching as well. To be sure, a critic's job is quite different from that of a teacher. Yet teachers function as critics do when they assess their pupils' performances. "A teacher is the personified conscience of the pupil, confirming him in his doubt, explaining his dissatisfactions, stimulating his urge to improve," as Thomas Mann so aptly put it in his music-based

---

[*] Heinrich Neuhaus, *The Art of Piano Playing* (New York: Hollowbrook, 1973) p. 88.

novel *Dr. Faustus*. Whether it comes from a teacher or a critic, good criticism achieves two ends: it points out weaknesses and errors of judgment, and it encourages and applauds all that is praiseworthy. Performers who sense that critics want them to do well, and will forgive them if they do not, will approach their performances more positively. Perhaps we can condense all of this into the following statement:

> Effective criticism requires an awareness of a person's positive accomplishments and an intellectual and compassionate understanding of his or her faults.

This statement holds true for friendship as well as music criticism. As understanding is the well-spring of compassion, so, too, is it the pathway to forgiveness.

Credentials

People who wield power to the extent that critics do should, one would think, have very impressive credentials to qualify for their influential positions. Yet no person I have spoken to on the subject is quite sure what those credentials might be, beyond a general knowledge of music and a command of journalistic skills. In fact, certain reviews I have read have led me to believe that the critics in question have not even met the first requirement — a general knowledge of music. Nor do they seem to have any idea of what is involved in its performance. Some performers who have been ill-treated by critics are indignant on the subject: "Let them know just what it feels like to be backstage during those agonizing moments before a performance, and they will never again treat performers so disdainfully." Yet most performers agree that professional critics are perfectly capable of writing sensitive and sensible reviews, whether they themselves have performed in public or not.

Interestingly, some critics have performed in public, and are well-acquainted with pre-performance anxiety. One can think of many reasons why a performer would turn to music criticism — a deep sensitivity for music coupled with a talent for writing, or insufficient talent for performing but a determination to remain in music in some capacity, to mention only two. And there may be another reason: If a performer happened to have failed on the concert stage or suffered guilt for not being able to practice properly, then he or she might have decided to shift to music criticism to punish other performers for these failings. For people often seek positions of power in order to rescue their wounded egos. Whatever their reasons for going into music criticism, all music critics ought to have one thing in common: a passion for music.

Some of the finest examples of controlled, informative, and altogether human music criticism were written by those great composer-pianists and literary figures of the "golden age of romanticism." I am thinking especially of Robert Schumann, Hector Berlioz, and Franz Liszt. Notable also were Heinrich Heine and E. T. A. Hoffman, the latter a musician, painter, novelist and poet. Heinrich Heine (1797-1856) was the first literary giant to write as a journalist about music and musicians. No one at that time made a greater contribution to Parisian musical life than he did. Considering his credentials, it is not surprising that his criticisms were infused with poetic imagery. Thus, to him, Chopin was the "Raphael of the piano":

> Hearing Chopin, I quite forget his mastery as a performer on the keyboard and sink into the sweet abyss of his music, into the hurting loveliness of his creations, as deep as they are tender. *

And about Thalberg:

> [He] seems to regard his talent as a royal grant.

In contrast to the above, Alan Rich, in reviewing a re-release of a recording of Jascha Heifetz, accused him of playing like "a café violinist." Notwithstanding Heifetz' revered and unchallenged position as one of the greatest violinists of the twentieth century, a critic has every right to quarrel with his interpretations. But to compare an artist of such stature to a café violinist is an affront to Heifetz, to music, and to common decency.

George Bernard Shaw was no less monstrous to performers than Alan Rich. The fact that he was a great writer made the poison of his pen that much more lethal. That he decided to turn to music criticism at one point in his career was certainly the misfortune of performers. Compassion? Forgiveness? Quite the contrary. See how he responds to a performer who had an off-night:

> ...when people do less than their best...I hate them, loathe them, detest them, and long to tear them limb from limb and strew them in gobbets about the stage or platform. †

---

* Max Graf, *Composer and Critic* (New York: W. W. Norton, 1981) p. 210.
† Graf, p. 295.

Essay: The Music Critic

Nor did Shaw have the slightest compunction about reviewing cellists, when, in fact, he confessed to loathing the cello:

> Ordinarily I had as soon hear a bee buzzing in a stone jug.

Some of our critics today fluctuate between the egomania of a Shaw and the eloquence of a Heine. From the following article, one would never know just how vicious and opinionated Bernard Holland could be:

> As to the art of music and how it will be rescued from the tense spirit which rules it now, one cannot predict. The spirit of music is never far from the spirit of the age which produces it. When we learn warmth and graciousness, ease and magnanimity, our music will certainly follow. These are problems no conservatory will ever solve.[*]

Joseph Horowitz, a particular favorite of mine, indeed projects "warmth and graciousness, ease and magnanimity" in his review of Nathan Milstein's 1963 recording of Saint-Saëns' 3rd Violin Concerto:

> He never forced or varnished his slender, silvery tone. He shunned the urgent vibrato of his onetime classmate Jascha Heifetz. He disdained what Virgil Thomson called the "wow effect." A performance more earnest than Milstein's would make this music sound sentimental. A more brilliant performance — from a less transcendental instrumentalist, incapable of Milstein's composure under fire — would make it sound trite. The vehemence of the Concerto's opening Allegro, the intoxication of its luminous, swaying slow movement, the élan and manqué religiosity of its tarantella and chorale finale — all, in Milstein's hands, are poised, but perfectly, between passion and refinement. The result is transformative: an exercise in elegance and craftsmanship become sublime.[†]

---

[*] Bernard Holland, "What Will All These Musicians Do?" *The New York Times,* June 16, 1985.
[†] Joseph Horowitz, "From Russia to the World: The Complete Cosmopolite," *The New York Times*, August 22, 1993.

Rare is the critic who can offer negative criticism with a sense of respect and compassion for the performer in question. In the following excerpt, the German pianist, teacher, writer, and critic Gerhard Schroth shows knowledge and understanding:

> In the seven movements of Bach's Partita in E minor, the pianist showed a feeling for polyphony as well as a deep sensibility for the character of the single movements. Yet she frequently gave the impression that pianistic considerations took priority over critical aspects of the baroque style. This was already in evidence in the exaggerated dynamic range of the fugal section of the opening Toccata, which began poetically and understated, and in her too violent approach to the extroverted character of the Corrente.[*]

To return to credentials, many music critics seem to have had their training in such diversified fields as art history, political science, mathematics, and philosophy. And Ross Parmenter, the former music critic of *The New York Times* who happened to review my New York City debut, was formerly a sports editor. Holding to the ancient dictum *scientia est potentia* (knowledge is power), diversified experience ought to contribute to a critic's expertise. For ideally, knowledge gained in one area ought to refine one's discernment in all other areas. Yet, as some of the above quotations from learned men undoubtedly suggest, the pursuit of knowledge may sharpen the mind, but it can bypass the sensibilities entirely.

Blunders and Witty Malice

Critics, like musicians or anyone else, cannot possibly know everything. For example, they often accuse pianists of over-pedaling in the Rondo of the *Waldstein* Sonata by Beethoven. Yet, if they would simply consult the score, they would see that Beethoven himself indicated daringly long pedal marks in this movement. Pianists, simply by being faithful to the score, risk being publicly chastised by ill-informed critics. On the other hand, if the adherence to Beethoven's long pedal indications results in a blurred effect, then the pianist is at fault. For following a composer's long pedal indications requires of the performer a skillful handling of the dynamics and textures. But critics ought to know what exactly is involved when something sounds wrong to their ears.

---

[*] Gerhard Schroth, *Frankfurter Allgemeine Zeitung*, September 10, 1991, translation by Gerhard Schroth and Seymour Bernstein.

Essay: The Music Critic

Not all critics know the subtle distinctions between various Italian terms used in musical notation. Even performers make serious blunders in this area. I was in my mid-forties, for example, when I discovered that I had been using the word *portamento* erroneously whenever I referred to half staccato. *Portamento*, which literally means "carrying," is best described as a slide between two pitches of a large interval in singing. The correct word for half staccato is *portato*. Curiously, some dictionaries sanction the use of *portamento* to mean both things — a slide and half staccato. But fundamentally, the two words *portamento* and *portato* are distinct in meaning.

To be sure, anyone can miss the distinctions between one word and another. But when a critic chastises a performer because of his own ignorance of a musical term, his faux pas has far-reaching consequences. One such word, *attacca*, means to go directly on to the following movement without pause. The cellist Ardyth Alton, being faithful to the meaning of this term in the Beethoven's Sonata No. 5 for cello and piano, went directly from the second movement to the third — a Fugato marked *piano*. Unfortunately, the *Washington Post* critic Paul Hume, thinking no doubt that *attacca* meant "attack," criticized her in his review for starting the Fugato *piano* instead of *forte*. Mr. Hume's misinterpretation of that one word caused a scandal in musical circles that reverberated for a long time afterwards.

Overindulging in technical ease and proficiency, whatever the medium, is a tendency that is hard to resist. Just as musicians may show off their virtuosity at the expense of music, critics having a flair for words coupled with a sardonic nature may indulge themselves in irony and witticisms at the expense of performers. A case in point is the final sentence of Harold Schonberg's unfavorable review in *The New York Times* of the late pianist Glenn Gould:

All that glitters is not Gould.

Quite obviously, Gould's career was not in the least affected by this altogether nasty play on words. He probably would have agreed with Beethoven's response to the critics of the *Allgemeine Musikalische Zeitung*:

As for the oxen from Leipzig they may say what they will. They will make nobody immortal with their talking, and, likewise, they will not take immortality from that man whom Apollo has destined for immortality.[*]

To turn critic, temporarily, I would unhesitatingly say that Glenn Gould's compartmentalized genius (I am thinking of his magnificent recordings of the *Goldberg* Variations and other works of Bach) existed alongside a nature that was as eccentric and virulent as it was forceful and communicative. If music critics ever doubted for one moment the power of the written word, they need only ponder to what extent Gould's statement about Mozart — that he "died too late rather than too soon" — has poisoned the minds of countless musicians and music lovers.[†] Some musicians feel that Gould, in this outrageous statement, was merely placing Mozart in historical perspective and not qualifying his musical output, while others suggest that Gould was referring to Mozart's last works, which Gould thought to be inferior to his earlier works. But anyone familiar with Gould's various attacks on Mozart and other musical giants would find it hard to side with the above rationalizations. One need only listen to Gould's recordings of Mozart sonatas to know the contempt with which he held the master. In a democracy, all people can say or write whatever they wish. But that Gould would flaunt his disdain for Mozart by recording his sonatas, and, moreover, that a recording company would cash in on such an affront to music, surely demotes them both — Gould and the recording company — to the ignoble status of hypocrites.

When thinking of Harold Schonberg's play on words, I am reminded of a snide witticism that was leveled at me by the chief monster of critics, Claudia Cassidy. The situation was made especially amusing by the fact that while my name was on the program, someone else was playing in my stead. As it happened, I was touring for a month in the United States as a substitute pianist with the Royal Shakespeare Company. It was their production of *The Hollow Crown*, which depicts the Kings and Queens of England in a series of readings. The musical score called for a pianist-harpsichordist to be onstage throughout the production, along with four actors and two singers. Besides playing both solos and accompaniments, the pianist had to move about the stage at pre-arranged intervals. Needless

---

[*] Graf, p. 118.
[†] "Of Mozart and Related Matters: Glenn Gould in Conversation with Bruno Monaingeon," originally published in *Piano Quarterly*, Fall 1976, quoted in *The Glenn Gould Reader*, ed. Tim Page (New York: Knopf, 1984) p. 32.

to say, this was rather a complicated procedure for someone who had never gone through the routine before. When I joined the troupe in Chicago, therefore, all agreed that it would be to my advantage to watch the production on opening night from the audience. One detail, however, had been overlooked: my name appeared in the program. With all of the excitement on opening night, no one remembered to announce to the sold out house that a different pianist would be playing that evening.

The pianist who did play was not the original pianist of *The Hollow Crown*, but rather a conductor temporarily serving as music director. I don't mean to slight conductors, for some of them, like George Szell, Leonard Bernstein, and Daniel Barenboim, are extraordinary pianists, but I am obliged to say that this particular conductor played as though he were wearing gloves. This of course aroused Claudia Cassidy's penchant for viciousness:

> At the end of the production, Queen Victoria reads from her diary on the day of her coronation, and Seymour Bernstein plays Beethoven's Variations on "God Save the King." But it wasn't the King who needed saving — it was Beethoven.[*]

Reading this over breakfast, I laughed until the tears streamed down my cheeks — a rather indiscreet thing to do considering that the conductor was sitting with a long face only a few tables away. The following day, however, when it was my turn to perform in the production, my vanity proved greater than my sense of humor. I telephoned Claudia Cassidy to inform her that through no fault of hers I had been the victim of her bad review. Charmed, and apologetic, she took the trouble to print a correction the next day.

The Queen Victoria scene was unquestionably the dramatic highlight of the production. Against a darkened stage, one spotlight fell upon the actress. At the end of her reading, a second spotlight engulfed the pianist, now making him the center of attention. The visual effect tended to heighten the aural one, perhaps making the playing on opening night seem worse than it actually was. Still, what could that conductor learn from Claudia Cassidy's witty malice? While making sport of a bad performance may give everyone a temporary chuckle, nothing constructive is achieved by it. If the pianist's technique was faulty, then say so. If his tone was wooden and inflexible, then point this out. And if there was just one good phrase, and I can testify to the fact that there were many, then this, too,

---

[*] Claudia Cassidy, *The Chicago Tribune*, February 4, 1964.

should be mentioned. Unfortunately, everyone had a good time at the expense of the conductor. While he should never have assumed the responsibilities of a full-fledged pianist to begin with, one could only feel sorry for him in the end.

Happily, music critics occasionally indulge in complimentary witticisms, such as the following:

> The only drawback to Mr. [Richard] Goode is the inappropriateness
> of his name. To me, he is Richard Great.*

"Tell me how wonderful I am."

Who among us likes to be criticized? With few exceptions, whatever we do, and regardless of the level on which we do it, something in our nature wants to be praised — if only for effort's sake. A verbal compliment will suffice, but written praise is far better. Because most of us secretly want to be told how wonderful we are, nothing disturbs us more than adverse criticism. Whether it is valid or not, such criticism evokes a wide range of emotional responses — anger, resentment, depression, defensiveness — all of which are tantamount to our saying that we have been misunderstood and deserve better. A bad review can even make the president of a country temporarily lose his diplomatic poise. As it happened, Margaret Truman, daughter of President Harry Truman, gave a recital in Washington, D.C., on December 6, 1950. The aforementioned critic of *The Washington Post,* thirty-four year old Paul Hume, thought that Margaret was "extremely attractive," but went on to say she "cannot sing very well" and "has not improved" over the years. The President was furious and freely vented his indignation:

> It seems to me that you are a frustrated old man who wishes he could
> have been successful. When you write such poppy-cock as was in the
> back section of the paper you work for it shows conclusively that
> you're off the beam and at least four of your ulcers are at work.
>
> Some day I hope to meet you. When that happens you'll need a
> new nose, a lot of beefsteak for black eyes, and perhaps a supporter
> below! †

To some musicians, the thought of a critic sitting in the audience can be so unnerving that they actually will them out of consciousness. In truth,

---

* John Ardoin, *The Dallas Morning News*, November 24, 1993.
† Letter in the Malcolm Forbes Collection.

though, the effort expended in doing this merely makes their presence felt all the more strongly It is far better to face the truth squarely: A critic *is* sitting out there in the darkness, and he may be even more "grizzled" than usual. Being criticized, and running the risk of eliciting a bad review from the critic, is simply one more occupational hazard in a profession that is already fraught with them. With good reason, then, many performers refer to the stage as a "battlefield."

The God Figure

When a critic actually does appear at a performance, he commands instant attention. An aura of magisterial power surrounds him. Whispers signal his presence: "Look who just walked in!" Audience members look surreptitiously at him so as not to make him uncomfortable. Heaven forbid that anyone knowing the artist should arouse a critic's displeasure, for he might express his annoyance by writing a bad review. To the family and friends of the performer, the critic is, for all intents and purposes, an authority sitting in judgment of the performer, the composer, and the audience as well. Even facial expressions are adjusted for his sake. And it certainly would not hurt to shout an extra bravo: "I hope he heard that. He would have to be made of stone not to write a rave review after such a wild and enthusiastic response!"

Absurd as it may seem, an enthusiastic audience response might be the very thing that causes a critic to write a scathing review of a performer. For it is possible that a neurotic critic might be driven to vie with the performer and the audience for supremacy: "So you like it, do you? Well, I decide the performer's fate, not you!" One of my friends who was especially attuned to this type of psychological aberration even went so far as to make a comparison between critics and those annoying people whose sudden fits of coughing seem calculated to coincide with the softest moment in a piece. According to my friend's analysis, both the critic and a certain type of cougher find ways to express unconscious competitive feelings by diverting attention away from the performer and towards themselves — the cougher by coughing, and the critic by writing a scathing review.

To many concert-goers, the critic is just as important as the performer. Nor does the attention given the critic cease when the concert has ended. At one extreme, it is the absence of a critic that stirs up passions. Thus, for days or weeks afterwards, the performer and his followers exchange heated telephone calls: "You mean to tell me no critic showed up!" Even when the critic is present, his subsequent review may arouse praise or blame depending on one's own reaction to the performance.

Being There

Nothing can arouse more anger and be more demoralizing to performers and their fans than the absence of any review at all. This is particularly heartbreaking to a young artist who has just made his debut in New York City. The *New York Times'* policy of always reviewing debut recitals, even those of unknown artists, is a thing of the past. Occasionally, though, a lesser known artist *is* reviewed, but only if well-known artists happen not to be performing on that particular day. But generally speaking, only newsworthy items are deemed worthy of review. Certainly the pitifully small staff of music critics assigned to the biggest newspaper in the world, *The New York Times*, and the limited space allotted to reviews in that paper contribute to the situation.

This leads me to raise the following question: Do artists who have a thriving career depend upon another review? Aren't their credentials such that they will continue to thrill audiences and sell out concert halls, whether a critic shows up or not? And would a leading newspaper such as *The New York Times* suffer a significant loss in sales if lesser known artists were reviewed? Since space is limited in *The New York Times,* I believe that the public would be far more interested in reading about newcomers to the music scene then seeing reviews only about superstars. The same thing might be said about publicity concerning forthcoming concert series: the constant appearance of the same superstars will always be greeted with enthusiasm, and rightly so; but new names stir tremendous interest and curiosity.

Certain people might influence *The New York Times* in reviewing lesser known artists — established artists in the concert field. To them I make the following plea:

> Stop for a moment and consider the plight of some of your less fortunate colleagues. You, who are standard-bearers of ultimate artistry, help now to perpetuate the art of which you yourselves are the masters. Request of your managers that they not invite critics to your concerts. Use your influence to encourage critics to attend, instead, performances of lesser-known musicians. They want only to establish a modest foothold in a world where you reign supreme. But do even more than that. Listen more frequently to young musicians, and take note of those in whom the spark of true artistry resides. Know in advance that given your position in the music world, you, more than your managers, can influence the direction of the

performing arts today. Use your formidable power and appeal to your managers to book lesser known artists on the very concert series graced by your names. Boldly refuse to accept certain engagements unless your wishes are honored. Needless to say, it would be a boon to lesser known artists to have the opportunity to perform more frequently and — an additional benefit — to be able to buy a good meal once in awhile. But beyond that, each engagement will symbolize your own trust in their abilities — no small thing when you consider that you are their musical heroes. The rest is predictable: Having the proof of your belief in them, and with the challenge of concert engagements to motivate their best work, such artists will practice ever more diligently and expand their artistry. The world, then, will be enriched, and you will have the distinctive honor and satisfaction of having brought this about.

Some well-known artists have been known to take young gifted musicians under their wings. But no musical figure of the twentieth century that I know of has done for pupils and colleagues what Liszt did for his. He had a musical and personal conscience that extended in all directions. He launched the careers of Grieg and MacDowell, for instance. And he promoted neglected musical masterpieces from both past and contemporary composers. It was he who conducted the first performance of Wagner's *Lohengrin* and various works by Berlioz. With all of this, he found the time to compose, perform, conduct and teach.

I would imagine that Liszt was no more gifted as a performer than the superstars of the twentieth century. But according to what we know of him, he certainly showed more regard for his colleagues. And he composed, too, which is something that few contemporary virtuosi even attempt. My hunch is that figures such as Horowitz and Rubinstein were powerfully endowed with creative gifts in addition to their instrumental ones. To confess my true feelings, I am angry with them. The legacy of their never-to-be-equaled live performances and recordings notwithstanding, I feel that they entrusted their lives to entrepreneurs who earned fortunes of money for them and for themselves. At the risk of offending their adoring public (and I am no less an admirer of their playing), I believe that they squandered their talent and energies on more performances than they ought to have given, and saved none for creative pursuits. I am angry with these artists most of all for failing to extend their formidable knowledge, as well as just plain human concern, to young musicians. While they may have shown a certain interest in a few young artists, I seriously doubt that any of them promoted the careers of young hopefuls as Liszt did.

Rarely have I known a public figure who would speak out forcefully on any of the issues concerning careers in music, issues which ultimately affect all musicians, including the superstars. The reasons for this lack of action and involvement are not difficult to imagine. Some artists with major careers work incessantly at keeping their names before the public. Like some magnates of big corporations, certain performers can never get enough of the big time. In the end, there is little time and energy left to invest in anyone or anything else. Other artists, neurotically worried about losing their hard-earned reputations in a cut-throat world, are forever fearful of incurring the displeasure of managers, critics and, paradoxically, their own colleagues. There is good cause to worry. For careers today are like quicksilver: managers cannot predict the number of engagements they can book for their artists from season to season; critics may damn performers even when they play their best; and some performers, peeved about the low status of their own careers, can find ways to make life just as miserable for their more successful colleagues. With the unpredictability of bookings being every performer's chief concern, one performer whom I know wonders and worries whether he should put down a deposit on a weekend retreat, a "dream place" that he and his wife have their hearts set upon. Unpredictability, then, becomes a way of life for most performing musicians. Small wonder that the majority of them are neurotic to the point of seeking professional help.

Recommendations

I would not want to change places with a critic. Even Haydn, who was often deeply hurt by critics, did not envy their position. But unlike Beethoven, he suffered their insults with a quiet patrician forbearance. For critics have overwhelming responsibilities — responsibilities to music, to the performer, to the public and to the high standard of writing which they have inherited from great literary figures. Just thinking of the large numbers of people who read *The New York Times* is quite enough to induce within a music critic something akin to pre-performance anxiety. This, coupled with the fact that critics have to meet deadlines, may well inspire our sympathy.

Yet do critics offer the same concern to performers? Who, in fact, is more at risk than performers, who have to perform their best in public within a limited time span? Nothing can be changed, nothing erased —

performers have only one chance at it. Because critics and performers have similar responsibilities, they ought to link their hands together, as true comrades do, and help one another — more for music's sake than for any other reason. In this spirit, then, I offer the following recommendation:

TO ALL MUSIC CRITICS:

1) Act upon the above plea and recommendations which I have made to world-renowned artists for improving the plight of lesser known performing musicians:

   If you believe that superstars no longer need reviews to sustain their careers, then write forcibly about this in articles. No one can be more effective than you.

2) Acknowledge that you cannot possibly know everything that concerns music and performers:

   I suggest that you draw from a list of distinguished musicians who are specialists in their field. Invite one of them to accompany you to a concert. Such a specialist can educate you in areas where you may be lacking. It is not difficult to imagine the benefits to be derived from such an exchange: You will be enriched with pertinent information; the performer, whose function and preservation ought to be your chief concern, will receive a fair and intelligent hearing; and finally, the specialist will enjoy the rewards reserved for those who share their knowledge with others.

3) Keep in mind that performers are also human. Take a few moments after the performance and speak with them backstage.

I have always been pleasantly surprised when critics introduced themselves to me after performances — always in smaller towns and never in major cities. By talking with me, they learned something of the person behind the performer. On occasion, I welcomed the opportunity of providing them with some facts, even extra-musical ones, which sometimes influenced their reviews. For example, I once used an edition which omitted certain measures. I was quick, therefore, to let the critic know that I had not had a memory slip. At another time, I had just left the sickbed after a week-long bout with the flu. Under the circumstances, I felt that I had not played my best, and I told this to the critic. She was surprised and insisted that my indisposition had not hampered my performance in the slightest. Much relieved, I thanked her for her vote of confidence. Then there was the time that my brother-in-law died on the morning of a performance. When a critic introduced himself to me at the reception, I shared my devastation with him, for whatever it was worth. He didn't mention it in his review, but it was a comfort to me to share my loss with someone who was going to review my concert.

Some Pet Gripes and Observations

I believe that there is a miraculous ingredient of the mind from which music itself stems, something that is potentially alive in all people — imagination. Music critics who lack imagination can neither identify with music nor the performer. They will not even hint to the public that discipline, courage, and all of the admirable qualities that performers reveal on the stage are the very qualities which bring music to life. Their powers of imagination long since deadened, these critics, like bored magistrates, sit safely in their seats. And with a scribble of their pens, they pass sentence upon performing musicians.

There are, of course, examples of music criticism of the highest calibre. Their authors possess the attributes I have been discussing — spiritual values and imaginative thinking, combined with a keen understanding of the musical language. Like a well-integrated and perceptive performance, a successful critique is a harmonious whole in which no one attribute stands out apart from the others. Critics who are capable of this kind of writing respond not only to what musicians actually do, but also to what they are trying to do. One beautiful phrase falling upon the ear, like the voice of truth, ought to be sufficient to dispel the critic's remembrance of temporary memory lapses or an occasional wrong note. To acknowledge what is beautiful in a performance is to learn forgiveness for minor mishaps. And no one deserves forgiveness more than performing musicians. For few activities in life are more difficult than reproducing musical masterpieces on the stage. The following review by Michael Kimmelman exemplifies the above:

> Sometimes frustratingly complacent, the music world is occasionally jarred by a strange and heartening twist of fate. Consider, for

503

instance, what has happened lately to Jorge Bolet. For decades, the pianist's career progressed at what might be called a respectable trot, never sprinting despite the combination of good looks and swift fingers that his artist possessed. Then a few years ago the Cuban-born musician, already in his late 70s, made a series of Liszt recordings and gave several recitals of Romantic favorites that brought him widespread praise and newfound popularity. There was nothing strikingly different about these performances from what Mr. Bolet had been doing all along on stage, and yet suddenly — rather inexplicably — the pianist found himself with more concert dates than ever.

Friday evening in Carnegie Hall, he presented to a large and highly appreciative audience the sort of program that has become his acknowledged specialty: Mendelssohn's Prelude and Fugue in E minor (Op. 35) and Rondo Capriccioso (Op. 14), Beethoven's "Appassionata," the Franck "Prelude, Chorale and Fugue," and Liszt's "Reminiscences of Bellini's 'Norma.'"

Mr. Bolet is not a heart-on-the-sleeve performer — his playing can seem a bit chilly, at times — but he brings to this music a mixture of elegance, power and sophistication. Though long recognized for his thundering octaves and blistering scales, he is more admirable for a supple sense of rhythm, a polished, singing tone in the service of long, arching melodies, and, perhaps most importantly, an instinct for when not to play loud and fast. The final movement of the Beethoven was taken at a slower pace than usual and sounded terrifically dramatic. The Franck built slowly and steadily to a great, forceful climax, and the Liszt flowed smoothly through passages of both considerable delicacy and grand theatricality. All in all, a splendid performance.[*]

For all of their heroism, performers are a vulnerable lot. Through experience, and with the help of caring people, they learn to build up their confidence and strengthen their determination. To be human, though, is to go beyond a belief in oneself and extend generosity towards others. Teachers demonstrate this by believing in their pupils' ability to make progress, whatever their degree of talent.

But how, in fact, can performers believe in or trust the judgment of critics who write gratuitously cruel and unfair reviews? Some critics seem actually to enjoy evoking the anger and resentment of performers and

---

[*] Michael Kimmelman, *The New York Times*, March 6, 1988.

their public. While this might temporarily satisfy their penchant for controversy, their baleful intent, nonetheless, reflects adversely upon their colleagues, among whom are the finest critics in the profession. Indeed, one bad apple spoils the whole barrel. Certainly, critics who express boredom with music and performers have nothing to recommend them. Whether they indulge in these feelings consciously or not is open to discussion. But I feel strongly about one thing: critics who have stifled their own dreams will be driven to thwart those of others.

Music touches the lives of a countless number of people. Yet few people can write or speak about music with the authority befitting a fine music critic. From wherever they are drawn, and whatever their credentials, music critics of the calibre I envision must have a strong point of view and demonstrate leadership on musical issues. In a sense, I see them functioning in the music profession as presidents and prime ministers function for their countries. As leaders in their field, I should like to see critics go beyond their responsibilities and lobby for increased federal support of the arts. I should also like to see them write articles about the importance of including lesser-known artists on concert series. Above all, musicians want critics to listen to them with intelligence and compassion.

There has never been a consensus as to what constitutes good musical criticism and what, exactly, is a critic's mission. I, personally, enjoy music criticisms that are imbued with the very qualities we admire in compelling performances — personality, temperament, education and experience. And just as performers are expected to have a technique equal to music's demands, so, too, ought critics to have a commendable writing style. This, of course, is asking a great deal of music critics. But, then, music critics ask no less of composers and performers. In regard to a critic's mission, I should think that critics who write for newspapers, and therefore speak to a large public, have a dual mission: to educate the public, and to critique performers in a style that reveals "a liberal, enlarged, and candid mind."[*]

It is in their responsibility to the public, however, that critics fall short most critically. When they demean certain master composers, they sway the public against serious music. Critics can turn all of this around by the very tone of their reviews. If, for example, they believe that music can have a profound effect upon the human condition, they ought to write articles about this. If they revere time-honored masterpieces, then the very way they write will encourage the public to revere them as well. Finally,

---

[*] Dr. Charles Burney, in his "Essay on Musical Criticism," prefixed to Book III of his *A General History of Music*, 1789, quoted in *Harvard Dictionary of Music*, 2nd ed., p. 554.

if they have even an inkling of what it means to practice a lifetime in order to control one phrase of music on the stage, then mention this in reviews. A good music critic should do all of these things while listening with "a liberal, enlarged and candid mind" to what a performer is trying to say.

Through the power of the written word, critics can strike awe in the hearts and minds of their readers, revealing to them the wonders of music, and elevating the musician to an heroic status. But if critics are no longer "moved by concord of sweet sounds," then, indeed, they are "fit for treasons, stratagems, and spoils," as Shakespeare put it. Perhaps one day a critic will inspire universal approval and thus make obsolete a statement attributed to Sibelius: "No statue has ever been put up to a critic."

About the Author

"Seymour Bernstein Triumphs at the Piano"
(Donal Henahan, *The New York Times*)

Seymour Bernstein has accrued scores of "triumphs" in a variety of activities — performing, composing, teaching, and lecturing. He studied with such notable musicians as Alexander Brailowsky, Sir Clifford Curzon, Jan Gorbaty, Nadia Boulanger, and Georges Enesco, both in this country and in Europe. His prizes and grants include the First Prize and Prix Jacques Durand from the international competition held at Fontainebleau, France, the National Federation of Music Clubs Award for Furthering American Music Abroad, a Beebe Foundation grant, two Martha Baird Rockefeller grants, and four State Department grants. His concert career has taken him to Asia, Europe, and throughout the Americas, where he has appeared in solo recitals and as guest artist with orchestras and chamber music groups. In 1969, he made his debut with the Chicago Symphony Orchestra, playing the world premiere of Concerto No. 2 by Villa-Lobos.

Acclaimed for his "...technical brilliance and penetrating interpretive skills," Seymour Bernstein is also an internationally known writer, composer, teacher, and lecturer. Many of his piano works are on the best-seller list. His books *With Your Own Two Hands*, *20 Lessons in Keyboard Choreography*, and *Musi-Physi-Cality* (the children's version), have been published in various languages including German, Japanese, Korean, and Russian. They, along with his videotape *You and the Piano*, have been hailed by critics as "...firsts of their kind," and "...landmarks in music education." In constant demand for masterclasses and educational programs, he is one of the most sought-after clinicians in this country and abroad. Performances of his piano works have earned him awards from ASCAP.

Seymour Bernstein maintains a private studio in New York City. In addition, he is an Adjunct Associate Professor of Piano and Music Education at New York University.